CANADIAN
HOME DOCTOR

CANADIAN
HOME
DOCTOR

The Complete Home Medical Guide for You and Your Family

McGraw-Hill Ryerson

Toronto   Montreal

Acknowledgements

The publishers and editors acknowledge with appreciation the consistent and ready co-operation of the many doctors and specialists who have assisted in this work.

Medical contributors
Editorial advice and authentication
J. S. Chan M.B., B.S., D.I.H.
John Dowsett M.B., B.S., F.R.A.C.G.P.
Major text contributions and advice
John Gambrill M.B., B.S. (U.N.S.W.), F.R.A.C.G.P. and
    L. P. Miller M.B., B.S., B.Sc. (Med.) both of the
    Department of Community Medicine, University of
    Sydney
Douglas Cohen A.M., M.B., M.S., F.R.A.C.S.
Kim Oates M.B., B.S., M.R.C.P. (U.K.), F.R.A.C.P.,
    D.C.H. (R.C.P.&S.)
John Yu M.B., F.R.A.C.P., D.C.H. (R.C.P.&S.)
    all of the Royal Alexandra Hospital for Children,
    Camperdown
Graeme Morgan M.B., B.S., F.R.A.C.P., of Prince of
    Wales Children's Hospital, Randwick
Eng-Kong Tan M.B., B.S., M.P.M., F.R.A.N.Z.C.P.
Jean R. Nairn M.D., M.B. ch.B., D.C.H.
Julian Gold M.B., B.S.
Contributions to the general text
Frances Black B.Sc. Med. (Hons.), M.B., B.S.,
    F.R.A.C.G.P., Department of Community Medicine,
    University of Sydney
Rhonda Brill Dip.Sp.Ed., Dip.Ed.St.
Heather L. Brotchie M.B., B.S.
Jane Carrick M.B., B.S.
R. J. Cassano M.B., B.S.
F. C. R. Cattell B.Sc., Ph.D., Dip.Env.Stud.
K. Christie M.B., B.S.
I. Collier B.App.Sci., Dip.Phty., M.A.P.A.
Joan Croll M.B., B.S.
Julie Dennis B.Sc., Dip.Phty., M.A.P.A.
Brian Gaynor M.B., B.S. (Syd.), F.R.A.C.P.,
    F.R.A.C.G.P., M.R.C.P. (U.K.), D.C.H. (Lond.)
Walter St. Goar M.D.
G. Goldberg B.A. Hons (Psych), Dip.Ed.M.Psych.
C. Greene M.D., F.A.C.E.P.
D. G. Hamilton A.M., M.B., B.S., F.R.A.C.G.P.
J. C. Johnson M.D., F.A.C.E.P.
E. F. Joyner M.B., B.S.
R. B. Kendall M.B., B.S., O.G.O. (Syd), F.R.A.C.O.G.
Suzanne L. Korbel M.B., B.S. (Syd.)
E. P. Kremer M.B., B.S. (Syd.), J.P.

Rosalind Lehane M.B., B.S.
K. C. McGrath
Julia A. McKeown M.B., B.S. (Syd.), D.A. (Lond.)
Margaret Mitchell M.B., B.S. (Hons.)
John Eryl Rees L.R.C.P. (Lond.), M.R.C.S. (England)
Margaret M. Rozea M.B., B.S.
Douglas Saunders M.R.A.C.O.G., F.R.A.C.O.G.
David Schottke
R. Smith M.D., F.A.C.E.P.
R. W. Strauss M.B., F.A.C.E.P.
St. John Ambulance Australia
Lynette Thew M.B., B.S. (Syd.)
L. M. R. Thomson M.B., B.S.
Christine Trevor M.B., B.S.
Ian Unsworth B.M., B.Ch., F.F.A.R.C.S.,
    F.F.A.R.A.C.S.
U. Vyas-Major M.D., F.A.C.E.P.
Alex Wodak F.R.A.C.P.
Pamela Woodroff M.B.B.S., F.A.C.E.M.

Contributions to the illustrators
Abbott Laboratories, North Chicago, Illinois, USA
    (*Abbottempo magazine*)
Aid Retarded Persons NSW
Asthma Foundation of NSW
Audio-Visual Department, Westmead Centre,
    Westmead, NSW
Blackmores Laboratories
Blind Society of NSW
Central District Ambulance Training School
Family Planning Association of NSW
H. J. Heinz Co Australia Ltd
Ralph Hockin M.B., B.S., F.R.A.C.M.A.
Little People's Association of Australia
Modern Medicine of Australia Pty Ltd
National Flying Doctor Service
New South Wales Drug and Alcohol Authority
New South Wales Metropolitan Water Sewerage and
    Drainage Board
Northcott School for Crippled Children, Sydney
Prince Henry Hospital, Sydney
Royal Alexandra Hospital for Children, Sydney
Sonicaid Limited, England
3M Australia Pty Ltd
Traffic Accident Research Section, NSW Department
    of Transport
UNICEF
I. R. Vanderfield O.B.E., M.B., B.S., F.R.A.C.M.A.,
    F.A.I.M.

Contents

Introduction

This book sets out to supply on the one hand a comprehensive introduction to health and how to maintain it and, on the other, a description of common illnesses and the possibilities of assessing and coping with them. It is not a specialized encyclopedia of medicine or a do-it-yourself medical manual. It is a useful, practical guide for everyone interested in maintaining optimum health and pursuing a health-promoting lifestyle, based on knowing about the needs of the body and how it functions. All sections of the book have been written by qualified doctors and medical specialists in language made as plain as possible for the layman.

Many common illnesses and minor disabilities are a part of family life, but even these must be dealt with in commonsense ways that cause no further damage to the health of the person. In accident and serious illness, an appreciation by the family of what is happening will help them to care for the patient with more skill and understanding, and reduce the dislocation of daily routine. It is important to know when you need the help of a doctor, for once severe illness strikes, its remedy is substantially in the hands of the medical profession. Even so, some knowledge on the part of the patient can be the basis of effective cooperation with the doctor.

The emphasis of the book is on the promotion of health rather than the treatment of disease, but a substantial guide to first aid is given in the last chapter. This is arranged alphabetically to make it possible to look up procedures quickly, whether it is mouth-to-mouth resuscitation or the treatment of burns, fractures, bites, or whatever. This chapter will enable you to help yourself and others in emergencies.

The book opens with a description of the way in which the body works, describing its various systems such as the cardiovascular system, the digestive system, the respiratory system, and the properties of the skin and the functioning of the senses. This first chapter tells you something of the resources and structures of the body so that you can maintain and protect them in good health. Preventive health also depends upon an informed and healthy approach to sex, child bearing and rearing, diet, fitness, exercise, and, eventually, the onset of the inevitable aging process.

A detailed explanation of human sexuality follows in Chapter 2, with sections dealing with libido, conception and contraception, puberty, and sexual variations and diseases.

The central chapters (Chapters 3 to 7) follow the course of human life from birth to old age, tracing the natural progression of development in the body and the complaints and diseases most likely to occur at various times. The chapters on infant and child care, adolescence and young adulthood will steer you through the years of parenthood, from breast feeding, temper tantrums or chicken pox, to the problems of puberty or teenage acne, with all the minor and major problems in between.

The descriptive sections on problems and diseases given at the end of these chapters will help you to assess what is happening and whether any professional help is needed. These descriptions are listed in alphabetical order within the chapter dealing with the age group in which the illness most commonly (although not always), occurs. A comprehensive index to the book enables you to make easy reference to any subject.

The features of a healthy lifestyle and questions of environment and health are discussed in Chapter 8. Subjects which should help you to resist poor living habits in our contemporary and usually urban environment include diet and the nutritional needs of the body, the impact of environment on health, the use of exercise, problems of occupational health and the effects of pollution.

It is important for everyone today to take a positive attitude to maintaining health because of the impact of illness upon the family and the community as a whole. The cost of health to a family, community and country is extremely high, and these resources should be used where possible to support those who are an unavoidable charge upon the state; to help the helpless. Just as mothers have a responsibility to care for the young, so the young must care for the old, for no health system can play the role of daily guardian. Those who are healthy must remain so if they can, and do their utmost for those who are not.

To accompany a healthy body it is necessary to have a healthy mind free from abnormal states of anxiety, depression, neuroses, and phobia. These states are dealt with in Chapter 9, as are the forms of therapy. In a world where stress is common, mental illness sometimes goes unnoticed or is unsympathetically dealt with and it is important for all of us to be able to recognize in ourselves and others the fine dividing line between a normal state and an emotional disturbance that calls for qualified help.

It is not possible in a book of this size to touch on all medical knowledge and only the commoner illnesses have been described. So that the book can be easily read and understood, and to avoid the daunting use of much medical terminology, descriptions and technical terms have been translated into plain English wherever possible.

In medicine, as in other fields, there are areas where knowledge is still limited or where one medical authority may take a different viewpoint from another. In regard to some statements within the book, it is therefore possible that others in the medical field would hold a different opinion. However, to attempt to include many alternative ideas would be confusing, and although every effort has been made to show alternative views where possible, the most popularly held or current medical viewpoints are the ones generally presented or preferred.

1 How the Body Works

— Systems and Senses

Learning to Understand the Body

The human body has been a source of wonder, interest and speculation for many hundreds of years. Primitive peoples attributed its strange, complex and marvelous workings to the magic of their gods, its ailments to their displeasure.

Slowly but surely the search for real knowledge progressed — with many setbacks. For every far-seeing pioneer in the history of anatomy and medicine there were dozens of the fainthearted who clung to old beliefs even in the face of irrefutable evidence.

In Europe, the dominance of the Church slowed the impetus of early modern science and, although the monasteries provided the Middle Ages with caring hospitals and effective herbal remedies, the actual study of the body itself was hampered by the Church's antagonism towards human dissection.

The voluminous medical works of the Greek physician Galen, who lived in the second century A.D., were regarded as the absolute authority on anatomy for well over a thousand years. Galen was a skilled and clever medical pioneer whose writings contain much accurate observation although apparently he had to rely mainly on the dissection of animals rather than humans.

Although the surgeon William of Saliceto (1215–1280) wrote a treatise on human dissection which was the first real evidence of the practice in 'modern' times, and official studies of human anatomy were underway by the end of the 1400s, very little further knowledge was gained, as Galen was still held to be absolutely accurate, even when first-hand evidence revealed discrepancies between the written word and the facts.

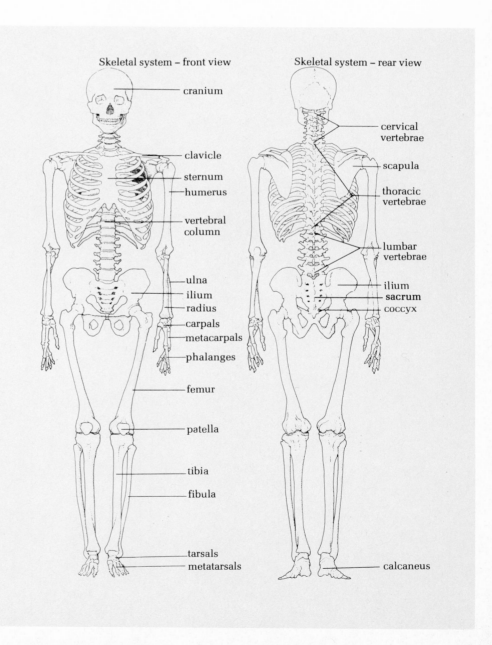

Skeletal system – front view

Skeletal system – rear view

- cranium
- clavicle
- sternum
- humerus
- vertebral column
- ulna
- ilium
- radius
- carpals
- metacarpals
- phalanges
- femur
- patella
- tibia
- fibula
- tarsals
- metatarsals

- cervical vertebrae
- scapula
- thoracic vertebrae
- lumbar vertebrae
- ilium
- **sacrum**
- coccyx
- calcaneus

Leonardo da Vinci (1452–1519) studied anatomy with a brilliant combination of artistic skill and scientific probing. He recorded his findings in profusely illustrated notebooks which were to have been the basis for an anatomical textbook he intended to produce in collaboration with Professor della Torre. Unfortunately the professor died at an early age and the book was never written; the notebooks were lost after Leonardo's death and rediscovered only in the twentieth century. Had they come to light when he died, the development of the study of anatomy would possibly have been advanced by many years.

While Leonardo's notebooks lay unnoticed over the years, it was left to Andreas Vesalius (1514–1564), a young and brilliant professor at the University of Padua, to dispense with unskilled assistants and, from observation while carrying out his own dissections, to confound the die-hard followers of Galen with his superb *De Humani Corporis Fabrica*, an exhaustive illustrated treatise on the human body.

In England also considerable difficulty was encountered in the early days by those doctors who wished to dissect human bodies, and although in 1540 licensed 'barber surgeons' were permitted to dissect on a limited scale, medicine mostly had to rely on second-hand anatomical information. John Bannister, who lectured the barber surgeons on anatomy, wrote an anatomical treatise (heavily influenced by Vesalius), and prepared a few independently researched drawings, but it was not until the seventeenth century that the great English doctor William Harvey evolved the system of detailed anatomical study which revolutionized the science all over the world.

The body can be trained to withstand enormous demands.

For something like two centuries thereafter anatomical study was largely an extension and refinement of these major developments of the fifteenth to seventeenth centuries, until the modern detailed study of cellular structure became the norm.

In the twentieth century most medical students in modern universities have continued to be required to dissect the human body as part of their early training. However, this type of training has decreased in recent years with the reduction in the length of most medical courses, and anatomy is taught more by lectures and the use of models than by requiring the students to dissect.

Nowadays, highly accurate and detailed anatomical photographs, many produced with the aid of sophisticated equipment such as the electron microscope, have replaced the painstaking drawings of earlier times. However, our modern scientific understanding of human anatomy owes a tremendous debt to Vesalius and Leonardo da Vinci, despite the loss of the latter's work for centuries, in making available accurate and artistic representations upon which our widespread general understanding of human anatomy and physiology is based today.

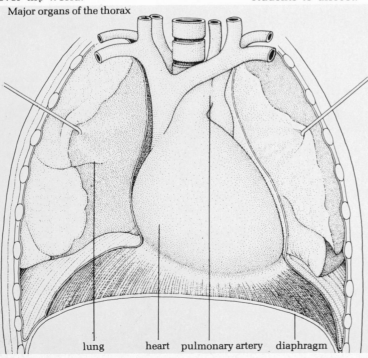

Major organs of the thorax

lung   heart   pulmonary artery   diaphragm

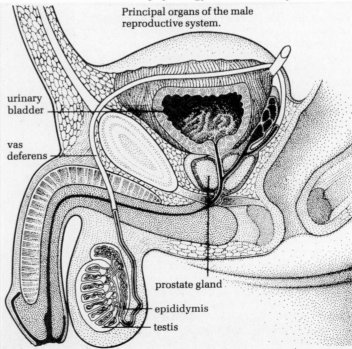

Principal organs of the male reproductive system.

urinary bladder

vas deferens

prostate gland

epididymis

testis

Looking at the body

It is possible to study the human body in many different ways. It could be discussed in terms of the individual organs; the heart, the liver, the stomach. It could be divided, for the purposes of anatomical description, into the major regions of head and neck; chest or thorax; abdomen; limbs. But as all the regions and organs are essentially interdependent, it is probably simplest to describe the body in terms of its systems, such as the musculoskeletal system expressed in the body's framework and muscles; the cardiovascular and respiratory systems expressed in the heart, blood vessels and lungs; and the nervous system expressed in the brain, nerves and spinal cord.

The following sections of this chapter will therefore describe in some detail the way in which the various body systems are made up and how they function, and also explain the way in which we relate to the outside world in terms of our senses of hearing, sight, smell, taste and touch, and through that major organ of sensation, the skin.

Cardiovascular System

There are three main components of the cardiovascular or circulatory system: the heart, the blood vessels, and the blood that flows within them.

The heart

The heart is the center of the system. It pumps about 10½ pints (5 L) of blood each minute and contracts about 70 times during that period. The number of beats per minute is called the heart rate. The fact that this process goes on continuously throughout life makes the heart a truly remarkable organ.

A muscular structure, about the size of a man's fist, the heart weighs, on average, 17½ ounces (500 grams). Situated within the chest cavity between the lungs and the breast bone (sternum), it lies predominantly on the left side, protected by the sternum and ribs.

The heart comprises three main layers. The middle layer or myocardium is by far the thickest and consists mostly of muscle. The contraction and relaxation of this muscle results in the heart's pumping action. The inner layer is called the endocardium; it is very thin and smooth and lines the inner surfaces of the heart chambers and the valves. The outer protective layer is more fibrous and tough and is called the pericardium. It is generally surrounded by a thin layer of fat.

The blood supply to the heart comes from the coronary arteries. These leave the aorta (the main artery that takes blood directly from the left ventricle) near its

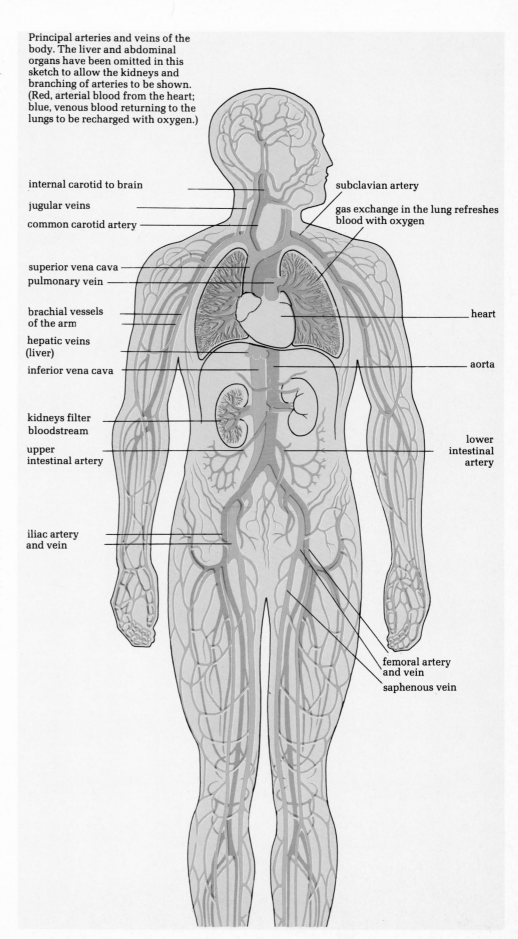

Principal arteries and veins of the body. The liver and abdominal organs have been omitted in this sketch to allow the kidneys and branching of arteries to be shown. (Red, arterial blood from the heart; blue, venous blood returning to the lungs to be recharged with oxygen.)

internal carotid to brain

jugular veins

common carotid artery

superior vena cava

pulmonary vein

brachial vessels of the arm

hepatic veins (liver)

inferior vena cava

kidneys filter bloodstream

upper intestinal artery

iliac artery and vein

subclavian artery

gas exchange in the lung refreshes blood with oxygen

heart

aorta

lower intestinal artery

femoral artery and vein

saphenous vein

origin and form a branching network over the surface of the heart.

The action of the heart The heart is usually described in terms of the 'left' and 'right' heart, each comprising two chambers, the atrium (inflow chamber), and the ventricle (outflow chamber). Blood from the body returns to the right atrium and then into the right ventricle to be 'squeezed' into the lungs to be oxygenated. From there it returns to the left atrium and then the left ventricle from where it circulates to all the other tissues and organs of the body.

The heart has its own special set of nerve fibers which regulate its action. The key to this action is a small area of nervous tissue called the sino-atrial (SA) node, situated in the tissues of the atrium. This so-called pacemaker fires off regularly some 60–80 impulses a minute, and these spread through the myocardium of the atria to initiate their contraction and through the atrio-ventricular node which transmits them to the special conductive tissue called the bundle of His. This is a branching network of specialized muscle cells through which electrical impulses are transmitted to all portions of the ventricles, causing them to contract.

The firing rate of the heart's pacemaker is partially controlled by the autonomic nervous system and may respond almost instantly to stress or exertion. A heart rate of over 180 beats per minute, increasing the output of blood by more than ten fold, can be achieved.

1 The heart develops from a tube in the neck of the embryo. Before birth, the fetus has a single circulation, the lung circulation being parallel to the general circulation. (*Zefa*)

2 Anterior view of the heart showing the network of blood supply vessels. (*John Watney Photo Library*)

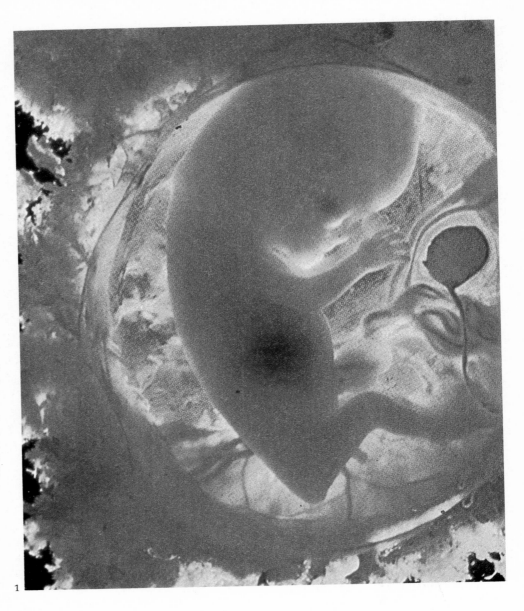

1

2

Blood

The life and health of every cell in the body depends on an adequate circulation of blood, a fluid which is pumped by the heart through the arteries, capillaries and veins of all tissues and organs. The fluid (about two-thirds plasma and one-third cells) carries into the tissues nutrients absorbed by the bowel from food, oxygen absorbed from the lungs, hormones manufactured by the endocrine glands, and anti-infective agents.

Waste products of cellular metabolism, such as carbon dioxide and urea, are conveyed in the blood from the tissues to the organs which effect their elimination from the body, namely the lungs and kidneys.

Human blood vessels contain about 12½ pints (6 L) of blood and, since the heart pumps at the rate of 10½ pints (5 L) per minute while the body is at rest, nearly all the blood supply circulates through the body every minute. During heavy exercise, the output of the heart increases four to five times and 42–53 pints (20–25 L) of blood are pumped around the body each minute.

This means that all the blood circulates through the body every 15–20 seconds during strenuous exercise, such is the demand for nutrients and oxygen and so rapid the accumulation of waste products in the tissues. Thus, the composition of blood varies continuously within certain limits according to the activities being performed, as the various tissues and organs take from it what they need and add waste products to it.

Blood is made up of a transparent, yellowish fluid (plasma), in which large numbers of different types of cells are suspended: red cells (erythrocytes), white cells (leukocytes) and platelets (thrombocytes). All the cells are being destroyed continuously and replaced by newly formed cells, and a finely regulated balance exists between the rate of formation and destruction, keeping the numbers of each cell type constant.

Red cells The body's cells are circular, non-nucleated, bi-concave discs about 7 microns in diameter. Their permeable membrane is very elastic and they are capable of considerable distortion as they squeeze along narrow capillaries. Male adults have about 5.5 million red cells in a cubic millimeter of blood, and females about 4.8 million.

Red cells are made in red bone marrow, most of which occurs in the ends of long bones, in flat bones like the skull and sternum, and in the vertebrae. The bone marrow is stimulated to make more red cells by a low oxygen level (as is found at high altitudes or in people with lung disease) and by the hormone erythropoietin.

Red cells live for about 120 days, old and damaged cells being destroyed mainly by the spleen. Therefore, approximately nine billion red cells are being destroyed and nine billion new ones are being made every hour.

About 30 per cent of each red cell consists of the substance which gives the cell its red color, the compound hemoglobin, a combination of an iron-containing pigment called heme with the protein globin. Male adults have approximately 0.6 ounce (15.8 gm) of hemoglobin in every 100 milliliters of blood, and females about 0.5 ounce (14 gm).

Hemoglobin combines reversibly with oxygen as it is carried in the red cells through the lungs. In the tissues, the hemoglobin releases the oxygen and combines with carbon dioxide, which it releases next time it passes through the lungs to take up another load of oxygen. A single ounce (28.3 gm) of hemoglobin, when fully saturated, has combined with 0.05 fluid ounces (1.34 mL) of oxygen. The amount of hemoglobin in the blood is therefore a direct measure of its oxygen-carrying capacity.

When red cells are destroyed (mostly by the spleen), the hemoglobin is broken down into the protein globin (which is re-used), iron (which is carefully stored in the body for re-use), and bilirubin. The bilirubin is joined to a plasma protein (globulin) which renders it soluble in the plasma. When red cell breakdown is excessive (as in sufferers from hemolytic anemia), large amounts of bilirubin accumulate in the blood, and impart a yellow tinge to the whites of the eyes and skin (jaundice).

The bilirubin-protein combination is removed from the blood by the liver, joined with glucuronic acid and excreted in the bile into the intestines where bacteria break it down into urobilinogen (stercobilinogen). Some urobilinogen is excreted in the feces and gives the characteristic brown colour; some is reabsorbed

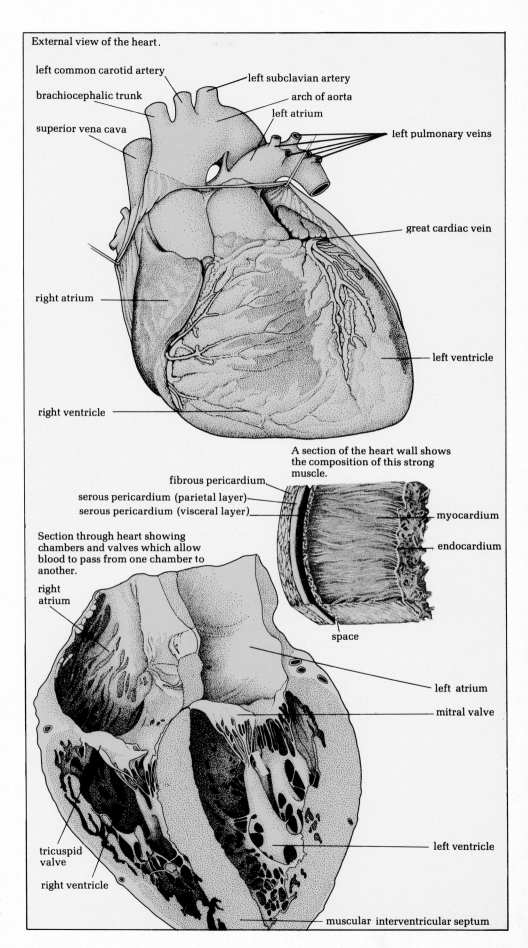

External view of the heart.

left common carotid artery
brachiocephalic trunk
superior vena cava
left subclavian artery
arch of aorta
left atrium
left pulmonary veins
great cardiac vein
right atrium
left ventricle
right ventricle

A section of the heart wall shows the composition of this strong muscle.

fibrous pericardium
serous pericardium (parietal layer)
serous pericardium (visceral layer)
myocardium
endocardium
space

Section through heart showing chambers and valves which allow blood to pass from one chamber to another.

right atrium
left atrium
mitral valve
left ventricle
tricuspid valve
right ventricle
muscular interventricular septum

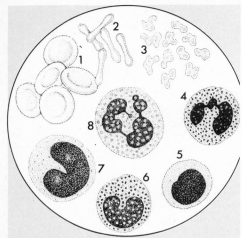

Cellular components of blood.

1 red corpuscles (front view) 5 lymphocyte
2 red corpuscles (side view)   6 basophil
3 platelets   7 monocyte
4 eosinophil   8 neutrophil

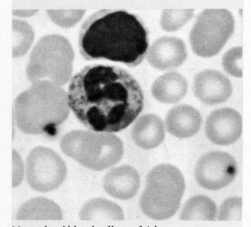

Normal red blood cells are fairly even in size and shape. A neutrophil polymorphonuclear leucocyte and a lymphocyte are seen. (Abbottempo)

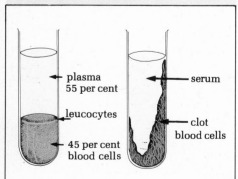

plasma 55 per cent

serum

leucocytes

clot blood cells

45 per cent blood cells

The difference between blood plasma and blood serum. Plasma is whole blood without cells and is made by centrifuging blood. Serum is whole blood without clotting agents and is made by clotting blood.

into the blood to be re-excreted in the bile and excreted by the kidneys in the urine.

The two common blood tests involving red cells are the red cell count per cubic millimeter, and the hemoglobin content of blood (in grams per 100 milliliters).

White cells The white blood cells are of three main types; the granulocytes, the lymphocytes, and the monocytes. In a normal circulation, the body has between 4 000 and 11 000 white cells in a cubic millimeter of blood, and they are very important in the defence of the body against infection.

Granulocytes are 10–14 microns in diameter and make up 50–70 per cent of the white cell count. They are characterized by a lobed nucleus and granules in their cytoplasm. Granulocytes are produced in the red bone marrow and destroyed and replaced in less than a week. When stained with Leishman's stain, three types of granulocytes can be distinguished:

(a) Neutrophils, also called polymorphonuclear leukocytes, make up 50–70 per cent of the white cell count, have fine red-brown granules and are sufficiently motile to pass through the walls of capillary blood vessels into the tissues and surround, engulf and destroy foreign material like invading micro-organisms.

(b) Eosinophils, which make up 1–4 per cent of the white cell count, are full of large red granules and contain histamine.

(c) Basophils, 0–1 per cent of the white cell count, contain purple-blue granules and are the chief carriers of histamine in the blood.

Lymphocytes vary from 7–14 microns in diameter and constitute 20–40 per cent of the white cell count. Round, non-granular cells with large nuclei, they are formed in the lymphoid tissue of the body (the lymph nodes, spleen, tonsils, etc.) and last only a few hours in the circulation. They are motile cells which make and transport antibodies.

Monocytes are 10–18 microns in diameter and make up 2–8 per cent of the white cell count. They are large pale cells which contribute to the defense of the body by destroying bacteria, foreign material, and debris like the remains of dead leucocytes.

Blood platelets are small, non-nucleated bodies with a concentration of 300 000 per cubic millimeter of blood. To prevent blood loss following injury, the platelets clump together to plug the damaged blood vessel before breaking up and liberating a variety of chemical factors which, with other factors present in the blood and tissues, begin a chain reaction which eventually converts circulating fibrinogen into insoluble threads of fibrin. These fibrin threads enmesh white and red cells, and a jelly-like mass, or clot results.

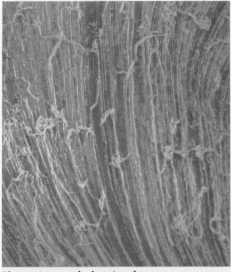

Photomicrograph showing the pattern of blood vessels in the kidneys. (Elsevier)

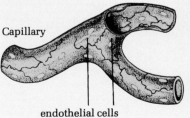

Artery

outer coat (tunica adventitia)

elastic and white fibrous tissue

muscle coat (tunica media) – thick in arteries and thin in veins

lining (tunica intima) of endothelium

Vein

valve

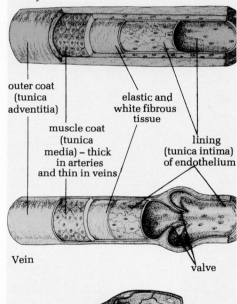

Capillary

endothelial cells

Comparison between artery, vein and capillary, showing difference in thicknesses of the coats: the muscle and outer coats are much thinner in veins than in arteries and the veins have valves. The walls of capillaries consist of only a single layer of endothelial cells. They have no smooth muscle layer, elastic fibres, or surrounding adventitia.

Plasma About one-half of the blood is a transparent yellowish fluid called plasma, composed of:

(*i*) water (90 per cent)

(*ii*) mineral salts and ions (such as sodium chloride and bicarbonate, potassium, magnesium, calcium, iron, copper, iodine)

(*iii*) plasma proteins (such as albumin, globulin, fibrinogen)

(*iv*) nutrient substances from digested food (glucose, fats, amino acids)

(*v*) organic wastes (urea, uric acid, creatinine)

(*vi*) gases (oxygen, nitrogen, carbon dioxide)

(*vii*) hormones, enzymes, antibodies.

Serum If blood is allowed to clot and the clot is removed, the remaining fluid is called serum. Its composition varies from that of plasma because the fibrinogen and other clotting factors have been removed.

Human red cells contain a number of inherited blood group substances known as blood group antigens. About ten groups of antigens have been discovered, but only the ABO and Rh systems are of major clinical significance.

Each person's serum contains the antibodies against the antigens lacking in his red cells. When blood containing an antigen is mixed with blood containing its specific antibody, clumping (agglutination) of the red cells or their dissolution (hemolysis) may occur. This is why, prior to giving a blood transfusion, the blood groups of the patient's and donor's blood must be determined, and donor blood of the recipient's group selected. Then samples of both bloods are mixed together (cross-matched) to see if clumping of the red cells occurs. If there is no reaction the donor blood is compatible with the blood of the recipient. Transfusing incompatible blood is often fatal, such is the severity of the antibody/antigen reaction.

Blood vessels

In the adult, approximately 12½ pints (6 L) of blood moves round the body constantly through a system of tubes called blood vessels. The heart is the pump which at rest has a stroke volume of 70 ml per beat, a rate of 70 beats per minute and an output of 10½ pints (5 L) per minute.

The function of the circulation of the blood is to deliver oxygen from the lungs to the other parts of the body, to collect waste and toxic substances from the tissues and deliver them to the lungs, kidneys and the liver for removal, and to carry nutrients from the gut to the liver and from there to the tissues to allow for their growth and maintenance.

The blood is allowed to flow in one direction only by a system of valves within the heart and the veins. Normally it takes only half a minute for a particular red cell to circulate completely round the body.

Arteries carry blood away from the heart and branch into minute vessels, the

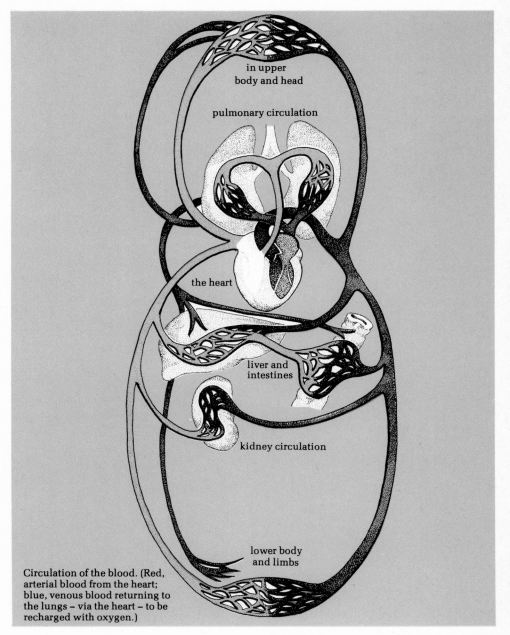

Circulation of the blood. (Red, arterial blood from the heart; blue, venous blood returning to the lungs – via the heart – to be recharged with oxygen.)

arterioles, which in their turn are continuous with microscopic vessels, the capillaries. The capillaries connect the smallest ramifications of the arteries with those of the veins, called venules; venules join with one another to form veins, which return blood to the heart.

The Vessels *Arteries* are made up of three layers: an internal intima, a middle media containing smooth muscle supported by a fibrous tissue, and an outer adventitia.

Capillaries lack the outer two layers and have a wall only one cell thick; they average less than 0.01 millimetres in diameter.

Veins have three layers but the muscular media is less well developed. Many veins also possess valves which prevent the backflow of blood.

Two systems of blood circulation function in the body, the pulmonary and systemic circulations.

The pulmonary circulation carries blood to and from the lungs. In the lung capillaries, the blood is brought into close relationship with air, it gives off some of its carbon dioxide and acquires a fresh supply of oxygen. Thus, the pulmonary arteries carry oxygen-poor blood from the right heart chambers to the lungs.

The systemic circulation distributes to, and collects from, all the other tissues and organs of the body. In the systemic capillaries, oxygen, nutritive materials and hormones are given to the tissues, and exchanged for carbon dioxide and other waste products.

Thus, the main systemic artery, the aorta, and its branches carry oxygen-rich blood from the left heart chambers to the tissues, and the veins return oxygen-poor blood to the right heart chambers, through the two major veins, the superior vena

The functioning of the heart cycle. *(Red, arterial blood from the heart; blue, venous blood returning to the lungs — via the heart — to be recharged with oxygen.)*

1 Diastole

Atria closed and filling with blood; the right heart with deoxygenated blood from the body, the left heart with oxygenated blood from the lungs.

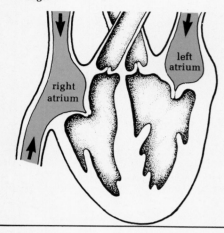

2 Diastole

Atria open and emptying of blood. Ventricles filling with blood.

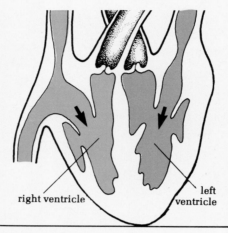

3 Systole

Ventricles open, sending blood from the right heart into the pulmonary artery and thence to the lungs, and the blood from the left heart into the aorta and thence to the body.

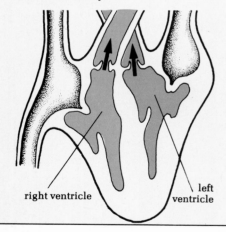

4 Systole

Atria closed and filling with blood from the body and lungs.

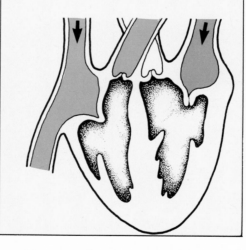

cava and inferior vena cava. It should be noted, however, that the circulation in the fetus is quite different.

The circulatory system In the normal person dark red de-oxygenated blood returns to the heart from all parts of the body in the upper and lower large veins (superior and inferior *venae cavae*). It enters the right-hand chambers of the heart (right atrium through the tricuspid valve to the right ventricle) from where it is ejected into the large artery leading to the lungs (pulmonary artery).

There the blood is re-oxygenated, becoming bright red in the process, and is returned to the left side of the heart (left atrium through the mitral valve to the left ventricle) from where it is ejected under greater pressure into the aorta and the rest of the arterial system which delivers blood to all organs, including heart muscle itself.

The arteries branch and rebranch, becoming smaller until they become fine-walled capillary vessels where gaseous exchange occurs, transferring oxygen from the blood to the tissues. The de-oxygenated blood then passes into small veins or venules which gradually join one another to form larger veins and finally the superior and inferior vena cava

vessels which discharge the blood back into the right atrium.

Regulation of blood flow The circulatory system is not fixed or static. To be effective it must be able to maintain an almost constant blood flow to vital organs during periods of exercise, regardless of changes (within limits) in posture and environmental temperature. The blood flow is controlled by many different nervous and hormonal mechanisms which are capable of varying flow under different circumstances.

In an emergency the blood flow to the kidneys, brain and liver is maintained at the expense of blood flow to the muscles or the gut. If the temperature of the environment alters, the blood flow through the skin is changed to maintain a constant body temperature.

The brain, which gets 15 per cent of the total cardiac output, requires a constant supply of oxygenated blood as otherwise the brain cells die very quickly. A special mechanism adjusts the blood pressure when the person is upright so that the brain receives a constant blood supply regardless of posture.

Oxygen and carbon dioxide exchange Gas exchange takes place at two sites, in the tiny vessels of the lungs (pulmonary capillaries) and in the capillary bed of the tissues. In the lungs oxygen is taken up from the air and enters the red blood cells combining with hemoglobin, while carbon dioxide is released from the plasma into the air in the lungs and expired. In the tissue capillary bed the reverse occurs; the blood loses its oxygen to the tissues which need it for their cells to function and carbon dioxide produced by cell metabolism enters the blood plasma in solution.

The gut has a large blood supply which allows the products of digestion to be taken through the bowel wall and conveyed in a special internal circuit called the portal venous system. The portal vein is the chief trunk to the liver where it divides and ends in a capillary system. The nutrients the system brings to the liver are metabolized there and either stored or used for synthesis of the body tissues.

Blood coagulation

The process by which fluid blood is changed into a more solid state or clot (thrombus) is called coagulation. In the event of an injury to any organ or tissue the bleeding is stopped by the small vessels contracting, the platelets in the blood plugging up the hole in the damaged vessel and by the process of blood coagulation which involves a chain of reactions of at least twelve different factors (proteins) in the blood.

Sometimes clots form inappropriately and can be life threatening when they travel about in the bloodstream and obstruct blood vessels in vital areas like the lungs, the brain or the heart. In other disorders a clot fails to form when it should, giving rise to continued bleeding. This is the case when there is a deficiency in one of the twelve clotting factors.

Coagulating systems Our knowledge of blood coagulation is limited, complicated and diverse and much is hypothetical. Different schemes have been put forward with variations. However, all the schemes distinguish between an *intrinsic system*, a series of biochemical reactions, which occurs in the blood itself and an *extrinsic system* which is a chain of reactions activated by chemicals released from damaged tissues.

Each clotting factor has an inactive precursor which, once the process of clotting commences, provides an active enzyme ('a') and this sets the next stage of the chain or cascade reaction going.

Blood clotting factors To identify the factors they are designated I to XIII. The following list gives their common names.

Factor I, fibrinogen.
Factor II, prothrombin.
Factor III, original tissue thromboplastin.
Factor IV, calcium.
Factor V, proaccelerin, labile factor, thrombogen.
Factor VI, the activated form of factor V.
Factor VII, proconvertin stable factor, serum prothrombin conversion acceleration (SPCA).
Factor VIII, antihemophilic factor (AHF), antihemophilic globulin (AHG), thromboplastinogen.
Factor IX, Christmas factor.
Factor X, Stuart factor, Prower factor.
Factor XI, plasma thromboplasmin antecedent (PTA).
Factor XII, Hageman factor.
Factor XIII, fibrin stabilizing factor, fibrinase, Laki-lorand factor.

Following the formation of a blood clot by the coagulation process, the next step in the clot formation is that of clot retraction, the result of shrinkage of the fibrin strands within the clot. If factors are missing or present in reduced quantities, as occurs in certain diseases such as hemophilia, bleeding is prevented with great difficulty and the smallest cut or injury may lead to great loss of blood.

Laboratory tests are available to test the functioning of the coagulation pathway and help to determine the cause of bleeding disorders. The tests of the function of blood coagulation include the partial thromboplastin time (PTT), the plasma prothrombin time, the clotting time of whole blood, the thromboplastin generation test, the prothrombin consumption test and the plasma thrombin time.

Drugs are available to lessen any tendency to the excessive coagulation of blood and the amount of drug required is monitored by using tests of blood coagulation.

Intrinsic system of blood clotting ('a' is the active form of the enzyme)

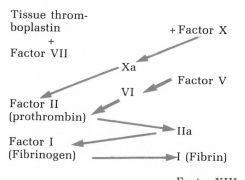

Factor XII → XIIa
Factor XI ← XIa
Factor IX (Christmas) ← IXa
Factor VIII (AHG) → VIIIa
Factor X → Xa ← Factor V
VI ← A platelet factor
Factor II (Prothrombin) → IIa
Factor I (Fibrinogen) → I as fibrin

CLOT

Factor XIII strengthens fibrin

Extrinsic system of blood clotting

Tissue thromboplastin
+
Factor VII   + Factor X

Xa
VI ← Factor V
Factor II (prothrombin)
IIa
Factor I (Fibrinogen) → I (Fibrin)

Factor XIII strengthens fibrin clot

Note: Factor IV (calcium ions) is required at various stages

Blood groups

When hemorrhage occurs, the body can usually cope with the fluid and blood cell loss if the volume removed from the circulation is less than 2 pints (1 L) (in an adult). A greater loss of blood requires replacement by blood transfusion to prevent the possible development of shock.

Attempts at blood transfusion were made in the last century, but problems often arose because the blood cells from the donor clumped together when they came in contact with the plasma of the other person. In 1900, Karl Landsteiner, an Austrian-born biologist, introduced the concept of blood groups, and this became the basis of matching blood for planned transfusions.

The many specific protein substances (antigens) on the surface of red blood cells are inherited from one's parents. Two systems of antigens are of particular importance in blood transfusions, the ABO system and the Rh system.

ABO antigen system The ABO system was identified first by Landsteiner and is based on determining whether the red blood cell has on its surface special types of antigen called A and B. The antigens may occur on their own, together, or be completely absent. These combinations are represented as groups A, B, AB (both present), and O (neither present).

In studies carried out among the Caucasian population, it has been ascertained that group A is present in about 42 per cent, group B in 9 per cent, group AB in 3 per cent, and group O accounts for the remaining 46 per cent.

In people who live at high altitudes, with low oxygen levels, bone marrow is stimulated to produce more red blood cells so that oxygen-carrying capacity is increased.

These diagrams show blood cells before and after agglutination or clumping together.

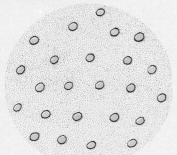

non-agglutination

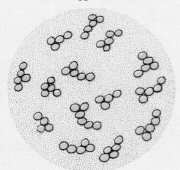

agglutination

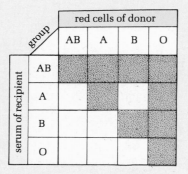

group	red cells of donor			
serum of recipient	AB	A	B	O
AB				
A				
B				
O				

Compatibility of blood cells. Red cells of donor are mixed with serum of recipient to test for agglutination. Colored areas show compatibility.

Group A blood has a special protein antibody, called anti-B, in its plasma which will attach to the B antigen on any red blood cells from a group B person and cause these cells to clump together. Similarly, group B blood contains a corresponding antibody called anti-A. Group AB people do not have any anti-A or anti-B. Group O people possess both anti-A and anti-B, although both these antibodies are normally present in very low levels.

To ensure that no clumping (agglutination) occurs during transfusion, it is best to have a blood donor and a recipient with the same ABO blood group. In an emergency, however, group O blood can be given to all other types because the levels of anti-A and anti-B are normally too low to cause any problems, and for

this reason Group O is known as the 'universal donor'. Group AB blood contains no anti-A or anti-B: it will not cause clumping in any donor blood of a different type and is therefore known as the 'universal recipient'.

RH antigen system The other major blood grouping system, the Rhesus or RH system, was discovered in 1940 and three antigens, called C, D and E, were identified. The antigen D is the most common, being present in 85 per cent of the Caucasian population, and blood with this antigen is called Rhesus (or RH) positive. The remaining 15 per cent have Rh negative blood.

There is normally no anti-D antibody in the blood of Rh negative people; however, transfusion of Rh positive blood into an Rh negative recipient will cause a slow development of anti-D antibodies. This production is too slow to cause problems during the initial transfusion. The level of anti-D remains high, so a second incorrect transfusion of Rh positive blood into an Rh negative person may produce severe agglutination.

The importance of recognizing the Rh blood types lies not only with matching blood for transfusions, but also becomes a vital piece of knowledge during pregnancy. When an Rh negative mother is carrying an Rh positive baby, a problem situation develops, because red cells from the fetus escape across the placenta to the mother. Because the mother's blood has no Rh factor, the cells appear as foreign matter to her bloodstream and she forms antibodies against the Rh factor. These antibodies pass back across the placenta to the baby's bloodstream where they destroy the baby's red cells and may cause death.

There are several ways of preventing such a disaster. For example, women who are found to be Rh negative can be immunized against Rh positive blood before they become pregnant, or the fetus may be transfused with Rh negative blood while it is still in the mother's uterus.

Other systems There are at least seven other blood grouping systems in man, including such groups as Kell, Lutheran, Duffy and Kidd. On the whole, incompatibility of these blood groups carries minor reactions, such as fever or rash.

The number of different antigens demonstrated to be on a red blood cell means that a person's overall blood grouping is as personal as his signature. An incompatibility in blood groups (particularly the ABO system) is one method used by forensic scientists to demonstrate that a man could not be the father of a child, although it is not yet possible to prove that a certain man is the father.

Blood pressure

Though the term blood pressure is often used to signify *elevated* blood pressure, this condition is more correctly known as hypertension. Blood pressure is measured in millimeters of mercury, and represents the pressure of blood within the vessels.

Because of the pumping action of the heart, the pressure levels have a wave form, falling in between heart beats. The peak pressure is called the *systolic pressure*, while the lowest point represents the *diastolic pressure*. Thus blood pressure is recorded as two numbers — for example 120/80 — the first (higher) pressure being the systolic, and the second being the diastolic.

Blood pressure can vary markedly, especially the systolic value, which usually rises with any increase in the heart rate or

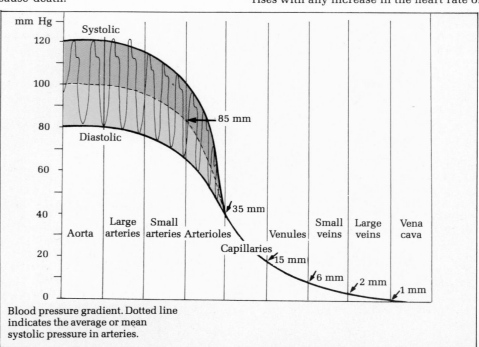

Blood pressure gradient. Dotted line indicates the average or mean systolic pressure in arteries.

output, such as occurs during exercise or times of increased emotion.

Blood pressure tends to increase slightly with advancing age. The normal range of blood pressure is 100 to 140 for systolic, and 70 to 90 for diastolic pressures. Older people tend to have a slightly higher diastolic pressure, usually between 90 and 95 millimeters of mercury. Their systolic pressure may extend up to 160 mm.

In many situations the blood pressure is clearly elevated, and is defined as hypertension. There is, however, a 'grey zone' between the lower levels of hypertension and the upper levels of normal blood pressure. In general, the blood pressure is considered to be abnormally elevated if the systolic value is 160 mm or above, and the diastolic is 90 mm or above.

How blood pressure is measured Blood pressure is measured with a sphygmomanometer and a stethoscope. An inflatable cuff is usually wrapped around the upper arm (but can be wrapped around the thigh), and then pumped up. The cuff is connected to a pressure-measuring device, and once the pressure is higher than the systolic value, no blood flow occurs.

When the pressure applied by the cuff is less than the diastolic pressure, blood flow is undisturbed. In both these situations no sounds will be heard by a stethoscope placed over the artery just below the cuff.

Between these two pressures, however, as the cuff is being deflated slowly there will be some narrowing of the blood vessel and the blood flow will be turbulent. This turbulence produces a clearly audible sound. Thus the pressure at which these sounds begin is the systolic pressure and the pressure when they cease is the diastolic pressure.

Body mechanisms which control blood pressure Muscle in the walls of the arteries and the arterioles contains nerve endings from the autonomic nervous system which control the tension in the muscle, and hence the diameter of the vessel's lumen. Not only does this control blood flow, but also the pressure of the blood within these vessels because of the altered resistance offered to the flow.

An important example of this process is shown when the skin's blood vessels constrict in response to cold or loss of blood. The blood vessels narrow down, not only to restrict heat loss from the body, but also to maintain adequate blood flow to essential tissues such as the brain, heart and kidneys.

Nerves from the autonomic nervous system also affect the heart muscle. Some of them can stimulate it to beat more rapidly and forcefully, while others have the opposite effect. When the output per minute from the heart is increased, the blood pressure is also increased.

Both the narrowing of vessels and increased activity of the heart are, therefore, normal body mechanisms used to maintain normal blood pressure and circulation even in the face of blood loss or dehydration.

A special set of nerve fibers is activated when the overall blood volume drops. Pituitary and adrenal gland activity is instituted by these nerves, and this decreases the loss of fluid from the kidneys. A feeling of thirst is also stimulated. Through their effect on monitoring blood volume, the glands have a role in the maintenance of normal blood pressure.

In some cases the control of these factors may become ineffective. The pressure may become abnormally high (high blood pressure or hypertension) or abnormally low (low blood pressure or hypotension).

Digestive System

Together with the alimentary canal (comprising the series of organs from the mouth to the anus through which food passes) the other organs of the digestive system are the salivary glands, liver, gall bladder and pancreas.

Common complaints

Even quite trivial disorders of the mouth and tongue can be distressing. Unsightly and unpleasant splits at the side of the mouth are usually the result of a vitamin deficiency while a furry tongue, apart from indicating a heavy smoker, usually has no medical significance. Mouth ulcers are unpleasant, and a nuisance, but should heal quickly. Any ulcer or sore that fails to heal should be regarded with suspicion and shown to a doctor. A dry mouth may be caused by breathing with an open mouth, high fever, dehydration or as a side effect of some medicines, particularly antihistamines.

A most distressing symptom is that of difficulty swallowing. Frequently the sensation of a 'lump in the throat' is a reflection of anxiety and stress; a physical manifestation of an emotional state. True swallowing difficulties, which generally become apparent more slowly, may indicate a serious disorder.

In almost any bodily upset, especially illnesses associated with fever, a feeling of nausea or even vomiting is common. Prolonged vomiting or vomiting blood, however, indicates a more serious condition.

When diarrhea accompanies vomiting the cause is often gastroenteritis. Diarrhea may also be the result of a viral or bacterial infection, failure to absorb food properly or a side effect of medicines, especially antibiotics. Pain which occurs an hour after eating may indicate a peptic ulcer. Ulcer pain may be relieved by vomiting, by eating or by drinking milk or antacids.

An obstruction of the small bowel may cause vomiting, pain and a blockage of the bowel motion. Frequently, a past abdominal operation may make adhesions of the bowel wall likely.

Constipation is largely the result of inadequate fiber intake, or poor bowel habits which develop because of being too busy or because of social embarrassment. Feces which contain blood may signify hemorrhoids or, if mixed with mucus, may be caused by inflammation of the bowel wall, dysentery or ulcerative colitis. Any change in bowel habit or loss of weight, especially if it is progressive and unexplained, is a significant symptom and should be investigated.

Digestive system function

Digestion is the process of breaking down food so that it can be absorbed through the wall of the stomach and small bowel. The main components of food that are absorbed are fats, carbohydrates, proteins, salts (or electrolytes), vitamins and water.

The initial stages of digestion, mechanical and chemical, occur in the mouth. The cutting and grinding action of the teeth allows easy access of digestive juices to the food. Saliva, produced by three pairs of salivary glands that open via

To a child, the sweet taste is more important than possible unpleasant after-effects.

ducts into the mouth, acts as a lubricant to facilitate swallowing but it also contains ptyalin, an enzyme which begins the chemical breakdown of food. As the food is mixed with saliva, ptyalin commences to break down starches (carbohydrates) into simple sugars. Lubricated, chewed food is swallowed via the pharynx into the esophagus (or gullet) as a soft mass called a bolus. Once food has passed through the upper third of the esophagus, the control of digestion and the physical transport of the food material occurs automatically under the control of the autonomic nervous system. The increasingly digested food, and later the residual feces, are moved along by the process of peristalsis. Alternating waves of contraction and relaxation of the smooth muscle in the wall of the alimentary canal squeeze the food material along its length. These waves of contraction and relaxation, when occurring in an empty stomach, produce the so-called hunger pangs.

Stomach Once the food has entered the stomach from the esophagus, it is rhythmically churned up by peristaltic action. A special band of muscle, or sphincter, at

the junction of the esophagus and stomach prevents food from being regurgitated back into the esophagus.

The cells that line the stomach produce a highly acidic fluid called *gastric juice* which further facilitates the process of digestion. The main enzymes contained in gastric juice are *pepsin* and *rennin*. Pepsin commences the breakdown of proteins into smaller units called polypeptides. Rennin, which aids in the digestion of milk products, is particularly important in early infancy.

As well as its role in the process of digestion, the stomach also acts as a reservoir. Although meals are taken infrequently, because of a strong sphincter or band of muscle at the lower end of the stomach, only small amounts of the partially digested food, now called chyme, are released intermittently into the duodenum, the first part of the small bowel. This process of slow release occurs for several hours after a large meal.

Small intestine A long, narrow tube, the small intestine is almost 23 feet (7 m) long, with a diameter of approximately 0.8–2 inches (2–5 cm) gradually decreasing

along its length. The first part, or duodenum, is only about 8–10 inches (20–25 cm) long; the second part, the jejunum is about 8 feet (2.5 m) long; and the final part, or ileum, measures almost 13 feet (4 m).

The small intestine occupies most of the abdominal cavity as a series of loosely packed loops. It is connected to the back wall of the abdomen by a fine web-like tissue called the mesentery, which carries the fine networks of blood vessels; the lymphatic vessels, which carry some of the nutrients from the food to body tissues; and the autonomic nerve fibres which regulate the process of peristalsis.

Secretions in the small intestine continue the chemical breakdown of the food. Once food has entered the duodenum, pancreatic juice from the pancreas gland is released, along with bile, which is produced by the liver and then stored in the gall bladder. Two ducts, called the pancreatic duct and the bile duct respectively, usually join just before entering the duodenum at the sphincter of Oddi. Occasionally these two ducts enter the duodenum separately.

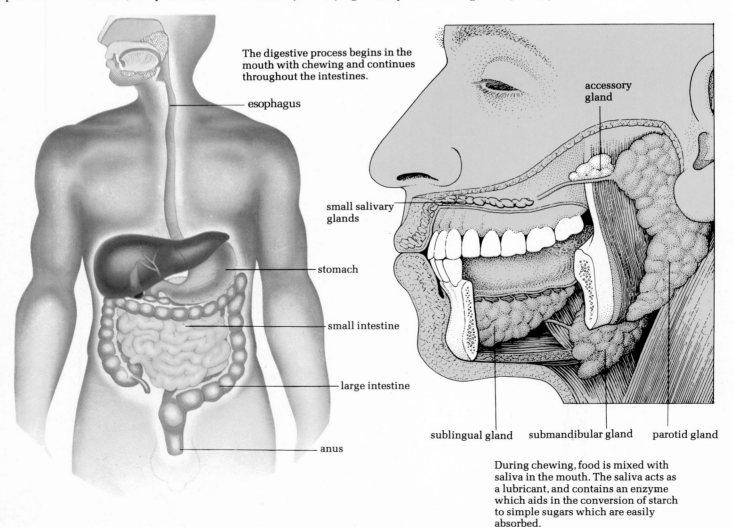

The digestive process begins in the mouth with chewing and continues throughout the intestines.

esophagus

stomach

small intestine

large intestine

anus

accessory gland

small salivary glands

sublingual gland   submandibular gland   parotid gland

During chewing, food is mixed with saliva in the mouth. The saliva acts as a lubricant, and contains an enzyme which aids in the conversion of starch to simple sugars which are easily absorbed.

Bile and pancreatic juice, which are both alkaline, help to neutralize the acidity of the chyme from the stomach. Bile consists of bile salts and pigments which include breakdown products of hemoglobin, an essential component of red blood cells. The gall bladder, which stores bile, contracts and releases a quantity of bile whenever food, especially fats, enters the duodenum.

The gall bladder, which is not an essential organ in man, may be removed surgically in certain conditions, particularly when it is severely inflamed (cholecystitis) or when gallstones develop (cholelithiasis). The bile salts combine with fats to make them soluble in water, and to prepare them for breakdown by enzymes in the pancreatic juice. This juice contains enzymes including trypsin which breaks down proteins; amylopsin which breaks down carbohydrates, particularly starches; and lipases which act on the emulsified fats and fatty acids.

Digestion and absorption of nutrients is completed within the small intestine. The internal lining of the intestine has millions of small projections called villi, approximately .025 inch (1 mm) in length and extending into the inner space of the bowel. The cells that line these villi absorb nutrients; over 95 per cent of the food's nutrient value is actually absorbed.

Further chemical changes occur once the nutrients have been absorbed into the cells lining the villi. They are then absorbed into the bloodstream to be transported to the liver or into lymphatic vessels which mainly carry the products of fat digestion.

The pancreas is a fleshy gland about 6 inches (15 cm) long, situated deep in the upper part of the abdomen. Its broadest portion, the head of the pancreas, is found on the right side in the curve of the duodenum. The gland narrows as it passes to the left forming the tail of the pancreas which extends upwards slightly, ending close to the spleen.

The exocrine (external) function of the pancreas is concerned with excreting various fluids into the duct. It daily produces between 2–8½ pints (1–4 L) of pancreatic juice, essential for the digestive process. Production of this fluid is largely precipitated by the hormones secretin and pancreozymin, released by the stomach acids from cells that line the upper part of the small intestine. The vagus nerve and gastrin (a hormone released from the stomach) also assist pancreatic secretion.

The pancreatic juice contains enzymes that help break down protein, fats and carbohydrates, as well as considerable amounts of sodium bicarbonate. The latter helps to neutralize the hydrochloric acid, secreted from the stomach into the duodenum, and found in the chyme.

Connected to small ductules that drain the varying segments of pancreas tissue,

the pancreatic duct extends throughout the gland's entire length carrying juices to the middle portion of the duodenum, usually via the bile duct where it penetrates the duodenal wall.

The gland's endocrine (internal) function involves the hormones insulin and glucagon which are produced by the so-called beta (β) and alpha (α) cells of the islets of Langerhans respectively. The pancreas' tissues contain approximately one million of these microscopic islets, or small cell clusters, and their secretions are released directly into the bloodstream.

Insulin affects metabolism in several ways, mainly by providing the tissue cells with energy by enabling them to absorb glucose. However, an insulin deficiency raises blood sugar levels creating the disorder known as diabetes mellitus. The lowering of blood glucose levels stimulates the secretion of glucagon which, amongst other things, produces glucose from fatty tissues and from glycogen which is derived from the liver. Consequently, the glucose levels return to normal counteracting the effects of insulin.

In its animal form the pancreatic tissue is used in several ways. A food delicacy known as sweetbread is the pancreas of cattle while insulin is extracted from the pancreas of pigs and cattle before being chemically modified for use by people with diabetes. Where natural human enzyme production is inadequate, causing chronic pancreatitis or fibrocystic disease, pancreatin, extracted from pig pancreatic tissue, is used.

The liver, the largest internal organ of the body, is situated in the upper part of the abdominal cavity, mainly on the right side, but extending to the left, beneath the lung and underlying the lower ribs. In the adult male the liver weighs approximately 3¼ pounds (1.5 kg), and in the female 2½ pounds (1.2 kg). It is normally red-brown in color.

Many functions are undertaken by the liver and it can be regarded as the 'chemical powerhouse' of the body. Most of the products of digestion are transported to this gland by the portal vein (which is formed from the smaller vessels leaving the intestines). These products are metabolized (altered chemically) for further use by other body tissues and many are stored in the liver. A large number of enzymes are present to enable these chemical processes to occur. Fats, proteins and carbohydrates (sugars) are all involved.

The manufacture of most of the plasma proteins, including the clotting factors that control bleeding, occurs within the liver. Many drugs and toxins are metabolized here, either to inactivate them or to allow them to be excreted by the kidney into the urine.

For children's parties it is wise to base the food, however exciting looking, on simple ingredients.

The digestive process is completed in the small intestine. Throughout its length of almost 23 feet (7 m), the millions of villi which line its walls absorb nutrients into their cells and convey them into the bloodstream or the lymphatic vessels.

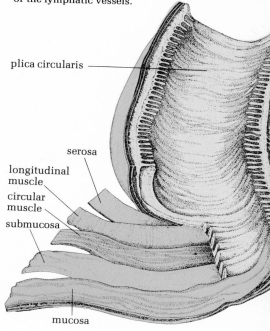

plica circularis

serosa

longitudinal muscle

circular muscle

submucosa

mucosa

This cross section of the intestine shows the muscular wall and inner lining with its millions of projecting villi which increase the area of absorption.

The liver is the largest abdominal organ. It has a vital role in the digestion of food through the formation and excretion of bile and the storage of the products of digestion.

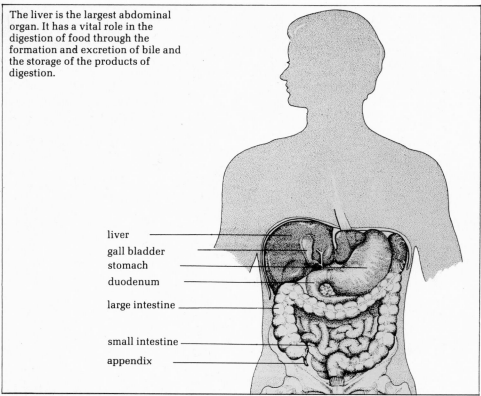

liver
gall bladder
stomach
duodenum
large intestine
small intestine
appendix

The liver, gall bladder and pancreas, showing their interrelationship and relative sizes.

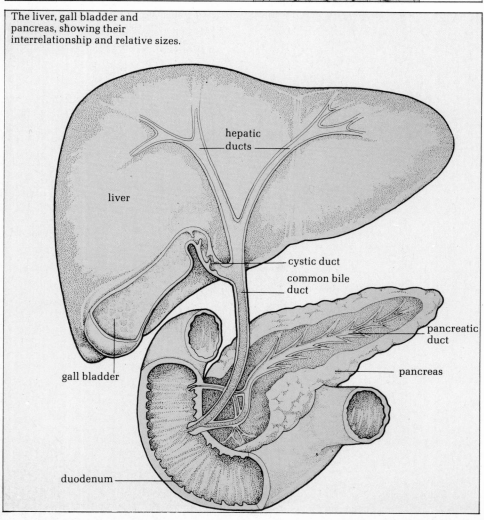

hepatic ducts

liver

cystic duct

common bile duct

pancreatic duct

gall bladder

pancreas

duodenum

One of the most important functions of the liver is the formation and excretion of bile. Bilirubin is formed as a breakdown product of the blood pigment hemoglobin. It is removed from the bloodstream by the liver, altered chemically and excreted in the bile. Bile is concentrated in the gall bladder and subsequently released into the upper part of the intestines, where it assists in the absorption of fats and fat-soluble vitamins. It is also the pigment that colors the feces.

Functional abnormalities A main feature of abnormal liver function is jaundice, resulting from the accumulation of bilirubin in the bloodstream and making the whites of the eyes (sclera) and the skin yellow. Apart from liver diseases such as hepatitis preventing the organ from handling the bilirubin adequately, excess bile production or any obstruction to the outflow of bile can also cause jaundice. Other functions of the liver may also be disturbed by disease processes.

Large bowel Unwanted substances that remain in the small intestine are transported into the large bowel by peristaltic action. During the progress of food through the small intestine, a significant amount of water is also absorbed. By the time the material has reached the large bowel, it has a semi-solid consistency, and is known as a stool or feces.

The large intestine extends from the small intestine to the anus and includes the cecum, the appendix, the colon, the rectum and the anus. The cecum, the first part of the large bowel, is a dilated pouch, into which the small pouch called the appendix opens. In grass-eating animals the appendix aids the digestion of cellulose, the main component of plant fiber. In man cellulose is not digested but forms the bulk of the stool. The appendix in man often becomes inflamed, a condition known as appendicitis.

The colon is approximately 5 feet (1.5 m) long, and four times as wide as the small intestine. Within the large intestine, water continues to be absorbed so that the feces become firmer. Feces consist of undigested fiber material or roughage, lining cells shed from the intestine and large numbers of bacteria that are normally present in the lower parts of the bowel. Bile pigments present in the feces produce its normal brown color.

Distension of the walls of the rectum by the fecal material produces the conscious desire to empty the bowel. During defecation the circular muscle that surrounds the anal canal and its external opening, the anus, relaxes, and the feces are evacuated.

Control of digestion

Although chewing, swallowing and defecation are under voluntary control, the process of digestion is largely controlled by the autonomic nervous system and by special local reactions, or reflexes,

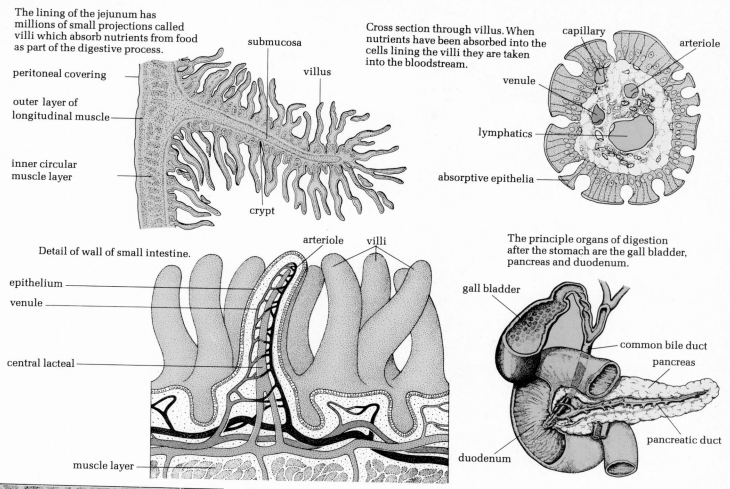

The lining of the jejunum has millions of small projections called villi which absorb nutrients from food as part of the digestive process.

submucosa

villus

peritoneal covering

outer layer of longitudinal muscle

inner circular muscle layer

crypt

Cross section through villus. When nutrients have been absorbed into the cells lining the villi they are taken into the bloodstream.

capillary

arteriole

venule

lymphatics

absorptive epithelia

Detail of wall of small intestine.

arteriole

villi

epithelium

venule

central lacteal

muscle layer

The principle organs of digestion after the stomach are the gall bladder, pancreas and duodenum.

gall bladder

common bile duct

pancreas

duodenum

pancreatic duct

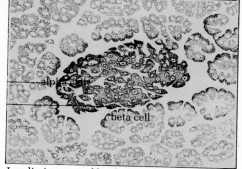

alpha cell

beta cell

Insulin is secreted by the beta cells of the pancreatic islets of Langerhans.

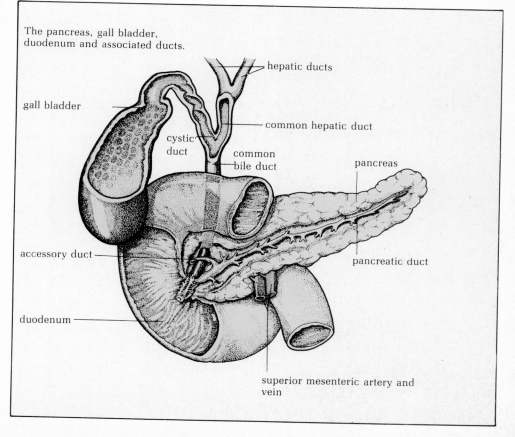

The pancreas, gall bladder, duodenum and associated ducts.

hepatic ducts

gall bladder

common hepatic duct

cystic duct

common bile duct

pancreas

accessory duct

pancreatic duct

duodenum

superior mesenteric artery and vein

under the control of hormones. Reflexes control the secretion of the various digestive juices and initiate the process of peristalsis within the alimentary system.

The sight, smell or, even, thought of food can initiate the flow of saliva and gastric juice. Secretion of these juices is further stimulated by the physical presence of food in the mouth or stomach.

Cholecystokinin, a hormone produced by the duodenum, stimulates the contraction of the gall bladder, which increases the flow of bile into the small bowel. Two other hormones, gastrin and secretin, produced by cells in the stomach directly stimulate the flow of pancreatic juice.

Similar increases in secretions are also stimulated by the vagus nerve, a part of the autonomic nervous system.

Diet

A well-balanced and healthy diet keeps the digestive system functioning adequately. Any disturbance of a particular part of the digestive system may affect the whole food breakdown process.

Adequate fiber and fluid content in the diet are important for regular bowel movement and relatively soft stools. A number of illnesses, particularly appendicitis and diverticular disease, may occur more frequently in populations where the normal diet has a low residue of fiber.

Endocrine System

Ductless glands, the endocrine glands secrete their products, called hormones, directly into the bloodstream. The hormones, which act as chemical messengers and produce their effects on tissues at distant sites, are concerned with the regulation and control of various biochemical reactions in the body.

The body is composed of billions of cells. Although each cell is a very complex functional unit, coordinating and controlling the activity of all cells demands an extensive communication network which is provided by the nervous system, and the hormones of the endocrine system.

Prolactin initiates and maintains lactation while luteotropic hormone stimulates milk secretion. (Zefa)

Unlike the exocrine glands (such as salivary glands) the endocrine glands release their secretions, or hormones, directly into the circulating blood. These chemical messengers are able to regulate the chemical activities of cells, ensuring all organs work together under various environmental conditions. Hormones may have different effects on different tissues and they may affect the same tissue in different ways, depending on prevailing conditions. They have an extremely wide range of functions, from controlling growth, reproduction and sexual characteristics to influencing mental attitudes and personality traits.

Knowledge about hormones has been acquired by various techniques: by observing what happens to an animal when a gland is removed and by administering extracts of the removed gland to see if the changes are reversed; and by chemically isolating the hormone to determine its chemical structure. Further studies have determined what controls the amount of hormone secreted and how a hormone exerts its effect. Excessive production or deficiency of a particular hormone produces a definite disease state. An excess of thyroid hormone causes hyperthyroidism and lack of it causes cretinism. An overproduction of hormones from the adrenal cortex causes Cushing's syndrome but an insufficient amount results in Addison's disease. The symptoms and effects of such diseases provide more information about hormones and their function.

Over-production of a hormone is caused by a tumor in the gland, or enlargement of the gland. The surgical removal of the tumor or part of the enlarged gland may correct the condition. The destruction of the gland by inflammation or cancer usually causes a hormone deficiency which may be corrected by administering the missing hormone, for example, a person with diabetes mellitus will require injections of insulin.

Distribution and function

The pituitary gland, or hypophysis, is often called the 'master gland' because it regulates other glands. A spherical gland about the size of a pea, the pituitary is situated under the brain, just above the roof of the mouth. A stalk attaches it to the hypothalamus, the part of the brain immediately above it. The secretions of the pituitary gland are controlled not only by nerve impulses from the brain but by the level of other hormones in the blood.

Posterior pituitary hormones The back portion of the pituitary, which has two separate secretions, is the neurohypophysis.

Antidiuretic hormone (ADH) controls the secretion of urine by the kidney, and so regulates the water and electrolyte, or salt, composition of body fluids.

Oxytocin, a hormone which causes secretion of milk from the breast during lactation may also be important during the birth process.

Anterior pituitary hormones The front part of the pituitary gland, the adenohypophysis, produces several hormones.

Growth hormone is a protein which controls growth, particularly of bones, muscles and body organs. Over-secretion of this hormone causes gigantism in children and acromegaly in adults.

Adrenocorticotropic hormone (ACTH) stimulates the cortex or outer shell of the adrenal glands to produce a group of hormones called adrenocorticosteroids.

Thyrotropic or thyroid stimulating hormone (TSH) stimulates the thyroid gland to produce its hormone, thyroxine.

Melanocyte stimulating hormone (MSH) stimulates the melanocyte cells in the skin to form the brown pigment melanin and deposit it in the skin, allowing it to tan in the sun.

Follicle stimulating hormone (FSH) converts a primary follicle in the ovary into a mature Graafian follicle. Before ovulation can occur, a small amount of luteinising hormone is required.

Luteinising hormone (LH) induces ovulation and the formation of the corpus luteum.

Luteotropic hormone stimulates the production of progesterone and the secretion of milk from the mammary glands.

Interstitial cell stimulating hormone (ICSH) is the same hormone as LH, which, in the male, stimulates the interstitial cells of the testes to produce the hormone testosterone.

Prolactin is a hormone which is responsible for the initiation and maintenance of lactation.

Symptoms of pituitary dysfunction When pituitary hormones are absent growth ceases, atrophy of the thyroid gland causes cretinism, atrophy of the adrenal cortex leads to symptoms of cortisone deficiency in one to three days, before puberty the gonads fail to develop and after puberty they atrophy, impotence and sterility occur, secondary sexual characteristics disappear, and diabetes insipidus develops.

In cases of advanced breast cancer, the pituitary gland is sometimes (but rarely) removed.

Adrenal cortex hormones The outer shell of the adrenal gland, the adrenal cortex which is essential to life, secretes a group of hormones called adrenocorticosteroids (abbreviated to steroids or corticoids) which regulate the general metabolism of the body, that is, the utilization of protein, carbohydrate and fat by all body cells. By their action on the kidneys, corticoids also control the water and electrolyte content of blood and tissue fluid. Corticoids are of two types.

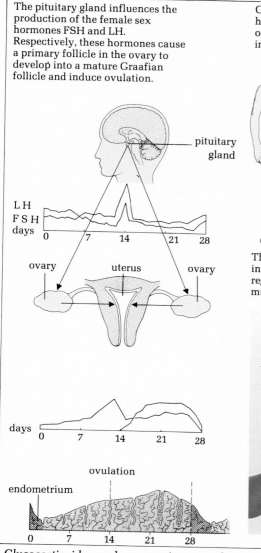

The pituitary gland influences the production of the female sex hormones FSH and LH. Respectively, these hormones cause a primary follicle in the ovary to develop into a mature Graafian follicle and induce ovulation.

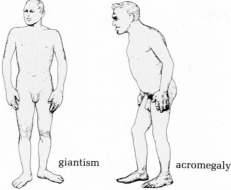

Over-production of the growth hormone causes giantism if it occurs in children and acromegaly in adults.

giantism   acromegaly

The growth hormone, directly influenced by the pituitary gland, regulates the growth of bones, muscles and body organs. (*Zefa*)

Glucocorticoids, such as cortisone and hydrocortisone, have a strong metabolic action but a weak action on water and electrolytes. They promote tissue breakdown, suppress inflammation and are essential for the body to cope with stress such as in adverse environmental conditions. Glucocorticoids are secreted according to the amount of circulating ACTH. A delicate feed-back control exists between the adrenal cortex and the anterior lobe of the pituitary gland which secretes ACTH. A fall in the amount of glucocorticoids circulating in the blood stimulates the anterior pituitary to secrete more ACTH, which makes the adrenal cortex produce more steroids. Similarly, a rise in the concentration of steroids in the blood inhibits ACTH production so that the adrenal cortex decreases the production of further steroids.

The mineralocorticoid, aldosterone, has a weak metabolic effect but a strong action on the kidney. By excreting less sodium and more potassium, the electrolyte balance of the blood and body fluids is main-

tained. The production of aldosterone is stimulated by a decrease in the blood volume within the blood vessels or by a high blood level of potassium and a low blood concentration of sodium. Its secretion is independent of ACTH from the pituitary gland.

A center in the brain stem may monitor the blood levels of sodium and potassium and by secreting another hormone, glomerulotropin, stimulates the secretion of aldosterone when it is required. Stretch receptors, probably in the right atrium of the heart, monitor blood volume and control aldosterone secretion via the nervous system.

Symptoms of adrenal cortex dysfunction A functioning tumor or enlargement of the adrenal cortex produces excessive amounts of steroid hormones. The resulting condition, Cushing's syndrome, causes obesity of the trunk, a fat 'moon' face, muscle weakness and thinning of the skin and bones. Cushing's syndrome also results in excessive hair growth, acne, diabetes mellitus, high blood pressure, impotence and suppression of menstruation.

Destruction of the adrenal cortex (either by disease or surgical removal for the treatment of breast cancer) results in a deficiency of steroid hormones, and the condition called Addison's disease. The main clinical features are muscular weakness, low blood pressure, pigmentation of the skin, complex changes in metabolism and in the composition of tissue fluids, which finally result in heart and kidney failure.

Adrenal medulla hormones The inner section of the adrenal gland, the medulla helps the body adapt to stress or emergency situations.

Adrenalin increases the rate and force of the heart beat, dilates the pupils of the eyes, constricts the arteries in the skin and internal organs and dilates the arteries supplying the heart and skeletal muscle, relaxes bronchial muscle, relaxes the intestinal muscles and closes the sphincters, causes the hair on the skin to stand erect, causes the liver to release stored glucose, and diminishes muscle fatigue.

Noradrenalin, which has similar effects, produces a greater rise in blood pressure and less relaxation of smooth muscle.

These hormones are secreted in response to nerve impulses generated by physical exertion, emotion, exposure to cold or a fall in arterial blood pressure. They are also secreted when the body is under threat to prepare it for 'fight or flight'. In an emergency situation adrenalin makes the heart pump more blood, the liver release more glucose for energy, the pupils dilate to enhance vision and the breathing passages dilate to let more air into the lungs. Blood is diverted from the skin (causing its pallor) and from the internal organs to the voluntary muscles and muscle fatigue diminishes.

Sex hormones In addition to the ovaries and testes producing ova and sperm, both organs are endocrine glands secreting hormones into the circulating blood. The pituitary gland and the adrenal cortex also contribute hormones to the sexual functioning of the body. After puberty males and females possess both male and female hormones in their bodies.

Estrogen is a steroid hormone produced by the ovary, the placenta, the adrenal cortex and the testis.

In girls at puberty, estrogen is responsible for the development of the vagina, uterus and breasts, the changes in body shape and contour, the growth of underarm and pubic hair and many features of the menstrual cycle.

Progesterone, a steroid secreted by the ovary, mainly from the corpus luteum during the second half of the menstrual cycle, is also secreted by the adrenal gland and placenta. It induces changes in the uterus, preparing the lining for the fertilized ovum and maintaining the pregnancy once it is embedded in the uterus. It stimulates proliferation of breast tissue, encourages salt and water retention, and relaxes smooth muscle, particularly in the uterus, bowel and veins.

Testosterone, responsible for the development of secondary sexual characteristics in boys at puberty, is a steroid hormone secreted by the testes. FSH (follicle stimulating hormone) from the anterior pituitary gland stimulates the sperm cells in the testes, allowing spermatozoa to form. ICSH (interstitial cell stimulating hormone) also from the anterior pituitary gland, stimulates the interstitial cells of the testes to secrete testosterone and other androgens.

Before puberty, testosterone increases formation of protein and has a number of other functions, as in the metabolism of cholesterol and cutaneous vessels. At puberty, it causes the growth of the penis and scrotum; the growth of the beard and of underarm, pubic and body hair; a rapid increase in height and the development of bones and skeletal muscles; the thickening of the skin; the proliferation of sebaceous glands which are prone to infection and may produce acne; and the deepening of the voice.

Thyroid hormone The thyroid gland which is located at the front of the throat, secretes a hormone, thyroxine, in response to thyrotropic or thyroid stimulating hormone (TSH) secreted by the anterior pituitary gland.

Thyroxine stimulates the activity and metabolism of all tissues by speeding up the chemical reactions inside the cells. Over-activity of the thyroid gland produces excess thyroxine and a condition called hyperthyroidism or Graves' disease. The affected person is over-active with a fine tremor, has a fast heart rate and loses weight. An under-active thyroid with reduced thyroxine levels causes cretinism or myxedema characterized by physical and mental slowness, loss of memory, slow speech, dry skin and hair, loss of energy, obesity, and a slow, sluggish heart rate.

Parathyroid hormone The parathyroid glands which secrete parathormone are usually about four pieces of tissue lying behind the thyroid gland.

Parathormone regulates phosphorus-calcium metabolism by causing phosphorus to be excreted in the urine. An increased level of parathormone which increases phosphorus excretion, causes an increase in calcium in the blood and calcium excretion by the kidneys. To maintain the high levels of calcium in the blood in response to the low level of phosphorus in the blood, calcium is stripped off the bones and then excreted in the urine. Thus, in hyperparathyroidism, the bones fracture or become deformed and calcium stones may form in the kidneys. If the parathyroid glands are removed or destroyed, the most notable effect of parathormone deficiency is the hyperexcitability of the nervous system caused by a low blood calcium. This may cause muscle spasms and, eventually, convulsions.

Pancreatic hormones As well as secreting pancreatic juice through ducts into the small intestine, the pancreas also has an endocrine function. The islets of Langerhans within the pancreatic tissue secrete insulin and glucagon directly into the bloodstream.

Glucagon, a hormone secreted by the alpha cells of the islets of Langerhans, acts on the liver like adrenalin to release stored glucose. It reduces intestinal mobility and gastric secretions, and increases the urinary excretion of sodium, potassium chloride and phosphate.

Insulin is a soluble protein hormone secreted by the beta cells of the islets of Langerhans. By acting on cell membranes, it allows glucose to enter the cells where it is metabolized to provide energy for other cellular activities. A deficiency of insulin results in diabetes mellitus. Because glucose can no longer enter the body cells, the blood concentration of glucose rises until it is lost by excretion in the urine. As a result, the metabolism of carbohydrate and fat and the balance of salts in the blood are disturbed. These changes may be reversed by the injection of appropriate doses of insulin.

Other hormones may be secreted by various glands or organs throughout the body, some of which include:

Gastrin The presence of food and resulting distension of the stomach stimulate the release of gastrin from the stomach. Released into the circulation, gastrin later reaches the gastric glands via the arterial blood supply, and stimulates the secretion of gastric juice.

Enterogastrone is a hormone released from the intestinal mucosa into the bloodstream when fat enters the duodenum. By acting on the glands of the stomach to inhibit the secretion of acid and pepsin and by reducing gastric movement, it regulates the release of food from the stomach into the duodenum.

Erythropoietin, a hormone which may be secreted by the kidney, stimulates the bone marrow to increase the rate of red blood cell production, maturation and release into the circulation.

Renin If kidney tissue runs short of oxygen, the tubule cells release the hormone, renin, into the blood where it acts on the circulating protein hypertensinogen, converting it to angiotensin. Angiotensin which causes constriction of arteries and elevates arterial blood pressure may be involved in high blood pressure.

The melanocyte stimulating hormone allows a suntan to develop.

Genitourinary System

The organs of the body that are responsible for the production and excretion of urine and the process of reproduction, are called the genitourinary system. They are grouped together because many of these organs developed from the same embryological structures. Some, such as the male urethra, are involved in both processes.

Kidneys

The kidneys have three main functions: the excretion of waste products, notably nitrogen in the form of urea; the regulation of the salt and water content and acidity of the body fluids; and the secretion of renin, which controls blood pressure and erythropoietin, which stimulates red blood cell production.

The kidneys are bean-shaped, approximately 4¼–4¾ inches (11–12 cm) long and half as wide, and lie at the back of the abdomen behind the peritoneum. They are protected by muscles at their rear and by the eleventh and twelfth ribs in their

upper halves. The right kidney lies a little lower than the left. The duodenum and some loops of intestine lie in front of the right kidney while the spleen, the tail of the pancreas and the stomach lie in front of the left kidney.

The concavity, or hilum, faces inwards and receives the renal artery, renal vein and pelvis of the ureter. The renal arteries supply the kidneys with a huge flow of blood, about 148 pints (70 L) an hour, or a quarter of the total circulation of blood through the body at rest. This reservoir of blood tends to remain steady despite fluctuations in flow.

Each kidney contains over a million nephrons which are necessary for filtration and reabsorption. Blood from a minute branch of a renal artery runs into a tuft of capillary vessels enclosed in a membraneous bag (Bowman's capsule). Here fluid is filtered from the blood before running into a long tubule 1¼–1½ inches (3–4 cm) in length. It is then concentrated by the selective reabsorption into the blood of water and essential substances such as glucose.

Each renal tubule ends by joining a collecting tube which conveys urine to the pelvis of the ureter. The first part of the nephron acts as a filter, letting water, salts, glucose and urea through but holding back blood cells and large protein molecules. This filtration takes place at the rate of about 15 pints (7 L) an hour, easily exceeding the outflow of urine. This difference in volume is accounted for by the reabsorption of more than 99 per cent of the filtrate by the tubules.

However, this reabsorption is selective. Water is reabsorbed at a rate depending on the body's needs: more is reabsorbed if the body is short of fluid, less if the body is well hydrated. Some salt is reabsorbed, while the excess is left in the urine. Glucose is almost completely reabsorbed, except when the blood level exceeds a threshold measure of about 180 milligrams per 100 millilitres, as in diabetes. Urea is allowed to escape in the urine, although about a third is reabsorbed. The kidney also eliminates many drugs and toxic substances.

The kidney also regulates the blood's acidity level. By secreting urine of greater or lesser acidity a constant acidity level is maintained. The hypothalamus, found in the floor of the brain, regulates urine production. It responds to changes in the blood by stimulating the pituitary gland to release antidiuretic (ADH) hormone which promotes reabsorption in the tubules, thus diminishing urinary output. Reduction in ADH secretion increases urine output. In the rare disease diabetes insipidus (not to be confused with the common diabetes mellitus), ADH is non-existent so that urine is passed in vast amounts, up to 42 pints (20 L) a day. ADH secretion is increased by emotion, sleep

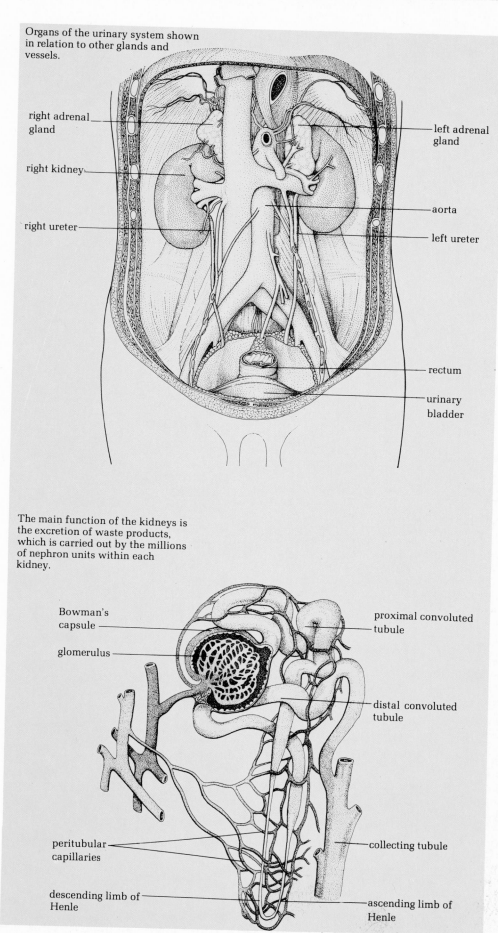

Organs of the urinary system shown in relation to other glands and vessels.

right adrenal gland

right kidney

right ureter

left adrenal gland

aorta

left ureter

rectum

urinary bladder

The main function of the kidneys is the excretion of waste products, which is carried out by the millions of nephron units within each kidney.

Bowman's capsule

glomerulus

proximal convoluted tubule

distal convoluted tubule

peritubular capillaries

collecting tubule

descending limb of Henle

ascending limb of Henle

and drugs such as the nicotine in tobacco.

Salt excretion is regulated by another hormone, aldosterone, which is secreted by the adrenal gland in response to lack of body salt or a lowered blood pressure. This hormone increases the reabsorption of sodium and then promotes the retention of salt. The drug spironolactone, which antagonises the action of aldosterone, is sometimes given to counteract excessive aldosterone activity. **Examining the kidneys** The kidneys are too deeply placed for ordinary clinical examination to be helpful so examination is usually indirect. Urine is tested to determine kidney disease, a condition which usually causes the protein, albumin to leak into the urine. Blood cells also may be present and may be seen by viewing a drop of urine under a microscope.

The volume of urine secreted is normally increased by a large fluid intake and scant sweating and abnormally increased by conditions such as certain kidney diseases in which the kidney cannot effectively reabsorb the fluid. Insufficient fluid intake, fevers that cause excessive fluid loss or vomiting and diarrhea all reduce the body's fluid. At least 21 fluid ounces (600 mL) of urine must be secreted daily to get rid of waste products. When only a small quantity of urine is passed, it is concentrated and characterized by a high specific gravity and a dark color.

Certain diseases, notably hepatitis or any obstructive jaundice where the urine becomes dark from bile pigments, alter the colour of urine. Stale urine smells because of the presence of ammonia formed from urea decomposed by the action of bacteria. Bacteria are not usually present in fresh urine. The appearance of blood in urine requires further investigation to determine its source while the presence of glucose raises the possibility of diabetes.

The kidneys are x-rayed using an iodine solution, which is opaque to x-rays. For an intravenous pyelogram, a suitable dye is injected into a vein. After being excreted by the kidneys it shows up in an x-ray picture. This shows the rate of excretion — an index of kidney function — and the anatomy of the kidney, ureters and bladder. In retrograde pyelography, dye is injected up the ureter by means of a cystoscope and fine tubes. This method gives a picture even if a kidney is not functioning. Kidney failure increases the level of waste products in the blood, and urea and creatinine are measured to assess the severity of renal failure.

Ureters

The tube conveying urine from each kidney to the bladder is called the ureter. Some 10–12 inches (25–30 cm) long, the ureters are narrow, thick-walled, muscular tubes commencing at the kidney as a funnel-shaped dilatation called the pelvis of the ureter. Each ureter runs down behind the abdominal cavity, passes

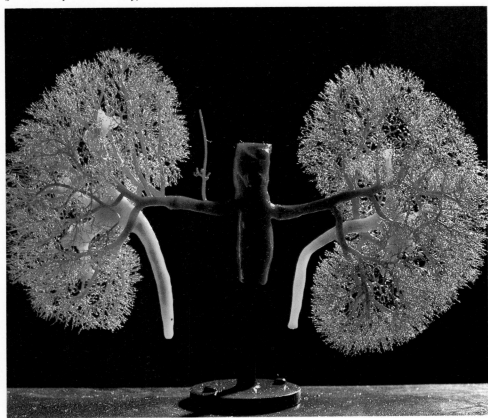

Corrosion cast of the blood vessels of the kidneys — posterior view.
(John Watney Photo Library)

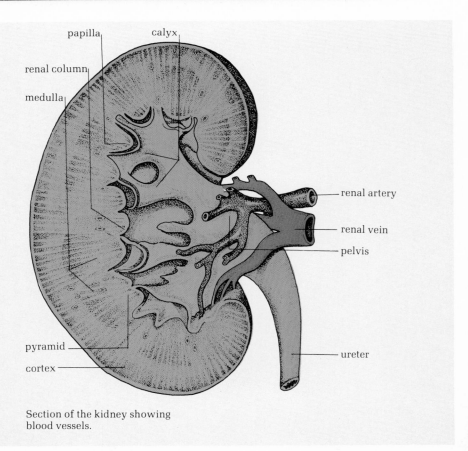

Section of the kidney showing blood vessels.

into the pelvic cavity and opens into the base of the bladder. The pelvis of the ureter divides into two or three large branches (major calyces), which in turn divide to form between seven and thirteen smaller branches (minor calyces). The minor calyces are indented at their expanded ends and moulded around one or more projections (papillae) of the kidney.

The abdominal part of the ureter lies behind the peritoneum on a muscle (psoas major) which comes between the ureter and the transverse processes of the lumbar vertebrae. Entering the pelvis by crossing the iliac vessels, the ureter runs down and turns towards the midline. At this juncture the male ureter is crossed by the vas deferens just before entering the bladder while the female ureter crosses the side of the cervix before reaching the bladder.

To prevent urine from backing up, the ends of the ureters are pressed together as they run obliquely through the bladder wall by slit-like apertures. With a full bladder the openings may be about 2 inches (5 cm) apart, but the distance is halved when the bladder empties. Reflux is also countered by waves of contraction that pass down the ureter.

Bladder

The bladder is the only part of the urinary system over which we have some voluntary control. As the bladder fills from the steady dribble of urine down the ureters, the bladder's muscular fibers relax to accommodate the extra volume. In time further relaxation cannot prevent a rise in pressure inside the bladder, and nervous impulses are sent to the spinal cord and brain.

The brain receives the information that the bladder is full, and that this condition is causing discomfort. The sacral region of the spinal cord is ready to take part in the reflex action causing the bladder to empty. But in appropriate circumstances, the brain will overrule the spinal reflex. An injury to the spinal cord may abolish this voluntary control over the bladder.

Urethra

The male urethra is a fibro-elastic tube about 8 inches (20 cm) long which runs from the bladder, through the middle of the prostate and the lower section of the penis, before opening to the exterior through the external urinary meatus (hole) in the end of the penis. It is used to convey urine from the bladder to the exterior.

The female urethra is approximately 1½ inches (4 cm) long and ¼ inch (6 mm) in diameter. After leaving the bladder it runs along the front of the vaginal wall, opening to the exterior through a small meatus just in front of the vagina. It is susceptible to the same infections, strictures and tumors as its male equivalent.

The flow of urine may be impeded if the meatus is narrowed, caused either by a developmental abnormality or infection.

Genitals — male

In the male the sex glands or gonads are the testes, which are situated in the pouch-like structure called the scrotum. Two groups of cells within the testes called Leydig and Sertoli cells produce the male hormone testosterone and develop into sperm cells. Each cell type is stimulated at puberty by different hormones produced by the pituitary gland. Testosterone produced by the Leydig cells initiates and maintains the secondary sexual characteristics of facial and pubic hair, deep voice and body development.

The sperm produced by the Sertoli cells are stored in the epididymis (which is a coiled tube-like structure attached to the back of the testis). This structure is also continuous with the vas deferens (also called the seminal or sperm duct).

The vas deferens conducts the sperm cells up to the groin and into the abdominal cavity where it penetrates the prostate gland.

Less than 10 per cent of the volume of ejaculated fluid is formed by the testes. The prostate and two other pairs of glands add their secretions to make up the remainder.

Just below the prostate there are a pair of glands called the seminal vesicles, and these provide the bulk of the seminal fluid. They are lobulated sacs about 2 inches (5 cm) long. Ducts from these glands join the vas deferens to form the ejaculatory duct. The two ejaculatory ducts join the urethra within the substance of the prostate gland. Small amounts of fluid are added to the semen by the prostate gland and also by the small pea-like bulbo-urethral or Cowper's glands whose small ducts penetrate the urethra.

The male genital organs are designed to allow deposition of sperm close to the opening of the cervix in the female as a result of erection and ejaculation during intercourse.

The shaft of the penis contains layers of spongy tissue filled with blood vessels. During sexual excitation these vessels become engorged with blood, and a special valvular mechanism traps the blood in the penis. This process enables erections to be maintained. The process of ejaculation

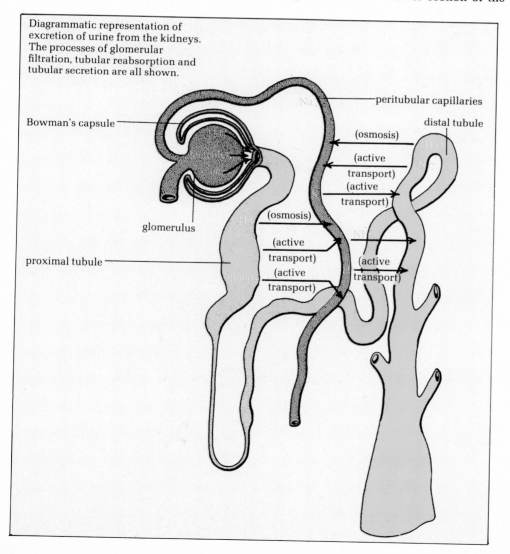

Diagrammatic representation of excretion of urine from the kidneys. The processes of glomerular filtration, tubular reabsorption and tubular secretion are all shown.

Bowman's capsule

glomerulus

proximal tubule

peritubular capillaries

distal tubule

(osmosis)

(active transport)

(active transport)

(osmosis)

(active transport)

(active transport)

(active transport)

occurs as a result of rhythmic contractions of the vas deferens and the seminal vesicles.

There is evidence that an increasing proportion of men over fifty years of age show signs of diminishing testicular function with decreasing size of testes, decreased libido and potency and loss of body hair. Lower blood testosterone levels accompany these signs. There also appears to be a decline in sperm production but both testicular functions show a very gradual decline. Symptoms of tiredness, lack of drive, loss of libido and potency, hot flushes and depression can accompany these physical changes.

Undescended testicle Very early in pregnancy, testicles develop in the male fetus, high up in the back of the abdominal cavity. They begin their 'descent' as early as the third month of pregnancy, but do not reach the bottom of the scrotum until the ninth month, just prior to birth.

This process of descent may cease at any stage causing cryptorchism or cryptorchidism, meaning 'hidden testis', from the Greek *kryptos* and *orchis*. This is

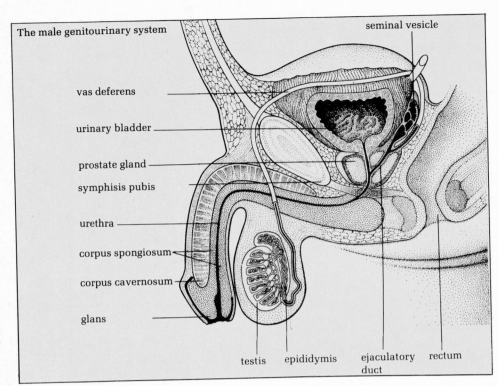

The male genitourinary system

- seminal vesicle
- vas deferens
- urinary bladder
- prostate gland
- symphisis pubis
- urethra
- corpus spongiosum
- corpus cavernosum
- glans
- testis
- epididymis
- ejaculatory duct
- rectum

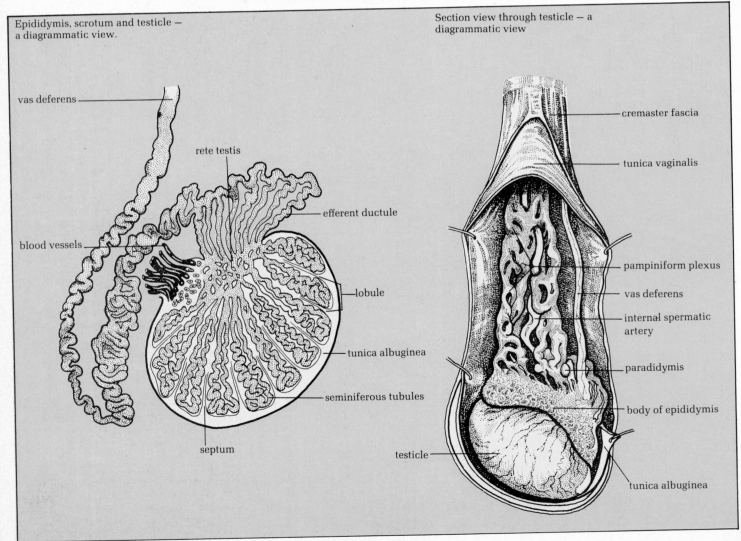

Epididymis, scrotum and testicle — a diagrammatic view.

- vas deferens
- rete testis
- efferent ductule
- blood vessels
- lobule
- tunica albuginea
- seminiferous tubules
- septum

Section view through testicle — a diagrammatic view

- cremaster fascia
- tunica vaginalis
- pampiniform plexus
- vas deferens
- internal spermatic artery
- paradidymis
- body of epididymis
- testicle
- tunica albuginea

the medical term for undescended testicles. It is one of the commonest conditions in children. At least 2 per cent of males will have at least one testicle inadequately descended at the age of one.

Although testosterone secretion is unaffected, sperm production is reduced if the testis remains in its abnormal position beyond the age of five or six. This relates in part, to the need of the testes to be one Celsius degree below body temperature for optimal functioning. This is normally achieved by their usual position in the scrotum.

Undescended testes are corrected surgically at the age of four or five. In about half the cases, a functioning testis is found and transferred to the scrotum. The remaining one is removed because it has failed to develop properly and, in its abnormal position is more prone to damage by injury and has a greater risk of developing a tumor.

Inguinal hernias, often present with undescended testicles, are repaired at the same time. Testicular prostheses may be inserted into the scrotum shortly before puberty.

Even with only one functioning testis, the chances of fertility are still very high.

Genitals — female

The female genital system, unlike that of the male, does not share any internal structures with the urinary system. The ovaries are the female sex organs or gonads and are situated within the abdominal cavity. Hormones from the pituitary stimulate the ovary to produce the female sex hormones, estrogens and progesterones, and to release an egg cell (or ovum) every four weeks. A cyclical pattern is established at puberty (or the menarche) and this continues until the menopause. During the maturation of the ovum within the ovary, increasing amounts of estrogen are produced. This in turn

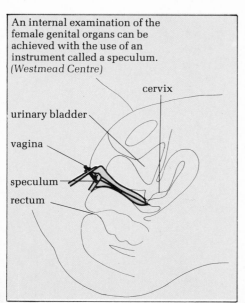

An internal examination of the female genital organs can be achieved with the use of an instrument called a speculum. *(Westmead Centre)*

cervix

urinary bladder

vagina

speculum

rectum

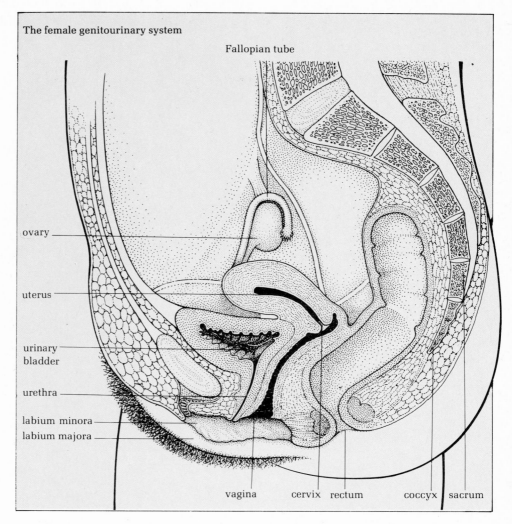

The female genitourinary system

Fallopian tube

ovary

uterus

urinary bladder

urethra

labium minora

labium majora

vagina   cervix   rectum   coccyx   sacrum

stimulates the lining of the uterus (or endometrium) making it thicker and more rich in blood supply.

If the ovum is fertilized after ovulation, this endometrial tissue is already prepared for implantation of the developing embryo and the establishment of pregnancy.

A pair of fallopian or uterine tubes convey ova to the uterus. They are approximately 4 inches (10 cm) in length, each with one broadened funnel-shaped end curling around an ovary. The other end of each tube enters a top corner of the uterus. The inside lining of the tubes is covered by fine hairs or cilia. Their rhythmical beating, together with contractions of muscle within the wall, aid the progress of the ovum towards the uterus. Fertilization, when it occurs, is usually in the part of the tube nearest to the ovary.

The uterus is normally pear-shaped and in the young adult female is about 3–4 inches (7–10 cm) long. At its lower end it narrows to form the cervix, which protrudes into the vagina and provides a passage for sperm. The wall of the uterus is made up of three separate layers. The outer tough fibrous covering overlies the myometrium, a relatively thick structure that consists of bands of muscle and fibrous tissue. The innermost layer is the endometrium.

In the two weeks prior to ovulation this layer is thickening in preparation for possible fertilization. Should this not eventuate, estrogen production from the ovum is decreased and the endometrium is shed. This process occurs 14 days after ovulation and is called the menses (or menstrual period). This four-weekly cycle is known as the menstrual cycle.

Should fertilization occur, the embryo implants in the wall of the uterus, and the fetal and maternal blood circulations become joined via the placenta. Throughout pregnancy the uterus continues to enlarge until at full term its upper edge is almost parallel with the edge of the lowest rib. Contractions of the myometrium are important components of the birth process.

Menstrual cycles cease at the menopause, and the endometrium becomes extremely thin.

The cervix or neck of the uterus is approximately 1¼ inches (3 cm) long. It is cylindrical in shape and extends into the vagina. The cervix consists mainly of hard fibrous tissue and has a small central (cervical) canal. A plug of mucus lies within

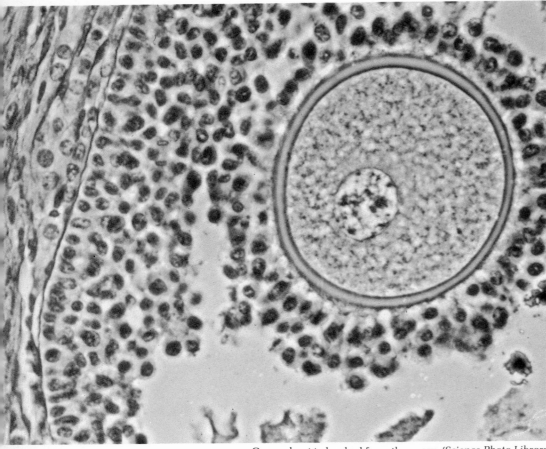

Ovum about to be shed from the ovary. *(Science Photo Library)*

Stages in the development of the ovum. *(Elsevier)*

1 primary follicle
a nucleus of the ovum
b granulosa cells
2 follicle with cubic follicle cells
3 follicle cells forming an ever-thickening layer around the follicle
4&5 maturing follicle
4a development of cavity
5b follicle cavity
6 ovum released from the ovary

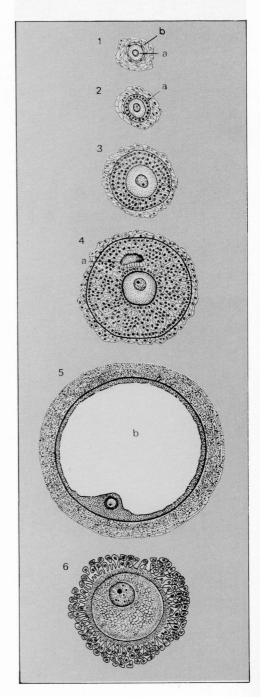

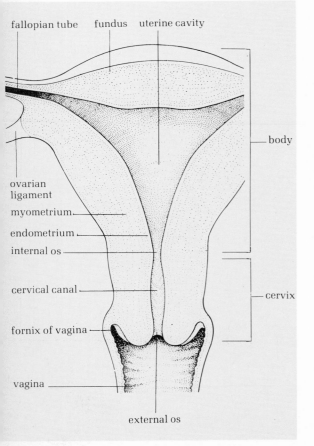

Left
Sectioned view of the uterus.

this canal and generally prevents the entry of sperm and bacteria into the uterine cavity. At the time of ovulation this cervical mucus (which is manufactured by glands lining the canal), becomes more profuse and stringy in consistency. This change facilitates the penetration of sperm for possible fertilization.

The vagina is a muscular tube that opens externally at the vulva, the region of the external genital organs and extends inwards to the cervix. It is normally 4–5 inches (10–13 cm) long but it enlarges during intercourse, and especially during childbirth. As well as being the site for normal coitus, it is also a channel for the menses. The rectum lies behind the vagina and the bladder.

In female virgins the external opening of the vagina is partially blocked by a relatively thin membrane called the hymen.

The vulva consists of two separate folds of tissue. The outer larger ones are called the labia majora, and the inner ones the labia minora. Above the urethral opening at the top of the vulva there is a small organ called the clitoris. This contains erectile tissue similar to that found in the male penis. As such it can be stimulated by touch and also during intercourse. A number of small glands are also present in the lower female genital tract. Their secretions are stimulated by sexual arousal and help to provide lubrication. They are the equivalent to the bulbo-urethral glands in the male and are situated on either side of the vaginal opening.

Urinary tract infection

This was commonly known as 'a chill in the bladder' and the symptoms are frequency and dysuria. That is, repeated and frequent urges to pass water accompanied by pain or a sensation of 'burning' or 'scalding'.

These infections occur in both sexes, but much more commonly in women, because the female urethra is only about 1½ inch long, compared to about 8 inches in men, and presents much less of a mechanical barrier to the entry of infection.

Women are also more prone to infection due to other mechanical factors, such as the wearing of sanitary napkins and the insertion of tampons. Also, during intercourse, the urethra dilates and allows the entry of bacteria.

Another common reason for infection is the incorrect method of wiping after passing water. This should be correctly taught from childhood. The method consists of wiping from the front backwards and not using again that piece of toilet paper.

Women should also get into the habit of passing water immediately after finishing intercourse. This empties the bladder of bacteria introduced during sex and helps to prevent infections from developing.

Lymphatic System

Lymph is the clear, protein-rich fluid which circulates in the lymphatic vessel system of the body, and which is formed by the filtration of tissue fluids into the lymphatic capillaries. In a broader sense, the term 'lymph' also includes the fluid bathing the cells (the interstitial fluid), which is formed by filtration of plasma through the walls of the small capillary blood vessels.

Lymph resembles plasma in many respects, but there are differences in mineral (electrolyte) concentrations, and the protein content is lower than that of plasma and variable, depending on its source. The highest protein concentration is in lymph from the liver (6 to 8 per cent). Glucose and urea are almost equally distributed in plasma and lymph.

The lymphatic system is composed of lymph vessels and lymph nodes. In most of the tissues of the body containing blood vessels there is a network of closed lymphatic vessels of microscopic dimensions. The lymph in these lymphatic capillaries flows into larger lymphatic vessels, which in turn unite to form two large vessels that empty into the great veins at the root of the neck. Fluid arising from the blood is thus returned to it.

Lymph vessels are delicate and transparent and contain valves which direct the flow of lymph. The lymph vessels of the small intestine which absorb fat after a fatty meal are called lacteals because of the milky appearance of their fluid (chyle) which contains fat globules.

There are no lymph vessels in the central nervous system, but the cerebrospinal fluid surrounding the brain and spinal cord may be considered equivalent to lymph. There are no lymph vessels in bloodless structures such as cartilage (gristle). Some lymph vessels run superficially, just under the skin, others run deeply, alongside veins and arteries.

Lymph vessels are more numerous than veins, though smaller. They intercommunicate with other lymph vessels and unite to form two large ducts: the right lymphatic duct draining the upper half of the right side of the body, and the thoracic duct draining the rest.

The right lymphatic duct is quite short, about 2/5 inch (1 cm) in length, and opens into the junction of two large veins at the root of the neck (the right subclavian and right internal jugular veins). Two half-moon shaped valves at the opening prevent the intrusion of blood into the duct.

The thoracic duct is a longer structure, arising from the upper end of a lymphatic sac (the cisterna chyli) lying in front of the first and second lumbar vertebrae. It passes upwards in front of the vertebral column and into the neck, forming an arch about 1¼ inches (3 cm) above the left collarbone (clavicle), and finally turns downwards to open into the junction of the left subclavian vein with the left internal jugular vein.

The thoracic duct is about 16 inches (40 cm) long and 1/5 inch (.5 cm) wide where it begins, its widest part. It has several valves, and like the right lymphatic duct is protected by a pair of valves where it terminates.

Lymph nodes The lymph vessels are interrupted by lymph nodes (lymph glands), of which there are several groups. They may be present in the neck, in the groin, in the armpit, behind the knee and in front of the elbow. Deep nodes are present in the abdomen and the chest.

The lymph nodes are small bean-shaped structures composed mainly of lymphoid tissue, which forms lymph cells (a type of white blood cell) and antibodies. Lymphoid tissue is also present in the tonsil, appendix and spleen.

Besides forming lymphocytes and antibodies, the lymphatic system is concerned with the collection (by the lacteals) of fatty globules from the intestine and its transmission through the mesenteric glands and the thoracic duct into the bloodstream.

The lymphatic system also prevents infection entering the bloodstream.

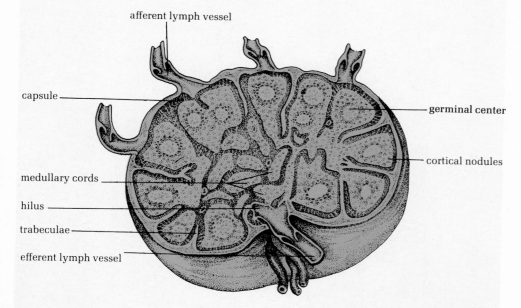

Structure of a lymph node. Lymph is delivered to the node by several lymph vessels and is collected by one vessel which is located at the hilus. The vein and artery also enter and leave at the hilus.

afferent lymph vessel

capsule

germinal center

cortical nodules

medullary cords

hilus

trabeculae

efferent lymph vessel

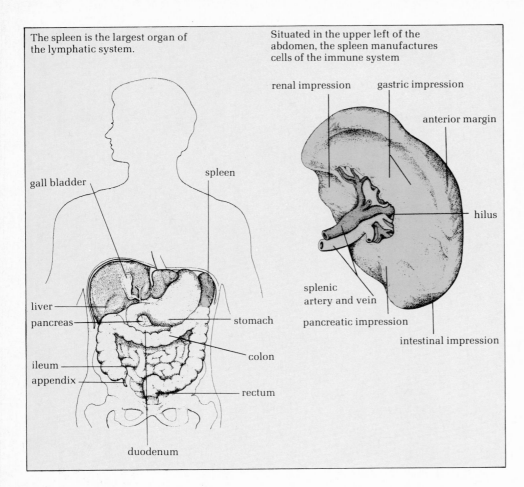

The spleen is the largest organ of the lymphatic system.

Situated in the upper left of the abdomen, the spleen manufactures cells of the immune system

gall bladder

spleen

liver

pancreas

ileum

appendix

stomach

colon

rectum

duodenum

renal impression

gastric impression

anterior margin

hilus

splenic artery and vein

pancreatic impression

intestinal impression

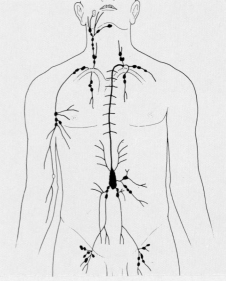

There are two major lymphatic ducts; the right lymphatic duct and the thoracic duct.

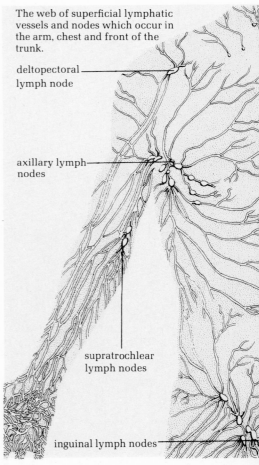

The web of superficial lymphatic vessels and nodes which occur in the arm, chest and front of the trunk.

deltopectoral lymph node

axillary lymph nodes

supratrochlear lymph nodes

inguinal lymph nodes

The spleen

A body organ located in the upper left of the abdomen, the spleen rests on the kidney and vessels at the back of the abdomen, and lies up under the diaphragm. It is not possible to feel the spleen below the front ribs except when it is enlarged in certain disorders.

The spleen is the largest single organ of the lymphatic system in the body. It is responsible for manufacturing cells of the immune system and for filtering from the bloodstream the aged and broken cells and foreign matter, such as bacteria, which circulate through its rich network of blood vessels.

The spleen may, if necessary, be removed surgically (splenectomy). This was common in times past when it was more difficult to control the severe bleeding which occured in cases of splenic rupture. Better techniques of blood replacement have led to attempts to conserve the spleen rather than proceeding to immediate removal. This can, however, only be done in certain cases and splenectomy still must be performed in severe cases of splenic laceration. This can be done without apparent damage to the immune system.

Abnormalities involving the spleen are most often detected due to its enlargement. Some congenital differences include total absence, multiple small spleens or a misplaced spleen elsewhere in the abdomen.

Injury to the spleen: accident victims are often shocked and complain of pain in the abdomen and left shoulder. This is due to irritation of the diaphragm by blood from a ruptured spleen. This type of injury can be caused by sudden deceleration or blunt compression of the abdomen, and is common in road accidents.

The spleen is an extremely vascular organ and death can be rapid if the rupture is large. Occasionally, the substance of the spleen is torn but the overlying capsule remains intact. The possibility of later rupture is high and a person complaining of pain referable to the spleen, even months after an accident, should be considered a serious risk.

Diseases Many diseases also affect the spleen. Infections such as septicemia may cause splenic abscesses. Malaria and other tropical parasites may cause it to enlarge. Syphilis and tuberculosis may also affect the spleen. Generalized bodily conditions, such as rheumatoid diseases and sarcoidosis can cause splenic enlargement, as can increased pressure in the veins draining the spleen, occurring in liver disease and heart failure.

The most widely known diseases affecting the spleen are blood disorders, for example various types of anemia, platelet abnormalities and the leukemias and lymphomas. In many cases, where the spleen is working to excess either breaking down or producing blood cells, it may be removed with good effect on the disease. In other cases, it may take over from the bone marrow which normally produces the cells but which may be invaded by abnormal cells as in leukemia and myelofibrosis.

Musculoskeletal System

The bone framework of the body and its associated muscles are collectively called the musculoskeletal system. The muscles arise from and insert into different parts of the skeleton, and it is through their attachment to bone that movement occurs.

Bone not only acts as a lever to which muscle and tendons are attached but also gives support to the softer tissues. In some places the skeleton forms a protective cage for internal organs such as the brain or heart and lungs. Bone also has a role in the production of blood cells and in storing important inorganic salts.

The skeletal system

The skeletal system is divided into two main sections: the axial skeleton and the appendicular skeleton. The axial skeleton comprises 80 bones in the head, face, neck and trunk. These include the backbone or vertebral column extending throughout the length of the neck and trunk, the breastbone or sternum, twelve pairs of ribs, the skull bones, the hyoid bone and three ossicles in each ear.

The appendicular skeleton consists of the bones in the limbs, of which there are 32 in each adult upper limb and 31 in each adult lower limb. These include the clavicles, the scapulae, the humerus, the radius and the ulna in each arm, the carpal bones of the wrists and the metacarpals and phalanges of the hands. The lower appendicular skeleton comprises the fused ilium, ischium and pubis forming each side of the pelvis and in each limb the femur, patella, tibia and fibula, the ankle bones, the metatarsal bones and the phalanges of the toes.

The bones belonging to the musculoskeletal system are divided into four classes according to their shape: long, short, flat and irregular.

The long bones are in the limbs and include the humerus of the upper arm and the femur or thigh bone. Each long bone has a shaft and two ends; the space inside this shaft is called the medullary cavity.

In contrast, short bones are fairly cubical in shape, consisting of a thin shell of compact bone with spongy bone inside. Examples of short bones include the eight bones of the wrist, the seven bones of the back part of the foot and the sesamoid bones such as the patella or kneecap.

Flat bones are thin rather than flat. They enclose a layer of spongy bone between two layers of compact bone. Included in this group are the ribs, the shoulder-blade and the skull bones.

All those bones that do not fall into one of the other classifications are known as irregular bones. These include the vertebrae and some of the skull bones.

Muscles require about fifty times more oxygen during exercise than at rest.

The interaction of bones, tendons and muscles gives the human body considerable strength and wide-ranging movement.

The features of bone Articular cartilage covers the articulating parts of most bones to help movement. However, many of the skull bones have no such articular cartilage and are united instead by fibrous tissue. *Periosteum*, a fibrous tissue, covers the whole of the bone except the articular part. The muscles are attached partly to the periosteum and partly to the bone itself. Red marrow fills the spongy bones and yellow the medullary cavity. Endosteum lines the spongy bone.

The growth of the skeleton The skeleton originates in 'ossification centers' in membrane and cartilage. The long bones of the limbs increase in length through the activity of the epiphyseal, or growth center near the end of each bone.

The rate of development depends on many factors and is particularly influenced by the growth hormone. Excessive growth hormone production by the pituitary gland produces either giant stature or acromegaly, while deficiency is the cause of many cases of extreme dwarfism. Lack of thyroid gland activity leads to stunting of growth and is associated with the retention of the proportions of an infant. Excessive sex hormone androgen stimulates growth, but also leads to earlier maturity with growth stopping years sooner than it would otherwise be expected.

The spine The backbone or spinal column is formed of a number of separate irregular bones called vertebrae which allow flexibility and movement. Although the vertebrae are firmly attached to one another, each can move a little on its neighbour, supplying a strong but flexible support for the trunk. The bony column also protects the spinal cord, the nervous tissue which runs down inside it from the base of the brain.

A typical vertebra consists of a substantial part in front, called the body, and an arch behind enclosing a space (the vertebral foramen) which houses the spinal cord. The body of a vertebra is cylindrical and separated from the one above and below by a disc of cartilage (intervertebral disc). An intervertebral disc is made up of a jelly-like centre enclosed in fibrous tissue attached to the vertebrae. The discs act as shock absorbers and allow movement between the vertebrae.

The vertebral arch consists of a bony stalk on each side and a pair of bony plates fused together behind. Each arch has a sharp projection of bone in the midline behind, and on each side where muscles and ligaments are attached. Four other projections connect with the corresponding processes of adjoining vertebrae.

Seven vertebrae are in the neck (cervical), twelve are in the chest region (thoracic), five are in the lumbar region, five fuse together to form the sacrum and three, four or five vestigal vertebrae unite to form the coccyx or tail bone.

The cervical vertebrae, not having much weight to support, have a small body, and to allow for the wide range of movement of the neck without damaging the spinal cord, the arch is larger than in other vertebrae. The thoracic vertebrae gradually increase in size consistent with the greater weight supported by vertebrae at a lower level. The ribs form joints with the sides of the thoracic vertebrae. The lumbar vertebrae are larger than the thoracic. The sacrum, comprising five fused bones, is a large triangular bone inserted like a wedge between the hip bones. It curves forming a hollow in front.

Before birth the vertebral column already has two primary curves and two compensating curves which become more pronounced as a child sits and walks.

In males the average length of the spinal column is about 27½ inches (70 cm) [neck 4¾ inches (12 cm), thoracic 11 inches (28 cm), lumbar 7 inches (18 cm), sacrum and coccyx 4¾ inches (12 cm)], the discs between the vertebrae contributing about a quarter of the length. In the female the average spine is about 23½ inches (60 cm). In old age the column tends to shorten because of softening of the bones (osteoporosis).

An abnormal curvature of the spine, spinal curvature may be congenital or caused by disease, fracture or abnormal posture.

Before birth the vertebral column already has two forward curves, one in the thoracic region, the other in the pelvis. Two secondary curves, one in the neck (cervical) and the other in the lumbar region compensate for these primary curves. The cervical curve is present before birth and is accentuated when the baby holds up his head at three or four months and sits up at about nine months. The lumbar curve appears when the child begins to walk, and becomes more pronounced in the female than in the male.

Undue curvature of the thoracic spine is kyphosis and excessive curvature of the lumbar spine is lordosis. Curvature from side to side is scoliosis.

The functions of the skeleton include the protection of vital organs such as the brain and the heart. Bones are composed of up to a third organic matter which contributes towards the toughness of the skeleton, and the remainder is mostly mineral matter, primarily calcium phosphate. Accordingly, the skeleton is also a reservoir of various minerals often required elsewhere in the body.

Perhaps the most important role of the skeleton is the formation of blood. This takes place in red marrow found in the cavity of certain bones, not only towards the ends of various long bones, but also in the vertebrae, ribs, sternum or breastbone, the skull and the pelvis.

The health of the skeleton The bones of children are less brittle and though easily damaged, they bend rather than break (greenstick fractures). Furthermore, the fractured bones of children rarely remain distorted but tend to grow straight again.

Ageing people have bones which become progressively less dense with a corresponding loss of calcium (osteoporosis). Due in part to lessening blood supply to the bones, partly to a decreased estrogen (female hormone) level in the blood after the menopause, as well as due to progressively less activity, such bones crack easily and spinal vertebrae may even crush with simple strain.

There are many other factors affecting the health of the skeleton. Lack of activity, such as follows fractures, produces local loss of mineral in the bones. Vitamin D influences the absorption of calcium and a deficiency can cause rickets.

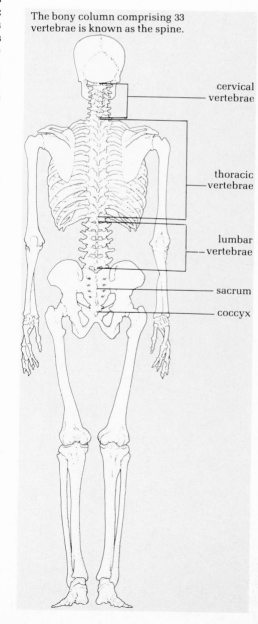

The bony column comprising 33 vertebrae is known as the spine.

cervical vertebrae

thoracic vertebrae

lumbar vertebrae

sacrum

coccyx

The bones of the skull, comprising the eight flat bones of the cranium and the bones of the face and jaw.

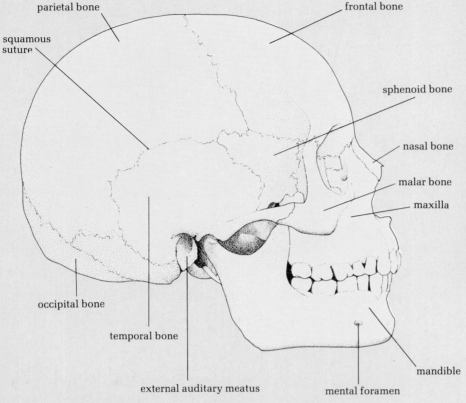

parietal bone

squamous suture

frontal bone

sphenoid bone

nasal bone

malar bone

maxilla

occipital bone

temporal bone

external auditary meatus

mandible

mental foramen

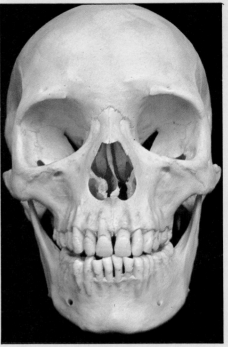

The frontal view of an adult skull clearly shows the bone structure of the face. (*John Watney Photo Library*)

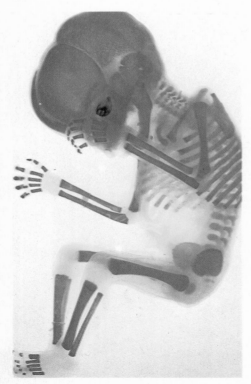

Sixteen-week foetus showing bone development. (*John Watney Photo Library*)

Prolonged fatty diarrhea (steatorrhea) also limits the absorption of bone-making material and may cause osteomalacia, with bent and softened bones. Inadequate vitamin C produces a weak bone matrix, the substance between the bone cells, as well as hemorrhage beneath the lining of the bones (periosteum).

The skull The bony framework of the head, the skull consists of the cranium or brain-case section, made up of eight bones, and the facial section which, including the jawbone (mandible), consists of fourteen small interconnected bones. Although the skull is basically the same in childhood, whatever the sex, after puberty the skull of the female is relatively lighter and has thinner bones.

The various bones develop either from condensations found in the mesenchyme (in which the connective tissues originate) or are preformed in cartilage. The newborn baby's cranium is composed of plates of very fine bone, well separated by suture lines, and the two soft spots, the anterior and posterior fontanelles. Gradually these are obscured and by the age of two years the fontanelles should no longer be felt. After the age of twenty-five the suture lines are also obliterated.

Hollows within the bones begin to form in various parts of the face soon after birth, producing the sinuses. Lined with mucus-producing membrane, the sinuses control the temperature and moisture of breathed air.

Problems The bones of the cranium may fracture as a result of direct blows, producing either split or depressed fractures. The vault or base of the skull is relatively elastic and fractures less easily.

The skull is prone to various diseases and complications. Paget's disease, or osteitis deformans, produces gross thickening and enlargement of the brain case, and with it an increased tendency to malignant changes. Coarsening of the features may follow certain pituitary gland tumours, associated with thickening of the bones of the face (acromegaly).

Occasionally hemolytic or blood-destroying disorders such as Mediterranean anemia (thalassemia) lead to greatly increased efforts by the body to regenerate sufficient blood to maintain life. To this end the marrow within the bones of the skull increases in amount and activity. The result is a peculiar 'oriental' appearance plus an increased widening of the various bones.

The sinuses around the face and the somewhat similar cavity behind the ear (mastoid cavity) are prone to infection from blockage of their drainage ducts or from nearby infection such as middle ear abscesses.

The teeth Each individual can expect to get two sets of natural teeth in a lifetime, the deciduous or primary dentition and the permanent or secondary dentition.

Eruption of primary teeth in the human infant occurs from about six to 24 months of age in a fairly regular pattern, but the time of arrival of each group is variable. In the first 18 months of life the average child has approximately six teeth less than his age in months. As the teeth are preparing to erupt, the gums thicken and the outline of the tooth in the gum margin can often be seen.

The front eight teeth (four upper and four lower) can appear at any time between birth and 15 months of age, but the sequence can also vary. The first molars appear between six and 18 months, followed soon after by the eye (canine) teeth. Second year molars erupt from 18 months to three years of age.

The primary or deciduous teeth are shed from about six or seven to 12 or 13 years and are replaced by the secondary or permanent teeth.

The 32 permanent teeth begin to erupt at approximately six years of age with the upper and lower first molars followed by the central and lateral upper and lower incisors between the ages of 7 and 9 years. These are followed by the canines, bicuspids and molars. The 'wisdom' teeth (back molars) are the last to appear, if they do so at all, at about 18 years of age, but often as late as the early twenties.

Composition of the teeth The hard outer surface of the teeth is called the enamel and the inner surface the dentine. Within the dentine in the center of the tooth is the pulp containing the nerves which originate from the root of the tooth which is embedded in the jawbone.

Possible problems Some types of behavior problems and infections at the time of primary tooth eruption are attributed to teething but many are coincidental and common to this stage of development. (Teething alone never causes fits or high fever.) There may be an increased tendency to certain infections such as gastroenteritis during the teething period although many children have no symptoms at all during teething while others become irritable and reluctant to eat.

Slow eruption of teeth may parallel a delay in bony development in some infants.

The permanent teeth may become discolored from tobacco smoking or because of poor hygiene. Teeth which have had the pulp removed (pulpotomy) and a root filling gradually become grey.

Cavities or dental decay is the most common tooth problem. Probably the largest single factor in reducing cavities in children in recent years has been the addition of fluoride to the water supply. Decay may also be greatly reduced by regular brushing to remove debris and by regular dental care.

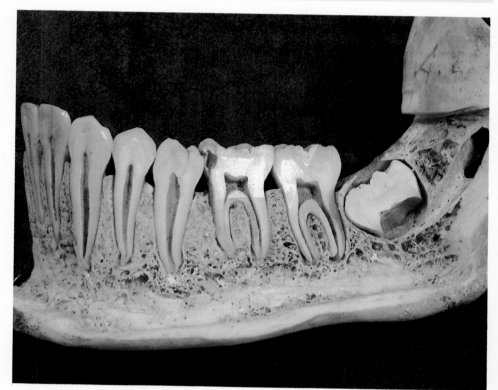

Diagram of section through a molar tooth.

crown — enamel — pulp — pulp cavity — neck — gingiva — root — dentin — periodontal membrane — cementin — root canal — spongy bone — nerve — vein — artery

Adult human lower mandible (jaw bone) showing root canals. Cavities are evident in 1st molar and a wisdom tooth is impacted. *(John Watney Photo Library)*

With proper care of gums and teeth and a nutritious diet it is possible for an adult to retain the permanent dentition throughout life. Missing teeth should always be replaced, not only to improve the facial appearance but because food must be bitten and chewed properly before swallowing.

33

Strenuous sports subject the muscles to considerable stress. (Zefa)

The structure of a muscle will depend on the arrangement and size of its fibers, which again will vary with the function. A more powerful muscle has a larger number of shorter fibers.

There are different types of fibers in muscle, such as the pale, thin, quickly contracting and easily tiring fibers that use a large amount of metabolic energy; and the red, thick, slowly contracting fibers which do not tire so easily. Some muscles are composed mainly of one sort of fiber. The amount of shortening that a muscle undergoes is related to its initial fiber length.

Mode of action Most skeletal muscles function by causing movement at the joint or joints over which they pass on their way from their origin to their insertion. The muscles may act either by relaxation or contraction according to whether they are acting with or against gravity or against resistance. Both relaxation and contraction of muscle may be important for its action.

Isometric contraction describes the situation in which muscle may contract voluntarily without movements occurring and without shortening, that is, the length of the muscle remains constant while the tension increases. In isotonic contraction the opposite occurs, the tension remaining constant while the muscle shortens.

In the musculoskeletal system the bones often act as levers for the muscles. In the limbs the muscles are usually attached just beyond the joint on which they act. This conveys the advantage of a small movement at the knee or elbow producing a wider movement at the corresponding foot or hand.

The different ways in which muscles function have been classified as follows: the prime movers, the antagonists, the fixation muscles and the synergists. One particular muscle can be classified in various ways at different times according to the particular movement involved.

The prime movers are responsible for the actual movements which take place. The antagonists are those muscles which, by relaxing, allow the movement to occur. If they were to contract they would produce the opposite movement. The fixation muscles provide a stable basis from which the muscles can act, steadying the part or joint. The synergists can be regarded as a special class of fixation muscle; they work by controlling the position of intermediate joints so that the prime movers which pass over several joints may exert their power in the movement of the joint required. Many movements require the simultaneous action of muscles from the four different groups.

All muscles are supplied by the vascular and nervous systems.

The muscular system

Comprising all the skeletal muscles, the muscular system does not include the cardiac or unstriated muscles which are found in the walls of organs, blood vessels and glands.

The skeletal muscles can be divided into two groups to correspond to the divisions in the skeleton: the axial muscles are grouped around the axial skeleton and comprise the muscles of the trunk, neck, head and face; the appendicular muscles are those of the limbs and correspond to the appendicular skeleton.

These skeletal muscles make up the 'red flesh' of the body, comprising approximately 42 per cent of body weight in the male and 36 per cent in the female. They are voluntary muscles, performing movement at will, and possess the characteristic of tone. Even at rest they are under a slight tension called *tonus*, a feature which is demonstrated by those muscles which maintain the normal posture of the body. Voluntary muscle is also known as striated muscle because of its characteristically striated appearance under the microscope.

Muscles derive their names from their structure, shape, location, direction, function or points of attachment.

A typical skeletal muscle comprises a number of muscle bundles (fasciculi)

which are covered by fibrous tissue (fascia). They connect at one or both ends to bundles of white fibrous tissues known as a tendon.

Attachments of muscle to bone Muscle fibers have the ability to contract. In order to do this they require a fairly fixed point of attachment, known as the origin, which is usually nearer the median plane of the body. In addition, an attachment known as an insertion is required, which may be relatively more movable.

Skeletal muscle is usually attached to bone through non-contractile fibrous tissue rather than muscle itself. Deep fascia, tendons, cartilage, ligaments or even skin may be the points of origin and insertion.

There are different sorts of muscular attachments — fleshy, tendinous and a combination of these. In a fleshy attachment the muscle appears to spring from the bone itself, although it is actually joined to the fibrous layer covering the bone. A tendinous attachment interposes some fibrous tissue (a tendon) between the muscle belly and the bone.

Tendons themselves can vary greatly in their appearance. They may be long and thin or broad. Aponeurosis describes a tendon which is sheet-like. A muscle consisting of two fleshy bellies is known as digastric or biventral. The two bellies may be set at angles to each other or in a straight line.

Nervous System

The system of the body which controls and coordinates all other body systems in response to environmental stimuli and the needs of the body is the nervous system. It comprises the central and the peripheral systems.

The central nervous system includes the brain and spinal cord which are continuous with one another at the large hole in the base of the skull (foramen magnum).

The peripheral nervous system, which connects the brain and spinal cord with all other parts of the body, includes the spinal and cranial nerves and also a special portion concerned with involuntary activity called the autonomic nervous system, itself composed of the sympathetic and parasympathetic nerves.

Nerve tissue is made up of cells or neurons and nerve fibers surrounded by supporting tissue (neuroglia) in a putty-like mass. Each neuron tapers at one end to form a long thin process called an axon; in addition most have other elongated branches called dendrites. Each one of these processes forms a nerve fiber, and a nerve is a bundle of nerve fibers.

The nerve fibers conduct electrical impulses or messages; fibers which convey impulses to the central nervous system are called sensory or afferent, and those carrying them away, motor or efferent.

The nerves

There are 12 pairs of cranial nerves and 31 pairs of spinal nerves. Cranial nerves are attached to the brain stem with the exception of the first two, the olfactory and optic, which are connected to the cerebral hemispheres. Some are purely motor, some sensory and some mixed.

Right
A model of the human body shows the nervous system network. *(Zefa)*

A single neuron, nerve cell, magnified 400 times. *(John Watney Photo Library)*

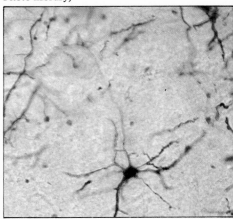

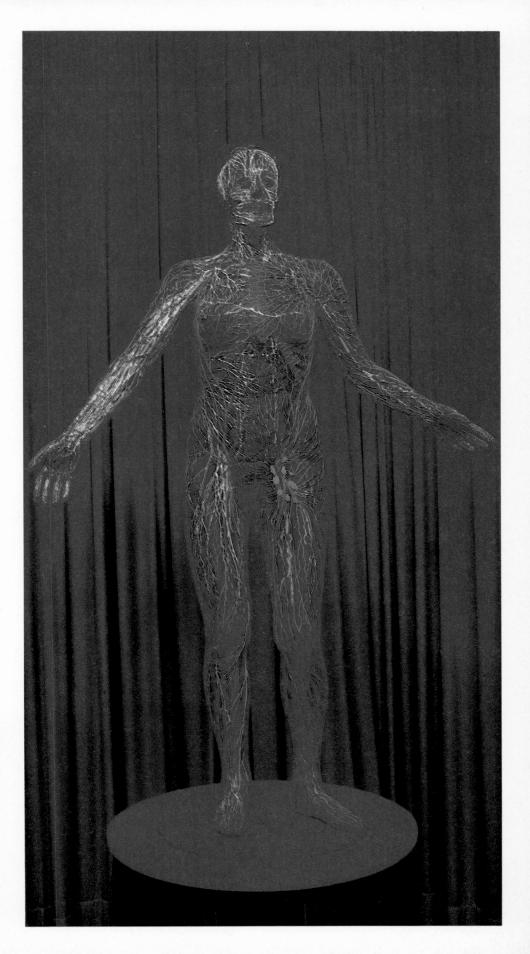

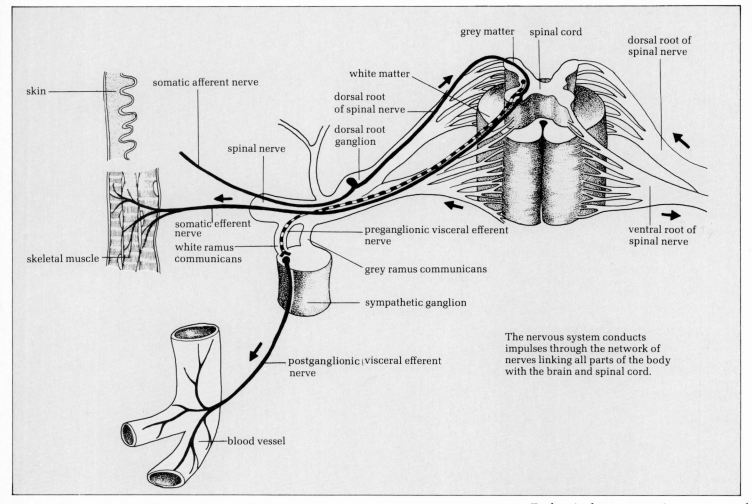

grey matter

spinal cord

dorsal root of spinal nerve

white matter

dorsal root of spinal nerve

dorsal root ganglion

skin

somatic afferent nerve

spinal nerve

somatic efferent nerve

white ramus communicans

skeletal muscle

preganglionic visceral efferent nerve

grey ramus communicans

ventral root of spinal nerve

sympathetic ganglion

postganglionic visceral efferent nerve

blood vessel

The nervous system conducts impulses through the network of nerves linking all parts of the body with the brain and spinal cord.

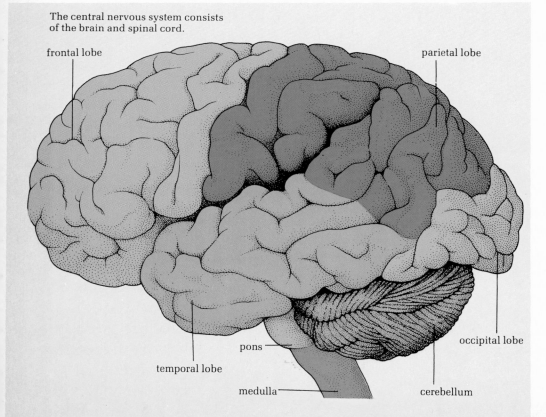

The central nervous system consists of the brain and spinal cord.

frontal lobe

parietal lobe

pons

temporal lobe

medulla

cerebellum

occipital lobe

Each spinal nerve contains sensory and motor fibers. The part of the nerve nearest the spinal cord is divided into two roots, anterior and posterior. The anterior root contains motor fibers, the posterior root, sensory fibers. The posterior root also has a ganglion from which the posterior root fibers emerge.

The spinal nerves are generally described according to the regions of the spine in which they join the spinal cord, thus cervical or neck (8); thoracic or chest (12); lumbar or lower back (5); sacral or hip region (5); and coccygeal at the root of the spine (1).

The brain

The expanded upper portion of the central nervous system is the brain. It is situated within the cranium or skull, and is the most important and most complex organ of the body. As well as controlling body functions and interpreting incoming signals the brain is the site of memory, learning, thinking and reasoning.

Within its mass of approximately 2¾ pounds (1.25 kg) are thousands of millions of nerve cells or neurons and their associated myriads of connections. These cells function at a level that is far more intricate than any computer

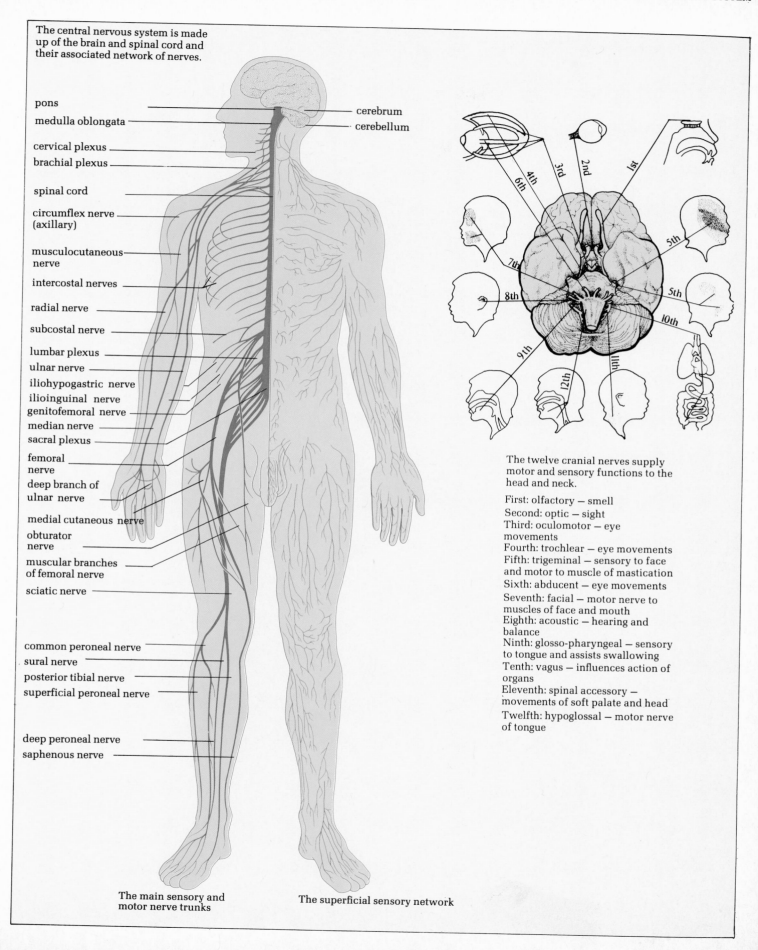

The central nervous system is made up of the brain and spinal cord and their associated network of nerves.

pons

medulla oblongata

cervical plexus

brachial plexus

spinal cord

circumflex nerve (axillary)

musculocutaneous nerve

intercostal nerves

radial nerve

subcostal nerve

lumbar plexus

ulnar nerve

iliohypogastric nerve

ilioinguinal nerve

genitofemoral nerve

median nerve

sacral plexus

femoral nerve

deep branch of ulnar nerve

medial cutaneous nerve

obturator nerve

muscular branches of femoral nerve

sciatic nerve

common peroneal nerve

sural nerve

posterior tibial nerve

superficial peroneal nerve

deep peroneal nerve

saphenous nerve

cerebrum

cerebellum

The main sensory and motor nerve trunks

The superficial sensory network

The twelve cranial nerves supply motor and sensory functions to the head and neck.

First: olfactory — smell
Second: optic — sight
Third: oculomotor — eye movements
Fourth: trochlear — eye movements
Fifth: trigeminal — sensory to face and motor to muscle of mastication
Sixth: abducent — eye movements
Seventh: facial — motor nerve to muscles of face and mouth
Eighth: acoustic — hearing and balance
Ninth: glosso-pharyngeal — sensory to tongue and assists swallowing
Tenth: vagus — influences action of organs
Eleventh: spinal accessory — movements of soft palate and head
Twelfth: hypoglossal — motor nerve of tongue

The brain comprises a number of regions or structures.

The brainstem is the part that extends upwards for about 4 inches (10 cm) from the spinal cord. It is comprised, in ascending order, of the *medulla oblongata*, the *pons*, and the *midbrain*. As well as providing the access for nerve fibers going to other parts of the brain, the brainstem controls most of the autonomic body functions.

These activities occur 'spontaneously', with the body exerting little conscious control over them, and include the beating of the heart, the processes of digestion and the production of urine.

The medulla oblongata contains masses of nerve cells or nuclei from which most of the cranial nerves arise. Many actions are controlled by these cells, including those of the heart, lungs and nervous system, and the muscles of the head and neck.

The pons (Latin for bridge) lies between the medulla oblongata and the midbrain. It acts as a conduit for nerve fibers that pass both upward to the brain and across to the two hemispheres of the cerebrum.

Complex activities requiring the simultaneous utilization and coordination of many different nerve fibers use the many connections within this structure. Gymnastics, which need balance and a very high degree of visual coordination, is but one example.

The *midbrain* expands in its upper region as its fibers enter the cerebrum (the major component of the brain). Within the midbrain is the *thalamus*, the chief 'relay station' of sensory fibers, which receives input from the cerebellum, the spinal cord, and the cranial nerves. These messages are then passed on to higher centers in the cerebrum, where all sensations such as touch, pain and temperature, and the basic senses such as hearing and sight are interpreted.

The hypothalamus, which regulates the body's temperature, appetite and also influences a number of aspects of metabolism (body chemistry) is also contained within the midbrain.

The cerebellum overlies the upper part of the brainstem. This structure is responsible for the maintenance of balance, muscular coordination and posture.

The cerebrum lies on top of the brainstem, and comprises about three-quarters of all brain tissue. It is composed of two hemispheres, each of which is responsible, in the main, for the actions of and sensations in the opposite side of the body. This is because most of the nerve fibers cross over as they traverse the medulla oblongata. One hemisphere is, however, dominant in many functions, such as speech and the relative usage of a particular hand or foot. Most right-handed people, for instance, have what is termed 'left-sided dominance'.

The different parts of the brain control particular body functions.

speech control · sensation · movement · consciousness

vision · hearing · taste · smell · olfactory nerves · intellectual activity

The cerebrum is the control center of all conscious activities and thought processes and receives continuous sensations from sensory nerve endings within the skin, and from other organs such as the ear and eye. A filtering or selection system operates so that only the information considered most important is perceived at a conscious level at any one time.

One common example of this process is the ability to concentrate on a conversation with one person in a crowded room while excluding all other chatter. The usual lack of awareness of clothes resting upon the skin, unless specifically thought about is another example.

Emotions, imagination, conscience and memory, and the control of motor activities such as walking and chewing are also functions of the cerebrum.

The pituitary gland, another important structure within the brain, is situated deep within the brain tissue. It releases a number of *hormones* that in turn control other glands of the body such as the adrenals, the thyroid and the sex glands.

The meninges are three membranes which cover the brain and spinal cord. The outermost is the *dura mater*, a tough membrane lining the inner surface of the skull bones. The middle layer is the *arachnoid*, and the innermost layer, the thinnest and most delicate, is the *pia mater*. The space between the pia and the arachnoid is filled with the *cerebrospinal fluid (CSF)*.

These coverings provide support for the brain and spinal cord, and for the blood vessels that run along the brain just beneath the pia. They also provide a space for the cushioning fluid that literally bathes the nervous tissue.

Cerebrospinal fluid is made by a special fold of the pia mater that lies within two cavities in the cerebrum known as the lateral ventricles. From here it circulates through two midline ventricles within the brainstem and the central canal of the spinal cord, and around the tissues within the subarachnoid space. As well as providing a protective cushion against any injury to or sudden movement of the brain and spinal cord within their bony enclosure, it equalizes any changes in pressure that may occur.

The outer surface of the cerebral hemispheres and cerebellum is composed of a series of ridges and grooves known respectively as gyri (convolutions) and sulci. This infolding pattern increases the surface area of the brain and makes the most efficient use of the space available in the skull.

Grey matter, which forms the outermost layer of the brain, is composed of nerve cells that both originate and receive nerve impulses or signals. This is the thinking or active portion and it overlies the *white matter*, which is made up predominantly of nerve fibers. These are the long thin extensions of the nerve cells that transmit impulses. Within the spinal cord the white matter forms the outer layer of the nervous system tissue.

The functioning of the brain and its connections is extremely complex. An increasing number of chemical systems and substances that play a role in the transmission of information and impulses from one nerve cell to another have been identified. A major breakthrough in this field was the identification of a specific transmitter called dopamine that was lacking in people suffering from Parkinson's disease.

The exact mechanism by which information is learned and stored as memory is far from being fully understood. The relative roles of heredity, previous experiences, the external environment, personality, intelligence and character are still debated.

Much research and investigation into the mechanism and functioning of the brain continues.

The spinal cord

The spinal cord is a column of nerve tissue extending down from the medulla and occupying the upper two-thirds of the spinal canal (the backbone). It is shaped somewhat like a cylinder, flattened on one side and thickened in the neck (cervical) and back (lumbar) areas.

The nerve tissue is composed of grey matter or nerve cells surrounded by white matter consisting of nerve fibers which convey impulses up and down the spinal cord. The core of grey matter divides the white matter into anterior (front), lateral (side) and posterior (back) bundles of

nerves. These connect the brain and the spinal cord in both directions to enable the transmission of impulses up and down the cord.

The somatic and autonomic aspects of the nervous system

On a functional basis, the nervous system can be regarded as two parts, the somatic nervous system concerned with the reception of sensory information and the execution of movements by somatic muscles, and the autonomic system which controls the activity of organs, glands and blood vessels. The functions of all the various parts are closely integrated.

The motor system for the control of muscular movements in the body arises in the neurons of the motor area of the cerebral cortex (precentral gyrus) where the cells have a strict anatomical arrangement. The fibers converge through various areas and continue their downward course through the midbrain, pons and medulla where most cross the midline and descend in the spinal cord, terminating in grey matter connected with the neurons from which the motor spinal nerves emerge. Motor impulses are then conveyed to the motor end-plate of the muscles. This system is regulated and influenced by many other impulses from the cerebellum and brainstem.

The sensory system. Superficial sensation has three primary modalities: touch, pain and temperature. The deeper sensations are deep pain, pressure, movement and position.

Sensory impulses arise in sensory receptors in skin and deeper structures and pass along sensory nerve fibers to their cell stations in the posterior root ganglia and then into the spinal cord along specific pathways in the ascending white matter, crossing over at some point to the

opposite side to the great cell relay station of the thalamus in the cerebrum. The impulses then pass to their final station in the sensory cortex (postcentral gyrus) where areas subserving different parts of the body are arranged in a similar way to the motor cortex. At the cortical level, appreciation, integration, localization and interpretation of sensory information occurs.

When a nerve is stimulated to conduct an impulse, a small but measurable amount of heat is produced. Nerves utilize carbohydrate almost exclusively for cellular respiration and energy needs. The carbohydrate stores (glycogen) of the brain are very small, thus a minute to minute supply of blood glucose is particularly important to the nervous system. At the junction of the nerve fiber and the organ or cell supplied, such as muscle, a chemical substance is released by the action of the nerve impulse. This substance, called neurotransmitter, actually brings about the activity of the effector organ. The known neurotransmitters include acetylcholine, adrenalin, noradrenalin and dopamine.

Respiratory System

The organs concerned with breathing and the interchange of gases in the lungs are known collectively as the respiratory system. Air is breathed in through the nose and passes through the nostrils, the hairs in the nose cleaning, warming and moistening it as it passes through, but the respiratory system proper begins with the pharynx (the passageway from the nose to the larynx).

Larynx The larynx or voice box is specially adapted to protect the entrance of the air passages to the lung. It is able to close so that solids, liquids, and even air if necessary, cannot pass.

The larynx contains the vocal folds used in voice production and has many muscles which change the position and thus the tension of the vocal folds.

The larynx is composed of the thyroid, cricoid, epiglottic, arytenoid, corniculate and cuneiform cartilages. Below, the larynx is continuous with the trachea or windpipe.

Trachea The tracheal structure includes a number of cartilaginous rings. At birth the trachea is about 1½ inches (4 cm) long, by adulthood it has extended to about 4¾ inches (12 cm).

The structure of the trachea comprises three layers. The innermost is the mucous layer, the next the submucous layer and then the supporting layer which comprises a network of elastic fibers including the tracheal cartilages. These prevent the collapse of the trachea. From the trachea the respiratory system branches into two

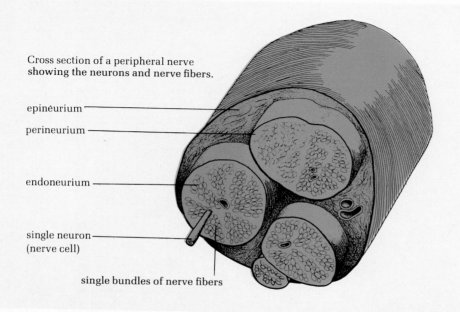

Cross section of a peripheral nerve showing the neurons and nerve fibers.

epineurium

perineurium

endoneurium

single neuron
(nerve cell)

single bundles of nerve fibers

bronchi. Like the trachea, the bronchi are supported by cartilage.

Bronchi The bronchi lead into the lungs, one main bronchus to the right lung and one to the left, each bronchus dividing into secondary or lobar bronchi with three on the right side and two on the left. Each of these bronchi divide into still smaller airways to supply segments or lobes of the lung. With further division into yet smaller bronchioles they extend to the alveoli or air sacs.

Lungs are the twin organs in which the blood gives up water and carbon dioxide and receives oxygen.

The thoracic cavity is divided into a pair of pleural cavities with an intervening region called the mediastinum. Each lung lies in a pleural cavity and is covered by a membrane called the pleura which is continuous with the pleural membrane lining the inner surface of each cavity. The pleural space thus enclosed is under negative pressure to allow for lung expansion during the act of breathing air into the lung (inspiration).

The lungs are soft, spongy, and pliable, and very light. In adults they have a dark mottled appearance but are pink in children. The overall shape is pyramidal with an apex lying above the clavicle in the web of the neck and grooved by a subclavian artery. The base is indented and semilunar in outline and lies on the diaphragm which separates the right lung from the liver and the left lung from the liver, stomach and spleen. The front border of the left lung, near its lower end, has a wide indentation or notch to allow for

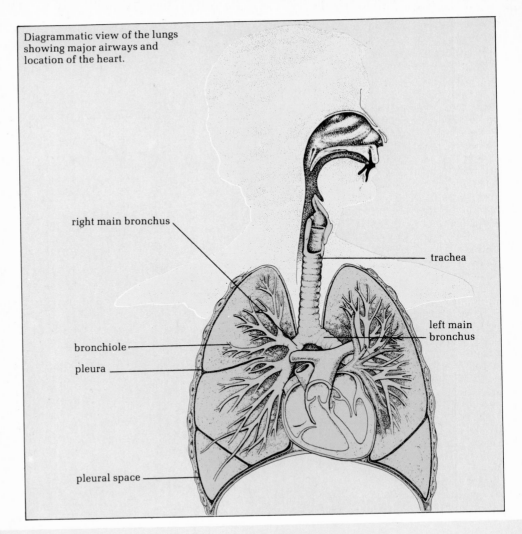

Diagrammatic view of the lungs showing major airways and location of the heart.

right main bronchus

trachea

bronchiole

left main bronchus

pleura

pleural space

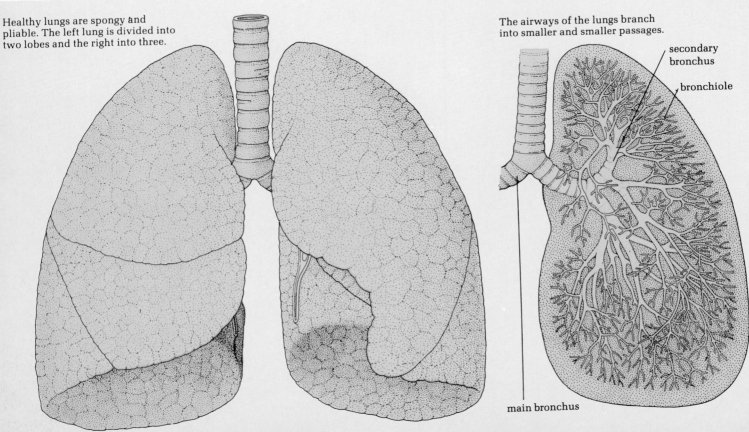

Healthy lungs are spongy and pliable. The left lung is divided into two lobes and the right into three.

The airways of the lungs branch into smaller and smaller passages.

secondary bronchus

bronchiole

main bronchus

the heart to be uncovered by lung in the front. All blood vessels, nerves and bronchial passages enter and emerge from the medial surface at an area called the hilum.

The left lung is divided into two lobes by an oblique fissure. The right is divided into three lobes by two fissures. Pulmonary arteries convey blood from the heart to the lungs for oxygenation and pulmonary veins convey it back again to the left side of the heart for ejection into the general circulation. Lung substance is supplied with oxygenated blood by bronchial arteries. Lymph vessels end in glands within the lung and its hilum.

Respiration The bronchial airways divide and subdivide within the lung substance ending in tiny, thin-walled, air-filled sacs called alveoli, where the gaseous exchange occurs.

Oxygen from the air in the alveoli diffuses into the capillary vessels on their outer wall where it is taken up and transported by red blood cells to all tissues. About one-quarter of the oxygen in inspired air passes into the blood and is replaced in the expired air by carbon dioxide leaving the blood. It is assumed that gaseous exchange occurs in accordance with the laws of simple diffusion of gases, or the difference in pressure of each particular gas on either side of the capillary membrane. The pressure of nitrogen is essentially the same in both venous blood and alveoli and the gas is therefore physiologically inert.

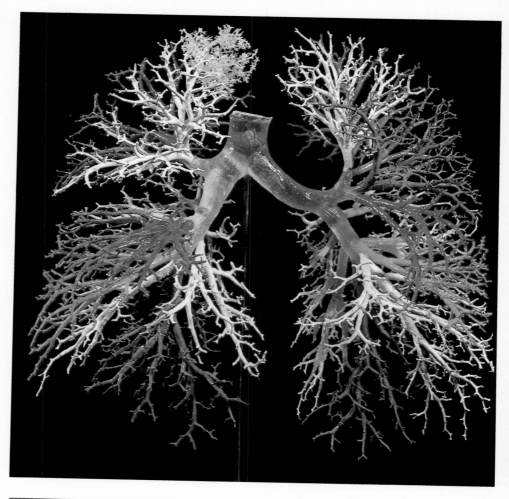

The airways of the lungs, showing the segmented bronchi and their main branches. (*John Watney Photo Library*)

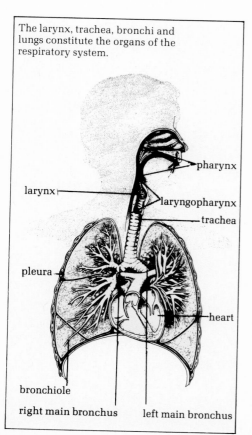

The larynx, trachea, bronchi and lungs constitute the organs of the respiratory system.

pharynx

larynx

laryngopharynx

trachea

pleura

heart

bronchiole

right main bronchus   left main bronchus

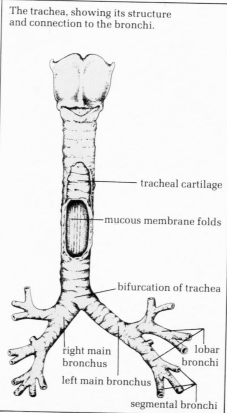

The trachea, showing its structure and connection to the bronchi.

tracheal cartilage

mucous membrane folds

bifurcation of trachea

right main bronchus

lobar bronchi

left main bronchus

segmental bronchi

Prior to birth, the fetal lung is unexpanded and receives only a very small blood supply to provide for lung growth and development. At the time of birth, with the first breath, lung by-pass routes close (foramen ovale and ductus arteriosus) with lung expansion, and thereafter the blood receives oxygenation in the usual manner.

Skin

As well as protecting the body from its external environment, the skin plays a key role in a number of body processes. It is the main organ of sensation, keeping each individual attuned to his external surroundings through the millions of sensitive nerve endings within its structure. Sweat glands and a rich network of blood vessels provide an efficient mechanism for temperature control and heat regulation.

There are two main layers of the skin proper, consisting of an outer epidermis and an inner dermis. Beneath these two outermost body coverings is a thicker subcutaneous region consisting primarily of fatty tissue. This layer provides insulation, support, a reserve of calories for times of need, and a 'buffer zone' for the minor injuries repeatedly suffered by the skin.

The epidermis is the cellular layer of the skin, varying in thickness from .003 inches (.1 mm) in the eyelid to over .03 inches (1 mm) on the palms of the hands and soles of the feet. It contains no nerves, blood vessels or connective tissue fibers, and derives its nutrition from the layer beneath.

Tall, columnar cells in the basal or germinal layer of the epidermis multiply continually. The cells produced are pushed towards the surface as newer ones are formed beneath them. As the cells move upwards, they flatten and eventually lose their nuclei. They die before reaching the surface and form keratin, a fibrous protein that acts as the final barrier to potentially damaging agents.

The rate at which keratin is abraded away generally equals the rate at which new cells are formed, so that the skin thickness remains constant. On average, a skin cell takes about one month to complete its life cycle from basal layer production to keratin flaking. Whenever there is any injury or damage to the skin, even relatively minor scratching, there is an increase in the rate of basal layer cell division and a compensatory thickening of the dermis. This process is clearly shown in the development of callus in response to continued friction.

A second cell division process occurs in the epidermis. Melanocytes derived from the nervous system are scattered throughout the basal layer and these cells are responsible for the pigmentation of the skin. The protective pigment contained within them is called melanin, and the amount in each cell increases following exposure to sunlight, particularly the ultraviolet component. Albinism is the condition in which there is an absence of this pigment.

The dermis A thin basement membrane separates the epidermis from the underlying dermis. The junction is wavy, with cone-shaped dermal papillae pointing towards the surface. These are larger in the palms and soles and create the ridges from which prints may be taken. Portions of the dermis extend downwards and attach to the connective tissue beneath the dermis. These areas form natural skin creases.

Collagen fibers make up the bulk of the dermis, although elastic fibers, occasional cells and a mucus-polysaccharide 'cement' complete the framework within which lie the many specialized structures of the skin. A rich supply of nerve fibers and blood vessels also lies within this layer. The main function of the dermis is to support and protect the structures within it.

Nerve fibers

A large number of nerve fibers is present in the deeper layers of the skin. They are one of the most important components of this organ. As well as providing the means of registering sensations, such as pain and temperature, the nerves also regulate, via the autonomic nervous system, the sweat glands and the blood vessels.

Blood vessels

The blood vessels provide nourishment for other structures within the dermis as well as the epidermal cells. Heat regulation and local immune defense mechanisms are also dependent upon this blood supply. The capillaries within the skin enable an exchange of nutrients and waste products to occur. These vessels become more permeable in response to tissue damage, particularly because of the release of histamine and other related chemicals from mast cells in the skin. The increase in permeability allows immune cells and proteins to leave the capillaries.

The arterioles (small arteries) of the skin contain smooth muscle in their walls. This muscle contracts in response to cold or shock and relaxes in response to heat. When these vessels constrict, the skin becomes white and cold and heat loss from the body is minimised. Adequate blood flow to more essential organs, such as the heart and brain, is maintained. This process is most marked during times of blood loss or circulatory collapse.

Hair

There are basically two types of hair. *Vellus* hairs are fine and downy, covering most of the body, except the palms and soles. *Terminal* hairs are longer and darker and are found in the scalp, eyebrows, eyelashes, the groin, the armpit and the male beard line. The terminal hairs are those of major concern for many people, because of their cosmetic importance.

Hair follicles are impouchings of the skin that extend into the dermis. One or more sebaceous glands open into them and their base is formed by a papilla from which the hair matrix develops. In the pigmented terminal hair follicles there is a layer of melanocytes in the papillae that provides the hair colouring. The hair filament is composed of keratin. It is formed in a method similar to the keratin that becomes the surface of the skin.

A full head of hair contains about 100 000 hairs. With an average lifespan of three years for the scalp hair, about 70 hairs are lost from the head each day. Once a hair has been shed, the growing phase of that particular follicle commences once more and a new one soon emerges.

Nails

These are hard keratin structures formed by special cells found at the end of fingers and toes. The cells of the nail bed contain no melanocytes, and the nail is able to grow indefinitely and regrow when cut. There is no cyclical shedding and regrowth as occurs in hairs.

Sebaceous glands

These structures are found only in association with hair follicles and their function is to provide a grease, or fatty-based product, called sebum, important in maintaining the moisture and suppleness of the skin. Although they are found predominantly on the scalp, face and

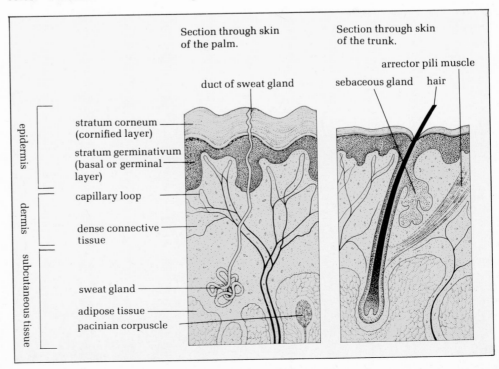

Section through skin of the palm.

Section through skin of the trunk.

epidermis

dermis

subcutaneous tissue

duct of sweat gland

arrector pili muscle

sebaceous gland   hair

stratum corneum (cornified layer)

stratum germinativum (basal or germinal layer)

capillary loop

dense connective tissue

sweat gland

adipose tissue

pacinian corpuscle

groin areas, sebaceous glands are found in lesser numbers in all parts of the skin except the palms and soles. There is no nerve supply to these glands although they are influenced by a number of hormones.

Sweat glands

These glands consist of coiled tubes deep in the dermis that extend upwards to open onto the skin surface. They are activated by the autonomic nervous system to release their watery secretions whenever the body starts to overheat. There is also increased perspiration or sweating during fear or anxiety.

Special Senses

We tend to take for granted the senses which give us our perception of the world around us, until perhaps one of these senses becomes impaired, cutting us off from a particular aspect of sensation and limiting our lifestyle. It is worth understanding something of how the sensory organs operate, how they keep us in communication with the environment.

Hearing

The ears provide one of the most important human senses. Apart from the most obvious benefit of communication with other people through hearing speech, there are many other crucial ways in which this sense is employed. When crossing the road, the noise of an oncoming car alerts us to danger as much as the sight of its approach. Many other warning sounds alert us throughout the day of impending danger, accidents or occurrences of which we would otherwise be unaware.

Enjoyment of music, dialogue, theater, the sounds of nature and familiar happy voices are all benefits to daily life gained through a functioning ear. In addition it is often not realized that the inner ear is intimately integrated with the brain to provide a sense of balance without which we would have difficulty walking steadily in a straight line or standing upright.

Outer ear On the outside of the head is the ear trumpet or auricle which leads down a curved passage about 1½ inches (4 cm) long, the external auditory canal, to the drum (the tympanic membrane). This is the external or outer ear which assists hearing by directing sound waves towards the central canal. This can be augmented by cupping the hand behind the ear to increase the sound-collecting area, the principle behind the first type of hearing aid, the ear trumpet.

Middle ear The drum is the side of an air-filled bony six-sided box lined with mucous membrane called the middle ear or tympanic cavity. Inside the box are three tiny bones (ossicles) which articulate with

The structure of the ear.

helix
temporal bone
antihelix
tympanic membrane
external acoustic meatus
facial nerve
lobe
semi-circular canals
cochlea
stapes (stirrup)
incus (anvil)
malleus (hammer)

The ear is able to pick up a wide range of sounds. *(Zefa)*

one another, the malleus (shaped like a hammer), the incus (shaped like an anvil) and the stapes (like a stirrup). The handle of the malleus touches the drum and the stapes abuts the 'oval window' on the opposite wall of the bony box which leads to the inner ear. Also opening into the tympanic cavity is the Eustachian tube, a 1½ inches (4 cm) long air passage which leads to the nose and the back of the throat. This tube allows equalization of pressure between the nasal passages (and outside atmospheric pressure) and the otherwise closed box of the middle ear.

Inner ear The inner ear (labyrinth) is divided into three parts; the vestibule, which is a fluid-filled chamber connected through the oval window with the middle ear; the semi-circular canals which are three fluid-filled curved tubes at different projections embedded in bone; and the cochlea which is the organ of hearing. The cochlea is so called because its spiral tube looks like a cockle or snail shell. Sound waves received by the oval window pass along the fluid-filled coils of the cochlea. Pressure changes induced in this way in the fluid stimulate special hair cells (in part of the cochlea called the organ of Corti) to produce electrical impulses. These are transmitted to the hearing center in the brain tissue by the vestibulocochlear nerve.

To prevent pressure waves reflecting back and re-stimulating the hair cells, another membrane-lined opening in the cochlea just below the stapes attachment absorbs the impulses that have passed through the cochlea. This is called the round window, and it expands and contracts in order to absorb the pressure waves.

The vestibule and canals are not concerned with hearing but with balance.

Ear drum It is possible to see the external ear canal and the drum in two ways. Either an auroscope, an instrument with a light source and attached shaped tube (speculum) to hold the curve of the external canal straight is used, or a head mirror, speculum and separate light is used.

The normal drum is a pearly grey colour. The handle of the malleus is visible lying nearly vertically near the centre of the drum. A cone of light is reflected from the lower end of the handle to the periphery. If the drum is inflamed it is reddish pink. If there is pus in the bony box of the middle ear, the drum is red, tense and bulging. Any holes in the drum where pus has burst through under pressure are seen as black holes (perforations), most frequently in the upper part of the drum.

Ear wax, also known as cerumen, is the soft brown secretion produced in the outer ear to protect the ear canal. This wax is carried forward through the outer ear canal to the exterior by lining cells which themselves turn over and carry the wax with them. It is therefore unnecessary to clean inside the ear canal; only the entrance and the outer part of the ear need to be cleaned. Inserting objects such as bobbypins or cotton buds into the ear canal itself is not advised as they may perforate the ear drum or scratch and infect the ear canal.

In some cases the ear wax dries out and impacts against the ear drum, causing deafness or blocked ears. Once the diagnosis is confirmed, ear drops or a few drops of olive oil put in the ear each day for about a week will help to soften the wax which can then be syringed out by a doctor.

Sound and sound measurement Sounds vary in their loudness, pitch and quality, and the ear is finely attuned to pick up a wide range of sounds. Loudness is measured in decibels, the scale of which is logarithmic, which means that a rise of 10 decibels (dB) means a tenfold increase in loudness. A barely audible whisper is 10 dB, while a normal conversation of 20 dB is ten times as loud. Persistent noise of over 100 dB (one thousand million whispers) can permanently damage the hearing mechanism. A jet taking off can produce a noise level equivalent to 130 dB.

The pitch or frequency of a sound is measured as the number of cycles per second or Hertz (Hz). The lower the Hz the deeper the sound. The normal range of human hearing lies between 15 and 30 000 Hz, but the upper limit falls rapidly with age. By adulthood this has often fallen to 15 000 Hz. Most speech is in the 40 to 4 000 Hz range.

The direction from which sounds come can be detected by the hearing center in the brain which interprets the difference in sound intensity or loudness received from each ear. It is therefore impossible, without other information such as that provided by the eyes, to detect whether sounds have come from exactly in front or behind.

Difficulty in hearing usually becomes obvious when the hearing loss, compared to the norm, becomes greater than 20 dB.

Sight

Eyesight is a complex and important function that begins when light rays enter the front of the eye through the cornea which is transparent, like a window. The cornea plays a major role in focusing the incoming light rays. The rays then pass through the lens, also a clear structure, normally. The lens acts as a 'fine tuner', and adjusts the light rays so that they form their image correctly at the surface of the retina.

Once light rays are focused on the retina, they are converted into nerve impulses that are taken via the optic nerve to the area of the brain where they are interpreted as 'sight'.

The eye is the organ of vision. In structural terms it can be considered as a special type of camera.

Light enters the eye through a transparent curved window called the cornea, which protects the eye's inner contents and focuses the light rays. The lens, a transparent curved structure, then transmits the light rays and focuses them on the surface of the retina.

The retina is a thin light-sensitive layer at the back of the eye and represents the innermost lining of the sheath of the eyeball. It contains special cells called rods and cones which convert light into electrical impulses. Each of these cell types connect with special nerve cells that make up the major component of the retinal tissue.

Normal vision is the result of many complex processes involving various parts of the brain. (*Zefa*)

These nerve fibers meet at a structure called the optic disc. This is also where the main blood vessels that supply the eye enter and subsequently branch. At the optic disc the nerve fibers aggregate to form the optic nerve. This nerve then runs along the bony orbit of the skull to enter the skull cavity, where it then forms part of the brain tissue.

The nerve impulses formed at the rods and cones are transferred by the optic nerve to a special area in the brain called the visual center. It is here that they are interpreted as the sensation of sight.

The iris gives the eye its color and controls the amount of light entering by varying the opening of the pupil.

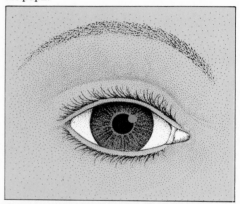

The amount of light that enters the eye is controlled by the iris. This, situated between the cornea and the lens tissue gives the eye its color. The actual center of the iris is called the pupil.

In controlling the amount of light entering the eye, the iris assists in the process of focusing it. When the opening (size of the pupil) is small, a greater depth of focus is obtained. This means that both near and far objects are in focus at the same time. When the pupil is wide open (fully dilated) distant objects become slightly out of focus. The same principle applies in the photographic camera where the size of the diaphragm is adjusted to alter the depth of focus. Pupil size is controlled by special muscle fibers in the iris, largely under control of nerves from the automatic nervous system.

The front part of the eye is divided into two major chambers. The anterior chamber comprises all the space in front of the iris, while the posterior chamber consists of the area between the iris and the lens.

The front of the eye is filled with a clear watery fluid called the aqueous humour, which is the equivalent of the 'lymph of the eye'. This fluid is produced by special cells in the ciliary body, a structure to which the lens attaches. There is persistent circulation of aqueous humour throughout the front of the eye. It is absorbed back into small blood vessels in the area between the cornea and iris (called the filtration angle). Glaucoma occurs when the absorption of aqueous humour is impaired, and pressure increases as a result.

The space behind the lens is filled with a clear jelly-like substance called the vitreous humour.

The sclera is the tough, fibrous, outermost covering of the eye; this is the 'white of the eye' as seen through the conjunctiva. It becomes continuous with the cornea and is made up of tightly entwined fibrous tissue bundles. The conjunctiva is the delicate membrane that lines the inside surface of the eyelids and extends to cover the exposed part of the sclera.

Beneath the sclera is the so-called 'middle layer' of the eyeball. This offers general support for the eye and helps it to keep its shape. Its medical name is the choroid. It is an extension of the ciliary body and iris, and these three structures are called the uvea or uveal tract. The choroid has a large number of blood vessels and also many pigment cells which give it a purple coloration.

Factors affecting vision Anything that causes damage to the retina, the optic nerve, or the part of the brain that interprets the nerve impulses may affect vision.

In dim lighting, the iris adjusts to give better perception.

For example, opacities in the lens (called cataracts), and opacities in the cornea resulting from trauma, infection, or metabolic defects can affect vision by preventing light rays from being adequately focused on the retina.

Sometimes the muscles used in focusing become fatigued producing a feeling of tiredness or pain known as asthenopia.

Normally, the distance from the lens to the retinal surface allows exact focusing of incoming rays. There are three main conditions that may affect this normal process.

Hyperopia (also called far-sightedness or long sightedness) occurs when the point of focus would be behind, not on, the retina. When this occurs the lens is able to focus on objects at a distance, but not on near objects. This is corrected by using a convex lens in a pair of glasses.

Myopia occurs when the light rays come to focus on a point in front of the retina. Near objects can be viewed clearly with appropriate adjustment of the lens, but this becomes impossible for distant ones. This is corrected by concave lenses in glasses.

Presbyopia occurs when the lens loses its elasticity, a feature that commonly develops in people over the age of 45. Both close and long-distance vision is affected, and glasses with two different types of lenses (bifocals) may be required.

Astigmatism. When the curvature of the cornea is significantly altered, the lens and brain center for sight may not be able to compensate adequately. Blurring and distortion of vision occurs. This abnormality in the corneal surface is called astigmatism.

Usually present from birth, astigmatism may be severe enough to affect a child's schoolwork. It should be suspected when a child tilts his head at an unusual angle to read. This maneuver, enabling light to enter through a part of the cornea with the normal curve, can sometimes minimize distortion.

In regular astigmatism, where the refractive power of the cornea (its ability to focus light) varies regularly, special cylindrical lens glasses can readily correct the problem.

Corneal transplantation. Previously some conditions, such as trachoma or trauma from chemicals, resulted in permanent damage to the cornea and blindness.

Corneal transplantation is now performed routinely, with a high rate of success, in most large medical centers.

Radial keratomy. This proceedure is relatively new. Extremely short-sighted (myopic) people used to have to wear very thick glasses to see effectively. Radial keratomy shaves away cornea so as to decrease the radius and allow much thinner spectacles to be worn. It is not suitable for mildly short-sighted people.

Binocular vision Within each orbit (the bony cavity that contains the eye) there is a layer of fat that helps to pad and protect the eyeball. Six muscles extend from the orbit to attach to the eyeball and thereby control eye movements. These muscles are normally coordinated in such a way that both eyes move in the same direction. A similar mechanism of nerve connections between the two eyes also controls the size of the pupil and the process of accommodation. As a result the latter processes also occur simultaneously in both eyes.

Stereoscopic vision When both eyes are open, these differences are not perceived because the visual cortex computes all the incoming signals and registers a composite picture. This 'fusion' of images enables depth and distance to be judged, and also provides a wider field of vision.

If there is malalignment of the eyes, known as a squint, binocular vision is lost and double vision occurs because the brain is no longer able to fuse the images. If no corrective treatment is undertaken, the weaker image is eventually suppressed entirely.

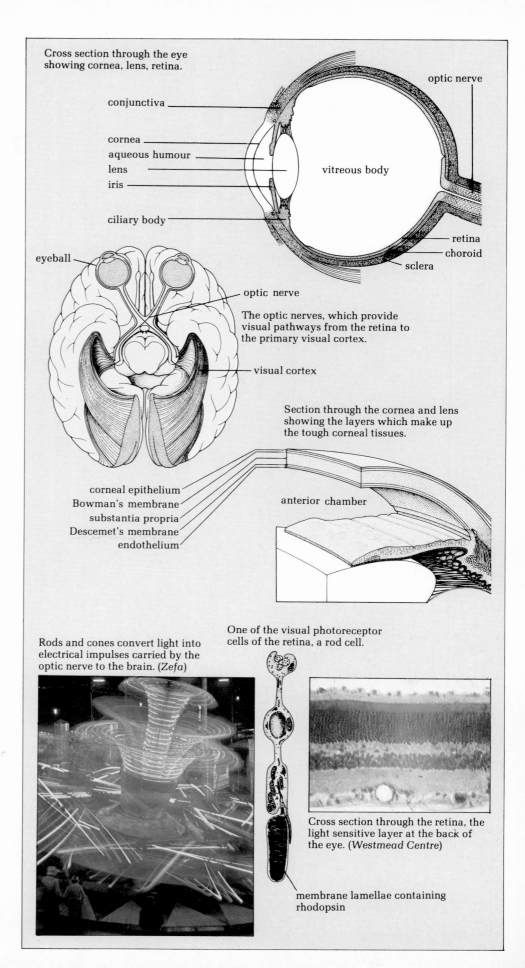

Cross section through the eye showing cornea, lens, retina.

conjunctiva

cornea

aqueous humour

lens

iris

ciliary body

optic nerve

vitreous body

retina

choroid

sclera

eyeball

optic nerve

The optic nerves, which provide visual pathways from the retina to the primary visual cortex.

visual cortex

Section through the cornea and lens showing the layers which make up the tough corneal tissues.

corneal epithelium

Bowman's membrane

substantia propria

Descemet's membrane

endothelium

anterior chamber

Rods and cones convert light into electrical impulses carried by the optic nerve to the brain. (*Zefa*)

One of the visual photoreceptor cells of the retina, a rod cell.

Cross section through the retina, the light sensitive layer at the back of the eye. (*Westmead Centre*)

membrane lamellae containing rhodopsin

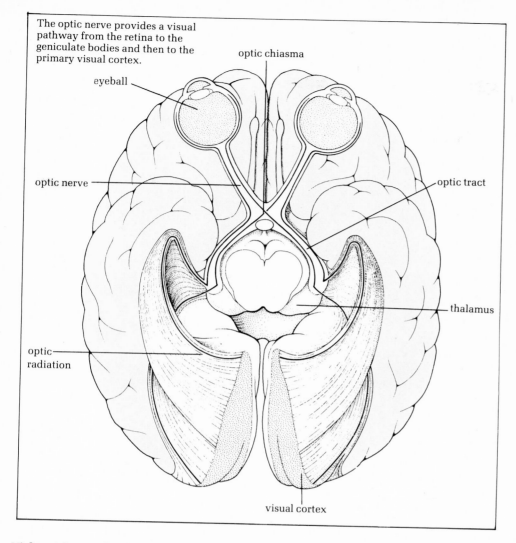

The optic nerve provides a visual pathway from the retina to the geniculate bodies and then to the primary visual cortex.

optic chiasma

eyeball

optic nerve

optic tract

optic radiation

thalamus

visual cortex

longed lack of this vitamin in the diet, the level of retinol falls and night blindness ensues. This is the relative failure of the rods to function in subdued light. Illumination needs to be quite strong for affected people to see adequately.

Visual fields and tunnel vision The visual field is the area within which objects will be seen by the eyes when they are in the straight ahead position. Because the retina is not distributed symmetrically around the optic nerve, the visual field is not circular even though the inner surface of the eye is spherical.

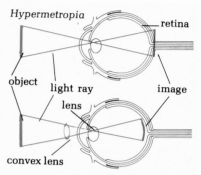

Hypermetropia

retina

object

light ray

lens

image

convex lens

In hypermetropia, or long-sightedness, distant images cannot be focused clearly on the retina. The natural point of focus would be behind the retina, but glasses with a convex lens correct this problem. *(Westmead Centre)*

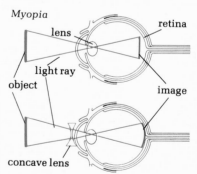

Myopia

lens

retina

object

light ray

image

concave lens

In myopia, or short-sightedness, glasses with a concave lens are prescribed so that the light rays are focused on the retina. Without glasses the natural point of focus would be in front of the retina, causing a blurred image. *(Westmead Centre)*

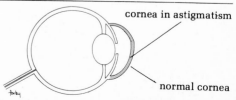

cornea in astigmatism

normal cornea

Cross-section of the eye showing uneven segments of the cornea. *(Westmead Centre)*

Night vision and color vision The rods and cones within the retina contain special pigments such as rhodopsin and iodopsin that are altered chemically when exposed to light. Such changes produce the nerve impulses which are subsequently transmitted to the visual cortex.

However, the distribution of rods and cones in the retina, their main functions, and the impact of various abnormalities upon them differ.

In the center of the retina is a small depression known as the macula, and this area contains only cones. Outwards towards the periphery of the retina the number of cones reduces. The relative distribution of rods is the reverse, being at its greatest at the edges of the retina. Whilst the cones are primarily concerned with color vision and function optimally in bright light, the rods are concerned with black-and-white vision and retain their function in subdued light.

Three types of cones are said to exist, each form being sensitive only to red, blue or green light. Combinations of these colors in varying proportions result in the visual appreciation of various 'hues'. The arrangement of three basic colors is also used in photography (three separate emulsions) and in color television (three separate signals).

Defects in the appreciation or interpretation of one or more of these colors results in color blindness. Such abnormalities are congenital and tend to run in a family. The loss of color appreciation is virtually never total. Almost 10 per cent of males are affected, whereas less than 1 per cent of females are color blind. Color blindness is inherited most frequently in a sex-linked pattern, with both X sex chromosomes in the female having to be affected.

Being color blind generally creates few problems in modern society. Many people do not realize that they have the disorder, and others tend to 'learn' colors like 'leaves are green' and 'stop signs are red'. Ishihara color charts are widely used to test color vision. Colored dots with differing depths of darkness and varied hues are arranged in various configurations, and the subsequent interpretation depends upon which, if any, color perception loss is present.

Retinol is a chemical in the retina derived from vitamin A. When there is a pro-

The shape and integrity of the visual fields may be determined by seating the subject in a darkened room, asking him to look straight ahead at a screen and to indicate when he can first see an illuminated spot as it moves slowly to the center of the screen. When this is repeated with the spot coming from various directions the visual field can be mapped out on a chart.

Various disturbances of the visual fields may occur, their features depending upon the nature and position of the lesion. When an optic nerve is severed, the visual field of one eye is blacked out completely whereas the other remains unaffected. Various lesions of the nerve fibers beyond the optic nerve may cause defects in the fields, the exact pattern depending on whether the nerves have crossed at the optic chiasma.

Peripheral vision occurs as a result of images falling on the outer part of the retina. This portion of the light-sensitive membrane may be damaged more severely than the central areas in a number of conditions such as long-standing glaucoma, a disorder associated with an increase in the pressure of the aqueous humor in the front of the eyeball.

When peripheral vision is lost the condition is like peering through a tube or tunnel and the term tunnel vision is used to describe it.

A scotoma or central patch of blindness is the other major type of field disturbance, which may result from a number of conditions that affect the central portion

Right
Much of our enjoyment of food is derived from our sense of smell.
(*Zefa*)

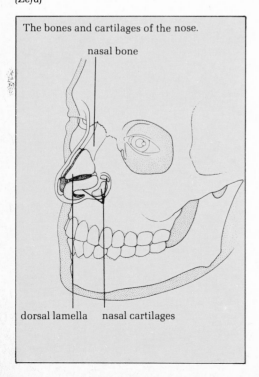

The bones and cartilages of the nose.

nasal bone

dorsal lamella   nasal cartilages

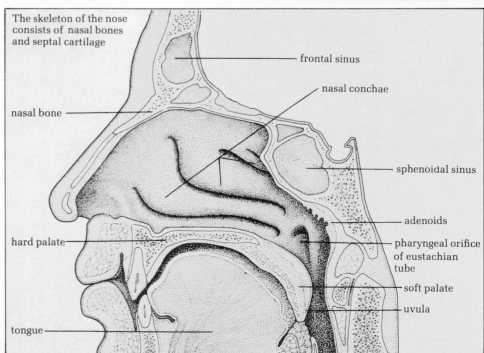

The skeleton of the nose consists of nasal bones and septal cartilage

frontal sinus

nasal conchae

nasal bone

sphenoidal sinus

adenoids

pharyngeal orifice of eustachian tube

hard palate

soft palate

uvula

tongue

of the retina. The main causes of a large scotoma are multiple sclerosis and brain tumour.

Treatment of visual field disturbances depends on the cause, although frequently little can be done because irreversible damage has occurred. Often the main aim is to prevent further progression of the visual loss.

Smell

The sensation of smell is experienced when odors are dissolved into the mucus which lines the olfactory (smell) plate in the upper nasal cavity. Fine hairs attached to the mucous cells excite nerve receptors, and individual odors are then identified in nerve tissues, the olfactory bulb and the olfactory area of the brain. Spicy, flowery, fruity, resinous, burnt and foul smells may all be recognized. Prolonged exposure to particular odors leads to 'fatigue', of which we can be unaware.

The nose is the prominent portion of the face above the mouth and below the eyes, in which the nostrils and olfactory nerve endings required for smell are located.

The skeleton of the nose consists of the nasal bones, the frontal processes of the maxilla and the upper and lower nasal cartilages. The skin is thin and movable over the upper part, but is thick and adheres to underlying cartilage and fibrous tissue of the expanded mobile wings round the edge of the nostrils. The septal cartilage divides the nostrils.

The cavity of the nose extends from the nostrils to the apertures at the back of the nose, which open into the nasal part of the pharynx, where the adenoids are located. The two halves of the nasal cavity are often unequal in width, if the septum bulges to one side. The adult nasal cavity is about 2 inches (5 cm) along the floor and approximately 3 inches (7.5 cm) along the roof.

The ducts for the drainage of tears from the eyes (nasolacrimal ducts) open into the lower part of each nasal cavity. Several sinuses (ethmoidal, frontal and maxillary) open into the middle and upper parts of each cavity. The vestibule is the dilated end of the nostril and is lined with skin bearing coarse hairs. The remainder of the cavity is lined with ciliated mucous membrane containing many blood vessels and glands.

The main functions of the nose are the sense of smell, and the warming, filtration and humidification of the inspired air for the lungs. Potentially harmful micro-organisms are attacked by powerful immune defense mechanisms in the mucous membrane and adenoidal tissue.

Taste

In medical terminology, taste refers to sensations perceived on the top of the tongue by sense organs called taste buds. Traditionally, taste sensations have been divided into various types such as sweet,

Diagrammatic representation of whole tongue viewed from above.

root of the tongue

foramen caecum

vallate papillae

dorsum   transverse mucosal folds

bitter, sour and salty. This, however, has no practical use and most taste sensations are a combination of these four tastes.

Nerve fibers on the top of the tongue perceive the various sensations and these are transmitted to the brain by two central nerves (cranial nerves). Loss of taste may occur if any of these structures are damaged by injury, or lack of blood supply. Any diseases of the tongue, cranial nerves or brain also may lead to decreased taste sensation.

The tongue A mobile organ in the floor of the oral cavity, the tongue is covered with mucous membrane and composed largely of voluntary muscle. It is attached to the periphery of the mouth by many external muscles which also help to maneuver food for more easy chewing and swallowing. The intrinsic, or internal, muscles primarily alter the shape of the tongue for both speech and swallowing.

Below the tip of the tongue is the frenulum, a fold of mucous membrane which helps hold it in place. Fine papillae, or projections, line the upper surface and sides, while over ten thousand taste buds are scattered over the tongue and on the palate and the pillars of the tonsils.

The taste buds are variously shaped and are described as filiform (hair-like), fungiform (mushroom-like), vallate (rimmed) and circumvallate (cupped). On the side of the tongue it is possible to distinguish salty and sour tastes, on the tip, sweet and at the back of the tongue, the circum-

vallate buds identify bitter tastes.

When humans reach the age of 45 the taste buds begin to decrease in number and this leads to lessened sensation and discrimination in tasting.

Sometimes the mucous membrane fold, or frenulum, under the tongue is attached to the tip of the tongue, preventing its protrusion from the mouth and inhibiting its movement. This condition is called tongue tie.

Only when the tongue tie interferes with the speech of a child more than one year old is it necessary to operate and cut the fold, for which a general anesthetic may be required.

The fold should not be clipped at birth because bleeding and infection may result. In any event, the fold will often stretch spontaneously to allow normal tongue movement later.

Touch

In addition to its other functions, the skin serves as the organ of touch. Its tactile sensibility includes the capacity to appreciate light touch (localization and discrimination), pressure, pain, heat and cold. The special skin receptors which subserve the different sensations vary in the complexity of their structure and in their distribution on the skin.

Touch is appreciated by receptors called Meissner's corpuscles which are distributed unevenly over the body. They are most numerous over the tips of the fingers, the palms, soles and lips and less so on other areas such as the back and shoulders. Their closeness depends on the discrimination or ability to recognize whether a contact is single or multiple. The finger tips can feel two separate contacts when the points are .04 inch (1 mm) apart, whereas on the back a separation of 2 inches (5 cm) may be required.

The very sensitive areas of the skin are hairless, but elsewhere the skin surface bears hairs which are either obvious or rudimentary. Tactile receptors are found round the bases of these hair follicles. Light contact with hair tips causes a sensation of touch since each hair acts like a tiny lever, transmitting movement to its base and stimulating the touch receptor. From these receptors the impulse is carried by nerves to the spinal cord and thence upwards to the brain and its sensory centres.

Other special receptors transmit the sensations of pressure, pain, heat (organ of Golgi-Mazzoni) and cold (end-bulbs of Krause).

Alterations of skin sensitivity, of which touch is only one component, provide important diagnostic clues. Departures from normal may be anesthesia (loss of sensation), hyperesthesia (increased sensitivity), or paresthesia (abnormal sensations such as burning, pricking or itching).

2 Human Sexuality

— Functions, Pleasures and Variations

Anatomy of Sex

In both men and women, sexual maturity marks the attainment of adulthood. At puberty, over a period of two or three years, the internal and external sex organs develop fully, giving the individual an adult physical appearance as well as the ability to reproduce.

Male sex organs

The male external genital organs comprise the penis and the scrotum which contains the testes or gonads. In its unexcited state the penis forms a soft cylinder about 3½ inches (9 cm) in length, which rests against the scrotum, usually with a slight incline to the left.

The head of the penis, the glans penis, is covered by the foreskin or prepuce. When erect, the penis rises at an angle in front of the body and measures on average about 6 inches (15 cm); the distended glans protrudes from the foreskin.

The skin of the penis is extremely thin, pinkish and hairless around the glans. On the body of the penis is the sheath, a supple skin which is able to slide freely over the erectile tissues. At the union of the sheath and glans is the fold called the prepuce or foreskin.

Some religions, such as Judaism and Mohammedanism, still require ritual circumcision of the prepuce in young boys, although there is no longer any medical reason for this custom, whose origin is supposed to lie in the requirements of primitive hygiene. All that is necessary is to clean the glans and the foreskin once daily to get rid of any excess of the lubricating sebaceous fluid (the smegma).

Opposite
The ability to reproduce marks the attainment of sexual maturity.
(Zefa)

Young children should have this area cleaned daily. Circumcision is only required in a condition called phimosis, where the preputial opening of the foreskin is too tight to allow retraction of the prepuce over the glans penis.

The scrotum is the sac suspended behind and beneath the penis. An internal partition completely separates the right testis from the left which in most men usually hangs a little lower. The outer skin of the scrotum is fine, supple, and wrinkled. Beneath the skin an involuntary muscle, the dartos, can contract to make the internal sacs tighten up, particularly under the effects of cold, fear, or sexual stimulation.

Masculine genital hair forms a roughly triangular shape on the pubis, around the base of the penis and on the scrotum. Hair often grows around the perineum, behind the scrotum, around the anus, and in the cleft between the buttocks.

The male testes are egg-shaped glands which measure on average about 2 inches (5 cm) in length. A tough protective membrane, the tunica albuginea, forms the external shell: within are the numerous seminiferous tubules that produce the spermatozoa. The cells between these ducts (Leydig's cells), produce the male hormone testosterone.

Immediately above each testicle is the epididymis a convoluted organ in which the ducts of the testis are gathered and grouped into the vas deferens, the single duct which emerges from the rear of the epididymis.

All the structures that enter and leave the testicle, the arteries, veins, lymphatic ducts, nerves and vas deferens, together form the spermatic cord which runs up through the scrotum and passes through the inguinal canal to the abdomen.

Within the abdomen, the two vas deferens pass along either side of the bladder to reach the prostate gland. Before they do, they swell to form the ampulla. Adjacent to each ampulla are the seminal vesicles, short sac-like structures which secrete part of the seminal fluid. The duct of the seminal vesicle joins the vas deferens to form the ejaculatory duct.

The prostate gland is situated underneath the bladder and the seminal vesicles just in front of the rectum; the urethra passes through it on its way from the bladder to the penis. In the prostate, the urinary and spermatic ducts meet within a structure which also allows the secretions from the prostate to enter the urethra. From this point, the mixture of fluids and spermatozoa called semen is carried by the urethra.

Female sex organs

In the female, the genital organs are primarily internal. Externally, the mons pubis, a pad of soft tissue and skin, covers the pubis. The vulva lying between the mons pubis and the anus comprises the labia majora, the labia minora, the clitoris, the vestibule and Bartholin's glands. The labia majora, beginning at the mons pubis, form the side lips of the vulva which is usually about 3½ inches (9 cm) long. Two smaller folds lying within the labia majora, the labia minora enclose the vestibule and the clitoris.

Like the penis, the clitoris has a shaft with a bulb or glans at the tip. The glans, which is covered by a hood, contains many sensitive nerve endings and on stimulation contributes greatly to heightening a woman's sexual response.

The deepest level of the vulva is the vestibule, the cavity containing the urethral and vaginal openings. The urethra, for the excretion of urine, opens into the vestibule just behind the clitoris. The vagina also opens into the vestibule. A membrane called the hymen may partially obstruct the opening to the vagina but often stretches particularly with the use of tampons during menstruation. A ruptured or absent hymen does not indicate loss of virginity.

On each side of the vaginal opening are

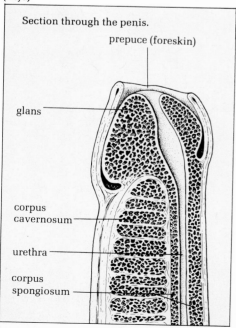

Section through the penis.

- prepuce (foreskin)
- glans
- corpus cavernosum
- urethra
- corpus spongiosum

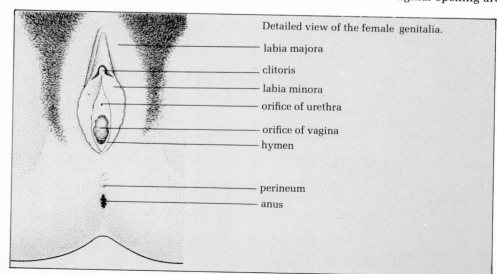

Detailed view of the female genitalia.

- labia majora
- clitoris
- labia minora
- orifice of urethra
- orifice of vagina
- hymen
- perineum
- anus

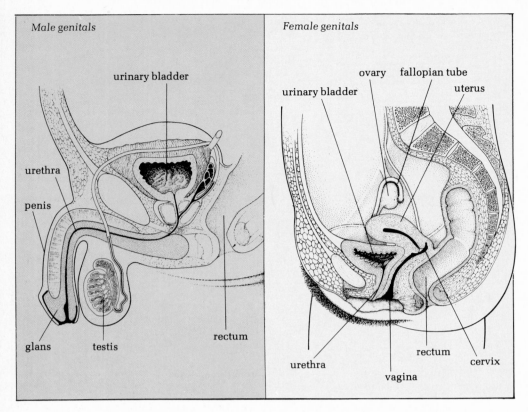

Male genitals

urinary bladder

urethra

penis

glans   testis

rectum

Female genitals

ovary   fallopian tube

urinary bladder

uterus

urethra

rectum   cervix

vagina

The nipple and areola have smooth muscle which enable them to contract. During pregnancy breasts increase in size, the areolae become darker and, when lactation begins, a number of small ducts open on the surface of the nipple.

Secondary sexual characteristics

The man is generally taller than the woman with greater breadth of shoulders than hips, while in the woman the shoulders are equal to or only slightly wider than the pelvis.

The male skeleton is taller than the female with a raised rib cage and a larger skull. The masculine bone structure is proportionately narrower, but the woman's pelvic opening is larger in order to allow the fetus to pass through.

The skin is thicker and rougher in the man, with more sebaceous and sweat glands. Baldness, often occurring at an early age, is common in men but is rare in women. A woman's hair is generally finer and silkier.

In a woman, hair also occurs around the genitals, under the arms, lightly upon the upper lip, on the legs and in the anal cleft. Female eyelashes are usually longer.

The man is much hairier, with heavy eyebrows, beard and mustache; hair may be present upon the front of the chest and abdomen and, sometimes, on the back as well; on the upper and lower limbs and on the feet. A man's teeth are larger than a woman's and toe nails are heavier and flatter.

In the male, the muscles are likely to be more fully developed and stronger than those of the female, although a woman's pelvic muscles are particularly strong. The larynx or Adam's apple is larger and more noticeable in the male and the voice is deeper.

Sexual hormones

Substances secreted internally by various glands, sexual hormones stimulate sexual development and functions. In human beings sexual hormones are secreted principally by the gonads, that is, the ovaries and testes.

Male hormones The cortex of the adrenal, or suprarenal, gland also produces small quantities of male hormone. The secretion of hormones is itself controlled by the hypothalamus in the brain.

The primary purpose of the testes is hormonal activity and production of spermatozoa. They continuously produce the male hormone, testosterone, which is responsible for the development of masculine characteristics. Production starts at puberty and remains fairly constant throughout adult life, though a lesser amount is probably produced as a man grows older.

Menstrual cycle

The activity of the ovaries is regulated by the menstrual cycle which lasts for about

the pea-sized Bartholin's glands. The vestibule is enclosed by the labia minora.

The vagina is the passage for insertion of the penis and reception of semen, for the discharge of the menstrual flow and is also the channel through which the fetus is delivered during birth. Stretching from the outer vestibule to the neck of the uterus and averaging some 3½ inches (9 cm) in length, the vagina rises up and back into the lower abdomen. Its lowest part is narrow and squeezed between the muscles of the perineum; the middle is canal-like and almost horizontal; and the upper section forms a cavity behind the neck of the uterus or cervix. Here the glans penis is accommodated during intercourse.

The vaginal walls which are normally in contact with each other, consist of a smooth muscular sleeve lined on the insides with a mucous membrane. Both membrane and muscles are thick, tough and extremely flexible, the walls measuring up to ½ inch (1 cm) in thickness. The cells of the surface layer of the membrane produce a whitish, mucous matter containing the natural organism called Döderlein's bacillus. Identical to *Lactobacillus acidophilus* found in milk, it produces lactic acid which acts as a chemical defence against infection.

The uterus or womb, in which the fertilized ovum grows to maturity, is pear shaped and almost entirely composed of smooth muscular tissue, forming a neck and a body joined by a narrow portion or isthmus. The neck of the uterus or cervix consists of an internal part and an exter-

nal part. The latter, containing the external os, is cone shaped, is longer in a woman who has borne children, and projects into the vaginal passage.

From the cervix, the uterus first narrows and then widens to form the triangular, flattish shape of the body. The body of the uterus is some ¾–1¼ inches (2–3 cm) thick, 2½ inches (6 cm) long and about 2 inches (5 cm) wide in the average woman who has borne children. The uterine cavity connects directly with the fallopian tubes. The interior of the uterus is lined with the endometrium, a special form of mucous membrane which varies in thickness during the menstrual cycle.

The fallopian tubes convey the ovum from the ovaries to the uterus and spermatozoa from the uterus towards the ovaries. Each is a smooth muscular duct lined with ciliated mucous membrane which conveys the ovum along the tube. The swollen lateral ends of the fallopian tubes open into the abdominal cavity by forming finger-like processes called fimbria, which lie above the ovary and, in the process of ovulation, receive the discharged ovum.

The two ovaries or gonads are located upon the lateral walls of the pelvis. Each is about the size of a pigeon's egg, and in a mature woman their greyish-white surface is covered with tiny scars caused by the breaking-out of ova.

The breasts or mammary glands, which develop fully at maturity, are of a generally rounded shape, each with a nipple surrounded by the circular areola. Milk is secreted from the nipple during lactation.

The female secondary sexual characteristics include the growth of hair under the arms and in the pubic area, enlargement of the breasts and enlargement and darkening of the areola around the nipple.

The male secondary sexual characteristics include the appearance of pubic and body hair and deepening of the voice.

28 days in two phases: the follicular and the luteinising stages.

On the first day of the menstrual period, the release of the follicle-stimulating hormone FSH from the pituitary gland causes a graafian follicle to be formed in the ovary; a tiny sac-like body forms around a reproductive cell. The maturing follicle in turn produces the hormone follicular estrogen, which prepares the lining of the womb for the implantation of the fertilized ovum.

On the fourteenth day ovulation occurs. The follicle ripens and the ovum is released from the ovary. This sometimes causes slight internal bleeding; and, occasionally, pain which may last for several hours enables some women to record their ovulation. The discharge of the ovum from the surface of the ovary leaves a hole which fills with new scar tissue. It has a yellowish appearance and is known as the corpus luteum (yellow body).

The luteinizing phase may be recognized by monitoring the morning body-temperature which, during ovulation, is generally two or three degrees higher than during the follicular phase. The corpus luteum produces the female hormone, progesterone or lutin. Progesterone completes the work begun by estrogen upon the endometrium, causing it to grow thicker; after conception, progesterone contributes to development of the placenta and the mammary glands. The gonadotrophic hormone B also contributes to the ovulation and to the production of the corpus luteum.

Premenstrual tension (PMT) It has been noted by many women that specific problems occur before a menstrual period. These problems, or symptoms, are uniform in women of different racial groups and are present in different geographical locations throughout the world. The symptoms include:

- fluid retention
- weight gain
- swelling of the fingers and toes
- swelling of the stomach, producing a 'pot-belly' effect
- enlargement of the breasts with soreness and tenderness
- constipation
- depression and headache, from mild to very severe migraine
- irritability and a tendency to 'snap' and become emotionally unstable
- unusual moodiness and a tendency to cry easily

It must be stressed that not all women experience all of these symptoms, and some lucky women do not get any. However, most women experience some of the symptoms during some stage of their reproductive life.

All of these symptoms are caused by hormones produced by the body. A woman who is free of chronic diseases, such as tuberculosis, and who has received good nutrition during childhood is in such good health that optimal physical development occurs. This results in large, healthy ovaries which produce their maximal potential of hormones. This, in turn, produces the symptoms described.

It must be stressed that 'PMT' is not a disease, that the symptoms felt are unpleasant and unwanted side effects produced by hormones, but they are quite natural and normal.

If the effects are severe and debilitating, a doctor will be able to prescribe specific medication to avoid or minimise these unpleasant and painful symptoms.

Should the ovum not be fertilized, the corpus luteum abruptly ceases to function around the twenty-eighth day, leading to the collapse of the endometrium. The unused uterine lining is expelled in the menstrual flow.

When the ovum has been fertilized, the corpus luteum continues to function and grow. The womb lining remains to receive the egg and the menstrual period does not occur. This is the first clinical sign of pregnancy.

Menopause In the average woman, the ovaries function for about 35 years, from puberty to the menopause, which usually takes place during the fifth decade. The menopause may last for one to two years and may be accompanied by the typical symptoms of hot flushes, dizziness, headaches, weight gain and other symptoms. After menopause some women show symptoms of estrogen deficiency including shrinking of the breasts and vulvo-vaginal dryness and irritation. Estrogen replacement therapy usually brings immediate relief of symptoms. Sexual activity after the menopause is not impaired. Emotional reactions such as anxiety, depression, emotional instability or reduction in sexual enjoyment usually respond to treatment.

A positive attitude minimizes any possible adverse manifestations of the menopause.

Growing up

Puberty or sexual maturation occurs gradually over two or three years. The genital organs develop the capacity for sexual intercourse and reproduction. The maturing ovaries of the woman become capable of producing ova, the male testes produce spermatozoa in seminal fluid. This period of rapid change commences between the ages of 13 and 15 in boys and earlier in girls.

Physical appearance takes on adult proportions; body hair will make its appearance, the length and size of the larynx increases resulting in a lowering of the voice tone in the girl and the 'breaking' of the voice in the boy.

In the male, the penis, testes and scrotum begin to take on adult proportions and the foreskin retracts to leave the end of the glans penis uncovered. Penile erections

A developing attraction towards the opposite sex is noticeable in most teenagers as their bodies become capable of expressing sexual feelings. (*Zefa*)

occur and the first ejaculations of semen usually take place at about thirteen to fourteen years of age. By the age of fifteen or sixteen the semen contains active spermatozoa. Hair growth occurs on the pubis, the face, and under the arms.

In the female, the mons pubis and the labia majora become plumper and labia minora develop around the vulva. The vagina lengthens and increases in size and the uterus develops fully. The first period, menarche, occurs at about twelve to fourteen years of age but menstruation is often irregular for the first two or three years. Ovulation becomes regular at about sixteen years of age, which is also the approximate age at which the breasts are fully developed. The growth of body hair and the development of subcutaneous fat also occur.

Sexual maturity is thus attained by boys at about eighteen years of age and by girls one or two years earlier.

Adolescent love As the adolescent begins to acquire the mature sexual organs which allow sexual intercourse, a developing attraction towards the opposite sex and the need to express sexual feeling and love become evident. But adolescence is an unstable period, when the physically mature person may be emotionally unsure and childlike. The boy remains a boy, though in a young man's body, and the situation is similar for girls. Adolescent erotic aspirations are most often expressed as 'crushes', 'love affairs' and other emotional adventures.

Although masturbation is common, satisfactory or regular sexual intercourse is not usual. Nevertheless unwanted pregnancies and anxieties about sexuality may be very disturbing for the adolescent.

Libido Derived from the Latin *libido*, lust, the term libido was first used by Sigmund Freud to describe a basic sexual desire or energy present in all people. According to Freud this desire motivates much of human behavior throughout the whole of life.

Modern day sexology defines sexual desire as the product of both biological and sociological forces. The hormone androgen is responsible for genital sensitivity and sexual arousal and is present in small quantity at infancy in boys and girls and increases greatly around age 8 or 9.

Although sexual arousal and desire has a biological basis the social environment will inhibit or encourage its expression. Differences in sexual desire are found between different individuals and between different cultures depending on the values, morals and taboos.

Freud theorized that child sexuality emerged in infancy as oral then anal (age 2) and later phallic (age 4) stages and that a latency non-sexual period occurred from age 5 to puberty. Kinsey (1948) found the majority of 5 year olds experience sexual build up and orgasm due to

Adolescence may be a time of emotional uncertainty. *(Zefa)*

genital stimulation. Sexual curiosity and activity continues throughout childhood, and reports from sexual therapists and people studying sexual behaviour in various countries all concur that masturbation, erotic self-stimulation, fantasy and heterosexual or homosexual experimentation continue from infancy, through puberty and the teenage years and into adult life. This is now considered to be perfectly normal.

Sex education

At the turn of the century formal sex education was non-existent, and in many homes discussion of the subject was taboo. As a result many people entered marriage with very little knowledge about reproduction and sexuality, a number of women having the idea that sexual intercourse was to be endured rather than enjoyed.

Since that time acceptance of discussion about sexuality, and the sexual life of adolescents in particular, has changed dramatically in the last 20 to 30 years. Despite these changes, the rate of effective contraception among people under the age of 20 is very low, and many parents are unable or unwilling to provide appropriate information or advice for their children. These are two of many

reasons why sex education is very important, both to assist parents to teach their children and for the children themselves.

The family In most societies the family has been the main source of information for children regarding sexuality. Children pick up much information concerning parental value systems merely by being part of the family, which remains the prime source of influence on a child's personality development and decision-making processes. In practice, however, much learning also comes from friends, from personal experience, and from various sections of the media.

The school An appropriate school program on sex instruction designed primarily to augment that which has already been provided by parents who have openly discussed such matters with their children is seen by many experts as being the most effective method.

An increasing interest is being shown in educating people for 'life' rather than merely to pass exams; as a result family life, health and sexuality programs are becoming integral components of the complete school curriculum.

Instruction concerning sexuality needs to be undertaken before puberty and before the occurrence of situations in which decisions concerning sexual behavior have to be made. Parents need to talk freely to their children and let them know their values and beliefs. The rate at which knowledge is imparted in the early years is best set by the child's own questioning. A child is usually seeking information so that he can progress one stage further in his understanding. He generally does not wish to know everything. Parents may help by defining exactly what the child understands and wants to know, by giving explanations in words that are readily understood and by never belittling the inquirer because of his lack of knowledge. Many books are available to assist parents in their important role as educators. For those parents who still feel unable to discuss sexual matters with their child, a suitable family friend with whom the child relates well may be a good alternative.

The origin of babies, their development and birth, and the organs of reproduction, together with the ways in which they function, are the main areas of interest for children. Correct information should always be given. Stories about storks and cabbage patches complicate matters and are unhelpful. By the time of puberty, information presented should have covered broad aspects of sexuality including reproduction, puberty and menstruation, contraception, emotional development and an individual's overall responsibilities within relationships.

Adolescents have to deal with their awakening sexuality and the emotional turmoil of this period of life, and to establish a personal code of sexual behavior. Such codes are best formulated in nonemotional situations by those with appropriate knowledge and attitudes.

Marriage

A lifelong, sexually exclusive and voluntary union of two people of the opposite sex is the accepted form of marriage in most Western countries. More recently, variants on the traditional form of association have emerged. Trial and de facto marriages are increasingly common and some couples sign contracts detailing obligations and property division if they separate. 'Open' marriages, which dismiss the concept of monogamy, have emerged, often in association with communal lifestyles where children are raised by several adults.

The growing divorce rate has created many single-parent families, often increasing the numbers of adults seeking 'alternative' forms of interpersonal union. Polygamy, where a person has more than one spouse, is common amongst Moslems and is practised in Asia, Africa and South America.

Marital disharmony occurs to some extent in all marriages and currently about almost half of marriages in Western societies end in divorce.

Problems in marriage frequently arise from inadequate preparation and immaturity, especially where the partners are young, which creates unreal expectations or needs. Conflict usually centers around sex and money, especially during the first two years of marriage when couples are still establishing their roles and learning to communicate effectively. Inadequate or crowded accommodation, the birth of children, their schooling and later their adolescence and departure from home, illness, loss of employment, financial difficulties, changing homes and retirement can also impose strain on a marriage, perhaps leading to separation and divorce. These factors can lead to a breakdown in communication between partners, the reason most frequently cited as causing marital breakdown. These problems sometimes continue in an unsatisfactory state for years before a divorce is sought.

Couples intending to marry can initially familiarize themselves with their roles and responsibilities within marriage. They should discuss their plans for children and their attitudes towards contraception, child care, including discipline, education and religion. They should also express their thoughts regarding finances, sexuality and the division of marital responsibilities. Problems within marriage can sometimes be dealt with by professional counseling and support from friends and may be alleviated if the partners involved are able to divide their responsibilities so that their respective roles are flexible and complementary. Individuals may of course have attitudes that are incompatible with a shared relationship and new patterns of behavior and coping methods will have to be adopted if the relationship is to work.

Many people happily choose marriage as a basis for their lifelong relationship.

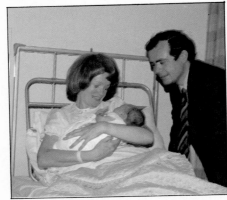

Intercourse

In advanced countries today each human being reproduces only a few times (on average once to four times) during a lifespan. Even in countries where the birth rate is a great deal higher, women rarely have more than fifteen children. These numbers are very low when compared to the number of times the average human being engages in sexual intercourse. Men and women use their genital organs much less often for procreation than for satisfaction or pleasure. Human emotions and memory make the agreeable sensations from the genital organs a special kind of pleasure, which reaches its zenith in orgasm.

Though erotic activity does not often have the immediate objective of procreation, it nevertheless depends upon the functions of the reproductive organs. Certain parts of the body when stimulated provide the sensation of sexual pleasure; these are the primary erogenous zones, which when excited can produce orgasm, and the secondary zones, which under stimulus may reinforce the action of the primary zones and make them more responsive.

Erogenous zones The man has only one primary zone: the glans of the penis. The woman has two primary zones: the clitoris and vagina. Stimulation of the clitoris alone is sufficient to cause orgasm. Vaginal stimulation during intercourse also contributes to orgasm.

The primary erogenous zones, though extremely sensitive to erotic stimulation, are less vulnerable to pressure, heat, cold and pain. The secondary zones by contrast are very sensitive, and often serve to trigger reactions in the primary zones.

In the man secondary zones are mostly to be found in the genital region: the sheath of the penis, the skin of the scrotum and the perineum and the upper part of the insides of the thighs.

Secondary zones in the woman are not limited to the genital area but are also found on the trunk (the spine, the small of the back and the stomach), the limbs (inside the arms and on the wrists, palms and ankles), the head (the lips, the area around the ears and the nape of the neck), the neck itself, and above all the breasts.

In the man, and depending on the individual, these zones are just as widespread, but are rather less sensitive.

The sexual response Erotic excitation need not be confined to the erogenous zones. A look or a word as well as touch may trigger off a reaction. Actual copulation leading to orgasm is often only the culminating part of an erotic experience.

The sexual reactions of the male are outwardly obvious. The penis becomes erect and stands upright; the scrotum tightens and the testicles increase in volume and

draw right up next to the perineum. A drop of fluid may appear at the end of the urethra.

The erection of the penis enables penetration of the female vagina and as the penis is moved in and out, friction between the skin of the penis and the vaginal lining is sufficient after some time (often only minutes) to excite the masculine glans to release an ejaculation. Ejaculation occurs at the moment of orgasm: propelled by a rhythmic contraction of the sperm ducts, the semen is ejected in three to five separate spurts, each separated from the other by less than a second. Although the orgasmic sensation coincides with ejaculation, it is not the emission of semen which causes it: men whose vas deferens have been surgically tied or who have undergone a prostate operation are able to experience orgasm in the almost complete absence of ejaculation.

Following ejaculation the penis deflates and the testicles slide down into their normal position at the bottom of the scrotum. Further sexual excitation is ineffectual for some time and may even be painful. The length of time before a further erection is possible depends upon the individual, the circumstances, and age and physical condition: it may be anything from five minutes to many days.

The woman's genital reactions, while less obvious are nonetheless distinct. During excitation, the principal response sign is increased production of vaginal fluid, which is released from the mucous membrane lubricating both the vaginal opening and the back of the vulva. The vagina expands even before penetration by the penis. The clitoris swells and the labia stand erect to allow easier access to the vagina. The vagina expands to a maximum and the uterus moves further into the pelvis. The breasts increase in size, the

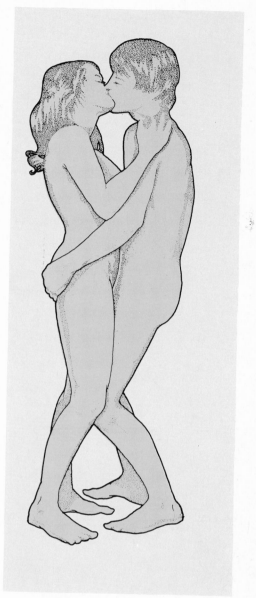

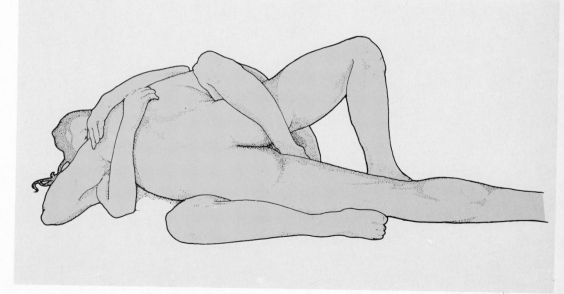

nipples harden and the areolae contract becoming more wrinkled.

During orgasm, rhythmic contractions of the muscles of the genital area occur, the first contractions being separated by less than a second, as with the man. The uterus also contracts more or less vigorously, depending on the intensity of the orgasm. The woman's orgasmic sensations coincide with her muscular contractions: they are generally more widespread involving more of her body and probably of greater intensity than those of the man.

The seminal vesicles lie along the lower part of the bladder. Union of the seminal vesicles with the vas deferens forms the ejaculatory ducts.

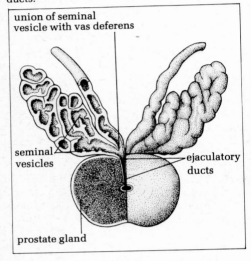

- union of seminal vesicle with vas deferens
- seminal vesicles
- ejaculatory ducts
- prostate gland

The bulk of fluid released at ejaculation arises from the seminal vesicles and serves to transport sperm produced in the testes.

Human spermatozoa, seen here under the electron microscope, may be present in millions in the seminal fluid. (John Watney Photo Library)

After orgasm, the vagina and clitoris gradually return to their usual size and position; the labia also return to their usual position and paler coloration; the body of the womb reverts to its customary place but the cervix remains open for a further 20 to 30 minutes. The nipples and the breasts also return to their normal dimensions.

Masturbation is stimulation or excitement of the genital organs without sexual intercourse. As a natural expression of pleasure, masturbation is common at all ages from infancy onwards.

The physiological mechanism of sexual excitement involves the swelling of the blood vessels in erectile organs and a heightening of muscular tone in involuntary or autonomic muscles of the perineum and lower pelvis; in particular the levator ani.

General physiological reactions are similar in both sexes. The respiratory and cardiac systems accelerate; the blood pressure rises and the skin flushes and perspires. The muscles of the body almost always contract in a universal spasm during orgasm and erotic feelings tend to become more and more dominant as the moment of orgasm approaches.

Conception

The process of conception occurs when a male sperm and a female ovum (egg) unite to form the first definitive cell from which a baby eventually develops.

The process begins when an ovum is released from the ovary, usually 14 days before the beginning of the normal menstrual period, and travels down the fallopian tube towards the uterus. The male sperm deposited during sexual intercourse travel up through the uterus to the fallopian tube where they meet the ovum and where fertilization occurs when one sperm penetrates the ovum.

In a normal menstrual period fertilization will occur on Day 15 (Day 1 being the first day of the preceding period) and is only possible in the first 12 to 24 hours after the ovum has been released.

Usually over 200 million sperm are present in one ejaculation, although only one sperm cell fertilizes the ovum. The others are thought to assist in the progress of the fertilizing sperm through the genital tract and in the chemical breakdown of the outer protective layer of the ovum. When the fertilizing sperm penetrates the ovum and fertilization takes place, a protective membrane which repels the other sperm is created around the ovum.

Union of the sex cells forms a single cell known as a zygote, which then proceeds along the fallopian tube where further cell divisions occur, leading to the formation of a morula (a mass of cells), followed by the development of a blastocyst which settles into the uterus where it remains during the pregnancy.

Recent advances in medical technology have been so rapid and varied that it is difficult to cover them all here. The results, in a practical sense, have been that couples who were unable to conceive a child previously, now have many alternatives open to them. These include:

1. Artificial insemination by the husband, or from a donor if the husband is infertile.

2. I.V.F (In Vitro Fertilization) when an egg from the woman is fertilized in a test-tube, either by the sperm of the husband or from a donor, and then the fertilized egg is replanted in the uterus of the mother.

3. G.I.F.T. (Gamete Intra-Fallopian Transfer), where an ovum fertilized in one woman is transferred into an infertile recipient.

The obstetric units at all large hospitals now have infertility clinics, where couples who are having trouble conceiving can be advised by experts in this field.

Preventing Unwanted Pregnancies

Family planning has come to be used as an alternative name for birth control or the use of contraceptives. The family is planned in the sense that rational non-use of contraception results in a planned pregnancy. The principles of family planning have gained widespread acceptance in the past few decades and, as it is now becoming apparent that the inability to become pregnant when desired is also a problem, family planning services have been expanded to include counseling of infertile couples.

Contraception is any process that prevents the establishment of pregnancy. Most women use some form of contraception during their child bearing period, yet many of them and their partners are unaware of the relative merits and disadvantages of the several different methods. Contraception which is suitable for a young couple to space their family may be quite unsuitable for an older couple who wish to have no more children. A woman with a regular sex life will require different contraceptive advice from that required by a woman with an irregular one.

A completely ideal method of contraception has not yet been found. Perfect contraception would be achieved with no discomfort, no side-effects, no long term repercussions, instant yet reversible action when required, complete medical safety and convenience, 100 per cent efficiency and very low cost.

There is no doubt that if a woman is to have a regular sex life, contraception in some form is desirable as there are risks involved in any pregnancy even with the best maternity services available. Statistically if one million young women without contraception have a regular sex life they will produce 600,000 babies annually and in 53 of the pregnancies the women will die. So, aside from the social problems that such a rising birth rate might entail, it is evident that the risk which pregnancy itself carries would justify some contraceptive practice in given instances where the woman's health does not fit her for child bearing. To be acceptable, any method of contraception used should have lower risks than pregnancy itself.

Coitus interruptus

Meaning interruption of the act of sexual intercourse, coitus interruptus, a form of contraception, requires withdrawal of the penis from the vagina before the ejaculation of semen. A worldwide form of contraception, the method is one of the earliest known, and is mentioned in the Old Testament.

Reliability When combined with avoidance of intercourse during the fertile part of the menstrual cycle, the method does limit conception. Compared with the other forms of contraception, such as the combination oral contraceptive pill, the mini-pill or an intra-uterine device, the rate of conception of around 20 per cent is considerably higher.

Disadvantages Because semen can be released from the penis during intercourse before ejaculation occurs, contraception is not reliable. Occasionally sperm deposited near the opening of the vagina may also cause pregnancy.

The abrupt interruption of the sexual act may be distressing to one or both of the partners, leaving feelings of tension or dissatisfaction. Further, the male partner may fail to withdraw at the appropriate moment.

Condom

This form of contraception is still frequently used despite the advent of oral contraceptives and modern intra-uterine devices (IUD). The condom is a thin sheath that is placed over the penis prior to intercourse to prevent escape of semen into the vagina. The semen is retained in the condom. The method is one of the oldest contraceptive practices though of course the materials of manufacture have

changed over time.

To avoid leakage of semen, the condom should be applied to the erect penis before intercourse, and the penis should be withdrawn from the vagina shortly after ejaculation with the condom being held in position. Unsheathing should occur well clear of the vaginal opening.

Spermicidal cream aids lubrication and increases efficiency of the condom as a method of contraception. A failure rate of less than 3 per cent can be attained with this combination, using the correct technique.

Condoms and spermicidal creams or foams may be used separately or in combination. *(Family Planning Association)*

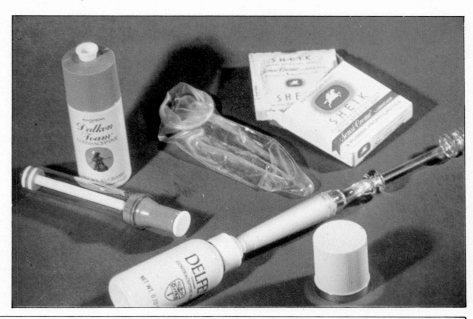

How to use condoms

The condom must be put on the penis before any sexual contact. The condom can only be put on AFTER the penis has become hard and erect.

Gently roll the condom onto the penis. Make sure that about 1.5 cm of the condom is left free beyond the tip of the penis to allow room for the fluid during ejaculation.

The loose end of the condom beyond the tip of the penis should be free of air to avoid bursting the condom during penetration.

After ejaculation, hold the rim of the condom when withdrawing the penis from the vagina (if possible before the erection is completely lost) to prevent the condom being left in the vagina. *(Family Planning Association)*

The advantages of the condom are that it is relatively cheap, readily available and involves no hormones or internal devices. It also reduces the risk of contracting venereal disease.

Studies in the United States have shown that condoms, if used properly, will stop organisms that cause sexually transmitted diseases, like syphilis, herpes, and gonorrhea. The most serious of these is AIDS. Health authorities strongly recommend the use of condoms in any situation where one partner suspects they may be infected.

Some people find that the condom is an unacceptable form of contraception and a nuisance when preparing for intercourse, especially if the partners prepare themselves independently. The distraction can be reduced by the partners sharing preparation, such as the man being responsible for the cream and the woman for the condom, a procedure which can be incorporated into foreplay.

The condom does involve some loss of sensitivity but with the thinness of modern sheaths, this is not marked.

Diaphragm

A contraceptive diaphragm is a thin, dome-shaped piece of rubber or synthetic material stretched over a flexible metal ring. It prevents sperm from entering the cervix and, if properly used, together with spermicidal cream, is quite an effective method of contraception.

Care should be taken to fit the diaphragm correctly. Because it remains in position for some time it is important that it is comfortable for the user; however it must be large enough to form an effective seal. The first fitting should be done by a skilled person who will demonstrate proper preparation, insertion and removal.

Spermicidal cream should be smeared on both sides of the diaphragm and around the rim. This acts as a lubricant as well as a chemical barrier to the sperm.

Many women are soon able to insert their diaphragm quite easily; for those who need it a specially designed inserter is also available. This is a thin rod with elevations over which the diaphragm may be stretched to allow easier insertion. Once in the vagina, the inserter is removed, and the diaphragm forms a seal by fitting over the cervix, the rim positioned above the bony bridge, (pubic symphysis) in the front, and in the space behind the cervix (posterior fornix) at the rear.

Diaphragms are inserted before intercourse and left in position for eight hours following coitus. This ensures that all sperm are killed prior to removal of the diaphragm. If intercourse occurs later than three hours after insertion, a further application of spermicidal foam should be placed in the vagina.

After removal, the diaphragm should be rinsed and dried carefully, ready for its

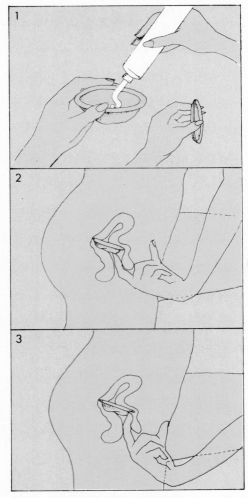

How to insert and remove a diaphragm.

1 Hold the diaphragm by the rim and cover both sides and the rim with a vaginal cream (spermicide). Squeeze diaphragm into a long narrow shape between thumb and first finger.
2 Insert while standing with one foot on a chair, squatting, or lying with knees bent. Spread the vaginal opening with your free hand while the other slides diaphragm in. Slant the diaphragm towards the small of the back, not straight in or up, and push in as far as it will go. Tuck the front rim up behind the pubic bone, just inside the opening of the vagina.
3 To remove the diaphragm put your forefinger behind the front rim and pull it down and out.

next use. With time, diaphragms tend to lose their shape and may become damaged or torn. It is important to regularly check that they are not torn, and also to replace them every two years. Also there should be a reassessment after childbirth as a different size of diaphragm may be required.

Other smaller forms of diaphragm, such as the cervical cap, are also available. These fit directly over the cervix, but are slightly less effective as they can be more readily dislodged. Caps are not generally as popular as the standard diaphragm.

If a diaphragm has been inserted properly, neither partner should be able to detect its presence during intercourse.

Douche

The application of water onto the body or into a cavity of the body is described as a douche. An internal douche is usually the application of water to the vagina.

Vaginal douches, containing various substances, have been used for centuries for different purposes: to maintain cleanliness, to induce abortion, to influence the sex of the child of a woman attempting to conceive, and as a form of contraception.

For the purpose of cleanliness a woman need not use a douche, normal methods of hygiene are sufficient.

In fact some of the substances used in douches can cause considerable damage to the vaginal lining. They may also alter the normal pH (the degree of alkalinity or acidity) of the vaginal secretions and destroy their naturally protective functions.

There is some uncertainty about the effect of acidity or alkalinity on the X (female) or the Y (male) sperm, but some authorities claim that mild acidic solutions (lactic or acetic acid) applied to the vagina before intercourse, increase the chances of conceiving a boy. On the other hand, alkaline solutions (sodium bicarbonate) increases the chance of having a girl.

As a form of contraception, douches are inefficient, given that sperm can enter the cervix within seconds of ejaculation and in some cases may be released before ejaculation. In any case douching does not remove all the sperm from the vagina.

Intra-uterine device

The small coils or loops of varying shapes that are placed in the uterus to prevent pregnancies are known as intra-uterine devices (IUDs). Except for the combined oral contraceptive pill or sterilization, IUDs are possibly the most effective form of contraception. Only about three out of every hundred women using it for one year become pregnant.

Effective intra-uterine devices were used early in this century, but they only became popular after World War II. It is now one of the most widely used forms of contraception, especially for those who cannot take the pill for medical reasons or who dislike having to regularly take something to prevent conception.

In recent years there have been increasing number of reports of women who contracted pelvic inflammatory disease (PID) while using IUD's. Some devices have been withdrawn from sale because of this risk and there are many lawsuits pending by women who used devices like the Dalkon Shield. It may be several years before clear evidence on the risks of IUD's is available.

The IUDs render the lining of the uterus unsuitable for implantation of the fertilized ovum. They also make fertilization of the ovum less likely, especially if they are copper coated, as copper reduces sperm motility.

Insertion Intra-uterine devices are inserted with the aid of a special introducer onto which they are stretched to ease passage through the cervical canal. Once within the uterus, their normal shape is regained. If the uterus is very small or has an unusual shape, insertion may be difficult. This is usually first determined by an examination using a uterine sound (a thin metal rod) which is inserted into the uterus.

The IUD is best inserted during menstruation, the time when it is certain that the woman is not pregnant. Also, at this time the cervix is slightly opened, making insertion easier. The slight spotting of blood that may occur for a few days after IUD insertion is no problem.

After an operation on the uterus it is desirable to wait three months before inserting an IUD. Also, an IUD inserted six weeks after giving birth is much less likely to be expelled than if inserted immediately after the birth.

An IUD should not be used if there is a recent or current history of pelvic inflammatory disease, as infection or inflammation of the uterus or fallopian tubes may be aggravated by an IUD.

An intra-uterine device should be inserted by a trained person, usually a doctor, with precautions to prevent the risk of infection. Because the instruments are so fine, an anesthetic is often not needed. A local anesthetic can be used if needed.

A thread attached to the IUD extends into the vagina making it easy to remove the IUD later. It is also an easy way of checking that the IUD is still in position. The IUD is most likely to be naturally expelled during the first period after insertion, if it happens at all. A follow-up visit for a check-up is desirable, but the patient can be shown how to make the check herself. Sometimes when it is reported as lost, it is actually curled up under the cervix. Its absence from the vagina indicates that it has either been expelled or turned within the uterus, drawing up the thread with it. This can be determined by an ultrasound scan or an x-ray of the pelvic area.

Problems The vast majority of women have no difficulties with IUDs. As the body adjusts to the device, there may be cramping, heavier bleeding, and spotting between periods in the first two to three cycles. Any abnormal vaginal bleeding should be fully investigated before an IUD is inserted. Some women continue to have pains and heavy periods after IUD insertion. An IUD is not usually recommended if a woman usually has heavy or painful periods.

It was once thought that IUDs were unsuitable for women who had never given birth to a child. It is now known, especially since the development of smaller IUDs, that many of these women have no problems at all.

Types There are a number of different types of IUDs, some containing copper and others a hormone. Both substances are slowly released and further reduce the suitability of the uterine lining for implantation. The advantages of these devices are that they are effective almost immediately and can be made slightly smaller so that problems of heavy periods and cramps are not so frequent. However, because of the smaller size, they can be expelled more easily. Copper IUDs should be replaced every second year and hormone types every 12 months. If inert IUDs (those without active chemicals) are inserted, alternative contraception is often recommended during the first two cycles.

Oral contraceptive

The combined oral contraceptive pill, containing both progestogen and estrogen, acts primarily by suppressing ovulation (release of an ovum or egg from the ovary). It is almost 100 per cent effective if taken correctly and has been a major medical advance, enabling planning of a family.

Estrogen and progestogen are present in sufficient levels to prevent the pituitary gland in the brain from releasing other hormones that stimulate the ovary, a process occurring naturally during pregnancy. The plug of mucus in the cervix of the uterus is also prevented from becoming permeable to sperm, a process which usually occurs just prior to ovulation.

One pill is taken each day for three weeks, followed by a break of one week. In some packs, seven chemically inert pills are included for this time. Several days after the active pills have been completed, there is a withdrawal bleed when the lining of the uterus is shed because of the sudden drop in the level of the hormones.

For the pill to be effective, it has to be taken routinely and also has to be absorbed. If one pill is missed, it should be taken as soon as it is remembered. Forgetting more than one pill in a cycle is an indication for using an alternative form of contraception for the rest of the month while continuing to take the pill.

Absorption may be reduced if there is diarrhea or vomiting. Drugs, including some antibiotics, barbiturates and anticonvulsants may interfere with the effects of the hormones. If bleeding occurs between periods while a woman is sick or on medication, she should consult her doctor and temporarily use other contraceptive measures as well as the pill. The bleeding may indicate a drop in the level of hormones.

Advantages of the pill are that it is effective, easy to take, and may improve a number of conditions. Periods are more regular, usually lighter and less painful. Premenstrual tension is often reduced or controlled, as is acne.

Contraindications There are, however, several medical contraindications to the use of the pill. These include breast cancer, a history of thrombosis (blood clots in the veins, particularly in the deeper veins of the leg), a history of stroke and some liver conditions. Those with hypertension, diabetes and some other diseases may need more than usually careful monitoring if they take the pill. Acne, vaginal thrush and obesity may be made worse by hormonal combinations in some pills.

Side effects Oral contraceptives have been available for about thirty years, and the levels of hormone in them since that time have been and are being reduced. Side effects and risks are thus being continually reduced as well.

Severe side effects are rare, most being related to clot formation in the veins. Age and cigarette smoking increase this risk; heavy smokers over the age of 35 and all women over the age of 40 should be carefully assessed. Cessation of smoking at any age is to be encouraged, as risks are increased slightly at all ages for smokers compared to non-smokers.

Symptoms which should be reported to a doctor include severe pain in the chest, a sudden onset of visual disturbance, and the occurrence of a painful and swollen calf with no obvious cause.

After cessation of the pill, one or two periods may be missed, but most women continue menstruating and are fully fertile. It is rare for periods not to have begun again within twelve months. In such cases, treatment is available which is successful in stimulating ovulation in the majority of those who wish to become pregnant.

Women with a history of very irregular periods before starting the pill are more likely to have difficulties later. It is generally thought that younger teenagers should have at least 12 months of regular periods before using oral contraceptives.

Difficulties in re-establishing regular periods are not related to times of amenorrhea (no blood loss) while on the pill; this is related to the effects of the pill on the uterus, not on the brain center that controls ovulation or the length of time that a woman has been on the pill.

Originally many doctors encouraged women to have a break from the pill every six to twelve months to allow ovulation to recommence and reduce the possibility of difficulties later. It is now known that such breaks are not needed.

Minor symptoms caused by the pill occur in less than 10 per cent of women. Many of them either settle over the first cycle or two or are prevented by a change to another pill. There are a number of different brands available, with varying levels and combinations of hormones. Since women vary in their reaction to different hormones and levels, a change is often beneficial. Common symptoms include nausea, breast tenderness and breakthrough bleeding (spotting or bleeding between periods).

Mini pills have been developed in recent years. Because these contain small amounts of progestogen and no estrogen, side effects, risks and contraindications are less than those for the combined pill. They have been used for women who are breast feeding or who have clotting problems. However there are more likely to be irregular or persistent bleeds, because one hormone used alone cannot control the shedding of the uterine lining as successfully.

The mini pill has to be taken every day without a break and preferably within the same three-hour period each day in order to prevent the plug of mucus in the cervix of the vagina from becoming permeable to sperm. To achieve this, a steady level of progestogen in the bloodstream needs to be maintained.

It is only about 97 per cent effective; 3 out of every 100 women using the mini pill for a year become pregnant.

Rhythm method

The method of contraception known as the rhythm method relies on identifying parts of the menstrual cycle in relation to possible fertilization, and restricting intercourse to the safe time.

The ovum (egg) is released from the ovary about fourteen days before the next period, and may be fertilized one to two days later. Sperm may remain viable (capable of fertilizing an ovum) in the female genital tract for up to three days.

In theory, abstinence from days ten to seventeen of a 28 day cycle (day one being the first day of the period) should ensure that no pregnancy occurs. Variability in the timing of ovulation, however, lengthens the unsafe time. Many couples abstain from day ten to day 20 of each cycle.

Most people find the rhythm method too bothersome, unsatisfying, and inefficient to use. Those with strong moral or religious objections to other forms of contraception have less choice if they wish to restrict the size of their families.

When periods are irregular, it is the first part of the menstrual cycle prior to ovulation that is variable in length. Once ovulation occurs (and there is no subsequent fertilization) the next period will follow fourteen days later.

Three main methods are used to try to define the safe and unsafe aspects of the menstrual cycle of the individual woman more accurately. Some effort is required, but a greater contraceptive efficiency is

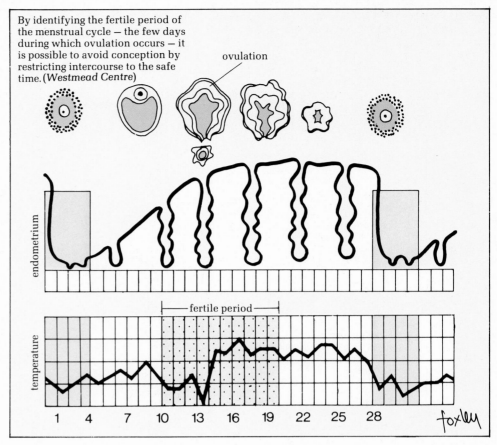

By identifying the fertile period of the menstrual cycle — the few days during which ovulation occurs — it is possible to avoid conception by restricting intercourse to the safe time. (Westmead Centre)

achieved by their use.

The calendar method initially involves the keeping of a diary, preferably for at least 12 months, documenting the days when menstruation occurs. Assuming that the unsafe time for a 28 day period is from day 10 to day 17, subtracting 18 days from the length of the shortest recorded cycle (four days prior to ovulation) gives the earliest time in a cycle that pregnancy may occur. Subtracting 11 days from the length of the longest cycle gives the latest time in a menstrual cycle that pregnancy could occur. Thus, if the time between periods varied from 26 to 30 days over a twelve-month period in one particular woman, the unsafe time would be between day 8 and day 19.

Body temperature Changes in hormonal levels that regulate the reproductive cycle in a woman regularly produce a small increase in the body temperature from approximately 36 hours after ovulation through to the end of the menstrual cycle. The increase in temperature is about 1°F (0.5°C), and is best detected first thing in the morning before getting out of bed.

The keeping of a temperature chart every morning for at least six months is desirable, to detect the rise readily and predict its appearance. Once the change is noted, intercourse can be recommenced two days subsequently. The temperature may be recorded orally or vaginally.

Temperature charting is used primarily

to determine the *end* of the unsafe time. It cannot identify the time that abstinence should begin.

Mucus observation Another physiological change brought about by the altered hormonal levels is the stimulation of the mucous glands in the cervix of the uterus. Shortly before ovulation, the cervical mucus increases in volume and becomes thin in consistency and more 'stringy'. Strands can be drawn out between the fingers. This change in thickness allows the sperm to penetrate through the mucus more readily.

After ovulation these changes are reversed and the mucus becomes scantier and thicker, and the stringiness is lost. By regularly assessing, and becoming used to these changes, the accuracy of predicting when ovulation occurs is enhanced.

In the fern test, a small sample of mucus from the vagina is placed on a glass slide and allowed to dry. As a result of hormonal changes around the time of ovulation, a tree-branch or fern-like pattern forms in the drying mucus.

The latter two procedures are also used by those women who are having difficulty in conceiving and want to know when intercourse will be most effective.

After childbirth, when nearing the menopause (when periods often occur infrequently and irregularly), and in women with persistently irregular periods, the rhythm method becomes much more difficult and unreliable.

Spermicides

Used alone, spermicidal creams, foams, gels and tablets have a high failure rate so are not advisable. Nevertheless, they have a place in contraception and should always be used with diaphragms and as an added safeguard in mid-cycle with IUDs.

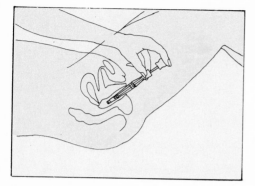

How to use spermicides.
Insert no more than twenty minutes before intercourse.
A new application must be inserted before each ejaculation.
Position for insertion should be one that is most comfortable for the woman.

Sterilization

The process of making a male or female incapable of reproduction is described as sterilization. It is a method of contraception being increasingly utilized by couples in today's society once they have completed their family. The choice lies between tubal ligation for the woman and vasectomy for the man.

Tubal ligation is the commonest method of sterilization in the female. The procedure involves dividing and tying off the fallopian tubes which carry the egg (ovum) from the ovary to the womb (uterus).

Sterilization has become popular in recent years among couples who do not wish to have any more children. As tubal ligation is considered to have a permanent and irreversible effect, despite a few recent successful reversal operations, surgeons always make sure that each partner is certain that the family is complete.

In the mid-1970s tubal ligation was performed much more often than vasectomy (sterilization in the male), but the trend is now being reversed.

The technique for a tubal ligation once involved giving a general anesthetic and surgically opening the abdomen. Nowadays a viewing tube called a laparoscope is passed through a small cut in the abdominal wall near the navel. A general anesthetic is used but the laparoscopy procedure is shorter than tubal ligation, and it is not necessary to stay in hospital for long after the operation. The small scar is usually hardly visible, indeed it is sometimes within the fold of the navel and cannot be seen. In a laparoscopy the

The most common sterilization procedure for the male is vasectomy, the removal of a small section of the vas deferens which transports the sperm from the testicles.

vas deferens is tied in two places prior to removal of segment

Using the procedure known as laparoscopy the surgeon locates the fallopian tubes, doubles up a segment of each and closes them off with a firm band.

grasping instrument   viewing scope

bladder   elastic band

testis

rectum uterus ovary

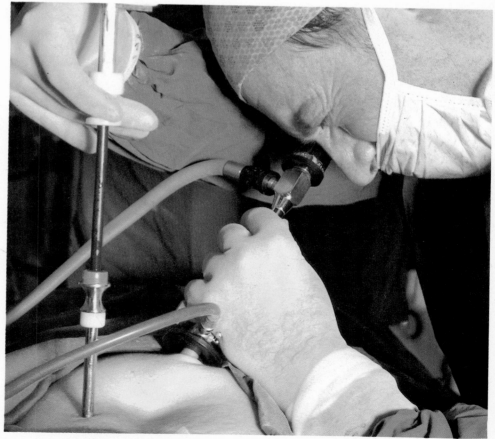

Laparoscopy operation. *(John Watney Photo Library)*

tubes are blocked off by either clips or rings. Sometimes diathermy (a small heat source) is used.

However, in patients who are obese or who have had previous abdominal surgery, standard operative procedures are used.

The advantages of tubal ligation are that while there is virtually no further risk of becoming pregnant, there is no change in menstruation or function or structure of the ovaries, womb or vagina or in the hormonal balance of the body.

A very small number of women become pregnant after tubal ligation, about 0.1 to 0.4 per cent of cases. Usually this is because the tube becomes open again despite apparently adequate surgical blockage. Because of this possibility some surgeons divide the tubes across as well as blocking both ends.

Vasectomy, the method most commonly used to achieve permanent sterilization in males, involves dividing and usually tying off the two vas deferens.

The vas deferens is the thin tube contained within the spermatic cord that transports sperm from the epididymis behind each testis up into the abdominal cavity through the inguinal canal, to eventually form the ejaculatory duct within the prostate gland. Just before entering the prostate, the vas deferens on each side is joined by a duct from the seminal vesicles.

The vas deferens carries less than 10 per cent of the ejaculate volume, the remainder coming from the accessory sex glands such as the seminal vesicles. Following vasectomy the volume reduction is thus not noticeable and the male's ability to have an erection, orgasm and satisfactory sexual intercourse is unaffected.

A vasectomy may be performed under local or general anesthetic, and usually takes less than half an hour. A small incision is made in the skin of the scrotum, and each vas, which lies just under the surface, is divided. Usually a small section is removed, and the two cut ends tied off.

Apart from slight tenderness and perhaps a little bruising for a few days, complications from vasectomy are uncommon. Taking a simple analgesic and wearing supportive underpants is usually all that is required.

Although sperm are no longer in the ejaculate, the production and body levels of the sex hormone testosterone remain unaffected.

Problems with Sex

An individual's sex is determined by genes. Female-determining genes are carried on the X chromosome, male-determining genes are carried on the Y chromosome. Normal females have two X

chromosomes in every cell; normal males have one X and one Y chromosome in each cell. At the time of fertilization, the ovum carries only one X chromosome and the sperm may carry either one X or one Y chromosome. When the ovum and the sperm unite an XX combination will result in a female and an XY combination will produce a male.

Although sex is determined at the time of fertilization, during the first five to six weeks of embryonic development, all human beings are structurally female. At the fifth or sixth week, if the cells contain the XY chromosome pair, the developing gonads become testes and produce the male hormone androgen, which stimulates the developing uro-genital ducts to form the male epididymis, vas deferens and seminal vesicles. If the cells carry the XX chromosome pair the female development proceeds without modification, and the ovaries stimulate the genital ducts to form the uterus and fallopian tubes. Only the male embryo is required to undergo a differentiating transformation of sexual anatomy, the penis developing from the undeveloped clitoris, the scrotum from the rudiments of the labia.

Embryonically, man comes from woman. The removal of the ovaries from a female fetus does not prevent the for-

Couples experiencing physical or psychological problems may be helped by a doctor or counselor. *(Salmer)*

mation of a female genital system, but the removal of the testes from a male fetus at an early stage arrests the development of male genitals and results in the development of female genitalia. Castrated female humans remain the same whereas castrated males tend to revert to femaleness. Where there is complete absence of gonads, for example in Turner's syndrome, the individual has female characteristics. All this indicates that the normal body state is that of femaleness, and that the male state is a hormonal modification of the female state.

Abnormalities — physical

Because the process of sexual development is so complex, depending on chromosomes, genes and hormone levels and being influenced by environmental factors, there are many ways in which it can go wrong and produce sexual abnormalities.

Hermaphrodites True hermaphrodites have both ovarian and testicular tissue; sometimes an ovary on one side and a testis on the other. Numerous variations in the external genitalia occur, but most have male genitalia and are reared as boys, although they later develop breasts. Treatment consists of removing organs which contradict the sex of rearing.

Total absence of gonads occurs in Turner's syndrome. Although the majority have a male chromosome pattern, all are reared as females. Their genitalia are infantile, but feminine, and cyclic treatment with estrogen produces development of breasts, vagina, uterus and menstruation.

Male hermaphrodites are genetic males with non-functioning testes. They are raised as females, but their genitalia are poorly developed with both male and female characteristics.

Some babies are born with an overdevelopment of the cortex of the adrenal glands (congenital adrenal hyperplasia) which produce male hormones (androgens). This makes the genitalia of female children resemble male, and is the commonest reason for an individual to have both male and female characteristics.

Hypogonadism In the male, hypogonadism or eunuchoidism usually refers to the failure of the interstitial cells of the testis to secrete testosterone (an androgen), although the failure of the seminiferous tubules of the testes to produce sperm is often associated with it and may even occur without changes in hormone production.

Hypogonadism in males can be caused by disorders of the testis (primary hypogonadism), or by disorders affecting the pituitary gland in which the pituitary no longer secretes adequate amounts of the gonadotrophic hormones interstitial cell stimulating hormone (ICSH) which is the same as luteinising hormone (LH), and follicle stimulating hormone (FSH). This is called secondary hypogonadism because, the testes being normal, their failure to function is secondary to the failure of the pituitary gland. Developmental abnormalities such as absent or uncorrected undescended testes and Klinefelter's syndrome and Turner's syndrome result in hypogonadism which is present from birth.

Symptoms of hypogonadism which develop before puberty are not apparent until the adolescent growth spurt or the development of secondary sexual characteristics fails to occur. These males have persistent infantile genitalia, female distribution of body hair, no seborrhea or acne and no deepening of the voice.

If hypogonadism develops in a man after puberty, it is usually because of the destruction of the testes by infection such as mumps, tuberculosis, gonorrhoea and syphilis, or because of the destruction of the pituitary gland by a tumor or infection. In young men the changes are minimal: beard growth diminishes, and axillary and other body hair thins, the skin becomes smooth, the prostate gland atrophies, and sexual desire and performance wanes. The genitalia may decrease in size and the breasts slightly increase (gynaecomastia), but the voice remains unchanged.

Primary hypogonadism in the male is treated with testosterone; secondary hypogonadism may be treated with human chorionic gonadotrophin or testosterone. A gonadotrophin rich in FSH prepared from human menopausal urine may even restore spermatogenesis (the formation of spermatozoa) to normal.

In *females*, hypogonadism means the failure of the ovaries to secrete adequate quantities of estrogen and progesterone, and occurs when the ovaries have failed to develop, are destroyed by disease or have reduced their function on reaching the menopause. Ovarian failure can also be secondarily induced by diseases of the pituitary gland, psychological trauma and general constitutional and metabolic disturbances. When it occurs prior to puberty, puberty does not occur and the female secondary sexual characteristics, the adolescent growth spurt and menstruation do not develop.

The menopause, which is experienced by all women in middle life, is the final cessation of menstruation, and is due to a decrease in the functions of the ovary. Preceded by a considerable decrease in fertility, it is accompanied by gradual regressive changes in the breasts, vagina and uterus; pubic and axillary hair becomes sparse and eventually some osteoporosis (increased porosity of bones) develops. Changes in the vasomotor and nervous systems sometimes cause nervousness, irritability, fatigue and lassitude. Occasionally the symptoms are sufficiently severe to justify estrogen therapy.

Emotional disturbances are among the commonest causes of amenorrhea (loss of menstrual periods) and sterility, although other signs of ovarian failure are usually absent. Nervous tension affects the hypothalamus (the part of the brain to which the pituitary gland is attached) and this inhibits gonadotrophin secretion by the pituitary.

Oral contraceptive tablets contain sex hormones and depress the secretion of gonadotrophin by the pituitary gland. Occasionally prolonged and even permanent amenorrhea and sterility follow when the contraceptive pill is stopped. Treatment with the drug clomiphene may reverse this condition. Women with previously irregular periods are more susceptible to hypogonadism following the contraceptive pill, and are better advised to use some other form of contraception.

Errors occurring in the embryonic development of the sex organs can result in diverse combinations of abnormalities, such as the complete absence or underdevelopment of the ovaries, uterus, tubes and vagina, or malformations of these organs, for example double uterus or double vagina.

In the male, the testis may be absent, abnormal or retained within the abdomen; the penis may be small or rudimentary, and the urethra, instead of opening onto the tip of the penis, may open onto its upper surface (epispadias) or anywhere along its lower surface (hypospadias) as far back as the scrotum.

Sexual precocity is generally defined as the development of puberty before the expected age, including the onset of menstruation, the production of sperm and the development of secondary sexual characteristics. The time is somewhat arbitrarily chosen, although 8 to 10 years is the generally accepted range. Although no abnormality can be detected in the majority of cases, serious organic disorder may be the cause. More often constitutional or inherited tendencies are responsible.

The development of all the features of puberty is controlled by hormones released by the pituitary gland in the brain. These gonadotrophins stimulate the ovaries in the female and testes in the male to produce sex hormones that are in turn responsible for secondary sexual characteristics including breast development in females, facial hair and deepening of the voice in males, an adult body contour and the growth of body hair. The exact mechanism which stimulates gonadotrophin production has not been identified, although its timing appears to be an individual or genetically inherited characteristic.

Although even collectively they are uncommon, several organic conditions may cause precocity. Disorders of the hypothalamus, midbrain or the pineal gland may result in the premature release of gonadatrophic hormones. Tumors of the ovaries, testes or the adrenal gland may also stimulate the production of various sex hormones. If a testosterone-secreting tumor develops in a young female, virilism, the development of male characteristics such as body and facial hair, may occur.

When sexual precocity occurs, physical examination, hormonal status assessment including tests for ovulation in females, x-rays, and sometimes laparotomy (investigative abdominal operation) are undertaken to find the cause, which is then treated accordingly. Those whose tests are all normal are kept under periodic observation in case later evidence of a tumour or some other lesion develops.

Early excessive sexual development causes premature closure of the growing ends of the long bones of the limbs and may result in an eventual relative shortness of stature. Mental capacity is unaffected by the premature or early occurrence of puberty. Sometimes protection against sexual exploitation is necessary for sexually precocious children.

Much has been written about Lina Medina of Peru who gave birth to a baby when she was only five years and eight months old.

Dyspareunia

Pain or difficulty experienced by the female partner during sexual intercourse is called dyspareunia.

Pain during sexual intercourse is usually caused by the presence of some painful condition in or close to the woman's vulva or vagina, such as inflammation, ulceration, infection, a cyst or abscess in Bartholin's glands or a urethral carbuncle. Atrophy of the vulva and vagina after menopause, changes in the anatomy of the region after surgery, a very rigid hymen and a small vaginal opening may also cause pain. Less common causes are a tender retroverted uterus, prolapsed ovaries, a tumor of an ovary or inflammation around the uterus and ovaries.

Fears and anxieties experienced by the female partner during sexual intercourse may cause dyspareunia. A sympathetic partner can help to overcome the psychological cause of this condition. (*Australian Picture Library*)

Difficulty during sexual intercourse is usually caused by a local condition, such as a very small vaginal opening, a rigid hymen membrane, a tumor or a congenital malformation of the vagina such as an absent, extremely small or deformed vagina.

Sometimes there is no local cause for pain or difficulty during intercourse. This can be because the participants are not performing the act correctly. Anxieties and fears on the part of the woman about sex, pregnancy or her partner can induce areas of increased sensation (hyperesthesia) in the genital area, or spasm of the muscles surrounding the vagina (vaginismus). These conditions make the act of sexual intercourse painful and difficult and provide the female partner with an excuse for avoiding sexual relations.

Often a combination of factors is responsible for dyspareunia. For example, local inflammation or a rigid hymen may have caused initial dyspareunia, and vigorous attempts at intercourse by an impatient and unsympathetic partner may cause a protective anxiety and vaginismus which persist long after the initial cause has resolved.

The treatment for dyspareunia is that of its cause. In this sensitive area even local inflammation causes some degree of anxiety, tension and even depression which must be recognized and treated. Infections are treated with the appropriate anti-bacterial and anti-fungal preparations; a small vaginal opening can be stretched or surgically enlarged; where the vagina is completely absent or seriously deformed, an artificial vagina can be created. The resolution of psychological problems requires the expert counseling of both partners.

Frigidity

The term frigidity is used to describe an absence or reduction of sexual desire in a woman. In a narrower sense, the term means the inability or relative inability to achieve orgasm.

Some cases of frigidity may be caused by a local condition or disease of the genitalia, by concurrent treatment or by ignorance of sexual technique. However, the great majority arise because of a psychological or emotional reason.

Many factors such as fatigue, illness, depression, fear of pregnancy, worry or anger may cause a temporary lack of desire.

In order to treat frigidity, a detailed sexual history must first be taken, including a description of the symptom, its first occurrence, any concurrent medication, the patient's attitudes and feelings about herself, her partner or partners, sex and family, and consideration as to how attitudes and behavior have arisen.

The treatment will then depend upon the cause. If the cause is local, physical treatment may be required. Where ignorance is the cause, explanation, education and reassurance can be given.

If a psychological cause is found, treatment will revolve around exploration of the feelings and issues involved. Behavioral techniques may be used, such as *sensate focus* a program which gradually increases the patient's sensitivity through participation in a series of graded exercises. These exercises may involve self-exploration of the body and exploration by the partner. Rate of progress is governed by the individual and the problems involved. The exercises usually proceed concurrently with sexual and general counseling. The success rate is reported to be high.

Impotence

Literally meaning a lack of power, impotence is most commonly related to the inability of a male to achieve and maintain an erection for the purpose of satisfactory sexual intercourse.

Causes Any illness, especially if associated with a general weakness such as anemia or malnutrition, may predispose to impotence. It may also be caused by damage to or diseases of the nerves or parts of the spinal cord that control erection. The most common predisposing illness is diabetes mellitus in which inflammation of the nerves produces a degree of impotence in at least half of the male diabetics over the age of 50.

The nerve fibers that control erection may also be affected by spinal injuries, tumors and multiple sclerosis. Impotence is infrequently caused by endocrine abnormalities, and occasionally by diseases of the thyroid gland, the pituitary gland and the testes. It may also occur as an unwanted side-effect of the use of certain tranquilizers, anti-depressants, some anti-hypertensive (high blood pressure) medications and alcohol.

By far the most common causes of impotence, accounting for over 90 per cent of cases, are psychological problems such as anxiety about the ability to perform adequately, fear, and guilt. Fear of sexual failure may in turn lead to even greater anxiety, setting up a vicious cycle. The sexual performance of an individual may be impaired by anger towards a sexual partner as in marital conflict, disinterest, or a partner's apparent lack of response to sexual advances. Also, males who achieve sexual satisfaction through unconventional forms of sex are less likely to do so in normal heterosexual activity.

In some cases, a man who is unable to engage in satisfactory sexual intercourse with his wife or regular partner may be quite potent with someone else.

It is thought that in some cases impotence is caused by a failure to resolve subconscious erotic attachments to the mother, who is subconsciously perceived as the woman with whom the subject is impotent.

Treatment The initial treatment should deal with any definitive disease, including depression, that is responsible for the problem. Hormone treatment is not recommended unless there is a specific deficiency.

If the problem involves a breakdown in the relationship between the two people concerned, professional counseling may be of some help in resolving it. In this regard it is important to establish good communication, trust and confidence within the relationship. This may then make it possible to discuss and deal with feelings of hostility, disinterest, doubts about the partner's love, and other problems.

Behavior therapy may be used to decrease the anxiety associated with intercourse. In most cases, with appropriate treatment, the outlook is good.

Infertility

After a couple have failed to achieve a pregnancy for a year or 18 months they generally seek specialist advice regarding infertility. Both partners require to be interviewed, examined and investigated, as a remedial cause of infertility may otherwise be missed.

Infrequent (say once a week or less) sexual intercourse without any regard for the possible time of ovulation (mid-menstrual cycle) is an obvious possible cause. Failure to form an erection or premature ejaculation in the man or vaginismus in the woman are psychological causes which can be also treated by counselling. Failure to reach an orgasm on the part of the woman is not a cause of infertility.

Infertility in the man Excessive smoking, excessive alcohol consumption or overwork all depress the formation of sperm. Any condition which raises the temperature of the testes in the scrotum is also liable to cause less sperm to be formed. Examples are thick underpants, regular sauna baths, hot occupations like working in a boiler house or varicose veins in the scrotum.

If the man has had maldescended or undescended testes in childhood which were not brought down into the scrotum surgically before he was five years old, the testes are liable not to function well. Torsion of a testis or its stalk, when it becomes twisted, cutting of the blood supply, in childhood also causes severe damage. Tuberculosis, gonococcal or syphilitic infections, mumps, any surgical operation in the groin or testes, bronze diabetes (hemochromatosis) or liver cirrhosis are liable to cause poor sperm production.

A specimen of seminal fluid should be obtained by masturbation and put in a sterile container for microscopic and chemical examination within 2 hours. Normally there is $^{1}/_{10}$–$^{1}/_{5}$ fl. oz. of fluid containing

around 350 million sperm, with more than 75 per cent of the sperm moving and less than 25 per cent abnormally formed. A low sperm count or, more important, too many abnormal slow-moving sperm reduce the chances of pregnancy. A sample of sperm taken after intercourse from the female can also be examined as this gives valuable information on any factors in the female mucus which may be harming the sperm before reaching the egg. In between 15 and 50 per cent of couples, infertility is attributable entirely to the male.

Infertility in the female The examination and investigation of the female partner is normally undertaken by a gynaecologist. If no obvious physical cause like large fibroids in the womb is found the first step is to do three or four tests to find out whether or not ovulation is taking place.

The woman must chart her oral temperature every morning before rising for three or four months. A rise of 0.5° occurs at ovulation in mid-cycle and is maintained until the next period. A blood test to measure the plasma progesterone on the twenty-first day of the cycle and a biopsy of the uterine wall taken with a fine suction tube in the second half of the cycle will show whether the womb surface is responding to the hormone usually released by the egg follicle (corpus luteum).

A sample of cervical mucus taken on the fourteenth day of the menstrual cycle. The fern-like pattern shows that ovulation has taken place. (John Watney Photo Library)

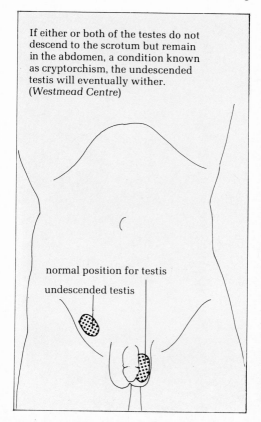

If either or both of the testes do not descend to the scrotum but remain in the abdomen, a condition known as cryptorchism, the undescended testis will eventually wither. (Westmead Centre)

normal position for testis

undescended testis

The last test entails putting mucus from the cervix on a microscopic slide on the tenth to fourteenth day of the cycle. A fern-like pattern indicates that ovulation has taken place.

If there is regular ovulation, tests for tubal patency are carried out. Obviously, if a tube is blocked conception is prevented. Under a general anesthetic a flexible thin tube is inserted through a small incision in the abdomen and the surgeon can see inside (laparoscopy).

At the same time a dye is injected through the cervix and if it is seen escaping through the laparoscope the tubes must be clear. Radiopaque substances can also be injected into the cervix and x-rays taken to outline the tubes and locate the block. Inflammation of the tubes (salpingitis) or fibrous bands or scars around the tubes (adhesions) caused by previous operations like an appendectomy, can cause kinks and blockages in the tubes. They also tend to damage the tube lining.

The tests of seminal fluid, post-coital fluid, ovulation, and tubal patency often reveal no abnormality and after reassurance the pregnancy follows.

Several additional causes of infertility should be mentioned. These are two rare inherited disorders of the chromosomes (Klinefelter's syndrome and Turner's syndrome) which cause complete untreatable sterility. Disorders of the endocrine system like thyrotoxicosis, Cushing's syndrome or pituitary tumors also cause infertility, but these can be treated with drugs with limited success.

Regular sauna baths, which raise the temperature of the testes, may inhibit the formation of sperm. (Zefa)

Treatment If an abnormality is found, treatment is possible in the following instances. In the male, varicose veins in the scrotum can be removed. If there are too few sperm, male sex hormone can be given for six months or artificial insemination with the husband's semen can be tried. Microsurgery has been successful in some instances with blocked male tubes (vas deferens).

In the female if there is a failure to ovulate the drug clomephene can be given to stimulate ovulation. 'Hostile' cervical mucus can be improved by estrogen therapy. If the tubes are blocked (which accounts for about 25 per cent of cases) a surgical operation may be attempted to free the blockage. In some specialist centres attempts are being made to 'catch' the egg before it enters the tube, fertilize it with the husband's sperm in a test tube and implant it in the uterus at a second operation. The first successful 'test tube' baby was widely reported by the media in 1978.

Until recently only about half the couples seeking treatment for lack of fertility could be treated successfully. New drugs and techniques such as those described will undoubtedly increase this proportion considerably.

Counseling for the infertile couple. The subject of infertility may create emotional problems as social and psychological pressures to have children may become significant. Sensitivity during any discussion is important. When a couple seek help with fertility difficulties, both should be involved. Mutual encouragement means that any adjustments that may be required are achieved more easily and the tendency for one to blame the other is also reduced.

Acceptance of sterility is, however, still a reality for a significant number of couples and the number of babies available for adoption is continuing to decrease. Waiting periods are often over five years and not every applicant is accepted as a prospective adoptive parent.

Premature ejaculation

Some medical authorities regard premature ejaculation as the inability of the male to delay ejaculation of sperm during sexual intercourse long enough for the woman to experience orgasm 50 per cent of the time. Others have defined it as the inability to delay ejaculation for a certain specified period of time after the penis has entered the vagina. Premature ejaculation has also been defined as pertaining to the satisfaction of both partners, rather than any arbitrary criteria.

It is one of the most common sexual problems in the male causing much distress. In most cases there is no physical cause, and treatment includes referral to psychologists for sexual therapy where sensate focus techniques with the

'squeeze technique' will be recommended.

Vaginismus

Involuntary spasm of the muscles forming the walls of the outermost part of the vagina, particularly the *levator ani* muscles, is called vaginismus. Depending upon the degree of spasm and the particular muscles involved, sexual intercourse may be rendered painful (dyspareunia) or even impossible, especially if the inner thigh muscles also go into spasm. Contraction of the muscles occurs as an involuntary reflex whenever attempts at vaginal penetration are made.

Causes Inflammation and other conditions that render intercourse painful may be responsible for vaginismus, although in most instances the underlying difficulty is psychological. Deep-seated fears are often present and these may be related to previous sexual trauma, inappropriate sex education, guilt in relation to intercourse, fear of pregnancy, or cancer.

Treatment In almost all cases, treatment is successful. Once any physical abnormality or condition has been excluded or treated, sympathetic understanding in a counseling situation is the first step towards identifying the cause of the difficulty. Sometimes fears are irrational and born out of ignorance or deep-seated anxiety and specialist psychotherapy may sometimes be required.

Confidence about having intercourse is built up slowly, usually in conjunction with support and specific treatment. Such programs generally involve teaching the patient how to relax the appropriate muscles, together with the use of vaginal dilators. These are a series of thin instruments in graduated sizes. A woman and her partner use a very thin one initially and gradually move up the scale until there is sufficient vaginal relaxation to allow regular and satisfying sexual intercourse.

Venereal Disease

In recent years, the term 'sexually transmitted diseases' (STD) has become an increasingly used alternative for 'venereal diseases', those transmitted most frequently by sexual intercourse.

Venereal disease was once primarily used to describe gonorrhea, syphilis and chancroid or soft chancre, but now also includes:

- genital herpes
- non-specific or non-gonococcal urethritis (NSU or NGU)
- trichomoniasis
- genital warts or human wart virus infections
- human papilloma virus
- chlamydia
- LGV or lymphogranuloma venerium
- granuloma inguinale
- AIDS, or HIV (human immuno-supressive virus)

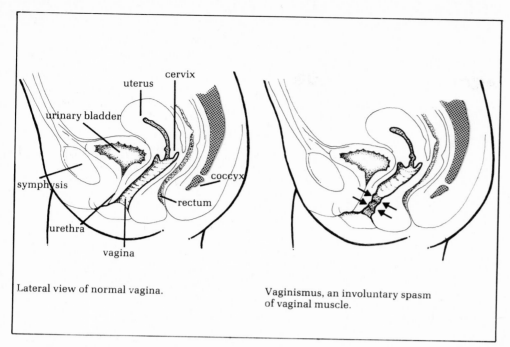

Lateral view of normal vagina.

Vaginismus, an involuntary spasm of vaginal muscle.

Syphilis Although syphilis is medically the most severe of the sexually transmitted or venereal diseases, it is not as common as gonorrhea, non-specific urethritis or genital herpes. Its name is derived from the name of an infected shepherd called Syphilus, the main character in a poem written by Fracastorius in 1530.

Although there are references to syphilis-like diseases dating back thousands of years, the condition was not clearly described until it came to prominence in Europe at the end of the fifteenth century. A particularly virulent form of the disease which killed many people emerged in Europe shortly after Christopher Columbus returned from his voyage of discovery and many historians feel that such strains had been brought back from the Americas. During the European pandemic, syphilis became known as the great pox to distinguish it from smallpox.

Syphilis is caused by the bacterium *Treponema pallidum*, a delicate, spiral-shaped, motile organism belonging to the spirochete group of bacteria, and first identified in 1905 by the German bacteriologist Fritz Schaudinn (1871-1906).

The bacterium, although usually transmitted during sexual intercourse, may occasionally be contracted by close contact with infective lesions, and can also be transferred by a pregnant woman across the placenta to her unborn baby. It penetrates the mucous membranes or the skin and enters the bloodstream. The incubation period varies between 10 and 90 days, although on average it is three weeks. The disease, if untreated, usually passes through three stages.

Primary stage. A chancre or painless papule heralds the first or primary syphilitic stage. It occurs most frequently on the external genitalia at the site of bacterial entry, although it may occasionally develop in or near the anus, on the lips or mouth, or on the cervix in the female. This papule soon ulcerates and local lymph nodes enlarge. In the absence of treatment resolution takes up to twelve weeks.

Secondary stage. The progress of the disease and the specific symptoms beyond the primary stage are quite variable. Secondary syphilis tends to develop one to three months after the chancre has healed, although at times it may commence while the primary stage is still present.

A generalized rash and painless enlargement of the lymph nodes are almost universal, while weight loss, fever, malaise and headache are common. The organism is present throughout the body and often causes inflammation of blood vessels so that virtually any organ or tissue can become affected. In the particularly virulent forms present in the great pox pandemic in Europe in 1494 many deaths occurred during this stage of the infection. Such severity is rare today and resolution generally occurs over two to six weeks.

About one-quarter of those with syphilis will undergo relapses of the secondary stage within the next one to two years. The usual symptoms are the presence of various types of rashes and *condyloma lata*, flat warts that usually develop in the groin or on the genitals.

Tertiary stage. The infection then remains latent for an indefinite period in the majority of people, although 20 to 30 per cent may develop symptoms of tertiary syphilis up to twenty years later.

A *gumma*, which is a collection of inflammatory cells that may occur in virtually any tissue of the body, is characteristic of the tertiary stage. Symptoms generally relate to its pressure on the surrounding structures.

Slowly progressive inflammation of small blood vessels and nervous tissue is the other main manifestation of tertiary syphilis. Tiny arteries called *vasa vasorum* supply the tissues of the walls of the largest arteries and when they become inflamed and blocked, the wall of the vessel that they supply weakens. The first part of the aorta and the valve between it and the left ventricle of the heart are the main areas affected. Leakage or incompetence of the aortic valve and dilatation or aneurysm formation of the aorta follow.

Neurosyphilis is the term used to describe a wide range of nerve tissue problems that may occur during the tertiary stage. Tabes dorsalis, which involves the motor nerves, is characterized by an unsteady gait, loss of reflexes and sometimes loss of bowel and bladder control. General paralysis of the insane, in which there is inflammation of both the membranes that cover the brain (meninges) and the parts of the brain itself, is characterised by gradual memory loss, personality deterioration, mood swings, dementia and eventual paralysis.

Congenital syphilis can develop in the fetus once the fourth month of intrauterine life has been reached. The infecting bacteria, having crossed the placenta, may lodge in any tissue or organ. Miscarriages or stillbirths are more frequent. In the infants surviving to birth, the *snuffles* are a common occurrence and other symptoms similar to secondary syphilis may also develop. Developmental abnormalities may be present, particularly of the teeth and facial bones.

Diagnosis of syphilis may be made by identifying the *Treponema* bacteria in the serum at the bottom of the chancre in the primary stage, or in the tissue that forms the condyloma lata in the secondary stage. A variety of serological blood tests such as the Wasserman reaction (WR) and the Venereal Diseases Research Laboratories (VDRL) test may be used to detect the presence of specific antibodies.

Treatment. Mercury, which is fairly toxic and not very effective, was the only specific treatment available for syphilis until the discovery of arsphenamine by Paul Erhlich in 1910. This arsenic-based compound was replaced in the 1940s by penicillin, which is still the preferred drug today.

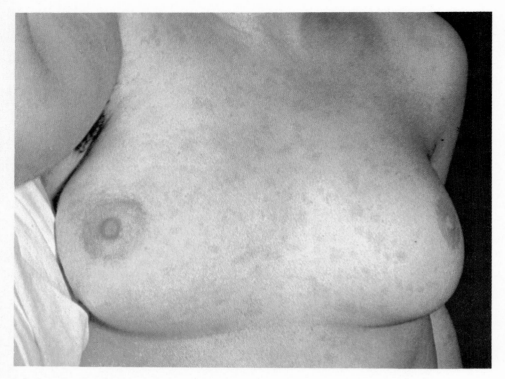

Some months after the primary infection of syphilis has healed, a generalized skin rash develops. *(Abbottempo)*

Primary and secondary stages of syphilis are readily curable and the resolution of gummas of tertiary syphilis is also aided by the use of penicillin. Although the progression of tabes dorsalis and general paralysis of the insane may be halted, the deterioration that has already occurred is irreversible.

Since the introduction of antibiotics the occurrence of tertiary syphilis has become rare. An initial reduction in the incidence of syphilis has, however, been followed by an increasing incidence over the last two decades. A delay in diagnosis is more likely in homesexual males and in females, as anal and vaginal chancres are more easily overlooked.

Because people can remain infectious for over twelve months during the primary and secondary stages and during the relapses, comprehensive follow-up of all sexual contacts is important in controlling the spread of syphilis.

Gonorrhea ("clap") is almost always transmitted between adults during sexual intercourse. The bacteria die within two hours if exposed to dry air, therefore it is rare for the disease to be spread by contaminated water or clothing.

A form of gonorrheal infection which is now much less common is ophthalmia neonatorum. This occurs in newly-born babies whose eyes have been contaminated by the gonorrhea bacteria present in the birth canal of the mother. If untreated it can cause blindness. However the condition is usually easily recognized and can be rapidly cured with antibiotic drops.

The initial infection in men usually occurs in the urethra, the tube that carries urine from the bladder through to the penis. Inflammation first occurs in the last part of the urethra near its opening at the end of the penis. When symptoms do occur they begin with a feeling of irritation. This is soon followed by a watery discharge which in turn usually soon becomes yellowy-green and thick in consistency. The inflammation also causes a burning feeling when passing urine. In homosexual males initial gonorrheal infection may develop in the throat or rectum, and in the female it may develop from orogenital contact.

Inflammation of the urethra also occurs in women during the early stages of infection. However the symptoms tend to be milder than in males and even may not appear. Only in very few cases is there a discharge.

Complications may occur if initial symptoms are untreated, with the disease spreading to other organs. In males infection may spread back along the urethra to the prostate, and sometimes to the epididymis, a tissue attached to the testis. In females the organism may be transferred via the vagina through the cervix into the womb and fallopian tubes. A long-standing or severe infection may permanently damage the epididymis or fallopian tubes, rendering them incapable of transporting the sex cells (sperm and ova), thereby causing infertility.

The *Neisseria gonorrhoeae* bacterium may occasionally be spread by the bloodstream to produce arthritis (inflammation of joints), and more rarely to the heart valves to produce an endocarditis (inflammation of the heart valves).

Diagnosis of gonorrhea is made by examining the discharge (usually urethral) under a microscope, and also by growing the organism in a special culture medium.

Because other venereal diseases, such as syphilis, may also be present, it is advisable to make blood tests to determine this.

The bacteria are fairly sensitive to antibiotics, although there is an alarming increase in the number of strains that are resistant to penicillin. Intercourse should be avoided during treatment.

The incidence of gonorrhea is increasing throughout the world. The widespread use of the pill and the intra-uterine device in preference to the older barrier methods such as the condom, which offered some protection against venereal disease, has influenced the spread of the disease.

Other factors which affect the spread of gonorrhea are delays in treatment because the mildness of the symptoms leads to lack of awareness of the disease, the increasing resistance of the bacteria to antibiotics, and the increase in promiscuity.

Chancroid Painful genital ulcers with tender, enlarged lymph nodes in the groin are the main features of chancroid. Generalised symptoms such as fever and joint pains (which occur with the painful genital ulcers of herpes simplex) are usually absent. The condition, being caused by a

The eyes of this infant have been infected by gonorrhoea at birth, during its passage through the mother's vagina. *(Family Planning Association NSW)*

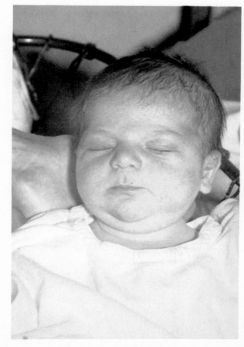

bacterium, responds to treatment with antibiotics.

Genital herpes Local blisters which soon ulcerate are an early symptom of genital herpes simplex. Dysuria (the painful passage of urine) is another common feature that is usually absent in chancroid. Other strains of this virus may also cause cold sores and it often remains asymptomatic in tissues for several years, being reactivated periodically to produce further crops of blisters.

Genital herpes is common, long-lasting and painful.

Curative treatment is available for genital herpes. A drug, Acyclovir has been shown to reduce the severity and frequency of attacks. Local application of ointments and oral analgesics also provide symptomatic relief.

Non-specific or non-gonococcal urethritis (NSU or NGU) is a condition associated with dysuria and a urethral discharge. The exact cause is uncertain, although species of *Mycoplasma* and *Chlamydia* bacteria are often isolated from cultures of the urethral discharge. Tetracycline antibiotics are generally effective against these types of organisms and are the preferred drugs.

Acquired Immune Deficiency Syndrome (AIDS) In 1981 a new disease was observed in young homosexual/bisexual men in Los Angeles, San Francisco and New York. Serious infections and unusual cancers were seen in these cases and they all had severely depressed immune systems. Over the next two years AIDS was reported in intravenous drug users who share needles, blood transfusion recipients and hemophiliacs, in male and female prostitutes and in their sexual partners. In 1984 the cause of AIDS was discovered by the National Institutes of Health to be a virus now called the Human Immunodeficiency Virus (HIV).

AIDS has become epidemic in many countries, especially in central Africa, Australia and in Europe. The fastest increase is in the United States where more than 5000 cases have already occurred and more than one million people are estimated to be infected. The major route of spread is through intravenous contamination. Anal intercourse probably increases the risk of infection as the lining of the rectum is very thin and easily broken, allowing the AIDS virus to enter the bloodstream. Condom use is very strongly advised for all people who are in high risk groups. AIDS has been widely reported in Africa where most cases are in heterosexual men and women and the virus is spread via vaginal intercourse. Once infected a person can probably pass the disease to others, for the rest of their lives. There is a very good scientific evidence that the AIDS virus is not spread by casual contact with an infected person. Food, inanimate objects, touching and any activity that does not involve exchange of body fluids (like blood, semen and vaginal secretions) will not result in infection with the AIDS virus.

The early signs and symptoms of the AIDS virus infection are similar to many common less serious illnesses. Diarrhea, fevers, night sweats, unexplained weight loss, persistent lethargy and general swelling of the lymph nodes may be associated with infection, especially if they persist for weeks or months. In the later stages of infection, the immune system is destroyed by the virus resulting in an overwhelming attack by different bacteria, parasites and other organisms. Unusual cancers are also commonly seen in persons with AIDS.

Exposure to the AIDS virus is diagnosed by a blood test which measures the presence of antibodies. This test is used to screen all blood donations in Western countries and the blood transfusion system is now considered to be safe.

There is no known treatment for the AIDS virus and the longterm outcome for people who are infected is not yet clear. However, it is estimated that by 1991 about 300 000 Americans will have AIDS and 180 000 will have died of the disease. Prevention and education are the most important ways that this epidemic will be stopped. Most STD clinics have detailed information about AIDS and they should be consulted by anybody who thinks they may have become infected.

There is still no "cure" for AIDS, but a new drug, "ATZ", is proving very promising. A great deal of work is being done on this problem.

Other venereal diseases Trichomoniasis is a protozoal infection that is a common cause of vaginal discharge. Males are often asymptomatic. Treatment with metronidazole or tinidazole is quite effective.

Lymphogranuloma venereum and granuloma inguinale are not common. Both produce genital sores or ulcers, although in lymphogranuloma venereum the local lymph nodes tend to form a mass of inflamed tissue that subsequently develops into an abscess. Both conditions respond to tetracycline.

There are a number of other conditions that may also be transmitted by sexual acitivity. Parasites of the skin, such a pubic lice and the scabies mite, transfer with close body contact. A variety of viral conditions also may be transferred by sexual intercourse because the organisms are present in the seminal fluid. Hepatitis B, glandular fever, and cytomegalovirus are among these. Anal intercourse, particularly by homosexual males, enables amebiasis, giardiasis, as well as various helminthic and bacterial diseases to be contracted sexually.

Candidiasis, or thrush, is a common source of vaginal discharge. It may affect the male and be passed on sexually, although most frequently the source of infection in the female is her own large bowel.

The last group of conditions, like thrush, while capable of being transmitted sexually, is most often transmitted in other ways.

Sexual Variations

The title of this section, 'sexual variations', rather than 'sexual deviations' reflects a profound change in thinking about sexuality by psychologists, psychiatrists and doctors. Sexuality is now considered to be more than just a sexual act, rather our ideas and definitions are reflections of: biological and physiological, sociological, economic, spiritual, cultural and psychological processes. Thus, our views on sexuality constantly change and are re-defined. In this process, conflicting viewpoints are often heard, for example, in regards to homosexuality.

Sexual attraction between opposite sexes is called heterosexuality and is the accepted norm. Only about 4 per cent of the world's population is exclusively homosexual. (Zefa)

The 'truth' is always clouded by 'moral' arguments and cultural differences.

It has always been known that human sexual expression has many variations. These occur in regards to (a) the length and type of relationships we experience; (b) the sex of the person we relate to; and (c) the form of our sexual expression.

The formation of sexual variation is generally considered to relate to an interaction between biology and learning. Although our society regards a heterosexual relationship culminating in coitus, as the most usual and acceptable form of sexual expression, there are many others.

Sexual preferences

The most common form of sexual expression is heterosexuality (male–female attraction). Sexual preferences are now considered a continuum heterosexuality-to-homosexuality. Although the majority of people tend towards being heterosexual a sizable minority also experience sexual activity with members of the same sex. In addition, there are sexual preferences held by a minority of individuals such as:

Children brought up in a stable, happy environment are generally unlikely to develop sexual problems or deviations in later life. (Zefa)

bestiality, pedophilia, necrophilia. In general, these are a result of maladjustments occurring early in life or as a result of an underlying illness.

1. Homosexuality

Sexual attraction between people of the same sex is homosexuality. When females are attracted to each other the term lesbianism is generally used. Actual sexual activity may not always be involved.

The direction and nature of our sexuality are complex. In conventional contemporary society, educational practices have the effect that from pre-school years to puberty, most people tend to be primarily in the company of their own sex. By the end of adolescence, heterosexuality is usually the established preference. During the exploratory phase of one's sexuality, when there is a corresponding search for identity and development of interactions with others, strong feelings for someone of the same sex are common, though usually not long lasting.

A number of these infatuations may be expressed in a physical way. In research into sexual behaviour Kinsey found that, usually during adolescence, over a third of adult American males had had physical contact with another male to the point of orgasm. Under varying degrees of psycho-

logical duress and female deprivation, such as in prison, a number of males who are normally heterosexual will become involved in homosexual acts. Only about four per cent of the population is exclusively homosexual in the physical expression of sexuality.

During adolescence, mutual masturbation, embracing and kissing are the main sexual activities. Later, oro-genital and anal intercourse become more common. Forms of abnormal sexuality such as pedophilia (a sexual interest in children) and exhibitionism *usually involve heterosexuals* and are very uncommon among the homosexual population.

Causes Many studies have been undertaken to discover the cause of homosexuality. No hormonal abnormality has been detected and genetic causes cannot be found. The influence of parents and family relationships is undermined. Most professional psychiatrists and psychologists and their professional associations consider homosexuality a natural human variation, as is lefthandedness.

Someone who has an established and exclusive pattern of homosexual behavior seldom wishes to change the direction of sexual expression. Psychological treatment may be sought if the individual is anxious about related issues, for example the intolerance of others or the apparent need for secrecy regarding homosexual activity.

2. Bestiality

This term describes individuals who have sex with animals. For those who do, it may be related to geographical circumstances (eg in the country) and the absence of other forms of sexual release. Few people have an exclusive interest in animals and where they do, it is usually related to a poor ability to form adult relationships.

3. Pedophilia

The sexual attraction of an adult, of either sex, to a pre-pubertal or immature child.

Most pedophiles satisfy their urges by using pornographic literature or videotapes while masturbating. Very few actually make advances to young children. Contrary to popular belief, sexual attacks on young children are not usually by pedophiles but by other types of psychopath, and the fact that the victim is a child is only incidental.

Because pedophilia is illegal in most countries it is rigidly controlled under legislation against general 'child abuse' and is controlled by both police agencies and pediatric units specializing in the treatment of this problem.

4. Necrophilia

Sexual intercourse with a corpse. An indication of severe mental illness or psychosis.

Sexual arousal

In addition to the continuum of sexual preferences, there are also various ways of becoming sexually aroused, such as exhibitionism; fetishism; masochism; sadism; voyeurism. Although it is normal to experience mild forms of these, for example, biting in sexual foreplay, or being sexually aroused by observing pornography, in the extreme forms, these activities may effect a maladjustment to unsatisfactory early experiences and relationships. In these cases the element of choice is usually absent, and the only way for the individual to become aroused is to act out and seek out the object of their sexual gratification.

Extreme forms of sexual behavior occurring for the first time in people over the age of 40, may be a reaction to a severe crisis or a symptom of an underlying illness. Treatment if sought is usually in the form of psychotherapy. As with other firmly established patterns of behavior, change requires the cooperation of the individual.

1. Exhibitionism

The sexual deviation in which a male exhibits his genitals, usually an erect penis, to females is known as exhibitionism. A reaction of shock or fear causes sexual excitement. Intercourse or physical violence are not features of exhibitionism and the man usually disappears quickly to achieve orgasm by masturbation.

Often the exhibitionist is insecure and is subconsciously seeking reassurance about his sexuality. The exhibitionism which is a relatively common feature of play in pre-adolescent children does not develop into an adult perversion.

2. Fetishism

Fetishism describes a form of sexual behavior where a particular object becomes central and essential to sexual arousal. Sexual excitement in fetishism is normally gained by handling the item concerned, but sometimes destroying or stealing it is part of the pattern. It is almost exclusively a male behavior.

Furs, leather boots, and female underwear are common items which may become fetish objects but a mere preference for certain clothing, perfume or surroundings for sexual activity does not, of course, amount to fetishism.

Fetishism is frequently an essential component of copulation rather than an alternative to it, requiring a partner compliant with the fetish to achieve orgasm.
Causes are usually psychological, relating both to the overall personality and to prior experiences. In some cases, brain damage or, rarely, temporal lobe epilepsy may be responsible.

Treatment In the majority of cases where no specific physical cause is found, treatment (if desired) involves psychotherapy. This may include counseling, with a marriage partner if one exists.

3. Masochism

The sexual behavior known as masochism was first described by the Austrian novelist Leopold von Sacher-Masoch (1836–1895). This form of behavior involves receiving pain in order to achieve orgasm and sexual gratification. It is often associated with sadism in the sexual partner and is then known as sado-masochism. Being whipped or beaten often forms part of the masochist's sexual foreplay.

Freud's view was that masochism represented the need for punishment to appease the guilt of repressed sexual desires for one's parents.

The milder form of pleasure felt when 'mastered' by the person who is the object of sexual desire is relatively common. Many psychologists regard this as normal rather than as a type of masochism.

Treatment mainly involves psychotherapy or behavioral modification therapy. However, unless the person wishes to change, the chances of success are slim.

4. Sadism

Sadism is a form of sexual perversion in which sexual pleasure is achieved by inflicting pain on another person. The name is derived from the Marquis de Sade (1740–1814), whose writings focused on sexual cruelty. Whipping and beating are common forms of sadism, but sometimes violent rape and sexual assault with associated mutilation may occur.

One theory is that the aggression is the inturning of feeling that is felt subconsciously towards others, particularly the parents.

Rudimentary forms of sadism in the form of erotic arousal in response to sadistic stories have been demonstrated in 10 per cent of men and three per cent of women. Biting or scratching associated with sexual foreplay is not uncommon.

5. Narcissism

A condition describing excessive self-love and self-admiration, 'narcissism' is derived from the Greek legendary character Narcissus, who fell in love with his own image. Extreme narcissism requires psychiatric treatment.

6. Voyeurism

The attainment of sexual satisfaction by observing the genitals or the sexual activities of others is described as voyeurism. To some extent this form of excitation is normal. Only in its extreme forms is it true voyeurism as, for example, in the case of the 'peeping Tom' who attempts to

Voyeurism, pleasure derived from observing the genitals or sexual activities of others, is sometimes the result of sexual inadequacy.
(Salmer)

gain sexual satisfaction from the unobserved watching, through a window or keyhole, of women undressing.

This is a predominantly male perversion, generally the result of sexual inadequacy and fear of rejection by the opposite sex. Early developmental psychological difficulties are usually responsible, and treatment by psychotherapy is often successful.

7. Transvestism

Transvestism involves dressing up in clothes of the opposite sex and acting out the appropriate role.

There are many forms of sexual expression which have been defined as 'abormal'. In general children growing up in a family in which sexuality is talked about openly and honestly, are less likely to internalize negative feelings about sexual expression. There is no evidence indicating that talking about sexuality in an honest way will have a negative effect on a child's sexual development. In addition behavior exhibited during childhood does not necessarily relate to adult sexual expression. However if you have any concerns or doubts, contact a general practitioner or psychologist/psychiatrist.

3 Pregnancy
Childbirth and Postnatal Care

Pregnancy

The human embryo is formed by the fusion of two reproductive cells, or gametes, one from each parent. The male supplies the sperm, usually by way of intercourse, while the female produces the ovum and provides the environment for fertilization and gestation; she also gives birth and produces milk to nourish the child.

The sperm and the ovum differ from other body cells, in that each possesses only half the necessary chromosomes. In the process of fertilization the male and female cells unite, re-establishing the correct number of chromosomes. The hereditary characteristics carried on the chromosomes are therefore determined half by the father and half by the mother.

Spermatozoa The testes commence to produce spermatozoa some months after the onset of puberty. Fertile sperm are normally produced from about the age of fifteen until death. The seminiferous tubules of the testes are filled with spermatogonia, the basic reproductive cells which, by dividing, assure continuing production of spermatozoa. From spermatogonia to spermatocyte, to spermatids, to spermatozoa, the cells gradually develop into the mature sperm consisting of a cellular nucleus, or head, and a tail.

Following conception the fetus develops in the uterus for 40 weeks.

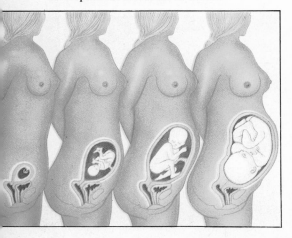

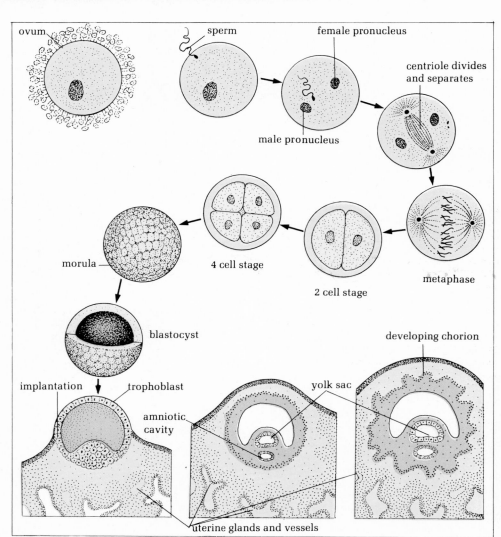

The first stages of pregnancy.

The tail propels the sperm along. In the testes, the epididymis and the vas deferens, the spermatozoa are packed tightly together forming a thick cloudy mass. The semen emitted during ejaculation is a fluid compounded of secretions contributed by various glands.

The seminal vesicles produce a liquid containing nutrients for the spermatozoa, while the prostate gland emits a substance which both dilutes the fluid and gives it an alkaline pH. The normal acidity of the vagina, which is fatal to sperm, is thus partially neutralized by the semen itself.

However, the volume of a typical male ejaculation is usually 3 to 5 milliliters with each milliliter containing up to 70 million spermatozoa, so although many will not survive the acidic environment, sufficient remain to fertilize the ovum.

Ovum A single ovum is released once during each menstrual cycle, except for the very rare cases of double ovulation which may result in non-identical twins. Each human female comes into the world with a non-replenishable stock of about 40 000 eggs in her ovaries. The ovum which is expelled from the graafian fol-

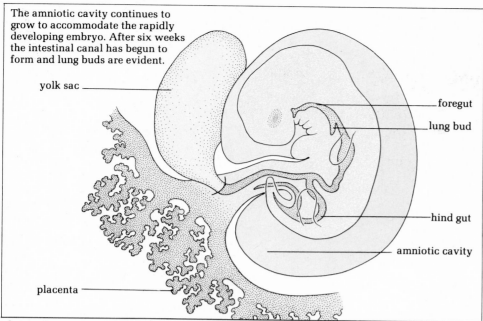

The amniotic cavity continues to grow to accommodate the rapidly developing embryo. After six weeks the intestinal canal has begun to form and lung buds are evident.

yolk sac

foregut

lung bud

hind gut

amniotic cavity

placenta

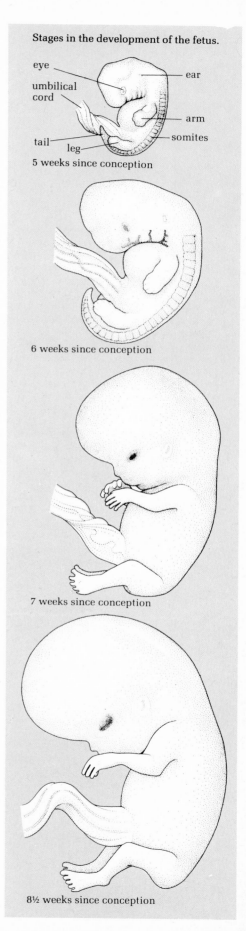

Stages in the development of the fetus.

eye

ear

umbilical cord

arm

tail

somites

leg

5 weeks since conception

6 weeks since conception

7 weeks since conception

8½ weeks since conception

icle is a large round cell just visible to the naked eye. Although it is inert and full of nutritional reserves, the ovum dies in 24 to 36 hours if it is not fertilized.

Conception Fertilization is normally the result of sexual intercourse, also termed coitus or copulation.

The ejaculated sperm lodge in the cul-de-sac at the top of the vagina. Unlike the man, it is not necessary for a woman to reach orgasm to procreate: for this she needs only appropriately timely intercourse with a fertile partner. The most active spermatozoa enter the neck of the womb, travelling through the uterus into the fallopian tubes. Although they may remain active for as long as four days, survival time is variable.

Human fetus at eleven weeks, 46 millimeters long. (*John Watney Photo Library*)

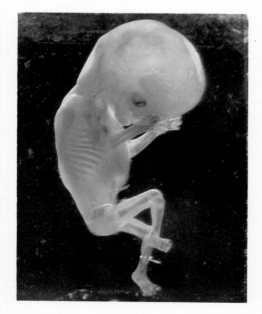

After expulsion from the graafian follicle the ovum is moved along the fallopian tube by hair-like processes lining the inside of the tubes. Fertilization usually occurs in the fallopian tube when one sperm penetrates the ovum. The tail of the sperm falls off and a membrane forms around the fertilized ovum preventing the entry of other sperm. The fertilized ovum then commences the cellular divisions which will gradually transform the egg into the embryo.

The fertilized ovum continues to move to the uterus where it becomes secured in the thick lining of the wall.

Development of the baby

Implantation is the attachment of the fertilized ovum to the wall of the uterus. By the eighth day after ovulation the ovum becomes partially implanted into the lining of the upper part of the uterus (the secretory endometrium) and about three to four days later the process of implantation is complete.

Sometimes implantation may occur in the lower part of the uterus, in which case the condition known as *placenta previa* develops. In some cases, implantation may not take place in the uterus at all, creating an ectopic pregnancy, the site of which may be the fallopian tubes, or the ovaries or the abdominal cavity.

Embryo During the first two weeks after fertilization (the union of the male and female sex cells), a rapid multiplication of cells occurs resulting in, first, a solid mass of cells (morula), and then a blastocyst. By the blastocyst stage the tissues have formed as two separate types. The outer layer of tissue is called the trophoblast and this attaches to the wall of the womb (uterus), eventually to form the afterbirth or placenta. The inner tissue is called the embryoblast and develops to form the so-called embryo.

The second to eighth week after fertilization is called the embryonic period. During this time the embryoblast tissue develops a longitudinal form. By the eighth week all the major structures of the body are represented and the embryo is recognizably human. From this stage the developing offspring is called a fetus.

Fetus The rapid development continues during the first two months of the fetal stage. By the third month after fertilization the heart has been formed and is pumping blood to other organs of the fetus. By the fourth month the kidneys have started to function as excreting organs.

During the early stages of development, especially the first 13 weeks, the growth and development of body tissues are most prone to abnormalities caused by drugs (such as thalidomide) or infections (such as rubella).

The last part of pregnancy is called the growth phase. All organs and tissues enlarge and the weight of the fetus is more than doubled in the last two months. During this period great demands for nutritional products are placed on the mother-to-be, and the need for an adequate and balanced diet is at its maximum.

At one time the fetus had no chance of surviving outside the womb before it had reached the 28-week stage (that is, 28 weeks after fertilization) and for this reason, 28 weeks was regarded as the age of fetal viability. Advances in medical techniques have meant that some babies could be cared for successfully in intensive care units following delivery as early as 26 weeks. By common agreement the age of fetal viability is now defined arbitrarily as 20 weeks subsequent to fertilization.

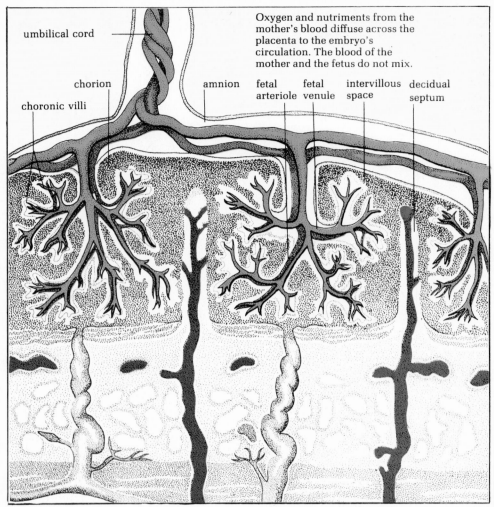

umbilical cord
chorion
choronic villi
amnion
fetal arteriole
fetal venule
intervillous space
decidual septum

Oxygen and nutriments from the mother's blood diffuse across the placenta to the embryo's circulation. The blood of the mother and the fetus do not mix.

Ultrasound equipment is used in fetal scanning. (*International General Electric*)

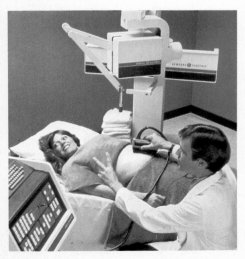

The placenta

The afterbirth or placenta is an organ which develops in the uterus after conception to provide an exchange of nutrients and wastes between the fetus and the mother and to secrete the hormones necessary to maintain the pregnancy. The fetus is attached to the placenta by the umbilical cord.

Fertilization of the ovum occurs in the fallopian tube and the resulting single cell (the zygote) divides rapidly to form a spherical mass of cells. During the second week of pregnancy the outer layer of cells (the chorion) penetrates the adjacent wall of the uterus, where they are bathed with maternal blood from open uterine blood capillaries. Large numbers of delicate finger-like processes (villi) which grow through into the wall of the uterus firmly anchor the embryo to the uterine wall and provide a most extensive contact with maternal blood. Initially the villi completely cover the embryo, but, as the embryo grows, the villi covering the outer part of the ovum atrophy, while those attached to the uterine wall develop into a very complex structure of blood vessels. The uterine wall adjacent to these highly developed villi also becomes modified into spongy tissue rich in blood vessels. The combination of the embryonic villi and spongy uterine wall, forms the placenta.

An adequate placenta is essential for the satisfactory development of the embryo. Poor implantation and poor placenta development may be one of the causes of spontaneous abortion. By the twelfth week of pregnancy the placenta is fully formed.

Exchange across the placenta Oxygen and nutrients pass from the mother's blood across the placenta into the embryo's circulation, while waste products diffuse back across the placenta and into the maternal circulation, to be excreted by the mother's kidneys into her urine. Oxygen, food and wastes pass across the placenta by diffusion: the blood of the mother and the fetus do not mix. However, many other substances do pass across the placenta and may harm the developing fetus, for example, drugs, products of tobacco smoke, alcohol, and some infections such as the syphilis bacillus and the German measles virus. Therefore during pregnancy, great care must be taken with diet, smoking and alcohol consumption should be discontinued and drugs should be avoided unless deemed absolutely essential by the doctor.

Afterbirth The placenta progressively enlarges as the fetus grows and its requirements for nutrition and excretion increase. Following the birth of the baby, the uterine contractions also expel the placenta which is then known as the afterbirth. It is a spongy mass weighing about half a kilogram, with a diameter of about 8 inches (20 cm) and a maximum thickness at its center of about 1¼ inches (3 cm). Occasionally the placenta does not separate spontaneously and has to be removed manually, by inserting the hand into the uterus and gently lifting it off the uterine wall. The fetus remains attached to the placenta by the umbilical cord.

The umbilical cord is composed mainly of a jelly-like substance called Wharton's jelly, which surrounds and supports the blood vessels (the umbilical vein and the umbilical arteries) of the umbilical cord.

The umbilical vein carries oxygenated blood from the placenta to the fetal liver where it branches and then divides, one branch joining the portal vein, the other branch continuing as the ductus venosus and joining the inferior vena cava.

The umbilical cord also contains the vitielline duct, a tubular outgrowth from the yolk-sac from which the gut develops. This has disappeared by the time the fetus is six weeks old but its vessels remain as the portal vein and the superior mesenteric artery.

The allantoic duct is also within the umbilical cord and this persists as a microscopic remnant.

The cord at full term is about 21½ inches (55 cm) long and appears as a twisted rope-like structure. The length of the cord varies and may be as short as 4 inches–6 inches (10–15 cm) or as long as 40 inches (100 cm). At birth the umbilical cord is divided carefully and ligated firmly. By the third or fourth day of life the stump of the umbilical cord has shriveled and the umbilicus becomes a scar. Internally the remnants shrink into obliterated cords.

In multiple pregnancies resulting from the fertilization of a single egg (for example identical twins) each fetus shares the one placenta. However, when the multiple pregnancy results from the fertilization of several eggs, each fetus has its own placenta.

Placental hormones The structure produced in the ovary following the release of an egg or ovum is the corpus luteum. The follicle releases the ovum and then becomes the corpus luteum. This acts for a time as a ductless gland which will shrivel and leave a scar unless the ovum is fertilized.

In every menstrual cycle the corpus luteum produces a hormone called progesterone in the latter half of the cycle, which reaches a peak at about the twentieth day.

Following fertilization, the corpus luteum is maintained until the fourth month of pregnancy and for most of this time it continues to secrete estrogen and progesterone, both of which are needed to maintain the lining of the uterus during pregnancy and prepare the mammary

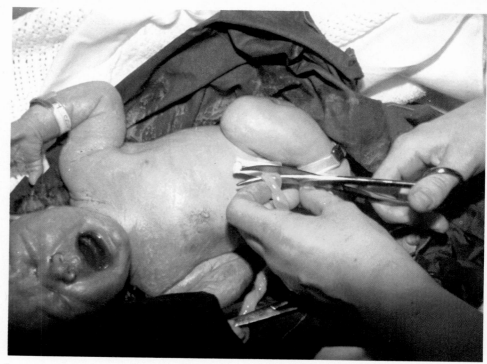

The umbilical cord being cut after delivery. (*John Watney Photo Library*)

glands in the breast to secrete milk. During the pregnancy the placenta secretes a hormone, human chorionic gonadotrophin (HCG), the excess of which is excreted in the urine of pregnant women from about the middle of the first month of pregnancy, reaching its peak of excretion during the third month and decreasing sharply during the fourth and fifth month. The measuring of HCG in the urine is the basis of some pregnancy tests.

The main function of HCG is to maintain the activity of the corpus luteum, since the continuing secretion of progesterone, in particular, is necessary to maintain the attachment of the fetus to the lining of the uterus. From the third month the placenta itself takes over the secretion of estrogen and progesterone, and high levels of HCG are no longer needed. Placental estrogen and progesterone increase, reaching their highest levels at the time of birth.

Artificial insemination

The introduction of semen into the genital tract of a female is called insemination. The usual way is by sexual intercourse, which deposits semen in the upper part of the vagina.

Artificial insemination may be used if the husband cannot perform sexual intercourse or is sterile. If he is fertile but sexually disabled, his semen may be injected by a syringe into his wife's womb, a method known as AIH (artificial insemination by the husband). If he is sterile, the couple may decide on artificial insemination by a donor (AID) rather than wait

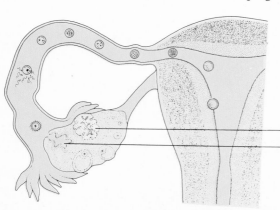

Diagrammatic representation showing the sequence of ovulation and fertilization, including formation of the corpus luteum.

corpus luteum after ovulation
corpus luteum at ovulation

in a lengthening line to adopt a child. Ideally the donor should resemble the husband. Anonymity is preserved between the couple and the donor. About three inseminations a month for three months are needed, and in most the procedure is successful.

There is a storage system of donor sperm known as the Sperm Bank. Donors remain anonymous but are rigidly screened to ensure that their semen is free of infection and that the sperm count is well within the normal limits. As far as possible the donor's physical characteristics are closely matched with those of the recipient's spouse.

In the United States the legitimacy and status of the artificially conceived child is regulated by the Uniform Parentage Act (1973). 25 states have adopted this legislation which places the presumption of paternity in favour of the social father rather than the biological father. If there is any uncertainty as to the laws governing your state it's best to contact the local justice department or the Department of Justice in Washington D.C.

Human embryo transfer

Should a woman's fallopian tubes be blocked, or should a man's sperm be deficient in number or motility, fertilization will not occur and the couple will be unable to have children. The technique of human embryo transfer was developed to enable such people to have children, the so-called 'test tube babies'.

When the time for ovulation approaches, the woman is admitted to hospital. Drugs such as clomiphene and human chorionic gonadotrophin are administered to stimulate ovarian follicles. The progress of follicle maturation is monitored by measuring the amount of plasma estradiol daily and by ultrasound scanning of the developing follicles. A newer technique allows for the follicles to be aspirated using the ultrasound technique, and a needle passed from the vagina. This technique requires minimal anesthesia.

When these tests indicate that ovulation will occur within a few hours a laparoscope (a thin, fiber-optically illuminated tube) is inserted into the abdomen through a small hole in the abdominal wall while the woman is under anesthetic. The abdomen is then filled via the laparoscope with carbon dioxide gas. The gas separates the abdominal organs, so that the doctor, when looking through the laparoscope, is able to see the abdominal organs clearly. The carbon dioxide is later absorbed into the tissues and blood vessels, and is excreted by the lungs.

The ovary is grasped with a pair of forceps inserted through the abdominal wall, and the contents of the larger follicles aspirated through a special needle into a test tube. This fluid is immediately examined microscopically to find a suitable ovum.

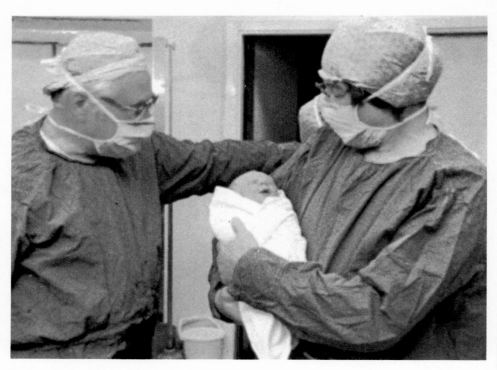

The world's first test tube baby soon after her birth in 1978. (Rex Features)

Sperm, provided by a fresh ejaculate by the husband, is added to the fertilization medium. Through the microscope, fertilization can be seen to have occurred within 24 hours and the growth of the zygote can be observed. At the 2 to 4-celled stage, the zygote, contained in a small amount of culture medium, is inserted via a plastic catheter through the vagina and into the uterus. This is the most difficult step in the procedure and is responsible for most of the failures. In the first reported series, only four pregnancies resulted from 32 embryo transfers, and in another series, only two from 14 transfers.

The technique is continually being improved. Researchers are trying to find a way of recovering the ovum by washing out the uterus) to avoid its removal by laparoscope under general anesthesia.

New concepts will follow embryo transfer, such as the possibility of banks of frozen human embryos and their potential use in controlling future populations. Animal embryos have been frozen, stored in banks, and then thawed at a convenient time and implanted to produce viable offspring.

Another new concept is that of the 'ovum donor'. When a wife is sterile because she cannot produce viable ova, an ovum can be taken from another woman, fertilized with sperm from the wife's husband, with the embryo being deep frozen

and transferred to the uterus of the infertile wife during the implantation stage of her menstrual cycle. Another technique involves freezing the ova themselves.

As with all new technology, various ethical, moral and legal questions are being raised and will be the subject of public debate for some time.

Testing for pregnancy

The tests available for the detection of pregnancy are now so sophisticated that pregnancy can be detected as early as forty-eight hours after conception.

The tests all consist of detecting the presence of specific hormones of pregnancy (HCG, human chorionic gonadotrophin) in either the urine or blood of the mother by agglutination with a specific antibody to that hormone. These antibodies are made artificially by injecting the hormones to be detected into an animal, such as a rabbit, which produces the antibody to the hormone. These antibodies are extracted and packaged in a detection kit, and form the basis of both the home test kits on sale at pharmacies, as well as the pregnancy tests used in commercial laboratories. Thus, a sample from the woman is mixed with the antibody, and if the hormones of pregnancy are present in sufficient titre, agglutination or clotting of the specimen occurs, and this is visible to the naked eye.

Although rare, 'false positives' can occur due to some drugs which may have been taken being present in the sample, or

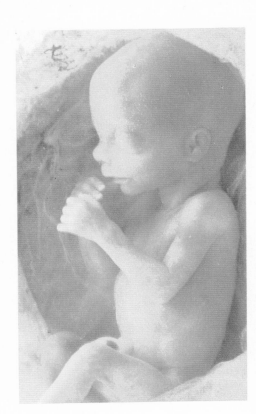

A 12 week old fetus

Central nervous system Some women may have difficulty with activities which require precision and coordination.

Cardiovascular system During pregnancy the volume and composition of blood changes, contributing to an increased incidence of blood clotting disorders. While the heart rate remains relatively normal, the heart itself may increase in size in response to the increased blood volume, which occurs early in the pregnancy and stabilizes at about 28 weeks. Blood pressure readings usually decrease during the first two trimesters of pregnancy, return-ing to normal during the third. Varicose veins are common.

Respiratory system Because the diaphragm movement is more restricted, the rib cage tends to flare out, not always returning to its normal position. Late in pregnancy, breathing becomes deeper and more frequent as the lungs become restricted.

The final weeks of pregnancy can be a time of some discomfort, tiredness and shortness of breath being relatively common. (*Zefa*)

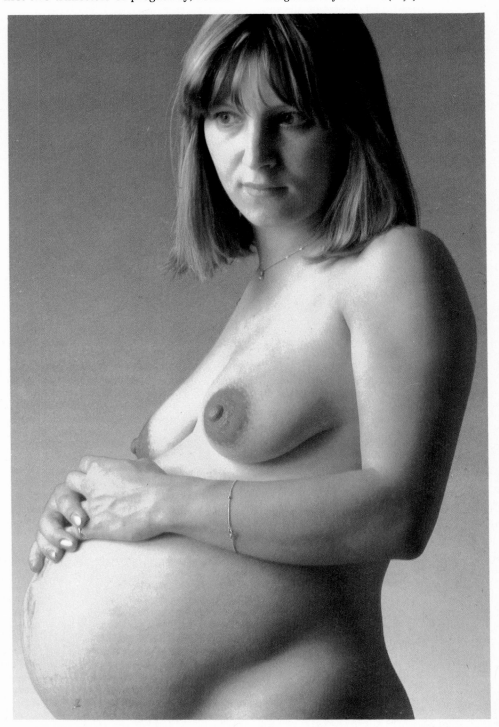

other chemical factors.

After a pregnancy test any woman should be able to talk to her doctor about the result and receive appropriate counseling.

Progress of pregnancy

A woman's condition from the time she has conceived a child or children to the time of delivery is called pregnancy. Traditionally divided into three parts, or trimesters, of roughly three months each, pregnancy usually lasts 266 days from conception or 280 days from the date of the beginning of the last menstrual period in a woman who has a normal cycle. The expected time of delivery is usually calculated from the last menstrual period using a variety of formulae such as adding one year and ten days to the date of the last menstrual period and then subtracting three months from the total.

During her first pregnancy a woman is called a primigravida. Multigravida refers to a woman during her second or subsequent pregnancies. Fewer risks are involved with later pregnancies as the mother is more familiar with the techniques of birth and is less likely to develop toxemia of pregnancy. However, the risks of toxemia and bleeding increase again after three pregnancies or when a woman is over the age of 35.

Numerous changes occur throughout the body during pregnancy. Although there is increased activity in the heart and lungs, the gastrointestinal and genitourinary systems slow down.

Gastrointestinal tract The muscles of the gastrointestinal tract tend to relax, sometimes resulting in heartburn, constipation and delayed emptying of the stomach.

Genitourinary system As the muscles of the bladder, ureters and renal pelvis relax, urine may accumulate, causing an increased incidence of urinary tract infections. The kidneys' ability to filter waste from the bloodstream increases. More water is excreted. Urination also becomes more frequent as the developing fetus restricts the bladder.

General changes in pregnancy may include increased pigmentation on the face and abdomen (chloasma); marks on the abdomen where the skin is stretched; enlarged breasts; changes in posture which may cause leg and back pain and spinal curvature in the lower back; and changes in body minerals particularly a decrease in iron. Weight usually increases by between 24¼–28½ pounds (11–13 kg).

With the development of the embryo, the womb increases in size and its neck softens, an early sign of pregnancy. The internal os muscle in the uterus dilates and the womb expands and rises, reaching the level of the navel about the middle of the fourth month. By the end of the pregnancy the uterus has expanded to about 14 inches (36 cm) above the pubis.

Hormones During pregnancy female hormones contribute to the healthy development of the embryo. At first hormones are secreted by the yellow body in the ovary; later they are produced in large quantities by the placenta. These hormones encourage the full development of the mammary glands; the breasts swell, the areolae increase in size and the nipples protrude.

The increased production of female hormones may be one of the causes of the troublesome symptoms which often accompany the onset of pregnancy: morn-

It is not uncommon for a woman to experience a sense of well-being during pregnancy despite the minor discomforts experienced by most expectant mothers. (PAF International)

Many dramatic changes occur in a woman's body during pregnancy.

ing sickness, dizziness and weariness. These symptoms tend to disappear around the third month, when the woman enters a fairly agreeable phase of pregnancy lasting for three to four months.

Quickening The first sign of life in the developing baby felt by a pregnant woman is called quickening. This is associated with early fetal movements and is often described as being like the fluttering of a bird in the hand, sometimes so faint that a mother may often be doubtful whether movements are in fact present during the first week or so. Although it is known that activity of the baby may begin as early as the tenth week of life, it is usually not until the mother is 16–18 weeks pregnant (or even later with first-born babies) that she is consciously aware of such activity.

The expected date of delivery can be estimated roughly from the date when the woman is first fully aware of quickening. With first-time mothers it is approximately 22 weeks to delivery, but with mothers of previous children, who are more aware of these early flutters from prior experience, 24 weeks to delivery is more realistic.

Fetal movements may diminish during emotional periods and sometimes seem to vanish for days or even weeks before reappearing, for no apparent reason.

Patterns of movement may occasionally be discerned when it is assumed that the baby is awake, particularly when the mother is lying in bed relaxing.

Prenatal care

The care given to the mother and her fetus during the term of pregnancy is known as prenatal care. Nowadays, such care is a large part of an obstetrician's job, but until about fifty years ago very little attention was paid to this time in a patient's life; all the care and concern tended to center around the actual birth. Since the introduction of adequate prenatal care there has been a very marked drop in the illness and death rate of both mothers and babies.

Prenatal care is basically an exercise in preventive medicine aimed at ensuring that both the mother and fetus remain healthy throughout the pregnancy and that a healthy baby is delivered from a healthy mother.

A patient must be seen regularly throughout the duration of pregnancy. The benefits are twofold: the patient has a chance to develop a relationship of confidence and trust in her obstetrician and the doctor can assess the progress of the pregnancy, detecting at the earliest opportunity any abnormalities which may require treatment.

Ideally, every pregnant woman should be seen within the first ten weeks of pregnancy, so that an assessment can be made, against which future physiological changes can be measured. At the initial visit the doctor usually orders a series of blood and urine tests. These are repeated at various stages during the prenatal period in order to detect and monitor changes that may arise.

Prenatal classes, which teach relaxation techniques to be practiced during labor, give the expectant mother a feeling of confidence. *(Zefa)*

Early in pregnancy the patient without complications is usually seen monthly, later biweekly and eventually weekly. Naturally this regime will vary with circumstances. More frequent visits may be deemed necessary should complications arise.

At each visit the patient will be assessed emotionally as well as physically, the obstetrician taking time to answer questions and, if necessary, provide reassurance. Physical assessment includes checking the patient's blood pressure and weight, assessing the size of the uterus, testing a specimen of urine and enquiring into the presence of any symptoms.

An examination which detects disorders in the fetus prior to birth is called a prenatal diagnosis. This may involve a physical examination of the mother or certain tests such as ultrasound, x-ray, amniocentesis and fetoscopy. Such tests are usually necessary if the mother's condition and health are liable to produce abnormalities in her child. For instance, women over forty have a higher than average chance of producing a mongoloid (Down's syndrome) child.

Information given to the mother during the prenatal care period will vary with the needs and expectations of the particular patient as well as the expectations, expertise and personality of the attendant doctor. Areas that may be covered include general hygiene, care of breasts, suitable diet and clothing, dental care, immunization, smoking and traveling. Nowadays the husband is likely to be included in some or all of the sessions. The actual birth and labor are discussed, including the husband's role at the various stages. The patient's expected date of confinement will have been assessed and she will have been booked into the hospital.

Many women, on becoming pregnant, particularly for the first time, wonder whether they should carry out an exercise program during their pregnancy. The woman with a normally active lifestyle, possibly with a job which in itself gives plenty of exercise, may find that her usual activities are quite sufficient. Provided the pregnancy is progressing without complications, her activities need not be curtailed, and if she is accustomed to sporting activities, these can be continued in moderation. Undue exertion to the point of exhaustion is, however, unwise, and very strenuous or hazardous sports such as water skiing, horse riding or skin diving are best avoided.

Those women who are normally very inactive could probably be encouraged to exercise gently, those who are extremely active, to slow down a little.

Apart from the exercise obtained during normal everyday activities, some women attend the special prenatal exercise classes which are conducted by physiotherapists in most maternity hospitals and encompass various aspects of preparation for the birth. Pelvic floor exercises strengthen the pelvic muscles, important during the birth process (they are often continued post-natally to help prevent prolapse of the vaginal walls). Breathing and relaxation exercises are also helpful. The expectant father often attends the exercise classes and can therefore help and encourage the mother to use these exercises during labor.

Naturally, no specific exercise program should be undertaken by an expectant mother without the consent of her doctor, who will advise each patient according to her particular situation.

Prenatal care can involve a hospital program to familiarize the mother with the procedures at her particular hospital. Lectures and films as well as discussion generally form part of the hospital prenatal program and the future mother may attend physiotherapy sessions where instructions on breathing and muscle control is given to enable an easy birth. Some parents may wish to enrol in 'Natural Childbirth' classes, in which the participation of both parents is an important factor, as the father is generally preparing to assist the mother during labor and delivery.

Problems in Pregnancy

Although most pregnancies proceed uneventfully and peacefully and many women 'bloom' during pregnancy, both looking and feeling unusually relaxed and well, problems may occasionally occur. It is emphasized, however, that the conditions mentioned here, such as eclampsia, ectopic pregnancy and miscarriage, are the exception rather than the rule.

Abortion and miscarriage

Interruption of pregnancy before the fetus can survive independently of the mother is known as abortion. It may be spontaneous or it can be artificially induced. The age at which the fetus can survive independently of the mother has previously been dated as the twenty-eighth week of gestation. However, recent advances in specialized care have meant that some babies survive earlier births. Twenty weeks has been suggested as the recognized age of viability and in time will probably be accepted.

Threatened abortion Significant bleeding from the uterus (womb) during the early stages of pregnancy is a sign of a threatened abortion or miscarriage. The bleeding may be associated with mild contractions of the uterus, resulting in slight, crampy lower abdominal pain. However, the canal within the cervix and the vagina does not widen (dilate).

A slight amount of *spotting* may occur around the time of the 'expected' menstrual flow (about two weeks after fertilization), but this is part of the process of implantation of the fertilized ovum into the uterine wall.

In most cases of threatened abortion, the bleeding will cease and the pregnancy progress satisfactorily. Leading a quiet

Nowadays, medical attention is available even in remote areas and adequate care in pregnancy will detect potential problems.

life, and avoiding sexual intercourse for a time to reduce the risk of infection being introduced are generally advocated. Strict bed rest and sedation with various drugs are not routinely advised today unless the bleeding is particularly heavy or prolonged.

If the bleeding persists, the uterine contractions increase, and the cervix starts to dilate, the situation is termed an *inevitable abortion* as expulsion of the developing embryo follows.

In pregnancies where threatened abortion occurs, no untoward effects on the developing embryo follow. Those embryos with significant abnormalities result in a rapidly progressing miscarriage, known medically as a *spontaneous abortion*.

Miscarriage A spontaneous expulsion of the developing egg from the womb before the twenty-eighth week of pregnancy is called a miscarriage although medically this is known as a spontaneous abortion. Most miscarriages happen during the first twelve weeks after conception.

The symptoms are vaginal bleeding, which can be heavy with large clots, and marked painful abdominal spasms. The consequent loss of blood and shock may cause collapse and sudden death so the

woman should be taken immediately to the nearest hospital.

Miscarriages are most commonly precipitated by malformation of the unborn child or fetus. Abnormalities of the womb (uterus), such as fibroids in the wall or deep in the neck of the womb (cervix); illness in the mother, like diabetes, syphilis, acute fevers or chronic disease of the kidneys, and major injuries, such as a car accident, can also cause miscarriages. A blow to the abdomen, a fall or some physical activity like swimming or tennis will rarely cause a miscarriage unless the uterus is actually penetrated.

Miscarriages sometimes occur without obvious cause and hormonal imbalances are usually blamed. Hormonal imbalances should be corrected in subsequent pregnancies if possible. Due to its small size the fetus is rarely subject to close pathological examination to look for abnormalities. Miscarriages are common in normal women and most have a normal pregnancy and baby when they next conceive.

The treatment is surgical. The neck of the womb is stretched and the womb emptied under a general anesthetic (dilatation and curettage). Unless this is done bleeding may continue and the womb may never empty itself spontaneously (incom-

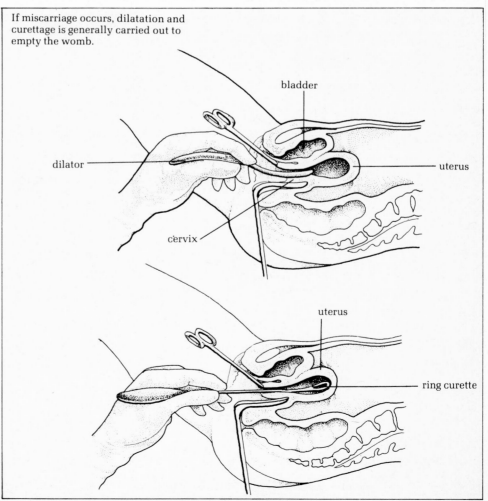

If miscarriage occurs, dilatation and curettage is generally carried out to empty the womb.

bladder

dilator

cervix

uterus

uterus

ring curette

plete abortion). The remaining vestiges of the pregnancy hence become infected. If the products of conception are completely expelled, resulting in a complete abortion, the bleeding stops spontaneously and no further intervention is required.

After a miscarriage women usually experience a feeling of anticlimax and emotional upheaval, which is at least partly due to sudden changes in hormone levels, and they should be treated with reassurance, kindness and counseling.

Losing an eagerly-awaited baby before its birth is most disappointing. Frequently the cause is not discovered, but women should be encouraged by the fact that having had one miscarriage does not necessarily mean another will follow — this is the exception rather than the rule.

Induced abortion Before the eighth week after conception abortion can be induced by introduction of a small plastic catheter through the cervix to suck out the uterine contents. Only a local anesthetic is used.

Thus usually, termination after the tenth week of pregnancy is performed under a general anaesthetic. The methods commonly used today involve a procedure called suction curettage, and here a tube or catheter is introduced into the uterus through the cervix, which has been dilated, and the products of conception are sucked out. The simultaneous administration of drugs, such as Syntocinon, cause rapid uterine contraction and prevent bleeding.

Pregnancies later than twenty weeks, or mid term, are terminated by surgical means which involve a procedure called hysterotomy, which involves opening the uterus to physically remove the fetus. Because of the availability of antibiotics, and generalised surgical sophistication, induced abortion today represents no risk to the mother, and certainly will not prevent pregnancies at a future date. These aspects must be stressed because in the past, when abortion was illegal, it became the province of backyard operators who often caused great damage to the mother, if not death, from perforation, hemorrhage and introduced infection. This does not happen today, when the procedure is carried out in a hospital under medical supervision, and the sequelae like sterility do not occur.

No matter how unwanted pregnancies are dealt with, a number of people experience emotional and psychological difficulties.

Eclampsia

A convulsion resulting from toxemia of pregnancy, eclampsia is a dangerous condition which threatens the life of mother and child. Blood pressure is high, protein is retained in the urine and swelling occurs as fluid accumulates in the tissues

Regular check-ups are important if toxemia in pregnancy is to be detected early. *(Zefa)*

(edema). A small number of patients with eclampsia may have a midbrain hemorrhage which is sometimes fatal. Other hemorrhages into the brain can cause repeated convulsions. Eclampsia often occurs suddenly. The woman becomes drowsy and complains of headache and not being able to see well. About half the cases occur before labor, a fifth after delivery and about a third during labor. When it occurs the eyes roll, the hands twitch and breathing becomes spasmodic. The major convulsion then follows. As about half the babies die, eclampsia is a calamity.

Eclampsia requires emergency treatment. Prompt lowering of the high blood pressure is possible by the injection of a drug such as diazoxide. Intravenous injection of diazepam is required to control the convulsion. Once eclampsia is controlled, immediate delivery is the most direct method of treatment. Early diagnosis and prompt treatment of pre-eclampsia or toxemia of pregnancy is the best way to avoid eclampsia itself.

Pre-eclampsia In a pregnant woman the combination of high blood pressure, protein in the urine and swelling of the ankles, legs, hands and face, is called toxemia of pregnancy or pre-eclampsia. On rare occasions pre-eclampsia may progress to convulsions and eventual coma (eclampsia). A woman with a raised blood pressure before pregnancy or with chronic inflammation of the kidneys (chronic nephritis) is particularly prone to pre-eclampsia and eclampsia.

Toxemia of pregnancy occurs in about 6 per cent of all pregnancies, with a higher incidence in women having their first baby (12 per cent) and in women who already have had six or more babies (9 per cent). The incidence of eclampsia has fallen markedly in the last 20 years because of better ante-natal care and hospitalisation with observation for early signs of eclampsia. Pre-eclampsia is more common in women in low socio-economic groups.

The cause of pre-eclampsia is unknown although there are several theories. Usually the raised blood pressure or swelling of the ankles and legs or face or hands is noticed during a routine prenatal visit and the woman admitted to hospital for bed rest and observation. Excessively salty foods should be avoided.

Regular checks on weight are made and a woman with excessive weight gain is watched carefully as this may be the prelude to the development of pre-eclampsia. The disorder usually begins slowly but then progresses steadily.

In pre-eclampsia the blood vessels of the placenta are narrowed, which can starve the baby of oxygen. The higher the blood pressure the more likely the baby is to die. Therefore, if there is a rapid or high rise in blood pressure, induction of labor or a cesarean section must be considered in order to save the baby. If possible this should not be done until after the 36th week, otherwise the baby will be very premature. An induced birth is necessary in about one in four cases of women with pre-eclampsia, most of the remainder continuing pregnancy without interference and giving birth spontaneously.

After delivery of the child the blood pressure falls to normal within six months, the swelling disappears and the urine no longer contains protein. There is no evidence that the condition causes permanent damage.

Ectopic pregnancy

An ectopic pregnancy occurs outside the uterus usually in one of the fallopian tubes. The egg (ovum) fertilized in the fallopian tube, normally passes into the uterus, where it becomes embedded. Occasionally, once in about 150 pregnancies, the fertilized ovum becomes embedded in the lining of the tube. As the embryo develops, the placenta may burst through the thin muscular wall of the tube into the abdominal cavity. Although rare instances have been reported of an infant surviving in the abdominal cavity long enough to be rescued by cesarean section, a tubal pregnancy usually does not develop past two or three months.

Symptoms A disrupted menstrual pattern, severe abdominal pain and slight loss of blood through the vagina may be the first indications of a tubal pregnancy. If the

Most pregnancies are uneventful, producing a happy, healthy baby.

tube ruptures, internal bleeding may be severe enough to cause collapse. The condition is not easy to diagnose and may not be definite until the abdomen is opened. Unlike some other methods of birth control, an intra-uterine device, though useful as a contraceptive, does not prevent ectopic pregnancy.

Treatment Surgery is essential to prevent further hemorrhage and terminate the pregnancy. It is usual to repair the tube (tuboplasty) using routine micro-surgical procedures.

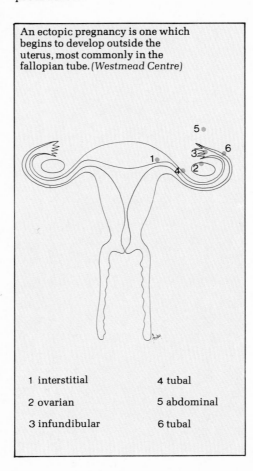

An ectopic pregnancy is one which begins to develop outside the uterus, most commonly in the fallopian tube. *(Westmead Centre)*

1 interstitial	4 tubal
2 ovarian	5 abdominal
3 infundibular	6 tubal

False pregnancy

The condition in which a woman believes herself to be pregnant when in fact she is not, is described as a false pregnancy. Known medically as pseudocyesis, this occurs in women who are anxious to conceive or who are unusually apprehensive about being pregnant.

Symptoms are similar to those of actual pregnancy and can make accurate diagnosis difficult. However, the real condition can be revealed by an ultrasound examination. The uterus is seen clearly and it can be judged whether the pregnancy is normal or not.

Once false pregnancy has been diagnosed it may still be difficult for the patient to believe that she is not pregnant and psychological treatment may occasionally be required.

Hydatidiform mole

Also known as chorionic myxoma or cystic degeneration of the chorion, a hydatidiform mole develops in the first three months of pregnancy as a result of degeneration of the chorion, the outer membrane that eventually envelops the fetus. It occurs approximately once in 2000 pregnancies and its cause is unknown. The embryo appears to die very early after fertilization and it is probable that the ovum was abnormal before fertilization.

The chorion develops into a mass of thin-walled fluid-filled cysts, resembling grapes. The term hydatidiform is used because the cysts are similar to those formed in hydatid disease.

Enlargement of the abnormal tissue frequently results in the uterus developing at a rate greater than would be expected during a normal pregnancy. Other symptoms of pregnancy such as amenorrhea and vomiting occur, and in over 20 per cent of cases, early pre-eclampsia also develops.

Diagnosis is based on the history of the pregnancy and the abnormal size of the uterus. The uterus has a doughy consistency, and the fetal parts are not usually palpable. Spontaneous evacuation of the mole tends to occur in the second or third month of pregnancy and the passage of grape-like cysts confirms suspicions. Diagnosis may also be made by special urine tests, since the tissue of the hydatidiform mole secretes high levels of a chorionic hormone.

Treatment The lining of the uterus is scraped to remove completely the abnormal tissue and to minimise the risks of hemorrhage.

Hydatidiform tissue may occasionally develop into a malignant choriocarcinoma. For this reason, follow-up tests are performed to ensure that everything has returned to normal after treatment.

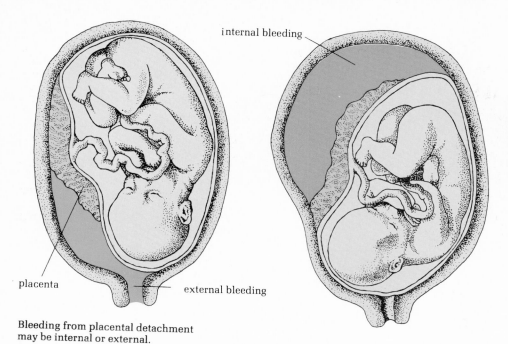

internal bleeding

placenta

external bleeding

Bleeding from placental detachment
may be internal or external.

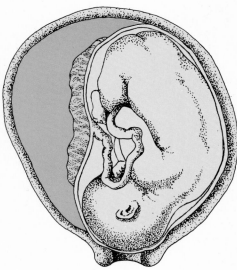

Obstruction of cervix by baby's
head, preventing escape of blood.

Hydramnios

An excessive amount of fluid surrounding
the fetus in the womb before birth is
called hydramnios. Hydramnios may
occur rapidly (acute) or it may progress
slowly (chronic). Acute hydramnios is
very rare and causes severe abdominal
pain and persistent vomiting. Chronic
hydramnios is more common and usually
occurs in the second half of pregnancy.
Symptoms The abdomen becomes greatly
distended and the uterus is larger than it
should be for the age of the pregnancy.
Indigestion, flatulence and breathlessness
are the main symptoms. Hydramnios may
accompany abnormalities in the mother
like toxemia, diabetes, or cardiac failure,
or fetal abnormalities like spina bifida (ex-
trusion of the spine to the surface of the
body), esophageal atrexia (absence of part
of the gullet) or anencephaly (lack of development of the brain). Hydramnios may
also occur in pregnancies with twins or
triplets.
Treatment of hydramnios depends on
whether or not any abnormality is found
when the mother and fetus are investigated and how far the pregnancy has progressed. With modern techniques of
amnioscopy, ultrasound and x-rays it is
often possible to identify multiple birth
and fetal abnormalities. So that the pregnancy can continue, some of the fluid can
be removed through the abdominal wall
to allow the patient some comfort. However, such a maneuver may increase the
risk of inducing early labor or of causing
internal bleeding.

Hyperemesis gravidarum

The vomiting associated with pregnancy
is described as hyperemesis gravidarum.
Traditionally it is called 'morning sickness', but it may occur at any time during
the day. It is caused by the increased
levels of hormones during pregnancy. It
can be relieved by eating or by taking
(carefully prescribed and monitored)
doses of appropriate drugs. It usually disappears by the twelfth week of pregnancy.

Placental disorders

Occasionally the fertilized ovum implants
in the lower part of the uterus causing
two problems. The placenta may cover or
obstruct the opening of the uterus (placenta praevia), preventing normal
childbirth and necessitating a cesarean
section; or the painless contractions of the
last two months of pregnancy may cause
areas of the placenta to separate from the
wall of the uterus, tearing open the blood
sinuses and causing vaginal bleeding.
Placenta praevia All episodes of vaginal
bleeding occurring prior to birth are not
necessarily caused by separation of a placenta praevia, but immediate medical advice must be sought because bleeding
caused by placenta praevia can endanger
the baby's life and even the mother's life.
Ultrasound or x-ray pictures are taken to
demonstrate the position of the placenta.
Should a placenta praevia be confirmed,
the mother is kept in hospital under observation until the baby is born, usually by
cesarean section.
Abruptio placentae An accidental separation of the implanted placenta, usually
during labor or near the time of delivery,
is referred to as *abruptio placentae*. This is
one of the causes of bleeding from the
birth canal after the twenty-eighth week
of pregnancy (ante partum hemorrhage).

The treatment of this condition depends on the amount of blood loss and the
presence of other symptoms such as pain

and tenderness, according to the degree
of separation of the placenta. If there is
severe hemorrhage so that the unborn
baby's life is in danger as judged by the
baby's heart rate or movements or staining of the fluid surrounding the baby, a
cesarean section is performed. If there is
only slight bleeding and no fetal distress,
pain-relieving drugs are used during
labor.

Version

A maneuver performed by an obstetrician, a version is an effort to change the
position of the fetus or developing baby.
The prime indication of need is an abnormal position of the baby which could
make ultimate delivery difficult or dangerous.

Although usually managed externally,
the doctor occasionally finds that bipolar
or internal version is required, necessitating one hand on the abdomen of the
mother pushing the baby into place, the
other in the vagina the better to maneuver
the baby's head.

Internal version is not something to be
undertaken lightly. Not only are there
hazards to the baby and the risk of partially separating the afterbirth (placenta)
from its attachment to the womb (uterus)
but, when performed too strenuously, the
wall of the womb may be damaged.

There are certain definite contraindications, such as when the mother is considered to be old (obstetrically speaking)
and having her first baby. A cesarean delivery may then be safer. With a mother
who has a history of bleeding during pregnancy (antepartum hemorrhage), or high
blood pressure, or who has previously
had a cesarean delivery, the risks in using
version are increased.

Childbirth

The birth of a baby is a completely natural process essential to the cycle of life. Nevertheless, to each new father and mother it is a dramatic and memorable experience and for them it is unique.

The process of birth is known by other terms: labor, confinement, accouchement and parturition. The birth may occur at home or in hospital, it may occur naturally or be induced by surgery.

The pregnant woman should ask questions and make up her own mind on which hospital, doctor and type of treatment she thinks would be best for her and her baby.

The choice of doctor, whether family doctor or specialist, is important. The doctor must be a person she can trust, can communicate with and who is prepared to impart information to her. Whether her husband can be with her throughout labor and at the birth may be important, and whether the baby will be given to her straight after the birth to cuddle or whisked away in a cot.

Inquiries should be made on the policy of the labor ward and nursery from either the Director of Nursing Services at the chosen hospital or the charge nurse in the labor ward. Many of the procedures will be explained during prenatal classes where the pregnant woman is informed of what is done and what choices she has.

Most doctors still prefer hospital delivery because of the back-up facilities for unforeseeable complications such as hemorrhage or a baby needing resuscitation. Hospitals are therefore adapting more to the feelings of mother and child. Some have established birth centers which simulate a home environment although emergency equipment and help are at hand.

Childbirth may be both shattering and exhilarating for mother, child and father. Hospitals are beginning to respect the need of all concerned for a quiet birth, with lighting dimmed to a level at which the child and its mother can make comfortable visual contact. Sometimes the father bathes the baby, all to aid in the bonding of the baby and its parents.

Labor

The onset of labor occurs about 280 days after the beginning of the last menstrual cycle. The process by which labor is started is not fully understood. Presumably it is due to some hormonal influence.

The mother goes to the hospital when she has regular contractions occurring every five minutes or when her membranes break or when she has a show. She is examined, has a shower and her pubic hair may be partly shaved off. Very occasionally she may be given an enema.

The birth of a child is divided into three stages.

The first stage is characterized by the progressive increase in frequency, strength and duration of the contractions of the womb which pull up the cervical canal and thus dilate the cervix to 4 inches (10 cm).

The contractions feel like stomach cramps, sometimes with backache. Breathing exercises help the mother to relax and thus cope more easily with the pain. The neck of the womb stretches and the mucus plug that fills it is dislodged: this is called the show.

Typically, the sac that holds the water bulges in front of the baby's head and ruptures on full dilation of the cervix at the end of the first stage (sometimes it may break before this, even before the contractions begin).

The first stage usually lasts about 16 hours in mothers giving birth for the first time, and four to eight hours in subsequent deliveries.

Sometimes a woman needs pain relief during this stage, and it may be given by gas breathed through a mask or by injection.

During labor the baby's heart rate is checked regularly (babies at risk are monitored throughout the labor) and the mother may be examined internally to see how labor is progressing.

The second stage During the second stage the baby is born. Some women deliver on the back, some on the side. Sometimes stirrups are used. When the neck of the womb is fully open the mother feels a desire to push down. As the baby passes through the birth canal the mother bears down by taking a deep breath, tightening the muscles of her abdomen and pushing down as if opening the bowel. Relaxation between contractions is important.

Right
The final moments of childbirth.
(Westmead Centre)

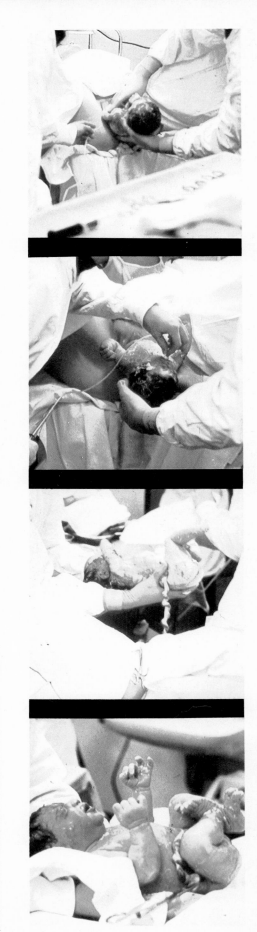

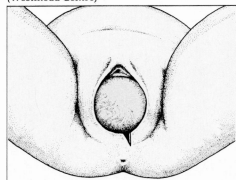

An episiotomy — a small cut made at the bottom of the vagina at the moment of delivery of the baby's head — is performed when there is a risk that the baby's head will tear the mother's perineal tissues. The cut is placed to avoid vital structures.

First the head appears (this is called the 'crowning'). The doctor controls the birth of the head in order to allow the mother's skin to stretch gradually, the mother assisting by taking short panting breaths until the head is delivered. Sometimes an episiotomy (a cut) is performed at this stage.

After the head is born the baby turns sideways as the shoulder comes down the birth canal and within a few minutes the baby is born.

At birth the cord throbs at the rate the baby's heart is beating, because until this moment the baby has relied on the blood passing through the cord for oxygen and nourishment. As soon as the first breath is taken the cord stops throbbing and is tied and cut. This is not painful for mother or baby.

The baby is usually covered with a white slippery material (vernix) which has protected the baby's skin in the womb and assisted the passage during the birth.

The third stage For another 10 to 15 minutes the womb continues to contract, but to a lesser degree. The afterbirth which has become detached is pushed from the womb and is finally delivered by the mother bearing down as before.

The above is a description of a normal birth. Sometimes complications occur, and labor may have to be induced; also delivery may need to be assisted by the use of forceps. In some cases a cesarean section may need to be performed.

Above right
During labor, the doctor, midwife and mother work together. *(Science Photo Library)*

The placenta. Here it has been stretched over a balloon in order to display it clearly. *(Westmead Centre)*

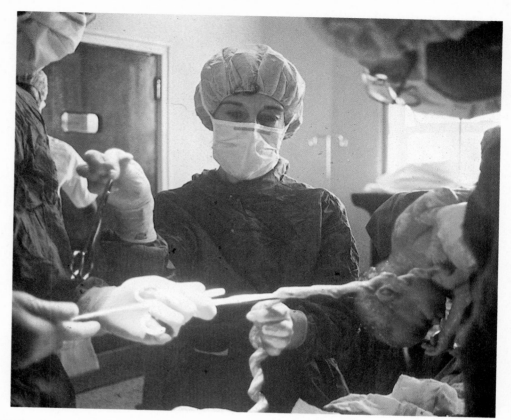

Help during labor The process is likely to be smoother if the mother has confidence, both in herself and in her doctor, and has learned to relax. Most confinements are straightforward but the slight risk of difficulties occurring is an argument for having the baby in hospital.

A pain-killer such as meperidine by injection or gas (nitrous oxide) and oxygen by inhalation may ease the pain. A well-timed episiotomy (cutting the stretched tissues at the vaginal outlet) prevents a tear and gives a neat wound which heals rapidly after being stitched. Obstetric forceps applied to the baby's head may also be used to ease it through the outlet; and in some cases cesarean section is safer for the baby than vaginal delivery. Ergometrine, a drug which stimulates the uterus, is given into a vein after the birth of the head in order to hasten the expulsion of the placenta and reduce blood loss.

During labor, the midwife monitors the uterine contractions, the progress of the opening of the neck of the womb, the blood pressure and the mental and physical state of the mother and baby. She identifies any abnormalities, for instance a breech birth, which is likely to occur during delivery. If this occurs she alerts the doctor in charge of the patient, keeping the doctor informed of the labor's progress.

During delivery the doctor, midwife and mother aim to deliver a normal baby in good condition. If emergencies or abnormalities exist they should be dealt with efficiently and promptly.

Home childbirth

The renewed interest in home births appears to be part of a generalized dissatisfaction with birth procedures in some major maternity hospitals. Women have complained that births are planned or induced to suit doctors and hospital staff and not the mother and child; that medical interference, in the form of drugs, instruments, surgical intervention and nursing procedure is too great; and that the birth atmosphere in hospitals is clinical, unfamiliar and somewhat forbidding. Most hospitals lack facilities or an atmosphere in which members of the family may comfortably be with the mother during labor and delivery.

Many doctors are, however, opposed to the growing tendency to and popularity of home births because of possible risks to the health of mother and child.

Even the most straightforward labor and birth can become problematical so that, no matter how experienced the midwife is, problems may occur which require expert medical attention.

Birth centers Much of the criticism regarding the birth procedures in hospitals refers to births which took place up to the early 1980s. Since this time much change and improvement have taken place.

In some major hospitals, birth centers, situated within hospitals, offer a more relaxed environment. These centers are well equipped with several beds, cooking facilities and television, and have a welcoming and non-threatening atmosphere. The entire family may come to visit, the

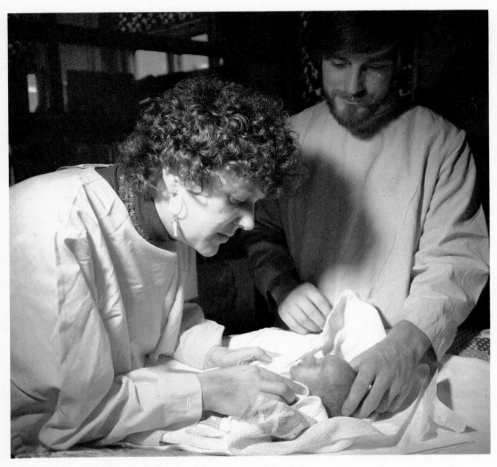

If a midwife is available to attend, a home birth may be approached confidently by the whole family. The father is likely to share much more of the experience than he would at a hospital birth. *(PAF International)*

woman calls the midwife who stays with her in the home until at least an hour after the birth.

Because of the different approach to birth, a prolonged labor is not regarded as a complication. Provided the baby's heart and the mother's condition are healthy, a prolonged second stage is also not seen as a complication. To prevent exhaustion the mother is encouraged not to push during labor. Massaging the perineal tissue in the month before labor and during labor may minimize the risk of tearing the tissues in the pelvic floor. The delivery position is chosen by the mother who is encouraged to change positions in order to feel more comfortable.

During the second stage of labor, when the cervix is dilated, a changed posture may help the baby move into a better position for birth. The mother is allowed to discover the baby's sex for herself. Massaging the infant stimulates breathing but the umbilical cord is not clamped until pulsation has stopped.

Even if it takes longer than the usual 15 minutes, the placenta is allowed to be expelled spontaneously if possible. Drugs which stimulate the uterus to contract (oxytocics) are administered only if the placenta is not expelled in 30 minutes or if the uterus fails to remain contracted or if more blood than normal is lost. Usually, stimulation of the woman's nipples while she is in a squatting posture controls the blood loss.

A *midwife* does not carry analgesics to relieve pain, but reinforces and supports the woman's breathing technique and gives general psychological support. Occasionally homeopathic remedies or acupuncture may be used. A midwife carries adequate sterile supplies, oxytocics and oxygen. All necessary tests are given to the baby and the midwife makes regular visits during the 10 days following the birth.

father may stay and assist with the birth, light refreshments can be made in the kitchen and the atmosphere has an air of friendliness and family involvement. Midwives and nurses are on hand and, of course, doctors are available if needed. The important advantage of these birth centers is that, should complications arise, expert attention is available in the adjoining wing or ward. After the birth, the mother keeps the baby in a crib beside her bed and establishes a feeding routine that suits both. Although such centers are not available in all hospitals, they do meet family and medical needs, avoiding the risks of a move to hospital should complications develop at home.

A family experience Despite the risks, more women are choosing to have their babies in their own homes, assisted by a midwife. The father of the child is usually present. In some instances the mother's other children, close friends or family may also be in attendance. The labor and birth become an experience shared by the family.

Deciding on a home birth is a very personal thing. It also tends to vary from country to country. In England, for example, home births have never lost popularity, while in Australia the renewal of interest is comparatively recent, and in the United States the vast majority of births take place in hospital.

Midwives will generally accept only women with low-risk pregnancies. These women show no evidence of anemia, toxemia, prematurity, placenta covering the cervical opening, breech or other unusual presentation or previous cesarean section or multiple birth. As birth is seldom predictable, a woman having her first child is unwise to plan a home birth unless she has the agreement of her physician.

The woman, frequently accompanied by her husband, is encouraged to attend classes to prepare her mentally and physically for childbirth. She also attends a medical practitioner and has the usual blood tests during the pregnancy.

Labor and delivery Once in labor, the

Complications A small number of home births have complications which require hospital care. Immediate transfer to hospital is required if descent of the baby is arrested or the baby is in a difficult position; if the membranes rupture without the onset of labor or hemorrhaging occurs during labor; if the placenta is retained or if the baby's condition after birth is not satisfactory.

A high quality experience Most women who have home births feel that they have a high quality experience, which is enhanced by support given at the time by family, friends, midwife and medical practitioner. Rather than the depression which may follow childbirth, mothers who give birth at home usually experience an increased sense of achievement and rise in self-esteem. Bonds within the family are also increased.

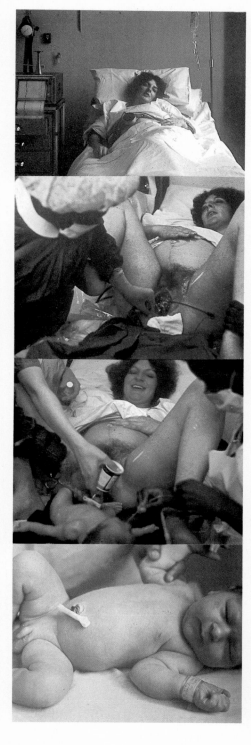

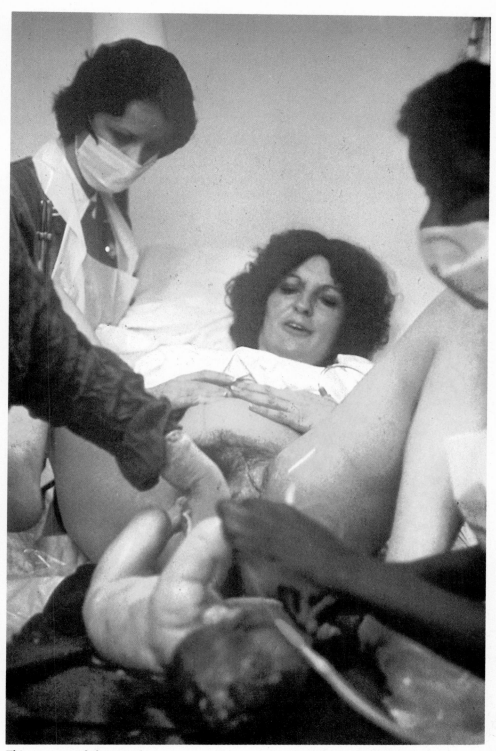

This sequence of photographs shows natural childbirth in a London hospital. The umbilical cord is clamped and cut immediately after delivery as the baby, which usually starts to breathe spontaneously, begins its independent life. *(Science Photo Library)*

Natural childbirth

Whether at home or in hospital, a natural childbirth is one which takes place without medical intervention. The renewed interest in natural childbirth began in response to the apparently excessive use of drugs and obstetric procedures by medical practitioners without considering the wishes of the parents.

Parent education Parents need to understand sufficiently the process of labor with its various stages and progress during a normal birth. They also need to be aware of the difficulties which can occur and to permit expert medical care when necessary.

Groups such as the Childbirth Education Association and Parent Centres have been formed to give prospective parents a basic education in the function of childbirth and there is some excellent literature which fully explains certain methods (psychoprophylaxis) of relaxation, breathing and psychology for overcoming the pain and anxiety of childbirth. Sometimes the inability to cope with the fear and anxiety can prolong labor.

The gentleness of delivery is emphasized by Dr Frederick Leboyer, who believes that this has a significant effect on the child.

The position adopted by the mother during labor and delivery should be the one that gives greatest comfort. Squatting is becoming more common and it has been shown that the action of gravity will aid the delivery and that in this position the birth canal can widen up to one-third greater than when lying, lessening the incidence of tearing and the need for an episiotomy (a cut made at the entrance to the birth canal).

Medical intervention in the natural progress of labor and delivery may have complications.

Epidural anesthetic was almost routine in some hospitals five or six years ago, but it caused increased bladder infections, prolonged labors and a sense of dissatisfaction among mothers.

Induction of labor, while necessary in cases of maternal illness, prolonged pregnancy and fetal distress, can cause birth complications such as prolapsed umbilical cord and delivery of premature infants when the expected date is incorrectly estimated.

Episiotomy is carried out in 75 to 90 per cent of cases to avoid a tear and is to a large extent avoidable. British midwives rarely use episiotomies and are taught to use massage and lubrication of the skin around the birth canal to help in the gradual delivery of the baby's head.

Drugs used during labor, whether to relieve pain or to stimulate the uterus to contract, can affect the unborn child to some extent.

Preparation for natural childbirth A natural childbirth can only take place when many factors acting together enable the mother to deliver successfully with only the gentle guidance of the birth attendant. Adequate education and preparation of both parents for the event, absence of any medical illness in mother or child, a normal course of labor without obstetric complications and a skilled birth attendant should make this possible. As each birth is unique a mother should not feel she has failed if she requires or requests aid.

After delivery, parents and child should be allowed to contact each other freely without artificial inducement or routine.

Problems in Childbirth

The birth of a child is the exciting and rewarding culmination of nine months of pregnancy and, in the vast majority of cases, proceeds in a trouble-free manner. The mother, whether at home or in hospital, will generally have the assistance of a doctor or midwife and in recent years the father frequently also helps at the birth.

Modern health care for mother and child before, during and after birth has greatly reduced the likelihood of serious infection or complication.

Nevertheless, in a minority of cases, the baby may suffer some injury, possibly if the birth must be instrument assisted. Generally such injuries are slight and self resolving. Parents may also be concerned about the physical hazards of birth including cesarean section, induction of labor and multiple birth.

Cesarean section

In birth by cesarean section the baby is delivered through an incision in the abdominal and uterine walls rather than through the natural birth canal. The generally accepted explanation of the term cesarean is that it derives from the name of Julius Caesar who was born in this manner, although other explanations are also current. For example, it is sometimes supposed to have survived from the edict of Augustus Caesar that all females killed on the battlefield must be cut open at the womb in order to save live unborn babies.

In general, cesarean section is the method of delivery used only when it is considered that vaginal delivery would in some way endanger the mother or the baby, for example if the mother's pelvis is too small for the baby's head to pass through or if the baby lies across the birth canal (transverse lie) instead of head or buttocks downwards.

Cesarean section is often favored in cases where the placenta is attached near to or over the cervix (placenta praevia) and excessive bleeding would be caused by vaginal delivery. If the mother's health is a risk to the fetus, such as in hypertension of pregnancy (pre-eclampsia), or if vaginal delivery is not progressing satisfactorily the doctor may elect to perform a cesarean section.

If a cesarean section is performed the surgeon will generally make the incision through the wall of the lower uterine segment.

Cesarean section usually involves a horizontal incision in the abdominal wall just above the pubic hair. The uterus is opened and the baby and placenta delivered. The operation, which is very safe, may be performed under a general anesthetic or with an epidural block. The latter is becoming more popular, because the mother is anesthetised only from the waist down and is thus able to have more involvement in the birth of her baby.

Although cesarean section is not normally a better alternative to vaginal delivery, it has made possible successful births where previously the mother or baby, or perhaps both, would have died.

Difficult presentation

The position of the fetus in the womb in relation to the body of the mother is described as the presentation or lie. In the most usual position the fetus is generally aligned with the mother's body, the head overlying the cervix in what is called the vertex or head-flexed presentation. Forehead and face-first positions also occur.

Breech (bottom first) presentations are the next most common. They are characterized by the extending of both legs with feet up over the shoulders with both legs in the squat position, or one in the squat position and the other extended.

Transverse presentations, with the fetus lying across the neck of the womb or with a shoulder coming first, are more common in women who have had several previous pregnancies. Babies cannot be delivered normally in such positions.

Any lie may result in a difficult birth and a forceps or cesarean delivery may be necessary. Fortunately about 80 per cent of presentations are of the vertex type which involves the least complication. Breech and transverse lies sometimes involve a cord presentation, whereby the umbilical cord is pushed through the cervix ahead of the baby, which is dangerous to the infant. Urgent intervention may be required to ensure the infant's blood supply and save its life.

Forceps delivery

Short, curved obstetric forceps, low forceps are used during birth to assist delivery of the baby's head. They are used when the head has already descended into the birth canal and lies at the vaginal opening, or vulva. A forceps delivery is needed in various circumstances: in cases of poor uterine action; poor pushing by the mother; maternal exhaustion or illness, such as heart problems; or in cases of fetal distress.

A general, epidural or, more usually a local nerve block anesthesia is required. The forceps are placed around the baby's head to assist passage through the birth canal. Often an episiotomy is necessary at this stage. There is little risk and few complications provided the forceps are used by an experienced practitioner and under appropriate conditions.

The care of mother and fetus
during pregnancy generally
precludes childbirth problems.

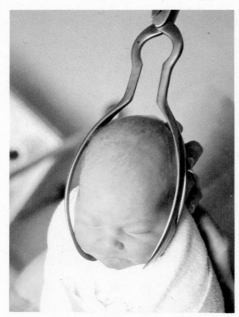

Forceps can be used to steady the
baby and prevent injury during a
difficult delivery. *(Westmead Centre)*

Induction of labor

Many women become nervous at the thought of having to undergo an induction of labor, but no doctor will decide to induce a birth without sound medical reasons, and the procedure is carried out in a well-equipped hospital, presenting minimal risk to mother and child.

Procedure The pregnant woman is admitted to hospital the day before induction is planned to take place. A small bowel enema is given and the cervix and position of the baby are checked. On the following morning the membranes are ruptured through the cervix (a painless procedure) and fluid is released. The woman is then allowed to walk about for four or five hours. If labor has not begun after this time she returns to bed and the intravenous administration of oxytocin (to start the contractions) begins. When labor begins, the contractions are timed and the baby's heart rate is monitored. Pain is relieved by injections of drugs either into a muscle or into the back (epidural anesthesia).

If the labor does not proceed normally, and delay or distress occurs, a lower segment cesarean section is performed.

Reasons Clear medical reasons for induction are toxemia of pregnancy, hemorrhage, kidney damage, or heart disease in the mother. In the case of a woman whose previous baby died in the womb, or where there was placental insufficiency or malfunction, induction at approximately 38 weeks will avoid a recurrence. In cases of multiple pregnancy labor should be induced by the fortieth week, and if toxemia is present it should be carried out at 38 weeks.

In some instances, social factors combined with medical reasons are sufficient to justify induction. For example, a mother who lives in the country, far from a hospital or doctor, and who has a large family (and is therefore at risk of having a hemorrhage after delivery) and a poor obstetric history, would be better admitted to a base hospital, where labor would be induced and properly managed with all facilities easily available. In this case, if the woman insisted on spontaneous labor, the only safe alternative would be to keep her in the hospital for the last three to four weeks of her confinement.

Induction is safest and easiest when it is carried out as near as possible to the fortieth week of gestation. Obstetricians usually do not attempt to induce labor until the thirty-eighth week; however they may be forced to do so before then to ensure a live birth. Before the thirty-eighth week the baby is more immature and at greater risk. Conversely, if pregnancy is allowed to continue beyond the forty-first or forty-second week, the baby is liable to suffer from lack of oxygen, either before or during delivery, because the blood vessels in the placenta deteriorate. The lack of oxygen may cause brain damage.

One of the main problems for the obstetrician is to establish that the actual maturity of the unborn child corresponds with the expected maturity as calculated from the date of the last menstrual period of the mother. Although x-rays, ultrasound and lung-maturity tests on the fetus help to gauge the maturity of an unborn child, clinical judgement remains the main basis for this decision.

Risks The main risks of induction are infection if labor is prolonged and delivery of a pre-term or low birth-weight infant. If induction fails, the obstetrician must be prepared to perform a cesarean section immediately.

Obstetricians are now much more easily able to determine when induction of labor is necessary and what the risks are, and they remain the best judges of the matter in the individual case. The decision to induce labor should be discussed by the mother and the obstetrician to resolve any anxieties and misconceptions that the mother may have.

Injuries

During the passage of a newborn baby from the mother into the world, various injuries may be inflicted inadvertently. Some injuries are reversible and cause no permanent damage, others may cause irreversible damage which will affect the baby for the rest of its life. The incidence of birth injury is increased when the delivery is abnormal, for example, breech birth, twins, use of forceps. It is also increased when the baby is premature or there has been poor care of mother and child before delivery. The possible injuries vary markedly in their effect.

Head injuries Trauma from forceps on the soft head may cause bleeding into the soft tissue of the scalp (cephalhematoma). This injury is common, occurring in 2 per cent of all births. It causes a soft lump which develops into a bruise where forceps have been applied, and can also occur in a normal delivery. It resolves without treatment over 2–3 weeks. Cephalhematoma occurs on the crown of the head if a vacuum extractor is applied to suck the baby down the birth canal.

Hemorrhage inside the skull may result from misuse of forceps, extremely rapid delivery or lack of oxygen (especially in premature babies) during and/or before delivery. The result of hemorrhage inside the skull varies from convulsions, shock, irritability and death in the short term, to cerebral palsy (the spastic child) and epilepsy in the long term.

Broken bones A fracture of the skull may occur when forceps are applied. Linear fractures (small splits) in the skull sometimes occur but are of little importance as they do no harm. Depressed fractures (when the fracture line is pushed in) which sometimes occur after forceps extraction usually correct themselves after 12–24 hours. If they do not then surgery is needed to elevate the fracture, that is lift the bits of bone up so they no longer press on the brain.

Occasionally other bones, most commonly the collarbone, are fractured during difficult deliveries.

Nerve injuries A nerve or nerve groups may be injured at birth due to unusual pressure. Nerve injuries account for about 5 per cent of all birth injuries. Such injuries may cause inability to close an eye on the affected side, a limp arm, inability to move a hand or wrist drop. These injuries usually resolve, and are most common in deliveries involving forceps, breech presentation, shoulder presentation or twins.

Fortunately, as modern obstetric techniques advance, with the aid of ever-improving monitoring machinery, and as the care during pregnancy improves, the incidence of birth injuries is decreasing.

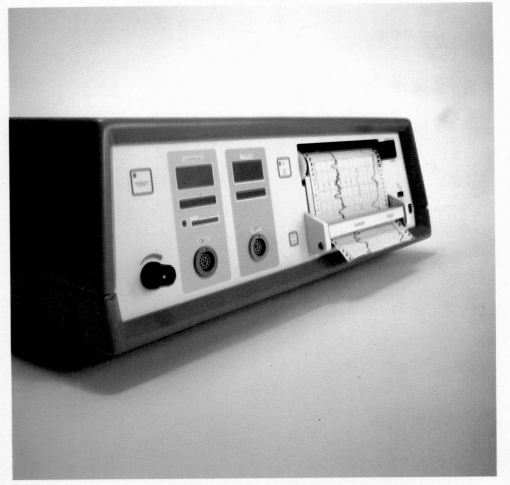

Following induction of labor, fetal monitoring assesses the baby's progress. (*Sonicaid Ltd*)

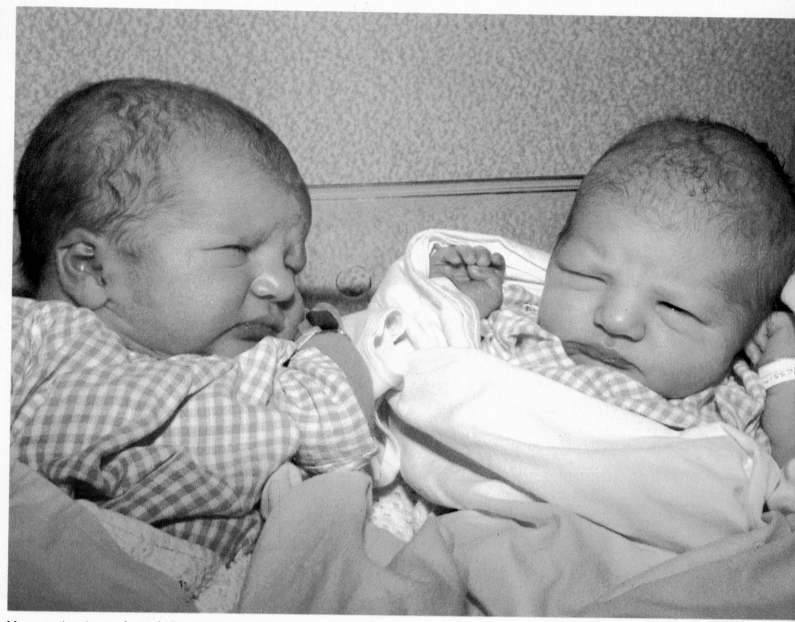

Monozygotic twins are those which have developed from a single fertilized egg. (John Watney Photo Library)

Dizygotic twins develop in the uterus from two fertilized eggs. They are not necessarily of the same sex and may differ considerably in size at birth.

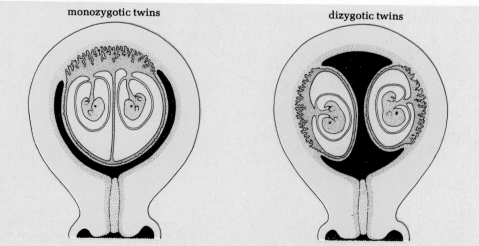

monozygotic twins   dizygotic twins

Multiple birth

If more than one baby is born of a single pregnancy this is known as a multiple birth.

Twins Fraternal (dizygotic or non-identical) twins develop when the mother produces two ova during the month (instead of the usual one), and both of these become fertilized. Each ovum is genetically different, as is each fertilizing sperm, so the developing babies are unalike and need not be of the same sex. Each fetus develops in the same way as a single fetus, within its own amniotic sac and with its own placenta.

Identical (or monozygotic) twins occur when a single egg is fertilized and very

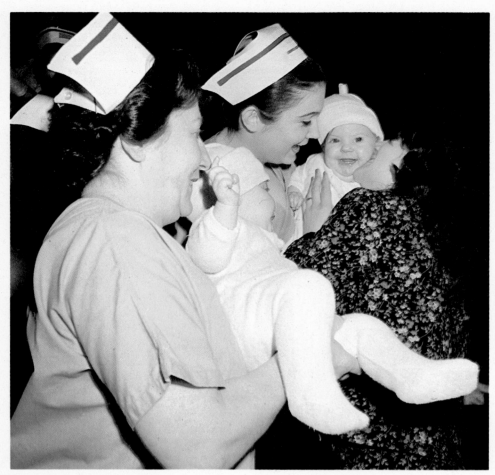

These girls, born conjoined at the skull, were successfully separated in Paris. (Rex Features)

early in the development process the resulting cell mass divides in two. These two cell masses are identical and have exactly the same genes. They go on to develop into two identical babies and share the same placenta and the same amniotic sac. Because they are genetically identical they are of course always the same sex.

It is estimated that one in about 50 000 births is of conjoined twins, many of whom die at birth or shortly thereafter. Much study is currently underway throughout the world into the problems posed by conjoined (sometimes called 'Siamese') twins. Generally, separation of such twins is not regarded as wise until the children are between one and two years old at the earliest, although the type of attachment and the condition of the particular children dictates each case.

The union may be as slight as a narrow band of flesh or as complex as shared abdominal organs or being joined skull to skull. Not all cases allow separation, but many such operations have been successful.

Modern techniques can now detect conjoined twins before birth and delivery of the babies by cesarean section lessens the risks to mother and children.

Triplets Three babies born from a single pregnancy are described as triplets. The babies may be identical when developed from the one fertilized egg (ovum). More common is the combination of either identical twins with the third baby a separate individual from a separate egg, or three non-identical babies born from three separate eggs. Whatever the combination, the size of individual babies may vary considerably. Usually the birth is premature, but even when the birth is full term each baby is smaller than most babies born from single pregnancies. When identical, the babies usually have individual fluid bags (amniotic sacs) surrounding each although they share a single afterbirth (placenta).

Diagnosis is usually confirmed before delivery by x-ray or ultrasonography. Because of excessive prematurity there is an increase in the risk of breathing difficulties and other life-threatening hazards. The first baby of the three appears to have the best outlook.

Because the womb (uterus) stretches excessively, it loses some of its general tone. Accordingly it may be difficult to stimulate the womb to contract firmly after delivery, resulting in bleeding. The mother is also more likely to experience longer labors and increased risk of infection.

Quadruplets Four babies born from the same pregnancy are known as quadruplets. This occurs approximately once in every 750 000 births in the Western world.

Quads may follow fertilization of separate ova (eggs) extruded at the same time (non-identical quadruplets) or else one, or two fertilized ova may split and duplicate into separate identical individuals before becoming embedded into the wall of the uterus.

Quintuplets Five babies from the same pregnancy (occurring naturally once in 15 000 000 pregnancies), are known as quintuplets. They are usually identical, from multiple splitting of a single fertilized egg (ovum) before it is implanted into the uterus.

Non-identical quintuplets have been recorded several times recently due to the use of the drug clomiphene.

Fertility drug For some years clomiphene has been prescribed for women with a particular form of infertility. The drug stimulates gonadotrophin — a hormone from the pituitary gland — to act upon the ovary, enlarging it and reflexly inducing it to extrude one or more eggs. Not infrequently, two or more eggs are extruded at the same time, and up to eight simultaneous pregnancies can occur.

Diagnosis Almost 10 per cent of multiple births are not suspected until they appear at delivery. Earlier diagnosis, which may be difficult, is based on an abnormal increase in uterine size, the finding of two or more heart beats in the uterus with a significant difference in rates, and possibly the discovery of extra body parts when feeling the uterus. If doubt remains, diagnosis can be confirmed by echograms (ultrasound) or x-rays.

When triplets are born the size of each baby may differ considerably. (Rex Features)

The birth of quadruplets is the result of four ova being fertilized together or of the splitting of one fertilized ovum into four. (Salmer)

Complications Infants of multiple pregnancies tend to be smaller than the average single birth and also vary in size themselves. For example, with twins one may be relatively large to the detriment of the other who has not received as satisfactory a blood supply. The total weight of a multiple pregnancy also seems to be limited by the mother's inability generally to carry more than 8–9 pounds (4 kg) of extra weight in the uterus.

Toxemia of pregnancy (pre-eclampsia), increased volumes of fluid around the infants (hydramnios) and anemia, caused particularly by lack of folic acid, are more common in multiple pregnancies. Other major difficulties occur because at least a third of all multiple babies are born a month or more prematurely.

Birth Usually the delivery of the infants is not difficult, although there may be a long delay between each birth. Over-stretching of the uterus may cause lack of muscle tone after birth; when the muscles do not contract properly, excessive bleeding may follow the removal of the placenta. About 7 per cent of mothers develop this complication.

Even under ideal conditions, between 100 and 150 twins per 1000 do not survive either childbirth or the first week of life. This is due mainly to prematurity, with the second twin being at greater risk. Triplets are lost twice as frequently as twins.

Fortunately the breasts produce extra milk to cope with the additional demands.

Post-maturity

When a baby is born after the expected date of delivery, it is said to be post-mature. These babies tend to have had some degree of hypoxemia (insufficient oxygenation of blood) while in the womb or during labor, and so are more liable to have brain damage.

Premature birth

An infant over 3 weeks early (less than 37 weeks developed) is considered premature. Premature birth is more common in very young mothers and those over 35 years of age, especially if they already have a large family, and in those with a history of premature births. Malformed babies tend to be both premature and smaller than average.

Premature birth is more likely to occur if the mother has a chronic kidney infection, cyanotic (that is blue blood) heart disease, diabetes or syphilis. Pregnancy-related causes include unexplained rupture of the membranes, excessive fluid around the baby (hydramnios), toxemia of pregnancy and placenta praevia (where the placenta lies over the opening of the womb).

Risks to the baby increase in proportion to the degree of prematurity, so every effort is made to delay labor. Factors such as increased protein in the mother's diet, extra folic acid during pregnancy and bed rest during the last two or three months for mothers who have a history of premature labor appear to reduce the risk of early labor.

By administering alcohol both by mouth and intravenously or by injecting the adrenalin-like drug salbutamol, it is frequently possible to slow down labor or even halt it for several days.

Safeguards If premature birth seems inevitable, certain safeguards are needed. Cortisone-like drugs may be given to the mother to help mature the baby's lungs, thus avoiding the often fatal hyaline membrane disease. Vitamin K injected during labor helps protect the baby against bleeding disorders.

Sedation to the mother should be limited as it can adversely affect the baby and excessively long labor is avoided so the baby is not overstressed. Because of the smallness of the baby, additional care must be taken during delivery to ensure that the cord does not drop down and thus be constricted by the baby's head, cutting off the blood supply.

Rhesus factor

A special protein on the surface of red blood cells called D antigen, the so-called Rhesus factor derives its name from the fact that its discovery in 1940 resulted from experimentation with rhesus monkeys. It is present on red blood cells in about 85 per cent of Caucasians and is the main antigen of the Rhesus system. Blood containing the D antigen is called Rhesus positive or Rh(+), and is usually transfused into people who also have this antigen. Blood without the D antigen is called Rhesus negative or Rh(−).

Specific antibodies may be produced in the plasma of people with Rh(−) blood should Rh(+) red blood cells enter their circulation. These antibodies are called anti-D, and can cause clumping of Rh(+) cells should they enter the circulation for a second time.

The main problem of this anti-D antibody production occurs when a second Rh(+) child is born of an Rh(−) mother. If antibodies are formed during the first pregnancy as some of the fetal cells enter the mother's circulation, subsequent pregnancies also involving a Rhesus positive fetus may result in anti-D producing hemolysis of the unborn baby's red blood cells. Such a condition is called Rh disease of the newborn.

Rh disease of the newborn In a baby who is born with this condition, the red cells break down or hemolyse causing anemia (too few red cells) and rapid onset of jaundice. This condition is sometimes called hemolytic disease of the newborn or hemolytic jaundice of the newborn. The degree of anemia and jaundice depends on the quantity of antibodies present.

The baby is pale and jaundiced at birth or within two days and tests show that there is antibody present. If the jaundice is severe an exchange transfusion may be needed in which the baby's blood is exchanged for normal cross-matched blood. This procedure is very gradual, taking several hours as only 20 ml of blood is exchanged at a time. Sometimes the exchange has to be repeated.

In the majority of babies no further treatment is required and the baby enjoys normal health thereafter. However, if an exchange transfusion is not done, the baby may be irreversibly brain damaged.

The mother should be given an injection of anti-D antibodies immediately after delivery to prevent further children being affected. In most cases the antibodies should be detected at routine pre-natal examination and the condition prevented altogether. No first-born babies get this disease.

Rh(+) blood is inherited in a dominant fashion, that is, if a person is 'carrying' the particular Rh(+) gene, it will always be expressed (all children will have it on their red blood cells too).

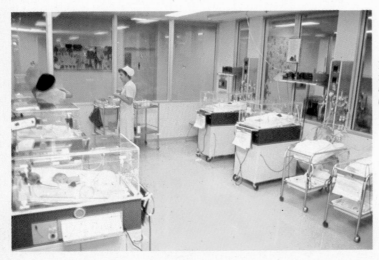

Humidicribs in the neo-natal unit of a large hospital. (*Westmead Center*)

Stillbirth

A baby which has never breathed, so that the lungs are bereft of air, and which is born dead after 28 weeks' gestation is called a stillborn baby. Death may occur several days before birth, a few hours before labor or during labor.

Death is diagnosed when the mother ceases to feel any movements and when the attendants are unable to hear or count the baby's heart beats. However it should be remembered that fetal movements usually diminish towards the end of the pregnancy anyway as there is not so much room for the baby to move.

Causes vary but lack of oxygen in the blood going to the baby is the basic reason for death. A hemorrhage between the placenta and the uterine wall with consequent raised blood pressure, and compression of the umbilical cord inside the uterus or prolapse of it through the neck (cervix) of the uterus will both cut off the baby's oxygen. The baby may have had a cerebral hemorrhage during labor.

Death may be averted by careful watchful prenatal care and care during labor to help spot and prevent these occurrences. Inadequate oxygen slows the baby's heart rate resulting in 'fetal distress'. This obstetric emergency demands immediate treatment, usually delivery by cesarean section or by forceps.

Unfortunately stillbirths are not always possible to avoid, especially in patients with high blood pressure, even with first-rate ante-natal care.

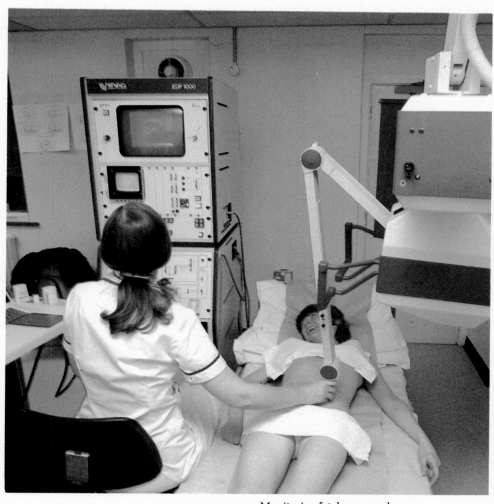

Monitoring fetal progress has helped reduce the number of still-births. *(John Watney Photo Library)*

Postnatal Care

The time from birth to about six to eight weeks afterwards is referred to as the postnatal period. Postnatal care involves consideration of the health and welfare of mother and infant within this period.

After the birth

Immediately after birth, the enlarged uterus weighs about 2¼ pounds (one kilogram), but shrinks over the ensuing four to six weeks to its normal non-pregnant size of 3 × 2 × 1 inches (7.6 × 5.0 × 2.5 centimetres) and weight of about 2 ounces (55 grams). For the first day after birth, the vaginal discharge, representing the discarded remnants of the specialized uterine lining tissue, is heavily blood-stained, gradually diminishing to a brown color by the end of a week, and white to yellow discharge by ten days. The latter persists for about one month.

The rich blood supply of the other pelvic organs during pregnancy diminishes to normal, and the stretched pelvic floor muscles and ligaments gradually regain their tone, aided by a special exercise program. The brown pigmentation of pregnancy (chloasma) disappears within four weeks and the abdominal wall muscles recover their tone and strength. Stretch marks persist as fine scars.

The breasts swell and enlarge further after delivery, first producing the pearly fluid called colostrum, which is especially suited in its composition to the needs of the newborn baby. Lactation is usually fully established by three to four days after birth, with production of normal breast milk, which the baby is now capable of digesting.

The cramping pains of the uterus, which occur in association with breast-feeding and are felt for a short time after childbirth, are known as afterpains.

The stimulation of the nipples during breast-feeding releases a hormone which helps the breast milk to flow. The hormone also makes the uterus contract, causing the pains. The contractions help the uterus to return to its non-pregnant state.

Following discharge from the maternity hospital, which in uncomplicated deliveries is about three to five days after birth, the mother will have been alerted by medical staff to report signs of infection, heavy, persistent, atypical vaginal bleeding, thrombosis, breast infection or cracked nipple, and undue anxiety or depression.

Each mother will have been given assistance and education on breast-feeding and advised to seek help if necessary. She should also have been advised about sensible nutrition, the need for adequate rest, and care of her infant.

Intercourse can be resumed when the usual blood discharge has ceased, at about three weeks if the delivery was uncomplicated. However, if there has been a forceps delivery, sutures or cesarean delivery, it is best to wait until the mother has been checked by her doctor at six weeks to ensure that all tissues have healed and that her uterus and vagina are back to normal.

Contraception If the baby is bottle-fed, it is possible for the mother to conceive again at four weeks. Therefore contraception will presumably be required as soon as intercourse is resumed. This could range from use of the ovulation mucus method, condom and spermicide cream method, diaphragm and spermicide, or intrauterina device inserted at the six-

week check, to resumption of the oral contraceptive pill at four weeks post-delivery, or at the time of the first period.

If the mother is completely breast-feeding, contraception is required from about four to six weeks and her choice ranges from condom and spermicide, diaphragm and spermicide, mucus ovulation method, or intra-uterine device fitted at six weeks, to the progestogen-only pill which does not affect the quality or quantity of breast milk.

Medical Checks A baby born in hospital will have its condition assessed immediately after delivery. Because pediatricians around the world wanted to be able to compare the condition of babies on an objective basis, a system called the APGAR rating was devised. This system takes into account five key factors of babies' condition which are directly indicative of its wellbeing: the heart rate, breathing, colour, muscle tone, and the baby's response to a stimulus. On each factor, the baby is given a score of 0, 1, or 2.

Each of these factors is very easily determined by observation and so does not depend on the presence of expensive or complicated equipment. Thus, for example, a baby's heart rate is either fast, normal or slow. A normal score in each category is two, so a perfectly healthy baby would have an APGAR rating of ten. A rating less than ten indicates to a specialist pediatrician that there is something slightly, or seriously, wrong with the baby.

The infant is usually examined at two weeks of age by the family doctor, who transfers the birth information to his records, notes any birth defects, records length, weight and head circumference,

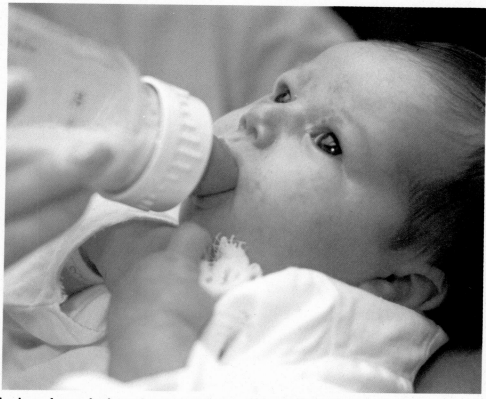

checks on breast-feeding, sleeping pattern and supports the mother and family. The value of regular clinic visits is discussed and the baby checked again at six weeks, with particular emphasis on head and nervous system development, heart sounds and hip joints (for evidence of dislocation). Length, weight, head circumference, birth marks, general development and milestones are also recorded. The in-

The care of an infant in its first few weeks of life should be a response to its need for food, warmth and a feeling of security. (Salmer)

fant immunization program is discussed and commenced at about eight weeks.

The mother At the four to six week medical check, weight, blood pressure, temperature, breasts, pelvis and urine are checked, PAP smear taken, abdominal and pelvic muscle exercises advised, adequate diet, rest, personal care, lactation and psychological support from family and friends discussed.

The family doctor and social worker have a particularly professional responsibility to provide support and assistance for the single mother and her infant.

Post-natal depression Many women develop a mild depression in the post-natal period, which subsides with normal family support and that of friends. Social isolation, previous psychological or psychiatric problems and, particularly, irritable, crying, vomiting babies with feeding and sleep disturbances, can aggravate this depression which requires skilled medical help. Infanticide and ill-treatment of the infant are more likely to occur under these circumstances, particularly if the mother herself has been a victim of emotional deprivation and violence.

With the loss of the extended family network in our culture, modern mothers are developing networks of supportive groups and services such as breast-feeding associations, mothercraft hospitals, play groups, tennis groups and babysitting clubs, which enable the young

Opposite
Very young babies are totally dependent on the loving care of the adults around them.

A hormone released during breast feeding makes the uterus contract, causing afterpains.

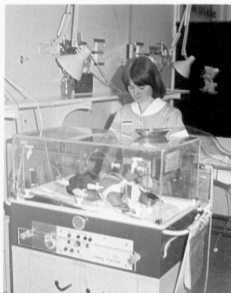

The humidicrib provides a safe environment for the prematurely-born infant. *(Royal Alexandra Hospital)*

A doctor checks the condition of a premature infant. *(Salmer)*

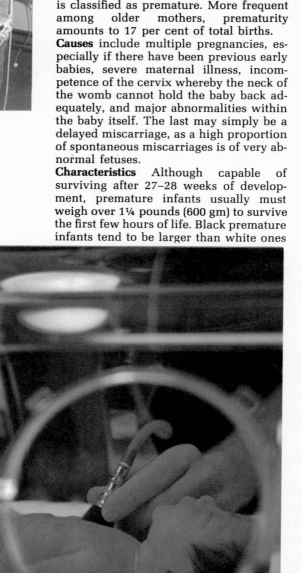

mother to feel a greater sense of personal freedom and self-esteem. This is achieved by the company of other young women in a similar situation, using shared resources and problem-solving methods. These arrangements can do much to prevent depression and inability to cope with the stresses and constant demands of motherhood.

Care of the premature infant

An infant apparently capable of maintaining life, born less than 37 weeks developed (full term is 40 weeks), and usually weighing less than 5½ pounds (2500 gm), is classified as premature. More frequent among older mothers, prematurity amounts to 17 per cent of total births.

Causes include multiple pregnancies, especially if there have been previous early babies, severe maternal illness, incompetence of the cervix whereby the neck of the womb cannot hold the baby back adequately, and major abnormalities within the baby itself. The last may simply be a delayed miscarriage, as a high proportion of spontaneous miscarriages is of very abnormal fetuses.

Characteristics Although capable of surviving after 27–28 weeks of development, premature infants usually must weigh over 1¼ pounds (600 gm) to survive the first few hours of life. Black premature infants tend to be larger than white ones

before 34 weeks, smaller in proportion thereafter.

Usually red, with proportionately large head, hands and feet, the premature infant has little fat cover and poor muscle mass. The skin is initially smooth, frequently wrinkling after a day or so, and may be covered with a cheesy white material, the vernix caseosa. Excessive body hair (lanugo), poorly developed nails, nipples and genitals, undescended testes and a pot-bellied abdomen are also common.

The internal organs are immature, and this usually causes most complications and deaths. Breathing difficulty (respiratory distress syndrome) with ultimate lung and heart failure due to the delayed development of surfactant, a chemical which lines the more mature airways, is the dominant problem. Numerous other problems frequently exist. Blood clotting factors are deficient, possibly causing brain hemorrhage or bleeding into other internal organs, food absorption is often poor and it may be weeks before the baby can suck adequately, while low blood sugar levels (hypoglycemia), an increased tendency to jaundice and occasionally brain damage can result from an immature liver.

Furthermore, the kidneys excrete body poisons poorly and have difficulty in concentrating the urine, leading to excessive loss of body fluids. Along with inefficient temperature control and underdeveloped defenses against disease, premature babies must also contend with the prospect of increased congenital heart disorders, especially patent ductus arteriosis.

Treatment Risks are minimized by specialized and good nursing, close monitoring of food intake, oxygen concentration in the baby's environment, and control over temperature and infection. Special cribs (humidicribs) are designed for this purpose, and minimal handling of the baby as well as quarantine against skin and other infections are imperative.

Most complications can be handled adequately by specialist doctors and various medical innovations, such as a synthetic surfactant material now being used experimentally.

Although very small infants, weighing less than 2¼ pounds (1000 gm), face considerable risk of brain damage, with subsequent retardation, behaviour problems, spasticity and deafness, prospects are good for most premature babies.

Possible postnatal problems

While most new mothers experience few problems apart from the common ones of tiredness and the occasional minor worry, in a minority of cases difficulties may occur.

Agalactia The inability to produce sufficient quantities of milk to allow adequate breast-feeding, in most cases agalactia results from anxiety or fear on the part of the mother who lacks confidence or encouragement.

Within a few days of birth the thin yellow fluid (colostrum) that had been coming from the nipples is replaced with milk. This process is controlled by two hormones produced by the pituitary gland, oxytocin and prolactin. Sucking of the nipple by the baby produces the *draught reflex*; stimulation results in the release of oxytocin hormones from the pituitary which in turn causes the milk glands in the breast to contract and commence lactation.

Anxiety and tension, or sometimes pain from a cracked nipple, inhibit this reflex and reduce the volume of milk. Specific diseases causing agalactia are rare. In most instances there is a generalized hormonal disturbance.

The size of the breast does not influence the amount of milk produced, as the number of milk glands is reasonably constant among most women. Certain disorders of the breast such as inverted nipples and abscesses may restrict the ability to breast-feed. While inversion of the nipple may affect as many as one mother in three during the first pregnancy, over 90 per cent of these will have achieved the normal everted position by the time of delivery. Regular massage before the birth and nipple shields may be of benefit in this regard.

A mother often stops breast-feeding when she feels that her baby is not getting enough, sometimes because of a demand for more frequent feeds. This is, however, the way that the breasts receive more stimulation and therefore produce more milk for the baby's increasing needs. A proportion of women who experience difficulty with breast-feeding during the first 2–3 months after delivery, may prefer to feed the baby by bottle.

Metritis An inflammation of the womb is described as metritis.

Acute metritis may result from infection after abortion or childbirth. The symptoms are fever and sometimes an offensive discharge. Treatment with antibiotics is usually effective within a day or two. 'Backyard' abortions are a source of this type of infection.

Chronic metritis is an enlarged uterus in a woman with heavy, prolonged menstruation. Continued loss of blood may make her anemic. A diagnostic curettage may be needed. This operation (popularly called a D & C, dilation of cervix and curettage of uterus), consists of lightly scraping the lining of the womb to obtain tissue for microscopic examination. This is usually recommended if the patient is over 35, in order to rule out the possibility of uterine cancer. Treatment is usually either by administering gestagen hormones or removing the womb (hysterectomy).

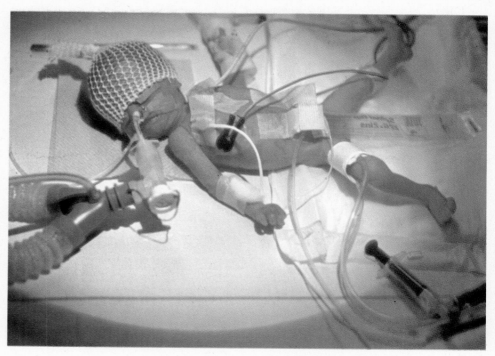

A premature infant being closely monitored in a neonatal intensive care unit. (*Westmead Center*)

Puerperal fever Often fatal in the days before doctors recognized the importance of cleanliness and antiseptics, puerperal fever occurs in women during the first ten days after giving birth.

Puerperal fever may be caused by an infection introduced during delivery into the birth canal although this is not certain. Unhygienic conditions are particularly dangerous at this time as even normally healthy women are especially vulnerable to disease at this stage. The raw wound on the inside of the womb, where the afterbirth or placenta was previously attached, is an ideal breeding ground for infectious organisms and disease will rapidly enter the bloodstream, precipitating death by blood poisoning (septicemia) a few days after delivery.

The introduction of simple cleanliness, antiseptics and sterile techniques has greatly reduced this disease and it rarely causes death today.

Temperature and pulse of the mother are checked regularly after delivery, and any evidence of infection is checked by a laboratory test of swabs from the vagina or appropriate organ. If an infection is detected the laboratory recommends the best antibiotic treatment, which will be continued for at least a week.

Prevention still depends on the hospital staff maintaining optimum sterility during labor and afterwards and they are regularly checked to ensure they are not carrying a particular organism that can inhabit the nose and respiratory tract without causing symptoms. Treatment is also necessary if the mother has an infection before labor. Women who have had prolonged, difficult labors or who are anemic, dehydrated or diabetic are most at risk.

White leg Usually occurring in the puerperium, the period following a baby's birth, the condition known as white leg was first described by François Mauriceau in 1668. He called it phlegmasia alba dolens, or milk leg, on the assumption that the associated swelling was caused by milk accumulating in the mother's leg after lactation had ceased.

Occurring approximately once every thousand deliveries, the condition begins in the veins of the mother's pelvis, initially with clotting. The clot soon spreads down into the leg and upwards to the vena cava, the main vein of the body.

At first there is a vague feeling of malaise, soon followed by mild fever. Shortly afterwards the fever rises rapidly, there is severe pain in the groin and thigh and the leg swells from edema or accumulation of fluid. Because the nearby arteries spasm, the blood supply diminishes and the leg becomes unusually white. Rarely, gangrene of the toes, or death, occurs.

The condition, which may last for weeks, often causes a swollen leg thereafter, and is occasionally complicated by clots moving to other parts of the body. These may flow to the lungs (pulmonary embolus) and can prove fatal.

The condition of white leg is less likely to occur if the mother is allowed to walk about soon after the baby's birth. Treatment is usually a combination of high doses of antibiotics and anticoagulants (drugs to thin the blood and make clot formation less likely). The leg is elevated and usually wrapped in elastic bandages.

4 Infant and Child Care

The Infant — to Two Years of Age

Infancy can be defined as the period between one month and two years of age. Babies can see and hear from the first few hours of life, and soon afterwards they begin to show definite characteristics of their own personality. In fact the baby is a far more complex individual than was previously thought.

Among children there is a very wide variation in normal development and behavior. Infants range from the quiet, placid baby who sleeps for much of the time and is very easy to care for, through to the active, eager baby who is always on the go and seems to need less sleep than his parents.

From the first weeks of life, physical contact with his parents is one of the baby's major needs. The infant enjoys being wrapped firmly, cuddled and talked to. A baby has very few ways of expressing his emotions and crying is one of these. Some episodes of crying, when the baby is distressed, are very intense. It is only as the infant grows older that he learns to have some control over his emotions.

By about six weeks the infant begins to have some social interaction with his parents, smiling in response to their talking to and smiling at him.

At about six months of age the infant becomes aware of the differences between his parents and other people. It is at this stage that he is likely to cry when being picked up by, or being left with strangers.

In early infancy the child is very attached to his mother and is not aware at this stage that he and his mother are two separate beings. An important part of later normal development is for the child to be able to cope with separation from his mother. In early infancy the infant feels that he has lost his mother when she is absent and becomes anxious, as he has not yet learned that when his mother goes away, she comes back.

Towards the end of the first year the infant is beginning to learn a variety of skills such as rolling, manipulating small objects, standing, and crawling or walking. An important part of mastering these skills is repetition and it is common to see infants repeatedly practice new skills until they have perfected them.

18 months to two years From about 18 months of age there is a rapid development of language and the child begins to express some of his feelings in words. Night waking is also common at this age, the child often needing to be reassured that he is not alone.

By the second year the infant starts to have some physical independence and to assert his own individuality, often by doing the opposite of whatever his parents ask. He has very few words at his command at this stage and 'no' is usually the favorite. This stage is often described as negativism, but the child is actually striving to assert his independence and become an individual in his own right. Children frequently choose to assert their independence by refusing to eat at meal times. The child is also curious about the shape and texture of things and will tend to handle his food, creating a mess. However this behavior tends to diminish once the child develops an ability to use language.

If too many choices are offered at one time, such as the choice from a large number of toys, the child will be confused. The concentration span is short; for example, the tendency is to play with one toy at a time but quickly change to another.

A baby begins to make definite responses to the surrounding world when only a few weeks old and by the age of twelve weeks generally recognizes its mother.

At this age the child cannot be induced by promises or bribery to obey the parent. However by the age of two the child is able to understand repeated, firm commands and can understand that certain things displease his parents.

Two to three years During the second year the child begins to show strong likes and dislikes, which are often most obvious at meal times. It is helpful to remember that this is a normal stage of development.

A few general guidelines are always helpful, particularly for the first-time mother, but it should always be remembered that, right from the beginning, each infant is an individual, with his own personality. With a calm, relaxed approach, a routine to suit both mother and baby will soon be worked out.

Bathing and dressing

Babies are bathed daily in many Western countries because it is socially accepted practice, not because they need to be washed so frequently. In winter when the weather is very cold a warm sponging may be all that is needed. What is important is that the baby's bottom should be gently and thoroughly cleaned at each diaper change and some soothing baby oil or cream applied.

Right
New experiences occur daily for the young baby.

Very small babies should be held with a support under the neck and head and a firm grasp around the upper arm. *(Heinz)*

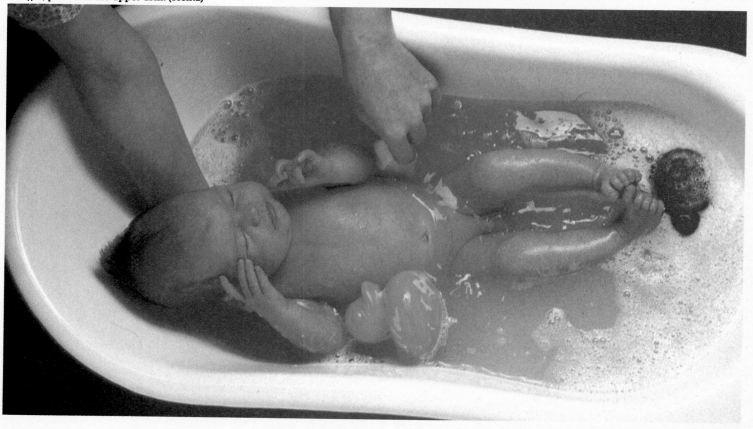

When bathing a baby make doubly sure that the water is not too hot by testing it with the inside of the wrist. It should be warm, never hot. Some very useful temperature testers which indicate the correct temperature are now available from pharmacies.

When preparing a bath for a baby, always put the cold water in first, adding the warm gradually until the required temperature is reached.

Cradle cap The condition of flaking discolored skin on the scalp is not so common nowadays and can be prevented with a weekly washing of the baby's scalp with soap. If it still occurs, oil the scalp about one hour before washing and then wash with soap and a washcloth. Brisk washing may make the scalp red, so after drying apply a little more oil.

Baby clothes are generally easy to care for. Many are made from synthetic fibers and, while these are hardwearing and easier to launder, in hot weather they are often uncomfortable for the baby. It is generally better to use a fabric where the synthetic fiber is mixed with cotton or wool. For small infants, one-piece baby garments are very sensible and easy to use both at night and in the day time.

When possible, buy baby clothes which are non-inflammable.

When washing either diapers or baby clothes, make sure that they are rinsed thoroughly. This will help reduce diaper rash and other allergies, particularly around the neck.

Suitable clothing and bedding will help to keep the baby comfortable and contented.

Coping with crying

A cry is the first sound that a baby makes when it takes its first breath. In children or adults, crying almost always represents distress, but in the case of young babies, crying is the main way of communicating some need.

The attempt by the baby to communicate its needs can lead to concern and frustration, especially for a new mother who at first finds it difficult to determine exactly what the need is. In time a mother will become adept at dealing with her crying baby. In fact within two days of giving birth, many women are able to distinguish the cry of their own child from those of others in the nursery and very soon learn to deal with their needs.

There are a number of causes of crying, and therefore each occurrence has to be assessed to discover the particular cause.

The need for physical contact In the first few months of life the baby needs to be frequently cuddled and have close physical contact with the parents, especially the mother. The baby will often cry simply to be picked up to receive close bodily contact.

Boredom is also a cause of crying. Beyond the age of four to six months babies will be interested in what goes on around them. Even as early as one month old a baby can be propped up to watch his mother doing things.

A bored baby is more likely to cry than one that has adequate interest during waking hours.

In both these cases the baby will stop crying for more than a minute or so after being picked up. If the child was crying because it wanted food it will begin crying again sooner.

The need for food Crying is the usual way in which a baby indicates its need for food. A common sense approach to feeding is needed in the first few months, when feedings are required most frequently. A modified demand feeding schedule is generally considered more appropriate than a rigid schedule dictated by specific feeding times.

The baby can be left crying for some time, though not for a prolonged period, before being fed, rather than being fed immediately at the expense of whatever else the mother is doing. A feeding regime which fits into the mother's plans for the day enables her to have short respites, visits, or trips to the shops, even if she is breast-feeding.

Inadequate feeding is often revealed by more frequent crying which cannot be stopped by cuddling. In such a case weight gain frequently slows down as well. If there is any doubt, test feeds should be undertaken (particularly for breast-fed babies). These involve weighing the baby immediately before and after each meal for a whole day to discover exactly the weight gained from each particular feeding time.

Wind Swallowed air seldom causes pain in babies and is less of a problem than is generally believed. Many books giving guidance on child care suggest that merely cuddling the baby for a minute or two after a meal allows any wind to come up and that no special maneuvers for 'burping the baby' are necessary.

Soiled clothing The discomfort of a wet or dirtied diaper may cause a baby to cry. It is inadvisable to leave a child for long periods with a wet or soiled diaper, as this may lead to diaper rash. However, if the baby is asleep there is no need to wake it to change a soiled diaper. When the child wakes and cries for whatever reason, this will be an appropriate opportunity to change the diaper.

Physical illness When children become physically ill they often lose appetite; other symptoms are also usually present. The quality of the crying is different from that of other causes; it is a continuous whimpering. If the mother is unsure of the cause of this crying, or is unable to deal with it, medical advice should be sought.

Other causes If a baby becomes too hot or too cold it will often cry. The usual solution is to change the number of clothes or bedclothes. Sudden noises, bright lights and other disturbances may also cause a baby to cry.

Babies cry at night for the same reasons as during the day. To treat the cause is important, but it is advisable not to spend excessive periods of time with the baby at this time or to take it back to the parental bed, or the baby will soon cry frequently in the night to gain attention or to be taken into bed with the parents.

There are times when a baby continues to cry without obvious cause. Incessant crying can create unnecessary tension in the mother. A vicious cycle may then be set up. As the baby becomes aware of this increased tension and cries more, the mother becomes more tense and less positively responsive to the baby's cries.

Sometimes when no obvious cause for the crying can be found, the baby may be left to cry. Alternatively the mother could arrange for the child to be cared for briefly by someone else or could shut herself off from the crying for a similar brief period to enable her to relax. A relaxed, calm mother is more easily able to comfort her distressed, crying infant.

As a baby grows up, crying mainly becomes associated with physical hurts and emotional upsets. For example, things may not turn out the way the child wants, or a child may fear that the mother is 'lost'. To deal with crying at any age needs common sense and affection.

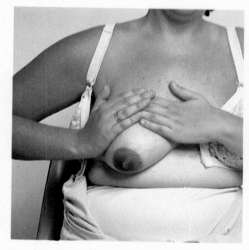

Feeding

One of the first problems many new mothers face is whether or not to breast-feed their baby. There are many advantages and conveniences in breast-feeding and this should be encouraged. However, if this is not possible, bottle-feeding can be very satisfactorily managed, particularly in well-developed countries where the water supply is clean and refrigeration readily available. Healthy, happy babies are possible whether they are breast or bottle-fed. The important thing is that the mother is doing what she wants to do and is comfortable in doing it.

Breast-feeding should be a rewarding experience for all mothers who choose to feed their babies this way. With appropriate preparation and support, over 90 per cent of mothers can successfully breast-feed their babies.

In some countries where hygiene is poor, there are significantly more deaths among artificially-fed babies but the advantages of breast-feeding are not so marked in advanced countries. There are, however, some differences in overall health between breast-fed and bottle-fed infants.

Feces are bulkier and more acidic in breast-fed babies and there are fewer digestive tract problems because the occurrence of some bowel infections is reduced by the acidity. Studies have also shown a reduction in the frequency and severity of respiratory infections in breast-fed infants. These observations are possibly explained by the presence of antibodies in the breast milk.

Preparation for breast-feeding should begin during the first pregnancy. Education about the values and advantages of different ways of feeding is important. If a woman decides that she would like to breast-feed, active support and encouragement should be given. An adequate diet for the mother is important, and special diets have been designed, with iron, protein and calcium particularly increased.

The flow of milk into the ducts of the breast, the 'let-down' or 'draught' reflex,

When a baby cannot be breast fed immediately, the mother can express her milk so that it can be given to the baby from a bottle. *(Westmead Centre)*

occurs when sucking on the nipple is begun. This causes the release of a special hormone (oxytocin) from the pituitary gland in the brain which, in turn, stimulates the milk secretion. This reflex is often reinforced by a conditioning that starts the milk flowing into the ducts when the baby cries for milk, or a feed is being prepared.

Advantages. Overfeeding with resultant excessive weight gain and the associated problems, is avoided during breast-feeding. Human breast milk is tailored to the baby's nutritional needs, providing the correct mixture and the correct volume. Convenience for the mother in breast feeding is an important practical point as preparation of bottle-feeding equipment can be a nuisance. The close physical contact between mother and baby which is provided by breast-feeding is undoubtedly one of the many factors in fostering bonding. The pleasure and satisfaction derived from the successful achievement of breast-feeding is important for many women.

Difficulties. Breast-feeding is not without its difficulties. The ability to delegate feeding to others, and periods of freedom from the baby, are not available. Breasts may become tender at times, and leakage of milk may be annoying or embarrassing.

Drugs or medications taken by the mother often appear in breast milk, so special precautions are taken with some of these as their presence may cause some problems in the baby.

A tendency to underfeeding can be detected by weighing the baby before and after meals. Insufficiency of milk is often due to inadequate emptying of the breasts, or to the mother being worried or tired.

Distension and pain in the breasts frequently occur in the few days following the birth. This is often remedied by allowing the baby to feed more frequently, or by expressing milk manually from the

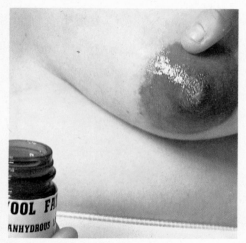

Cracked or sore nipples should be treated with a soothing ointment such as lanolin. *(Westmead Centre)*

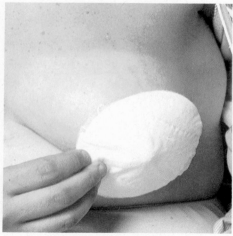

A pad fitted over the nipple will absorb any milk leaking from the breasts. *(Westmead Centre)*

Encouraging a baby to burp after every feed is a common practice as it makes the baby more comfortable.

breasts after feeds, to relieve the discomfort and maintain the supply. Sedatives and pain relief are sometimes needed.

Sore or cracked nipples can be a problem. Feeding the baby on the unaffected side first, giving shorter, more frequent feeds, applying lanolin or healing cream, and exposing the affected breast to air and a little sunshine all help. In more severe cases, the baby may have to be taken from the affected breast, and milk expressed manually until the nipple is healed.

Excessive washing or use of drying agents on the nipple, feeding a hungry baby later than needed, and pulling the baby off the breast may all cause sore nipples. The feed is best terminated by inserting a finger gently into the corner of the baby's mouth so that the seal is broken.

Periodically the baby needs more milk than is coming and for a period of one or two days feeds may be demanded very frequently. This is a normal occurrence and women should be forewarned about it. This may be exhausting, but a more regular pattern of feeding occurs as the supply increases. A commonsense approach to the feeding schedule is important. Feeding strictly by the clock rather than to the baby's needs is frequently inappropriate, as is demand feeding which allows no planning for the day's activities.

Bottle-feeding of infants may either supplement or replace breast-feeding. Some women may have difficulties with breast-feeding. In many cases bottle-feeding is chosen by the mother before the delivery of the baby as being the most appropriate method, either for convenience or to enable her to return to work early.

Modern proprietary preparations, although more expensive than goat's milk and cow's milk, reflect the composition of human breast milk very closely. They are more convenient to prepare because nutrients present in inadequate quantities in

goat's or cow's milk have been added.

If cow's milk is used as the basis of feeding, water must be added to dilute the high levels of protein and sodium. A sugar, preferably the non-sweet lactose, is also needed to elevate the low carbohydrate level (the major source of energy).

Selection and preparation of the equipment is important. Unbreakable bottles are best. A top with a seal which fits over an inverted nipple allows several bottles to be prepared at the same time for use when needed.

The hole in the nipple must be the correct size, and should be checked before every meal to make sure that there is no clogging. When the bottle is held upside down, milk should drip out fairly readily but not so fast that the drops cannot be counted.

A bottle-brush, funnel, sterilising equipment, and possibly a measuring glass are also needed.

It is important, especially in the first two to three months, for the mixture, bottle and nipple to be as sterile as possible. Boiling bottle and nipple in water for several minutes or leaving them to soak in a proprietary disinfectant are equally effective.

Feeding intake. The amount of fluid needed by babies varies and depends on their size, age, the weather (more fluid is needed in hot weather), and other factors. An approximate volume is 150 milliliters per kilogram (5 fl oz per 2.2 lbs) of body weight per day. Babies tend to drink more if the formula is too weak.

A formula should, however, not be made stronger than the recommendation on the container as excessive salt intake can cause difficulties. As long as the baby is generally contented and putting on weight satisfactorily, he should be able to dictate his own feeding needs.

In some societies there is a belief that a baby must be fat to be happy and healthy. Babies that are significantly overweight,

however, even if only one to two months of age, are much more likely to become obese children and adults. Many health problems in adults are related directly to being overweight as babies.

Underfeeding can also be a problem, and unhappy, crying, underfed children are more susceptible to infection. When underfeeding is severe, problems in general development may ensue. The best way of assessing the overall adequacy of feeding is by the amount of weight that a baby is gaining. During the first three months a healthy baby that was not born prematurely should be gaining 6¼ ounces (175 gm) each week.

In some cases the mother's milk production may be excessive or associated with an exaggerated let-down reflex as soon as the baby grasps the nipple, delivering too much milk too quickly. This can frighten the infant and cause him to cough and splutter and draw away or fight the breast. Expressing some milk prior to feeding or posture feeding can alleviate this problem.

The baby who is underfed usually cries continually in the first few weeks. A common problem is an apparent insufficiency of the mother's milk supply, which can usually be dealt with by psychological support, relief of anxiety, increased fluid intake and frequent, complete emptying of the breasts after feeding. The Nursing Mothers Association and the LeLeche League provide excellent counseling on this subject.

Soreness and cracked nipples can also cause feeding problems which can be overcome easily with prompt attention to the feeding situation, and the use of creams and other protective measures.

The healthy bottle-fed baby can have problems with nipple size or blockage, or strength and type of milk formula, resulting in an inadequate intake and a restless, crying, unhappy baby.

Too strict an adherence to formulas and time schedules can result in the same problem in particular babies because of the variation in individual requirements. If swallowed air is not expelled during or immediately after feeds, the baby may acquire a premature sense of fullness and cry shortly after feeds because it is hungry.

Allergy to cow's milk, resulting in vomiting, diarrhea or skin rashes, occasionally causes failure to thrive; the baby will generally respond to change of milk formula.

It may be necessary to add vitamins C and D to some formulas, although most of the preparations developed recently contain adequate quantities. Be guided by a trained nursing sister or your doctor.

Feeding techniques. Several factors can help the feeding technique. Minimizing air swallowing is important, and one way of achieving this is to hold the bottle up high enough so that the baby sucks milk and not air.

It also helps to remove the nipple periodically from the baby's mouth to allow air to enter the bottle and ensure continued even milk flow. The nipple should be replaced when it becomes excessively soft, a condition that causes the nipple to collapse inwards to prevent adequate outflow of milk.

If you are bottle-feeding your baby, give yourself and the baby a chance to enjoy it and each other. Nurse your baby close to you when feeding; never leave a baby alone with the bottle propped up. Not only is it not much fun eating alone but there are the real dangers that the baby may splutter and choke or that milk may get into the middle ear from the eustachian tube which joins the back of the mouth and the ears.

A commonsense approach to the feeding routine applies just as much to bottle-feeding as to breast-feeding. Some scheduling of feeds is important as this allows the mother to organise some of her time, but it should be flexible enough to cater for the baby's varying needs, too.

Thickening of feeds is normally commenced some time in the second month. Weaning from the bottle (or breast) has usually begun by the age of six months. Generally it should be completed by the time the baby reaches 12 months, although there are no hard and fast rules.

Although it appears that fewer women nowadays bottle-feed their babies than was the case in recent years, it must be realized that, for a variety of reasons, not all women *can* breast-feed. There is certainly no evidence that bottle-feeding causes major physical or psychological problems to the baby.

How much milk should baby be given? Your baby will generally tell you if he is

still hungry and will stop feeding when he has had enough. Most babies take about 2½ fluid ounces per pound of body weight per day in five to six feedings. It is usual to give this about every four hours, but some babies demand more frequent feedings during one part of the day and leave longer intervening periods at other times. Do not worry if your baby is different from others.

Babies are generally about eight weeks or older before they sleep through the night without waking. If your baby seems slow at achieving this do not try to force him, as most tricks designed to give you those extra hours of sleep do not seem to work. Be patient and let the baby decide for himself when he can do without the night feed.

Small vomits are very common and normal, particularly when the baby brings up wind. If you have any doubts, check with your family doctor as persistent vomiting may be the first sign of illness.

Feeding problems Poor feeding, wind, irritability, little weight gain and diarrhea, all fall into the broad category of feeding problems.

The first thing to do is to seek advice from your doctor or baby health center nurse, who will help unravel the many factors which might be involved. Do not be satisfied with a pat on the head and a change of feedings. If this happens, find a different advisor who will take more time and care to help. Sometimes a minor upset creates anxiety and concern which leads to a tense baby who gulps his milk, also taking in a large amount of air, causing pain, vomiting and a reluctance to feed. In some cases a short stay in hos-

pital may be needed to resolve the problems.

Vitamin supplements Whether you are breast or bottle-feeding, it is a good idea to give your baby some additional vitamins.

A preparation containing vitamins A, B, C, D and E should be used and the dosage instructions on the bottle followed exactly. Vitamins are beneficial, but excessive amounts of vitamins A and D can be very dangerous.

Weaning A baby is ideally breast fed for at least six months. By that time he will have developed reasonable immunity against infections and various allergies; he will have been protected from many virus infections, particularly those of the gut, and bonding between mother and child will have become well established.

The advantages and convenience of breast feeding can be enjoyed by both mother and baby. *(Heinz)*

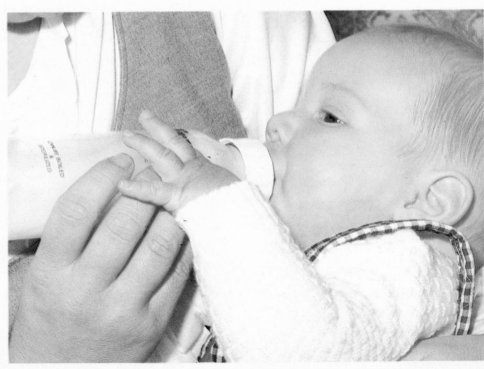

Bottle feeding can be comforting and satisfying if the formula is warmed to the right temperature and the baby is held close.

As the baby grows, the demands on the mother can become excessive and if no supplements to breast milk are offered, an infant over six months may become deficient in both vitamin C and iron, leading to irritability and anemia.

Weaning of the baby from total breast-feeding often begins between the fifth and sixth months of age. Initially whole cow's milk is offered either at the end of, or as a substitute for, a particular feeding. Gradually, as the mother's milk supply becomes progressively less adequate in relation to the baby's needs increasing amounts of cow's milk and then solids are substituted.

The weaning may be a gradual and relaxed process, continuing over a period of months. Often a baby will be eating normal family meals and drinking cow's milk by nine or ten months but still needing the comfort of a breast-feed last thing at night.

The first solids offered to the baby at around six months should be soft, bland and in small amounts. Suitable foods are purées of stewed fruit, mashed ripe banana, wheat or rice cereals and puréed cooked vegetables with mashed tender cuts of meat. Excessive fats, pork products, dried fruits, skin and peel of vegetables and fruit as well as peas and beans, are better avoided during the first year of feeding.

It is wise to avoid sweetened drinks, such as many proprietary vitamin C concentrates, as the baby may well reject more sensible, but less sweet, foodstuffs later. The baby should be offered rusks or crusts on which to chew, so that the introduction of more solid food which requires chewing then becomes easier, particularly once the teeth have appeared.

If the mother has to wean the baby onto a commercial milk formula, the family doctor or baby health centre will be able to recommend a suitable brand appropriate for the baby's age and weight.

Full cow's milk should not be offered before the baby is at least five or six months old. The baby from a family with a tendency to allergies often may not tol-

Regular weighing helps to establish whether or not the baby is gaining weight adequately. (*Royal Alexandra Hospital*)

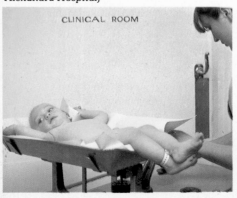

When solids are introduced into the baby's diet only a small spoonful should be offered at first.

erate cow's milk and will probably be more contented with soya bean formula.

The mother who weans her baby rapidly may have swollen tender breasts for some days. A firm bra is necessary, but binding and ice packs probably have little effect. Fluid restriction and the taking of excessive coffee or diuretic drugs (to increase the output of urine) are of little value in drying up the breasts. Various medicines will help, particularly bromocriptine which stops the action of prolactin, the milk-producing hormone.

The sex hormones estrogen and testosterone will both suppress milk production after several days of therapy. Unfortunately, about a third of mothers so treated resume lactating once the course has been completed and a further week or so of treatment may prove necessary.

Play

It is very important for children to engage in play so that they can learn new skills and stimulate their mental and social development. Children have to learn basic skills like reading and writing, holding a pencil, building with blocks and experiencing differences in taste, texture and color.

They are learning constantly through play; trying out new ideas, discovering how things fit together, making new patterns and designs and developing their imagination.

Very young children do play by themselves, and all they need from adults at this early stage is supervision, a steady supply of different simple toys and a little help if they become frustrated. They do not want to do things the way the parent thinks they should be done.

Play teaches a child to socialize and to

give and take in dealing with other children. This is a necessary part of growing up and the child who does not have adequate early contact with other children will often be at a disadvantage when trying to establish comfortable relationships later on.

Parents often worry when children fight over play things, but it is usually best to let them sort out their own differences without too much interference, unless one particular child is being hurt or always loses. In this way children learn to work with others and to resolve conflicts.

The first year At the crib stage the child can be introduced to bright, single-colored rattles that are light, unbreakable and washable, and to large wooden beads or rings which can be strung across the crib. Also the child can be given strong, soft plastic toys that can be chewed but are unbreakable and washable.

As soon as a baby begins to crawl, a large play-pen, preferably with a floor, will provide a safe playing area. It should be placed so that the baby has a good view of the room and can watch other members of the family.

At this stage, soft, brightly colored balls, preferably washable, are popular with children. This is also the time to introduce a teddy bear, or rag dolls and floating bath toys.

One to two years At this stage the child will tend to be interested in hollow blocks or beakers and empty plastic cartons, and toys to push and pull. The child should also be introduced to building blocks, especially large, brightly colored blocks, and if possible should have the opportunity to play in a sand pit with suitable sand toys, a bucket and spade.

Books and stories play a very important part in a child's education. The child should begin at about the age of one year with rag books or sturdy cardboard books that are difficult to tear, and the best are those with large, bright-colored pictures that are easily recognized by the child. Young children also enjoy counting, the ABC, and simple picture books.

Small problems of infancy

A majority of the so-called common behavior problems of childhood are really only natural reactions to the various situations that children face as they grow up and learn to fit into the community in which they live.

Most of the common reactions relate to activities which, earlier in infancy, are associated with comfort or sensations of pleasure or to the natural curiosity that all children have about their own bodies and their immediate surroundings.

Imitative play is performed with great seriousness. Children enjoy being busy.

Thumb-sucking by small children is not uncommon but the habit usually stops by the age of five or six. *(Zefa)*

Thumb sucking With very few exceptions, all babies suck their thumbs or fingers for a variable period of time. In some children the habit continues for many years, particularly when they are shy or tired.

Most children will stop sucking their thumbs by the age of three without any special effort being made by the parents, but it will do no harm if the habit continues for much longer than this. The example of friends is the best dissuader, although many children will continue to suck their thumbs at night in bed after they have stopped doing so in public.

It is important never to use any form of restraint as this will only frustrate and upset the child and will cause much more harm than the habit itself. Correspondingly, being cross with the child or removing the thumb by force is undesirable and will not help in any way.

Pacifiers and other comforters. Provided pacifiers are kept clean there is no real objection to their use, though most children can manage perfectly well without them. However, if you prefer your child to suck a pacifier rather than his thumb, by all means allow him to do so for a few months.

The tendency of many mothers to give their babies pacifiers coated with honey or jam greatly increases the risk of cavities and encourages the child to refuse unsweetened foodstuffs or milk from its bottle.

Pacifiers should have a wide flange and ideally be pinned by a ribbon to the clothing as babies have been known to swallow and choke on them.

There is a popular belief that thumb sucking or the use of a pacifier will cause the teeth to protrude. However, any effect that the habit has is negligible; in any case, it could only affect the milk teeth, since by the time the permanent teeth have emerged the child will usually no longer be sucking his thumb or pacifier.

While some infants comfort themselves by thumb sucking, others become attached to a particular object such as a soft toy, a teddy bear or a piece of soft cloth or blanket. Such children insist on having their comforter with them before they will settle down to sleep and, indeed, sometimes the attachment is so strong that they will carry the object around with them during the day. Some children retain their comforter for several years while others discard it very quickly. As with thumb sucking, there is no reason to interfere with a child's attachment to a comforter as no harm can result and in due course it will be discarded naturally.

Temper tantrums Most children cry or put on some sort of a performance if they are frustrated. Occasionally some children will lie on the ground, scream, kick and throw their arms around.

Frequent temper tantrums often indicate that the parents do not know how to handle the children. Occasional temper tantrums will always occur and the best way to deal with them is to ignore them. Persistent or prolonged tantrums are best dealt with by putting the child in his room and telling him he can come out when he is ready to behave himself. When he does so it is important to restore affection.

The most effective measure for temper tantrums is prevention. The parent should make sure the child has adequate opportunity to use up his energy in play without frequent and unnecessary restrictions and that he is not confronted with too many choices when he is not yet mature enough to make decisions; rather he should be told clearly what he is expected to do. If children want to express their independence by trying to do up their shoes or feed themselves, let them do so, providing judicious and tactful advice at the right time.

Breath holding and head banging Breath holding most commonly occurs in young babies as a form of temper tantrum. These babies cry vigorously with anger, then hold their breath and sometimes turn blue and even lose consciousness for a brief period. Older children sometimes bang their heads repeatedly on the wall or ground during a temper tantrum.

Although these symptoms are very frightening for the parent they never seem to cause any harm. However, if they do occur, it is wise to consult a doctor to make sure no serious abnormality is being overlooked.

A teething child may derive some comfort from chewing on a toy.

Dirt eating Many infants eat dirt, grass and a variety of garden flora and fauna. In most cases they are only exploring their environment and their behavior does not mean that there is an emotional disturbance. However, if the habit tends to persist it is usually a response to continuing stress and the parent should consult a pediatric specialist. Care should be taken that no poisonous plants are within reach.

Teething

Although the baby teeth may appear without trouble, in most cases the appearance of each tooth is preceded by a period of drooling, sometimes with irritability and fretfulness. In some cases, bowel movements become a little loose for a few days.

Many babies get obvious comfort during teething from chewing on a rattle or soft toy. A soft teething ring at this time may be of help.

Although teething certainly produces the minor signs referred to above, it is easy to blame it for all sorts of symptoms. Teething, by itself, will not make a child sick. So if a child develops a high fever, continuing diarrhea or any other symptoms or signs other than the minor ones listed above, a doctor should be consulted.

Toilet-training

The young infant has no real sensation of the need to empty bowels or bladder. Although some parents claim to have toilet-trained their baby before one year of age, what they have actually done is to take advantage of the baby's normal reflexes. The baby will pass a bowel movement automatically after a feed and if placed on a pot at this time will appear to be toilet-trained. It is only between 18 months and two years that the child will mature enough to develop some control over bowels and bladder. The infant often makes some sign of this need by indicating to his parents that he has a wet or dirtied diaper.

The attention of brothers or sisters makes life interesting for the small baby. (*Zefa*)

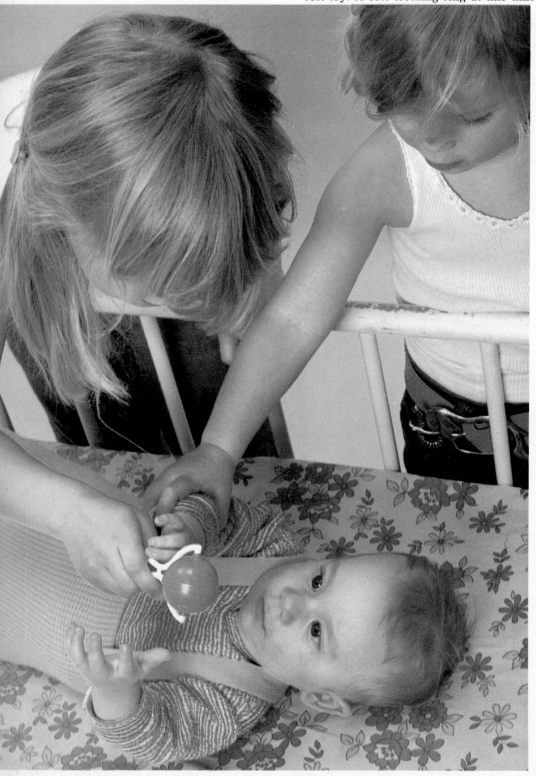

Bowel control is usually achieved during the second year of life, but the occasional involuntary passage of feces, encopresis, may occur for some years afterwards.

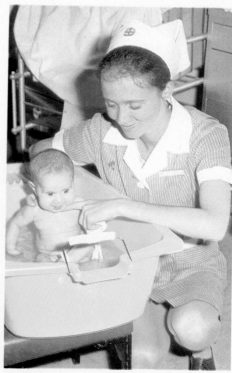

Sympathetic care is most important for very young patients. *(Royal Alexandra Hospital)*

Even one familiar toy can make a small infant feel comforted in the strange surroundings of a hospital. *(Zefa)*

Welfare

The rapid development of neonatology during the last twenty years, the improvements in facilities, the greater knowledge of the problems affecting the unborn fetus, and the greater prospects for surgical correction of defects, has led to a considerable decline in infant mortality rates worldwide over the last 30 years. A large proportion of the decline has been due to a reduction in death from infectious diseases. Better medical care for mothers and children and higher standards of living have also contributed to the drop in infant mortality rate.

Many handicaps can be resolved or greatly relieved, although some cannot. It is important for the parents to know what can be done for the child, so that optimal use may be made of whatever abilities he has.

Many organizations can help, some having been formed by parents who share the same problems. Your pediatrician can put you in touch with them.

Residential care of handicapped babies and infants is less common than in the case of older children. There are, however, some excellent private nursing homes for babies.

Special school facilities, state and private, exist for pre-school age handicapped children.

Just as early diagnosis of disease is important, so is the early referral of families with handicapped children to special skilled services designed to provide a total service.

Hospitalization of infants Infants are very vulnerable and need their parents and families. If an infant needs hospital treatment, every effort should be made by the parents to spend a lot of time with him, and if possible to stay in the hospital with him. Many children's hospitals have some type of facility to allow this. Familiar toys will help to minimize the effect of being in a strange place. Also the mother should discuss the problems with the family doctor who may be able to advise on how to make things easier.

Immunization is very important to prevent diseases such as diphtheria, tetanus and poliomyelitis. Always make sure that the immunization course is completed.

Immunization is generally available at baby health centers, at special immunization clinics conducted by local municipal councils, and at children's hospitals or by the family doctor.

A common timetable would be:

2 months:	Diphtheria, tetanus, whooping cough (DTP), polio (sabin)
4 months:	Diphtheria, tetanus, whooping cough (DTP), polio (sabin)
6 months:	Diphtheria, tetanus, whooping cough (DTP), polio (sabin)
15 months:	Measles, mumps and rubella (MMR)

(A further immunization is needed against diphtheria, tetanus and polio at 4–5 years, before a child enters pre-school or kindergarten.)

The Child — from Two Years of Age

With so much written and projected through the mass media about child care, it is understandable that many parents are confused and lack confidence in their ability to raise children. The first important rule about child care is that there are no rules, but rather common sense and guidelines. The greatest need for all children is a stable family situation in which they know that they are loved and wanted.

It should also be recognized that every growing child undergoes a conflict between his need for being mothered and his growing urge for independence. Each child is an individual personality who responds in individual ways to problems and stresses. Parents may find it difficult to understand why one of their children seems to over-react to stresses with which other members of the family cope without difficulty. Such variations in response are normal both within families and in the community generally.

Throughout childhood there is a strong need to belong and to conform. Initially families are important, but as children progress so the youth group and the school also become important. Children do not like to be different from their peer group. They have a great need to be loved and noticed, particularly by those who are important to them. In general, they have a clear sense of justice and are acutely aware of deception. Most children have much more awareness than we ascribe to them.

Height and weight A child's ultimate height and weight are determined by a number of factors, such as parental build, nutrition and general health. It is quite impossible to predict the future adult height and weight of young children. Most children weigh 31–33 pounds (14–15 kg) at the age of two years and then gain approximately 5½ pounds (2.5 kg) per year until puberty when there is a sudden growth spurt in height and weight.

Bowel and bladder control By the age of two years, a child has matured sufficiently to be toilet-trained; it is appropriate to

start training when a child gives some indication that he has wet or dirtied his diaper. Use a potty or training chair rather than a special toilet seat so that his feet are on the ground. Bowel control usually comes first and a considerable time may elapse after toilet training is started before full control is achieved; this has no relationship to intelligence or discipline. Toilet training should never become a battle between parent and child and if attempts to introduce training are resisted, the child should not be forced.

Once a child starts kindergarten, he will take his cue from other children or from older brothers and sisters. Children over three years of age usually have reasonable bladder and bowel control although accidents may still occur, particularly if they are absorbed in play activity. Bed wetting often continues for another year or more. If a child over the age of five years is still wetting the bed, it is wise to seek medical advice.

Social and emotional development No children under the age of two have any real concept of right and wrong, good and

bad. From this age, they start to understand firm commands like 'no' and 'don't touch', and that antisocial behavior such as bringing the garden indoors or unrolling all the toilet paper is displeasing. Young children become confused if given too many choices at once and they cannot concentrate for any length of time. They like to play with one toy at a time but quickly change from one to another. As speech develops, the world of their imagination and the real world often become intermingled. Children at this age do not tell lies deliberately.

By the age of three, a child needs the company of other children and may be introduced to the local kindergarten. At this age, play activities become more complex. Whereas young children play by themselves, children over three will participate in simple games with adults or other children. They may start treating a special toy or teddy bear as a real person. Some children form a close attachment to pieces of cuddly cloth or blanket. Such special toys are very important to the child and he should be allowed to take

them with him when he goes to bed, particularly if he is away from home.

Feeding By the age of three, most children are graduating to dining with the family and to eating the usual family meals. There is a lot of nonsense and confusion about what constitutes a balanced diet. Provided children have a reasonable intake of meat, fish, poultry and eggs to supply body-building protein, vegetables and fruit for vitamins and roughage, milk, butter or margarine, cheese, bread and cereals, they will have a balanced diet containing all the necessary ingredients. Milk and dairy products should feature prominently in the diet of all children.

If a child tends to be overweight, the calorie content of the diet can be reduced by cutting down on bread, cereal, and potatoes or by eliminating sweets, cookies, cake and snacks.

The only child Parents of an only child need to ensure that their child mixes regularly with other children. The single child experiences a great deal of adult company which must be balanced by play and association with peers. The child should be

A child's personality develops over the years as a combination of inherited characteristics and outside influences. (*The Sunday Times Magazine*)

A stable, loving family situation helps produce happy, well-adjusted children.

encouraged to engage in as many group activities as possible, for example pre-school groups and sporting teams.

This encourages the sharing of property and feelings, which is a way of learning to play, work and communicate effectively with other children.

Problems. The risk exists that the only child will mature too early. Childhood experiences include having fantasies, enjoying story-telling, rough games, shouting, gibberish and other 'childish' behavior. A child who spends too much time with his parents and other adults is in danger of unbalanced development, perhaps becoming a 'little adult' at the age of five or six.

Over-dependence is probably the greatest problem in rearing an only child. Although most parents are at least prepared for it, this does not eliminate the problem. Some single children are timorous, fearful and shy. A child who is not allowed to make some mistakes, to

Shared experiences, pleasures and activities are a vital part of the child's learning experience.

An only child may benefit from joining groups such as kindergartens and playgroups.
(Zefa)

ever, are emotional and intellectual; for example, they do not have to compete for the parents' affection.

The evidence indicates that single children are high-achievers (as are first-borns) in most careers. In general, they learn to walk and talk early so that as they grow older and attend school they are good conversationalists, do well in school work and are average in sports. The difference between academic and sporting performance may be the result of the single child's tendency to amuse itself reading, drawing and talking when alone, whereas excellence in sport is often influenced by physical play with other children at a very early age.

All children on their own will tend towards quiet activities involving dolls, trains, reading, writing, painting and so on. The only child spends far more time on his own than do most and by eight or nine years old is often a prodigious reader, regarding books and their characters as 'friends'. It is obvious, therefore, that being an only child tends to encourage intellectual prowess, creative activities, good language skills and mature social responses.

Behavioral problems

Most of the so-called 'problems' of behavior are simply the natural reaction of a small child to a new situation encountered as growing up proceeds. The vast majority of such situations are self-resolving.

Bad language Four and five-year-olds often go through a 'swearing' phase. They know that they are being naughty without really understanding the meaning of the words they use. The object of the exercise is to disturb the parent, who should try not to be upset but should make it quite clear that the use of these terms is not approved. If they persist, one short sharp smack usually has the desired effect.

conquer his fears without adult assistance, who is constantly protected from any unpleasantness or who does not have to accept discipline or punishment when in the wrong, grows up into the sort of adult who perceives reality as harsh. Life without the protection of one or both parents is extremely difficult for such adults. They are often neurotic, extremely anxious and have very little self-esteem. The best they hope for is marriage or a relationship with a person who will also fulfill a protective role thus keeping them 'safe'.

Over-protection is especially common in the relationship between the single parent and the only child, especially between mother and child, and must be

avoided, no matter how hard it is for the parent to 'let go' at certain times.

All children need the protection, security and love of their parents. The danger is that a surplus of love will stifle normal development. Most parents know, by comparing with their children's friends, whether they are tending to over-protect their child. If they feel they are, they should endeavor to allow the child, through everyday experiences, to develop its own resources so that normal self-confidence develops.

Advantages. The parents of an only child can often afford to provide more material aids and comforts than would be possible if there were other children in the family. However, the only child is no more liable to be 'spoiled' in this sense than other children are. Emotional indulgence is far more damaging to the only child and much more common. The main advantages in being an only child, how-

Although most children are toilet trained by the age of two and a half years, a few remain bed wetters up to the age of nine.

The same approach should be used for other antisocial habits such as kicking and biting. If handled in this way these habits rarely last long.

Bed-wetting The condition of bed-wetting is estimated to occur in 15 per cent of boys and 10 per cent of girls at the age of five, but only 5 per cent of all children remain bed-wetters by the age of nine. Most children who are subject to bed-wetting remain dry by the time they are teenagers.

Bed-wetting is taken to mean involuntary or unintentional passing of urine at night, and as described below it may result from physical causes including illness. The term 'enuresis', sometimes used to describe bed-wetting, strictly applies where there are no such causes.

The passing of urine in infants is a simple reflex action. During the second year of life the nervous system matures and it is usually during this year that children are able to exert control over the emptying of the bladder. Most children are toilet-trained by the age of two and a half years.

Bed-wetting may occur after a period of initial control, possibly as a result of physical or emotional problems. There is no one cause and each case needs full investigation of the circumstances and development of the particular child.

Children who are bed-wetters as a result of some physical cause are usually wet during the day as well as at night, but many enuretic children also may not have perfect control during the day.

The psychological and emotional factors which appear to cause bed-wetting are varied. The child's home situation, including such aspects as relationships between parents, parents and child and the child and other family members, may need to be understood. Parents should be aware of all these factors and be prepared to discuss them fully with the family doctor if the case demands medical advice. The possibility that an affected child may be a particularly heavy sleeper should not be overlooked.

In most cases, punishment of the child will only serve to worsen the situation. With young children, a reward system might be advised. Stars could be placed on a calendar to denote 'dry' nights, and a suitable reward be given to the child when a certain goal — like a dry week — is reached. Often an understanding approach coupled with a simple reward system works very well.

Among other methods are the use of alarm systems which work on the psychological principle of a conditioned reflex. Every time the child urinates in bed the alarm awakens him. Suitable drugs may also be prescribed to help the child cope with the problem. All methods meet with a degree of success but it is important to discover and deal appropriately with any underlying causes.

Possible physical causes. Bed-wetting may be a sign of several conditions, including diabetes and certain kidney diseases, particularly those which result in increased production of urine. If infection is involved, testing of urine will establish this. Some neurological conditions may be associated, and occasionally some forms of epilepsy may be identified through bed-wetting symptoms.

When bed-wetting is characteristic of several members of a family, it may sometimes be due to an inherited limitation on the ability of the bladder to hold urine. Such a condition will usually correct itself with age, assisted by the fact that children require fewer hours of sleep as they get older.

Day dreaming The vague unrealistic thinking of day-dreamers is often a substitute for unrewarding real experiences. Some day-dreaming is natural, especially in childhood, but when indulged in to excess, or when a child fails to distinguish between dreams and reality, it may be a symptom of a psychiatric illness. The child should be given interesting and rational occupations in a happy environment; if the problem persists, expert help should be sought.

Day-dreaming is often confused with *petit mal* epilepsy as in each case the child looks vacant. In day-dreaming the child can easily be brought back to his surroundings but in *petit mal* this does not occur until the episode is over.

Feeding problems Mealtimes often become a trial of strength between parent and child; some children use mealtime battles as a means of asserting their independence. As children are sensitive to atmosphere, mealtimes should be happy and relaxed.

Small servings with the option of more are better than large helpings; favorite foods and finger foods for young children can be included; meals should be served at regular times as a tired child cannot be expected to enjoy his meals; and snacks, particularly sweets, cookies and soft drinks, should be avoided.

Sometimes a favorite story helps, with appropriate pauses for mouthfuls. If a child refuses to eat after a reasonable time and a sympathetic approach, parents should desist and wait for the next meal. No child ever starves itself to death.

Hyperactivity There are two types of hyperactivity. In one sense it is a sign of overactivity, the other includes the inability to pay attention and the inclination to impulsive behavior.

In the case of primary school children the incidence of the hyperactivity syndrome varies from 4 to 10 per cent, the sex ratio being nine boys to every girl. These children are persistently overactive without good reason or excuse. This hyperactivity persists from an early age, only becoming recognized as abnormal at around the age of three or four.

The inability to attend to anything for very long is a key feature. The child is easily distracted and finds it difficult to learn his lessons. He may also have difficulty in

The hyperactive child may play in very energetic ways and resist sleep.

A child should not be made to feel guilty because he wets the bed. A calm and understanding approach is best.

getting on with people and his behavior may be impulsive, though not purposefully antisocial.

Another feature is clumsiness. Any indication of minimal brain damage (such as increased tone of the muscles or difficulty with rapid repetitive movements) will only be revealed on medical examination of the central nervous system. Any brain damage could have occurred before or during birth, or later from encephalitis or meningitis.

Hyperactivity, or hyperkinesis as it is sometimes called, must be distinguished from other conditions such as mental retardation, an anxiety state and defective hearing or eyesight.

There are several theories about the causes of hyperactivity. The theory that it is inborn is supported by the observation that infants are overactive from their earliest days and that their parents were also overactive as children.

Another theory is that it is a reaction to early separation from the mother or to her mental depression after giving birth. This theory is difficult to test. Critics suggest that the mother's dejection may be the result, not the cause, of the hyperactivity of her offspring.

A third theory is that it is caused by minimal brain damage. This is supported by the electroencephalogrammic (EEG) evidence showing abnormality in more than half the cases and by central nervous system examination revealing mild abnormalities in one-third of cases.

As part of the medical examination a child may be examined by a pediatric neurologist for any brain damage, and by a psychologist for assessment of intelligence and to advise on educational problems. Vision or hearing may also be checked. Parents are advised not to set too high a standard for their children, as this can cause harm. They should provide an outlet for their energy. For example, toys should be unbreakable and harmless. Only a few firmly enforced rules to guide behavior are necessary. Parents should encourage their children with praise and rewards for good behavior. And they should try to give themselves a break from the child, often enough to enable them to tolerate him.

Medical treatment is based on drugs or diet. The drugs are either stimulants or antidepressants. Stimulants increase the ability to pay attention. Antidepressants perhaps work in the same way. Both pro-

One of the treatments for hyperactivity is a diet which excludes artificial dyes such as those found in many sweets. *(Zefa)*

duce the side effect of a slight slowing down of body growth. Every year or so the drugs are withdrawn to determine whether the child can do without them.

A popular, and perhaps valuable, form of treatment is the diet proposed by Dr Ben Feingold. The diet excludes artificial dyes and other additives, and also certain foods. There are reports of improvements following this treatment. However, research continues to determine whether improvements are due to the diet and to discover how the diet is effective.

Some of the findings of research do support the theory that some children are hyperactive because of certain chemicals in their diet. Details of the Feingold diet and advice on treatment can be obtained from pediatricians and hyperactivity societies.

It is important that the hyperactive child is thoroughly assessed and that the parents, the teacher and the child are made aware of the disability. A hyperactive child who is unjustly blamed for

poor performance at school may react by misbehaving, for example by soiling himself.

Parents may be consoled by the knowledge that hyperactive children tend to improve with age. Although some children with minimal brain damage may have problems in adjusting to society, most hyperactive children improve.

Jealousy is very common in the child who is confronted with the arrival of a new baby in the household. The parent should anticipate the problem by informing the child well ahead of time that there is going to be a new arrival and should allow the child to help with preparations for the new baby.

Also the child should be prepared for the inevitable period of separation while the mother is in hospital. The child should be told why the mother has to leave and that she will return, and he should be allowed to stay for short periods with whoever will be looking after him at this time so that he will not feel deserted. When the mother returns with the new baby she should take good care to give the older child sufficient affection and attention.

Nail biting A majority of children bite their nails for a time and most will stop after a few years. There is usually no obvious reason for the habit, which disturbs parents rather than the children. Sometimes the habit reflects emotional stress and this possibility should always be considered.

A child should never be scolded for nail biting and bitter substances should never be painted on the nails to stop the child biting them. It is helpful to keep the nails short, otherwise the habit should be ignored. In the case of older girls, the gift of a pretty manicure set may help.

Nervousness A timid, fearful child may sometimes show nervous mannerisms such as tics, nail-biting, speech disturbance, phobias and sleep disturbance. This pattern usually indicates a high level of emotional tension and anxiety in the child, often associated with maladjustment to family, school and social pressures. When parents are either over-protective or expect too much independence on the part of the child, then excessive fear or timidity may occur.

Abnormal fears or phobias usually represent displacement of internal fears or anxiety to an external object. For example, school phobia can be caused by a marked separation anxiety from the mother.

However, transient fears are very common in the pre-school age group when the child is experiencing and learning about danger, strange people and animals, and parental absence.

Treatment involves understanding the particular basis for fear and timidity in each child. Discussion of the family situation, stresses, school problems and social interactions usually pinpoints the problem. A team approach to treatment is often required, involving parents and teachers as well as health professionals.

Sleep disturbances There are a number of common minor bedtime problems such as repeated requests for a drink of water or a trip to the bathroom. Another common problem is that of the child who is put to bed and promptly reappears for a chat and a cuddle. Firmness and consistency usually solve the problem: a quick cuddle, then back to bed. Sometimes fear of the dark or of the closed bedroom door is the underlying reason for this behavior and a subdued light seen through a partly opened door may be of help.

Speech problems It is worth remembering that speech commences with single words around one year of age and progresses to simple sentences by two years. At this age children also chatter away in a totally incomprehensible language of their own. This is a perfectly normal stage of speech development.

There is considerable individual variation in the age at which speech develops. If a child is slow to speak this does not necessarily mean that mental development is slow, unless there is an obvious slowness in passing other milestones such as sitting up, walking and self-feeding.

It is important for parents to talk to their children in order to stimulate normal speech development, and it also helps if there are other children in the family or if there are friends' and neighbors' children of approximately the same age.

Speech will be delayed if a child has a hearing defect, and emotional stresses such as separation from parents or the arrival of a new baby will often cause a child to revert to baby talk. The latter is a sign of insecurity and what the child usually needs is a little extra affection and attention.

Stammering is quite common around the age of two to three when children are rapidly increasing their vocabulary and only occasionally does it persist. Such children tend to be rather tense and excitable and the stammer is more obvious whenever they are upset. If stammering persists and is obviously embarrassing to the child the parent should seek expert advice.

Tongue tie. A rather prominent fold of skin joining the bottom of the tongue to the floor of the mouth may be referred to as 'tongue tie'. Only occasionally does it interfere with tongue movement and with speech. However, if there is any concern about it consult a doctor.

Discipline

An important part of growing up is learning to develop a degree of self-control and respect for the rights of others. One aim of training should be to help the child to develop these values in order to be able to function effectively and happily in society.

It is important to have some understanding of the way children develop. The new-born baby is completely self-centered and incapable of controlling its feelings or considering the needs of others. As the child grows older it becomes capable of distinguishing right from wrong and learning which behavior will please or displease its parents.

Learning new skills Much behavior in young children that sometimes irritates parents is really the young child practicing a new skill. Whenever a child learns a new skill, he practices this until he has perfected it. A common example is the child who at ten months learns to let go of objects spontaneously. He generally practices this when sitting in his high chair, dropping food, plate and utensils over the side! This is often irritating to parents but it is the child's way of perfecting a newly-found skill.

Left
Normal speech development is stimulated by play with other children.

Right
Parental firmness, reassurance and consistency will ensure that a child goes willingly to bed.

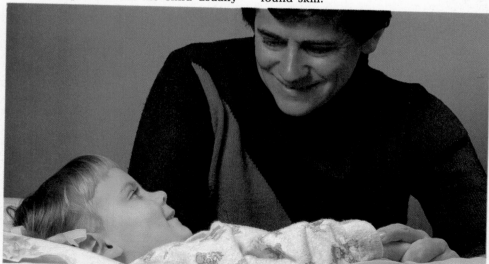

Imagination Children have a very vivid imagination and often have difficulty distinguishing their fantasy world from the real world. Their play often involves fictional friends and pets and they are notorious for making up stories and embellishing stories with vivid detail. This should not be regarded as lying for it is the child's attempt to reconcile the fantasy world with the real world.

Temper tantrums are a common response to frustration in the toddler age group. These children have not yet learned to contain their anger and are unable to put their problems into words, so they often take the more direct approach of lying on the ground and screaming. The best way to handle the occasional temper tantrum is to ignore it; the child soon learns that there is no point in a performance without an audience. Also, as tantrums are extremely frustrating to parents it is often best for the parent to withdraw physically from the situation.

Assertion of identity A common frustration for the parent is the attitude of a child in the two year age group who becomes negative and says 'no' to almost every suggestion. However this may not be an act of defiance but rather a sign that the child is beginning to find and assert his own identity.

Parental example By far the most effective training is the example of the parents.

It is important for parents to have realistic expectations for their children so that the level of behavior that they expect is appropriate to a child's age and ability. It is unreasonable to expect a child under one year of age to be able to know right from wrong, but it is quite reasonable to expect such knowledge in a three-year-old.

It is important for parents to be consistent in their attitudes to discipline and child-rearing so that the child has some firm guidelines for behavior. There is nothing more confusing for a child than to be allowed to do a particular thing one day and then be punished for the same action the next. Also, if the parents make unrealistic threats which are not carried out the child soon learns not to believe the threats and therefore not to be worried by them.

Many parents are concerned about the role and effects of television. A powerful educational tool, television may limit the child's opportunities for normal play and other learning activities. Suitable programs should be selected and a limit placed on the amount of time spent watching television.

Punishment There is considerable dispute over whether a child should be spanked. In general a child should be encouraged in his good behavior because he wants to

Parental guidance and supervision should be consistent and dependable.

please his parents and follow their example. However there will be occasions when the system will break down and the parent may resort to spanking. It is important that this should hurt the child's dignity rather than inflict pain and that the child realizes that the spanking is an extreme measure.

Whatever form of punishment is used it is important that it follows soon after the misbehavior. Young children have a poor concept of time so if the punishment is delayed for several hours it is usually meaningless to the child.

There is no one correct way to bring up a child. The most important thing is that the child should be surrounded with an atmosphere of love and security. If this is achieved, then variations in the exact method of child-rearing, including discipline, will not be likely to interfere significantly with the proper emotional development of the child.

Above
A family doctor can often help with simple child guidance problems.
(Royal Alexandra Hospital)

Below
A baby is given a simple hearing test at an infant welfare center.
(Royal Alexandra Hospital)

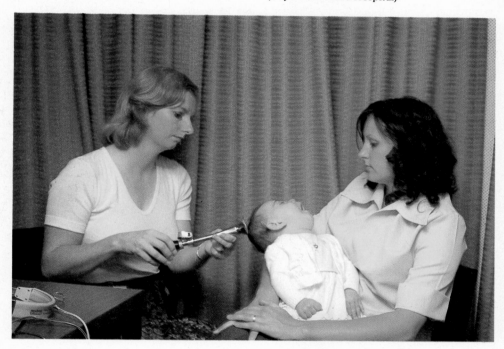

Health services

Health services for children vary from country to country in their availability, their scope and their mode of operation. But, within broad limits, the aim is universal, to provide: infant welfare facilities; school health services; guidance and services for the sick, the handicapped and the emotionally disturbed; the preventive care to ensure healthier citizens of the future.

Pediatricians are specialists with extensive training in children's diseases and in child care and development. Pediatricians are responsible for most child care including health screening immunizations, and care of the sick child. The speciality of pediatrics has grown so rapidly that subspecialities have evolved and some pediatricians practice entirely in particular areas of childhood problems.

Pediatric surgery is now a well recognized speciality. The knowledge and skills required to operate on a child, especially a baby, are signficantly different from those required for adult surgery. There is a trend for children's surgery to be performed by trained pediatric surgeons in hospitals accustomed to caring for sick children.

Children's hospitals provide a whole range of child health services. Their emergency sections may see few real emergencies but are generally busy with children brought directly to the hospital for a variety of problems ranging from sudden acute illness to skin rashes and behavior problems.

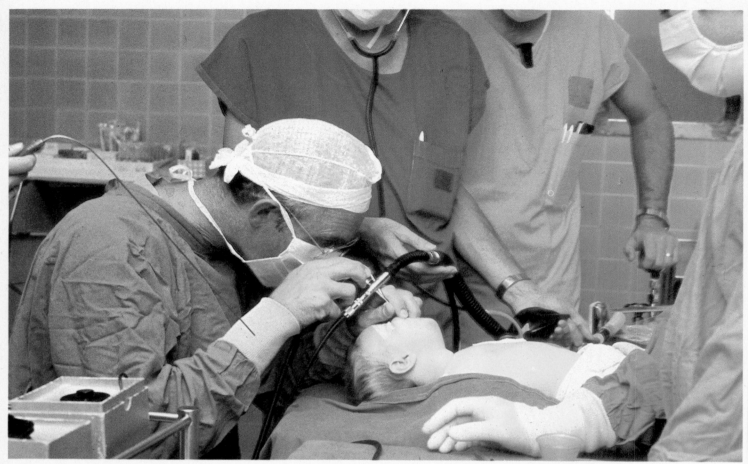

Pediatric surgery requires skills quite different from those used for adults. (Royal Alexandra Hospital)

Children's hospitals realize the importance of treating children out of hospital wherever possible, and of the need for parents to visit child patients at any time, or even stay with them in the hospital. Play leaders, occupational therapists and play areas are provided to meet the emotional needs of the child while in the hospital. The average length of stay is between five and seven days.

For children who can be treated without being admitted, the outpatient services of children's hospitals provide a wide range of pediatric speciality services as well as physical therapy, social work, occupational therapy, dietary, psychology, and psychiatry services. Referrals are usually made to outpatient services by the family doctor or directly from the children's hospital casualty department.

Child guidance services Parents often require help with behavior problems in children, including refusal to attend school, conduct disorders or problems in family relationships. The family doctor can often help with advice about simple problems but in more complex cases it may be necessary for a child psychiatrist to see the child.

A specialist in childhood emotional disorders, the child psychiatrist may be visited privately on referral from another doctor, at a child guidance clinic attached to a child health center, or in a department of child and family psychiatry in a children's hospital. Childhood emotional disorders are quite common and there should be no stigma attached to seeking help from a child psychiatrist, as early intervention can often prevent a problem progressing.

Child psychiatrists often work in close cooperation with a social worker and a clinical psychologist and may enlist their assistance in providing regular help for the child and the family.

Services for handicapped children Children with physical or mental handicaps have a variety of organizations available to help them. Most countries have centers for those affected by cerebral palsy and organizations to help other physically handicapped children. Children with mental handicaps require special schooling which may generally be arranged through education authorities.

It is most important that a thorough assessment be made of the disabilities and abilities of the handicapped child. This should be followed by a careful explanation to the parents and the provision of a practical plan to help the child achieve

Specialist teaching services, such as for the deaf, are available for school children. (Mosman Park School for the Deaf, Western Australia)

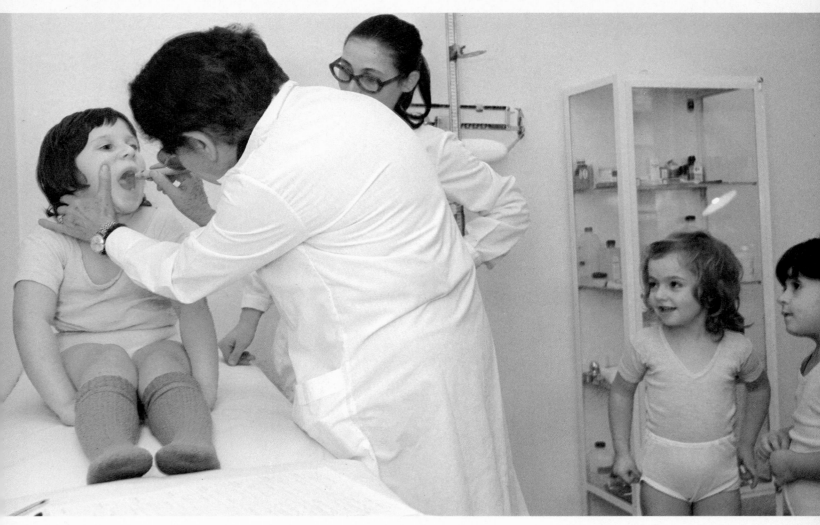

The school medical officer plays an important part in the early detection of developmental abnormalities. *(Salmer)*

Left
Mobile dental services may be available to school children in isolated areas.

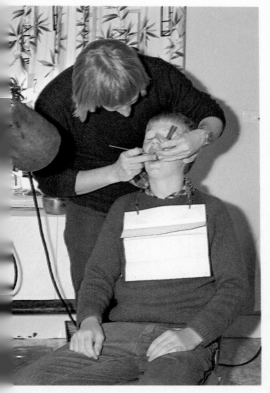

his fullest potential. All children's hospitals and many child health services have assessment centres for this purpose.

School health services The organization and type of free health services available to school children differs according to location.

Funded by state or local governments, school health services provide free medical assessment for preschool and primary school children at regular intervals. It is usual to request parents' approval before screening any child. Doctors and nurses based in regional centers visit local schools and clinics to examine children and interview parents. A more detailed assessment is available if necessary. Parents who are concerned about their child's development may usually contact the center directly at any time to arrange an examination.

Although no treatment is offered for acute or chronic illness, treatment may be available for speech disorders, hearing loss, learning difficulties and emotional problems.

The child's general condition is noted and some or all of the following tests are carried out. Eyes are tested for squint or other vision defects.

If a simple screening test of hearing is abnormal, a more accurate test of each ear with a portable audiometer will indicate the degree of hearing loss. Referral for a full audiometric assessment at a specialist hearing clinic may be necessary.

The nose, throat and neck glands are examined. The hair is examined for any infestation such as lice. Skin rashes, thyroid enlargement, abnormalities in the heart or large blood vessels, hernias and undescended testes are noted. Any abnormalities in the legs and feet or difficulty walking will also be noted.

The child's speech, educational progress, behavior and physical development are also assessed. The parents are usually interviewed. If any problems are detected, further assessment through the school health service or treatment by the family doctor may be recommended.

Facilities for the treatment of speech, learning or emotional problems may be available at a regional center or clinic.

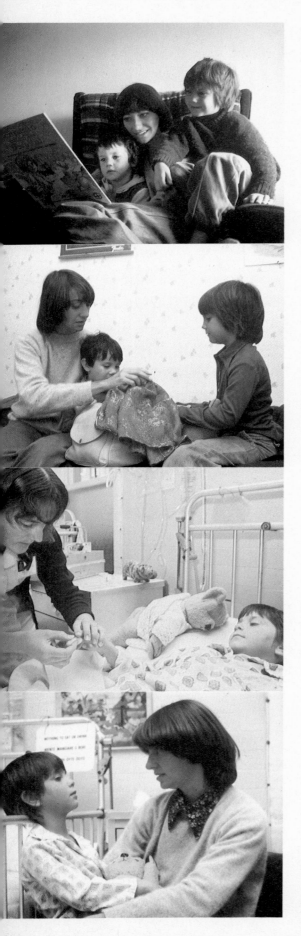

The child who enters hospital with an understanding of what to expect is better able to cope with hospitalization. Visits from parents are vitally important, never more so than on the day of the operation. *(Royal Alexandra Hospital)*

A speech therapist, social worker, psychologist and psychiatrist may be available to assess and treat a child.

The child's family may all be interviewed in the case of behavior difficulties since these are often the result of a wider disruption within the family. During a period of bereavement, separation, or divorce, for example, the center may be able to provide counseling to help a single parent and children through a difficult time in their lives.

Clinics staffed by dental therapists may be available in some areas for infant or primary school children. Mobile dental clinics provide service in some country areas. The clinics provide free examination, treatment and dental education.

Hospitalization

The preparation of children for the hospital should start in the doctor's office. Parents should be told in simple terms what is wrong, what treatment is needed and why this is best carried out in hospital. If an operation is necessary, it should be described in simple terms and the approximate length of stay in the hospital given.

The child should be included in the discussion, if he is old enough and some simple explanation is necessary for young children. When admission to the hospital is urgent and unexpected, support is best given by a parent escorting the child to provide a sense of security and to answer questions.

Preparation by play can be helpful. Parents can play hospital games with the child and his toys to help him understand what will happen. Coloring books and story books about going to the hospital are also useful.

All questions should be answered as truthfully and factually as possible. For example, if a child asks about 'needles', tell him that doctors may need to give drugs or take samples of blood in this way. He should not be told that they do not hurt but be reassured that it stings only for a moment. If x-rays or laboratory tests are likely, include a simple description of what is to be expected.

Some hospitals provide slide and tape programs about going to the hospital so that both parents and child have a clearer understanding of what to expect. It can also be helpful to visit the hospital and the ward before the child is admitted to meet staff and see where the child will eat, sleep and play. Most large children's hospitals welcome such visits by parents and children. When the time comes to enter the hospital the child can help pack his own bag and include special toys and other reminders of home.

The child receives the best hospital care when parents and staff work together; parents know and understand their children and the hospital staff have special knowledge and skills. Parents, particularly the mother, should spend as much time as possible with the child, helping with feeding, washing and play, and brothers and sisters should also visit. If the child is having an operation, it is particularly important to be with him on that day, preferably both before and after the operation.

When the time comes to leave, it is important for the parent to say goodbye, even though this may be upsetting, and to tell the child when to expect the next visit. It is reassuring to leave something for the child to 'mind', such as a scarf or a handkerchief. When preparing to leave, tell a member of the nursing staff so that there is someone to comfort the child if necessary. Departure should be prompt.

In some cases, living in at the hospital may help to reduce the emotional stress of separation and aid recovery, particularly with young children who find it difficult to understand the need for hospitalization

A favourite toy provides comfort to a child who is separated from the family whilst in hospital. *(Royal Alexandra Hospital)*

and separation, and with babies.

Day stay surgery Following a growing re-alization of the importance of reducing the time that a child is separated from his family, most major children's hospitals and units provide day stay surgery. The child is admitted in the morning for the operation and goes home in the afternoon after being checked by his doctor. Experience has shown that most minor procedures can be done on this basis. Not only does it reduce the emotional trauma of hospitalization but there is considerable saving in travel and hospital expenses to parents and less disruption to the family.

Coming home Fortunately, children recover much more quickly than adults; after minor surgery they are often walking and playing the next day. If uncertain, parents should ask their doctor about any advisable limitation of activity and when the child may have a bath.

Children often take time to settle down after a stay in the hospital, particularly young children who may become more babyish and demanding. Even with care and understanding, changes in behavior are common. Nightmares, fear of the dark or a closed door and bed-wetting are all signs of anxiety, but such problems usually subside if parents provide reassurance and security.

A visit to the hospital for treatment, particularly if anesthesia and surgery are involved, will always have some emotional effect on a child. However, with adequate and truthful preparation by parents, doctors and hospital staff and by participation of both parents and brothers and sisters in the hospital experience, the undesirable effects of hospitalization can be minimized.

Intelligence and learning difficulties

Intelligence is defined as the general ability to learn, understand and reason. This is reflected in the way we adapt to different situations and work out a plan of action. The effective use of intelligence requires judgement in evaluating the current physical surroundings and estimating possible results from any intended action, the recollection and application of previous experiences, and imagination.

The ability to reason and think situations out is regarded as the cardinal feature of intelligence that separates man from other species. Many animals can learn specific tasks and modify their behavior in varying circumstances, but this generally appears to develop from 'trial and error', that is learning from previous experience. Only a few of the higher animals appear to be able to work out new situations.

IQ scores are often interpreted as a mental age. (*Zefa*)

Teachers are trained to recognize learning difficulties.

Every person is born with abilities which comprise intelligence, but the development and efficient use of these depends on the social and cultural environment in which a person develops, as well as on the various experiences that occur throughout life.

The relative roles of heredity and environment are still the subject of debate and continuing research.

Intelligence Quotient I.Q. A desire by researchers and psychologists to quantify, measure, and compare people's intelligence necessitated the invention of some way of measuring this elusive quality. In many ways it is like trying to measure pain or love, but, because intelligence can be linked to the performance of specific functions, it was possible to create so-called 'intelligence tests'.

Because the questions are constant, comparison of the performance of different individuals over the same time span is possible.

Many such IQ tests have been created, and those most frequently used are the Stanford-Binet for children, and the Wechsler Adult Intelligence Scale for adults.

These tests involve recognition, rep-etition, rearrangement, and the probing of degree of vocabulary, arithmetic, reasoning, and conceptualisation.

As testing became more sophisticated, and 'norms' were established, the concepts of chronological and mental age were established, and this became the basis of the so-called IQ.

For example, a person whose actual, or chronological, age was twenty, and whose score in the test matched the average for twenty year olds, was said to have a normal IQ. If his score matched the average for ten year olds, then he was said to have a mental age of ten, and was retarded, or had a low IQ.

Conversely, a ten year old whose score approximated the average for twenty year olds, had a mental age of twenty, and consequently, a high IQ.

The IQ was thus defined to be the ratio of the mental age to the chronological age, multiplied by one hundred. A normal, or average, must therefore be one hundred, because if the mental and chronological ages match, the ratio is one, and the score is one hundred. A mental age of forty with a chronological age of twenty gives an IQ of 200.

About half the population have an IQ between 90 and 110. About half a percent has an IQ of 140 or over.

It is important to stress that an IQ is really a measure of capability to learn and perform, and the possession of a 'high IQ', will not in itself, guarantee success in any field without work and application.

Specific learning difficulties Problems experienced by children and adults with specific learning difficulties (SLD) relate particularly to understanding or using the written or spoken word. Reading, writing, spelling, arithmetic, talking and thinking processes may be affected, and often more than one is involved. Sometimes poor attention span, emotional lability, and clumsiness when performing fine motor skills such as using scissors are associated features.

By definition, mental retardation, emotional disturbances, inadequate teaching, difficulties in muscular co-ordination, and auditory or visual handicaps must first be excluded as primary causes of the problem before a diagnosis of SLD can be made.

The incidence of SLD depends upon the specific way in which the condition is defined, although it is generally accepted that about 10 per cent of children probably have some degree of delay in skill attainment in the absence of any detectable cause such as deprivation or mental or physical handicap.

More emphasis has recently been placed upon looking at the specific difficulties and defining them rather than seeking a specific cause. Not only is the

Remedial tuition will help overcome some learning disabilities. (*Zefa*)

latter usually not easy to find, but also historical information such as 'meningitis at the age of one' does not generally indicate what needs to be taught or how to teach it.

Thus learning difficulties tend to be dealt with according to their degree of severity rather than their cause. Individualization of programs for the child within the normal class setting is aimed at wherever possible, as the greater the degree of disruption to the normal educational setting the greater is the difficulty in returning the child to a normal educational environment. When a problem cannot be dealt with adequately in the normal classroom setting, affected children may spend some of the time in a special class, or have a short intensive program under a specialist remedial teacher. It is only the most severely affected child who is taught in a special class for the whole time.

Teachers, especially in primary schools, are learning more about special education as part of their general training, and increasing numbers of full-time specialist remedial teachers are being trained. It is important that teachers are not only able to detect and diagnose SLD,

but also learn to deal with such children successfully through the establishment and implementation of programs of remediation. Continuous evaluation of the child's progress towards attaining the set objectives is also important.

Screening, detection and treatment should ideally begin in kindergarten or in the first year of school when reading or writing is commenced. With appropriate management the vast majority of such disorders can be overcome successfully within one or two years.

Research is continuing into the improvement of detection and treatment techniques as well as that of prevention; although the exact cause is unknown, subtle neurological and hereditary factors are probably involved.

Dyslexia Sometimes called 'word blindness', dyslexia is a condition in which there is a specific difficulty in learning to read, despite an average intelligence and usually adequate teaching. This is often also accompanied by difficulty in writing and spelling correctly.

Dyslexic children may suffer from one of several problems of word expression or interpretation. Letters may be seen as reversed, reading 'b' as 'd' or 'p' as 'q'. This may be reflected in writing difficulties,

Leisure activities give twice the enjoyment when they're shared.

The specific reading difficulty, dyslexia, may be evidenced by a tendency to reverse the sequence of letters in reading.

such as writing some letters back to front (mirror image). Some have difficulty in discriminating between right and left, or mix the order of letters such as reading 'mat' as 'tam'. There may be reduced fine motor control such as in threading a needle or tying a knot. A family history of reading difficulties is not uncommon.

Other problems that may impair a child's ability to learn to read, such as hearing or visual disturbances or emotional difficulties, must first be excluded before a diagnosis of dyslexia can be made. Special reading charts that detect the presence of dyslexia have greatly facilitated its diagnosis.

Up to 5 per cent of children are thought to suffer from dyslexia. Such children are sometimes erroneously labeled as 'slow learners' or lazy. This labeling, combined with an inability to keep pace with other children in the development of reading skills, may lead to behavioral disorders as the child attempts to cope with his frustrations.

Treatment of the disorder is best begun early, and involves individual or small class tuition by an experienced teacher. Parents are encouraged to participate in the program. They play an important role, as does the teacher, in helping the child to maintain or regain a sense of self-worth and to prevent or deal with any tendency to anti-social behavior.

Opposite
Water is a source of amusement for both children and animals.

Because of the variation in difficulties of learning that exist in those with the condition, some experts believe that dyslexia covers a number of abnormalities rather than being a single problem.

Play

By the age of two, although children begin to play together, they actually tend to play side by side but individually. At this age they have not developed sufficient social grace to share their toys with another child and it is unreasonable to expect a child under three to understand the concept of sharing. If a dispute develops over the toys, the best policy, usually, is not to intervene, unless, of course, one of the children is getting hurt, and then the offer of another toy to one or both children will usually resolve the crisis.

The kind of toys and activities that will interest a child at two to four years of age will include large wooden blocks, simple puzzles and building sets; a dinky or similar push-along toys; coloring-books and colored pencils, finger painting or brush painting with water soluble poster paints, under supervision; dolls, puppets and cuddly toys. By now the child should have a toy box and be taught to put the toys away after play. If there is a play room, it

A faithful animal makes a great playmate.

Left
Fantasy is a vivid part of the child's world.

suggested that one hour of selected viewing is sufficient for pre-school children.

Safety

Most children's accidents occur at home between 4 and 6 p.m. on weekdays, and during the weekend. The most dangerous areas are the backyard and the kitchen and the most common accidents are falls, cuts, poisoning, burns and scalds, drowning, and motor vehicle and bicycle injuries.

After the home, the next most frequent sites of children's accidents are the road, the school and playgrounds. Children under the age of five are at greatest risk.

Falls Common causes of falls are bad lighting, slippery floors, worn floor coverings, defective footwear and household articles, and tools and toys left lying about. Young infants, once they become mobile, are particularly liable to fall from one level to another, such as down the stairs or from the crib if they are left with the side of the crib down, or from a bed to a table if left unattended, even for a moment. A baby is safest in a playpen on the floor with mother close by.

Cuts Keep knives, scissors and razor blades where they belong, out of the reach of young children. Use non-glass containers whenever possible, for example milk cartons instead of milk bottles. Sweep up broken glass immediately and wrap it securely before placing it in the garbage bin. Make sure glass doors are clearly marked.

Never allow small children near lawn mowers.

Burns and scalds Scalds are much commoner than burns but flame burns tend to be more serious.

Matches and flammable substances like gasoline, methylated spirits and kerosene are responsible for most flame burns. Keep matches out of the reach of children. Never use flammable liquids on barbecue fires. Do not store gasoline in the house or garage and keep all flammable liquids securely stored in child-resistant closures

Even the daily journey home from school can provide lots of fun.

should have a blackboard or drawing board.

This is the age of swings, jungle gyms and adventure playgrounds, but under supervision.

The two-year-old is usually eager to be told stories. At first, these should be short, no more than five minutes as young children tend not to concentrate for long. The child may want the same favorite story repeated.

Children tend to enjoy fairy stories and stories about animals, and the old favorites, such as the Three Bears, The Three Little Pigs, Red Riding Hood and Cinderella, are always popular.

Between the ages of four and seven children gradually begin to read for themselves. Suitable books have large print and many illustrations; picture-story books, simple non-fiction material and traditional stories are good. Often children will return to a book that has been read to them before so it is a good idea to read books that children can go back to later. But it is also important to read books at a level above the child's reading ability because their level of understanding is more developed. Six and seven year olds devour books; they particularly like stories they can relate to their own experiences.

Television Although children do learn from television, it should not be regarded as a subsitute for formative play. As many programs are unsuitable for children viewing should be selective, and to ensure that the amount of television watched forms a relatively small part of a child's pleasure and play time the parents should impose a time limit. As a useful rule, it is

Care should be taken to store poisonous substances out of the reach of children.

and out of reach of young children.

Household heaters should be properly guarded. Never leave young children unsupervised near an open fire inside or outside the house. Young children should always have track-suit style pyjamas. Nightgowns and long flowing dresses are dangerous.

Never leave your child unattended in a car. Do you know that the cigarette lighter works when the ignition is off? Even if you don't, the child probably does.

To avoid the risk of scalds, always check the temperature of bath water and put in cold water before hot. Never leave a young child unattended in the bathroom, even for a moment.

Turn saucepan handles away from the edge of the stove. Never place cups or pots of hot tea or coffee near the edge of the table. If you have young children in the home, use table mats instead of table cloths.

Poisons Keep household cleaners, detergents, bleaches and pesticides safely out of the reach of young children. Never store them with food and never store them in the cupboard under the sink.

Always keep kerosene or paint cleaners in their original containers. Never store

them in soft drink bottles.

Caustics such as sink and oven cleaners are particularly dangerous. Do not keep them in the house at all if you have young children.

Always put pills and medicines away in a cupboard with a childproof catch immediately after use, and do not keep half empty bottles of medicine and pills once they are no longer required.

Inhaled foreign bodies The most commonly inhaled foreign body is a peanut. Children under five should not be given nuts to eat.

Do not permit your child to play with small objects like beads or nuts and bolts. All little children put things in their mouth and small things can be inhaled.

Water safety Never leave your child alone or unsupervised near water. Small children can drown in very shallow water. Never allow your child to swim alone. Your child should learn to swim but don't let this be a license to drown.

Domestic swimming pools should be surrounded by a childproof fence and self-closing gate. Make sure there is a nonslip surface around the pool and always have something that will float near the pool — a ball, a cushion or a rope. It is safer to throw something that will float to anyone in difficulty rather than jump in to help them.

All members of the family should know how to perform heart massage and mouth to mouth resuscitation.

Electrical safety Have a qualified electrician inspect the electrical system of your home and carry out any recommended repairs.

Fit safety plugs to electrical outlets not in regular use and never permit your child to play with electrical outlets. Turn off electrical outlets when not in use.

Keep cords of toasters, jugs and electrical appliances out of reach of young children and replace frayed cords and broken plugs promptly.

Road safety On the road, motor vehicle and pedestrian accidents are the most common causes of the death of children.

When travelling by car, children should always ride in the back seat and be restrained in a properly designed car seat or harness.

Remember that drinking and driving do not mix. This is doubly important when you are responsible for children as passengers or pedestrians.

Teach children the rules of the road and about traffic lights and pedestrian crossings but do not expect young children to be able to cross roads or cope with traffic on their own. Children under school age require constant supervision.

If you are prepared to let your child have a bicycle, you should be responsible

Riverside beaches look inviting, but
the water can conceal tree-trunks
which make diving dangerous.
(*Royal Alexandra Hospital*)

for seeing he knows how to use and maintain it.

Most bicycle injuries involve children between the ages of five and fourteen years. No child under the age of twelve years should be allowed to ride a bicycle on the road.

Emergency treatment *General.* If your child has suffered an accident, do not give him anything to eat or drink in case he needs an anesthetic.

Most bleeding will stop with direct pressure applied to the bleeding point. Then apply a firm pad and bandage.

All head injuries are potentially serious. Seek urgent medical advice. Do not move a child with a suspected neck or spinal injury.

If a child is unconscious, make sure that the airway is kept clear by turning him face downwards and keeping the chin firmly forwards.

Make sure tetanus immunization is kept up to date.

Cuts and falls. A firm bandage will control most bleeding. A tourniquet is rarely necessary and can be dangerous unless applied expertly.

Seek medical advice without delay for: any cuts or laceration that might require stitching; any loss of movement or function in a limb; continuing pain or swelling; any loss of consciousness; continuing or increasing drowsiness; persistent vomiting; pallor or shock.

Burns and scalds. Wrap the child in a rug, blanket or cape to put out the flame. With a scald, immediately apply plenty of cold water.

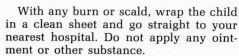

Stairs, matches and fragile toys
with parts small enough
to swallow are all potential
sources of danger to young
children.

With any burn or scald, wrap the child in a clean sheet and go straight to your nearest hospital. Do not apply any ointment or other substance.

Poisoning. Call the Poison Control Center or its corresponding organization immediately for urgent advice. Always keep a bottle of Ipecac syrup in the house to induce vomiting as soon as possible.

If your child has swallowed a caustic like sink or oven cleaner or paint stripper, *do not induce vomiting.* Offer milk or water to drink and take your child straight to the nearest hospital.

If poisoning is suspected, if possible take the container from which your child has taken drugs or poison with you to the hospital.

Inhaled foreign bodies. In the case of very young children, turn the child upside down and slap *gently* but firmly between the shoulder blades to dislodge the article. If a cough and wheeze persist, seek urgent medical advice.

Seizures. A sudden loss of consciousness, with or without convulsions, is known as a seizure. The convulsions may be generalized or localized as a series of jerks, twitches or muscle spasms.

A generalized convulsion in a child or baby is most likely to be present in a feverish illness such as pneumonia, tonsillitis, ear infections, influenza or blood poisoning. The child suddenly becomes very stiff, does not breathe or move and turns a greyish-blue color around the mouth and nose. After half a minute or so the child begins to move the limbs and head in a jerky repetitive way and to breathe again, and normal color returns. After a minute or two the child wakes briefly and then drifts off to sleep. If there is a fever it is important to give acetaminophen to reduce it, and to sponge the child with tepid water to increase the loss of heat through the skin. This will help prevent another fit.

Common Childhood Illnesses and Conditions

A parent may be able to identify one of the common illnesses of childhood if the symptoms are the obvious ones such as skin rash, diarrhea or vomiting, but if the signs are less obvious, for example when the child becomes fretful, listless, and loses interest in food and in play, then the temperature should be checked.

In doing this it is better to place the thermometer in the groin or armpit than in the mouth or rectum. A very easy thermometer to use is the plastic strip type which is simply placed on the child's forehead.

To reduce fever, the child should be sponged all over with lukewarm water, and covered with a light sheet or left completely uncovered if the weather is warm, until his temperature begins to fall. The child should be offered small amounts of water or any clear fluid frequently, and there is no need to worry if the child does not want to eat. An appropriate dose of acetaminophen will often help a child to sleep and will bring down the temperature.

A child should not be given tablets and medicines that have been prescribed for someone else unless it is known exactly

If a small child appears to be feverish an underarm temperature should be taken and checked again every hour if it is over 99°F (37.2°C). *(Royal Alexandra Hospital)*

what they are for and proper advice has been taken. Antibiotics should never be given without medical advice. Medicines and tablets should be kept out of the reach of children; every house in which there are young children should have a child-proof medicine cupboard.

Common infectious diseases

The infectious diseases common in childhood all start with an incubation period during which a child is vaguely unwell, often with a low-grade fever. As it is at this time that the disease is most highly infectious other members of the household should be kept away from the infected child once the diagnosis is obvious, unless they have already suffered from the particular disease. It is always wise to avoid contact with other children during the isolation period.

Chicken pox An infectious viral disease, chicken pox (or varicella) is characterized by fever and the eruption of lesions which appear on the body in crops. A person with chicken pox is infectious from a day or two before the appearance of the rash until six days after the last lesions have appeared. The virus is spread by the respiratory route or by skin contact, and the incubation period is from 10 to 21 days. Before the rash appears, the patient may feel unwell and have a fever for a day or two.

The most commonly affected are children aged five to eight years, although in adults the illness may be more severe. The rash is very itchy and begins as elevated nodules which become filled with fluid and surrounded by a red margin. The redness decreases and the lesions collapse

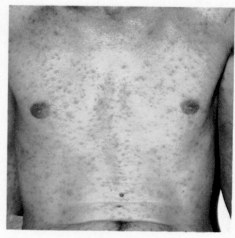

Chicken pox lesions usually appear in concentrated crops on the trunk of the body. *(Westmead Centre)*

to form crusts which then fall off without scarring unless secondary infection occurs. The trunk of the body tends to have the highest concentration of lesions, but they also occur on the face and scalp and occasionally on the eyes, palms, soles and in the mouth.

Complications can occur with this disease. Scratching the lesions may cause secondary infection by bacteria which delays healing and produces scarring. Occasionally the bacteria can spread to the blood causing bacteremia. Pneumonia may develop from one to six days after the rash has started, more commonly in adults than in children. A rare compli-

Vaccination of teenage girls reduces the risk of German measles occurring during a pregnancy.

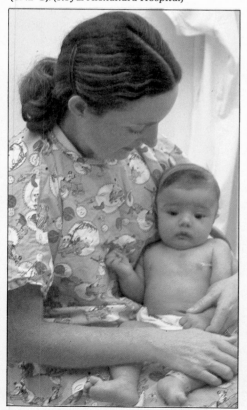

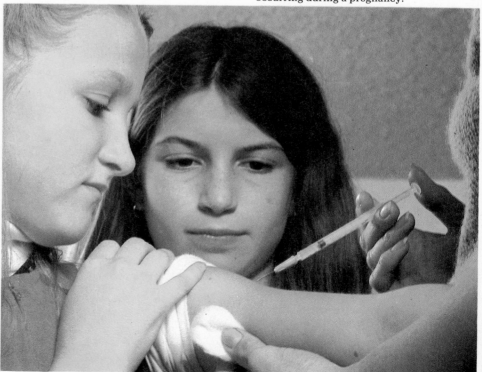

cation, encephalomyelitis (inflammation of the brain and spinal column), which is less common in chicken pox than in measles, begins three to fourteen days after the rash has begun. The patient may feel irritable and drowsy and then experience vomiting, fits and loss of consciousness.

Chicken pox can be prevented by a vaccine, although it is not usually given to healthy children. Patients with uncomplicated chicken pox should be isolated and symptoms are best treated as they arise, with sponging and medication to reduce fever and local soothing applications to the spots to reduce itching.

The varicella virus which causes chicken pox also causes herpes zoster (shingles).

German measles or rubella is a relatively mild infection caused by the rubella virus.

There is usually a two to three week incubation period from the time of exposure to the onset of symptoms. Virus particles are normally present in the throat for one week before and two weeks after the onset of symptoms. Spread of virus is by droplet infection from the mouth.

The main feature is the appearance of a very fine red rash that spreads rapidly from the face to the rest of the body. The other common features of the infection are a mild fever and some enlargement of lymph nodes (or glands), particularly around the neck. Symptoms of general viral infection such as malaise, tiredness, headache, and general aches and pains may precede the rash.

German measles is often called 'three day measles' because symptoms classically only persist for this period and then cause no subsequent problems.

The infection predominantly affects children under 10 years of age. Often the mildness of the rash (which may occasionally be absent) results in the disease being mistaken for a common cold or influenza. It is not very contagious and as a result many children reach adult life without ever contracting the disease.

The fine rash of rubella or German measles. *(Royal Alexandra Hospital)*

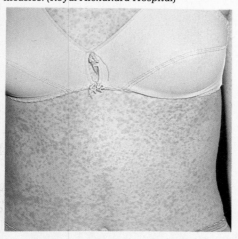

Rubella causes few problems to adults, although they may suffer from temporary arthrytis.

The main danger of German measles is its ability to cause fetal abnormalities should a woman develop the infection during the early stages of pregnancy (particularly the first three months). The relationship between German measles and birth defects was first recorded by an Australian, Dr Norman Gregg, in 1941, when he noted a higher incidence of cataracts (opacities of the lens of the eye) in the babies of mothers who had developed rubella infection early in pregnancy. Deafness, other problems of the eyes, heart abnormalities, and sometimes mental deficiency may occur. The extent and severity of defects varies greatly.

Prevention. The risks of developing German measles have been reduced since the introduction of widespread vaccination of girls in their early teens. This vaccination entails the injection of a live virus preparation that has been modified from the actual rubella virus. Despite this modification, the altered virus may still be able to cause birth defects, so it is never given to women who are pregnant or who are contemplating pregnancy in the subsequent two to three months.

Vaccination is successful in only 95 per cent of cases, so it is desirable for specific antibodies to be measured before pregnancy to ensure that adequate immunity has been achieved. If the levels are high, this will confirm a successful vaccination or proof of a previous infection.

Should a susceptible woman in early pregnancy possibly come in contact with German measles and develop a nonspecific rash plus fever that could be rubella, the antibody levels should be measured immediately and again two weeks later. If there is a significant increase, then the presence of rubella infection in the woman is likely.

Should the presence of rubella infection in early pregnancy be confirmed, the possibility of terminating the pregnancy may be considered, because of the risk of the baby being born with defects.

Measles A viral illness which spreads by the inhalation of droplets from the respiratory tract of an infected person, measles is experienced by many children. One attack of measles produces a high degree of immunity, making it very unusual for a person to have more than one attack in his lifetime. A mother who has had the disease provides partial immunity for her infant for the first six months of its life.

The incubation period (that is, the time from which infection occurs to when symptoms become manifest) is about ten days.

Measles begins in much the same way as a common cold. There is a sudden onset of fever, with nasal blocking and catarrh, sneezing, redness of the eyes, some

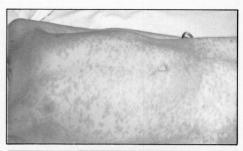

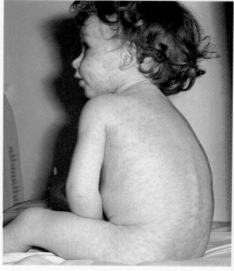

Measles is an infectious viral disease usually transmitted from one person to another in close contact, by droplets from the mouth or nose. *(Salmer)*

swelling of the eyelids and watering of the eyes. In addition, a cough, hoarseness of the voice (laryngitis) and pain on looking at light (photophobia) usually appear by the second day.

At this stage, diagnosis may be made from the presence in the mouth of small white spots surrounded by a narrow zone of redness and inflammation. These are known as Koplik's spots and are numerous on the inside of the cheeks.

The disease is infectious during this stage and the child is miserable and irritable. After three or four days of this cold-like illness, the Koplik's spots disappear, and the dark red, flat (macular) or slightly raised (maculo-papular) skin rash develops.

The rash first appears at the back of the ears and at the junction of the forehead and the hair. Within a few hours it covers all the skin area, and there is usually an increase in fever.

As the spots rapidly become more numerous, they fuse to form the characteristic blotchy appearance of measles. The face is usually the most densely covered area. When the rash has fully erupted in two or three days, it tends to deepen in color and then fade into a faint brown staining. The fever and the feeling of being unwell subside as the rash fades.

Part of the treatment is to isolate the

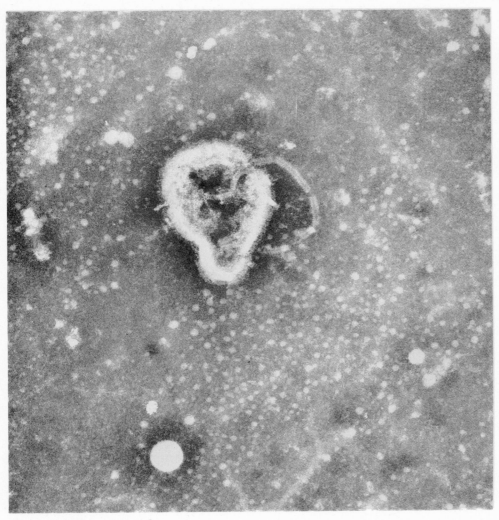

The virus which causes measles, found in nasal secretions. *(Science Photo Library)*

child if possible and keep him away from school for 14 days from the appearance of the rash. Rest, and simple measures such as reducing fever and good nursing care, usually prevent complications.

Immunization against measles is now available and is advised by many doctors. It involves one injection just below the skin surface (subcutaneous) and should be given to children over one year old who have not had the disease. An immunized child may get measles subsequently but it will be only a mild attack.

Complications. Most cases of measles, in spite of the high temperature, remain uncomplicated. However, in a few cases problems do occur.

In young children the commonest complication is convulsions, which occur as the rash is appearing. Pneumonia and secondary infection by bacteria (as opposed to viruses), which sometimes causes a middle ear infection (otitis media), are particularly dangerous in the first eighteen months of life. Persistent conjunctivitis, gastroenteritis and appendicitis may also occur.

Encephalitis (inflammation and infection of the brain tissue) is perhaps the most serious complication. Acute headache and disturbance of consciousness (from mild drowsiness to deep coma) usually occurs early and may sometimes advance dramatically. Various other symptoms may occur, for example weakness of certain nerves, sensory disturbances and epilepsy. With rest, recovery is usual, although certain weaknesses may remain.

Mumps Epidemic parotitis, more commonly called mumps, is an acute, highly infectious viral illness, usually of childhood, which characteristically begins with painful swelling of the parotid salivary glands. First described by Hippocrates in the fifth century B.C., it is caused by a member of the paramyxovirus group. More common in winter and spring, the condition is endemic (constantly present) in most communities.

During an epidemic it has been found that about 40 per cent of people who contract the disease have no symptoms. For those who do become ill, the course follows a common pattern. After two or three weeks incubation there may be moderate fever, muscle pain and headaches,

although most people affected wake with an obvious painful swelling behind one ear as the first symptom of the illness. The swelling continues to enlarge over a period of two to three days, after which the fever subsides. Sometimes there is a secondary appearance of temperature rise, usually denoting either a developing complication or that the gland on the other side is becoming swollen.

During the swelling of the glands, pain is worsened by chewing, and particularly if sour fluids (which stimulate the flow of saliva), are drunk. Occasionally the other salivary glands beneath the jaw (submandibular and sublingual) may also become swollen and painful.

The glands usually subside within a week or so but the condition is considered infectious from seven days before the onset of swelling until nine days after it first appears.

In most cases, the course of the disease is uncomplicated. The possible complications tend to occur in adults rather than young children.

Meningoencephalomyelitis, or mumps meningitis, appears in 10 per cent of patients whose parotid glands are involved. However, two-thirds of all patients with mumps in any form are found to have an infection involving the brain and spinal cord, mostly without symptoms.

1 The symptoms of mumps may include swelling of the parotid glands and swelling and reddening of the parotid duct (located in the lining of the cheek opposite the second upper molar).

2 Glandular swelling and tissue edema distort the features in a severe case of mumps. In the second picture the edema has subsided but glandular swelling is still evident.

1
2

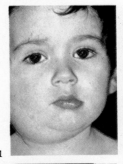
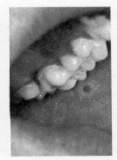
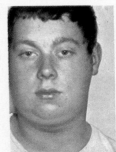
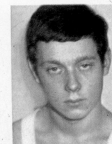

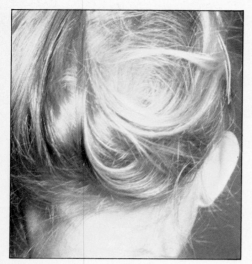

This child with mumps shows prominent swelling on the right side of the neck. *(Royal Alexandra Hospital)*

Usually mild, mumps meningitis very occasionally can be fatal. Initially it develops with a rise in temperature, headache, irritability and vomiting, together with some stiffness of the neck when bending forwards. In the great majority of cases it subsides without any residual problems after a few days.

Orchitis, or swelling of the testicle, is rare before puberty, but up to one-third of all males past this age develop acutely painful swelling of one or both testes. After three or four days the inflammation subsides. Sometimes one testis may end up smaller than the other because of some degree of atrophy. Sterility is unusual, although partial diminution of fertility occurs in about 10 per cent of cases. Complete sterility will not occur unless both testes are inflamed and even then in probably less than 3 per cent of cases. A similar condition affects the ovaries of young women, causing moderately severe lower abdominal pain. Female fertility is not affected.

Pancreatitis, in which the pancreas becomes acutely inflamed, is uncommon. Attacks with gross pain in the upper abdomen, fever and prostration are known but rare. It is possible that sugar diabetes (diabetes mellitus) may follow some of these attacks.

Deafness caused by damage to the auditory or hearing nerve is reasonably rare, but is a not uncommon cause of unilateral (one-sided) deafness found among children.

Other complications can include thyroid, heart and kidney inflammation, arthritis and purpura (bleeding into and bruising of the skin and tissues). The eyes may also be damaged in various ways. In early pregnancy the possibility of miscarriage is increased, but there is no firm evidence that mumps damages the growing embryo.

Not all swellings of the parotid glands are necessarily caused by mumps, as certain other viruses (parainfluenza and Cocksackie) can produce similar symptoms. Repeated swelling of these glands may occasionally be caused by allergies or stones in the canals of the glands, leading ultimately to infection.

Treatment is not needed for the simple uncomplicated attack of mumps, beyond avoiding sour foods and fluids and food requiring hard chewing. Cortisone-like drugs may limit the pain and swelling of testicular inflammation, although local heat, pain relievers and adequate support for the affected testis will probably give as much benefit.

Prevention. One attack of mumps generally produces lifelong immunity against further attacks. It is now possible to immunize against mumps, as a vaccine (given at fifteen months of age) is now available in some countries. If there is any doubt about whether a person has had a previous attack of mumps or if it is necessary to determine whether the vaccine has produced adequate immunity, a skin test can be carried out to check this. Levels of immunity also can be checked by blood testing.

Scarlet fever A bacterial infection caused by *Streptococcus pyogenes*, scarlet fever (also known as scarlatina) occurs most commonly in children between the ages of 3 and 10. The condition is much less common in adults, most likely because of increased resistance to the bacteria as a result of previous exposure.

The bacteria most commonly become established in the tonsils or throat, although sometimes a skin wound or burn is the initial area of infection. About four days later there is sudden development of a high fever, often to 104°F (40°C), and a sore throat. Soon after, most people develop a headache, malaise and various gastrointestinal symptoms. In adults the main symptoms are pharyngitis and tonsillitis, with only minimal generalized malaise and rash.

Up to five days after the onset of symptoms, a generalized fine scarlet rash occurs over the body. It begins on the neck and upper part of the trunk, and then extends downwards. Although all parts of the skin may redden or 'blush' from the time of the fever, the rash itself does not involve the face, and a pallor around the edge of the lips (circumoral pallor) is usually prominent. The spots soon begin to fade, but there is a peeling of the skin about a week later, the hands and feet being most prominently affected.

A so-called erythrogenic toxin released by the bacteria is responsible for most of the symptoms. Dilation (widening) of capillaries just under the skin causes the 'blushing', which classically blanches with pressure. Small hemorrhages into the skin (petechiae) may also occur

although these lesions do not lighten on pressure.

Other physical symptoms include enlargement of the lymph nodes of the neck, redness of the tonsils and throat, often with an associated exudate (accumulation of fluid), and white spots within the mouth where the surface cells are peeling, as well as changes in the tongue. Early in the condition the tongue appears as a 'white strawberry' as it becomes coated, leaving the papillae reddened. Later these papillae become more swollen and the coating peels away to give the classic 'red strawberry' appearance.

This condition is much milder and less prevalent today than earlier in the century, with most children returning to good health within a week. Complications such as otitis media (inflammation in the middle ear cavity), rheumatic fever, and post-streptococcal glomerulonephritis are today quite rare.

Penicillin most rapidly relieves the symptoms, and for anyone allergic to penicillin, erythromycin is generally used.

Whooping cough Pertussis or whooping cough is a highly infectious disease in which paroxysms of coughing end in a noisy indrawing of breath which sounds like a whoop. It is caused by the bacillus *Bordetella pertussis*. About 90 per cent of those affected are children under the age of five years.

Whooping cough is spread by droplets of moisture in the air breathed out by an infected person or one who is unknowingly incubating the disease. The incubation period is from seven to fourteen days.

A runny nose, slightly reddish eyes and a cough are the first symptoms. After a week, typical paroxysms of coughing begin. These are more frequent at night with a succession of progressively more rapid short sharp coughs followed by a deep inward breath when the whoop can be heard. During the paroxysm, the child's face becomes red and sometimes bluish, the eyes bulge and the tongue sticks out. Sticky phlegm may be spat up and often vomiting occurs. The paroxysms may occur as often as 40 times a day or only occasionally. This stage continues for one or several weeks and gradually decreases with paroxysms becoming less frequent.

Whooping cough is often accompanied by pressure effects from coughing such as hemorrhage around the eyes or prolapse of the rectum. Although uncomfortable, these conditions are not really serious and the affected person usually recovers without treatment. Pneumonia, lung collapse and repeated convulsions are more serious complications. Even without complications a child with whooping cough may become debilitated and undernourished and can be ill for six to eight weeks or longer.

Severe cases of whooping cough, es-

Common infectious diseases

DISEASE	INCUBATION	INFECTIOUS PERIOD	EXCLUSION FROM SCHOOL
Chicken pox	14–16 days	From about 24 hours before the spots appear until they are converted to scabs.	For 7 days or until all the spots have turned to scabs. Some schools do not permit children to return until all the scabs have fallen off.
German measles (Rubella)	14–21 days	From the start of symptoms, usually 1–2 days before the rash appears.	For 7 days from appearance of rash. Avoid contact with pregnant women.
Measles	10–15 days	From the start of symptoms, usually 3–4 days before the rash appears.	For 10 days from appearance of rash.
Mumps	18–21 days	From the start of symptoms, usually 1–2 days before the swelling appears.	Until swelling subsides, usually about 10 days.
Whooping cough	7–10 days	From the start of symptoms, usually the cough.	For 28 days from the start of symptoms.

pecially in children under two years of age, should be treated in the hospital where meticulous nursing care, small frequent feedings and, if necessary, oxygen, can be administered. Antibiotics are usually given only when pneumonia or other infections are present. Sometimes cough mixtures are given to suppress the cough. Immunization of children is desirable, starting at two or three months of age with the first of three monthly injections. If an immunized child gets whooping cough the attack will be very mild. Children exposed to the disease who are not immunized can have an injection of concentrated hyperimmune serum from a person who has recently had whooping cough.

Although the vaccine sometimes causes a reaction with a mild fever, fractiousness, and loss of appetite the night and day after the injection, this is preferable to the severe debilitating illness which can be fatal, especially in children under a year old. Furthermore, when the disease is at its most infectious during the first stage of the illness, it is very difficult to diagnose, and the infected child may therefore not be isolated until it has infected many others, causing an epidemic.

Immunization It is important that all children should be immunized against the serious infectious diseases of childhood. For example, diphtheria and poliomyelitis (infantile paralysis) had been almost eradicated, but because some parents neglected to have their children immunized, diphtheria is now beginning to appear again more frequently.

Diphtheria, whooping cough and tetanus can be prevented by administering triple antigen in three injections given at two months, four months and six months of age. A further injection of triple antigen should be given as a booster at 18 months, and when the child reaches the age of about five to six a further booster of combined toxoid against diphtheria and tetanus should be given. Children who have been immunized against tetanus should still be given an injection of tetanus toxoid after any significant laceration or burn.

Poliomyelitis can be prevented by administering Sabin vaccine by mouth. This is given at two months, four months and six months of age, when the baby receives the triple antigen, and a booster should be given at five to six years of age.

Measles vaccination should be given at about 15 months of age, and all girls should be immunized against German measles at 12 to 14 years.

Smallpox vaccination is no longer recommended, even when going overseas, as the disease has now been eradicated, except in a very few isolated communities.

Ear problems

Acute ear infections are common in children up to about the age of eight years. Infants will be feverish and irritable and often pull at their ears or rub them, while older children who are affected may complain of earache, particularly at night, and experience fever and loss of appetite.

Such infections are sometimes caused by contamination in a swimming pool. Whatever the cause, the treatment of the infection should be determined by a doctor who will usually prescribe a suitable antibiotic.

Sometimes the drum will perforate and the ear will discharge, and if this persists there may be progressive loss of hearing.

Secretory otitis media ("glue ear") is a condition which most commonly affects children between the ages of three and six. It occurs when there is an accumulation of thick fluid in the middle ear, which causes earache and partial loss of hearing.

The treatment requires the services of an ear, nose and throat specialist who will drain away the fluid through a tiny plastic tube which is inserted into the ear drum.

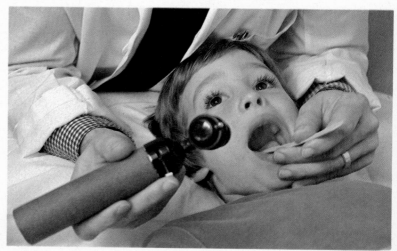

Inflammation of the middle ear, otitis media, may occur in conjunction with tonsillitis.

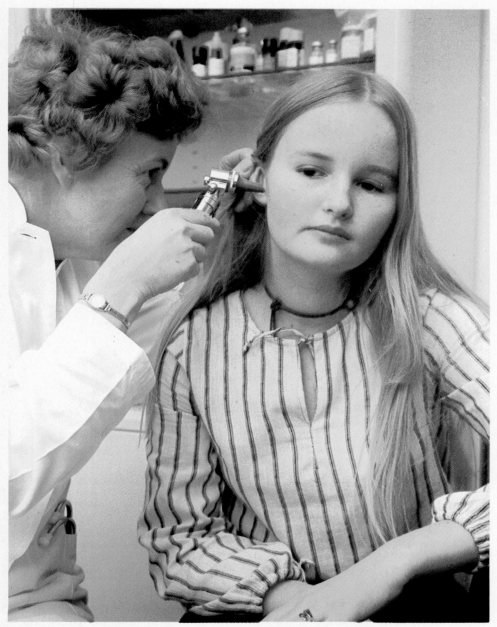

Middle ear disease must be treated
carefully to avoid the risk of
complications. *(PAF International)*

ear (mastoid). There is a discharge from
the ear, which changes from a mucousy
colour to thick and yellow. The treatment
depends on whether the infection is detected early, whether the middle ear drum
is bulging, or whether it is discharging
fluid.

A mother who suspects that her child
has a middle ear infection, should consult
her local doctor or hospital immediately.
In the early stage of the condition antibiotics are used to control the infection,
and analgesics such as aspirin are given to
control pain. It is also sometimes useful to
give a decongestant to promote eustachian drainage and prevent the ear-drum
from bursting.

If treatment has been administered
early and antibiotics given in an adequate
dosage and for sufficient time, most cases
resolve and hearing returns to normal. If
a child has had one bout of otitis media,
subsequent colds which may give rise to
another attack should be treated promptly.

Occasionally the pain and temperature
subside but discharge and deafness persist. This may indicate that there is still an
infection in the nose. Occasionally there
may be a low grade infection in the
middle ear and the mastoid cells. A mixed
bacterial infection is now present. As the
damage to the middle ear increases, so
does the degree of conductive deafness.

Antibiotics may eradicate the infection.
The general state of health must be improved by diet and exercise, and special
cleaning of the ear must be carried out
two or three times a day. Surgery is indicated only when conservative measures
have failed.

Glue ear is not always preceded by an
episode of acute otitis media, and the
exact cause of the condition is uncertain.
Middle ear disease Inflammation of the
middle ear, caused by bacteria, is known
as otitis media.

It occurs most commonly in children
when infection travels from the tonsils, or
adenoids and sinuses, up the eustachian
tube at the back of the nose to the middle
ear. In many children the eustachian tube
is almost horizontal and it is thought that
this enables organisms to reach the
middle ear very readily. The eustachian
tubes in a child are also relatively shorter
and wider when compared with those of
an adult providing the bacterial organisms
easy access to the middle ear.

The most common causes of otitis
media are acute tonsillitis, common cold,
influenza, or early measles. It begins by
the bacteria invading the membrane of
the middle ear (the eardrum). This causes
redness, edema and profuse exudate. The
edema prevents drainage through the
eustachian tube. The pressure in the
middle ear increases until the ear drum
bursts, and discharge continues to escape
through the perforation until the infection
is cleared up.

There is earache, which is usually severe
and throbbing. A young child may cry and
scream for hours until it falls into a fitful
sleep in a state of exhaustion. Deafness
and ringing in the ears are also symptoms,
and in an adult these may be the first complaints.

The child is flushed and often has a high
temperature. There is usually some tenderness on the bony point just behind the

Otitis externa Inflammation of the skin
lining the external ear, caused by bacteria
or fungus, is known as otitis externa.

Certain people are predisposed to otitis
externa, especially those with a tendency
to eczema. For these people, failure to dry
the ear after washing or swimming causes
the problem. Damage also occurs if there
is excessive drying with a towel. Scratching with a fingernail can also damage the
ear and introduce new organisms, setting
up a vicious circle as the bacteria causes
itching. Otitis externa occasionally occurs
in the case of ear syringing.

Symptoms include irritation of the ear,
with a slight, clear discharge. A moderate
amount of pain occurs which is increased
by jaw movement. Slight deafness may
also be present. There is tenderness on
pressure to the area and there is moist
debris which, when removed, shows the

underlying skin to be red, raw and edematous.

Treatment consists of meticulous removal of every particle of debris in the ear. A medicated dressing, with an antibiotic and fungicide combined, is then inserted and left in place for 24 hours. It should be renewed daily until the skin has returned to normal. In mild cases, no dressing is necessary and the use of ear drops will allow free drainage and assist the skin in returning to normal.

Wax, which is produced by the ear canal, sometimes accumulates and interferes with the hearing. Usually it can be removed with the corner of a handkerchief or a cotton swab used carefully. A bobby pin or match, which may damage the delicate lining of the ear, must never be used. If the wax is difficult to remove, a doctor should be consulted as the ear can easily be syringed clear.

Eye conditions

Conjunctivitis In older children, redness and discharge from the eyes is usually the result of conjunctivitis which is most commonly caused by a germ, sometimes contracted from contaminated swimming pools. A doctor will usually prescribe bathing and antibiotic eye drops.

Discharge or persistent watering If babies have a persistent watering or discharge from one or both eyes it is usually due to blockage of the tear duct. Some cases will respond to massage over the tear sac, and a doctor can easily demonstrate how to do this. If it persists for several months a minor operation to probe the tear ducts clear may be necessary.

Foreign body Sometimes a red, irritable eye is due to a small foreign body lodged on the surface of the eyeball. The parent should take the child to the doctor rather than attempt to remove the foreign body.

Squint Many infants appear to be cross-eyed, particularly the child that has a broad, flat bridge to the nose. Also, it takes some time for babies to learn to co-ordinate their eyes so that they move together. If there is any doubt, it is wise to seek early advice from a doctor. If a crossed eye is neglected the squint may become worse.

Eye movements are controlled by six muscles within each orbit or eye socket, which are in turn regulated by three different cranial nerves. Interconnecting nerve pathways within the brain ensure that pupil size, lens shape and eye movements all occur in synchrony on each side. A squint may be classified as paralytic or non-paralytic.

Paralytic squint. In this type of squint there is an abnormality in one of the muscles or one of the nerves; as a result the muscle either functions poorly or is paralysed. Most paralytic squints are present at birth, although head injuries, tumors, infections and other conditions

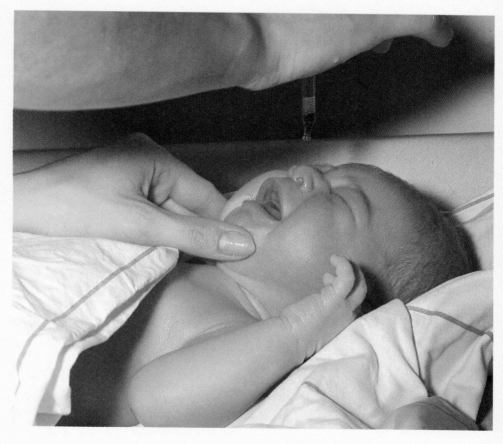

may be repsonsible for their development in later life.

Non-paralytic squint. Whereas a paralytic squint becomes marked when the gaze is in the direction of the affected muscle, a non-paralytic squint tends to have a degree of malalignment. Inadequate development of eye co-ordination and accommodation (the alteration of the lens shape to allow precise focusing of the image onto the retina) is often responsible for non-paralytic squint; however, other abnormalities such as a cataract, corneal scarring and retinal disorders need first to be excluded as causes. In such circumstances there is no stimulus to keep the eyes straight because double vision is not registered, resulting in a squint.

Complications. Vision is normally very poor at birth and develops over the first four years of life. Part of this development relates to the visual cortex, the part of the brain responsible for co-ordinating visual and other input. By this mechanism the two separate images for each eye are fused to form a single picture. Even when both eyes are in perfect alignment, each one has a slightly different view of an object. This can be demonstrated by alternately closing one eye and then the other, and noting changes in the relative positions of various objects within the field of vision.

When a squint occurs, the two images are too dissimilar to integrate and as a result, *diplopia* or double vision occurs. If

Treatment such as the application of eye drops may be necessary for minor infections. *(Salmer)*

the condition is not treated, the image of the weaker eye tends to be suppressed and lack of vision develops on that side.

The aim of treatment is to prevent such a loss of vision (amblyopia) from occurring and to enable binocular vision to be established. This is the coordinated use of both eyes that results in a fusion of the separate retinal images, allowing visual depth to be discerned and accurate judgement of distances to develop.

Surgery is usually required to correct paralytic squints although different forms of treatment are generally successful in the other cases. Once specific diseases have been excluded, the sound eye may be covered to encourage the squinting eye to take over. Glasses may be used to correct any error of refraction, the most common being hypermetropia (long-sightedness). When the visual acuity in the amblyopic or squinting eye has improved sufficiently, orthoptic exercises may be commenced to help in the attainment of binocular (stereoscopic) vision.

Medical assessment should be sought for any recurrent or persistent malalignment of a child's eyes.

Stye A small boil at the base of an eyelash, a stye may be caused by bacterial infection. Bathing with warm water and the use of a local antibiotic ointment usually clears it up quickly.

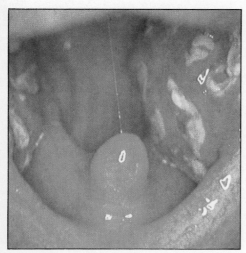

Inflammation of the tonsils may
lead to their having to be removed.
(Royal Alexandra Hospital)

Mouth and throat conditions

Enlarged adenoids Sometimes the adenoids become enlarged because of infection and obstruct breathing, leading to snoring and a tendency to breathe through the mouth. If they block the auditory tube the eardrums may be affected and so the child's hearing.

Usually the child naturally grows out of enlargement of the adenoids, but in some cases the condition is severe enough to justify their removal.

Tooth problems For various reasons, the permanent teeth sometimes come through in incorrect positions. Sometimes, there is a gap between the central incisors. Sometimes the teeth overlap and, not infrequently, the third permanent molars or wisdom teeth come through on the skew. Such a tooth is known as an impacted wisdom tooth and usually ultimately requires removal.

Sometimes the upper teeth do not bite correctly against the lower teeth or they project prominently to form so-called buck teeth.

Regular dental check-ups are
recommended after the age of four.

These abnormalities in eruption of the permanent teeth can be corrected by appropriate braces. A dentist will advise about this and will refer the patient to an orthodontist at the appropriate time.

It should be understood that the tooth buds start to form by about the sixth month of pregnancy. The quality of the teeth will be very much influenced by the expectant mother's diet. It is important that the mother should take plenty of milk, meat, fresh fruit and vegetables at this time so that there will be an adequate intake of vitamins, calcium and phosphorus.

The baby's permanent tooth buds begin forming very soon after birth, although the first permanent teeth do not break through for some years. Children normally get plenty of calcium, phosphorus and vitamins in the milk supply whether they are breast-fed or artificially-fed, but any major illness, particularly if it interferes with the child's nutrition, can affect the development of the permanent teeth.

Some parents think that the milk teeth are unimportant and that it does not matter if they decay. This is not so. It is important to retain the milk teeth in good condition until the permanent teeth start to erupt in their correct positions.

In order to reduce the likelihood of dental decay, a child should be encouraged to avoid foods containing sugar, especially sticky sweets.

For snacks between meals a child should be encouraged to eat fresh or dried fruits and drink unsweetened fruit juices. If the child wants something to chew, raw celery or carrots or cheese are better than chips or sweets.

The child should always clean the teeth after meals, particularly if any sweet or sugary items have been served.

Children are great imitators, especially of their parents, and by the age of two they usually want to clean their own teeth like their parents. However, this habit can start before the growth of teeth, using a soft tooth brush and once the child has its first few teeth, a piece of apple to chew at the end of the meal will help clean them.

Even when a child wants to clean its own teeth, it should be remembered that before the age of five or six children do not develop sufficient coordination to enable them to clean their teeth properly. They should be allowed to try, but the parent should always check the child's teeth and clean them again.

By the age of four a child should be examined by a dentist to check that the teeth are coming through evenly and that the bite is normal.

Tonsillitis is an inflammation of the tonsils usually caused by a germ. The child with tonsillitis usually has a high fever and feels sick, has difficulty in swallowing, and may experience headaches and vomiting. The glands in the neck often become swollen and tender.

Treatment with a suitable antibiotic is often required to overcome the infection. The symptoms can be relieved by the use of moderately hot throat washes and gargles.

The tonsils, which help to build up immunity to various diseases, very occasionally become infected and need to be surgically removed, though this is uncommon and rarely happens before the age of seven or eight years.

Physical problems

Bow leg or *genu varum* is an outward bending of the knee. Although the condition is common to a mild degree in children up to three years of age, in the vast majority there is no underlying disease and no treatment is needed; the abnormal bending disappears spontaneously.

More severe or persistent examples may be due to injury or disease, for example a mal-united fracture of the bones just above or below the knee, or bone-softening diseases such as rickets or Paget's disease.

Flat foot If either or both of the arches of the foot flatten out, the condition is known as flat foot.

When a person stands normally, the inner border of the foot is raised off the ground to form a lengthwise arch while the outer border rests on the ground. Another arch lies across the foot under the heads of the bones nearest to the toes (metatarsal bones). The arches of the foot act as shock absorbers when the foot bears the body weight, and give spring to the act of stepping.

Flat foot or loss of one or both of the arches of the foot occurs in children and adults. It is so common as to be almost

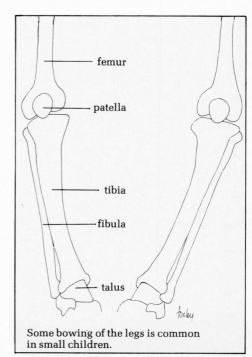

femur

patella

tibia

fibula

talus

Some bowing of the legs is common
in small children.

normal, but it may be caused by an abnormality of the leg muscles caused by poliomyelitis. The ankle turns in so that the inner edge of the heel and sole of the shoe become worn. If the condition is very pronounced in children, the inner border of the upper shoe may get scuffed.

As flat feet frequently cause no pain and seem to right themselves as the child grows older, no treatment is required. Sometimes, however, intensive exercises with a physical therapist are recommended for children when the feet are particularly flat. Some children appear to walk a great deal better with special shoes and arch supports.

It is doubtful if either of these treatments improve flat feet. In any event, even if flat feet persist through adult life they usually cause no pain or trouble. If an adult has flat feet which ache after long walks or when standing for lengthy

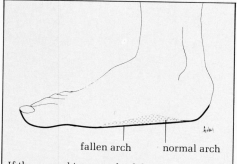

If the normal inner arch of the foot is not apparent and the sole of the foot rests flat, the condition is known as flat foot. (*Westmead Centre*)

fallen arch   normal arch

periods, it may be advisable to wear special supportive shoes if these relieve the symptoms.

Retractile testes The cremasteric reflex is one of many tests used to evaluate the adequacy of the nervous system affecting withdrawal of the testes. The test is performed by stroking the skin of the lower abdomen from the base of the penis upwards and outwards. When the test is positive the cremaster muscle contracts, twitching the overlying skin and momentarily retracting the testis up on that side. A retractile testis may also be activated by cold, emotional stress or by gentle handling of the scrotum; it is particularly active in the very young.

The testis may be drawn completely into the inguinal canal in the groin, often remaining there for prolonged periods if the stimulus, such as cold, continues. Because of this many boys with excessively retractile testes are wrongly diagnosed as being cryptorchid (having undescended testicles).

The condition may be distinguished by asking the child to squat. If the testes are normal they will descend into the scrotum. If held firmly between two fingers at that point, they should not pull upwards into the inguinal canal when the child stands up. Conversely, the testes will normally both descend into the scrotum when the child has been sitting for a few minutes in a hot bath. For the worried parent, a medical examination will usually resolve the problem.

Respiratory illnesses

Illnesses which involve the lungs and respiratory tract range from those that are mild enough to treat at home without ex-

Left
Flat feet tend to improve as children grow older.

pert medical supervision to those of far greater severity which may require hospital treatment.

Asthma An allergy to certain substances is undoubtedly important in some cases of asthma, but it is often difficult to define the specific substance that is responsible for the illness. Moreover, although some children are allergic to certain foods this will only cause skin rashes or diarrhea. For an allergen to cause asthma it must be inhaled into the lungs.

The most common symptom of asthma is a severe shortness of breath.

The illness is much more common in children than in adults, and boys are affected more frequently than girls. Fortunately, most children who suffer from asthma grow out of it as they grow older. In general, allergy injections are not of much help for childhood asthma.

Bronchitis An inflammation of the bronchial tubes, bronchitis is caused by a viral infection.

The major feature of bronchitis is a cough which at first is usually dry and rasping but after a few days may become loose and rattling. The child also usually has a fever, may complain of some tightness and discomfort in the chest, and is generally more unwell than in the case of a simple cold. If a child has recurrent bouts of bronchitis, particularly if it is associated with wheezing, then asthma may be the underlying cause.

The treatment for bronchitis includes rest, a constant room temperature and humidity, drinking fluids, and perhaps antibiotics prescribed by a doctor to prevent secondary infection.

The oxygen tent can be a valuable aid in relieving respiratory problems. (*Royal Alexandra Hospital*)

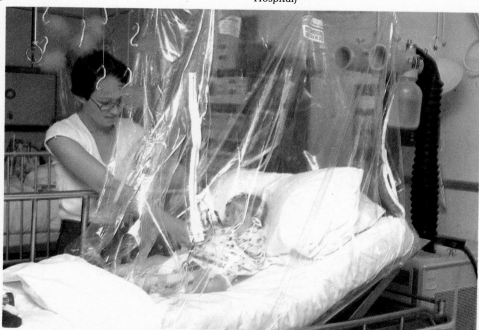

Various breathing tests help to assess the condition of the child with respiratory illness. This child is breathing into a spirometer which will test how effectively she can breathe out. (*Royal Alexandra Hospital*)

Coughs and colds More than half the illnesses in young children are the result of the common cold, which is caused by a virus. Antibiotics have no effect on viruses and should not be used; fortunately the body naturally overcomes the viruses within a few days.

Colds and coughs are spread from one child to another by coughing and sneezing, which is why children so commonly get colds and bronchitis when they first go to school and mix with other children.

When a cough is troublesome, a cough syrup may help the child to sleep at night. If a child seems to suffer from an excessive number of coughs and colds a doctor should be consulted.

Croup is caused by a spasm of the larynx which gives rise to a sudden attack of noisy breathing, usually at night. In the common type of croup the child is not usually very sick and the noisy breathing

Croup is an inflammation of the air passages including some obstruction of the larynx, which causes breathing difficulty and a barking cough. (*Westmead Centre*)

pharynx

obstruction

trachea

bronchus

lung

can be easily treated by steam inhalation. A simple way to achieve a steamy atmosphere is to close the bathroom door and window and let the hot tap run for a while. Always stay with the child, both for reassurance and to avoid accidents.

Some cases of croup are more severe, and if the noisy breathing becomes worse in spite of the simple treatment outlined above, or if the child is obviously becoming sicker, a doctor should be called without delay or the child taken to the nearest hospital.

Skin problems

There are a variety of minor skin rashes in the first few months of a child's life. Some of the commonest are fine, white, pearl-like pimples on the face and small red spots on the cheek and neck. Some infants, if the skin is a little dry, develop rough, red patches on the cheeks.

Vigorous sucking sometimes produces little white blisters or loose skin in the center of the lips. Many babies have salmon-pink marks on their upper eyelids, on the center of the forehead and on the nape of the neck. None of these are of any significance and they all disappear completely within the first few months of life.

Birth marks Medically termed a *nevus*, a so-called 'birth' mark is not necessarily apparent at birth but may appear during the first few months of life. There are two main groups of nevi: vascular, which are due to an overgrowth of the blood vessels; and non-vascular, which are due to an overgrowth of the connective tissues.

Vascular nevi may be subdivided into three main varieties.

The simple flat type is commonly seen on the back of the neck or the bridge of the nose in young babies. Most of this type disappear spontaneously within a few months.

The port wine stain (*Naevus flammeus*) which is always flat and may be widespread, is quite common and does not always respond well to treatment.

It appears as a bluish-red patch that resembles port wine in color and several may be present together.

Port wine stains occur most commonly on the face, and tend to enlarge in the first few years of life. The appearance, plus the enlargement of these lesions, is often an embarrassment to the child affected and to the parents. Usually significant regression occurs, and this is completed before puberty. The eventual appearance depends largely on the size of the port wine stain at birth.

In previous years, low dose x-rays were applied to the stain in an attempt to shrink the abnormal blood vessels. Results were generally unsatisfactory and such treatment is not used today.

Usually port wine stains are left alone to allow natural regression to occur, which provides the best result. Surgical removal is seldom required. Various cosmetic pow-

ders and creams that blend in excellently with the surrounding skin are often used.

The strawberry mark (*Naevus vascularis*) is perhaps the best known birth mark; it is raised, bright red and often lobulated resembling a strawberry, and can occur on any part of the body. Strawberry marks often disappear with age and generally require no treatment.

Non-vascular nevi include a group of pigmented moles (*Naevus pigmentosus*). A mole consists of a deposit of pigment in a circumscribed area. It may occur alone or with hairs and/or an overgrowth of connective tissue.

Naevus spilus is a smooth flat nevus without hair, *Naevus pilosus* is a pigmented mole covered with soft, downy or stiff hairs, and *Naevus verrucosus* is a pigmented nevus with a warty surface. *Naevus linearis* is a pigmented warty nevus which is arranged in patches or streaks and *Naevus linearis comedonicus* is one associated with blackheads (comedones).

Flat moles need not be removed unless they are in an area which is subjected to injury, such as on the waistline where there is constant friction from a belt or waistband. Elevated moles may be removed. If a mole is very dark in color or changes in any way, either in color or by bleeding or growing larger, medical attention should be sought without delay.

Cradlecap, which is quite common in early infancy, is caused by oily secretions from the scalp, and is best treated by washing daily with a mild soap and water followed by a little baby oil.

In hot weather some babies develop clusters of small pink pimples surrounded by red blotches on the neck and upper part of the chest and back. This is usually due to using warm woolly clothing in hot weather, so a parent should not be afraid to dress the child in light clothes during the summer.

Chronic eczema may cause rashes on the arms and legs. (*Westmead Centre*)

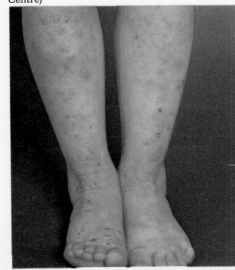

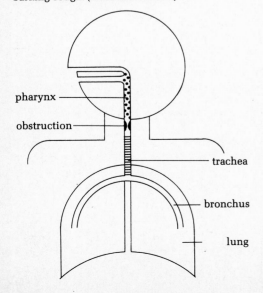

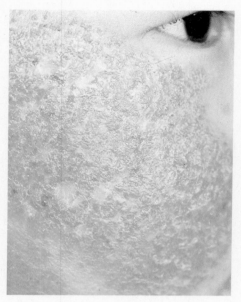

Infantile eczema commonly occurs on the cheeks. *(Royal Alexandra Hospital)*

Some babies will develop red areas on the neck or in the armpits and groins if care is not taken to dry these areas after bathing and to apply a mild dusting powder.

Eczema A word derived from the Greek, meaning to boil out, eczema is an inflammatory condition of the skin. Initially the skin is red and itchy with oozing blistery lesions, but later it becomes scaly, crusted or hardened. Because the eczema rash appears without much outside provocation, it is usually distinguished from dermatitis in which the skin reacts to an external irritant.

Usually appearing in the second three months of life, *atopic eczema* initially affects the face. By the third year, half those affected will have recovered. If it persists, the skin behind the knees, in front of the elbows, around the wrists and ankles and behind the ears is affected. In adolescence the eczema may spread to the face, neck and trunk or it may persist to the age of 30 as a dermatitis of the hands or feet.

Hay fever and asthma often occur with atopic eczema. About 3 per cent of infants have this form of eczema. In 70 per cent of these, there is a family history of these related diseases. These patients produce excessive antibodies and often react badly to insect bites. Although the importance of psychological causes is controversial, emotional upsets can cause a flare-up of eczema. The skin readily becomes itchy and may be sensitive to wool, nylon or satin. The skin may be red, oozy and scaly with some thickening from continual scratching.

Itching may be eased by an antihistamine. A sedative may be useful at night when the itching is worse. Rough material like wool should not be worn next to the skin. Excessive soap and other irritants should be avoided.

It is important to seek medical attention since treatment may be prolonged and recurrence is common.

Impetigo Commonly known as 'school sores', impetigo is a contagious infection of the skin caused by staphylococci or streptococci bacteria.

Impetigo is more common in childhood. It is spread by direct contact with infected skin, so that exposed areas such as the hands, arms and face are most likely to be affected. In Britain, its high prevalence in boys' schools where rugby is played (because of the greater body contact than in other forms of sport) resulted in impetigo sometimes being called 'scrum pox' or 'football itch'.

The condition begins with the appearance of small blisters which rapidly become filled with pus and then break. Hard yellow scabs or crusts soon develop on the surface.

Impetigo

1 Small blisters appear first.
2 Blisters discharge pus.
3 Pus-filled eruptions spread and scabs form.
4 Infection spread by scratching.

Young children are particularly vulnerable to impetigo infecting the skin. *(Royal Alexandra Hospital)*

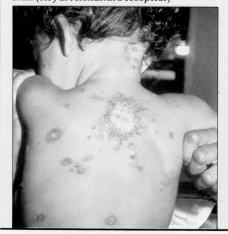

Infection may invade previously healthy skin, or enter through a minor injury, or develop in an area of inflamed skin as in dermatitis or eczema. The degree of spread depends both on the virulence (infecting ability) of the bacteria, and the general health and resistance of the individual affected.

Because impetigo is more common among young children, it is thought that they have a lower resistance to it. People with diabetes mellitus may also be more susceptible to impetigo. When babies are infected, the condition is often more severe and blisters or bullae are a more prominent feature (bullous impetigo).

Treatment involves both the use of local applications of topical antibiotic creams and sometimes antibiotics by mouth.

Some doctors recommend the removal of very thick scabs to increase the effectiveness of antibiotic creams. A well-tried method of scab removal involves the use of a simple starch poultice. The poultice is applied to the affected area, left to dry and then removed, taking with it most of the scabs. Paraffin solutions can hasten softening of the crusts or scabs, and weak Condy's crystals solution and various antiseptic creams may both soften scabs and destroy some of the bacteria.

Many cases respond to the immediate application of specific antibiotic creams or ointments used several times a day. Antibiotic tablets or injections are sometimes used in more widespread cases.

The lesions of impetigo are contagious and affected school children are therefore required to stay at home until the sores are fully healed.

Diaper rash Most babies develop diaper rash from time to time. It is most commonly caused by the continuous contact of tender skin with a wet diaper.

Ammonia dermatitis is the most common kind of diaper rash. It starts around the genitals rather than the anus and there is often a strong smell of ammonia in the diaper, particularly one worn overnight. At first the skin is red and spotty, becoming wrinkled and peeling. Ulcers may form.

The extreme inflammation of diaper rash shown here is caused by ammonia in the urine. *(Westmead Center)*

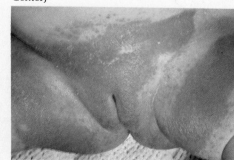

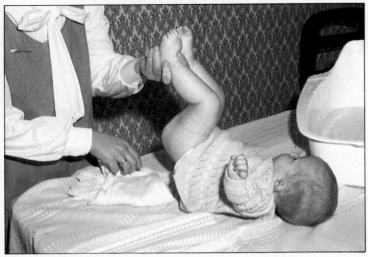

Wet diapers should always be changed promptly to avoid skin irritation. (*Westmead Center*)

If left untreated, ammonia dermatitis can spread all over the diaper area, groin and lower abdomen.

Diaper rash caused by thrush. If a baby gets oral thrush, the infection caused by the fungus *Candida albicans*, this can produce a rash around the anus, as the stools contain the thrush fungus.

Seborrheic dermatitis. Diaper rash is occasionally caused by seborrhea, the brownish dandruff that babies tend to get on the scalp. This may spread to other areas causing an extensive rash, brownish-red in color. The rash may be found in the groin and on the genitals and buttocks.

At the first sign of a rash, the use of disposable diapers and plastic pants should be avoided as the plastic tends to cling to the skin, keeping the moisture in. Toweling diapers with liners are advised, and they should be changed frequently. If possible, the area should be exposed to fresh air and sunlight. Creams such as zinc and castor oil cream or petroleum jelly may help by forming a barrier between skin and diaper.

There are several anti-bacterial preparations available which can be used for soaking the diapers, or if diapers are given a final rinse in diluted vinegar (approximately 1.8 fl oz [50 mL] of vinegar to 17 pints [8 L] of water), the acetic acid in the vinegar will prevent the bacteria making the ammonia. Diapers should be dried in the sun when possible.

If the rash worsens or does not clear up within two or three days, the advice of a doctor should be sought.

If thrush is causing the rash, an antibiotic is given by mouth to clear up the infection and gentian violet painted on the rash.

Perlèche Derived from the French *lécher*, to lick, perlèche is an inflammatory condition affecting the corners of the mouth, usually in children. Fissures appear and there is a burning sensation, causing the patient to lick the area.

The condition is thought to be caused by infection, either bacterial or fungal, transmitted directly from another person or via cups and towels. Infection may also develop in those with badly fitting dentures which can alter the angle where the lips meet, thus creating a warm moist folded area of skin suitable for the growth of organisms. Some doctors feel that it is caused by a deficiency of riboflavin (part of the vitamin B group).

With adequate hygiene, attention to dentures and diet and the use of steroid ointment, combined with the appropriate antibiotic or antifungus, the condition disappears, usually without scarring.

Prickly heat or heat rash appears on the skin as small pimples surrounded by pink blotches. The condition is very common in small babies in hot humid weather. The rash is usually found on the face, neck and upper body and blisters may form on the pimples. White adults in tropical areas are also afflicted with a similar condition usually around the waist and inside knees and elbows.

The rash is apparently caused by a keratin plug (dead skin cells) blocking the sweat ducts. When sweating occurs, the duct swells to produce pimples and may rupture into surrounding skin to produce blisters.

Babies appear little troubled by the condition, which can produce a strong irritant effect in adults. The condition is aggravated by too much clothing and hot humid weather.

The treatment consists of reducing the skin temperature by removing excess clothing and cooling by fans or air conditioning. Very rarely secondary infection of blistered areas may require treatment with antibiotics.

Thrush This is due to a fungus and occurs in the mouth or in the diaper area. In the mouth it looks as if patches of milk are stuck to the tongue and inside the cheeks, in the diaper area it looks like a diaper rash. The treatment prescribed by a doctor will quickly control the condition.

Warts are caused by a virus, and children

are quite often affected, with the fingers or legs the areas most commonly involved. After a variable time they will always disappear spontaneously. If they are troublesome a doctor can prescribe a caustic ointment which will often accelerate their disappearance.

Stomach and bowel disorders

Most stomach pains in childhood are not caused by disease but are expressions of emotional upset, similar to headache in adults.

If there are other symptoms, such as vomiting, fever or diarrhea, or if the pain is severe enough to wake the child at night, it is wise to seek medical advice.

If the doctor considers that the pain is caused by emotional stresses it is important to understand that the child is not deliberately playing for sympathy; subconsciously the child is trying to tell the parent that something is troubling him. It should be remembered that growing up means learning to cope with all sorts of problems and a child will need the parent's understanding and support to help him to do this.

Medical examination of all cases of repeated abdominal pain, however mild, is essential as there are treatable conditions, such as mild urinary infections or even worms, which can produce this type of pain. Medical practitioners may recommend urine testing and blood counts as part of the investigation.

Colic Spasmodic abdominal pain arising in hollow or tubular soft organs, colic is caused by the spasm of smooth muscle. The pain typically occurs as a symptom of many conditions: infection such as that associated with appendicitis; inflammation in colonic diseases such as ulcerative colitis; and gallstone migration (biliary colic) or kidney stone migration

Colic, the painful spasm of smooth muscle in hollow abdominal organs, may be a symptom of many conditions. (*Westmead Centre*)

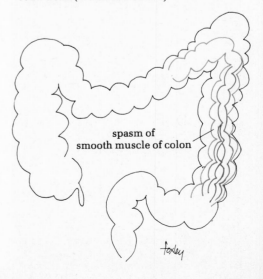

spasm of smooth muscle of colon

(renal colic). Colic can also be produced by poisons, such as in lead poisoning, by swallowing air, overeating or by indigestion from emotional factors.

Treatment is usually directed to alleviating the cause, for example by removing renal stones. However, drugs may be used to alleviate the pain, which is often severe.

A baby who cries and pulls up his legs is often described as suffering from colic or having wind, and this is usually attributed to the baby swallowing large quantities of air during feeding. Often no real cause is found. Attention to feeding habits and an antispasmodic drug are used to treat the condition.

Constipation Sometimes when parents place too much stress on regular bowel action children become aware of this and may use it in order to gain attention. However, not all children have a bowel action every day, and a child will be suffering from constipation only if the motions are abnormally hard. In the case of babies, infrequent bowel action can be helped by a little extra orange or prune juice. If this is not effective the doctor will prescribe a softening agent to add to a feeding.

In older children the commonest cause of constipation is insufficient bulk or fluid in the diet. This can be corrected by providing a suitable cereal containing bran; fruit and vegetables and plenty of fluids also help.

If constipation is marked or persistent, or associated with pain or vomiting, then medical advice is needed.

Diarrhea Small babies commonly suffer from diarrhea with frequent green motions. This can be caused by teething, a cold, or the introduction of new items into the diet for the first time. Such attacks are usually mild and settle down within a day or so.

Gastroenteritis usually produces vomiting as well as watery, greenish diarrhea, and motions may also contain blood or mucus. The infant is usually feverish and looks sick and listless.

Gastroenteritis can cause considerable fluid loss, and whenever diarrhea is severe or persistent medical advice should be promptly sought. If the condition is severe, the baby may require admission to hospital. In less serious cases, the most important part of treatment is replacement of the fluid that is being lost. It is best to give the child small amounts of glucose and water or diluted orange juice frequently, and to substitute sweetened condensed milk diluted to a strength of one part milk to seven parts of water instead of the usual feedings.

The condition is especially common among children under the age of two. In underdeveloped areas where general hygiene is low and available medical services are inadequate, gastroenteritis causes many deaths among young children.

Gastroenteritis occurs less commonly in breast-fed babies than bottle-fed ones. Maternal milk contains antibodies, special proteins that destroy any potentially infecting bacteria in the baby's intestines. Breast milk also contains large numbers of harmless bacteria called *Lactobacilli* which colonize the baby's bowel and help to prevent the establishment of any harmful organisms. Contamination of the nipple during preparation of the bottle is another occasional cause of gastroenteritis. The prevalence of bottle-feeding in Third World countries may explain a similar rise in the occurrence of gastroenteritis.

Umbilical hernia An umbilical hernia occurs when an internal organ or part of an internal organ such as the gut protrudes through the umbilicus. The hernia is due to weakness or faulty closure of the umbilical ring. Umbilical hernias are fairly common and are usually seen in male infants.

The hernia generally causes no problems but occasionally crying or straining enlarges the hernia, causing some pain. The part of the organ causing the hernia can usually be pushed gently back into the abdomen and the hernia is then said to be reducible. If the contents cannot easily be pushed gently back into the abdomen, pain occurs and the hernia is said to be obstructed. It is extremely uncommon for this to happen under three years of age.

Most umbilical hernias clear spontaneously during the first eighteen months of life but occasionally a small operation is necessary to effect a cure. If obstruction occurs, immediate surgery is required.

Worm infestation In most instances worms do not cause any symptoms unless they are present in large numbers. Threadworms are the common type and may cause irritation around the anus and sometimes redness and vaginal discharge in little girls. Roundworm are less common and usually do not cause any symptoms.

Threadworms. Resembling small threads of cotton, pinworms or threadworms (*Enterobius vermicularis*) are less than 1 inch in length (4–10 millimeters), the female being longer than the male. Common parasites, they readily infect the intestines of human beings.

The worms reside in the cecum and ascending colon. The female, however, migrates down the length of the large bowel during the night to lay thousands of eggs on the skin around the anus. This often results in itching, and scratching leads to the fingers becoming contaminated. The eggs may remain alive and infective for several weeks, and are usually ingested via contaminated fingers. After being swallowed, the eggs move to the large intestine where they mature. Although the adult worm only lives for about a month, auto-infection ensures that infestation continues.

Pinworms obtain their nourishment from the fecal residue and do not penetrate the intestinal lining.

Symptoms are usually restricted to an itch around the anal area.

If the worms are not apparent to the eye, the most effective way to diagnose the condition is to collect the eggs from the skin around the anus with a piece of sticky tape several hours after the person has gone to bed. The tape can then be examined under a microscope.

Infestation is easily eradicated from the intestine by the drugs pyrantel, piperazine or vipyrium. Usually all members of the household are treated simultaneously because of the risk of reinfection. Careful washing of hands before eating and after defecation reduces the risk of spread and there is little point in dosing all members of the family for worms at regular intervals in the absence of symptoms.

Severe Conditions of Childhood

While the vast majority of infants are born healthy and grow up to be healthy adults, suffering only the minor expected illnesses along the way, there are, of course, the exceptional cases where children are either born with a problem or else develop one as they grow.

Parents of such unlucky children should be reassured by several factors. Medical science is advancing so rapidly that many conditions considered untreatable as little as five or ten years ago, are now either curable or at least controllable. Also, as media coverage of medical matters becomes more widespread, many parents find they have support and friendship from self-help societies formed by people in the same situation. Common burdens are lightened, helpful tips passed on and courage gained from the knowledge that others are sharing the same load.

Prevention

Many congenital defects can be prevented by measures such as good nutrition and medical care throughout pregnancy. The pregnant woman should avoid smoking and the use of drugs and chemicals (for example, insecticides). The pregnancy should be observed by x-rays, used with caution, there should be some genetic counseling, and prior to pregnancy there should be immunization against German measles.

Cerebral palsy

Children and adults with cerebral palsy may be totally incapacitated or affected only to a minor degree with abnormal movements and posturings and trouble in speaking, hearing and seeing. The sufferers are not necessarily mentally retarded.

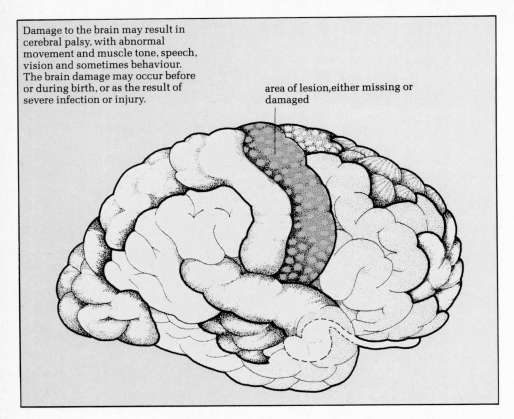

Damage to the brain may result in cerebral palsy, with abnormal movement and muscle tone, speech, vision and sometimes behaviour. The brain damage may occur before or during birth, or as the result of severe infection or injury.

area of lesion, either missing or damaged

Resulting from damage to the brain before, during or immediately after birth, cerebral palsy is non-progressive and characterized by abnormal patterns of posture, movement and muscle tone. Disturbances of speech and language, hearing, vision and behavior may result. Epileptic seizures and various degrees of mental retardation may also occur.

Causes Maternal infections such as German measles (rubella), acute virus infections or any very severe illness during pregnancy, including asthma, may also cause damage to or abnormal development of the baby's brain. Rh and other blood group incompatibilities may interfere with normal development of the brain. During labor and delivery any condition which interferes with the oxygen supply to the baby may cause brain damage.

In the period following birth, brain damage may be the result of failure to establish independent respiration, infection, respiratory distress syndrome, hypothermia or an inability to maintain normal body temperature, and metabolic disorders. Brain damage leading to cerebral palsy may be caused by infections such as meningitis, head injuries, partial suffocation or near drowning.

Types Classified according to the characteristics of muscle disorder, cerebral palsy can vary from a mild form involving one or two limbs to a severe form involving the whole body.

The *spastic* form is characterised by an increase of muscle tone which restricts movement and, if untreated, results in skeletal deformity. A child with a severe form of spastic cerebral palsy will have great difficulty making voluntary movements and may only be able to move in certain abnormal patterns. In spastic diplegia, although the whole body is involved, the lower limbs are more severely involved than the upper limbs. Good head control and normal speech are common with this form of the disorder.

In quadriplegia the whole body is affected, in hemiplegia one side, either right or left, and in monoplegia, which frequently occurs, only one limb is involved.

Athetosis describes slow and uncontrolled movements caused by fluctuations in muscle tone. Although athetosis may involve all of the body, the upper limbs, particularly the hands and fingers, are most often affected. It is often seen in conjunction with some spasticity.

Although pure *ataxia* is not commonly seen in cerebral palsy, an ataxic element, or incoordination, quite frequently accompanies athetosis and some cases of spasticity. Incoordination is most marked when voluntary movement is attempted.

In the *hypotonic* form of cerebral palsy the normal muscle tone is decreased. The body remains floppy, making sitting up or holding up the head against gravity very difficult. Most common in babies and very young children, hypotonia may be a stage through which a child with another form of cerebral palsy passes: many hypotonic babies later develop athetosis or the spastic form of cerebral palsy.

Treatment The treatment of cerebral palsy is directed at reducing the deformity which can result from the constant tension and spasm of muscles, and at discouraging the abnormal patterns of movement, muscle tone and posture. Because treatment should be started very early and continued through the growing years if best results are to be achieved, a range of professional help may be required.

Various associations provide medical, educational and work facilities for affected children and adults. At special schools and work places people with cerebral palsy are educated and helped to socialize and to live with their handicaps.

Celiac disease

A condition in which faulty absorption of food occurs in the small bowel is known as celiac disease. Sometimes non-tropical sprue, a condition with similar symptoms, appears in adults.

Although the features of the disease were first described in the nineteenth century the nature of the disorder was not fully understood until the 1950s. The bowel rapidly develops a sensitivity to gluten, a protein found in cereal foods. For this reason celiac disease is also known as gluten-sensitive enteropathy.

As a result of the reaction to gluten, the cells lining the small bowel change shape and lose the fine finger-like projections, or villi, which aid digestion by providing a larger surface area for nutrients to be absorbed. Because the cell surface becomes completely flat, nutrient absorption is poor.

Symptoms Shortly after feeding with solids is introduced, often between 6 and 20 months of age, infants first develop symptoms. As a result of the malabsorption of fats, feces are foul smelling, clay colored and sloppy. As many other essential nutrients are also not absorbed in adequate amounts, affected children fail to thrive. If the condition is not treated, various vitamin deficiencies and anemia often develop. Although the condition tends to recur in families, a specific pattern of inheritance has not been determined.

Diagnosis and treatment A fine tube is swallowed to obtain a sample of the lining of the bowel which is examined under a microscope. Once a definite diagnosis is made, gluten is removed from the diet. Until the bowel recovers sufficiently to absorb adequate amounts, fats are restricted and additional vitamins given.

Once the sensitivity to gluten has developed, it will remain present, in varying degrees, for life. Although symptoms occurring later often appear less striking, a lifelong adherence to a gluten-free diet is advocated, as problems with vitamin absorption may persist.

Celiac societies have been formed in several large cities to act as self-help organizations. They provide social support, interesting gluten-free recipes, and

Sufferers from celiac disease are unable to absorb gluten, but they may eat foods which have been made with gluten-free cereals.

helpful information such as where to obtain gluten-free food most cheaply.

Congenital conditions

A congenital condition is one that is present from the moment of birth. Hereditary diseases, some of which do not appear until some time — weeks, months or even years — after birth, therefore may or may not be congenital.

An individual may be rendered more susceptible to trauma, infections, toxins and stresses, and therefore to disease, by specific defects. For example, a chronic kidney infection may be the result of deformity or obstruction of part of the urinary tract, and surgical correction may be necessary to cure the infection.

In most cases the cause of the defect or malformation is not clear. What is known is that the condition may arise in the womb during the first few weeks of pregnancy and may be caused by a variety of agents such as the excessive use of x-rays, certain drugs (for example quinine and thalidomide), an abnormality in a gene or combination of genes, infection (for example German measles), and tobacco smoke.

The damage caused to an embryo in the early stage of development can be so severe as to cause the death of the embryo and a miscarriage. In later stages of development the damage will be more localized, perhaps confined to a single organ.

Some congenital malformations can be detected early in pregnancy by sampling the fluid around the baby in the womb (amniocentesis). In such cases a therapeutic abortion can be offered if the test is positive.

Congenital dislocation of the hip

All newborn babies are now checked for this potentially crippling condition. If it is detected early it can usually be completely corrected.

Congenital heart disease

This is one of the most common major congenital malformations. The causes are not fully understood. German measles and viral diseases in pregnant women cause some defects. Others may be caused by certain drugs, chemicals, and agents in the environment.

In some infants there may be a deficiency of oxygen in the blood which becomes bluish-red, causing cyanosis or 'blue babies'. The blueness appears in the lips, fingernails and tip of the nose.

In other cases there may be a hole between two of the chambers of the heart, or severe narrowing of the origin of one of the major blood vessels leading from the heart.

Some forms of congenital heart disease may not be obvious at birth.

Because of the remarkable developments in heart surgery over the past 20 years most children with congenital heart disease can be operated on with complete success.

Crib Death

Sudden infant death syndrome (SIDS) or crib death is the unexpected death of an apparently healthy baby without obvious cause. SIDS is not a new condition: it is a well documented, worldwide disease of infancy recognized by the World Health Organization.

The mother finds the baby dead in the crib, commonly early in the morning. There is usually no sign of a struggle. The baby was not ill when put to sleep, although in retrospect a mild respiratory infection is often recalled. The parents are shocked at first and later have feelings of guilt. They need to be reassured that nobody is to blame for their infant's death.

Sometimes infants are found to be not breathing, limp and pale, but begin to breathe again when stimulated or resuscitated. These infants are said to be abortive SIDS or 'near misses' and a small proportion (less than 10 per cent) subsequently die.

To provide support for bereaved parents and to stimulate interest and research into crib death parent groups have been formed in several countries, including the United States, England and Australia.

The cause is not known but a great deal of research is being undertaken to establish the nature of the condition. At the present state of knowledge it is possible to say that a crib death may be the final process in a long-standing disorder of the control of breathing. This disorder, however, is not one that can yet be recognized during life.

Many misleading press stories and articles purport to explain the cause of crib deaths. It has now been shown conclusively for instance, that neither lack of vitamin C, lack of vitamin E, lack of sel-

Unlike the parents of this delightful baby, some unfortunate families have to face the heartbreak of an inexplicable infant death.

enium, nor allergy to house dust mites, cow's milk or pets causes SIDS. Nor is the type of bedding the cause.

Facts about crib deaths A number of facts about the dead babies are recorded. Eighty per cent of babies who die are less than six months of age with a peak incidence at two to three months old. More babies die in the winter months than in summer. Most of the babies who die do so during sleep and do not show any sign of struggle. Twins and siblings of crib death infants have a higher incidence of crib death than usual. Both artificially-fed and breast-fed babies die of SIDS. Large families and small families are equally affected. Poor families are just as likely to have a crib death as rich families. Well cared for babies die as frequently of crib deaths as do neglected babies. They die in cribs, bassinets, car baskets and beds, both indoors and out of doors.

Retrospective studies on the dead babies have shown that they had diminished growth in weight and length for two or three months before they died. At birth they had a lower score for breathing immediately compared with babies who did not die. More of the SIDS babies required resuscitation at birth and more were breathless and blue in the first few weeks (respiratory distress syndrome). The SIDS infant has been found to be less responsive to needle pricks and to be more floppy and less active before death. It has also been shown that there are changes in the lungs, heart, brain, brain stem and liver which may be caused by a chronically low amount of oxygen in the tissues.

Cystic fibrosis

Also known as mucoviscidosis or fibrocystic disease of the pancreas, cystic fibrosis is one of the most common inherited conditions seen in Western populations. It is inherited as an 'autosomal recessive' trait, that is, the sufferer inherits from both parents the gene that causes the condition. There is a one in four chance of a subsequent child of the family having cystic fibrosis.

One person in every 2000 live births suffers from cystic fibrosis and about one person in 25 is a carrier of the abnormal gene. Recently it was claimed that a test to determine a carrier had been developed in which samples of skin cells are treated with the drug ouabin. Sodium levels in the cells are normally significantly elevated, whereas cystic fibrosis patients show little change.

Characteristics and complications The disease was first described by Dorothy Andersen in the late 1930s. Despite intensive research since then, the exact mechanism and basic defect causing cystic fibrosis remains a mystery. Cystic fibrosis is characterised by widespread abnormalities in the function of exocrine glands, the glands which secrete directly into body

Cystic fibrosis is an inherited condition. The sufferer inherits from both parents the gene that causes the condition. (*Westmead Centre*)

cavities such as the mouth, or onto a surface, such as the skin, rather than into the bloodstream. Most of the clinical features of cystic fibrosis relate to malfunction of the respiratory and digestive systems.

In the lungs the main problem lies in the amount of transport of mucous secretions. These normally assist in preventing infections by keeping invading bacteria as well as other debris 'moving' but in cystic fibrosis, infections can easily arise because of mucus stagnation. Recurrent and often severe chest infections are common features. Damage to the lung tissues follows and chronic bronchitis, emphysema and sometimes pneumonia may develop because of reduced defenses.

Deficiency in the functioning of the pancreas gland is the other major difficulty related to cystic fibrosis. Cysts and thick fibrous tissue rapidly replace normal tissue in the pancreas. As a result, the production of normal digestive enzymes falls off markedly. This leads to non-absorption of a great proportion of fats in the diet and an associated malnutrition develops if this remains unchecked. Because of the excessive fat in the stools they are usually pale and pasty, bulky and foul-smelling.

In the new-born, the excessively thick mucus formed in the bowel may cause obstruction, and surgery may be required to correct the problem.

Diagnosis An abnormality in the sweat glands of the skin is also present, and is used to confirm the diagnosis of cystic fibrosis, as the concentrations of the salts sodium and potassium in the perspiration are increased. By measuring the concentrations of these salts (called the Sweat Test), a diagnosis can be made once a child is over two weeks old. Other factors that may provide a clue to diagnosis are family history of the condition, special changes seen in the lining of the bowel (a diagnosis which is achieved by a bowel biopsy in which a special instrument is swallowed), and by the features related to the lungs and the pancreas mentioned above.

Treatment One of the major aims of treat-

ment is to control respiratory infection and reduce damage to the lungs as much as possible. Regular physical therapy is applied to the chest to help drain secretions that may block small airways and predispose to infections. Parents of children with cystic fibrosis are taught the correct procedures which will effectively drain all areas in the lungs. Special aerosols that liquify the mucus are helpful when used shortly before physical therapy. These sprays often contain antibiotics to further reduce the chance of infection.

Long courses of antibiotics taken by mouth are needed to treat any established lung infection. Such therapy used to be given continually to cystic fibrosis patients.

Dietary management is the other major area of treatment. Preparations containing pancreatic enzymes are routinely given. The degree of fat restriction is variable, and depends on the extent of malabsorption present. Fat-soluble vitamins and extra salts are also needed in the diet.

Outlook Children with cystic fibrosis used seldom to reach teenage years. The major causes of death were fulminating infections in the lung or respiratory failure from gross lung damage. However, significant advances in treatment have now meant that sufferers often survive to early adult life, although by this stage significant lung tissue damage is likely. Adults often develop the special form of heart failure called *cor pulmonale*, which is related to the problem of trying to pump blood through the damaged lungs. Cirrhosis of the liver and diabetes mellitus from pancreatic damage may also develop.

Special cystic fibrosis clinics have been developed in many major hospitals where a team consisting of physicians, dietitians, physical therapists and other health workers provides optimal care. Cystic fibrosis associations provide information to doctors, patients and their families and supply equipment and resources to affected families.

Glomerulonephritis

Inflammation of kidney tissue which primarily affects the glomeruli is called glomerulonephritis. Glomeruli are tufts of capillary blood vessel loops, closely surrounded by tubules, which collect fluid excreted through the capillary walls. Most of this fluid, called glomerular filtrate, is reabsorbed into the bloodstream, with only about 1 per cent being lost from the body as urine.

Glomerulonephritis was once called Bright's disease, a vague term used to describe all inflammations of kidney tissue in which no obvious infection was present. Bacterial infection of the kidney is called *pyelonephritis*.

Post-streptococcal glomerulonephritis The main form of short-term glomerulonephritis is that which usually begins two to three weeks after an infection (usually in the throat) caused by the *Streptococci* bacteria. This so-called 'post-streptococcal glomerulonephritis' occurs most frequently in children. Weakness, fever, and aches and pains in the loins (over the kidneys) are common symptoms. Protein and red blood cells are often found in the urine. Elevation of the blood pressure, with swelling of the ankles and fingers and a 'puffiness' around the face also occur. This accumulation of fluid in the body tissues is called edema.

Whenever glomeruli become damaged or inflamed, quantities of protein and a variable number of blood cells, particularly red blood cells, can escape through the capillaries into the glomerular filtrate, and into the urine. The persistent loss of protein from the blood, and the increased retention of salts, leads to a loss of fluid from the blood vessels to the surrounding tissues (edema). For reasons not fully understood, this change results in an elevated blood pressure.

In post-streptococcal glomerulonephritis, the presence of a previous bacterial infection can usually be confirmed by special blood tests. The condition usually lasts for two to three weeks and then settles completely. Sometimes, however, persistent inflammation and impaired kidney function occur. Occasionally there is complete kidney failure.

Other forms There are many other forms of glomerulonephritis which are not associated with a previous streptococcal infection. Most frequently affected are young adults or those in early middle life. Diseases such as disseminated lupus erythematosus and certain other autoimmune diseases may all cause a chronic glomerulonephritis.

Diagnosis Specific diagnosis is usually made by microscopic analysis of small pieces of kidney tissue, obtained by renal biopsy. In the past, the normal or light microscope alone was used. Often the glomeruli appeared completely normal (nil disease), sometimes patchy inflam-

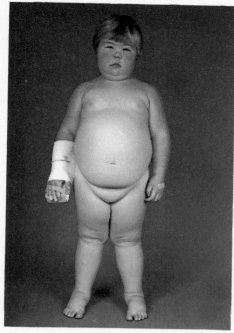

mation of glomeruli was noted (focal glomerulonephritis), and in others, only thickening of the capillary membranes was seen (membranous glomerulonephritis).

In recent years, there has been an ever-increasing understanding of the exact processes involved in the inflammation of glomeruli. Specific structural changes have been clarified by refinements in microscopic analysis of renal tissue. The electron microscope allows much greater magnification and can detect changes not visible under the normal microscope. The use of special antibody solutions is another advance. These are placed on kidney tissue and the antibodies 'stick' to it in various patterns which can be detected under fluorescent light (immunofluorescence). These techniques aid in classification.

In children, biopsy of the kidney (often performed to assess the type and degree of glomerulonephritis involved) is often delayed a couple of weeks to see if the condition resolves naturally.

Nephrotic syndrome is characterized by a lowered level of protein in the blood, a high level of protein in the urine, and edema of the tissues. Glomerulonephritis is the most common cause.

Treatment General treatment of glomerulonephritis involves bed rest, and the use of diuretics to control edema and antihypertensive drugs to manage any associated elevation of blood pressure. A close watch needs to be kept on fluid, salt and protein levels in the body. In those types of glomerulonephritis in which autoimmune problems are considered to be the main cause, corticosteroid or immuno-suppressive drugs are sometimes of value in shortening the severity and course of the disease.

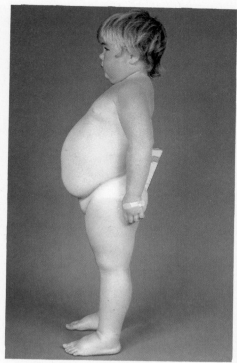

This child has nephrotic syndrome, an illness in which the tubes of the kidney malfunction, causing too much protein material (albumin) to be excreted in the urine.
The body swells from the massive accumulation of fluid in tissues.
Treatment is usually a high protein, low salt diet, with blood transfusions and steroid therapy.

In the most severe cases of the condition, the kidney may stop functioning completely. When this fails to resolve, renal dialysis or kidney machines are needed to keep these patients alive. In some cases, when a suitable kidney donor is available, a kidney transplant is performed.

Epilepsy

When a child experiences repeated convulsions, occurring without any obvious cause, the child will be suffering from a form of epilepsy.

Symptoms The child suddenly becomes unconscious, the muscles become rigid and, after a short interval, generalized jerking of the body and limbs commences. The child often passes urine or opens his bowels during a fit. The convulsion may last for several minutes after which the child relaxes and usually falls into a deep sleep.

In minor epilepsy there is no convulsion. The child simply stops what he is doing and stares vacantly. The attacks will usually only last a few seconds.

Treatment The same procedure would be adopted that has already been described for febrile convulsions. The child should never be left alone during a fit and the head and jaw should be supported so that there is no obstruction to breathing.

A special examination, an EEG (electroencephalogram), of the brain's electrical activity is necessary to diagnose epilepsy. In some cases more specialized investigations will be necessary.

Children with epilepsy require long-term treatment with anti-convulsant drugs, which will control the convulsions in the great majority of cases. Such children can then lead normal lives.

Hernia and hydrocele

An inguinal hernia is a swelling in the groin which may extend into the scrotum. It may be present at birth but sometimes is not noticed until later in childhood. Usually it occurs on the right side.

A protrusion of the navel is common, more so in the female than the male, and is known as umbilical hernia. It usually occurs at birth and in most cases resolves naturally during the first two years of life. There are no complications associated with umbilical hernia, but if the swelling is still present by the age of three it can be corrected by a simple operation.

A hydrocele is an abnormal collection of fluid around the testicle. In small infants such collections of fluid are often absorbed naturally, but if this does not occur, or if such a swelling appears in older children, surgery may be necessary.

If there is any swelling in the groin of a child a doctor should be consulted.

Infantile paralysis

Also known as poliomyelitis, infantile paralysis is an acute infectious disease caused by a virus which invades the spinal cord. Children and young adults are most commonly affected with more than 90 per cent of those paralyzed less than 5 years old.

The incidence of infantile paralysis has greatly decreased in the past 20 years due to the widespread, effective use of a safe oral vaccine, introduced about 1952. It is now possible to prevent poliomyelitis with oral immunization of babies, but epidemics still occur in areas where this immunization is not undertaken.

Dr Jonas Salk and Dr Byron L. Bennett whose work on the anti-polio vaccine first provided protection against poliomyelitis in the 1950s. *(Popperfoto)*

Cause The virus which causes polio has three immunological types. Usually infection by the virus occurs through the nose and mouth. Thereafter the virus lives and multiplies in the walls of the mouth and the gut. It is excreted in the feces for up to six weeks after infection. The virus is liable to enter the gray matter of the spinal cord which contains the nerve cells that control movement of muscles. It destroys these cells, leaving paralysis. The lumbar spine is particularly affected, causing paralyzed legs, but any part of the cord or the brain can be damaged.

In an epidemic, infection with the virus is very common, but in only a small proportion of infections (possibly less than 1 per cent) is there any illness or paralysis.

Symptoms At the beginning of the illness there is a slight fever and headache which disappear after a few days. In many people there are no further symptoms. However, in others, a week or so later the headache and fever recur, with a stiff sore neck and feeling of irritability. Pain in the muscles and paralysis of variable extent may occur later. The muscles of swallowing and speech may be affected but the commonest muscle groups involved are those of the legs.

Treatment If there is even a suspicion of poliomyelitis, bed rest is imperative. There is no curative treatment but the fever can be reduced with aspirin and plenty of fluids. Muscle pain and spasm can be relieved with hot moist packs directly applied to the affected area.

When the respiratory muscles are paralyzed, breathing is maintained by a variety of respirators which assist or take over completely. The earliest type of machine was the 'iron lung' or negative pressure machine. This consisted of a box which completely encased the body and limbs with an air-tight aperture for the neck. Pulmonary ventilation was produced by rhythmical lowering of the pressure inside the box, drawing air into the patient's lungs. It had two serious disadvantages; difficulty in nursing care and danger of accidental inhalation of food and drinks into the lungs.

This led to the development of intermittent positive pressure respirators which inflate the lungs at a rate of 14–20 cycles per minute, expiration being allowed to occur passively between each phase of positive pressure. Some respirators are driven by an electric motor, others by compressed air or oxygen. More complex machines have a mechanism whereby the action is controlled by whatever spontaneous breathing is still retained (patient-cycled respirators).

The paralysis is at its worst at the end of the first week of its presence. Thereafter it gradually improves for up to six

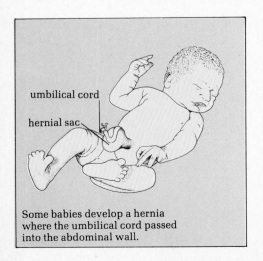

umbilical cord

hernial sac

Some babies develop a hernia where the umbilical cord passed into the abdominal wall.

months. Often other muscle groups take over the function of the paralyzed muscles, minimizing the overall effect of the paralysis.

Control and prevention of poliomyelitis are undoubtedly dependent on immunization. This is recommended for all children and young adults. Live (but altered to render it safe) virus is given orally in three separate doses one month apart, preferably to children at 3 months of age. A booster is required at 5 years of age on entering school. The Sabin vaccine, which is taken orally, is better than the original Salk formalin inactivated vaccine administered by injection because it induces rapid long-lasting immunity even in the very young. It is also effective in stopping epidemics if given to a large segment of the population. It causes an actual infection of the gut which means it is unlikely that the gut itself will become reinfected.

Meningitis

An infection of the meninges, the membranes lining the brain and spinal cord, is known as meningitis. The infection may be caused by a bacterium, a virus, or a fungus, which usually invades the meninges direct from the bloodstream, and which mostly follows a cold or flu-like virus. Occasionally, the infection spreads from the middle ear or sinuses. Sometimes, infection of the meninges may follow severe injury to the skull.

Symptoms The initial symptoms of meningitis are so varied that it is often extremely difficult to make a correct diagnosis. The infection may begin with a fever. In very young children, fever may be the only sign until the child suddenly becomes critically ill. Because the infection irritates the meningeal tissues, stiffness of the neck may develop. Confusion, coma, blurred vision, paralysis or other signs of disturbance to the brain or spinal cord may occur.

Treatment A lumbar puncture is used to identify the organism causing the infection.

A young patient with meningococcal meningitis, showing the characteristic star-like eruptions on the body. Each eruption contains thousands of meningococcal bacteria.

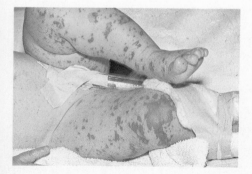

If a virus is responsible, the disorder is usually mild and with rest in bed and control of the fever the patient recovers rapidly and completely.

If bacteria are responsible, antibiotics will control the infection. Bacterial meningitis can be far more serious and, if no antibiotics are given, the patient may recover with a residual paralysis or blindness. Severe infection may lead to coma and death. With early diagnosis, good hospital care and effective antibiotic treatment, meningitis may be treated successfully.

Meningococcal meningitis Also known as cerebrospinal fever or spotted fever, meningococcal meningitis is a potentially serious infection of the membranes lining the brain. The organism responsible is the meningococcus bacterium *Neisseria meningitidis*.

This bacteria normally resides in the throats of many people, causing no symptoms but those who are susceptible may suddenly become infected. Those most frequently affected are young children, and occasionally the old and debilitated. Certain strains of the bacteria are more invasive than others, and occasionally epidemics of the disease occur.

Symptoms Because of the short incubation period of one to three days, most cases of meningococcal fever begin suddenly. Initial symptoms include a severe headache, an extreme intolerance to light, a high temperature, and often a degree of delirium. Other indications of meningitis include vomiting and stiffness of the neck. A red spotty rash characteristic of a meningococcal infection may develop over the body. Early diagnosis and immediate treatment usually limit the spread of infection beyond the meninges to other organs, particularly the brain.

Because of the possibility of permanent brain damage, emergency treatment is usually indicated.

Treatment The patient requires isolation and intensive nursing care. High-dose antibiotics are given through a vein.

Antibiotic treatment may be needed for several weeks to ensure complete eradication of bacteria. With prompt and expert attention, recovery is usually good.

Prevention In conditions of overcrowding and poor hygiene, the condition may be spread to others. Contacts of those infected should be checked to ensure that they are not harboring the organism in the nose or throat. In some cases, contacts are given antibiotics to ensure that the infection does not spread.

Poliomyelitis

See *Infantile paralysis*

Rheumatic fever

A less common disease in the Western world than it used to be, rheumatic fever usually occurs in children; about 90 per cent of cases begin in children between 5

and 15 years of age. It is more common in lower income groups; poor housing and overcrowded conditions seem to contribute to its occurrence.

Evidence suggests that rheumatic fever is related to an infection with group A hemolytic streptococcus, often following tonsillitis or pharyngitis. The disease can affect many different areas of the body including joints, muscles, tendons, heart valves, blood vessels and subcutaneous tissues.

Symptoms include the sudden onset of pain, swelling and stiffness in one or more joints. There may also be fever, excessive perspiration, a fast heart beat, and painless nodules under the skin around the joints. In some cases symptoms may be milder; the patient may just feel unwell and lose weight.

The main joints affected by rheumatic fever are the larger joints, those at the knees, ankles, shoulders and wrist. A rash is sometimes seen.

Involvement of the heart The most important area of the body affected by rheumatic fever is the heart. The heart valves, the heart muscle or the surrounding pericardium may all be involved. Often patients in later life are found to have disease of the heart valves which has been caused by rheumatic fever, although in many cases there is no history of the disease. There is also a close relationship between rheumatic fever and Sydenham's chorea.

Diagnosis and treatment It may be difficult to reach the diagnosis of rheumatic fever; studies of the blood can assist.

Acute rheumatic fever is treated with complete bed rest, and penicillin and aspirin. Sometimes corticosteroids are also used. It is important that the child remains in bed until all signs of fever, changes in heart murmurs, and joint pains and swellings have completely disappeared; this may take months in a severe case.

If the heart has been affected, some physicians believe that the child should take a low daily dose of penicillin for the rest of his life. Any recurrence of joint pains or fever should be taken very seriously and full treatment started again.

Before dental extractions or any surgical operations, the full dose of penicillin should be given. In this way acute bacterial endocarditis, which could be fatal, will be prevented.

5 Adolescents
and Young Adults

Changes and Development

The phase of development that extends from childhood to adulthood is adolescence. The length of the period varies according to the culture; it has been increasing in modern western civilization because of a continued lowering in the age of puberty, probably resulting from improvement in nutrition and exercise as compared with earlier generations. There is also a lengthening of formal education, with prolonged financial dependence on parents. Problems of unemployment which particularly affect young people have introduced new barriers to the adolescent in his endeavors to establish himself independently of his family.

Many major physical and social changes occur during the period of adolescence. These include bodily growth and changes occurring at puberty, the development of a sexual identity and mature relationships with others, as well as the establishment of self-determination and responsibility within the framework of the particular cultural values.

Adolescence is a period of mental and physical development and a readjustment of values. It is often a time when people need to be alone to work out their problems.

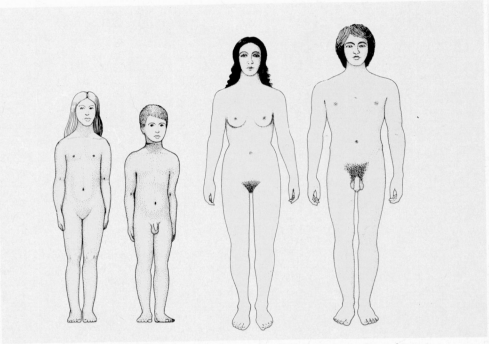

Physical appearance of boys and girls approaching puberty.

Physical appearance after puberty with the development of male and female secondary sexual characteristics.

The changes of puberty

The physical changes that occur during puberty are the results of hormonal changes. The pituitary gland secretes hormones that stimulate the sex glands, the ovaries or testes, which then secrete the sex hormones estrogen, progesterone and testosterone. It is these hormones that are directly responsible for the body changes that occur during puberty. The adrenal glands produce a variety of hormones including small amounts of the sex hormones. These glands are stimulated by pituitary hormones and also contribute to the developments in the body.

There is much variation in the timing of specific physical changes and the attainment of secondary sexual characteristics. Menstruation in females may begin at any time between the ages of ten and seventeen. The changes that accompany puberty also develop over a long period of time. A boy's voice may begin to deepen five years before the development of his full adult complement of facial hair.

In females Physical changes usually begin about a year earlier in females than males. Early features usually include sudden growth spurts, breast development and an increase in nipple size and pigmentation. The commencement of menstruation is often a little later.

During the growth spurt in which body height and width both increase, disproportionate growth in the arms and legs, as compared with the rest of the body, often leads to awkwardness, lack of poise and embarrassment. In females, the hips widen and the vagina and uterus develop further. Hair growth that occurs in females during puberty is in the armpits and pubic region. A little very fine hair often develops on the forearms, parts of the legs and the upper lip. Accessory glands that supply secretions develop in the vulval area.

In males there is enlargement of the penis and testes. Accessory sexual glands which produce seminal fluid also develop. 'Wet dreams', or involuntary emissions of seminal fluid that occur during sleep are not uncommon. Growth spurts also occur in boys and the shoulders in particular broaden as part of a general muscular development. The vocal cords and larynx enlarge to cause a deepening of the voice. Thick hair develops in the armpits and pubic area and to varying extents on other parts of the body. Facial hair first appears on the upper lip and cheek and later extends over much of the face.

Development of sexual identity and relationships with others

Together with the physical changes of adolescence, body awareness and developing sexual feelings and interest in the opposite sex become prominent. During the first part of adolescence, self-awareness and friendships with the same sex usually predominate. While girls often have one or two special girlfriends, boys more frequently socialize in groups.

At some stage during the development of a mature, balanced sexual identity, most people have a period where they are attracted to a member of the same sex. Some degree of physical involvement or mutual exploration is fairly common. This phase is a normal part of sexual development and these relationships usually do not last very long. If an older person is involved, the situation may be different. Masturbation is sometimes presented as a behavioral problem. It is almost universal among boys and quite common among girls, often commencing before puberty. Of itself it causes no physical or psychological abnormalities, being a normal part of growing up.

Social development, like physical development, varies considerably from person to person in its timing, but the sequence of stages is usually the same. Frequently, heterosexual friendships begin to become more important between the ages of fourteen and seventeen years. After a stage of having a number of friends of the opposite sex, more exclusive friendships occur. Girls often go out with boys who are one or two years older than themselves.

These early relationships tend to have a strong element of infatuation, the so called 'puppy love', when the loved one is seen as having no faults and being capable of doing no wrong. If these relationships are extended into an early marriage, later disillusionment often occurs. Statistically, the chances of disharmony and divorce are much higher among teenage marriages.

It is often through the 'heartbreaks' of these early friendships that ideas about the qualities and make-up of a suitable life mate are formed. In the process, one's own needs, strengths and weaknesses usually become more clearly understood as well.

Maturity — psychological

Maturing is a process begun very early in life and continuing indefinitely. Adolescence is certainly an important phase in the attainment of maturity, which appears to be best achieved when members of the family, those dealing with teenagers, and adolescents themselves understand and are each prepared for the processes that occur during this period of development.

During adolescence there is an increasing acceptance of personal responsibility. This includes finances, accommodation, employment, interpersonal relationships and the system of beliefs and values that a person has to develop for himself. The process of transferring responsibility from parental shoulders to the maturing adolescent should reach completion at adulthood, which is best attained when the transfer is smooth and gradual and, ideally, continuous from infancy onwards.

Modeling, that is imitation of an admired personality, occurs throughout life and is important in determining one's identity. Parents and special family friends and, later, teachers, peer-group members and public figures are the models. There is both the positive healthy modeling of characteristics which are to be valued and the negative aspect, borne

Some adolescents find that their problems disappear with companionship. *(Australian Picture Library)*

of insecurity, of modeling upon others indiscriminately.

Persons able to value themselves (self-esteem) and establish an identity (self-awareness) are far better equipped to deal with adolescence and its difficulties.

At times there is tremendous pressure on the adolescent to conform to standards of behavior of other people in the same age group (peer-group pressure and peer-group expectations) often with great intolerance of individual variation. Awareness of one's own strengths, weaknesses, goals and desires enables a person to make individual decisions, rather than merely trying to please others. There is a strong association between low self-esteem and sexual exploitation by others.

A phase of intense questioning and uncertainty usually occurs during the period when parental and community values, beliefs and biases are being reappraised. No longer are they accepted without question. Each one has to be personally accepted or rejected to become part of each person's own value system. Parents are sometimes fearful of this increasing questioning and the increasing freedom and independence of adolescents.

Peer group pressure may influence
the adolescent's taste in dress,
music, sports and other pastimes.

Maturity — physical

Reaching physical maturity later than average can be disturbing for both boys and girls. Breast development for girls and hair growth and a deepening voice for boys are often important in the development and maintenance of self-esteem. Rebellion against authority and withdrawal into personal isolation are two ways in which some react to delayed development. There is a desire to be fully adult and this often leads to resentment of implications that the adolescent is still a child, particularly when expressed through parental controls and domination.

With the many learning experiences of adolescence, fluctuation of attitude is common. There are occasions where insight and maturity are evident and other times when childish responses occur. Periods of marked emotional variation (lability) are common; highs and lows of mood often appear as periods of excitement and achievement suddenly giving way to confusion and a sense of inadequacy.

Delinquency

The term delinquency is most often, though not exclusively, used to describe antisocial behavior of children and adolescents (juvenile delinquency). Antisocial behavior becomes evident with the challenging or flouting of the social customs and laws that are conventionally observed in the particular society. Delinquency in modern Western society and among African Bushmen may not be the same, but both will violate customary ways of behaving.

Hostility and aggression towards parents or other people in authority, demonstrations of contempt for social customs and restrictive rules or laws may be forerunners of more actively delinquent behavior. When hostility originates from a poor relationship with parents, it tends to become built into the child's personality and to be directed towards all authority figures, for example school teachers, police, employers, referees.

The developing individual wishes to be free and independent, but, bewildered by the rapidity of physical, sexual, intellectual and social growth, experiences a strong need for security, control and guidance. This may emerge as a tendency to seek a sympathetic social group which can provide an additional feeling of security. This is the basis of the teenage gang with its restricted membership and distinctive forms of initiation, dress, language and behavior.

Lack of understanding, excess of opposition and failure of sympathetic support and guidance within the family may cause the adolescent to become excessively dependent or lead to rejection of family and society and to aggressive antisocial behavior.

Shoplifting and other forms of stealing, running away and truancy, lying, outbursts of temper and bad language, violence toward people and property, setting fires, making a public nuisance, sexual promiscuity and so on may all be forms of delinquency. It may be displayed on an individual basis, or only when in the company of peers in a gang.

Juvenile delinquency is a significant social problem, resulting in destruction of property, unhappiness and injury to people, litigation and the restraint of juvenile offenders in jail and other corrective institutions.

Treatment Where delinquency is the result of an adjustment reaction to family and environmental stress, the services of a psychiatrist, psychologist or other specialist may be sought. Such professionals attempt to demonstrate to the whole family the psychological processes behind delinquent behavior and suggest ways in which the family as a unit can seek to resolve the problem.

Coping with changes

Most adolescents and parents cope fairly well with this period of growing up. Adequate preparation of a person to achieve understanding of some of the things that will occur in adolescence, and the establishment of good communication channels in the late pre-teens, are important and worthwhile. Sometimes it is difficult to remember, during times of turmoil, that adolescence is only a stage in development; normality will return. Even in the

Right
Activities like this provide a satisfying outlet for energy that might otherwise be misdirected.
(Australian Picture Library)

most disruptive cases, few juvenile delinquents grow up to become adult criminals.

Adequate understanding, support and encouragement from those who are important to the teenager help the development of coping skills which enable problems of adolescence such as peer group pressure and minor variations in the timing of physical changes to be dealt with effectively. The adolescent struggle towards confident adulthood involves a good deal of effort in readjustment for both parents and teenager. Parents who express firm confidence in their adolescents by steadily increasing their freedom and responsibility give them the best chance of achieving mature, integrated personalities.

Generous parental affection can help adolescents cope with the problems of growing up.

Health Problems

Adolescence is usually marked by periods of energetic activity and by times of fatigue. Fatigue results both from the physical exertion and the increased energy used up in the period of accelerated growth. As a result, nutritional and sleep requirements of adolescents are both increased compared to those for adults.

A number of other difficulties can arise out of the physical changes that occur during adolescence and the timing of their appearance. The first menstrual period can be a devastating experience for a girl who has had no prior explanation of what will happen, although nowadays most girls are adequately informed in good time. Not only is preparatory explanation important, but it is also helpful for it to be presented with a sense of confidence and even excitement, rather than as a burden to be borne for much of life.

Initially, menstrual periods may occur at irregular intervals until the delicately balanced hormonal system becomes fully functional, with the ovaries releasing ova. This usually occurs one to two years after periods begin. At this stage menstruation becomes more regular, but some pain may be experienced during the first part of the flow. If it becomes troublesome, medical attention should be sought.

Some degree of breast tissue enlargement is quite common in boys during adolescence. It is usually minimal and transitory but can be the cause of slight physical discomfort and much embarrassment. No treatment is generally required but, if necessary, excellent results are achieved by surgical removal of the offending tissue from behind the nipple.

One common problem in adolescence is the response of the sebaceous and other skin glands to testosterone and progesterone. The secretions become thicker and more plentiful. Pores block, stagnant secretions become infected, and acne flares up. Unfortunately, quick cures are not possible and treatment is aimed at controlling the situation until the condition is 'grown out of'. Much concern and attention is often paid to the effects acne has on personal appearance.

The conditions described in the following paragraphs are those which commonly occur or have their onset during adolescence and young adulthood.

A happy relationship brings warmth to the sometimes stormy years of growing up. (Australian Picture Library)

Ankylosing spondylitis

A chronic and progressive inflammatory disease of the spine and surrounding soft tissue, ankylosing spondylitis usually affects the sacroiliac joints in the lower back first. The shoulder and hip joints are commonly affected, and sometimes also the peripheral weight-bearing joints. The condition may be confused with rheumatoid arthritis in the young, when the peripheral joints may be affected first. The disease eventually causes fusion (ankylosis) of the spine with consequent restricted spinal movement.

Causes The cause is unknown but hereditary factors play an important role. Generally the disease occurs in young men (ten times more frequently than in women), usually in their third decade; only a small number of people develop symptoms after the age of 45.

Symptoms Back pain and stiffness are common, usually worse in the mornings and tending to wear off with exercise. There may be pain in the shoulders and hips and the disease can occasionally resemble sciatica. The pain usually disappears with ankylosis. Pain in the chest can occur, sometimes on deep breathing, due to involvement of the costo-vertebral joints. Other symptoms occur only rarely, such as anterior uveitis (painful red eye, with a small sluggish pupil) and aortic incompetence (disease in the aortic valve and first part of the aorta).

As the disease progresses, the spinal movements become restricted but only a small proportion of patients develop severe fusion of the spine with the classical, rigid, bent posture.

Treatment The aims of treatment are to prevent or minimize the deformities of the spine which could develop. Exercise is encouraged to maintain spinal mobility. Deformity is prevented by maintaining an erect posture when walking, standing or sitting. The patient is encouraged to sleep face-down, or, if this is not possible, at least to sleep on a flat, firm mattress, using a small pillow or none. Breathing exercises are encouraged to prevent restriction of chest movement.

Anti-inflammatory drugs provide relief and allow normal daily activities. Surgery is sometimes performed to correct a severe degree of fixed flexion deformity of the spine, but this can pose a risk of damage to the spinal cord. Total hip replacement is carried out in patients with incapacitating hip disease.

Anorexia nervosa

Eating disorders, of which anorexia nervosa is the best known example, are most common in young women. Although a refusal to eat sufficiently resulting in a drastic loss of weight is the most obvious presentation of this problem there may be attempts to conceal the reduced intake of food. Self-induced vomiting may follow apparently normal meals. Sometimes excessive dieting is punctuated by eating 'binges'. Laxative and diuretic abuse may also be present.

The underlying problem in anorexia nervosa is a distorted view of the person's normal or desirable body image. The cultural emphasis in Western society on slimness as a desirable attribute, especially in women, is an obvious contributing factor to the creation of a vulnerable population. The disorder is not seen in underdeveloped countries, is uncommon in males, and is seen more in the more affluent socio-economic groups. Female dancers are an 'at risk' group. Despite popular belief anorexia nervosa is not a new phenomenon. The illness was given its name well over a hundred years ago by the British physician Sir William Gull and doubtless existed, nameless, before that.

Consequences Frequently, the patient is a normal young woman or girl who embarks on a diet to lose a pound or two. When the initial weight goal is reached she continues to diet, becoming terrified by the prospect of regaining even a few ounces. Eventually she resembles a skeleton, with hip, pelvic and shoulder bones clearly visible, the ribs standing out clearly and the face having a taut, stretched appearance with the eyes sunk in their sockets. Menstruation usually ceases and behavior is obsessional, erratic or depressed.

Causes Events in adolescence which may precipitate anorexia in an already vulnerable individual include the stress of establishing or breaking off new relationships; pressures related to studies, jobs or moving away from home; and conflicts in family interactions, particularly where parents are domineering. It has been suggested that some sufferers may be rejecting their own sexual maturity and developing womanhood choosing starvation as a way of prolonging and exaggerating their childish contours. When menstruation ceases it further emphasizes the return to childhood.

Many anorexic patients come from outwardly stable, affluent families in which there is really considerable inner conflict. It is surprising how many victims are devoted to their fathers and regard themselves as 'Daddy's little girl'. Parallel with this relationship is the fact that the patient's mother is often antagonistic to her, though the mother may not be conscious of this. Mothers of anorexic girls are frequently found to be over-obsessed with diet and slimness themselves. For such reasons, often one of the first steps taken in treatment is the separation of the patient from the immediate family.

Not all sufferers have disturbed home lives. Some girls begin dieting to emulate the appearance of a favorite model, actress or pop singer and continue losing weight well after the desired goal, despite the genuine protestations of caring and concerned parents.

Treatment Treatment for anorexia nervosa should be sought early since in established cases the physical changes may cause physiological disturbances and lowered resistance. The aim is two-fold — to restore normal body weight and to gain acceptance of a more normal body image concept. The combined efforts of a physician, psychiatrist and dietitian may be required. Psychotherapy either individually or in a group may be helpful. Some patients appear to benefit from antidepressant medication. Some patients appear to recover, regain weight and discontinue therapy, only to relapse later. This should not be regarded as total failure as treatment can be recommenced.

Appendicitis

Inflammation of the appendix, appendicitis, is a common condition in highly civilized countries.

The appendix A worm-like, narrow, blind tube about 3–4 inches (8–10 cm) long, the appendix opens into the cecum (the first part of the large bowel) where the small intestine joins the large intestine. It has no known function in man and is probably a vestigial structure.

Causes and occurrence of appendicitis Acute appendicitis occurs most commonly in susceptible families and the cause is generally unknown. However, in a large number of cases, obstruction of the appendix seems to be a contributing factor, for obstruction makes infection more likely to occur. Usually the obstruction is caused by a small hard piece of fecal matter (fecilith); occasionally by intestinal parasites such as worms.

Acute appendicitis is most common between the ages of twenty and thirty years but it can occur at any age. In infants and the elderly it may be more serious because peritonitis develops quickly and often resistance to the infection is lower.

Symptoms and diagnosis The first symptom of acute appendicitis is usually abdominal pain which initially is vague and centered around the navel (umbilicus). After a few hours the pain moves to the right and is constant and located over the area where the appendix lies. There is a lack of desire to eat food and often a feeling of nausea and even vomiting. Usually constipation is present but diarrhea can occur, especially in the very young. Early in appendicitis the temperature is normal but after about six to eight hours it often becomes slightly raised. On examination there is an area of tenderness over the area of the appendix and the muscles tend to become tight in that region.

Occasionally the appendix is not in the typical position. It may be lower down and lying in the pelvis or higher up than usual and tucked behind the caecum. In these cases the symptoms and signs of ap-

pendicitis may vary slightly. When an obstruction to the appendix is present the illness often progresses at a faster rate. Although acute appendicitis is a common cause of severe abdominal pain, it is not always easy to diagnose as many other conditions can have very similar symptoms and signs.

Treatment It is important that laxatives never be given to an undiagnosed severe abdominal pain as these cause strong movements of the muscles of the large bowel wall and if appendicitis is present this can lead to perforation and thence peritonitis.

When diagnosis is made early the treatment for acute appendicitis is removal of the appendix by surgery. This operation is known as appendectomy. Surgery is usually carried out early because there is a risk of the appendix perforating and either forming an abscess or causing peritonitis (infection and inflammation of the membrane lining the abdominal cavity and enfolding the viscera).

Sometimes when a patient with appendicitis is examined a lump or mass is felt in the area of the appendix. Such patients have usually had symptoms for several days. This lump is formed by a process localizing the infection and preventing it from spreading and causing peritonitis. When this occurs surgery is usually not carried out as an emergency. Instead, the patient is confined to bed and given no food by mouth while treatment with antibiotics is closely watched. If symptoms worsen, emergency appendectomy may be needed. The patient usually recovers in a few days and the appendix can be removed at a later date with less risk. Removal is still necessary to prevent a further attack.

Should an appendiceal abscess form, the abscess must be drained and time allowed for healing to occur before the appendix is removed.

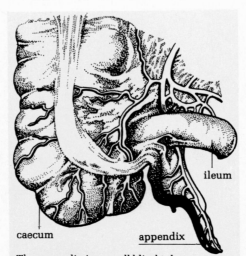

The appendix is a small blind tube, 3–4 inches (8–10 cm) long, leading from the cecum at the junction of the small and large intestines.

Pleurodynia

Also known as epidemic myalgia, Bornholm disease and devil's grip, pleurodynia is a non-recurrent (benign) viral infection occurring in minor epidemics. The outbreak was first described on the Baltic island of Bornholm. The infection can occur in any age group, but usually affects children and young adults.

Transmission Fecal-oral contact is the usual method of spread, and personal hygiene (particularly hand washing) inhibits the cycle. Small children often bring the virus into the household and infected family members may show varying degrees of the illness. Insects such as flies and mosquitoes may also act as carriers.

Symptoms The illness first appears, like any viral illness, with weakness, sore throat and loss of appetite. The patient may then develop muscular, abdominal and chest pain, which can be quite severe, often coming and going inexplicably.

The chest pain, situated over the lower ribs and upper abdomen, is sharp and is made worse by breathing, coughing, sneezing, movement and hiccuping. Pain may also be felt in the shoulders, neck and back and spasm of the abdominal muscles may also occur. The illness usually lasts about three to seven days, but the patient may experience relapses.

The pain of this illness can be confused with that of heart disease or with the abdominal pain of some emergency condition such as a ruptured appendix. On rare occasions a patient may develop complications, for example meningitis, hepatitis, inflammation of the heart or inflammation of the testes (orchitis).

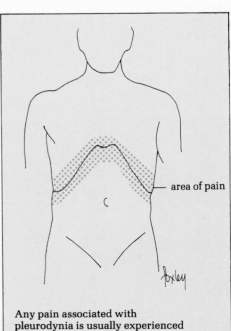

Any pain associated with pleurodynia is usually experienced in the chest and abdomen and is aggravated by movements such as coughing or sneezing. (*Westmead Center*)

Treatment The illness usually runs a benign course with complete recovery following treatment. Rest is advised with fluids encouraged, and aspirin to relieve the symptoms.

Tonsillectomy and inoculations are probably best delayed if there is an outbreak of pleurodynia. There are no antiviral drugs available at present and immunization against the virus is impractical because there are so many different strains and it is difficult to incorporate them all into the vaccine.

Cryptomenorrhea

The condition of cryptomenorrhea occurs when bleeding from the uterus during the normal monthly period (menstruation) is not discharged externally from the vagina, due to a congenital abnormality in the vagina. The abnormality may involve the complete absence of the vagina or the formation of a membrane of variable thickness across the vagina, closing it off. The latter abnormality is called imperforate vagina. Less commonly, the hymen may form completely across the vagina; this is called imperforate hymen.

The blood which would normally be discharged builds up in the vagina, in the uterus and then in the fallopian tubes. Some of this blood is reabsorbed so that the remaining blood becomes quite thick.

Symptoms and treatment The symptoms may begin at puberty, and sometimes not until a year or so after menstruation has started. The young woman affected will not realize that menstruation has commenced, though sometimes abdominal pains occur at monthly intervals. If it is some time before the condition is detected a mass of retained blood can cause discomfort and even press on the bladder,

An obstruction or congenital abnormality in the vagina can cause menstrual flow to build up in the vagina, uterus and even the fallopian tubes. This condition, cryptomenorrhea, may exist for some time without detection.
(Westmead Center)

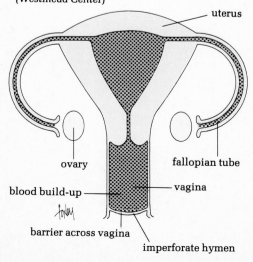

making the passage of urine difficult. If the retained blood has built up in the uterus and fallopian tubes, fertility may be affected.

The treatment of cryptomenorrhea is surgery to remove the retained blood and correct the deformity.

Dysmenorrhea

Painful menstruation is known as dysmenorrhea. Many healthy women experience some discomfort during menstruation but in only one in twenty is it severe enough for the woman to consult a doctor. Usually dysmenorrhea is considered to be of two types, primary and secondary.

Primary dysmenorrhea is the most common, starting soon after the onset of puberty. There is intermittent spasmodic pain in the back, lower abdomen and sometimes in front of the thighs, often referred to as 'cramps'. Usually the woman recognizes that the pain is associated with menstruation even if it starts before the menstrual flow as it sometimes does.

The pain usually lasts only a few hours and is a result of strong uterine contractions, the cause of which is not known. Primary dysmenorrhea may be severe enough to cause fainting, sweating, dizziness and vomiting, making the patient quite ill.

Often this type of dysmenorrhea stops after a pregnancy or it may be relieved by dilation of the cervix. The incidence of primary dysmenorrhea is much less than it used to be mainly because of sensible health education and the avoidance of unnecessary restriction of physical activities advised thirty years ago.

Treatment is to give pain relieving drugs which are not habit forming such as acetaminophen and aspirin in full doses. Non-steroidal anti-inflammatory drugs may afford relief. If these fail a diuretic such as hydrodiurnil taken for a couple of days before the menstrual period may be useful. The most effective treatment is an oral contraceptive pill with low estrogen content which inhibits ovulation. Today many young girls and women are on 'the pill' primarily for treating painful periods rather than for contraception.

As dilation of the cervix carries a risk of damaging the cervix and so causing later miscarriages, it is not so popular a treatment now.

Secondary dysmenorrhea occurs some years after painless periods. It is caused by fibroids, endometriosis or inflammatory disease of the tubes and ovaries (salpingo-oophoritis). The pain is more constant and less spasmodic and is liable to continue throughout the menstrual period and not for just a few hours.

Gynecological advice should be sought for this type of period pain.

Epilepsy

Epilepsy is a short, sudden, periodic dis-

Strong uterine contractions at the time of menstruation are part of dysmenorrhea. There may be severe pain and some treatment is necessary for relief.

uterus   cervix

vagina

turbance of the function of the cells of the brain; it is caused by abnormal electrical activity. The sudden electrical discharge results in an epileptic seizure which is usually associated with some disturbance in consciousness. The seizures may affect the whole body in a generalized fashion or they may affect only part of the body (focal seizures). Epilepsy occurs in 0.5 per cent of the population with more than 70 per cent of epileptics having a seizure before they are 20 years old.

In most people with epilepsy, no cause can be found though any disease of the brain, particularly tumors, head injuries and disorders of the blood supply, can cause seizures. Many diseases outside the brain, such as a block in the conducting mechanism of the heart, a low blood sugar level, accumulation of soluble waste products in the blood, or sudden ingestion or withdrawal of alcohol or drugs can also cause seizures.

Generalized epilepsy Generalized seizures are commonly called 'grand mal' or 'petit mal' according to their observed pattern. Grand mal seizures may occasionally be preceded by a change in mood which may warn the person of an impending attack. The seizure invariably occurs in three stages.

The first is the tonic phase, when the subject loses consciousness and all the muscles tighten, including the throat muscles and respiratory muscles so that often a cry is emitted. Breathing ceases and the patient goes blue. This phase lasts only 30 seconds.

Then there is the clonic phase, when the muscles of the limbs, face and body jerk intermittently. Foaming or frothing at the mouth may occur. This stage may also last half a minute.

In the third stage the person becomes relaxed, is still and in a state of coma, and eventually will sleep normally. A headache may be experienced on waking half an hour or so later.

Petit mal seizures are commonly a short loss of consciousness when the affected person just stops any activity and stares blankly ahead. These absences or interruptions may occur very frequently. Sometimes the arms jerk at the same time.
Focal epilepsy Focal seizures always start with a localized disturbance and may spread and become generalized. The most common site of focal epilepsy is the temporal lobe of the brain which produces a dreamlike state and hallucinations of smell, taste, hearing or sight.

Sometimes the focal seizure starts in the surface of the brain and develops into involuntary twitching of a limb or part of a limb which spreads to other parts of the body. This is called Jacksonian epilepsy.

A diagnosis of epilepsy can be made from the occurrence of a fit. An electroencephalogram (EEG) will confirm the diagnosis and can often identify a local cause or the focus of the attack.
Treatment During a seizure, care should be taken to move the person away from fires and hard, sharp objects. If it is easy to position, a padded gag between the teeth is helpful. Otherwise little fuss should be made.

Sometimes several seizures occur one after the other with no recovery to normality. This is known as status epilepticus and must be treated promptly with intravenous anticonvulsant drugs, otherwise the person may die.

The cause of a seizure may be a disease which may be cured or helped by surgery or other treatment.

Anticonvulsant drugs, sometimes used in combinations, can be used to suppress, or reduce the number of seizures, or eliminate them completely. Grand mal is frequently treated with the drug phenytoin which, unfortunately, can produce unwanted side-effects, so that in some cases other drugs may have to be used.

Only a few epileptics have frequent seizures when adequately treated by anticonvulsant drugs. In most cases the seizures are completely eliminated or only occur occasionally, provided the drugs are continued. Most persons with epilepsy can lead normal lives with few restrictions.

Eunuchoidism

Also known as hypogonadism, eunuchoidism describes any condition in which the testes (gonads) produce insufficient amounts of the male sex hormone, androgen. As well as a lack of fer-

Glandular fever is generally mild in children. The symptoms may be vague, such as occasional headache and tiredness. (*Zefa*)

tility, secondary sexual characteristics fail to develop.

In the male, secondary sexual changes at puberty include a deepening of the voice, the development of facial, body and pubic hair and an increase in muscle bulk.
Causes As well as abnormalities in the structure and function of the testes, abnormalities of pituitary gland function may also produce eunuchoidism. In these cases, inadequate production of various stimulating hormones from the pituitary gland affect the functioning of the testes. Tumours involving the pituitary gland, while rare, are the most likely cause. The inherited condition known as Klinefelter's syndrome also results in a general failure of gonadal development.
Treatment depends primarily on the cause. Although fertility may not be achieved, injections of the appropriate male hormones may help the development of secondary sexual characteristics.

The failure to develop such characteristics often causes psychological problems which may need special consideration. Adolescents, particularly, may require intensive counseling to cope with embarrassment about their condition.

Mononucleosis

An infectious disease first described in 1889, glandular fever or infectious mononucleosis is caused by the Epstein-Barr virus. It is spread by infected drop-

lets from the mouth. Studies have shown that the virus remains in the saliva for several months after the initial infection has subsided. However, the disease is not highly contagious, and is usually spread by close contact, the reason why it is sometimes called the 'kissing disease'.

Mononucleosis occurs most commonly in adolescents and young adults. The condition is fairly mild in children, and about half the adolescents and young adults affected do not develop significant symptoms.

Symptoms usually commence four to seven weeks after contact, with headache, tiredness and a general feeling of malaise the most common initial symptoms. Lymph gland (node) enlargement, especially in the neck, fever, and sore throat soon follow.

There is mild inflammation of the liver (hepatitis) in most cases, but actual tenderness of the organ and the development of jaundice, common in other types of hepatitis, are only present in the minority of cases. Enlargement of the spleen and the appearance of a vague rash for a few days are other occasional symptoms of the disease.

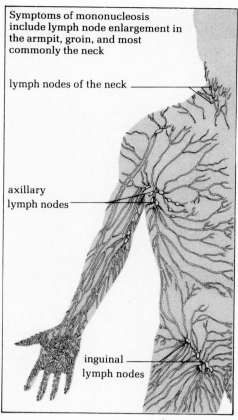

Symptoms of mononucleosis include lymph node enlargement in the armpit, groin, and most commonly the neck

lymph nodes of the neck

axillary lymph nodes

inguinal lymph nodes

Diagnosis is by examination of the blood. The lymphocytes in the blood increase in number, and many develop an abnormally shaped nucleus and are sometimes called virocytes. As these changes may occur in other similar diseases, especially cytomegalovirus infection, two other blood tests — the 'monospot' test and the Paul-Bunnell test — may be performed to measure the levels of specific antibodies and to confirm the diagnosis.

Treatment involves rest, general care, and the treatment of specific symptoms as they arise. As with other viral infections, antibiotics are of no value. Paracetamol or similar medications to relieve the pain and fever are usually the only medications needed.

Recovery Most patients recover within four weeks of first developing the fever, but a small percentage may remain unwell for several months. Symptoms tend to diminish with rest and then flare up when the patient becomes active again. Tiredness, loss of concentration, fever, and generalized aches and pains are the main symptoms of these recurrences. At times depression becomes a marked feature.

Sometimes a post-viral asthenia (a period of general tiredness and lethargy) may persist for up to six months. The exact cause for this is not known.

Prevention No immunization is available. Because of its relatively low infectivity, stringent measures to prevent its spread are usually not enforced, despite the persistence of the virus in the saliva.

Hay fever

Allergic rhinitis or hay fever is characterized by repeated sneezing and a blocked, running nose. There is often itching of the nose and palate, running eyes (allergic conjunctivitis) and bluish bags under the eyes. The lining of the nose has a boggy blue-grey appearance. The symptoms are worse at night and in the early morning. In young children, nasal obstruction is usually accompanied by nasal infection, which may have an underlying allergic cause.

The condition usually begins sometime in the first twenty years of an individual's life. It can occur only in spring and early summer (the true hay fever), or continuously throughout the year, or throughout the year but most severely in spring, or intermittently (from time to time).

The acute form is usually seasonal and is caused by an allergy to pollens from grasses and plants. Whether it is caused by an allergy can be determined by a nasal smear and skin tests.

Many people with hay fever are potential asthmatics. It has been estimated that as many as 40 per cent of people who have hay fever, but no clinical signs of asthma, suffer from a lung abnormality.

Treatment The use of nasal decongestant drops for long periods should be avoided as they tend to cause atrophy of the nasal mucosa.

Antihistamine tablets taken orally prevent histamine acting on the blood vessels in the nose and sinuses, and so can prevent the symptoms of hay fever developing. However, once histamine has produced its effects and the symptoms are well established, antihistamines are of little use. Unfortunately, antihistamines cause drowsiness, therefore it is unwise to drive a car or to engage in other activity, such as operating machinery, which may be potentially dangerous to oneself or others.

Sodium cromoglycate is effective in preventing the allergen producing the hay fever reaction in up to 70 per cent of people with true hay fever (seasonal allergic rhinitis). It has to be sniffed into the nose either as a powder or as a spray, but cannot be used until the nose is unblocked, for example by decongestant drops or steroids.

Grass seeds are known to cause allergic reactions. (*Zefa*)

Topical corticosteroids (cortisone derivatives) are available as a pressurized spray and relieve the symptoms in up to 70 per cent of hay fever victims. However it is not known whether their long term use might cause damage to the nasal mucosa, as may be caused to skin by long term use of steroids.

Avoiding the allergen is the best and safest treatment. The individual should avoid foods that precipitate the condition, replace feather pillows and quilts, keep domestic pets outside, and minimize the presence of house mites and dust.

Desensitization to some allergens, especially pollens, is now possible. Very weak solutions of the allergens to which the person is sensitive are injected at regular intervals over a long period of time. Sometimes this is very effective.

A spontaneous improvement and a change in allergen sensitivity does sometimes occur.

Migraine

A distinctive condition distinguishable from other forms of headache, a migraine tends to be severe, periodic in nature, and it commences prior to the age of 25. In over two-thirds of cases the headache is restricted to one side, explaining the migraine's alternative name, *hemicrania*.

Types Two distinct forms of migraine, which affect up to 5 per cent of the population, are recognized. The classical type is associated with an aura, which occurs for up to an hour before the onset of the pain. Lasting for minutes, the aura often involves visual disturbances, including the appearance of bright spots, zigzag lines or black areas (scotomata), tingling of the lips and hands, disturbances of walking or speech and general confusion. The small arteries within the brain tissue and the scalp narrow, causing the aura, and then widen, settling it and precipitating the development of the classical throbbing pain.

The common or atypical migraine pattern has no aura, but the pain produced is identical to the classical form. The pain varies, ranging from a mild discomfort to intense pain associated with nausea, vomiting and photophobia (a strong dislike of light), and may affect either or both sides of the head. Resting in bed in a darkened room and silence is recommended as a treatment.

This pain can last from several hours to several days and a reflex contraction of neck and scalp muscles may lead to a prolonged, superimposed 'tension headache'. Between attacks no abnormality is detectable.

The cause of migraines is complex and not yet fully understood. Many sufferers have a family history of the disorder while specific factors, such as intense prolonged focusing of the eyes, fatigue, eating specific foods like chocolates, and hormonal changes, can trigger migraines.

Hemicrania, pain on one side of the head, is a common symptom of migraine. (Zefa)

Women can have migraines immediately prior to a period.

Altering the levels of specific nervous system chemicals, such as serotonin, may cause the narrowing and subsequent widening of the arteries necessary for an attack.

Cluster headaches, characterized by a throbbing pain that occurs as a series of 'bouts' or 'clusters' often after several hours' sleep, are related to migraines.

Treatment involves dealing with the actual attack and attempting to prevent further occurrences. The aura is too brief to require specific treatment, although ergotamine-based preparations are best taken during this phase to prevent the pain from following on. Such medications work by narrowing blood vessels, thereby preventing the dilatation that triggers the pain. These drugs should be used sparingly and not at all by people who are pregnant or who have blood vessel, liver or kidney diseases. Deliberate constriction can cause nausea and vomiting so mild attacks are often best treated with antiemetic (to reduce nausea and vomiting) and analgesic (pain relieving) drugs.

Explaining the migraine's mechanism and reassuring the sufferer that no tissue damage is occurring are both important aspects of treatment. Identifying and avoiding specific triggering factors when they are present is also useful.

If migraines occur more than once a fortnight preventive medications, including pizotifen, cyproheptadine and clonidine, are often taken. In resistant cases methysergide or antidepressant medications are often used.

Because of the recurrent nature of this condition, narcotic pain-relieving drugs and similar preparations are generally avoided to prevent addiction.

Multiple sclerosis

A chronic, slowly progressive disorder of the central nervous system, multiple sclerosis is a condition in which degeneration of patches of white matter (myelin) occurs within the tissue of the brain and spinal cord. Myelin is the main component of the insulating sheath that surrounds nerve cells and fibres, and assists in the transmission of nerve impulses along the cells.

Multiple sclerosis is the commonest of the demyelinating diseases. The exact cause of the disease is unknown, although it is believed to be viral in origin, initially contracted in childhood, but without obvious symptoms for many years. It most often affects adults between the ages of 20–40 years. It rarely occurs among people who live near the equator.

Symptoms In over one-third of people with multiple sclerosis, the first symtoms are due to demyelination, resulting in visual disturbances caused by inflammation of one of the optic nerves. Partial or total blindness in the affected eye (often associated with pain upon movement) usually develops over a 48 hour period. In the majority of those affected there will be recovery within the next fortnight, many having an apparently complete recovery.

Other common symptoms include weakness or numbness, a tremor or shaking in the limbs and an unsteady walk; difficulties with speech and with control of the bladder. In most cases there are periods of improvement or remission, alternating with periods of worsening.

Although pregnancy is definitely associated with an increase in the number of flare-ups (exacerbations) of the illness, other possible triggering factors may be

In a normal nerve, as seen here, the nerve sheath insulates the nerve fibres from each other with the myelin in the sheath. Demyelinating diseases such as multiple sclerosis disrupt this insulation. (*John Watney Photo Library*)

infections, injury, or stress (both physical and emotional).

Diagnosis The effects of multiple sclerosis differ with the part of the nervous system affected and the location and duration of symptoms varies to such an extent that it is difficult to diagnose a typical case, especially in the initial stages. Generally, it is the particular pattern of the condition, in which unrelated symptoms occur at different points in time, that confirms the diagnosis. Several special tests, such as x-rays and blood tests, are often required to rule out other causes.

Treatment Many treatment regimes have been tried with little success, in an attempt to reduce the progression of the disease. It appears that the use of ACTH (a hormone secreted from the pituitary gland) is of benefit in some cases.

Rest and avoidance of strenuous activity are important during relapses, with supportive care including good nursing and physical therapy to prevent skin problems such as bed sores or muscle contraction during periods of paralysis.

Multiple sclerosis is a long-term illness, and encouragement and reassurance of both the affected person and the family are essential. The progression of the disease is generally slow, although some patients have frequent attacks and are incapacitated rapidly, while others have extended remissions and are still working some twenty years after the onset of the disease.

The break-down of the myelin sheath which surrounds the nerves prevents the transmission of nerve impulses, causing diseases such as multiple sclerosis. (*Westmead Centre*)

axon
nucleus
degeneration of sheath
Schwann cell
myelin sheath

In some cases, affected persons suffer personality changes, loss of memory and physical deterioration to the extent of needing a wheelchair for mobility. Multiple sclerosis societies have been established in many countries to provide information about the illness, and appliances and devices are available to help people cope with disabilities. General support and encouragement, with the aid of physical therapists, speech therapists and other health professionals expert in this particular field is also available through these societies.

Muscular dystrophy

The muscular dystrophies are a group of inherited diseases which primarily affect the muscles. Weakness and wasting of muscles are progressive to a variable extent and are usually symmetrical. Depending on the type of muscular dystrophy, the patient may be unable to walk, to raise the arms above the head, to sit up or to move the facial muscles normally. Severity ranges from mild to totally disabling.

Muscular dystrophies are categorized according to their mode of inheritance, usual age of onset, severity, rate of progression and distribution of weakness. The four most frequently seen categories are the Duchenne type, the limb-girdle dystrophies, facio-scapulo-humeral muscular dystrophy and myotonic muscular dystrophy (also called dystrophia myotonica). Not all dystrophic patients fall into one of these categories and less common types are recognized.

The Duchenne type used to be called pseudohypertrophic muscular dystrophy, a term which referred to the conspicuous enlargement of some muscle groups, especially the calf muscles, which is seen in affected patients. It is inherited through a sex-linked recessive gene, like hemophilia, and with rare exceptions affects only

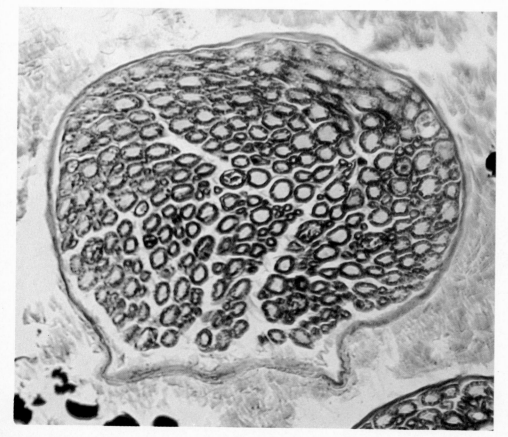

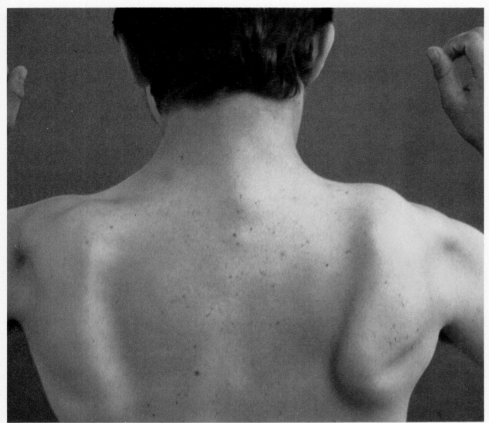

Facio-scapulo-humeral muscular dystrophy affects the muscles of the face and shoulder girdle, preventing the sufferer from raising the arms above shoulder level. (*Westmead Center*)

boys. These boys are usually brought to the doctor at between three and five years of age because of an abnormal gait and a tendency to fall frequently.

Weakness is first evident in the muscles of the pelvis and lower limbs, so that the child has a waddling gait and tends to walk on his toes. He is unable to rise from lying flat on his back by sitting up but has to roll over, get onto his hands and knees and push himself up with his arms. The disease is relentlessly progressive, leading to confinement in a wheelchair in adolescence and then to death, usually from a chest infection, in the late teens or early twenties.

The limb-girdle dystrophies are a group of diseases in which weakness starts in the shoulder girdle or the pelvic girdle. This type of dystrophy is most often, but not invariably, inherited in an autosomal recessive manner. Males and females are equally likely to be affected and the siblings of affected people are at risk. The onset is most often in childhood or adolescence and the rate of progression is variable but sometimes very slow, so that patients may have close to a normal lifespan.

Facio-scapulo-humeral muscular dystrophy is inherited as an autosomal dominant,

affecting both males and females and nearly always affecting one generation after the other. The onset is usually in adolescence or early adulthood. The muscles of the face and the shoulder girdle are affected early so that the patient has an unusual smile, cannot whistle, cannot close the eyes tightly and has difficulty raising the arms above shoulder level. The rate of progression is sometimes so slow as to be unnoticeable and the severity of disability is extremely variable. Only a small proportion of patients are gravely disabled. Some have a moderate degree of disability and others are so mildly affected that they are unaware of any disability. For many who are mildly affected the main worry is the genetic risk to their children.

Myotonic muscular dystrophy is characterised by weakness of the muscles of the face, neck, feet and hands, and also by the phenomenon called myotonia. This is a delayed relaxation of muscle so that after clenching the fist or shaking hands the grip cannot be released quickly. Like facio-scapulo-humeral dystrophy, it is inherited as an autosomal dominant, affecting both sexes in succeeding generations; the disease usually starts in adolescence or early adulthood and is very variable in its severity and rate of progression.

It is unlike the other muscular dystrophies in that it affects many other organs and tissues. There may be cataracts in the eyes, frontal baldness is common

and in males the testes may become small. When it is moderately severe or worse the face is lacking in expression, the eyes are half closed and the speech may become indistinct.

Treatment There is at present no cure for any of the muscular dystrophies. The aim of treatment is to delay or prevent the development of complications and to maintain the best possible functional capability. This is usually best undertaken at a special clinic and involves physical therapy, occupational therapy, advice on nutrition and the avoidance of obesity, educational and vocational guidance, general counseling and sometimes orthopedic surgery to correct deformities of the joints. Immobility may lead to rapid progression of weakness and patients are kept as active as possible.

Precise identification of the type of dystrophy is important in the light of the need for genetic counseling of members of affected families and because other causes of weakness, which may not be progressive and may even be curable, are occasionally mistaken for muscular dystrophy.

Skin problems

Acne A common chronic inflammatory disorder which affects the hair follicle and its related sebaceous gland, acne is characterized by blackheads (comedones), papules, pustules and cysts, mostly on the face, chest and upper back. Commencing at or about puberty, it affects adolescent and young adult males and females equally.

The cause of acne is still not well understood. The hair follicle becomes blocked, forming a comedo, but continues to secrete sebum (an oily secretion that lubricates the skin) which is changed to pus. The normal skin organisms split the neutral fat in sebum into free fatty acids, which sets up an intense inflammatory reaction; this reaction can be aggravated by pressure caused by the patient trying to express the lesion which then heals with scar formation. Hormones and psychological factors seem to have some role: acne is often worse before menstrual periods and in times of stress, for example during school or university examinations.

Treatment begins with skin care: gentle washing with hot water and soap, scalp hygiene, and avoiding greasy cosmetics and cleansing lotions and picking and squeezing. Sunlight seems to improve the condition. There is little evidence that certain foods aggravate acne, but restriction of chocolate, cocoa-bean products and nuts may help.

Acne lotions and creams reduce bacteria or enhance peeling of the surface layer of the skin; there are many preparations available. Oral antibiotics have been the major advance in acne control. The tetracyclines are most often used: these inhibit the growth of normal skin organisms and thus decrease the amount of free fatty acids, which cause the irritation. Low doses can be used over a long term, but there are side effects in some people. Oral contraceptives may help some women, but some types can themselves aggravate acne. Doctors may use a comedo expressor, or drain cystic lesions by needle, or use ultraviolet light or superficial x-rays. Bad scarring may need specialist treatment.

Blackheads Frequently a characteristic of adolescence, a blackhead or comedo is a black, blocked opening to the duct of a

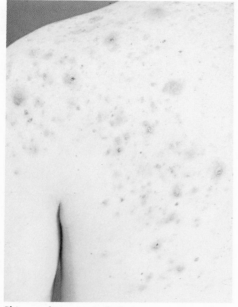

Skin condition typical of acne.

Not all teenagers suffer from acne but even if they do, the condition diminishes as hormones stabilize in adulthood.

Pimples develop when sebum blocks the opening of a sebaceous follicle. Washing with mild soap and water can be helpful.

sebaceous gland on the skin. Sebaceous glands secrete an oily skin lubricant known as sebum. Blackheads are the result of over production of sebum which becomes oxidized to a black color at the dilated opening of the duct, and of an altered androgen hormone balance, particularly during adolescence.

When the duct becomes blocked, the release of sebum into surrounding tissue may start inflammation and the typical pimples that occur with acne. The reaction will be aggravated by attempts to squeeze the blackhead which then heals with scar tissue. In some people, blackheads, which may appear as early as the age of nine or ten, may persist into later adult years.

The skin should be kept as clean as possible. In the case of isolated blackheads an extractor may be used to unblock the duct but if large areas are affected, chemical treatment is generally preferred. Antibiotics are sometimes effective.

Whiteheads Adolescent acne, or pimples, is generally caused by comedones or blackheads when they open onto the skin surface. Where there is no such opening, the comedo lacks pigment and is called a whitehead. Whiteheads occur as early as the eighth or ninth year of age, particularly amongst girls. Comedones develop in the smaller hair follicles when there is an associated relatively large sebaceous or oil gland. These glands become more active at the approach of puberty, producing cheese-like sebum in increasing quantities.

Whiteheads first appear beside the nose, on the chin and on the forehead. They are 0.04–0.01 inch (1–3 mm) deep and cone-shaped, narrowing towards the surface. Only rarely do they become infected, leading to 'blind' pimples. Usually they can be safely ignored.

The Abuse of Drugs

While by no means restricted to the adolescent or young adult, the abuse of drugs does frequently involve the teenager and concerns not only the widely publicized misuse of marijuana and narcotics but also the consumption of alcohol and the smoking of tobacco.

The use of drugs in our society is universal. Some drugs, such as cough mixtures or aspirins, which are used to treat illnesses, are available in the supermarket or the pharmacy 'over the counter'; others, such as morphine, pethidine or barbiturates, are available only on prescription. Tobacco and alcohol are easily available drugs which have no medical application.

The abuse of drugs generally occurs when a drug is taken regularly and in excessive quantities. In many cases the social and economic cost to the individual and to the community is considerable. Drug abuse may be an international, national, social, family or personal problem, largely depending on the drug involved. In some cases an individual may put others at risk. For example, a person driving under the influence of alcohol is a danger not only to himself but to his passengers and to the other road users.

Abuse of a drug often, but not always, implies dependence on the drug to some extent. Dependence is the result of repeated use of the drug. The form of dependence may be psychological or physical. Psychological dependence is an overwhelming compulsion to continue using a drug because of its pleasant effects. This can develop into a habit with a psychological need for the drug. Physical dependence is most obvious in the use of narcotics, where withdrawal of a drug produces physical symptoms such as sweating and a fast pulse rate.

The reasons for drug abuse appear to vary according to the age group and the drug itself. The abuse of drugs by adolescents and young adults results from a combination of factors such as peer group pressure, advertising, anxieties, social pressures, personality problems, and an ignorance of the dangers involved. The middle-aged man with an alcohol problem and the young married woman who chain smokes or takes six compound analgesic powders every day do so for different reasons. The man may regularly have to attend business lunches where alcohol is consumed. As for the woman, the harassments and loneliness of a day spent isolated with young children could be the reason for the pattern of drug abuse.

The abuser of narcotics develops an overwhelming compulsion after only a few experimental doses of the drug.

There is nothing new about drug abuse. From time to time in different cultures fashions have changed in drug taking.

The drugs which seem to be particularly abused at present can be divided into the following groups: alcohol, tobacco, opiates and narcotics, analgesics, marijuana and other forms of cannabis, barbiturates, and amphetamines. Each group must be considered separately according to the scale of abuse, the effects on the individual, the community and the nation, and the measures to restrict their consumption.

There is no easy or universal solution to the abuse of so many different drugs. Measures to control the problem have been taken by some governments. The total elimination of drugs which are abused is most unlikely. However, their

Emotional problems can lead to excessive drinking, which is a major cause of ill health and is often associated with violent behavior. (Drug and Alcohol Authority)

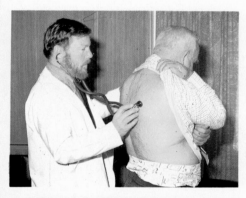

availability can be controlled and some of the adverse effects eliminated by modifying people's habits, for example through advertising. It is vital that the effects of educational programs about the dangers of drug abuse are monitored to determine whether they contribute to the solution of the problem and do not inadvertently advertise drugs or provide ludicrously inaccurate information. Similarly, the results of rehabilitation programs need to be evaluated periodically.

Alcohol It is estimated that 10.6 million Americans are alcoholics, and another 7.3 million abusers of alcohol, making alcohol the leading drug problem in the United States. The long-term physical effects of alcohol abuse can be disastrous, with infiltration of fat into the liver and hardening or scarring of the liver (cirrhosis). Also, drinking alcohol to excess over a long period can cause stomach ulcers, inflammation of the stomach, loss of appetite and therefore deficiency of vitamins in the diet, nerve damage, and weakened heart muscle. Alcohol abuse affects not only the drinker himself but his family and workmates. Marriages break up, children are alienated and abused physically, jobs are lost, normal social and economic functioning becomes impossible, until finally the alcoholic reaches such a state of moral and physical deterioration that he becomes estranged from the rest of the community.

Measures to curb the abuse of alcohol vary according to local laws and regulations. Examples include cancellation of driver's license, auto insurance penalties, mandatory jail sentences, fines and educational programs or convicted drunken drivers and blood alcohol testing.

Amphetamines The significant widespread abuse of amphetamines (pep pills) in the 1960s, which resulted in many psychiatric illnesses, no longer occurs. The use of amphetamines has been drastically reduced by about 90 per cent. It is now rare for a person to be admitted to a psychiatric hospital with amphetamine induced psychosis. This is largely because it is no longer possible to prescribe these drugs for illnesses other than narcolepsy and brain damage in childhood. Previously the drugs were used for treating depression, fatigue, obesity, and epilepsy, and consequently were easy to obtain.

Barbiturates The abuse of barbiturate drugs, leading to dependence, was a major problem years ago, particularly among middle-aged women. The major effects were chronic intoxication and withdrawal symptoms. This problem has been greatly reduced, largely because barbiturates have been replaced as a sedative and hypnotic by the benzodiazapine

drugs. Most doctors are now aware of the danger of dependence.

Cocaine Cocaine is a white powder produced from the leaves of the coca plant grown in South America. Cocaine is a local anesthetic and potent stimulant of the central nervous system.

It first became popular in the United States in the late 19th century and had a resurgence in the mid-1970s. Today, cocaine represents a serious problem. While previously thought not to be dangerous or addictive, it is now thought to be the most addictive and popular drug, both physically and psychologically. It can be lethal, causing cardiac arrest, respiratory failure, or brain hemorrhage, even in small doses.

Cocaine is used a number of ways: it can be sniffed, injected, or smoked. 'Crack' is a very potent smokable form of cocaine that has 10 times the effect of sniffing and is much more addictive.

LSD Lysergic acid diethylamide, or LSD, is perhaps the best known hallucinogenic drug. First discovered in the 1940s, it did not come into prominence until the 'flower power and love culture' period of the late 1960s and early 1970s.

Older adolescents and people in their early twenties are those who use it most frequently, its use is not as widespread as a number of other illegal drugs. Commonly, it is referred to as 'acid' or 'sugar', the latter term being used because a drop of LSD solution is sometimes swallowed in a sugar cube. The drug is not physically

LSD is a powerful man-made drug which produces striking, sometimes terrifying distortions in sight, sound and smell. It is available in various forms.

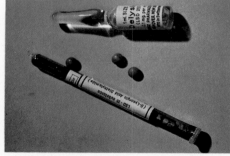

addictive as are a number of the other illegal drugs, although tolerance may develop very readily.

The effect of LSD varies greatly from person to person so there is no typical 'trip'. Some people, seeking to experience expanded consciousness and heightened perception, can suffer a 'bad trip'. Dramatic illusions may occur with an allied false sense of perception, so that colors become more vivid and immobile objects seem to change shape or to move.

Delusions can result so that the LSD user thinks he is able to fly or that he is immune to normal dangers. The perception of time may be altered and moods may change from euphoric to intense anxiety or sheer terror.

In a severe case of hallucination and terror while under the influence of LSD, the experience can be cut short by an intramuscular injection of sedative by a doctor.

Marijuana is produced from the dried leaves, stems and flowering tops of the hemp plant, *Cannabis sativa* and is usually smoked as 'reefers'. It is not a narcotic drug.

The acute toxicity of marijuana is very low compared with most drugs, but acute intoxication is possible through smoking, with a loss of psychomotor skills rather

1 *Cannabis sativa*, the plant from which marijuana is obtained.
2 A bottle of hash oil, one of the purest forms of marijuana. (*Drug and Alcohol Authority*)

1

2

1

2

3

Above
1 'Gray rocks', a form of heroin.
2 Morphine base prepared in block form.
3 The leaves of the coca plant from which the drug cocaine is derived. *Drug and Alcohol Authority*)

like the effect of alcohol. This acute intoxication certainly reduces the efficiency of the individual. There is no satisfactory evidence regarding the presence or absence of long-term effects.

Narcotic drugs such as morphine, heroin, codeine, opium, pethidine and methadone are abused by a very small proportion of the population (less than 0.5 per cent). The repeated use of these drugs rapidly leads to physical dependence, when the individual cannot withdraw from using the drug without experiencing unpleasant symptoms. The individual may also become psychologically dependent on the drug and craving may lead to stealing or even murder for another dose of the drug.

The cost of narcotic addiction is high

and the money is generally acquired through means such as prostitution, drug smuggling or trading, robbery and other criminal acts. The risks of narcotic abuse are huge largely because of the uncertain composition and doubtful purity of the drug and the use of contaminated syringe needles to inject the drug into the vein.

Some of the diseases that are caused by narcotic addiction include blood borne virus infections of the liver (hepatitis), and multiple abscesses infecting heart valves, kidneys and lungs. There is always the danger that a lethal overdose may be unwittingly self-administered.

Below
1 Smoking contributes to the deaths of thousands annually.
2 Even non-smokers may suffer eye, nose and lung irritations if near smokers.
3 More young women are taking up smoking. (*Drug and Alcohol Authority*)

1

2

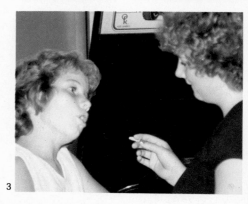

3

Few narcotic addicts live beyond 30 years of age. They will only increase their chance of doing so if they manage to stabilize their consumption on a small dose of the drug or cease using it completely.

It is a criminal offence to possess opiates and narcotics unless they are obtained on prescription. Drug abusers are frequently involved in other crimes. Although prison sentences are not an ideal form of treatment, in some instances the lives of addicts are saved by compulsory abstinence during confinement.

Drug referral and treatment centers use different methods of trying to wean the addict from the drug, sometimes substituting methadone for the original drug of addiction. Group and behavior therapy is used with varying degrees of success. Some centers are independently controlled and others are government sponsored. The British method is to reduce the dose gradually while providing the addict with a limited but constant supply which is maintained for years while the addict lives a normal life. This method is not universally favored.

Tobacco smoking is a form of drug abuse which contributes to death from heart disease and lung cancer. There is absolutely no doubt that smoking is a health hazard.

Recent surveys have shown that the heaviest smokers are those in the 20–35 year age group, and that smoking among young women is rising. Men over 50 years of age have a greater tendency to stop smoking.

Smoking is a causative factor in the following conditions: cancer of the lung, cancer of other respiratory sites (for example, the larynx), chronic bronchitis and emphysema, non-syphilitic aortic aneurysm, ischemic heart disease, cancer of the esophagus (gullet), tuberculosis of the lung, heart disease due to lung disease, ulcers of the stomach, cancer of the bladder, pneumonia, arteriosclerosis, and cerebral thrombosis. It has also been found that the following are associated with smoking: cancer of the pancreas, hypertension (high blood pressure), cancer of the rectum, suicide, cirrhosis of the liver and poisoning.

The effect of smoking on non-smokers (so called 'passive smokers') include eye irritation, nose irritation, coughing and wheezing. Children under one year old whose parents are heavy smokers are twice as likely to suffer pneumonia and bronchitis as children whose families are non-smokers. The stillbirth and death rate of babies in the first week of life is 30 per cent more than in non or passive smokers and they have lower than normal birth weight for their gestation.

In some countries there are restrictions on smoking on public transport and in public places such as hospitals, theatres and cinemas. There are also non-smoking areas in public places.

It is important that high tar cigarettes should be progressively banned until only low tar cigarettes are available. The tar and nicotine contents of cigarettes should be stated on cigarette packets. In some countries and states television and radio advertising of cigarettes is banned at certain times. The sale of cigarettes to children under 16 years of age is legally prohibited. Unfortunately, antismoking education campaigns have not been very effective in discouraging the young from smoking.

In most countries there are clinics and groups which help people to stop smoking.

Drug addiction

A person who uses drugs as a habit or to relieve unpleasant withdrawal symptoms is described as being drug dependent or addicted. Dependence on a drug is influenced by the personality of the drug-taker, circumstances, and the drug itself.

Certain kinds of personality, especially the psychopathic, the immature and the unstable, readily become addicted to drugs and will use any drug that is available, indicating that the nature of the person is more significant than the nature of the drug. If one drug becomes difficult to obtain the addict will use another.

A drug may be used simply because it is easily accessible. For example, in certain occupations there is frequent exposure to certain kinds of drugs. In some cases people become addicted to sleeping tablets first given to them in hospital as a sedative.

A drug itself may have certain attractions, and produce certain desired effects. For example, alcohol may be used to reduce inhibitions, morphine to kill pain, and barbiturates to produce 'highs'. Also some drugs are more likely to lead to dependence than others. There is considerably greater psychological dependence on heroin, morphine, cocaine, and amphetamine than on marijuana, and there is greater physical dependence on heroin and morphine than on barbiturates, alcohol and amphetamine, and physical dependence is even less on cocaine and marijuana.

The most common addictive drugs are cocaine and the opiates or narcotics such as heroin and morphine. Morphine can be prescribed to relieve pain without fear of addiction, though if taken often enough it will lead to addiction. Heroin, which is a derivative of morphine, is even more likely to cause addiction. If heroin is withdrawn from the addict he will experience restlessness and sweating.

Physical dependence is a state of addiction which develops from taking increasing amounts of the drug as tolerance increases. Eventually it is impossible to withdraw the drug without severe withdrawal symptoms, in some cases leading to death. The need to relieve these symptoms is a feature of physical addiction.

Psychological dependence is the formation of a habit involving milder forms of addictive drugs such as tobacco, alcohol, and amphetamines. A person develops a habit of taking a particular drug because it produces a certain effect or change in mood. The habit is established when the individual takes the drug irrespective of mood. This indicates the psychological need and the individual becomes disturbed if the drug is not available when needed.

Addiction to tobacco nicotine is more psychological than physical. The withdrawal symptoms include craving for a cigarette, sleeplessness, coughing, and increase in appetite. The dependence of alcohol, which has been described as a liquid barbiturate, is less likely than dependence on other barbiturates such as amphetamines. The use of solid barbiturates has now been largely replaced by the use of tranquilizers such as diazepam and oxazepam.

Drug addiction is responsible for thousands of deaths by suicide and accidental overdosage, for considerable private suffering, for reduced working efficiency and for the loss of millions of working hours.

The eventual effects on the individual vary with the drug. In the case of cigarette smoking there may be damage to the lungs and arteries, and in the case of alcoholism, brain damage.

Illegal drug-taking can lead to conflict with the legal authorities and to danger from association with criminals. A heroin addict risks being sold a sample of indeterminate strength, with the consequent dangers of overdosage.

Treatment of addiction is extremely difficult. Psychotherapy is often used, though it is seldom successful. Alcoholics can be helped by Alcoholics Anonymous. Dependency on cocaine or amphetamine is treated by withdrawal of the drug. Heroin addicts may need a steady supply of a drug, a situation that is dealt with in different ways in different countries.

Despite an increasing body of knowledge about the harmful effects of drug taking and the tightening of criminal penalties for drug possession and abuse, the spread of drugs in Western societies continues relatively unabated. The problems of drug dependence are still controversial and the treatment of drug addicts is similarly an open question.

Drug withdrawal

When an individual who is physically or psychologically dependent on a drug suddenly abstains from using it, he will experience the physical and psychological symptoms of drug withdrawal. As these

Young people injecting themselves with heroin. The men are in their early twenties — but are already confirmed users of narcotics. The girl is just 16 years old. She has taken cocaine and heroin for a year after first 'getting hooked' at a teenagers' party. *(Abbottempo)*

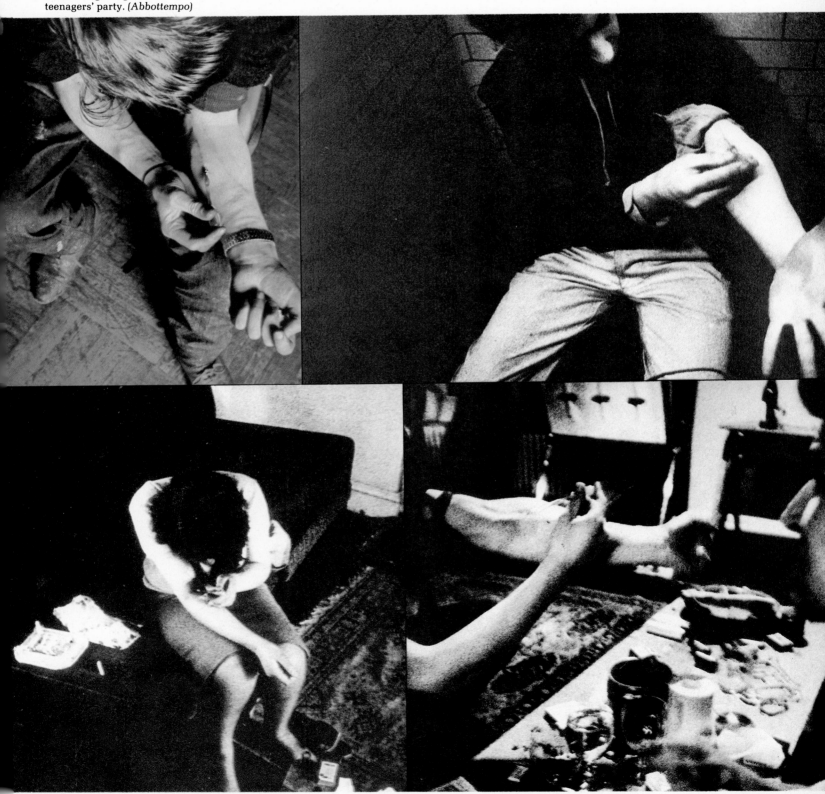

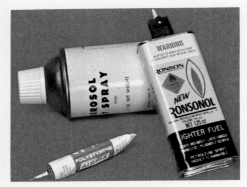

Various preparations have been used by addicts in an effort to experience 'highs'. (*Drug and Alcohol Authority*)

symptoms are often unpleasant, and because the condition may become dangerous, the patient will require close supervision. The severity of the symptoms and the potential outcome varies according to the drug.

In the case of the chronic alcoholic, the withdrawal symptoms are often those of delirium tremens, that is, extreme anxiety, shaking, agitation, irritability, and inability to sleep. Sometimes there are hallucinations involving animals and shapes, and sound and touch. A person in this state may be panic-stricken, confused, and unable to remember much of what has happened. This often continues for two to seven days. Treatment is possible with vitamins and sedatives.

Cocaine is a very dangerous drug not only because of its addictive properties but also the difficulty of breaking that addiction. It is estimated that only one third of first attempts at rehabilitation are successful. The monetary cost of cocaine is high, and the user must often resort to crime to support the habit. Withdrawal from cocaine causes apathy, long periods of sleep, irritability and depression.

The sudden withdrawal from barbitu-

rates can cause similar effects, namely, anxiety, restlessness and shaking, and after a short time delirium and convulsions. As this condition can be fatal if not promptly treated, it is imperative that the withdrawal from barbiturates is strictly supervised by medical staff. Other sedatives, such as meprobamate and chloridiazepoxide, produce effects which include anxiety, sleeplessness, loss of appetite, vomiting, unsteadiness, shakiness, muscle spasms, and seizures.

The outcome of barbiturate withdrawal can be much more serious than that of heroin. Heroin withdrawal symptoms begin with streaming of eyes and nose, yawning, itching, perspiring, and restlessness. If withdrawal continues the symptoms become more severe, with cramp, nausea, vomiting, diarrhea, chills and muscle spasms. Although this is an unpleasant experience, it is not fatal.

In the case of LSD (lysergic acid diethylamide) and mescaline, the withdrawal symptoms are panic, and feelings of derealization and depersonalization. It is vital for this condition to be closely supervised. In some cases tranquilizers may be helpful.

6 The Mature Adult

Middle Age Changes and Health

The period between youth and old age when the peak of physical maturity is reached and the gains in life are consolidated, is referred to as middle age. Psychologically it is usually characterized by a subsidence of youthful ardor, sexual aggression and ambition as the individual accepts his status in life.

Characteristics of middle age

Physical changes Beginning somewhere between the mid-thirties and late forties in women and in men perhaps slightly later, middle age is characterized physically by widening of the girth and hips, lining of the face and reduced energy. Hair, already thinner, recedes from the forehead, particularly in men, and gradually loses its color and tone. With decreased skin elasticity the face becomes more lined and female breasts sag. Degenerative skin lesions, the so-called 'liver spots' and red raised papules may appear for the first time.

Diet often increases in both quality and quantity as income rises or stabilizes and the responsibilities to children lessen. Stress is also less prevalent but degenerative and malignant diseases can rapidly become more apparent. Infections, accidents and congenital disorders are usually less hazardous, while blood pressure, stomach ulcers and similar stress-related diseases become much more difficult to reverse and overcome.

Intellectual changes Memory loss slowly occurs and new learning seems more difficult, perhaps because of a general lack of stimulus. A wide and varied interest can slow this deterioration. A gradual narrowing and hardening of all arteries to all tissues is caused by the slow deposition of lipids or fatty substances onto the inner lining of blood vessels. Heavy smoking can accelerate this and progressively limit the degree of blood flow to the brain and other vital tissues. Middle age depression and apathy may be partly caused by such changes.

Diseases Coronary heart disease usually first appears in mid to late middle age. People become more sedentary and heart attacks become more likely as a result of a decrease in blood supply to the arteries supplying the heart muscle. The result is chest pain (angina) and increased effort by the heart to maintain fitness. Such attacks are usually more common in men under 45, and become increasingly common among women after the female menopause. Diminishing blood supply to the gut may lead to decreased food absorption, causing discomfort from bulky meals. Also decreased blood supply to the legs may cause muscle pain after strenuous walking.

Gastric ulcers are most likely to occur in people of the 40–50 year age group.

Movement is limited when joints deteriorate and stiffen, particularly if they were damaged by extreme activities in youth. Osteoporosis, or diminished bone density caused by hormonal changes and a decrease in general activity, first appears at this time.

The pituitary gland may slowly become less active, possibly causing a decrease in thyroid and other glandular activity which in turn, if the pancreatic gland is affected, can lead to diabetes mellitus.

Malignant cancers, affecting the breasts, uterus, prostate and large bowel, become more apparent and more frequent from middle age onwards. This may be the result of a deterioration in the activity of the immune system.

Menopause Various glandular or endocrine changes occur. On reaching menopause, women experience a decline in fertility and their bodies begin to thicken. Their periods decline in frequency and amount, and they experience hot flushing caused by the instability of the vasomotor system which controls the constricting and dilating of blood vessels. Women may experience emotional changes for several months as the various female hormones readjust to different levels, and agitated outbursts and depression are more likely.

An understanding and sensible family doctor, through counseling and reassurance, can often resolve the worries and bewilderment of a woman at this time. Vaginal jellies, sometimes containing estrogens, can help vaginal dryness and stop the itching. If the flushes are frequent and severe some doctors give short courses of estrogen, the female sex hormone, which is very effective in reducing their number and severity. Most doctors agree that there is no perfect replacement available for human estrogen and side effects are lessened by short courses rather than long-term treatment.

After menopause women generally become far more relaxed and happy. Although pregnancy is no longer possible sexual awareness or enjoyment should not decline and may improve as the fear of pregnancy is eradicated. Because of a reduction in natural secretions the vagina

Above
An understanding family may allay
the depression sometimes caused by
the menopause. *(Zefa)*

Left
Middle-age may be a time of
relaxation and enjoyment. *(Zefa)*

becomes less acid and more prone to infection, and its linings tend to become dry and thin (atrophic). Pelvic muscle tone may also diminish and cause prolapse or dropping down of the womb, which might require surgical repair.

Male menopause Authorities cannot agree on an average age for the falling level of male hormone (testosterone) to affect sexual function and drive. Flushing and other physical or psychological symptoms are less obvious and are seen less often in the male.

Over half of the middle-aged men have some degree of prostate gland enlargement and a few ultimately have difficulty in emptying the bladder. In rare cases this can cause satyrism or excessive sexual desire and associated painful and protracted erection. Testicles may decline in size although this is apparently arrested by greater sexual activity. Associated psychological depression is not uncommon.

Ways of dealing with middle age

Several steps are advisable to counter po-

tential health problems. Regular medical check-ups are often considered advisable. Attention is given to urine tests, various blood tests, the blood count, blood pressure, and the heart and lungs. A pelvic examination, chest x-ray, a cardiograph to check the heart, plus sigmoidoscopy for deep examination of the bowel, may be considered important.

Secondly, daily physical exercise to induce heavy breathing, sweating and almost doubling the pulse rate may be regarded as essential. Walking, jogging, swimming and squash are recommended. Exercise should be gradually increased, otherwise there may be undue stress on the heart.

Care must be taken to control diet and weight, which is difficult to lose with increasing age.

The importance of positive thinking

Despite the fact that potential health problems exist in middle age and onwards, there is absolutely no reason, in the vast majority of cases, to be gloomy about advancing years.

Personal interests should be maintained — there will probably be more time for them now that the children are growing up. Many middle-aged people with time

Many forms of sport can be played
with enjoyment by the middle-aged.

on their hands find that a return to study, even to college, is most rewarding. Helping the less fortunate gives purpose and warmth to life. Keeping up with old friends, and making new ones, is all part of a positive attitude which will give validity to the often-quoted 'Life begins at 40'.

Medical Problems and Conditions

The conditions, problems and diseases described in the following pages are those which, if they occur, generally, but by no means always, do so in the middle years. The reader will, of course, know of exceptions in many cases, and more importantly, should be aware that most people will encounter very few, if any, of the conditions mentioned. It is, however, of interest to know something of problems which may arise. Difficulties and ailments, great and small, are always less alarming if faced with some knowledge about their probable form and outcome.

Anemia

A blood disorder, anemia is characterized by a reduction in circulating red blood cells. Red blood cells contain a special iron-containing pigment called hemoglobin which gives blood its color. During the time that it takes blood to pass through the lungs, hemoglobin combines with oxygen, producing a bright red color. Once this oxygen has been released in the small vessels (capillaries) of the body, the blood takes on a darker, bluish appearance.

Hemoglobin is measured according to its concentration in the blood (as millimoles per liter). The normal range in men is 8.7 to 11.2 mmol/L, and for women 7.8 to 10.5 mmol/L. The slightly lower range in women is the result of the persistent blood loss that occurs during menstruation. Anemia is considered to occur when the level of hemoglobin falls below these values.

There are many causes of anemia but clinically it is the result of three main processes; loss of blood, inadequate production of red blood cells and excessive destruction of hemoglobin or whole red blood cells.

Loss of red blood cells Blood loss can occur in many ways. Hemorrhage from external wounds is an obvious cause but slow bleeding inside the body may proceed unnoticed and result in anemia. Disorders in the gastrointestinal tract such as peptic ulcers, cancers and diverticular disease are the commonest causes of unnoticed blood loss. Abnormally heavy or frequent menstrual periods is another cause. Although rare, nose bleeds, blood in the urine and coughing up blood from the lungs can occasionally cause anemia.

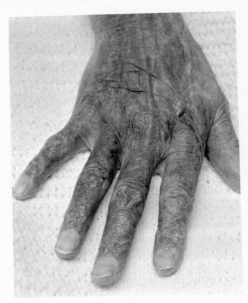

The hands of a patient suffering from pernicious anemia.
(Westmead Center)

Diagnosis The main clinical feature of anemia is pallor of the skin, although this may easily be masked by suntan or natural pigmentation. The color of the lining membrane of the lips, mouth and tongue and the conjunctiva of the eyes is a much better guide. In severe anemia, the creases in the palms of the hands lose color. Physical complaints are related to the reduced oxygen-carrying capacity of the blood; tiredness, particularly on exertion, is common. Headaches, dizziness, loss of appetite, and increased sensitivity to cold may also be noticed. The pulse rate is usually rapid, especially on exertion. Occasionally the amount of oxygen that can be carried by the blood to the heart is so reduced that a severe chest pain (anginal pain) is produced.

Several physical signs may help distinguish the particular cause of anemia; for example iron-deficiency anemia may produce a sore tongue, flat brittle nails and coarse hair.

The presence of anemia is confirmed by examination of the blood, in particular the concentration of the hemoglobin. The shape and size of the red blood cells may be altered in various forms of anemia. For example, iron deficiency produces abnormally small red blood cells, whereas a reduced level of folic acid or vitamin B_{12} will result in abnormally large cells called macrocytes. Special examination of the bone marrow, where red blood cells are formed, may further help in identifying the cause. A special needle to remove a portion of marrow is inserted into the center of the breast bone.

Inadequate production of red blood cells Three main vitamins and minerals are required for the production of red blood cells; iron, vitamin B_{12} and folic acid.

1 Normal blood. (Abbottempo)

2 Pernicious anemia. The red blood cells are irregular in size and shape but the hemoglobin content and volume are greater than normal. (Abbottempo)

3 Normal marrow. (Abbottempo)

4 Pernicious anemia. Megaloblasts, large cells with finely stippled chromatin in the nucleus, are presented in the marrow. (Abbottempo)

1

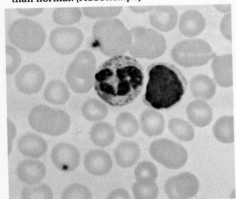

2

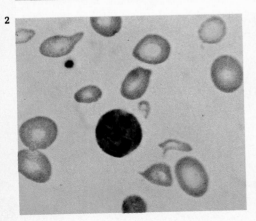

3

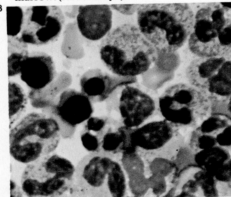

4

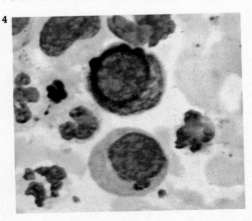

A deficiency of iron in the body may result from an insufficient amount in the diet. This occurs particularly during infancy or pregnancy when demands are greater, and in the adolescent female when the combination of increased needs for growth and the onset of loss via menstruation may reduce iron levels in the body. Any persistent blood loss may reduce the body's iron stores.

A lack of vitamin B_{12} can be the result of an inadequate diet, usually a lack of animal products, resulting in *nutritional anemia*; a special inflammatory condition in the stomach called *pernicious anemia*; and certain diseases of the bowel that produce malabsorption or reduced absorption of vitamins and other compounds.

Folic acid deficiency is most commonly caused by an inadequate dietary intake. Deficiencies of other substances such as protein and copper, and some other vitamins such as pyridoxine and nicotinic acid, may produce anemia, but these are more likely to cause more prominent clinical abnormalities.

Various chemicals and toxins may affect the production of red blood cells in the marrow. Heavy metals, such as lead and mercury, and antibiotic drugs like chloramphenicol and the cytotoxics (toxins which attack the cells of specific organs) are occasional causes of anemia. Such agents may affect the production of other components of blood (white blood cells and platelets). The term *aplastic anemia* is used to describe a depressed production of all types of blood cells.

Conditions such as leukemia, lymphoma and multiple myeloma may infiltrate into the bone marrow and reduce production of red blood cells. Chronic infections and inflammations such as collagen diseases and liver and kidney disease may also produce anemia.

Defects in red blood cells There are several conditions that cause the red blood cells to break down excessively. These are grouped together as the *hemolytic anemias*. Defects in the red blood cells can be in the lining membrane of the cell, as in spherocytosis; in the enzymes in the cell, as in glucose-6-phosphate dehydrogenase deficiency; or in the structure of the hemoglobin molecule itself, as in the *thalassemias*.

Treatment of anemia varies according to the cause. Deficiencies of iron, folic acid or vitamin B_{12} are the commonest causes of anemia. Once serious conditions that may be producing these low levels have been excluded anemia can be treated by replacing the levels of iron, folic acid or vitamin B_{12} in the body.

Angina Pectoris

Angina pectoris is a severe chest pain located behind the breast bone, usually brought on by exertion but, in some cases, it may occur at rest. The pain may spread down into the arms or up into the jaw and is so severe that it causes the person to stop whatever they are doing.

The pain is the result of the blood flow to the heart muscle being inadequate to meet the need for oxygen. This can be caused by a blockage of the veins supplying the heart itself, as in arteriosclerosis, or can be caused by other factors, such as

Causes of anemia

1 *Excessive blood loss*
Menorrhagia (excessive menstrual bleeding)
Bleeding in the digestive tract
    peptic ulcer
    cancer

2 *Inadequate production of blood cells*
Deficiency of essential components
    iron, B_{12}
    folic acid
    protein
    copper
    other vitamins
Infiltration into the marrow
    leukemia
    lymphoma
    multiple myeloma
    carcinoma (cancer)
    myelofibrosis
Depression of red blood cell production
    heavy metals
    cytotoxic drugs
    chloramphenicol

Disorders of endocrine glands
    thyrotoxicosis
    myxedema
    Addison's disease
Severe chronic inflammations and diseases
    collagen diseases
    chronic kidney disease
    chronic liver disease

3 *Excessive destruction of red blood cells (hemolytic anemia)*
    thalassemia
    glucose-6-phosphate
     dehydrogenase deficiency
    spherocytosis
    drugs
    porphyria
    sickle cell anemia

Angina pectoris may be brought on by stress situations such as the frustration of driving in heavy traffic.

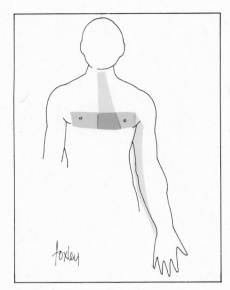

Areas of pain experienced in angina pectoris. *(Westmead Centre)*

severe emotional upsets or conditions which cause an increase in the heart rate. The pain is characteristically described as a 'tight band around the chest'.

The treatment of angina may be as easy as getting rid of excess weight and stopping smoking, which plays a great role in decreasing the coronary blood flow. However, if vessel disease is present, as in arteriosclerosis, then anticoagulant medication may be required. The regular use of aspirin 'thins' the blood and may be used in regular treatment.

If coronary arterial disease is severe, the blockages may have to be dilated by the use of a technique called 'balloon angioplasty', or by using a laser to literally melt the blockages. In many cases this treatment will not work and a surgical procedure called 'bypass surgery' is required. Here veins from a leg are used to replace or bypass the diseased and blocked coronary arteries which feed the heart.

In many cases the angina may be controlled very well by medication, the commonest being Anginine or glyceryl trinitrate, which is a tablet taken when an attack occurs. This is an old but very effective treatment.

Newer medications are available which work in various ways, the commonest being a group of drugs called 'calcium blockers', also available in tablet form. Another form of treatment consists of a patch, impregnated with medication, which is stuck on the skin. The medication is absorbed through the skin over 24 hours. There are also topical ointments which are widely used.

This disease has become much more amenable to treatment, especially over the last ten years.

Many seeds and pollens, particularly of grasses, will trigger an asthma attack.

Asthma

Asthma is common in children and more common in males than in females. But while children tend to grow out of it, in adults it tends to recur.

A condition in which the bronchial tubes narrow, causing difficulty in breathing, asthma is episodic in nature and largely reversible. Between attacks of asthma there is usually no difficulty in breathing. Up to 10 per cent of children are reported to have episodes of wheezing, but the vast majority grow out of it. Only 1 per cent or less of adults suffer such attacks.

During an episode of asthma, there is difficulty in drawing air into the lungs, and even more in blowing it out (expiration). The latter difficulty occurs because the bronchi and the smaller bronchioles become shorter and narrower during expiration, with the contraction of muscle in their walls; thus, any pre-existing narrowing is made worse. Wheezing, which is one of the main features of asthma, results. It is a high-pitched musical sound, occurring during expiration, and is heard even in relatively mild asthma attacks. Expiration, which is louder because of the bronchial narrowing, is also considerably lengthened.

The presence of wheezing, however, does not necessarily indicate asthma. Young children may develop a wheeze during an attack of respiratory infection such as bronchitis and certain diseases such as emphysema may produce a persistent wheeze in older people.

Breathlessness and a feeling of tightness across the chest are also features of asthma. Coughing is common, as a result of bronchial mucosal irritation and excess mucus production, both frequently present together. In a severe attack, the

One agent that is known to trigger some asthma attacks is the dust mite.

sufferer can become exhausted, as the amount of effort needed to maintain an adequate level of oxygen in the blood can be quite significant. A further problem is that extra oxygen is needed to maintain the effort of breathing, so that a cycle is set up, which, on occasions, can lead to extreme exhaustion.

Attacks of asthma usually begin suddenly and their duration and severity vary. An extremely severe episode of asthma that persists for many hours, or even days, is termed *status asthmaticus*. Such attacks are often resistant to therapy and occasionally may lead to death. Mechanical respirators are sometimes needed to help breathing when exhaustion is so severe that respiration becomes ineffective. Medical attention is essential, and hospitalization is usually needed for these severe attacks of asthma.

Causes The reason why some people develop asthma is only partially understood. Asthmatics appear to have bronchi that are particularly sensitive. Possibly they lack some of the defense mechanisms that normally protect the mucosal lining from irritants. Similar abnormal mechanisms are seen in other allergic diseases. The specific agent (allergen) that triggers an asthma attack can be identified in only 50 per cent of sufferers.

Heredity. Asthma has an hereditary component that appears to be associated with allergies in general. Childhood eczema, hay fever and other associated conditions are more common in both asthma sufferers and their close relatives than in the general population.

Allergens. Direct contact with a specific allergen is a frequent initiating factor. Common allergens are the house dust mite (dermatophagoides), house dust itself, grass pollens, other plant material and animal fur. Environmental pollution, including soot, smog and tobacco smoke are also well known bronchial irritants. In some cases, hypersensitivity occurs only after prolonged or repeated exposure to an allergen.

Respiratory infection is commonly associated with asthma, but the exact sequence of events is uncertain. Whether swelling of the bronchial lining in a hypersensitive reaction predisposes to attack by invading bacteria, or whether inflamed or infected mucosa lead to accumulation of the allergen is unclear.

Psychological and emotional factors can also precipitate an attack of asthma. Children may initiate episodes of wheezing 'voluntarily' to obtain extra attention.

Exercise, especially if it is sudden and energetic, such as a burst of running, can also be troublesome. Swimming, however, usually causes no problems and is, in fact, often recommended as a sport and form of physical therapy for asthmatic patients, because of the slow, regular and deep breathing required.

Effects of an attack When an attack of asthma occurs, several factors are usually involved simultaneously. In asthmatics with a definite allergic background, there is usually an increased blood level of a particular antibody (immunoglobulin gamma E or IgE). This combines with the irritating allergen, causing the release of chemicals from the mast cells found in the walls of the bronchi and bronchioles. The substances released include histamine and serotonin, which cause contraction of the bronchial muscle.

In longstanding asthma, persistent changes occur and do not revert when the episode of wheezing is over. Because of the difficulty in getting air out of the lungs, the latter often remain overinflated. This may lead to a mild 'pigeon chest' deformity. Changes also occur in the bronchial walls. Muscle fibers become enlarged, parts of the bronchial lining thicken, and an increased number of special 'allergic' cells are present in the lining.

Direct contact with an allergen such as animal fur is frequently an initiating factor in asthma attack.

Treatment consists of relieving symptoms and controlling factors likely to cause further asthma attacks. Triggering factors are sought by careful history taking. In some cases, special measures to reduce the amount of dust in the house, and avoidance of certain animals and occasionally certain foodstuffs may be of value. Patch testing (where substances are placed on, or injected into, the skin, to see if a reaction occurs) may be used to confirm that certain antigens are responsible for attacks. Desensitization is occasionally of benefit, especially if pollen or house dust mites are the main allergens triggering attacks.

If there is a strong association between asthma and attacks of infection, especially of bronchitis in those with other underlying lung diseases, use of antibiotics at the first sign of infection, or occasionally the longterm use of antibiotics such as tetracycline to prevent infections is helpful. Psychological factors may, in certain circumstances, require specific consideration.

A number of drugs are used to treat asthma. *Bronchodilators*, which reverse the muscle spasm of the bronchi consist mainly of two chemical groups. Sympathomimetics, which stimulate the nerve endings of the sympathetic nervous system, causing the bronchial muscle to relax, now include such new compounds as salbutamol and terbutaline which are less likely to cause rapid or irregular heart rhythm than earlier drugs such as adrenalin, because their action is more specific to the lungs.

Theophylline drugs, such as aminophylline, have a direct relaxing effect on bronchial smooth muscle, and are often used in combination with the bronchodilators. Bronchodilators may either be used in the acute attack, or on a regular basis to maintain adequate breathing. The presence of a wheeze, even if heard only through the stethoscope, indicates a degree of constriction. Keeping a person continually free from wheezing is the ideal.

Drugs can be taken as tablets, liquids, rectal suppositories or inhalations from aerosol packs. The last method delivers the medication direct to the bronchi, with more rapid results and reduced side effects, as smaller amounts of the drug are needed. When these methods of self administration fail to give adequate relief, medical aid should be sought. Generally injected medications are then given.

Steroids are a group of powerful and effective drugs. Hydrocortisone is often given by injection in very severe attacks of asthma, and prednisolone tablets are prescribed for chronic asthma which cannot be controlled adequately by other means. Significant side effects can occur with steroids so they are used only if absolutely necessary, and then in the smallest possible doses.

Advances in the treatment of asthma have occurred with the development of a preventive medication and a steroid in aerosol form. Sodium cromoglycate is an inhaled drug that acts on the surface of the bronchi to block allergic reactions. As this drug must be present before the allergen in order to prevent the reaction, it must be taken on a regular basis, usually three to four times a day, and is of little use once an attack of wheezing has begun. Beclomethasone is the inhaled steroid and is also often used between wheezing attacks as a preventative. Though this form of steroid administration produces minimal side effects, it is best reserved for use in those cases which have failed to respond to both simple bronchodilators and cromoglycate.

Although histamine is one of the chemicals involved in the asthma process, the value of the anti-histamine group of drugs in treating wheezing is negligible. Sedatives in general should not be used either, as they may further depress an already labored respiration.

Breathing exercises are advocated by a number of doctors. As mentioned earlier, swimming, which may be preceded by a dose of bronchodilator, is a very beneficial way of obtaining this exercise. Many people with asthma are encouraged to swim all the year round.

Various organizations have been established to help asthma sufferers and their families deal with asthma, and to promote increased public knowledge and awareness of the disease.

Backache
Although a number of disease processes may be responsible for backache, injury is the commonest cause. Backache may involve one or more of the many structures and tissues in the lumbar area including the discs, the intervertebral joints, the ligaments that lie alongside these joints and several layers of muscle.

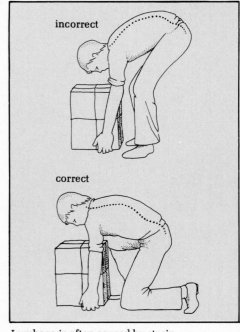

Lumbago is often caused by strain from heavy lifting or stretching. People whose jobs involve continued stress on the back should lift and bend in a way which causes them the least possible strain.

Lumbago A low back pain which does not radiate to other areas is often called lumbago. This type of sudden backache occurs most frequently in the 25 to 55 year age group, and is mostly caused by heavy lifting or stretching. Pain begins within a quarter of an hour, and gradually worsens over the next six hours. Mild cases may recover in a few days, but some persist for several weeks.

In some cases the cause of lumbago may be a mild degree of injury to a disc, which is not severe enough to irritate the surrounding spinal nerves. This type of injury is more likely to occur when a person lifts a heavy object and turns at the same time.

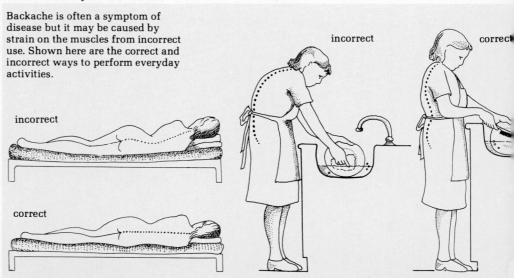

Backache is often a symptom of disease but it may be caused by strain on the muscles from incorrect use. Shown here are the correct and incorrect ways to perform everyday activities.

Lumbosacral strain, in which fibers of a ligament are stretched or torn, is the other likely cause of lumbago. When ligament or muscle strain occurs predominantly on one side of the back, bending sideways away from the injury causes pain as the damaged tissues stretch. Leaning backwards is painless as there is no stretching of these tissues. These two maneuvers are used to distinguish between damage to ligaments or muscles and disorders of the vertebral bones and discs, which produce pain on all movement of the back.

A prolapsed or 'slipped' disc is another major cause of sudden back pain. Cartilagenous discs which lie between the vertebral bodies act as flexible cushions, giving the spinal column its mobility in bending forward and sideways. With increasing age these discs degenerate and when an injury is sustained, this degeneration is often a factor, causing the protrusion (prolapse) of some of the disc contents from the normal position.

The discs between the two lowermost lumbar vertebrae (called L4 and L5) and between the fifth lumbar vertebra and the sacrum are most often affected. Not only is pain felt locally, but in many cases the disc presses on the nerve coming from the vertebral column. Pain is then felt in the nerves down the back of the leg and sometimes in the foot. This sharp and intense pain is called *sciatica*. Movements that stretch the nerve fibers aggravate the pain. The straight leg raising test is the classic method of diagnosis of disc protrusion. The patient lies on his back and the leg on the affected side is raised in the air. When protrusion has occurred the nerves are stretched over the inflamed disc, exacerbating the pain. Normally the leg can be lifted almost 90° from the horizontal but in severe sciatica pain may be extreme at an angle of only 30°.

Other sudden backaches The specific cause of backache is sometimes difficult to define. If the spine or deep structures

are involved, localized tenderness is less marked because of the intervening layers of unaffected muscles and ligaments. Protective muscle spasm, which usually occurs at the site of most disturbances, often causes a dull ache which may complicate diagnosis.

Congenital structural variations of the vertebral column are quite common and because of the increased movement and abnormal postures that they allow, these structure faults may predispose to backache even after relatively minor trauma. Spondylolysis, in which there is a defect of a lumbar vertebra, is a common example. Fractures of the vertebral bodies or their transverse processes by severe injury such as a motor vehicle accident or a major fall is another cause of sudden backache.

Long-term or chronic backache may be caused by degeneration of discs of facetal joints or by ligamentous strain. Poor posture, obesity, pregnancy or childbirth may also predispose o the condition.

Coccydynia, pain in the region of the coccyx, often follows local injury. It may

When pushing or lifting heavy objects the weight should be taken by arms, legs and back to minimize back strain.

persist for several months, but then tends to resolve spontaneously. Sacroiliac joint damage or inflammation may also occasionally cause backache.

Diseases that affect other bones and joints of the body may also involve those of the lumbar or thoracic vertebrae and cause backache. Tumor deposits and infections such as Pott's disease (tuberculosis of the spine) may cause bone collapse. Rheumatoid arthritis, osteoarthritis and ankylosing spondylitis are the most common forms of arthritis that affect the back.

Diagnosis and treatment Apart from recording a careful history and examining the back, a doctor often needs to search further before making a firm diagnosis. Rectal and vaginal examination can exclude pelvic and gynecological causes of back pain. Kidney pain such as renal colic and acute infections causing muscle pain

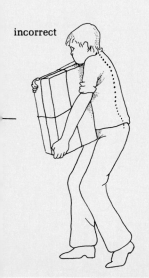

incorrect

correct

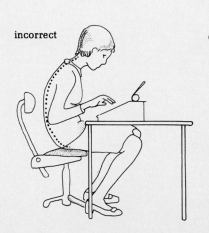

incorrect

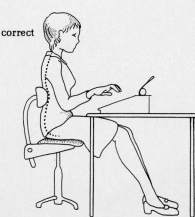

correct

usually have associated abnormalities such as protein and blood in the urine, or general malaise and fever.

X-rays are often taken to detect any bone injury, congenital abnormality, bony collapse, or narrowing of the space between the vertebrae as a result of disc prolapse. Newer x-ray techniques such as computerized axial tomography (cat scanning) are better able to reveal the soft-tissue abnormality. Sometimes invasive procedures such as a myelogram in which a dye is injected into the vertebral canal may be performed to demonstrate disc prolapse by x-ray.

If injury is the cause of backache, cooling the injured area to minimize initial swelling is helpful. After a few days, warmth from ray lamps, warm compresses and local applications of liniments are often of value by decreasing associated muscle spasm and improving the circulation, thus lessening inflammation.

Analgesics may be needed to relieve the pain.

Rest is important for all back injuries as is removing pressure on the injured part. A firm mattress is preferable. Lying on the side with the knees drawn upwards, lying face down, or having a small pillow or padding placed under the hollow of the back may give some comfort, depending on the injury.

Recovery The time required for the pain to resolve is dependent upon the severity and type of injury. Muscle strains resolve within four weeks, but ligament damage may take twice as long to heal. Disc injuries often require several weeks in bed. Mobilization should be gradual, and sometimes strapping or a back brace may be required. After the pain has subsided, muscle strengthening exercises help to protect the spine and its associated structures from further injury and to improve posture. Activities that are likely to put

strain on the back should be avoided for a period.

In some disc lesions, and if pain from other injuries does not resolve as rapidly as expected, traction may be needed. Weights are attached to the legs to 'pull' the vertebrae apart slowly.

Relief of pressure on a nerve or the spinal cord, removal of part of a vertebral bone (a procedure called laminectomy) or spinal fusion are surgical procedures occasionally utilized.

General fitness, good posture, keeping the back straight when lifting and using a firm mattress are important factors in preventing backache.

Breast conditions

Benign tumors Tumors, or abnormal growths of tissue, can be classified as harmless (benign) or harmful (malignant). Benign tumors of the breast are fairly common, particularly the fibroadenoma, which is usually found in young women and is noticed as a breast lump which is firm, distinct and easily movable. Sometimes in middle-aged women the fibroadenoma can be softer and deeper in the breast. The treatment is removal by minor surgery.

In older women (aged 30–50) the commonest tumors are fluid filled cavities or cysts. These are most often emptied by draining through a fine needle (aspiration) without the need for an operation. A benign tumor can also develop in the passages or ducts which carry the milk. This type, usually also found in older women, may occasionally be felt as a small lump near the nipple but often the first sign is

Breast examination. While lying down, the woman feels around each breast and nipple, using the flat parts of the fingers, not the tips. Self-examination should be practised monthly, just after menstruation.

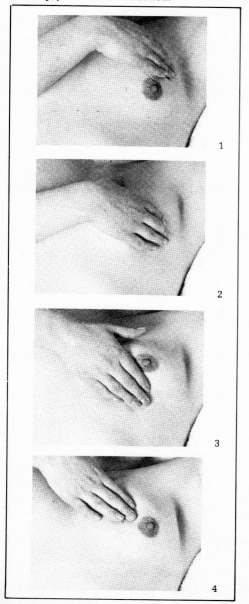

discharge from the nipple. The tumor should be removed by excising the relevant duct.

Some benign tumors which occur in other parts of the body can also appear in the breast. An example is the lipoma which is composed of fatty tissue and is felt as a soft round lump just beneath the skin. It is not attached to the skin or deeper tissues.

Breast cancer is the commonest cancer in women representing 25 per cent of all female cancers. While it is uncommon in men, it can occur. (1 per cent of all breast cancers are found in men.)

The disease most commonly occurs after the age of 40 in women, and the incidence continues to increase with age, being six times more common at 70 than at 40 years of age. The cause remains unknown, but various associations between breast cancer and certain lifestyles and personal factors have been observed.

Having had cancer in one breast increases the risk of cancer in the other. Risk increases where there is a family history of breast cancer, especially in close relatives who developed the disease before or around the time of the menopause, or if they had cancer in both breasts. Those women who have no children are also at increased risk and those who have their first child relatively late (28 or over) have a slightly higher risk again.

Women who have their first child at or before the age of 20 halve their risk for the rest of their life and those who have both their ovaries removed before the age of 40 are also at reduced risk.

The reasons behind this distribution of the disease are not understood, but they are thought to be due to hormonal changes.

It has also been suggested that the environment may play a part in the development of breast cancer. A higher incidence was noted in Japanese women living in the United States when compared with their mothers and grandmothers living at home. Finnish women have a lower incidence than Danish, and fat women a higher incidence than thin.

One of the most important factors in determining the long-term outlook for the disease is detecting the disease at an early stage, before it has spread to the glands under the arm. The less advanced the disease the better the chance for long-term survival. For this reason, breast clinics have been set up specializing in the detection and treatment of breast cancer.

Regular breast self-examination is the best way for each woman to learn what is normal for her, helping her to notice any abnormality at a very early stage. Every woman should ask her doctor to teach her this technique. A number of pamphlets illustrating breast self-examination are available.

Other diagnostic methods which aim at

early diagnosis include screening x-rays of the breasts (mammography) and aspiration biopsy of breast lumps using a fine needle to obtain cells which are examined under the microscope.

There are a number of different ways of treating breast cancer, and these are chosen according to the degree of spread of the tumor and the general state of the woman's health. It is important that the stage to which the cancer has advanced be assessed by removal and examination of the glands under the arm, to ascertain whether or not there are tumor cells present outside the breast tissue.

One of the following surgical procedures will be the usual initial treatment.

Partial mastectomy: in which the breast tissue is removed together with the glands under the arm, but the muscle on the chest is preserved as is the muscle at the front of the armpit. This is the most usual operation performed at this time, the patient retaining both full movement of the shoulder joint and a good appearance. This enables her to wear sleeveless or low-necked clothes and swimming costumes.

Wide lumpectomy: in which the tumor together with a large segment of breast tissue is removed on one piece. The glands under the arm are removed at the same time so that the development of the tumor can be assessed ('staging'). This operation is gaining acceptance.

Simple mastectomy: in which only the breast tissue is removed.

Radical mastectomy: in which the breast tissue, the glands under the arm, and the muscles on the chest are all removed. This operation is not common now.

Subcutaneous mastectomy: in which the breast tissue is removed, but the skin of the breast and nipple are left intact.

Deep x-ray therapy may be used before or after any of the surgical procedures. Sometimes it is the only treatment recommended, but in tumors which measure less than ¾ inch (2 cm) and which have not spread to the glands it is rarely used. The exception is when radiotherapy is used after lumpectomy for a small localized cancer.

Chemotherapy is used after surgery in some cases, and newer drugs and combinations of drugs which give fewer unpleasant side-effects are constantly undergoing trials.

Hormone therapy is another form of treatment. This is either given as drugs, or achieved by removal of hormone-producing glands such as the ovaries or the small glands on top of the kidneys called the adrenals.

Immunotherapy is also gaining popularity.

Meditation is thought by some to contribute to the patient's recovery and much interesting work is being done in this field.

Breast replacement. With modern forms of surgical treatment, an artificial replacement (prosthesis) may be inserted under the skin of the chest wall. Usually the normal breast needs to be reduced in size at the same time, so that it matches the size of the prosthesis.

Each patient is treated by her surgeon according to her individual needs. She should be reassured that the most suitable procedures for her particular case will be taken.

Bronchitis

An acute or chronic condition, bronchitis means inflammation of the bronchi; these are the largest of the tubes which extend from the division of the trachea (windpipe) and take air to the air sacs of the lungs. Inflammation of bronchial mucosa (the lining of the bronchi) can be initiated by irritant vapors or chemicals as well as by invasion of viruses or bacteria. Acute bronchitis, a short-term inflammation, is common, and in most cases, clears within ten days.

Symptoms Coughing, the principal symptom of bronchitis, results from irritation to the mucosal lining. Malaise and fever are other initial signs of infection. Vague chest pains and the production of phlegm (sputum), which at times may contain pus or blood, often develops later. The discomfort may range from a scratchy type of pain caused by the inflammation to a racking muscular pain caused by the strain of repeated coughing. Breathlessness may also be present.

Acute bronchitis is usually part of a general infection involving the upper respiratory tract. This includes the pharynx, larynx, nose and trachea. Occasionally infection later extends downwards to the lung tissue and bronchopneumonia occurs.

Percussion drainage is frequently used as part of the treatment for respiratory illnesses. *(Royal Alexandra Hospital)*

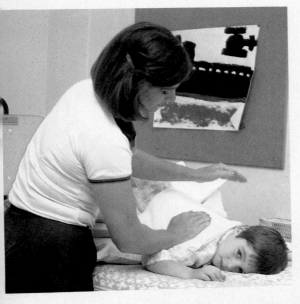

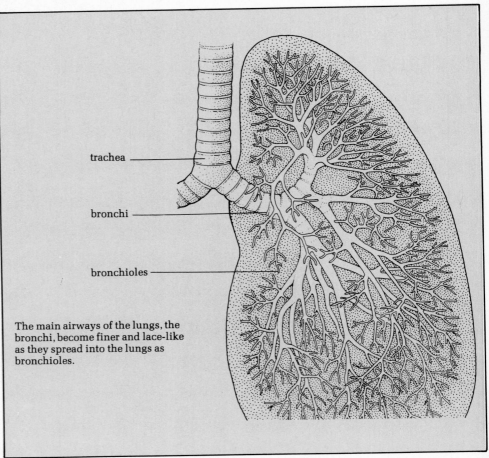

The main airways of the lungs, the bronchi, become finer and lace-like as they spread into the lungs as bronchioles.

Viruses, probably the commonest infective agents, produce a dry cough with little or no sputum. In children and healthy adults this usually settles quickly. In those with longstanding lung diseases, the development of secondary bacterial infection occurs far more frequently. Often the symptoms of the upper respiratory tract may be settling a little when symptoms of more severe infection, such as breathlessness and fatigue, become more pronounced. The sputum becomes much more profuse and is often yellow or green.

At this stage, cough suppression, which may have been helpful earlier, may be dangerous because of possible retention of excess infected sputum. Humidification of inhaled air, rest and antibiotics are usual treatments at this point. In those with other lung or heart diseases, the condition can become serious enough to require hospitalization.

Bronchitis can also be part of a general viral infection such as measles or chicken pox.

Chronic bronchitis Persistent and recurrent infection in the bronchial tubes is described as chronic bronchitis. Clinically it is defined as coughing that is present on most days for at least three months per year for more than two years.

One of the main causes of chronic bronchitis is thought to be smoking, but the condition does occur in non-smokers. As air pollution also aggravates the condition, city dwellers, and those in dusty occupations such as coal mining, are more severely affected. Childhood infections and hereditary factors may play small roles in the development of chronic bronchitis.

The initial change in chronic bronchitis is related to alterations in the mucosal lining. Cilia are hair-like projections that extend up from this lining and wave in sequence to move a thin film of mucus up towards the throat where it is swallowed. This is an important defence mechanism to remove bacteria and small particles that have descended into the bronchi.

In chronic bronchitis, cilia become shorter and fewer in number, and they also function less effectively. Mucus-producing cells increase in both size and number. The amount of mucus increases markedly and becomes much stickier.

Smaller bronchi tend to become blocked, producing breathlessness (particularly on exertion) because the expulsion of air becomes more difficult, but also reducing the drainage of the respiratory tract and therefore increasing the likelihood of infection. In later stages the amount of muscle in the wall of the bronchi increases.

Although there is much individual variation, damage from the condition is progressive, and it is accordingly important for the patient to obtain a full understanding of the process of chronic bronchitis.

Cessation of smoking, prompt treatment of any episodes of acute bronchitis, and avoidance of inhaled irritants may help slow the deterioration. Loss of excess weight and increasing general fitness may reduce the severity of the symptoms. Occasionally long-term antibiotics to prevent infection and the use of oxygen at home may also be of benefit.

Emphysema and asthma are other forms of chronic respiratory obstruction and features of these diseases may also be present in people suffering from chronic bronchitis.

Candidiasis

An infection of the skin or mucous membranes such as the lining of the mouth and the vagina, candidiasis (or moniliasis) is caused by the fungus *Candida albicans*. Infection of internal organs is uncommon.

The fungus is widespread and over 10 per cent of the population has candida organisms in the mouth or feces. Candida and other organisms, mainly bacteria, which are resident in these sites and cause no symptoms are known as commensals and are in competition with each other for space. If this balance is upset, an overgrowth of candida may occur.

Factors likely to contribute to an imbalance include lowered immunity from a long or severe illness, anti-tumor treatment (chemotherapy), or a course of antibiotics which may remove many of the commensal bacteria as well as those causing disease. However, symptoms are not common and are usually restricted to the mouth or vagina. Candidal inflammation in the bowel is very unusual.

When candida infects the mucous membranes it is called thrush. Oral thrush most frequently occurs in young children, probably because of a lower natural immunity and their habit of putting many objects, especially unclean fingers, in the mouth. Thrush is also one of the most common causes of vaginal irritation. As it is not mainly transmitted by intercourse it is not a true venereal disease; the source of infection is usually the bowel.

Candida grows more readily in the presence of sugar, so women with poorly controlled diabetes are more prone to infection in the vagina and surrounding skin of the vulva because of sugar in the urine. Genital thrush is sometimes the first sign of diabetes.

Female sex hormones increase the amount of sugar in the cells lining the vagina and thus the risk of infection is increased when levels of these hormones are elevated, such as during pregnancy or when the oral contraceptive pill is being taken.

Moist, warm conditions favour candidal growth. For this reason skin infections most frequently occur in the groin, armpits and under the breasts. Occasionally the web spaces between fingers

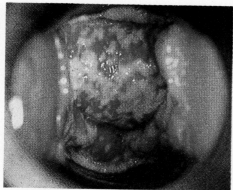

A thick white discharge is usually present with candidal infection. (*Modern Medicine*)

and toes, the umbilicus and under the nails may also become infected.

Symptoms In vaginal infection, a burning pain with passage of urine, discomfort along the walls of the vagina especially during intercourse and soreness are the main symptoms. Discharge is not a prominent feature because the fungus forms white patches on mucous membranes. These look like clotted cream and can be readily removed, leaving a red inflamed area beneath.

Infected skin often has a dull red appearance and blisters may appear. Clinically, it is sometimes difficult to distinguish the condition from a general eczema.

Treatment The aims of treatment are twofold. The first is to treat the infection by local application of one of several agents that destroy the fungus. Nystatin oral suspension, tablets, cream and vaginal applications are effective and have long been the treatment of choice. A number of newer antifungal preparations are now available such as amphotericin and miconazole. The old-fashioned treatment of gentian violet paint is effective but the residual stain makes it less popular.

The second aim of treatment is to assess and control possible predisposing causes of infection. Skin areas likely to be affected should be kept clean and dry; this may entail losing weight and powdering after bathing. The wearing of tight jeans, nylon underwear and panty hose should be avoided by women who are susceptible to vaginal thrush as these may create conditions favorable to candidal growth. Cotton is preferable to nylon.

Other measures which reduce the likelihood of candidal growth include the restrictive use of antibiotics, attention to hygiene to reduce the chances of bacteria from the bowel contaminating the vagina and changing to a contraceptive pill with a different hormonal balance or to a different form of contraception. Testing urine to see if sugar is present is advised after more than one episode of thrush.

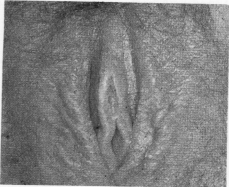

The mucous membranes of the vagina are a common site for candidiasis infection, which can cause redness and swelling. (*Modern Medicine*)

Sometimes nystatin tablets are given to a woman and her partner to clear the bowels as potential reservoirs of reinfection. The routine prescribing of antifungal vaginal suppositories whenever antibiotics are needed may also be helpful in persistent cases.

Cervical cancer

Cancer of the neck of the womb (cervix) is easy to detect early in its course by routine PAP smears (the Papanicolaou test). The cause of cervical cancer is not known and certain circumstances which tend to be associated with a higher incidence of the disease are controversial. They include a higher incidence of cervical cancer in women who commence sexual intercourse at an early age, women who have multiple sexual partners and those who suffer the infection of herpes genitalis (type II). At various times other factors have been deemed important, such as lower socio-economic status, urban living and venereal disease as well as certain racial groups.

Cancer detected by routine PAP smear is usually found in women in their late thirties who have no symptoms. The more advanced form tends to occur in older patients at the average age of forty-eight.

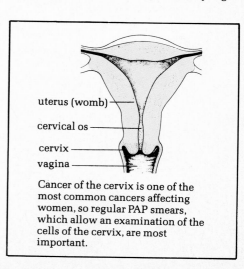

uterus (womb)

cervical os

cervix

vagina

Cancer of the cervix is one of the most common cancers affecting women, so regular PAP smears, which allow an examination of the cells of the cervix, are most important.

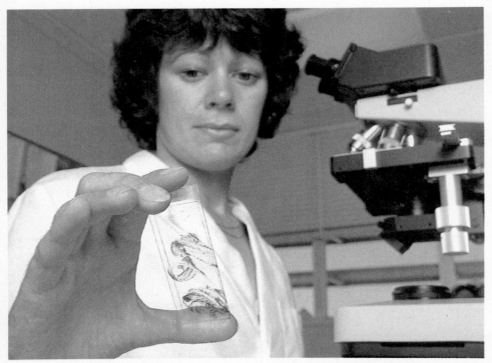

Regular smear tests will detect cervical cancer in its very early stages when treatment may be only relatively minor surgery. (*Westmead Center*)

This group tends to be picked up because of symptoms such as bleeding, usually slight, which may be noticed after straining, after coitus or strenuous exercise. The patient may also have abnormal vaginal discharge. If the disease has gone beyond these early stages the patient may complain of ulceration and infection of the discharge giving it a bad smell. Pain and discomfort in the rectum or bladder, or both, may be experienced.

Diagnosis and treatment Diagnosis of the condition can be accomplished by a variety of methods, including a PAP smear, colposcopy biopsy and local excision (conisation).

Treatment varies from local excision in an early-stage cancer to use of radiation and more extensive surgery at later stages.

Cholecystitis

Inflammation of the gall bladder, cholecystitis is usually associated with gallstones and occurs most frequently in the over-forty age group. Predisposing causes include obesity and disorders of cholesterol and bilirubin excretion. Cholecystitis may be acute or chronic.

Acute cholecystitis is usually secondary to a chronic process and is often triggered by a stone obstructing the gall bladder duct which causes the gall bladder to become inflamed. Infection may occur. Symptoms of an acute attack often follow a heavy meal and start with right upper abdominal pain radiating to below the right shoulder blade. The pain is severe and associated with sweating and tenderness over the gall bladder, which can itself often be felt. Mild jaundice and fever usually occur. Blood tests and x-rays confirm the diagnosis. Complications include perforation, infection, gangrene of the gall bladder and distension with mucoid material.

Treatment of acute cholecystitis usually involves settling the inflammation and infection with bowel rest, antibiotics, intravenous fluids and possible later removal of the gall bladder. An early operation is performed if gangrene or perforation is likely.

Chronic cholecystitis causes long-term indigestion which is aggravated by fatty food and heavy meals, flatulence, nausea and recurrent episodes of colicky upper right abdominal pain. X-rays confirm the diagnosis. Complications include acute attacks, stone in the common bile duct, and pancreatitis.

Treatment involves removal of the gall bladder or dissolution of the stones with bile acids. The latter method is suitable in only a small proportion of cases where there are small x-ray-translucent stones in a functioning gall bladder and where the patient is prepared to take oral treatment with bile acid for a long period. Surgical removal of the gall bladder is usually preferred unless there are serious conditions making the patient unsuitable for surgery.

Cirrhosis

A disease of the liver, cirrhosis is characterized by small areas of degenerative liver tissue and other areas of regenerating tissue. The name is derived from the Greek *kirrhos* which means 'tawny', the color of many of the forms of the disease.

Causes Various factors are associated with the disease. The most commonly known is the heavy consumption of alcohol over a long period of time. Alcoholism is associated with most cases of cirrhosis, although only a very small percentage of alcoholics (less than 10 per cent) develop cirrhosis of the liver and the disease can occur in someone who is a life-long teetotaller.

Cirrhosis may also occur in association with a protein deficient diet, infections such as viral hepatitis and serum hepatitis, long-standing obstruction of the bile ducts (for example, gallstones), chronic heart failure, and 'storage' diseases such as hemochromatosis (excess deposits of iron in the body) and Wilson's disease.

Symptoms When cirrhosis of the liver develops, many of the normal functions of the liver break down. For example, the patient may become jaundiced (yellow skinned), because the substance bilirubin is no longer being metabolized by the liver, and instead is deposited in the skin tissues. The liver stops making necessary blood-clotting substances, and thus the patient will bleed and bruise more easily.

The scar tissue of cirrhosis may also exert pressure on the liver blood vessels, and this can result in a back-up blood flow in many of the veins of the abdomen. Thus, vessels under high pressure will bleed, particularly in the esophagus (esophageal varices) and in the anus (hemorrhoids). This pressure build-up may also cause 'ascites', when the abdomen swells as in a pregnancy.

Diagnosis of cirrhosis may be made from the observation of symptoms such as those above, but a definitive diagnosis is made by a liver biopsy. A needle is inserted into the liver substance and a tiny piece of liver is removed and examined under the microscope for signs of cirrhosis.

Treatment Careful medical treatment can have a significant effect on how cirrhosis will develop in the long-term. If alcohol is the cause, then abstinence is necessary if the liver is to recover. For those who cease drinking there is a good (65 per cent) chance of recovery; for those who continue to drink, the end is total liver failure and death.

Malnutrition may be corrected with an adequate protein rich diet, except where mental changes are noted. Fluid retention is corrected with a low salt diet, restricted fluid intake and medication to increase fluid loss. In cases of blood loss, blood transfusions are often necessary and steps are taken to avoid further blood loss from veins in which the pressure is high.

In the terminal stages a confused state develops, often precipitated by hemorrhage, infection or an imbalance of salts in the body. Death from cirrhosis is the result of hemorrhage in about 20 per cent of cases; the remainder die from total liver failure.

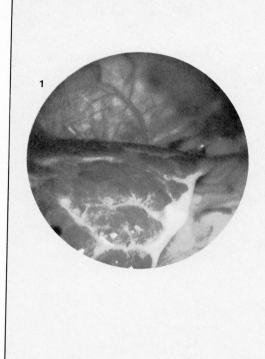

1 Cirrhosis has caused the death of this liver tissue, which shows extensive scarring. *(Abbottempo)*

2 The fine nodulation on the surface of this liver is typical of cirrhosis. *(Abbottempo)*

3 Cirrhosis of the liver showing fine nodules, found in association with a diseased gall bladder in a 70-year-old barbiturate addict. *(Abbottempo)*

4 Advanced cirrhosis of the liver in a 65-year-old alcoholic. *(Abbottempo)*

5 Alcoholism has caused 'hob-nail' liver in this case of cirrhosis and fatty degeneration. *(Abbottempo)*

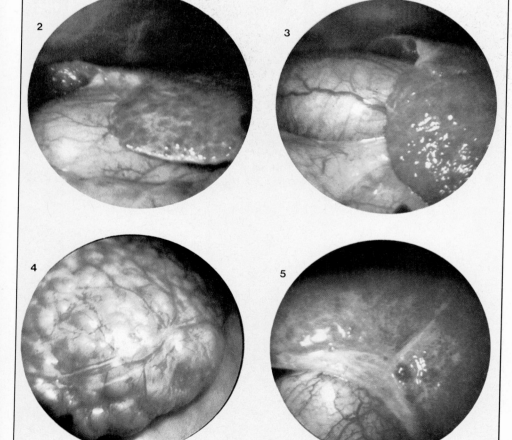

Conjunctivitis

Inflammation of the conjunctiva of the eye is known as conjunctivitis. The conjunctiva is the mucous membrane which covers the eyeball and the inner surface of the eyelids. Inflammation may be caused by infection with virus or bacteria, by allergic reactions to pollens, or by irritation due to dust, smoke or dandruff.

Symptoms Both eyes are usually affected although one may be worse than the other. The usual complaint is of discomfort and grittiness rather than pain.

There is also some sort of discharge, usually yellow, thick mucus which tends to stick the eyelids together, though sometimes it is pus or simply an increase in the amount of tears.

The eye appears red because of dilatation of the blood vessels and this is more pronounced towards the outer part of the eyeball, fading towards the iris, which is the colored part of the eye.

Vision is not affected apart from transient blurring with the discharge, the pupil reacts normally to light being shone into it and is clear rather than hazy. These last points are important to differentiate the red eye of conjunctivitis from more serious conditions, such as iritis, acute glaucoma, keratitis and episcleritis.

Treatment Sometimes, before treatment begins, a swab of the discharge is taken for culture of the offending organism and to establish whether there is sensitivity to antibiotics. In many cases treatment with an antibiotic is likely to be effective. Often the condition will respond to bathing with a normal saline solution (fresh cotton swabs dipped in a warm solution made up by adding half a teaspoon of salt to a cup of warm water). If this is not effective, antibiotic drops instilled hourly through the day with ointment used at night will usually be quickly effective. If the conjunctivitis is the effect of an allergy antihistamine drops may be used.

Cystitis

Bacterial infection or inflammation of the bladder, known as cystitis, is a common condition, particularly among women. In the female, the urethra is very short compared with that of the male, being only .8–1.2 inches (2–3 cm) long. The inside of the bladder is sterile but the female urethra opens out to the same area as the vagina and the rectum, both of which have a large bacterial population. Micro-organisms have, therefore, only a very short journey up the female urethra and it is thought that this is the reason for the frequency of cystitis in women.

Cystitis also often occurs after intercourse for the same reasons. Infection is more liable to occur if there is incomplete emptying of the bladder and when there is a reduced urinary output. Both circumstances encourage the growth of organisms and account for cystitis occurring in pregnant women and those with stones.

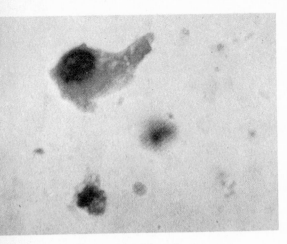

Any inflammation of the urinary tract will cause the presence of abnormal cells in the urine. *(Abbottempo)*

Where there is cystitis the desire to pass urine becomes more frequent and passing it causes scalding pain which can vary from mild to severe. The urine is often cloudy, has an unpleasant odour and may be blood-stained.

A clean sample of urine is needed to test for infection, and treatment with antibiotics and an alkalyzing agent is started. Within 24 hours of starting treatment there should be a marked improvement.

In the majority of cases, cystitis will be completely cured after the completion of the course of antibiotics. If it recurs frequently, special x-rays are required to investigate the possibility of bladder and kidney malformations which could predispose such recurrent infection.

Recurrent cystitis sometimes occurs in association with sexual intercourse in young women. Antibiotics are not always necessary and often an organism is not found in the urine. Emptying the bladder before and after intercourse, scrupulous attention to hygiene of the private parts and keeping up a good output of urine by frequent drinking often alleviates this distressing problem.

Dermatitis

Dermatitis is an inflammation of the skin. The inflammation begins when small blood vessels deep in the layers of the skin dilate, producing redness or irritation. There will also be some degree of swelling.

In the deeper layers of the skin, cells multiply and move towards the surface as cells beneath them continue to divide. The cells on the surface layers are shed continually as part of the normal 'wear and tear' on the skin. This process may be disturbed if there is inflammation. If the inflammation persists, scaling of the skin often occurs, that is, small masses of dead skin cells are shed from the outermost layers.

In more severe cases fluid leaks from the small blood vessels to produce fluid-filled blisters or vesicles. An example of this is the formation of blisters following relatively minor burns or scalds.

If the damage is severe, persistent weeping of serum through the inflamed skin may develop. This could eventually lead to bacterial infection which results in the formation of pustules (blisters containing pus).

The long-term irritation of the skin, with itching and scratching causes a thickening of the skin (lichenification) which becomes hard and leathery.

In general, the treatment of dermatitis is determined by the cause. A detailed history of the patient is needed. Once the cause is identified the patient should avoid further contact with it.

Further treatment depends on the stage of the inflammation. In the early stages when there is redness and swelling but little or no scaling, cooling lotions may be all that is required. Calamine lotion, menthol creams and several preparations containing coal tar are frequently used.

If there is marked weeping, special preparations that dry up secretions may be needed. Scaling and inflammation generally can be controlled with the use of special creams or ointments containing corticosteroids. These are potent and should be used only under medical supervision. The long-term use of these may cause a number of problems, particularly on the delicate skin of the face.

Contact dermatitis The direct contact of an irritant substance with the skin can produce contact dermatitis. In most cases this sensitivity to a substance is peculiar to the individual and therefore has an allergic basis. Some examples of irritants are soaps, hair dyes, and nickel (as in buckles and necklaces). When contact with the irritant substance is primarily at the place of employment the condition is described as industrial or occupational dermatitis.

A careful examination of the history of a patient is necessary to discover the most likely cause of the dermatitis. The cause may be confirmed by patch testing, which

Contact dermatitis is caused by the direct contact of the skin with an irritant substance, resulting in redness, swelling, scaliness and blisters. *(Westmead Centre)*

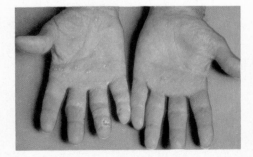

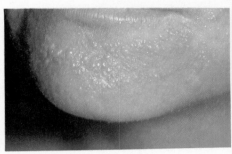

In severe cases, such as this perioral dermatitis, fluid leaks from the small blood vessels to produce blisters. *(Westmead Centre)*

involves exposing an area of the skin to the suspected substance in order to determine the reaction. The most important part of the treatment is to avoid the irritant. Also various creams or lotions can be applied directly to the affected area, usually resulting in rapid recovery.

Housewives' dermatitis An itchy localized inflammation of the skin of the hands, housewives' dermatitis is caused primarily by excessive contact with soap or other detergents which irritate the skin. Classically the hands become red and cracked in appearance, particularly the fingers, often with a mild degree of scaling round the nails.

Over-exposure to soaps and detergents results in the fatty contents from the superficial layers of the skin being leached out, making the skin more likely to become cracked and inflamed. Certain individuals are more likely to develop the condition; those affected often have a family history of dry skin or some other dermatological disorder.

It is most important to minimize contact with detergents and other skin irritants. Although rubber gloves prevent direct contact with detergents when washing and cleaning, they induce sweating which can aggravate the condition. Cotton-lined gloves are therefore preferable. In milder cases, silicone-based ointments, which are water repellent, may be of benefit.

Treatment of established cases is sometimes difficult because of the long-standing nature of the condition. Antibiotic or antifungal treatment is required when infection, which often develops round the nails, is present. The liberal and frequent use of creams, or ointments which have a higher fat content, is important as a means of preventing excessive drying of the skin. Inflammation may be further controlled by the addition of a low strength corticosteroid such as hydrocortisone to the cream or ointment.

Intertrigo Any type of dermatitis or inflammation of the skin that involves skin surfaces which lie in apposition to one another is known as intertrigo. It occurs most commonly in skin folds, as in the groin, armpits (axillae), beneath pendulous female breasts, and between the toes.

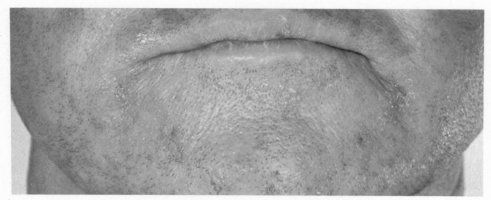

Contact with any irritant substance can cause the inflammation of the skin known as contact dermatitis. (Westmead Centre)

In most cases the initiating cause of the dermatitis is the physical rubbing of the skin surfaces across each other, with aggravation when the areas are warm and moist because sweat cannot evaporate.

Once inflammation has begun and the skin becomes macerated, infection with bacteria or fungi (particularly *Candida*) may complicate the condition further. Obesity also predisposes to the development of intertrigo.

The usual appearance of intertrigo is a patch of red shiny skin, often with some scaling, that corresponds exactly with the skin areas that are touching. Weeping may be present, particularly if there is associated infection. The affected skin is often itchy and sore; in more severe cases it becomes quite painful, producing a burning sensation.

The treatment of intertrigo depends partly on the situation. Minimizing irritating factors is an important first step, not only in accelerating the cure, but also to prevent recurrence. Separation of the opposing skin surfaces is important. Weight loss, and some form of dressing or support may help. Keeping the area dry also assists in healing. This can be achieved by gentle but thorough drying after bathing; the liberal use of non-irritant powders to reduce moisture and friction of opposing skin surfaces; and the use of cotton rather than nylon garments, where applicable, to reduce sweat retention and allow adequate aeration of the affected area.

When infection is present, appropriate antibiotic or antifungal preparations should be used. Corticosteroid creams may assist in the healing process, and mild keratolytic (scale-removing) creams may be used in dry forms of intertrigo.

Unless the above measures are persisted with, and predisposing factors controlled, recurrence is likely.

Neurodermatitis The condition which begins as a minor skin reaction with scratching and eventually becomes an unconscious habit, is described as neurodermatitis or lichen simplex. Persistent scratching produces a reddened area that becomes thick and scarred (lichenified).

As the habit of scratching is often difficult to break, treatment includes specific anti-itch tablets and creams, sometimes sedative drugs, and occlusive dressings. Supportive psychotherapy may also be needed.

Other skin disorders also have features of dermatitis. Psoriasis is the excessive multiplication of skin cells which produces patches of inflamed skin with redness, swelling and scaling. Skin infections such as ringworm and candidiasis sometimes produce patches of dermatitis.

Pompholyx A dermatitis or inflammation of the skin, pompholyx affects the palms of the hands, the front and sides of the fingers and the front of the wrist, as well as the soles of the feet and the sides of the toes.

The name is derived from the Greek word for blisters, because of the appearance of small white blisters in the deep layers of the skin. These blisters do not have a surrounding red, inflamed area and they do not tend to rupture.

Excessive sweating due to a disturbed sweating mechanism is thought to be responsible, because pompholyx occurs at times when the climate is hot and humid, or in association with emotional stress, tension and anxiety in certain susceptible people.

Treatment involves adequate protection against hot and humid conditions and avoiding contact with non-porous materials for hand and foot wear. Leather and cotton are satisfactory materials. In times of emotional tension and anxiety, a tranquillizing drug may be helpful.

Steroid creams are generally used in treatment. Sometimes the blisters may be pricked with a sterile needle, followed by bathing in a weak antiseptic solution of potassium permanganate (Condy's crystals) for a few days, prior to the use of the steriod cream.

Seborrheic dermatitis Scaling of the scalp is the typical condition of seborrheic dermatitis. The scaling also frequently occurs on the chest and armpits. This form of dermatitis is caused when sebaceous gland activity increases during and shortly after puberty. This build-up of sebum increases the likelihood of greasy skin, scaling (dandruff is a form of seborrheic dermatitis), and secondary bacterial infection of blocked skin pores which produces acne vulgaris. For those with an inherited tendency to persistent sebaceous gland overactivity, these conditions may be present throughout life.

The most common feature is patchy areas of dermatitis that appear and disappear over long periods of time. These areas are much more prone to infection by invading bacteria. Psychological factors such as mental stress may also produce 'flare-ups' of the condition.

To control the problem various anti-inflammatory lotions and creams are used. Also certain creams that prevent the build-up of sebum are often used in between the major attacks.

Solar dermatitis Inflammation of the skin in response to normal exposure to sunlight is known as solar dermatitis. This is an abnormal or excessive response to normal sunshine and should not be confused with sunburn, which is a normal response to excessive exposure. Many features are, however, similar.

Patchy reddening of the skin, swelling, and sometimes blisters occur on the affected areas, with shaded areas such as the upper eyelids and under the chin being unaffected. The skin of the face, neck, back of the hands and forearms is affected most frequently.

The most common cause of solar dermatitis is the entry of photosensitizing chemicals into the skin, either from ingested materials or from externally applied creams or lotions. They absorb extra energy from the sun's rays and skin damage may be caused by the release of this energy or by the chemical reactions thus triggered between these chemicals and the components of the skin.

A number of cosmetics, soaps, industrial products and various medications may cause this reaction in susceptible individuals.

Treatment entails identifying and then avoiding the triggering substance, staying out of the sun when vulnerable to such a reaction, using sunscreen creams and wearing protective clothing.

Diabetes

An incurable disease, diabetes mellitus, generally simply called diabetes, is caused by inadequate levels or reduced effectiveness of insulin. This hormone is produced by special cells in the pancreas, a gland that is situated in the abdomen, tucked into the first loop of the small intestine. Insulin is essential for the proper metabolism of blood sugar and the maintenance of blood sugar level.

The disease affects many aspects of the body's metabolism such as fat, protein, water and salts, but the main problem relates to carbohydrate (sugar) metabolism.

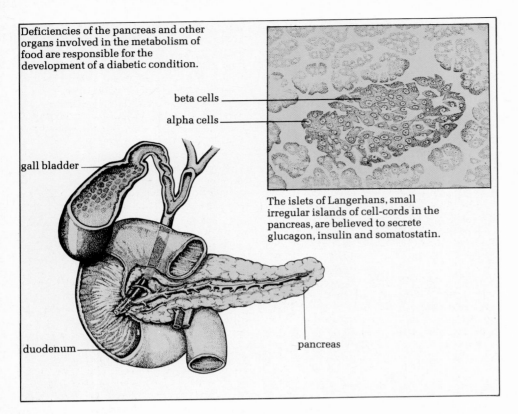

Deficiencies of the pancreas and other organs involved in the metabolism of food are responsible for the development of a diabetic condition.

beta cells

alpha cells

gall bladder

duodenum

pancreas

The islets of Langerhans, small irregular islands of cell-cords in the pancreas, are believed to secrete glucagon, insulin and somatostatin.

Diabetes is a very common illness and is the third leading cause of death in the United States. It is estimated that half those with diabetes in the older age group are unaware that they have the condition.

Cause The vast majority of cases of diabetes are caused by a degeneration of the pancreatic cells which produce insulin. The exact mechanism is not fully understood but there is a complex genetic factor involved; children of diabetics are more likely to develop diabetes than those whose parents are not diabetic. Those who develop this so-called 'primary' diabetes fall into one of two major categories. *Juvenile-onset diabetes* A, now often called Insulin Dependent or Type I, DM, or IDDM, is quite sudden and severe, occurring before the age of thirty, with the majority of these cases developing in the early teens. Insulin production from the pancreas is minimal and becomes entirely absent shortly after the onset of symptoms. In such cases, insulin given by injection is necessary for survival. Dietary control is also important.

In 80 per cent of patients who develop diabetes there are few initial symptoms. They are over the age of thirty and have less severe fluctuations of sugar levels in the blood. This group is termed *maturity-onset diabetes* B or Non-Insulin Dependent, Type II, NIDDM. There is still a degree of insulin production, but the overall levels are insufficient to meet the needs of the body. Dietary restriction is crucial. Drugs which stimulate the pancreas to make a little more insulin may also be of benefit. In both cases however, the same

underlying abnormality exists and the prime concern of treatment is directed largely to controlling the blood levels of sugar.

Other precipitating factors Diabetes may also be precipitated by illness or destruction of the pancreas such as in cancer, hemochromatosis or following surgical removal of the gland. Even with a normally functioning pancreas, excessive levels of other hormones that normally counteract the effects of insulin may also cause diabetes. Such conditions include acromegaly, Cushing's syndrome and hyperthyroidism (excessive activity of the thyroid gland).

There are a number of situations in which the body needs for insulin are increased, and their occurrence may cause an underlying tendency for diabetes (minimal reserve capacity of insulin production) to be unmasked as the level of insulin produced becomes inadequate. Obesity makes some tissues of the body more resistant to the effects of insulin and causes an elevation in the blood glucose levels. This in turn increases the amount of insulin needed to allow a normal blood sugar level to be maintained.

A number of hormones and other substances have chemical actions that counter the effects of insulin. Some diuretic drugs (those causing increased production of urine), noradrenalin and steroids which are produced in the body in greater amounts during times of physical or emotional stress, or infection are examples of situations which increase the

body's insulin needs. Pregnancy is associated with the release of hormones and with metabolic changes which have the same effect.

Effects in the body Insulin allows the cells of the body to take up glucose, the basic unit of carbohydrate metabolism. Subsequent chemical breakdown (metabolism) of glucose provides energy for the body to function. The permanent elevation of sugar levels in the bloodstream associated with inadequate insulin amounts accounts for many of the symptoms of diabetes.

Immediate effects Once the level of glucose in the bloodstream rises above 160 mgm per 100 ml (9 millimole per litre), the kidneys are no longer able to absorb it all, leading to loss of sugar in the urine. This sugar in turn tends to draw more water out with it, increasing the urine volume (polyuria). There is an increased feeling of thirst followed by a greater intake of fluid (polydipsia) as the body tries to maintain a normal fluid balance. These symptoms are the commonest initial features of the diabetes before the age of thirty.

Because the cells of the body are unable to obtain glucose from the bloodstream, protein and fats are metabolized in an effort to obtain satisfactory alternative sources of energy. This in turn leads to tissue breakdown and weight loss, particularly in juvenile-onset diabetes.

There are some increased risks for a baby if the mother has diabetes, but close supervision during the pregnancy is usually all that is needed.

Some of the fat which is broken down may be used for energy, although there are some body tissues that can only utilize glucose, particularly the brain. Fatty acids, the breakdown product from fats, that cannot be fully utilized are converted into potentially toxic substances called *ketones*. As the level of ketones builds up in the bloodstream, they too are excreted into the urine. The presence of ketones in the urine as well as sugar generally indicates that the condition is getting out of control.

If at this stage insulin is not given in sufficient quantities, the condition of the person with diabetes can deteriorate rapidly. Ketoacidotic coma may occur, and if this remains untreated death will follow. Ketones are strong acids and the blood becomes mildly acidic, hence the term ketoacidosis. Increasing drowsiness and coma occur largely because of the brain's almost total dependence on glucose as its source of energy. Dehydration develops rapidly and is usually quite severe. Another major feature is a deep sighing respiration caused by the body attempting to exhale as much carbon dioxide as possible in an effort to chemically counter the acidifying effects of the ketones in the blood. This is a medical emergency which occurs almost solely in the primary form of diabetes. Admission to hospital is necessary so that insulin, fluids, and electrolytes can be given and their levels closely monitored.

Longterm effect Although many of the symptoms of juvenile-onset diabetes relate to the blood levels of glucose, long-term effects of diabetes and the early symptoms of many cases of mature-onset diabetes relate to the vascular (blood vessel) changes associated with the condition. Changes in the blood vessels, although widespread throughout the body, mainly present difficulties in the eye, kidney and foot. Other complications of diabetes may affect the nervous system and the eye as well.

Complications The eyes may be affected by cataracts (clouding of the normally clear lens of the eye) and retinopathy (a degeneration of the retina, the light sensitive layer at the back of the eye). Retinal changes occur as a result of leakages from locally affected vessels. However, eye symptoms as a result of these changes do not usually appear until ten to fifteen years after the onset of the diabetes. The rate of progression and final degree of visual difficulty is quite variable, although in some cases blindness may occur.

Abnormalities of both small and large blood vessels occur. Atherosclerosis (thickening of the walls of arteries and narrowing of their lumen size) may cause angina, an increased risk of suffering from a heart attack or a stroke, kidney problems and reduced circulation to the legs.

The circulation of blood to the feet is normally not as efficient as it is to other parts of the body, so in people with diabetes good foot care is especially important. Intermittent lameness and skin ulcers on the legs occasionally leading to gangrene are more common in diabetics.

Problems in the functioning of nerves, both peripheral and autonomic, are problems that occur later in those with diabetes. Areas of numbness in the legs are the most frequent feature. Some males suffer from impotency — one of the autonomic nervous system symptoms that may occur.

Those with untreated diabetes are more prone to infection. In some cases the infection may be the first sign of diabetes. Urine infection, balanitis (infection of the glans of the penis) or vulvitis are especially common because of the sugar in the urine providing a good breeding ground for infective agents, especially the fungus *Candida albicans*.

It appears that careful treatment and strict control of blood sugar levels helps to delay the onset and severity of many complications. This particularly applies to people who develop diabetes early in life, when the chances of developing complications later are greater.

Detection Testing of urine for the presence of sugar is the normal screening method used to detect diabetes. Many authorities feel that adults, especially those over the age of forty, should have their urine tested for sugar at least every two years.

There are, however, a number of different causes of sugar being in the urine, such as pregnancy or kidney diseases. For this reason, anyone with sugar in the urine usually has a blood test to measure directly the blood level of sugar. If this is markedly elevated it probably indicates the presence of diabetes. The most accurate method is to measure the blood sugar levels at half hourly intervals for two hours after a standard sugar-rich fluid has been drunk. This is called a glucose tolerance test.

Screening urine tests are often performed at regular checkups and at insurance examinations.

The main aims of treatment are to prevent symptoms from developing and to limit the development of complications. Treatment is directed at keeping the blood sugar level as close to normal as possible throughout the whole day, particularly avoiding any marked deviations.

Insulin Those who develop diabetes early in life nearly always need injections of insulin. Insulin is given by injection because it is destroyed by the gastric juice in the stomach if taken orally. Chemically manufactured 'slow-release' preparations of insulin mean that only one or two injections are required each day; chemically unaltered insulin will only work for up to six hours when injected into the body. The insulins available today are obtained from the pancreas gland of pigs (porcine insulin) or cattle (bovine insulin). Synthetic human insulin produced by use of recombinant DNA techniques has recently become available.

Diet is an important factor in the treatment of people with diabetes. Those with maturity-onset diabetes should be on a low carbohydrate diet and also restrict the

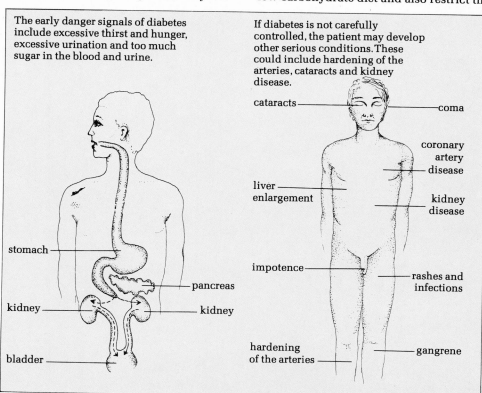

The early danger signals of diabetes include excessive thirst and hunger, excessive urination and too much sugar in the blood and urine.

stomach
pancreas
kidney
kidney
bladder

If diabetes is not carefully controlled, the patient may develop other serious conditions. These could include hardening of the arteries, cataracts and kidney disease.

cataracts
coma
coronary artery disease
liver enlargement
kidney disease
impotence
rashes and infections
hardening of the arteries
gangrene

total number of calories, particularly if overweight. In those who have diabetes and need regular insulin injections, the amount of carbohydrates, particularly sugars, in the diet needs to be fairly strictly controlled.

For many years the 'portion concept' of diabetic diets was in widespread use. A portion represented 0.5 ounce (15 gm) of sugar, and various amounts of carbohydrate-containing foodstuffs were given a value representing the number of portions they contained. For instance an average slice of white bread contained approximately one portion. The diabetic patient would be restricted to a certain number of portions each day.

Today a newer concept of the carbohydrate or sugar content of food has been adopted. This divides all foods into three categories: off-limits (high carbohydrate content), restricted (moderate carbohydrate content), and unrestricted (low carbohydrate content).

The assistance of a dietitian is often required in order to determine a person's daily calorie, carbohydrate and protein needs. The dietitian can then instruct the patient about suitable dietary programs. Special allowances both of food intake and insulin dose (if appropriate) usually need to be made before any degree of exertion, particularly sport. Exercise lowers blood sugar levels so that more carbohydrate or a reduced dosage of insulin may be required to adjust for this.

Drugs Where some insulin is still being produced by the pancreas in those with maturity-onset diabetes, insulin output may be increased by the use of special hypoglycemic drugs (usually sulphonylureas) that help to lower the blood sugar levels. Diet is also controlled.

Special care Instructions are also given to diabetic patients regarding the regular testing of urine for sugar (glucose) and ketones. This is usually done once a day, with extra testing (3–4 times per day) once or twice a week. Home blood testing for glucose levels is now possible using reagent strips. The color changes may be compared with a color chart or measured using a reflectance meter. This type of monitoring is advised when diabetes is unstable, in pregnancy and where urine tests are unreliable. Based on these results, dietary and insulin needs are adjusted. Infections often cause an increase in insulin requirements and more frequent urine testing is usually undertaken and the insulin dose increased. Too much insulin or excessive exercise can produce an abnormally low level of sugar in the bloodstream (hypoglycemia) causing symptoms such as tiredness and weakness. A tremor and sweating may also develop. In more severe hypoglycemia, extreme drowsiness and loss of consciousness may occur. Convulsions may be precipitated.

Early symptoms of hypoglycemia can be controlled if sugar, for example barley sugar or a sweet drink, is taken by mouth. People with diabetes are generally ad-

Regular testing of the urine, with a special kit, is a necessary procedure for diabetics. The level of sugar or ketones in the urine indicates the degree of treatment needed. (*John Watney Photo Library*)

vised to carry sugar tablets with them.

If hypoglycemic coma occurs, a special hormone called glucagon injected just under the skin (subcutaneously) will allow a short-term elevation of the blood sugar, often enough for the patient to regain consciousness and take some sugar by mouth. In other cases injection of a concentrated sugar solution (50 per cent dextrose) directly into the veins is necessary.

Sometimes it is difficult to distinguish between ketoacidotic and hypoglycemic coma.

Personal aspects Diabetes is a life-long disease and although it is common, there is much about it that people do not understand. The diagnosis of diabetes often comes as a shock to the patient and the family.

A full explanation given by the doctor in terms that the patient can understand is important. It often takes some time before all the questions are answered and confidence and understanding about the condition achieved. The vast amount of information that has to be given to the patient and the family during the initial stages of treatment takes time to be understood and learnt.

Those people who have juvenile-onset or insulin-dependent diabetes usually have the greatest adjustment to make. Learning to inject oneself daily for life is a concept that cannot be dealt with easily. Because of the hereditary factors in diabetes, parents sometimes have feelings of guilt and anxiety which need to be dealt with to minimize the risk of problems developing within the family unit.

In children and adolescents, pressure from peers may at times create difficulties. At school it is helpful if the child's teacher is aware of some of the problems of diabetes, especially emerg-

A daily injection of insulin

A record of medication and urinalysis

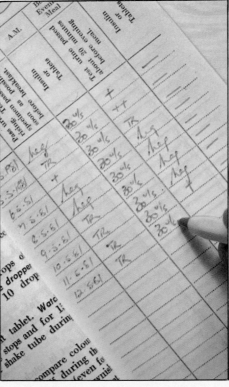

ency situations such as hypoglycemic reactions. Opportunities for parents and teachers to discuss potential problems are extremely useful, and assistance in this area may be obtained from the family doctor.

Counseling and support is important in relation to suitable employment and a knowledge of those occupations not available to diabetics is helpful in career planning.

Pregnancy used to be a problem for diabetic women, but careful supervision of the diabetic state and the unborn baby, early delivery and modern obstetric facilities have greatly reduced the risks.

Special services available to those with diabetes Diabetic associations provide educational programs and material for people with diabetes as well as their families. Public seminars to increase community awareness about the conditon are also held.

Interaction with other sufferers of diabetes, summer vacations, and the supply of equipment such as syringes at near cost price are some of the other activities provided by the associations.

Many of the larger hospitals run assessment clinics for people suffering from diabetes. Some have discussion groups where adolescents and others can share experiences, thereby gaining support and confidence.

Diabetes insipidus is an uncommon disease that causes excessive thirst and the passage of large quantities of dilute urine because of damage to the pituitary gland. Unlike diabetes mellitus, which is much more common, diabetes insipidus involves no disturbance in the metabolism of sugar, insulin or the pancreas.

Normally, a substance called vasopressin or antidiuretic hormone is produced by the pituitary gland and has the effect of controlling the amount of water excreted by the kidney. In diabetes insipidus there is a lack of vasopressin occurring from any one of a variety of causes: from a pituitary tumor; after a surgical operation on the pituitary; from encephalitis, viral meningitis or syphilis; from fractures at the base of the skull; or from secondary cancer deposits in pituitary fossa.

The treatment is to give a synthetic equivalent to vasopressin as snuff once or twice daily, which controls the thirst and high urinary output.

Diverticular disease

Formerly known as diverticulitis, diverticular disease is the inflammation of diverticula. The presence of diverticula without inflammation was formerly called diverticulosis or diverticulosis coli.

Diverticula are small sacs or pouches in the walls of a canal or organ, in this case the large bowel or colon. They mostly occur where an artery passes through the muscle layer in the wall, which creates a relative weakness.

Diverticula are thought to form as a result of increased pressure within the colon. Pressure is highest within the sigmoid colon which is narrower and has more muscle in its wall. Diverticula occur more commonly in this area.

Diet as a factor A diet low in fiber is thought to be a major factor in the development of diverticula. Diverticular disease is almost unknown in non-Western civilizations where the diet contains much higher levels of roughage and fiber. A high fiber diet results in a greater volume of material in the feces, which in turn stretches the rectum and ensures a more rapid passage. The greater amount of fiber also retains moisture more easily, and the feces passed are much softer.

When the amount of fecal material is low, its passage is slower, more water is absorbed, and the feces become dry and hard. As a result, greater pressure needs to be exerted by the muscle in the large bowel to expel the feces.

Complications The majority of those with diverticular disease remain symptom free but complications, sometimes severe, may occur.

Inflammation of a diverticulum is the most common complication. This can range from an extremely mild inflammation that settles spontaneously to a rupture of the diverticulum which may in turn result in a generalized peritonitis from leakage of fecal material into the abdominal cavity.

The inflammation is thought to be caused by inadequate emptying of the colon, allowing feces to enter the diverticulum and damage the wall. Bacteria which are normally present in the colon in extremely large numbers then invade the wall and produce inflammation. This inflammation may spread forming a localized abscess or peritonitis, or settle down. Occasionally during the healing process thick scar tissue may form which can produce more problems at a later date, particularly obstruction or blockage of the bowel.

Rarely, a diverticulum may attach to a neighboring organ and rupture into its cavity, producing a *fistula*. This may occur in the bladder (vesicocolic fistula) or the vagina (colovaginal fistula).

The other major complication of diverticular disease is hemorrhage, usually from a sudden rupture of a blood vessel within the wall of a diverticulum. Bleeding is often severe and shock may rapidly develop. Bright red blood is usually passed through the rectum. If bleeding persists after initial resuscitation of the patient, urgent surgical intervention may be required.

Symptoms of inflamed diverticula vary according to the complications which may arise. On most occasions the patient simply feels mildly unwell, and there is some degree of pain and tenderness in the

abdomen over the site of the inflamed diverticulum. This pain occurs most frequently in the lower right hand side of the abdomen and is often made worse by defecation (the passing of feces). If an abscess has formed round the diverticulum or there has been some scarring of surrounding tissue, a definite lump may be felt by the examining doctor.

If there is more widespread inflammation, the patient is usually extremely unwell. Pain in the abdomen may be severe, and it may be extremely tender to touch. Some degree of constipation is usually present.

Diagnosis of diverticular disease is usually made by the use of a barium enema which shows up the diverticula on x-ray.

It is important in diagnosis first to establish that more serious diseases such as cancer of the large bowel are absent.

Treatment Milder cases of diverticular inflammation are treated with antibiotics and by resting the bowel with a light or fluid-only diet. Sometimes fluids are given totally through the veins, with the patient having nothing to eat or drink.

The rarer, more severe cases often require surgical intervention, either to drain an abscess or to remove fecal material in the abdominal cavity if peritonitis has developed. Occasionally the inflamed part of the bowel has to be removed surgically.

Prevention In recent years the value of increased fiber and roughage in the diet has been increasingly recognized. Epidemiological studies have shown that a number of diseases are much less common in societies where there is a high fiber content in the diet. It is hoped that growing awareness will lead to the inclusion of more roughage in the diet, and thus reduce the incidence of diverticular disease and its complications.

Fibrositis

Pain and stiffness in the muscles or tendons on movement is known as fibrositis, or sometimes, in lay terms as 'rheumatism'. It occurs among the middle-aged and old. The condition is without any real pathological basis and has not been shown to be definitely associated with inflammation of the fibrous tissues, which its name suggests.

Causes and occurrence The cause of fibrositis is not known for certain. It is possible that a loss of muscular efficiency makes the individual more prone to strain and injury of muscles, tendons and ligaments. It is also possible that there may be a loss of resiliency and elasticity in the shock absorbers, the intervertebral discs in the spine, long before the changes are detectable. This makes the joints of the spine more susceptible to strains and sprains. In the case of an obese person the repeated stress on flabby muscles is likely to produce acute sprain or chronic damage.

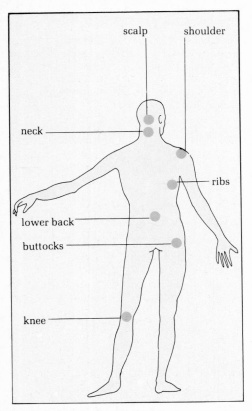

Sites where pain commonly occurs in fibrositis. (*Westmead Center*)

Fibrositis often occurs after unaccustomed physical effort, fatigue, minor injuries or exposure to damp or cold.

Symptoms Fibrositis begins as bouts of pain and stiffness, particularly in the shoulders, spine, neck and buttocks. This may happen suddenly or develop gradually. There may be muscle spasm, revealed in a tightness and hardness of the muscles. No joint damage shows up on x-rays and there is no accompanying fever or general ill health. In these respects fibrositis can be differentiated from rheumatoid arthritis, osteoarthritis and other forms of arthritis.

Fibrositis occurs more frequently among workers like miners, dockers and foundry workers in heavy industry, than among those with more sedentary jobs. It is one of the most common causes of absenteeism from work in people in the over 50 year age group. In these cases the condition is described by some doctors as muscular rheumatism.

Treatment Heat should be applied to the area of pain. This can be done with a hot water bottle or a heat ray lamp. It may also help to massage the area and the pain can be relieved with aspirin or acetaminophen. In general the symptoms will disappear in a few days, and provided the precipitating factors are avoided in the future, the fibrositis may not recur. If it does recur there will be discomfort but nothing more serious.

Foot and leg ailments

Bunion Inflammation and thickening of the bursa of the big toe, bunions are commoner in women as they are encouraged by the wearing of tight pointed shoes with raised heels. Repeated pressure from the shoes pushes the big toe laterally; this tends to be progressive as the muscle which extends the big toe pulls it over further. The bursa is subject to bouts of infection, and the underlying toe joint may become arthritic.

An acute attack is treated by local heat, rest and elevation of the foot, and antibiotics; the patient is advised to wear wide-fronted shoes. If the pain is severe an operation to remove the bunion and realign the toe is performed. The foot will not tolerate an ordinary shoe until three months after the operation and the patient may not feel the full benefit of the operation for six months.

Bursitis Inflammation of a bursa is called bursitis and may be of two types, irritative or infective.

Irritative bursitis is caused by excessive friction such as a shoe rubbing against the big toe, causing a bunion. 'Housemaid's knee', where excess pressure and friction over the kneecaps causes inflammation of the bursa, is called prepatellar bursitis.

Irritative bursitis can be difficult to cure. Some cases respond to rest, but some require injections of hydrocortisone into the bursa or removal of the fluid either by inserting a needle or by operating to open the bursa.

Infective bursitis may occur when a bursa becomes invaded by bacteria causing a hot, red and very painful swelling. Common sites are again the knee and the big toe. Treatment consists of antibiotics and possibly an operation to open the bursa and drain out the purulent fluid.

Ingrown toenail Almost always affecting the big (great) toe, an ingrown toenail is a painful growth of tissues over the side of a nail which has curled into the flesh, usually with a spike of nail at its edge. Often the area becomes inflamed, and a mild purulent (pus-containing) discharge results.

The condition is most likely to develop when excessively tight footwear is worn and the nail is trimmed incorrectly. Unlike fingernails which are cut parallel to

Formation of a bunion. *(Westmead Center)*

pressure forces big toe towards other toes, bursa becomes inflamed, causing bunion to form

the contour of the end of the finger, the toenail should be trimmed with the edges as long as or longer than the central part, to ensure that the edge extends beyond the fleshy tissue beneath.

The inflamed margin of tissue around the nail should be massaged back from the nail several times each day. Packing a small amount of gauze or cotton under the corner of the nail helps keep the tissue back as well as reducing or preventing further downgrowth of the nail into the tissue. Nail flexibility may be increased by thinning it with a file, enabling easier packing and assisting the nail to grow flat. Antibiotics may be required when significant infection is present.

Another method of treatment used by chiropodists (podiatrists) is a special fine metal spring clip attached to each side of the nail. This clip pulls the nail edges away from the inflamed skin and helps to flatten the nail.

Persistence is the key to success, but if these measures fail, excision of a portion of the nail, a wedge resection, is generally required.

Sometimes the excision is extended beyond the lower edge of the nail to include the nail bed, the area from which growth occurs. This procedure prevents that part of the nail from regrowing and is usually performed when there have been repeated episodes of inflammation at one particular edge. Resection allows adequate time for the inflammation to settle and for the tissues to harden. During regrowth of the nail, the growing corner must be packed with a little gauze or wisp of cotton wool, to prevent it from curling back again into the flesh.

Occasionally the whole nail is removed.

Night cramps Painful spasms, usually in the muscles of the calf or foot, waking the individual, night cramps are more common in old age and in pregnancy and are often associated with arthritis and varicose veins. Lack of salt in the body is not a common cause of cramps unless there has been prolonged and profuse sweating or severe vomiting and diarrhea, depleting the body of salt. Usually the cause of night cramps is not obvious.

Night cramps can generally be prevented by taking a quinine tablet at bedtime. Keeping warm in bed is also a worthwhile preventive measure.

Treatment involves stretching the painful muscle. For example, a calf muscle is stretched by pressing the front part of the foot on the floor to bend the back of the foot upwards.

Plantar fasciitis A painful heel condition, plantar fasciitis is characterized by marked tenderness beneath the front part of the heel bone on standing and walking. The site of pain corresponds to the area of attachment of connective tissue and the long plantar ligament.

The precise cause is unknown but the condition most often affects runners and those whose occupations involve continual walking and standing. Sometimes it appears to be related to poorly designed footwear.

X-rays are usually normal, but sometimes a sharp calcaneal spur of bone is evident at the site of greatest tenderness and may require surgical excision. Many orthopedic specialists, however, dispute the significance of a bony spur.

Treatment involves protection of the heel from pressure by a foam or felt insole, rest from activity, and injection of steroid drugs, which are often effective in younger patients.

Restless legs syndrome Also known as *anxietes tibialis*, the restless legs syndrome is a mild though irritating condition characterised by a creeping or aching sensation in the region of the tibia between the knee and the ankle. Usually occurring in bed, it either prevents the sufferer from going to sleep or wakes him up. Repeated movement of the leg or actually going for a walk are the usual solutions to the problem.

The cause of the condition is unknown, although those with diabetes, kidney disease and iron deficiency states are believed to be affected more frequently. Excessive fatigue and mild psychological disturbances are other triggering factors that have been implicated.

The sharp pains associated with leg cramps and the cold feet and 'pins and needles' associated with circulatory problems are absent, clearly distinguishing the restless legs syndrome from these two conditions.

Avoiding excessive fatigue, and relaxing before going to bed, such as by soaking in a hot bath, are often helpful. When simple measures such as these fail, a short period of treatment with diazepam or a related drug may be beneficial, usually taken as a single dose shortly before retiring.

Gastritis

A common condition, gastritis is inflammation of the wall of the stomach. The condition may be acute and short lasting or it may be chronic.

Acute gastritis Irritant substances like alcohol or aspirin may cause acute gastritis. It also accompanies many acute fevers such as an upper respiratory virus infection, influenza or diphtheria.

An inflamed stomach lining causes loss of appetite and nausea at the sight, smell or thought of food. An aching pain in the upper part of the abdomen and a more acute burning pain in the middle of the chest (heartburn) is often present. Vomiting is common in acute gastritis.

Treatment of acute gastritis is usually supportive. Only clear fluids are taken for 24 hours. Simple non-greasy bland foods are recommended for a further day before a light diet is resumed. The stomach lining quickly regenerates once the irritant or infection has gone. Although a child who is feverish and vomiting often has only a brief illness, dehydration caused by the combined vomiting and fever may require urgent hospital admission to allow fluids to be given intravenously.

A form of acute gastritis, causing nausea, loss of appetite and abdominal pain, may be caused when bile flows back into the stomach after eating or drinking hot liquids. Small, frequent, dry meals may help relieve the symptoms which may be aggravated by cigarettes and alcohol. Surgery to prevent the backward flow of bile may be required.

Chronic gastritis Other diseases often accompany chronic gastritis, including cancer of the stomach, pernicious anemia, gastric ulcer and polyps, diabetes, iron deficiency and a number of diseases of the endocrine glands. Ageing and the use of certain drugs may also be related to chronic gastritis. Frequent attacks of acute gastritis may also lead to a chronic form of the disease. The condition may be classified according to the appearance of the stomach wall.

Chronic superficial gastritis, which is often found with gastric ulcer, will recover as the gastric ulcer heals. Most gastric ulcers respond to treatment.

Chronic atrophic gastritis may occur in those who have previously had anemia. Patches of atrophic gastritis may accompany gastric cancer.

Other forms of gastritis include benign giant hypertrophic gastritis, corrosive gastritis caused by iron poisoning or swallowing strong acid or alkalis which can cause holes in the stomach (perforation) and obstruction.

Symptoms of chronic gastritis, if present at all, are usually vague and include loss of appetite, pain while eating, satisfaction with small meals, a bad taste in the mouth, vomiting after eating and some pain and discomfort.

Treatment, which depends on the cause, may only be aimed at relieving any symptoms which are present. In atrophic gastritis, no regeneration of the damaged stomach lining is possible.

Glaucoma

A condition of the eye, glaucoma is characterized by an excessive rise in *intraocular pressure*.

The front part of the eye is filled with a clear, watery fluid called *aqueous humor*, which is produced by the ciliary body and reabsorbed into the small vessels in the area between the iris and the cornea. This fluid bathes the structures in the front of the eye. The pressure of aqueous humor is normally about 0.3 inch (15 mm) of mercury and is called the intraocular pressure. Pressures greater than 0.4 inch (20 mm) may be associated with damage to structures within the eye.

Alcohol can create irritation in the stomach wall and may cause acute gastritis.

1 The end result of untreated glaucoma. Intraocular tension is high and the eye is blind. (Abbottempo)

2 The case of infantile glaucoma seen here shows a greatly enlarged cornea. The child has had a goniopuncture performed; the site of the operation is shown by the white dots on the corneal margin. (Abbottempo)

3 This patient has chronic glaucoma, which is being treated with drops which have caused the pupil to constrict. (Abbottempo)

1

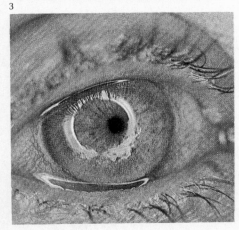

2

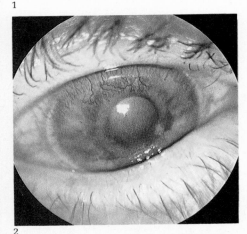

3

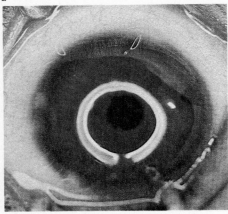

Glaucoma is a common condition, occurring in about 2 per cent of those over forty. Although raised intraocular pressure mainly affects older people, there is also a congenital form. Glaucoma is responsible for 10 to 15 per cent of blindness in Western societies.

The way in which the condition develops is not only affected by the actual cause but also by inherent properties within the eye. For reasons that are not yet fully understood, some eyes cannot tolerate even a mildly elevated intraocular pressure. The condition is then called low-tension glaucoma.

Although in many cases the cause is obscure, there are a number of abnormalities which may cause glaucoma, the treatment and likely outcome being dependent on the specific cause. However, the rapidity of symptom onset and the size of the filtration angle (the area between the root of the iris and the edge of the cornea) do provide broad guidelines, and so glaucoma may be classified according to these factors.

Acute glaucoma occurs when there is a rapid increase in the pressure of the aqueous humor. This is almost always caused by a sudden blockage of the flow of fluid at the filtration angle.

The major symptom is a sudden, severe pain in the affected eye. Blurring of vision and nausea and vomiting often occur. The patient feels very unwell. The eye becomes red and the pupil (the hole in the iris) remains dilated (fully open).

If left untreated, the increased pressure significantly affects the retina and optic nerve, and blindness may result.

Chronic glaucoma In approximately 90 per cent of cases of glaucoma, no specific blockage to the outflow of aqueous humor is demonstrable. The filtration angle is wide and causes no obstruction. Intraocular pressure is often only mildly elevated, and the progression of damage to the eye is slow. Symptoms may not become noticeable for several years, during which considerable damage will occur. Acuteness of vision begins to deteriorate rapidly. This is called chronic glaucoma because of its slow progression, or sometimes open angle glaucoma.

The initial symptoms of open angle glaucoma often include seeing haloes or rainbows around lights, vague headaches, and changing errors of refraction which necessitate a change in eye glasses much more frequently than in previous years.

If this elevation of intraocular pressure is left untreated, damage to parts of the retina and optic nerve may occur, leading to blurring or patchy loss of vision, and sometimes eventual blindness.

Closed angle glaucoma In the other 10 per cent of cases there is either a narrow filtration angle which predisposes to a slow blockage of the aqueous humor circulation, or a blockage caused by some

other problem such as blood cells from a small hemorrhage in the anterior chamber of the eye.

When the filtration angle is narrowed, acute attacks may occur. Often, however, there are brief attacks of milder symptoms, when the angle temporarily closes, which tend to resolve spontaneously. If these repeated attacks remain unnoticed, the angle may become permanently closed as a result of fibrosis occurring. This is called closed angle glaucoma, which may be either acute or chronic.

Diagnosis Because of the importance of early diagnosis, especially in chronic open angle glaucoma, and the fact that symptoms may be minimal or absent for a number of years, regular assessment of intraocular pressure is recommended, especially for those over the age of 40 and those with a family history of glaucoma. This can be done with a *tonometer*. The patient lies down and looks upwards, local anesthetic drops are applied to the eyes, and the instrument is placed gently on the eye surface. A measurement of the pressure is then made.

If glaucoma is diagnosed, a *gonioscope* is used to look directly at the angle in the anterior chamber of the eye (the filtration angle). A diagnosis of wide angle or closed angle glaucoma can then be made. Specific diagnosis is important as it directly influences the type of treatment used.

Treatment Open angle glaucoma is generally treated satisfactorily with drugs and seldom requires surgery, but closed angle or acute glaucoma usually needs surgical intervention. Occasionally in cases of acute glaucoma, obstruction is caused entirely by inflammation of the iris and the ciliary body; in such cases treatment with drugs may be successful.

Specific anti-glaucoma drugs are given initially in virtually all cases of acute glaucoma in an attempt to minimize the production of aqueous humor. The main drug used is acetazolamide. This substance is a 'carbonic anhydrase inhibitor' which blocks the enzyme that controls the production of aqueous humor by the ciliary body. In the first instance it can be given intravenously to produce a rapid effect; treatment is then continued with the tablet form.

Meiotic drugs are also commonly used. By making the pupil smaller, the angle between the iris and cornea is widened in an attempt to facilitate the outflow of aqueous humor.

A recent development is the use of eye drops that contain beta-blocking drugs (generally timolol). It is thought that these preparations work primarily by reducing aqueous humor production, although they may have a mild stimulatory effect on outflow.

The main surgical procedure used

either to treat acute glaucoma or to prevent recurrences in the chronic form, is peripheral (or partial) iridectomy (removal of the iris). This involves the creation of an artificial 'channel' in the iris to produce a new outflow tract.

It is important that glaucoma be detected and treated early because damage to structures within the eye as a result of the elevation in pressure is irreversible. When glaucoma is not detected until a late stage, further deterioration of acuteness of vision may occur. To minimize the risk of progression occurring, medication and eye drops should be taken exactly as prescribed.

The effect of glaucoma on lifestyle depends upon the extent of visual loss and whether it continues to increase. The patient's accustomed lifestyle and activities, his capacity for adaptation and the amount of outside support are other factors involved. Many small modifications in the home may be of value in reducing the inconvenience of decreased vision.

Gout

The disorder of the metabolism (body chemistry) in which there is an excessive amount of uric acid in the blood is known as gout. The word is derived from the Latin word 'gutta', meaning a drop. It is a fairly common condition being more common in males and usually first appearing in the 30 to 35 year old age group.

Gout, a condition most common in men over the age of 35, can be provoked by exposure to cold.

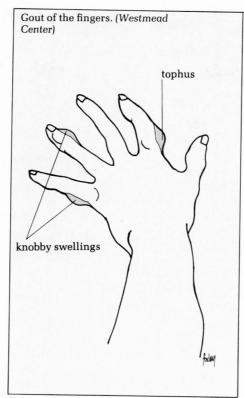

Gout of the fingers. (Westmead Center)

tophus

knobby swellings

Causes Gout is usually inherited. The excessive amount of uric acid in the blood is either the result of over-production of uric acid by the body or the body's inability to excrete sufficient amounts of uric acid to maintain a normally balanced level.

Other factors may also increase the amount of urate in the blood. For example, food like kidney, liver, sweetbread and anchovies have a high level of purines (components of protein) which produce uric acid. Therefore a diet in which these foods are prominent will tend to increase the level of uric acid in the blood. Some drugs, particularly diuretics and cytotoxics (anti-cancer drugs), may also increase the level of uric acid.

Symptoms In some people with a higher than average level of uric acid symptoms may not develop. However, in the case of very high levels, the condition will almost certainly develop.

The most striking feature of gout is sudden extremely painful arthritis. The symptoms are the same no matter what the cause. The classic symptoms begin early in the morning. The pain most frequently affects the big toe, where circulation is most sluggish, and uric acid may pass from the bloodstream into the joint. The pain can be so severe that the person is unable to tolerate the area being touched. The joint and surrounding area become red, hot and swollen. The area is described as the 'tomato joint' because of its appearance.

In addition, sweating and rigors (shaking) are often experienced. An attack can be triggered by dietary changes, stress, local trauma, and prolonged exposure to

heat or cold. Other parts of the foot, and more rarely more distant joints, can also be affected. However, the initial attack is almost always confined to one joint.

Complications If adequate treatment is not available, the uric acid passes into other tissues of the body. After several attacks of gout, joints may become thickened and deformed, and masses of hard urate deposits called tophi frequently accumulate in the cartilage around the outer edge of the ear. It is also possible that kidney disease will occur, particularly the formation of uric acid stones (with renal colic).

Diagnosis and treatment Usually gout can be diagnosed easily from the classic symptoms and diagnosis can be confirmed by detecting a raised uric acid level in the blood. In less obvious cases, when it cannot be distinguished from other forms of arthritis, a microscopic analysis of fluid from the joint space may be required.

Without treatment an attack of gout will pass spontaneously over a period, which can be from 2 to 20 days. However, the tendency is for attacks to recur.

There are certain signs that can warn of an impending attack of gout. These include indigestion, tiredness, and vague aches and pains. If medications are taken at this time they may help to control the actual attack more effectively than if not taken until the pain develops.

Anti-inflammatory preparations such as phenylbutazone and indomethacin are used in preference to the previous treatment with colchicine, which produced unpleasant side effects. These preparations often produce dramatic relief, with symptoms disappearing within 24 hours.

Once an acute attack has subsided, the main object of treatment is then to prevent future attacks. Measures that help are a reduction in weight if a person is obese, and avoiding or minimizing foods that contain a high level of purine.

The drug probenecid greatly increases the amount of uric acid excreted from the kidney, but is only effective in some cases. A much more effective medication is allopurinol. It produces relatively few side effects, and works by inhibiting the body's production of uric acid. However, treatment with allopurinol usually continues for life.

The introduction of effective drugs to treat and prevent gout has substantially reduced the number of joint destruction and kidney problems caused by the deposition of uric acid in the tissues of the body.

Hemorrhoids

Piles, or hemorrhoids, are a mass of swollen venous tissue near the anus, the outlet to the rectum. Two communicating networks of veins lie near the rectum: one is beneath the lining of the rectum, and the other is under the skin layer just outside the anus. When the veins of either of these networks become distended (varicose), they form a localized swelling consisting of the dilated vein and its overlying tissue. Internal hemorrhoids arise from within the rectum, and external hemorrhoids underlie the skin.

Causes Conditions that cause increased pressure of the blood within these veins give rise to hemorrhoid formation. Local conditions such as diarrhea or laxative abuse, tumors of the colon, and situations where there is a general increase in the pressure within the abdomen may all result in hemorrhoid formation.

Common causes of a raised intra-abdominal pressure include excessive straining to evacuate the rectum as a result of constipation, pregnancy and obesity. Liver disease, which causes an increased pressure within all abdominal veins, and even prolonged sitting, have also been implicated.

Symptoms *Internal hemorrhoids* do not usually cause symptoms unless they become infected or the surface breaks down and they start to bleed. This latter occurrence is alarming to the person concerned, and is often detected as blood spots on the toilet paper. The bleeding is generally free of pain.

If the hemorrhoids enlarge to the extent that they extend down through the anus, they are termed prolapsed hemorrhoids. Pressure on the base of the prolapsed hemorrhoid often causes swelling, and sometimes the circulation of the blood to the tissue is restricted (strangulated hemorrhoid) which, in turn, causes much pain.

Constipation can be a cause of hemorrhoids, so an adequate fiber content in the diet, using such foods as shown here, can help to avoid the condition.

External hemorrhoids are generally painful and appear as swellings under the skin. All dilated veins have an altered blood flow pattern which may give rise to blood clot formation. This occurs commonly in both types of hemorrhoid and results in increased discomfort. In many cases the swelling of an external hemorrhoid is probably caused by rupture of a small non-dilated vein, the blood that leaks out being responsible for the swelling.

Diagnosis Observation, rectal examination, and visualization of the lower portion of the rectum by a short instrument called a proctoscope are ways in which hemorrhoids may be diagnosed.

Persistent rectal bleeding should be investigated further. Direct examination using a sigmoidoscope or colonoscope, and a special x-ray (barium enema) are means of excluding the possibility of a cancer of the large bowel being the cause of the bleeding, particularly in people aged more than forty.

Treatment Mild cases of internal hemorrhoids may be managed by increasing the natural fiber content in the diet to reduce the likelihood of constipation. Larger hemorrhoids may be shrunk by injecting a sclerosand liquid (one that causes inflammation and fibrosis), or by placing a small elastic band around the base which cuts off the blood supply to the hemorrhoid tissue relatively slowly, causing it to die and drop off. Large hemorrhoids may require surgery. The offending tissue is cut out, along with a small section of skin around its base, and the area allowed to heal naturally.

External hemorrhoids may be cut out and the clot removed. A clot within an internal hemorrhoid may be dealt with in a similar fashion should it protrude through the anus.

Headache

The pain that is felt in the skull or upper part of the head is generally described as headache. It is extremely common: between 5 and 10 per cent of the adult population experience a headache at least once each week.

There are various causes of headaches. The stretching, pulling or dilation (widening) of blood vessels (both within and outside the bony skull) and spasm of scalp muscles are the most common causes. Headache is also caused by irritation or inflammation of the meninges (the membranes that line brain tissue), inflammation or pressure on sensory nerves, and an increase in the pressure of the cerebrospinal fluid, the liquid that bathes the brain and spinal cord.

Tension headaches The most common headache is the tension or muscle contraction headache. Virtually everyone suffers from it at some time. It affects both sides of the head and tends to be fairly constant. In most cases it begins slowly.

A headache may be caused by fatigue, as in the case of eyestrain.
(John Watney Photo Library)

The ache is usually most prominent above the eyes, and there is a feeling of tightness across the forehead.

It is said to be caused by persistent contraction and spasm of scalp muscles as well as by psychological factors. It usually occurs when there is anxiety, stress (especially prolonged concentration), or tension. It is most common in people who tend to be compulsive or competitive, in whom anxiety or tension is more likely. Also those with minor psychological or psychosocial problems are more prone.

The persistence of this kind of headache is a common feature. It may occur on most days for many months.

The treatment of repeated or longstanding tension headaches is most successful when the individual adopts a lifestyle in which he experiences less tension. Simple pain-relieving tablets such as aspirin are usually ineffective. More important are relaxation therapy and the minimization of stress, occasionally with the use of mild tranquilizers.

Vascular headaches Migraine is the commonest type of vascular headache. In about two-thirds of cases the pain is restricted to one side (this is sometimes described as hemicrania). The pain is preceded by an aura, usually a disturbance of vision. At times there may be weakness or tingling (described as 'pins and needles') down one side of the body. These symptoms may settle when the headache begins. An intolerance to bright light almost always develops with nausea and vomiting in about half the cases.

The aura is probably caused by a narrowing of blood vessels, followed by dilation (widening) causing the pain. These vascular changes may be precipitated by stress, certain foods or beverages, exercise, trauma to the head, and even the smell of strong perfume.

The treatment is to prevent further attacks and to rapidly relieve pain. Wherever possible avoid those things that will

A tension headache, the result of anxiety or stress, is one of the most common headaches. (*Zefa*)

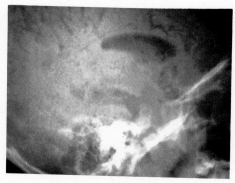

This arteriogram reveals a large aneurysm in the brain. (*Westmead Center*)

cause the headache. Various drugs such as methysergide, piztifen, clonidine and propranolol may be taken on a regular basis to prevent migraine attacks. Also ergotamine taken as soon as symptoms occur may prevent the pain by minimizing the dilation of the scalp blood vessels. Once the headache has become established, strong pain-killing drugs may be needed.

Cluster headache is a rarer form of vascular headache with pain occurring while the person is in bed. It lasts for several hours, and tends to occur regularly for weeks in bouts or 'clusters'.

The distinction between vascular and tension headaches is not always clear, and a number of people suffer from headaches that exhibit features of both.

Other headaches In the case of longstanding headache, the pain may be caused by a tumor growth stretching the blood vessels or meninges. The headache varies in intensity and frequency but tends to recur with increasing regularity and severity. In these cases it is important to establish whether the headache is caused by a tumor. Fortunately this is not a common cause of headache.

A trauma or head injury can cause headache. For example, concussion (bruising of brain tissue within the skull) can lead to the stretching and dilation of the blood vessels. The headaches associated with a hangover and those caused by

hypertension (high blood pressure) are also caused by blood vessel dilation. In the latter the headache is most severe on wakening.

A headache is one of the prominent symptoms of meningitis (inflammation of the meninges). A sudden hemorrhage within the skull (especially into the subarachnoid space between the pia and the arachnoid meningeal layers) produces a sudden, severe, generalized headache, usually with a rapid loss of consciousness. This may be caused by trauma, or the rupture of an aneurysm.

A headache often occurs with a fever, particularly in children. This is thought to be caused by a combination of a mild irritation of the meninges and a dilation and stretching of blood vessels caused by an increased blood flow.

Temporal arteritis, also called giant cell arteritis, is an inflammation of the scalp arteries. It mainly affects those over 65 years of age. If it is left untreated there may be permanent loss of eyesight. When generalized muscle aches and pains also occur the condition is described as polymyalgia rheumatica.

A headache sometimes occurs when there is disorder of nearby organs or tissues. For example, in the case of sinusitis (the inflammation of the nasal sinuses) there will tend to be dull headache and tenderness over the affected area. The head often feels stuffed up. Glaucoma, which is caused by increased pressure of the fluid within the eye, may produce a severe local pain that spreads out to the

forehead. A headache may also be produced by eyestrain probably as a result of persistent contraction of nearby muscles. Other causes of headache include diseases of the ears, jaw, throat and neck.

Diagnosis of the exact cause of headache can usually be made from the history and an examination of the individual. Sometimes special investigations may be needed to rule out serious causes. Any detected cause requires specific treatment, but frequently the minimization of stress and other triggering factors is an important part of treatment.

Heartburn

An uncomfortable burning sensation felt behind the sternum or breast bone, heartburn is often initiated or made worse by stooping as in tying up shoelaces. It also can be precipitated by lying down.

Associated symptoms are belching and sometimes regurgitation of sour fluid into the mouth.

Causes The pain is the result of irritation of the lining of the lower esophagus by the highly acidic contents of the stomach or by duodenal juices. Heartburn commonly occurs when a large amount of food or fluid is consumed rapidly, especially carbonated water.

Obesity, pregnancy, and recurrent constipation are all conditions in which there is an increased pressure within the abdominal cavity, which in turn often results in regurgitation of juices into the lower esophagus. Hiatus hernia is also frequently associated with heartburn.

Treatment may involve losing any excessive weight and preventing constipation. Various antacid tablets or mixtures may help. An agent such as cimetidine which blocks the formation of hydrochloric acid by the stomach may be helpful.

Slight elevation of the head of the bed and modifying activities to minimize bending over may also reduce the occurrence of heartburn.

Unfortunately treatment is often unrewarding.

Hepatitis

Inflammation of the liver is most commonly called hepatitis. It may be caused by a number of virus infections, or by excessive alcohol intake, and is an unwanted side-effect of certain drugs including phenylbutazone, sulphonamides, halothane and methyldopa. This so-called drug-induced hepatitis is relatively rare.

Viral hepatitis is fairly common. For many years it was classified as either 'infectious hepatitis' (which was spread by fecal contamination of food or fluid), or 'serum hepatitis' which was spread by infected blood. The investigation of the specific viruses causing these conditions led to the identification of a special protein or antigen, called the Australia antigen, associated with the virus causing serum hepatitis. It was found that both types of virus could cause infection by either way (fecal-oral or serum spread).

The terms hepatitis A and hepatitis B are now used instead of infectious hepatitis and serum hepatitis.

Type A hepatitis is the more common form. It occurs world wide, and primarily affects children and young adults, particularly in the winter months. Spread is usually via contaminated food, so the disease is especially prevalent in developing countries where hygiene is poor.

Once the virus has been ingested, it multiplies in the intestine. The symptoms first appear two to six weeks later. Probably more than half of those infected do not develop any symptoms and, as the virus is excreted in the feces shortly after initial contamination, the condition may spread rapidly throughout a community.

Type B hepatitis is spread most commonly by infected blood or serum. It became prominent about the time of World War II when there was a considerable increase in the number of blood transfusions performed. Before transfusion, blood is tested to determine whether the Australia antigen is present.

The virus may also be spread through kidney dialysis, drug addicts sharing needles, tattooing and contaminated surgical instruments. The virus may be present in other body secretions, particularly during the acute stage of the illness. These include the feces and the seminal fluid, so that fecal-oral and venereal spread are possible. It is a particularly common sexually-transmitted disease amongst homosexual males.

Type B hepatitis occurs world wide. It can affect any age group and has a longer incubation period than hepatitis A. Symptoms usually do not develop for a period ranging from six weeks to six months after initial contact.

1 The hepatitis A virus. (*Science Photo Library*)

2 The hepatitis B virus. (*Science Photo Library*)

1

2

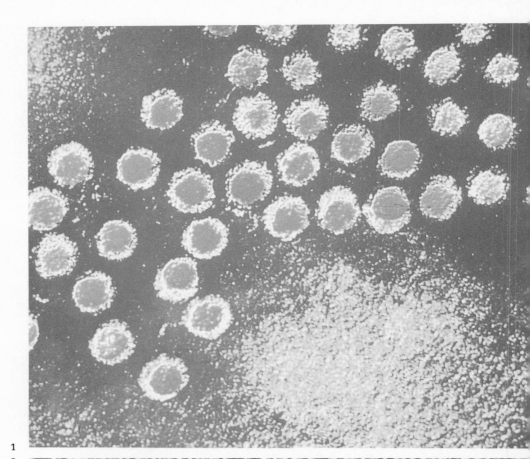

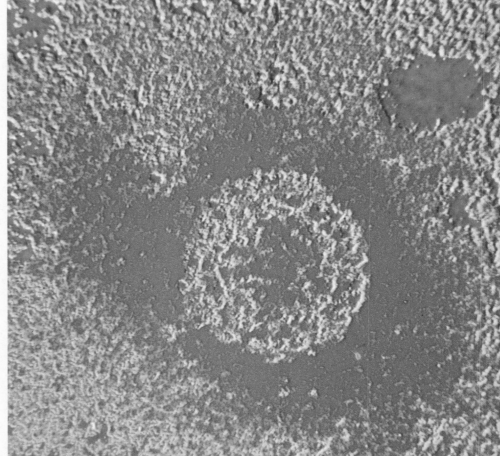

Symptoms Both types of infection and their associated symptoms have similar effects upon the liver. A period of malaise, lassitude, fever and loss of appetite usually precedes the development of jaundice. Gastrointestinal symptoms are often present, including nausea, vomiting, diarrhea, and general abdominal discomfort. When the virus spreads to the liver, the damage to the hepatocytes (liver cells), plus the general inflammation set up in the organ, leads to changes in bilirubin metabolism.

Once jaundice has appeared, the whites of the eyes become yellow, as does the skin, and a darkening of the urine and the appearance of clay-colored feces may occur. The liver is generally enlarged, and becomes tender to touch. Vague aches and pains in the muscles and a fine rash over the body are other symptoms, particularly in hepatitis B.

In hepatitis B symptoms tend to develop more slowly, and the flu-like symptoms of hepatitis A are usually less noticeable in B. Once jaundice develops, both infections follow similar patterns. Gastrointestinal symptoms soon settle and the jaundice itself subsides over a four to six week period. A transient period of generalized itching (pruritus) may be associated with the jaundice.

Treatment of both types of hepatitis is mainly directed at relieving the symptoms. Rest, a light diet and adequate fluid intake are the normal measures. Alcohol, marijuana and estrogen-containing preparations such as oral contraceptives must be avoided for six months, because of their potentially harmful effects on the recovering liver. In severe cases of hepatitis, admission to hospital may be required, particularly if the fluid intake becomes inadequate.

Hepatitis A is more contagious than hepatitis B but, because the virus has usually been excreted in the feces for some time prior to diagnosis, strict isolation is usually not undertaken. Careful hygiene is quite important, however, to minimize fecal contamination. Frequent washing of the hands, and thorough cleaning of linen and eating utensils are necessary.

Close contacts (those in the same household) of people with hepatitis A should be injected with gamma globulin as soon as the diagnosis has been made to protect them against the illness. The injection contains antibodies obtained from blood donors and these compounds will attack any hepatitis A virus present and facilitate destruction by the body's own defence mechanisms. Normal gamma globulin does not provide protection against hepatitis B.

Immunization is available against hepatitis B. The vaccine is costly and its use is advised only in persons identified as being at risk of exposure e.g. hospital staff,

Hepatitis may develop after the use of contaminated needles for such purposes as tattooing.

dentists. A special hyperimmune globulin is also available for administration to those who are exposed to the disease.

After the jaundice has settled most people generally feel well, but for a number of weeks they may complain of becoming excessively fatigued after even mild exertion. Total recovery usually takes several months. In 10 per cent of cases some degree of relapse, usually minor, may occur. Occasionally the condition may progress to more severe liver damage.

Diagnosis and progress can be monitored by clinical assessment and by blood tests including one for the detection of Australia antigen and some that assess liver function.

It is now possible to identify several antigens or antibodies that are associated with either hepatitis A or hepatitis B infection. However, a number of viruses causing hepatitis are, according to antigen and antibody studies, neither type A nor type B. Often the clinical features of the hepatitis produced lie between the

Cirrhosis with damage and scarring of the liver may be the end result of alcoholic hepatitis. Here the liver surface is seen through a laparascope. (*Abbottempo*)

classical type A and type B pictures. Such a condition is called 'non-A non-B hepatitis', as the exact number of different virus types is still unknown.

Hepatitis may also occur as part of other infectious diseases such as mononucleosis (glandular fever), cytomegalovirus infection and leptospirosis (Weil's disease), the latter being caused by a bacterium. Associated features specific to these illnesses usually assist in the diagnosis. Two blood tests used to confirm the presence of infectious mononucleosis are the Paul Bunnell test and the Monospot test.

The possibility of toxic hepatitis resulting from alcohol, drugs and noxious industrial and other chemicals needs to be accounted for in the process of diagnosis of hepatitis. As in the above conditions, the liver symptoms are usually only a part of the overall toxic effects on the body tissues.

Alcohol is the most commonly ingested toxin that can cause hepatitis. Alcoholic hepatitis is at times a very serious condition and may result in liver failure and death or progress to cirrhosis with destruction of liver tissue and resultant scarring. Liver function tests usually show a different pattern from that of viral hepatitis.

Chronic hepatitis occurs when inflammation of the liver tissue persists. It may follow from any of the other forms of hepatitis. Diagnosis is made by microscopic examination of liver tissue obtained by biopsy. Abnormalities of the immune system are probably involved and treatment includes the use of corticosteroid drugs or cytotoxics.

Control The key to control of hepatitis is the maintenance of a high standard of personal hygiene. Laboratory workers must be particularly careful when handling blood that could be contaminated by hepatitis B virus.

Hernia

The protrusion of an organ or part of an organ or tissue through any abnormal opening or defect in the wall of the cavity that normally contains it is a hernia. An external hernia is one which protrudes towards the skin surface. The vast majority of hernias occur in the abdominal wall. An inguinal hernia occurs in the groin and is commonly known as a rupture.

Sometimes a weakness in the cavity wall develops, for example above the scrotum where the testes descend during fetal development. Some hernias are the result of developmental abnormalities (for example, congenital diaphragmatic hernia) or weakness following an operation (for example, incisional hernia).

Repeated straining of the muscles of the abdominal wall increases the chance of developing a hernia. Some examples are whooping cough in children, obesity and

direct inguinal hernia protruding directly through the muscles of the abdominal wall, or it may first traverse the inguinal canal (the canal through which the vas deferens and other associated nerves and blood vessels pass from the scrotum into the abdominal cavity) and then reach the surface. This is called an indirect inguinal hernia. In some cases of indirect hernia the bowel may extend down into the scrotum.

Incisional hernia is the second most common one. It occurs through the deeper layers of an operation scar, usually soon after the operation. If a person is very obese, has a persistent cough, or has an infected wound, there is extra strain and the wound may not heal effectively. In these cases an incisional hernia is most likely to develop.

Femoral hernias are the next most common, and occur more frequently in females. They extend through the femoral ring, an opening in the lower part of the abdominal wall below the inguinal canal and at the upper border of the thigh. Normally only the major blood vessels of the leg (femoral artery and vein) pass through this opening. The opening is relatively narrow, and strangulation is more likely to occur here than elsewhere.

Umbilical hernias occur in infants through a weakened umbilicus or navel (where the umbilical cord was connected to the fetus to provide nourishment from the mother). Some degree of herniation occurs in about one in five newborn babies, but well over 90 per cent of these are cured spontaneously.

Para-umbilical hernias occur among adults. This is a protrusion between the

pregnancy in adults, and repeated straining associated with long-term constipation or partial urinary blockage (especially enlargement of the prostate gland in elderly men).

A hernia consists of a sac (in the abdominal hernias this is usually the peritoneum), its contents (often part of the small intestine), and its coverings (the layers of the abdominal wall).

In most cases the hernial sac, together with its contents, can be pushed back into place. This sort of hernia is described as reducible. Sometimes fibrous adhesions occur, or the hernia becomes 'overcrowded' with contents and cannot be pushed back. This is known as an irreducible hernia.

Occasionally the intestine within the hernia twists upon itself and becomes obstructed. If the blood supply is impeded, that portion of bowel may die and general toxicity result. This is called strangulated hernia and requires emergency surgical treatment to avert more generalized difficulties. If gangrene of the portion of the bowel occurs and its obstruction is not relieved, the pain becomes more generalized and the person affected becomes gravely ill.

Inguinal hernia is the commonest type of hernia, and occurs particularly in middle-aged men, often after heavy lifting or straining. Part of the bowel usually penetrates through an opening in the abdominal wall just above the groin. It may be a

Obesity contributes to the development of an incisional hernia. (*Zefa*)

An inguinal hernia often develops in middle-aged men who have been lifting heavy weights.

muscle fibers just above the navel. Women are affected more frequently than men, and multiple pregnancies and increasing obesity are important contributing factors.

Hiatal hernia occurs when a portion of the stomach protrudes into the chest cavity through the opening in the diaphragm that is normally reserved for the esophagus. Heartburn may be a symptom, but in the vast majority of cases there are no problems.

Congenital diaphragmatic hernia normally occurs shortly after birth. The contents of the abdominal cavity, particularly the small intestine, penetrate through a large defect in the diaphragm and enter the chest. They press on the lungs causing marked breathlessness. A severe trauma, most often after a motor vehicle accident, may produce a similar problem caused by a tear in the muscular diaphragm.

Hives

Urticaria is the medical term for hives, a condition characterized by white or red raised areas of skin which are often extremely itchy. The condition develops when the body releases chemical substances in the skin. The swellings most often appear in those parts of the body covered by clothes, though they can appear in any part of the body. The condition may also involve mucous membrane tissue, such as the stomach and mouth.

The condition may occur together with hay fever and allergic asthma or serum sickness, and can be aggravated by heat, physical exercise and emotion. The cause is not easy to determine, for it can occur

Contact with feathers may cause an allergic response resulting in hives.

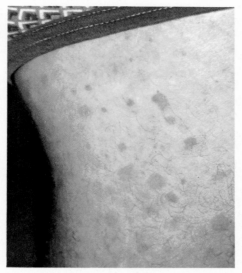

A crop of hives affecting the back. Hives may be confused with insect bites but the latter are more common on exposed areas.
(Westmead Center)

as an allergic response to a number of substances including foods, drugs, pollen, dust, feathers, certain clothes or cosmetics. When a specific cause is found the appropriate action may be to eradicate it from the environment.

The condition varies in severity from being a mild nuisance to being a threat to life. Treatment is possible with various drugs which can be given by mouth or injection. However, the chronic form, for which the cause is unknown, may be very difficult to treat.

Hodgkin's disease

One of a group of diseases called lymphomas, Hodgkin's disease is a malignant tumor of lymphatic tissue, particularly the lymph nodes or glands. A progressive but painless enlargement of lymph nodes occurs throughout the body.

The lymphatic system carries nutrients and fluid from the tissues to the bloodstream. Although lymph nodes varying in size are found at intervals along the lymphatic vessels, collections of nodes may be found in the neck, the armpits and groin.

The condition was first described by Thomas Hodgkin in 1832. For many years the exact cause, which is still unknown, was a source of controversy. Malignancy, chronic inflammation and an infection were all implicated.

Symptoms Hodgkin's disease commences inconspicuously, usually with a painless enlargement of some lymph nodes, most frequently those in the neck. More common in males, it almost always commences in the 30 to 45 year-old age group. As the condition progresses, the glands in the neck, armpits and groins get bigger and eventually matt together and become attached to the overlying skin. There is also enlargement of both the spleen and liver. Early in the disease the patient feels

weak and tired, loses weight and has an intermittent mild fever. Anemia, which gets progressively worse, is nearly always present. Some people also complain of a persistent skin itch (pruritus).

Diagnosis is initially confirmed by removing an enlarged lymph node and examining it under a microscope (a lymph node biopsy).

To predict the likely outcome of the condition and to select the most appropriate method of treatment, the extent of the disease must be accurately defined. X-rays and biopsies from bone marrow are often taken. Surgical exploration of the abdominal cavity (laparotomy) determines whether the liver, spleen or lymph nodes around the intestine are affected.

Untreated, the condition is often fatal within two years, resulting from invasion of vital tissues or the development of an overwhelming infection such as pneumonia or septicemia.

Treatment In the past twenty years remarkable advances have been made in the treatment of Hodgkin's disease. Two major forms of treatment are used; radiotherapy and specific anti-cancer (cytotoxic) drugs.

Radiotherapy is used when all the lymph nodes affected by the disease are relatively close together, for example all above the diaphragm. Cytotoxic drugs are used if the disease is more widespread. The main preparations used are the nitrogen mustards, which are given in short, repeated courses. If any lymph nodes are causing mechanical obstruction to neighbouring ducts or tissues, they are usually removed.

With treatment, the disease progresses very slowly in most patients. Today the three-year-survival rate of Hodgkin's disease is around 90 per cent and many patients can expect to go on with no recurrence of the disease for ten to twenty years, possibly never.

Hyperthyroidism

A disorder of the thyroid gland resulting in excessive secretion of thyroid hormone is known as hyperthyroidism. There are many causes, but Graves' disease (diffuse toxic goiter) and nodular toxic goiter account for over 99 per cent of cases. Rare causes include tumors of pituitary gland, placenta, testes, ovary and thyroid, inflammatory disease of the thyroid and administration of excessive amounts of thyroid hormone.

In Graves' disease, the thyroid is generally enlarged and overactive because of the excessive stimulation by abnormal circulating immune proteins. It occurs mostly in younger age groups and appears as a thyroid swelling or goiter, often with eye prominence (exophthalmos). Nodular toxic goiter tends to occur in older age groups without the prominent eyes, and only nodular, asymmetric gland enlargement.

Symptoms of hyperthyroidism are numerous and include intolerance of heat, weight loss, loose motions, tremor, warm sweaty palms, palpitations, emotional lability, breathlessness, and increased appetite.

The common signs are thyroid swelling, evidence of increased blood flow to the organ, prominent eyes, overactive movements, hot moist hands, and disturbances of cardiac rhythm and circulation.

Complications, if untreated, may involve heart rhythm disturbances, leading to cardiac failure and audible murmurs. Enlargement of lymph nodes and spleen may occur. Wasting of muscle and bone (osteoporosis) are common features in long-standing cases. Rarely, nausea, vomiting, and even fever and jaundice occur. Mental changes vary from nervousness and mild exhilaration to delirium and exhaustion, progressing to severe depression.

The thyroid storm, rare today, is an extreme form of hyperthyroidism marked by delirium, rapid pulse, vomiting, diarrhea, dehydration and high fever. The mortality rate is high.

Diagnosis and treatment Diagnosis depends on the clinical history of the patient, and the examination and estimation of serum thyroid hormones.

Treatment may be medical or surgical. Choice of therapy may depend on patient preference, influenced by proximity of medical care, sick leave arrangements, demands of a young family and the expertise of available surgeons. Surgery is often preferred if the goiter is large and, in expert hands, offers prompt, effective cure of hyperthyroidism with little risk of complications. Recurrence is possible, as is thyroid hormone deficiency, but these are relatively rare. Surgery is also best if there is compression of surrounding structures. Drug therapy is also used to reduce overactivity of the thyroid before surgery is undertaken. Medical treatment is usually used to prepare the patient for surgery.

Medical treatment involves the use of antithyroid drugs to suppress the thyroid overactivity for about 12–18 months, in the hope of natural remission. More than 50 per cent relapse, however, usually within a few months. The frequent medical visits, the duration of treatment and supervision, and the risk of side-effects from drugs used, lead some patients to reject this method.

Antithyroid drugs are usually administered to children and young adults, especially if the disease is mild with a small goitre. Radioactive iodine treatment cures hyperthyroidism by destroying the thyroid tissue, and is particularly useful when the patients are unsuitable for surgery, or they are older patients, with recurrent disease. It is not used in pregnancy.

Deficiency of thyroid hormone is a major complication of radioactive iodine

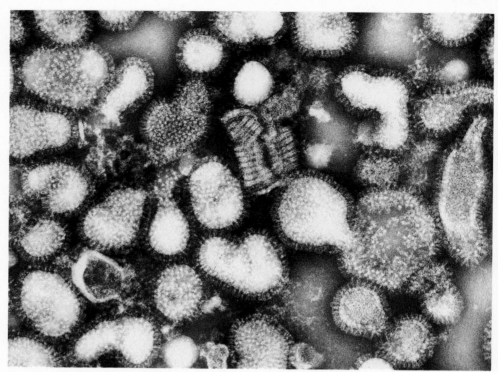

Particles of influenza virus showing its aspherical form with spikes protruding from the surface.
(Science Photo Library)

treatment as it is very difficult to determine the critical dose needed to destroy only a certain amount of tissue.

Hyperthyroidism in the newborn may be caused by the mother having hyperthyroidism during pregnancy. The condition at this stage is often very severe but self-limiting. Energetic treatment is required.

Influenza

A common and highly contagious viral illness, influenza primarily affects the respiratory tract. The first major influenza epidemic was recorded in the twelfth century, but the most devastating one occurred in 1918–19. It was responsible for more deaths than the war which immediately preceded it. Other pandemics (widespread epidemics) include the 1957 'Asian flu' and the 1968 'Hong Kong' variety.

At one stage a bacterium was thought to be responsible, and it was labelled 'Pfeiffer's bacillus', later to be called *Haemophilus influenzae*. In the 1918–19 pandemic this organism was a common secondary invader of the inflamed respiratory tissue. It was not until 1933 that the influenza virus itself was first isolated. Since then three distinct types have been differentiated, called Types A, B and C. Type A is the one responsible for pandemics, while type B occurs in isolated outbreaks. Type C infection is quite common, but is so mild that usually no symptoms are noted.

Epidemics of varying severity occur every two to four years, primarily as a result of structural changes in the *antigens* on the surface of the virus. These changes render people who were previously resistant to the virus sensitive again as *antibodies* produced from previous exposure are now less effective against the new antigens. At times viruses with antigenic structures similar to those causing previous epidemics will reappear.

Pandemics are associated with major antigenic changes. Mutation or accidental genetic changes are involved in this process, but the exact mechanism, and the role of animal influenzal viruses which sometimes share a portion of the antigens present on human ones, is still not clear.

Symptoms In each epidemic, the symptoms and the clinical course of uncomplicated influenza are quite predictable. The condition is contracted by the inhalation of infected droplets and the acute or sudden onset, especially in adults, is a common and distinctive feature. Symptoms occur abruptly some 24 hours after exposure, severe headache behind the eyes being the most common. A fever develops rapidly, its length and severity matching that of the illness. Tiredness and general malaise are always present and other common symptoms include generalized aches and pains, loss of appetite, nausea, and respiratory symptoms. Watering of the eyes and nose (rhinorrhea) and a dry cough are also frequent.

In uncomplicated influenza, symptoms tend to subside after several days, but tiredness and depression may at times last for weeks.

Complications of influenza are most likely to occur in the elderly, babies, and any person with underlying heart or lung disease. During the infection the lining of the respiratory tract becomes swollen and inflamed, and the protective action of the cilia is often lost. This may predispose this weakened and damaged tissue to secondary bacterial infection. Bronchitis or pneumonia are the main complications, usually indicated by the development of a productive cough (associated with thick sputum or phlegm) and breathing difficulties. Bacterial infection of the sinuses (sinusitis) and middle ear (otitis media) are other associated conditions. The influenza virus itself may cause penumonia, although this is not usual.

Fatalities occur more commonly in epidemics; an overwhelming pneumonia is the usual cause.

Treatment The main treatment of uncomplicated influenza is rest, adequate fluids, and analgesia for the muscle pains. Codeine-based compounds have the added advantage of suppressing any associated irritating dry cough. Initial bed rest is advisable, with a gradual return to full activity. Antibiotics do not affect the course of uncomplicated influenza, but are necessary if secondary bacterial infection develops.

Vaccination against influenza is now available; it is helpful for those most likely to develop complications. Because of the significant and frequent antigen changes of the virus, annual injections may be required. Because of this and the relative mildness of the illness in most cases, mass immunization is not usually undertaken.

Influenza vaccines are continually updated from the information provided by the World Health Organization's monitoring of the prevalence of various antigenic types of viruses in different countries.

An inhaler can help clear the nasal passages and afford considerable relief from symptoms of influenza.

Insomnia

The inability to sleep or to obtain sufficient sleep, affects most people at some time in their lives.

The problem may be the inability to fall asleep after going to bed, an inadequate depth of sleep, disturbed sleep with frequent awakenings, habitually waking in the early hours of the morning and being unable to go back to sleep, or a feeling of tiredness on awakening.

One of the greatest problems with insomnia is that it tends to be self-perpetuating: we cannot go to sleep and thus we lie in bed worrying because we cannot sleep. Sleeplessness then becomes a vicious circle. This sort of pattern exists in most chronic insomniacs.

Right
Anxiety or stress frequently cause insomnia but long walks may help to relax the body.
Below
Insomnia may cause constant very early awakening.

Sleep has several physiological levels. 'Orthodox sleep' is the first level. Here the heart rate and breathing rate are regular, eye movement is minimal, and the muscles become increasingly relaxed. Brain activity, as shown on an electroencephalogram (EEG, a tracing of the electrical activity of the brain) is reduced. This can be subdivided further into four stages, the fourth and final one representing the deepest sleep. At this level decreasing body movement and increasing muscle relaxation occur.

'Paradoxical sleep' follows, usually for about one-quarter the length of time of orthodox sleep. During this period there are both rapid eye movements and increased blood flow through the brain, with an associated acceleration of electrical activity. The heart rate and breathing rate become irregular and the body muscles totally relaxed.

The role of sleep and dreams The exact role of sleep is not fully understood, but a restorative or 'body recharging' function is certainly part of it. Prolonged deprivation of sleep leads to both physical and mental problems.

Dreams are thought to occur during paradoxical sleep which is also called REM sleep, from the rapid eye movement that occurs at this level. When people awake during this period they can vividly recall dreams just experienced. Some authorities propose that orthodox sleep is used to restore the body, whereas REM sleep is used primarily to restore the mind.

Sleep patterns change considerably with age. The failure to understand this and adapt to it often causes so-called insomnia. A young baby may sleep for about twenty hours a day, whereas many elderly people manage well on five hours. The relative amount of depth of orthodox sleep also decreases with increasing age. As people grow older, they may awaken more readily.

Even among people of the same age there is considerable variation in the amount of sleep required. Some still feel tired after eight hours' sleep a night, while others seem to manage well on four to five hours.

There appears to be a small group of people who have a lifetime of difficult sleep patterns, in the absence of any specific triggering factors. They sleep for shorter periods, their sleep is lighter, and they seem to have a higher level of arousal, a more rapid pulse, and a higher body temperature than most people.

Sleep is controlled by part of the brainstem (deep structure within the brain tissue) called the reticular activating system (RAS), which affects nerve fibers of the reticular formation. Each fiber apparently has one of two antagonistic functions, each with its own chemical transmitter. It is thought that the overall balance of these two actions determines the presence and depth of sleep. Perhaps in those people with difficult sleep patterns, the 'setting' of the RAS is altered.

Causes Most people experiencing insomnia can attribute it to a particular factor. Many older people fail to adjust to their decreasing sleep needs and possibly expect to continue to sleep for as long and as deeply as they did in former years. Experiments have shown that many people concerned about not having sufficient sleep and feeling lethargic, do in fact have adequate sleep and underestimate the amount of sleep they are having.

Environmental influences such as bright lights, loud noises, uncomfortable bedding and a too high or too low environmental temperature can also affect sleep.

Physical symptoms are another major cause of insomnia. Common examples are leg cramps, increased passing of urine (particularly from an enlarged prostate gland in males, or from a urinary tract infection), indigestion pains and headaches.

Psychological factors may also cause insomnia, particularly depression which often causes so-called 'early morning awakening', that is, waking in the early hours of the morning and being unable to get back to sleep. Those with schizophrenia may also have difficulty sleeping.

Anxiety and tension most frequently cause difficulty in falling asleep. Stress or excitement tend to arouse the reticular activating system, making the initiation of sleep difficult. Those who do stimulating mental work during the day frequently have trouble 'turning off' at night. The anticipation of a pleasurable or threatening event the next day will sometimes keep a person awake.

Insomnia is also produced by over-use of alcohol, drugs or stimulants such as tea and coffee.

Treatment Despite a feeling of tiredness the next day, insomnia is not dangerous to physical health. It is a symptom rather than a cause.

Environmental influences can usually be remedied. The bed should be comfortable, the amount of bedclothes and room temperature appropriate to the weather and ventilation adequate. Making a quiet back room the bedroom or using ear plugs may minimize traffic noise, and curtains or blinds may control the amount of light.

If insomnia is caused by stress or excitement, it is important to relax physically and mentally as much as possible before going to bed. Some of the successful techniques for relaxing include soaking in a hot bath, reading, drinking a cup of hot milk or camomile tea, or exercising. Relaxation therapy may help. The procedure is to relax by first tensing and then relaxing different groups of muscles in a particular sequence. With practice, it is possible to become calm and to lower the tone of the muscles quite rapidly.

Paradoxically, tablets which are initially prescribed for insomnia (hypnotics) may actually cause difficulty in sleeping. A physician may prescribe sleeping tablets when there is unbearable stress, tension or grief, but it is unwise to take them for lengthy periods. At best they are a synthetic 'crutch' and at worst they may produce psychological dependence. Most hypnotics reduce the amount of REM sleep, and thus disturb the normal sleep pattern. They also often lose their effectiveness after two or three weeks. Slow withdrawal, with appropriate counseling, support and explanation is important. Several weeks may be needed before a normal and satisfying sleep routine is re-established.

A person with chronic insomnia should consult a physician. Explanation as to the changes in sleep patterns and reassurance that the body almost always regulates its sleep patterns may be all that is needed. The physician may examine present lifestyle and health and, if ill health is a cause, provide appropriate treatment.

The human body has a far greater reserve than is generally recognized — eventually and inevitably it will put itself to sleep when it is sufficiently tired.

Irritable bowel syndrome

A disorder of intestinal function, the irritable bowel syndrome is also called spastic colitis, mucous colitis or irritable colon. It takes the form either of a disorder of movement of the bowel resulting in painful spasm or diarrhea or, less frequently, a secretory dysfunction of the colon with the passage of large amounts of mucus or slime in the stools. As there is no inflammation of the colon, the term colitis is not really correct. The exact cause of the condition is not known. Some studies have shown excessively high air pressures within the large bowel during an attack and it is presumed that this results from the muscle in the bowel wall contracting irregularly, causing pain or diarrhea.

The cause may be mental or physical fatigue, allergy or some other stress.

Irritable bowel syndrome affects both sexes, mainly in the 25 to 45 age group, and is more common in females.

Symptoms Recurrent attacks of moderate to dull lower abdominal pain occur for several hours. The pain is accompanied by a change in bowel habit, which may be in the form of diarrhea caused by taking purgatives, or as hard constipated stools covered with mucus. Large quantities of mucus may be passed in the stools. Between these attacks the bowel habit and stools are normal.

Diagnosis must first exclude the presence of other conditions. A general physical examination, microscopic examination of the feces, sigmoidoscopy (looking at the lower bowel through a tube) and barium enema are needed to exclude the possibility of disease such as infection or malignancy. Recurrent episodes connected with stress, but in the absence of any overall deterioration, are likely indications that irritable bowel syndrome rather than any other condition is present.

Treatment involves reassuring the patient that the problem is not malignant nor caused by some other disease. Stress should be minimized where possible, skill in coping should be improved and support may be needed. In some cases antispasmodic drugs and sedatives may be of benefit. The long-term use of antidiarrheal or laxative drugs should be avoided as they often cause irritation of the bowel. Changes in dietary habits are usually not successful, although increasing the fiber content may be of benefit in some cases.

Jaundice

Also known as *icterus*, jaundice is characterized by a yellow discoloration of the skin, the whites of the eyes (sclera) and other tissues as a result of excessive levels of bilirubin in the blood and tissue fluids.

Other causes of skin yellowing such as excessive levels of carotene in the blood are distinguishable from jaundice because the sclera are generally unaffected.

Red blood cells (erythrocytes) have a life span of about 120 days. Old and damaged erythrocytes are broken down by the reticulo-endothelial system, particularly in the liver, spleen and bone marrow. Bilirubin is formed from the breakdown of the hemoglobin from the destroyed erythrocytes, and is released into the circulating blood. As the blood passes through the liver, liver cells remove the bilirubin, conjugate it (add to it a salt so that it becomes water soluble and able to be excreted), and release it in the bile. The bile duct takes this fluid via the gall bladder to the small intestine, where it assists in the absorption of fats and is then excreted in the feces.

Bilirubin gives the bile its characteristic yellow-green hue, and after being converted to *stercobilinogen* and *stercobilin* by bacteria in the small bowel, gives the feces their brown color.

The normal blood level of bilirubin is 5 to 17 mmol per liter. Jaundice is usually not apparent until the level has reached 35 mmol per liter.

There are three major causes of jaundice: excessive breakdown of red blood cells (hemolytic jaundice), damage to the cells in the liver (hepatocellular jaundice), and obstruction of the bile ducts (obstructive jaundice).

Hemolytic jaundice In this form, overproduction of bilirubin results from excessive breakdown of red blood cells (hemolysis). For this process to cause jaundice, the degree of hemolysis usually has to be severe enough to produce a degree of anemia as well.

Causes are many and include defects in the structure of the hemoglobin (thalassemia), faulty red blood cell membranes (spherocytosis) and infection in the blood cells (malaria). Each of these make the red blood cells more fragile and susceptible to hemolysis. Normal red cells may also occasionally be 'attacked' by abnormal antibodies; this may be triggered by drugs, by incompatible blood transfusions, or be part of Rhesus disease of the newborn.

Hepatocellular jaundice Damaged liver cells cannot remove and conjugate the normal quantity of bilirubin circulating in the blood, thus causing the level of bilirubin in the blood to rise. Viral hepatitis is the most common liver disease that causes jaundice. Liver inflammation caused by certain toxic chemicals, alcohol (alcoholic hepatitis), and mononucleosis may also be associated with jaundice.

Obstructive jaundice When the bile duct is blocked, bilirubin builds up in the liver. As it is no longer being excreted from the body the level in the bloodstream then rises and produces jaundice. The most common cause of obstructive jaundice is a gallstone leaving the gall bladder and becoming lodged in the bile duct. In older people, cancers of the gall bladder and pancreas may also obstruct the duct. Occasionally, hydatid cysts and liver tumors may become large enough to block off bile excretion before it leaves the liver.

Some drugs, particularly the phenothiazines and the sex hormones may occasionally produce obstruction by causing a 'stasis' of bile within the liver itself.

Diagnosis The history, clinical findings and special blood tests usually enable the mechanism and specific cause of the jaundice to be identified. Hemolytic jaundice is associated with dark feces, anemia, a normal liver and abnormal blood films which show the increased destruction and turnover of red blood cells.

Diseases of the liver usually result in that organ becoming enlarged and tender to touch. Special liver function tests become abnormal and show elevated levels of certain enzymes in the presence of specific liver diseases.

Obstructive jaundice is associated with light colored feces and dark urine, as some bilirubin is excreted through the kidneys. The blood level of an enzyme, serum alkaline phosphatase, becomes elevated and the bilirubin level tends to be higher than in other forms of jaundice.

Treatment of jaundice depends on the cause. Surgical relief of bile duct obstruction may be required.

Where the jaundice is the result of hepatic disease, the diet is important. Patients are generally prescribed a high protein, high carbohydrate, low fat, high energy diet, except where there is liver failure, when protein intake may have to be restricted. Drugs which are known to be inactivated by the liver (such as oral contra-

ceptives) are best avoided as are potential hepatotoxic agents such as alcohol. Supplemental vitamins may be required.

Legionnaire's disease

A recently recognized respiratory illness caused by the bacterium *Legionella pneumophila*, Legionnaire's disease was discovered in 1977 following a lung infection epidemic among American war veterans who had attended a Philadelphia Legion convention in July 1976. Ten per cent of those affected became ill, setting off intensive investigations into the cause of the disease. In 1978 the first case was detected in Australia and over 1000 others have been diagnosed throughout the world.

Retrospective evidence indicates that the condition, usually with mild symptoms, has been reasonably common for many years, primarily appearing as an atypical pneumonia (a pneumonia with general symptoms and a prolonged recovery, and caused by an unknown agent).

Symptoms A flu-like illness with fever, malaise, and generalized aches and pains are the first symptoms, appearing about a week after the infection has been contracted. They usually disappear without specific treatment but the illness can worsen, causing mental confusion and disorientation followed by a persistent cough, with progressive difficulty in breathing as pneumonia (inflammation of lung tissue) develops. Kidney failure, bleeding disorders and liver changes can occur.

Droplets of sputum and lung secretions, infected by the *Legionella pneumophila* bacteria, most probably spread the disease, and it is thought that air conditioning may be a means of spreading the disease during epidemics. Research continues into how human beings become infected, though it is thought that the bacteria may be spread from the soil or from animals.

Diagnosis The easiest method of diagnosis is that which involves taking two samples of serum about two weeks apart. In these with the disease there will be a significant increase in the level of antibody against *Legionella pneumophila*. The bacterium can be detected only through a microscope.

Treatment In mild cases, only the symptoms need to be treated. In severe cases, hospital treatment is necessary. This involves administering high doses of the antibiotic erythromycin, respiratory assistance if required, and close monitoring of fluid and electrolyte (salt) levels.

Ménière's disease

Named after the French physician Prosper Ménière (1799–1862), Ménière's disease is a condition affecting the labyrinth, the part of the inner ear that controls the sense of balance. The labyrinth consists of three semi-circular canals each one lying in a different plane. Each canal is filled with clear fluid, or endolymph, and lined with sensitive cells that readily detect any changes in fluid movement which results from a change in posture.

In Ménière's disease, the volume and pressure of fluid within these canals increases periodically. Most often the condition first develops between the ages of 40 and 60. The precise cause and mechanism are not known, although they are probably related to a reduction in the rate of reabsorption of endolymph fluid, which is normally produced and resorbed at a constant rate. At first only one ear is affected but about one out of five people will subsequently develop the same problem in the other side.

Symptoms Bouts of vertigo, nausea and vomiting are the main initial features, sometimes preceded by a period of malaise and a 'fullness' in the ear. Vertigo is a form of dizziness in which the surroundings seem to be revolving, often violently, around the affected person, resulting in loss of balance and a very unsteady gait. Tinnitus, a persistent, high-pitched ringing or hissing in the ear, and deafness to external sounds may be absent in early attacks but become prominent later.

The frequency of attacks is variable, and sometimes months pass between bouts. In most cases the deafness increases, becoming apparent between attacks. Total perceptive (nerve) deafness is the final outcome: this is accompanied by cessation of other symptoms. The increased pressure in the canals is thought to damage progressively the cells in the middle ear that convert incoming sound waves into electrical impulses.

Diagnosis and treatment Diagnosis is usually based on the history of the patient's illness, and can be confirmed by tests, including a hearing test. During an acute attack, bed rest is usually required to maintain a head position that minimizes the vertigo. Drugs such as antihistamine medications or chlorpromazine may control the vertigo. Injections or suppositories may also be needed to prevent vomiting.

Between the bouts of vertigo, a low fluid and a low salt diet may reduce fluid production within the labyrinth. Drugs to facilitate fluid absorption may also be used. The dilation of small blood vessels by drugs such as nicotinic acid, cyclandelate and betahistine, increases the blood supply to the labyrinth, and may cause an increase in fluid resorption. Results, however, are variable.

In severe and persisting cases, the vestibular nerve may be divided surgically, eliminating the vertigo but maintaining hearing. However this is a major operation, and does not eliminate the tinnitus. Ultrasonic irradiation may be used to destroy vestibular function but some hearing loss results in about one-third of patients.

A surgical technique has been developed to reduce the pressure of endolymph fluid by shunting excess fluid through a plastic tube into the subarachnoid space (which contains cerebrospinal fluid).

Nasal disorders

The most common disorders associated with the nose are blocking, bleeding, discharging, and conditions caused by injury.

Blockage The nose may be blocked by a foreign body (particularly some small object pushed up by a child), by the septum being pushed to one side (deviated) in an accident, by a boggy lining with a polyp in the cavity, or by a swollen lining. Foreign bodies and polyps should be surgically removed, sometimes septums should be straightened, and a swollen lining should be reduced to normal size with the proper drugs or nasal sprays. Tumors of the nose may block the nose, sometimes only on one side, and should be removed.

Catarrh A stuffy nose, or nasal catarrh, describes a blocked, running or irritated nose. Sneezing, eye irritation or headache may be associated with the condition. It is very common and recurrent in adults and children.

The main causes are a local blockage of the nasal airway, or a swollen membrane lining the nose, narrowing the air passages.

Local blocking may be caused by a foreign body, a deviated nasal septum, a collection of pus in the nose, a polyp in the lining of the nose, or a growth. If the

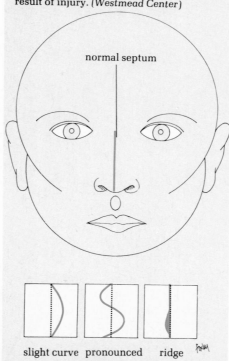

The septum, a ridge of cartilage which divides the nostrils, may be broken or become deviated as a result of injury. *(Westmead Center)*

normal septum

slight curve   pronounced curve   ridge

The nasal passages, which usually become blocked during a cold, may be cleared by inhalation of steam.

nose is blocked, whatever the cause, an ear, nose and throat surgeon should remove the blockage. Before doing so, it is important that some simple investigations be done so that the exact problem can be discovered. These include radiographs of the sinuses and a culture of any discharge from the nose.

The lining of the nose may be swollen and red as a result of excess alcohol, tobacco or chemicals in the air or at work. The lining may be a violet color in response to allergies to pollens, grasses or some other substance, or a blue-gray if the allergy has been present for a long time.

Treatment is to avoid the chemicals, alcohol and tobacco and to have specific treatment for the allergy.

Injury In a nose injury the nasal bone may be broken. The septum, which is made of cartilage and divides the nostrils, may be pushed to one side blocking the nose. Profuse bleeding may occur. The fracture must be reduced and the nose straightened. If the septum is deviated it can be straightened in a simple procedure later by an ear, nose and throat specialist or a plastic surgeon.

Nasal discharge may be watery, or greenish or blood stained. It may occur from only one nostril or from both. The most common cause is acute viral infection of the lining of the nose (rhinitis). In acute rhinitis the discharge is at first watery and later may become green. Other common causes are chronic rhinitis, a nasal allergy or a reaction of the lining of the nose to nasal sprays, tobacco or alcohol. Blood-stained nasal discharges occur in severe acute infections and from tumors of the nose.

Nose bleeds are often caused by injury but they frequently occur spontaneously and suddenly. The bleeding occurs after a rupture of a small blood vessel in the lining of the nose usually at the front of the septum.

Nose bleeds may be associated with diseases of the blood, with defects in clotting (hemophilia), defects in blood cells (leukemia), or defects in blood platelets (purpura). High blood pressure is a common cause of dramatic nose bleeds. If there is acute or chronic inflammation of the lining of the nose, as in sinusitis, hay fever, glandular fever, measles, chicken pox, syphilis or tuberculosis, the nose may bleed spontaneously.

Treatment of a nosebleed While sitting upright (do not lie down or tilt the head back), pinch the nostrils with the thumb and index finger for 5 minutes by the clock. Do not blow the nose afterwards. No ice is required over the bridge of the nose but a cold cloth (such as a handkerchief) might help to reduce blood flow. If this fails to stop bleeding, repeat the treatment. Should a second repeat be unsuccessful, call a doctor.

Rhinitis Inflammation of the mucosal lining of the nasal cavity is described as rhinitis. Because this lining is continuous with that of the sinuses that drain into the nose, a degree of *sinusitis* is often present as well.

There are a number of specific causes of rhinitis, but they can be classified into two main groups. In the first group, rhinitis occurs when a normal mucosa reacts to an infection or to some other irritation. In the second group, an over-reactive or abnormal mucosa causes the inflammation.

Infective rhinitis. The common cold, or *coryza*, is perhaps the most frequent cause of rhinitis. Viral infection results in swelling and inflammation of the mucosa followed by a profuse watery discharge. Bacteria normally present in the nose rapidly multiply to produce a thick, mucopurulent secretion and nasal blockage; the patient often compensates by mouth breathing. A wide variety of viruses and bacteria has been implicated in such situations. A fever is a common feature of infective rhinitis.

Other infections that may be associated with rhinitis include influenza, measles, congenital syphilis and diphtheria. Other features of these disorders are usually present as well.

Persistent, or *chronic infective rhinitis*, may be associated with anosmia (loss of smell), a post-nasal drip, where a thickened secretion trickles down the back of the throat, a thickened or heavy feeling within the nose and sometimes a reduction in the ability to concentrate.

1 A warm drink can do much to alleviate the effects of a cold.

2 The rhinovirus of the common cold. *(Science Photo Library)*

3 The coronavirus of the common cold. *(Science Photo Library)*

1

2
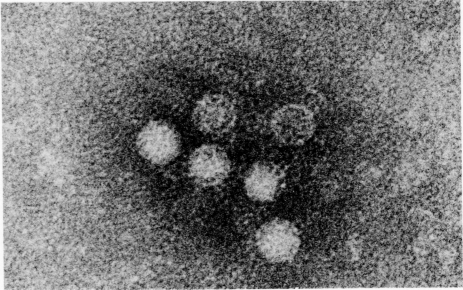

3
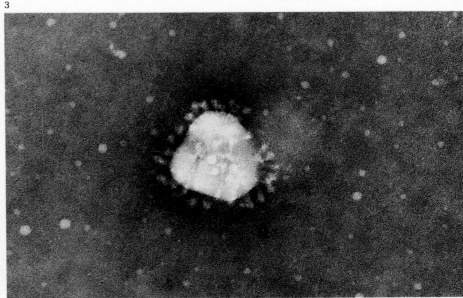

Allergens such as pollens or grass may cause rhinitis.

The common cold with its associated inflammation of the mucosa is one cause of rhinitis.

Other causes of chronic, infective rhinitis may be longstanding infections in the sinuses or adenoids; nasal obstruction due to a foreign body (particularly in children), a nasal polyp or a deviated septum; chronic irritation from cigarette smoke, fumes or industrial dust; reduced resistance due to dietary, immunological or hormonal abnormalities; and excessive use of locally-applied decongestant drugs. Chemical, or irritant rhinitis also may result from various fumes and from decongestant abuse.

Allergic rhinitis results from susceptible individuals reacting to allergens, such as pollens and grass, to which they have become sensitised. This term is preferred to 'hay fever', as hay is seldom involved and fever is not a feature. Other allergic conditions are often associated with allergic rhinitis, possibly affecting other members of the family as well as the patient.

Nasal obstruction and a watery discharge occur, as with infective rhinitis, although sneezing, and involvement of the eyes with itching and watering, are more prominent features. The symptoms may be seasonal or perennial and tend to alter in severity from day to day, and sometimes hour to hour.

Inhalation of dusts or pollens, ingestion of certain foodstuffs, fumes, drugs such as aspirin, and infections may sometimes precipitate attacks. Psychological stress, altered atmospheric humidity and exhaustion are among many situations in which people are more susceptible to the action of the precipitating allergens.

Vasomotor rhinitis is a term that describes an over-reactive mucosa. This responds to certain stimuli, such as dust, to produce symptoms similar to allergic rhinitis. Special tests however, indicate that there is no allergic basis to the reaction.

Treatment of rhinitis depends on the cause. Factors predisposing to infection need correction, and associated conditions such as sinusitis need to be treated specifically. Infective rhinitis usually settles over a few days, although local nasal douches and decongestants are often helpful if secretions are thick and are blocking the nostrils.

Allergic and vasomotor rhinitis may be prevented by avoiding precipitating factors where possible. Medications such as antihistamines, steroids and sodium cromoglycate may be prescribed and desensitization programs may be beneficial in some cases of allergy. Antibiotics are used if there is evidence of bacterial infection.

Peptic ulcer

An ulcer is a cavity which occurs as the result of the gradual erosion of a surface or lining. An ulcer similar to an ulcer in the skin can occur in the lining of the acid-secreting areas of the gastrointestinal tract (mainly the stomach and first part of the duodenum), and is called a peptic ulcer. Here the wall of the stomach or duodenum is eroded by the stomach's own digestive juices.

The way an ulcer forms is not well understood, but the main factors include the erosive power of the acid and pepsin in the stomach secretions (gastric juice) and the lack of resistance of the lining of

Pain from a duodenal ulcer usually occurs between meals. (Zefa)

the stomach and duodenum to this erosion. Many people who are subject to duodenal ulcers secrete more gastric acid than normal, but those with a stomach ulcer produce no more than normal quantities of acid, and often a good deal less than normal, so that decreased tissue resistance seems to be more important than the amount of acid and pepsin secretion.

One in every five men and one in every ten women develop a peptic ulcer at some time in their lives. Duodenal ulcers are two or three times as common as gastric (or stomach) ulcers and peptic ulcers are commoner in people with blood group O. It has not been proved that stress is important in causing ulcers, but tobacco smoking is harmful.

An ulcer may be acute or chronic.

Acute ulcers tend to be multiple, and chronic ulcers usually occur singly in well-defined sites, for example on or near the lesser curve of the stomach or near the pylorus. In the duodenum they usually occur in the first part on the anterior or posterior walls.

Duodenal ulcer The most common symptom of the presence of an ulcer is pain which may be felt high in the center of the abdomen or on the upper right side. The pain may be gnawing, or steady and burning and may awaken the sufferer very early in the morning.

Pain frequently occurs between meals and is relieved with food or medication. In many cases the patient tends to overeat and increase in weight is common.

There may be periods of painful symptoms and at times the patient has remissions and remains symptom free. Often there is no pain unless complications occur. The ulcers may only be discovered in later years when a duodenal scar is found in the course of other investigations.

Other gastrointestinal symptoms such as heartburn or regurgitation of acid fluid into the mouth may also be present.

Tests which can be performed to confirm the presence of a duodenal ulcer include the use of the gastroscope, an instrument with special lenses, which is passed down the food pipe (the esophagus) into the stomach and the duodenum, making it possible for the operator to see directly if an ulcer is present.

The causes of peptic ulcer seem to be varied but it is known that particular foods and also alcohol will worsen the symptoms. (Zefa)

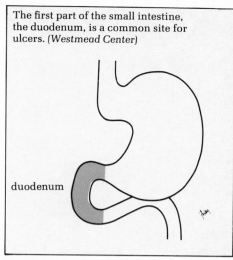

The first part of the small intestine, the duodenum, is a common site for ulcers. (Westmead Center)

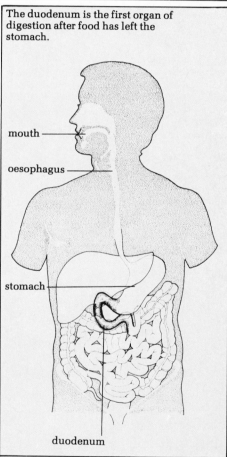

The duodenum is the first organ of digestion after food has left the stomach.

mouth

oesophagus

stomach

duodenum

Another test involves the ingestion of a barium meal followed by x-rays. The barium will then appear in outline in the organs in which it is present.

Earlier medical treatment involved complete bed rest and special diets. Nowadays major advances in the treatment of peptic ulcers have been made with modern drugs. Medication is usually given for a number of weeks, with follow-up tests to ensure that the condition is healing.

Only a minority of cases require surgical treatment. Usually these are instances involving complications such as heavy bleeding (hemorrhage), penetration of other organs, perforation and obstruction of the outlet of the stomach. Surgery may involve removal of part of the stomach or severing of the nerves which stimulate the production of acid.

It is important that a person with an ulcer, or past history of one, maintains a sensible lifestyle and avoids the use of drugs such as tobacco and alcohol which are known to aggravate the condition.

Stomach ulcer A stomach or gastric ulcer may produce a gnawing, burning or aching in the centre of the upper abdomen which occurs an hour after meals, and is relieved by food, antacids or vomiting. Nausea, vomiting, weight loss, poor appetite, constipation and fatigue are common. The symptoms tend to remit and then recur.

When a stomach ulcer is suspected a barium meal x-ray is given. Before the x-ray is taken, the person drinks a solution of barium salts which are opaque to x-rays. The barium fills the stomach and outlines its walls and usually shows up the ulcer. If necessary, the stomach may be further examined through a gastroscope.

The *gastroscope* is a slender, flexible tube of optic fibers which the patient swallows. When the end reaches the stomach it illuminates the stomach so that by looking through the gastroscope the doctor is able to see the walls of the

A stomach ulcer may cause a gnawing, burning or aching pain in the center of the abdomen an hour after meals.

stomach. If he finds an abnormality, he is able to nip a piece off for examination under the microscope. Gastroscopy allows the doctor to see the nature, size and location of the ulcer. Gastroscopic examinations can be repeated to observe the healing of the ulcer.

Stomach ulcers may produce complications such as bleeding, perforation, narrowing of the outlet of the stomach, and perhaps malignant degeneration. If the ulcer erodes a blood vessel in the stomach wall, uncontrollable bleeding may occur. The patient vomits blood (hematemesis) and passes altered blood in the feces (melena). This necessitates immediate blood transfusion and an urgent operation in which the bleeding vessel is stitched together.

When an ulcer erodes right through the stomach wall (perforation), the stomach contents and secretions escape into the abdominal cavity and cause intense abdominal pain, rigidity and shock. An emergency operation is performed to sew up the perforated ulcer.

An ulcer occurring near the outlet of the stomach (the pylorus) can cause scarring and narrowing of the outlet, and obstruction to the passage of food. This usually necessitates some form of drainage operation, for example joining a loop of jejunum (small bowel) to a hole in the stomach so that the stomach contents pass directly into the jejunum, by-passing the duodenum. A vagotomy, which is the cutting of the branches of the vagus nerve which supply the stomach, also may be required. Stimulation of the vagus nerve increases the secretion of acid and pepsin. Therefore, cutting the vagus nerve greatly reduces acid and pepsin production, promoting the healing of the ulcer and preventing recurrence.

The possibility of cancerous change occurring in a stomach ulcer is still disputed. Certainly some stomach cancers appear as ulcers, but whether they are the result of a malignant change in a peptic ulcer or arise as a separate condition has not been determined. When the cancer has not spread beyond the stomach, the malignant ulcer is usually treated by the complete surgical removal of the stomach (total gastrectomy).

Bed rest and the cessation of smoking have both been proved to accelerate the healing of gastric ulcers (but not duodenal ulcers). Sedation and ulcer diets do not appear to help ulcers heal, although small frequent meals and the avoidance of fried foods may ease the symptoms. Milk and antacids quickly relieve the discomfort and pain for reasons which are unclear. The traditional anticholinergic drugs which reduce acid secretion are often prescribed, but their value is also unproven. However, the new histamine H_2 receptor antagonist cimetidine does promote the healing of stomach ulcers while it is being

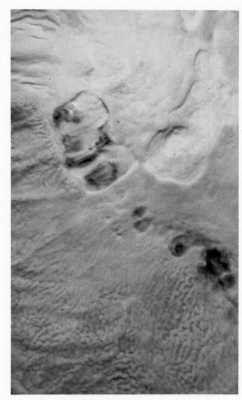

The lining of the stomach may be viewed through an instrument known as a gastroscope to reveal the presence of conditions such as this gastric ulcer. *(Salmer)*

taken, but the ulcer and symptoms may reappear when treatment ceases.

Drugs which strengthen the resistance of the lining of the stomach also promote the healing of a stomach ulcer. Such drugs are licorice derivatives such as carbenoxolone, and colloidal bismuth salts. At present cimetidine appears to be the most popular medical treatment for stomach ulcer.

The medical treatment of stomach ulcer often provides only temporary relief. Therefore, when a person is disabled by the symptoms of recurrent stomach ulcers which medical treatment fails to control, surgical treatment may be justified. Certainly the occurrence of life-threatening complications, such as bleeding, perforation and stenosis, justify surgical treatment to remove the ulcer and prevent further ulceration.

The commonest surgical approach is the removal of the affected portion of the stomach (partial gastrectomy) and the rejoining of the remainder of the stomach to the duodenum. As most of the acid-secreting cells occur in the lower third of the stomach, its removal greatly reduces the acid-secreting capacity of the stomach. Often a vagotomy is performed simultaneously in which the vagus nerve which stimulates gastric secretion is cut to ensure a further large reduction in acid secretion. Sometimes a vagotomy alone is effective.

Occasionally surgical treatment produces long-term complications including nausea, fullness, regurgitation and faintness after meals (dumping syndrome) and diarrhea. Chronic nutritional disturbances may result in weight loss, iron deficiency, anemia, vitamin B_{12} deficiency, pernicious anemia and premature ageing of bones (osteoporosis).

Pharyngitis

The passageway which conveys air from the nose to the larynx, the pharynx is commonly known as the throat, although in fact it forms only part of it.

Continuous with the food pipe or esophagus, measuring from 5–5½ inches (12.5–14 cm) in length and wider above than below, the pharynx is composed of fibromuscular tissue lined with mucous membrane.

The pharyngeal cavity or opening is divided into the upper or nasal area, which contains the adenoids, and the lower or oral and laryngeal areas. The tonsils are located in the oral pharynx.

The movements of the pharynx include closing to separate the nasal and oral areas; closing, in a different way, to separate the mouth from the pharynx; and swallowing.

Inflammation of the pharynx is described as pharyngitis.
Causes include viral infections, bacterial infections and an allergic reaction. Pharyngitis also may appear as one of the symptoms of other diseases such as glandular fever.
Symptoms are a sore throat and pain on swallowing. The degree of inconvenience and discomfort varies with the person.
Treatment Medications are available to eradicate bacterial infections and to help combat allergies. However, there is no definitive treatment for most cases, which are caused by viruses. The most that can be done is to alleviate the symptoms of pain and discomfort with appropriate lozenges and sprays. Gargling and simple analgesics (that is, pain killers) may help make the patient more comfortable.

Sometimes it is difficult to distinguish between infections caused by viruses and those caused by bacteria. Throat swabs help identify the cause which may be significant in determining the treatment needed to restore a patient's health.

Pleurisy

Inflammation of the pleura is known as pleurisy or pleuritis.
The pleura The serous membrane which covers the lungs is the visceral pleura and that lining the chest wall is the parietal pleura. Separating these two layers is a thin film of fluid, enabling them to glide smoothly over each other as the lungs expand during inspiration.
Causes of pleurisy Various viral infections are the most frequent cause,

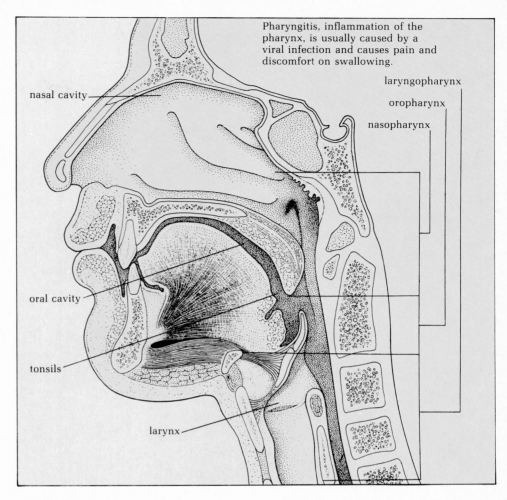

Pharyngitis, inflammation of the pharynx, is usually caused by a viral infection and causes pain and discomfort on swallowing.

laryngopharynx
oropharynx
nasopharynx
nasal cavity
oral cavity
tonsils
larynx

although bacterial bronchitis or pneumonia may extend to involve the pleura. Tuberculosis, lung cancer and pulmonary embolus are also occasionally associated with pleurisy.

Dry pleurisy The most prominent symptom is a sharp, stabbing or knife-like pain, brought on by a deep breath, coughing or sneezing. Such actions cause movement of the inflamed membranes across each other. Exudate and fibrinous deposits cause a stickiness of the membranes. In this condition, known as dry pleurisy, a harsh sounding rubbing is often readily audible through a stethoscope when the patient breathes in, being loudest over the site of the pain. Other symptoms depend on the primary condition but fever, malaise and a dry cough are common.
Adhesive pleurisy The pain of pleurisy often disappears within a week, although the condition may fail to heal and progress to adhesive pleurisy, where the pleural layers become joined by fibrous bands. This is more likely if bacterial invasion leads to pus formation between the membranes.
Wet pleurisy In response to the irritation, the inflamed pleural surfaces may exude much fluid, leading to a *hydrothorax* or wet pleurisy. Because the inflamed surfaces are now separated by fluid the pain

settles, although increasing difficulty with breathing follows.
Treatment of pleurisy is directed mainly at the primary cause, but antibiotics, cough suppressants and analgesics to relieve pain are often used. If fluid accumulation is causing difficulties in breathing, it is removed by a needle inserted in the chest wall between the ribs, and examined under the microscope. Surgical removal of extremely thickened pleura is occasionally needed if, after long and severe pleurisy, the membranes are restricting lung movements.

After disappearance of the symptoms, a chest x-ray may be needed to establish that underlying conditions such as tuberculosis or cancer are not present. If the symptoms are severe or do not resolve, an x-ray is usually taken earlier.

Pneumonia

An inflammation in the lung is described as pneumonia. There are many different causes of this condition and also a number of ways of classifying the different types.

Generally, pneumonias can be divided into two broad groups. Specific pneumonias are caused by specific organisms, while aspiration pneumonias involve some circumstance which predisposes the sufferer to the invasion of the lung by less virulent organisms.

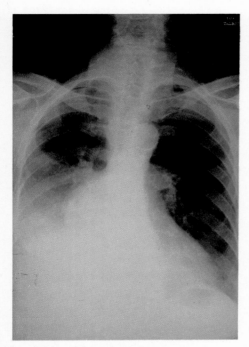

Pneumonia of the right lung shows
up as a white shadow on x-ray.
(John Watney Photo Library)

Specific pneumonias can be caused by a
very large variety of organisms. These
may be bacteria, viruses, fungi or other
agents. One of the most common of the
specific pneumonias is caused by an organism bearing the same name. This is the
pneumococcus bacterium, which causes
pneumococcal pneumonia.

Aspiration pneumonias The infection in
aspiration pneumonia may reach the
lungs in various ways. Pus may be inhaled
from the sinuses or perhaps during a
throat operation. Vomit may be inhaled,
for example in cases of intoxication, and
this too can be responsible for setting up
an infection. The aspiration pneumonias
can be divided into four major groups:

Acute lobular pneumonia is often preceded by bronchial infection, and occurs
most often in children or the elderly. In
children, it is often a complication of
measles or whooping cough, while in
adults it can occur after conditions such
as acute bronchitis or influenza. It commonly occurs in those with chronic bronchitis and emphysema.

Benign aspiration pneumonia occurs most
often as a result of the inhalation of infected material during an upper respiratory tract infection. The organisms that
cause the condition are not very virulent.

Hypostatic pneumonia A common cause
of death, this is a particular form of aspiration pneumonia which tends to occur in
the elderly or debilitated. Because such
people are weak and are unable to move
much, they have difficulty in coughing up
the secretions produced by the lung. Thus,
infection may occur. The condition is best
avoided by careful attention to preventive
measures.

Post-operative pneumonia is not a true
pneumonia but a pulmonary collapse due
to obstruction of a large bronchus by a secretion which causes infection. It is likely
to occur after an operation where the pain
experienced may make it difficult to
cough.

Pneumonia symptoms depend on the type
of pneumonia. There is often fever, cough,
sputum production and possibly pain. The
doctor will listen to and inspect the chest
and x-rays may be used to assist diagnosis.
A culture of the sputum will help to identify the organisms causing the pneumonia,
and this will aid the choice of correct
treatment.

Treatment will vary with the cause. In
bacterial pneumonia, antibiotics are the
mainstay of treatment. There are many
different types of antibiotics, each being
effective against a particular range of organisms. In addition, the patient should
rest, the fever should be reduced and the
pain relieved. Sometimes special exercises and physical therapy may be
required to help the patient cough up the
secretions. Drugs can also help in this respect. X-rays at repeated intervals will
help determine the response to treatment.

With modern treatment, the prognosis
for recovery from pneumonia is very good
in the majority of cases.

Polyp

A small, smooth growth from a mucous
membrane, to which it is attached by a
stalk, is known as a polyp. Polyps occur in
the nose, nasal sinuses, ear, bladder and
bowel, and in the womb.

Polyps of the nose and nasal sinuses are a
result of congestion of the mucous membrane caused by an allergy or infection
and are not regarded as true tumors.
Symptoms are produced by the blocking
effect.

A polyp may arise in a chronically infected middle ear and grow through a hole
in the drum, filling the external canal of
the ear. The infection must be treated and
the polyp removed with a snare.

Polyposis of the colon, showing the
multiple polyps which have
developed in the mucous lining of
the large intestine. *(Zefa)*

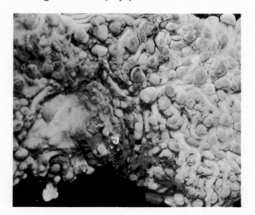

Polyps of the large intestine and bladder
are true tumors and cause bleeding (the
blood appearing in the feces or urine).
The polyps can be observed when the
bowel is viewed through a sigmoidoscope
or the bladder through a cystoscope.

A rectal polyp, more common in children than in adults, is a round tumor the
size of a raspberry, which may protrude
through the anus, bleed, and be mistaken
for a pile. It must be tied off at its stalk
and removed. Some polyps of the bowel
are prone to become malignant; they must
be removed, and subsequently the interior
of the bowel should be checked from time
to time, by sigmoidoscopy, to detect any
recurrence.

Polyps of the bladder are more common
in men than in women. A polyp at the
neck of the bladder may block the outflow
of urine. A bladder which has produced
polyps must be checked regularly for recurrence.

Polyps of the uterus A uterine polyp is
more likely to form at the neck of the
womb than in the body of the uterus.
These cervical polyps are associated with
chronic infection. They bleed readily and
rarely become malignant. Surgical removal is the simple treatment.

Other types of polyps of the womb are
a *placental polyp*, a rare growth from a
fragment of retained after-birth, and a
fibroid polyp, a benign growth.

Polyposis of the colon is a rare, hereditary
disease. A profusion of polyps appears in
childhood or early adult life. There may
be pain, diarrhea and bleeding, resulting
in anemia. The disease is pre-cancerous
and treatment involves removing the
affected segment, sometimes the entire
colon. Other members of the patient's
family must be checked immediately so
that those affected may receive early treatment.

Psoriasis

A common skin disorder affecting 1 or 2
per cent of the population, psoriasis, derived from *psora*, itch, is a lifelong condition usually beginning before the age of
25 and characterized by remissions and
exacerbations. Children are especially
susceptible to psoriasis which is often
triggered by infections like a cold or sore
throat.

Cause Its exact cause is unknown
although an hereditary pattern exists and
about a third of the sufferers have a close
relative with psoriasis. Cold weather,
psychological stress, hormone changes,
infections and drug reactions have all
been implicated as causes.

Symptoms The distribution and severity
of psoriasis vary greatly and excessive
multiplication of skin cells in the affected
areas occurs. Affected skin displays
sharply defined borders, pink to red
colors and silvery scales, formed when
increased cell numbers in the deeper skin
layers create a thickened outer layer that

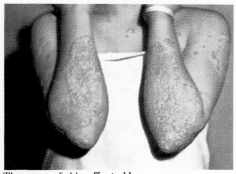

The areas of skin affected by psoriasis often have sharply-defined borders, contributing to the description 'geographic psoriasis'. The outer surface of the elbow is a common site. (*Abbottempo*)

exhibits numerous dead cells or scales. The amount of scale often increases when the scalp becomes affected.

Several types of this condition exist. *Guttate psoriasis* is characterized by small tear-like patches of scale that develop over the trunk and limbs. It usually clears over several months, but may be followed by *conventional psoriasis*, characterized by larger scales, between .7–3 inches (2–8 cm) in diameter, which appear, often in a symmetrical pattern, on the outer surfaces of the elbows and knees and on the scalp.

Flexural psoriasis occurs in skin folds, particularly in the groin, armpits and under pendulous breasts, whereas *pustular psoriasis*, characterized by small pus-filled lumps (pustules), occurs primarily on the palms of the hands or the soles of the feet.

Nail changes, characterized by an increased growth rate, thickening and the development of ridges and pitting affect some 20 per cent of psoriasis sufferers. Usually the distal joints of the fingers are involved, possibly causing joint deformities with these nail changes, which may also be associated with arthritis.

Normally symptoms are minor and are often ignored, although changes may be severe, as in joint deformities, in pustular psoriasis if the condition complicates, or if the skin of the entire body is involved.

Treatment Although no cure is available much can be done to control the lesions. Excess scale can be soaked in warm water or, if particularly thick, coated with dithranol cream or paste, salicylic acid or sulphur preparations and removed with a soft brush.

Locally applied steroid creams, coal tar preparations, or exposure to sunshine or ray-lamps, which improve about 90 per cent of cases are used to settle inflammation. Severe cases are treated with the cytotoxic drug methotrexate, and high doses of corticosteroids taken orally. Both treatments are potentially hazardous. Careful explanation of the condition

to the sufferer and an optimistic outlook about treatment are necessary with this life-long condition.

Raynaud's disease

Named after the French physician Maurice Raynaud (1834–81), Raynaud's disease is characterized by Raynaud's syndrome.

Raynaud's syndrome In this condition there are repeated periods of *ischemia* or reduced blood supply (and hence oxygen) to the fingers and toes. Occasionally the ears and the nose may also become affected.

The fingers or other tissues involved become suddenly white, cold and numb, usually with a 'pins and needles' sensation as their arteries go into spasm. Bluish discoloration and pain follow as the tissues become congested and deprived of adequate oxygen. Within a few minutes there is a sudden increase in blood flow, and the fingers become red, flushed and warm, often with an associated throbbing ache. This phase generally settles within an hour. Ulceration of the skin and gangrene of the ends of the fingers and toes occurs in some instances when the vascular spasm is particularly severe.

There is a wide range of causes for the syndrome and the overall prognosis or outcome depends largely on the nature of the underlying condition. Previous exposure to cold, strong emotion, poisoning with lead or arsenic, collagen diseases such as *scleroderma* or *systemic lupus erythematosus*, ingestion of drugs like methysergide and ergotamine, long-term vibration injury such as from the repeated use of jackhammers, and some specific arterial diseases are among the many causes of Raynaud's syndrome.

Diagnosis When no specific cause for the intermittent arterial spasm can be found, the diagnosis of Raynaud's disease is made. It is uncertain whether the main problem is in the nerves supplying the vessels, an abnormality in the vessels themselves, or a circulating chemical in the bloodstream acting upon them.

Most frequently women are affected, with symptoms occurring in early adult life. The hands are more often involved than the feet, and the distribution of vessels affected is symmetrical. Ulceration of the skin seldom occurs.

Treatment Minimizing exposure to excessive cold, and the use of various drugs that dilate the blood vessels are helpful aspects of treatment. When conservative measures fail to control the disease satisfactorily, surgery may be undertaken. The procedure used is a sympathectomy, which involves the excision of sympathetic nerves which constrict small blood vessels when they are stimulated.

Renal colic

Also called ureteric colic, renal colic is a severe cramping pain caused by a kidney

stone passing into the ureter, the tube which carries urine from the kidney to the bladder. The stone causes irritation and inflammation in the ureter as well as obstruction to urine flow.

Symptoms The pain usually commences in the lower back overlying the kidney and moves down towards the groin. In males pain may also be felt in the testes or penis.

Other symptoms include sweating, a rapid pulse and tenderness, especially deep in the abdomen over the ureter. Attempts to pass urine are often painful and unproductive because of a spasm of the muscle in the wall of the ureter.

The pain is usually severe and constant, but with spasms of increased intensity. The affected person frequently rolls over or moves round in an attempt to ease the pain. Often the knees are drawn upwards to try to provide some relief. The urine may be blood-stained because of damage caused by the stone to the lining of the ureter.

Treatment Strong pain-killing drugs are needed to relieve the colic. With rest, pain relief and subsequent consumption of large volumes of fluid most of those affected will be able to pass the kidney stone out with the urine.

Intravenous pyelograms are x-rays which are not only used to check kidney function but also to follow the progress of the stone.

The urine should be strained so that any solid material passed can be analyzed and the underlying cause of the problem diagnosed and treated.

If a stone remains lodged in the ureter, surgical removal becomes necessary.

A kidney stone, calculus, may pass from the kidney into the ureter and then to the bladder, causing blockage and considerable pain. (*Westmead Center*)

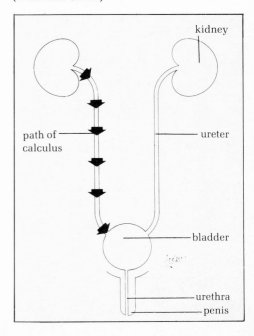

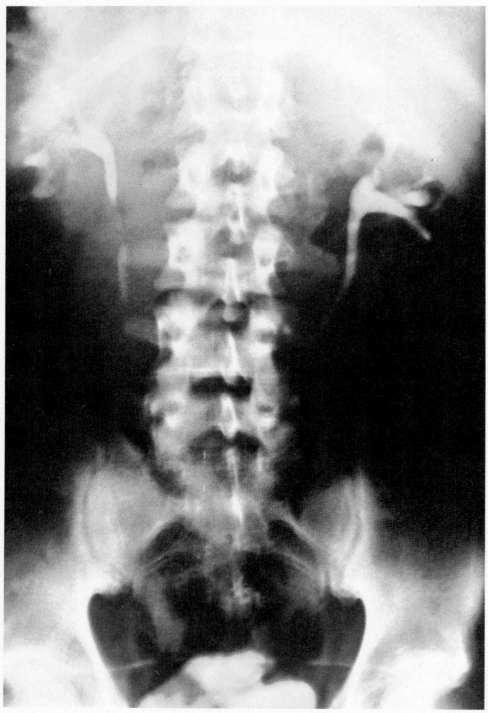

An intravenous pyelogram. (Abbottempo)

If treatment to improve kidney function is not successful or the kidney has been irreparably damaged, waste materials may be artificially filtered from the bloodstream (renal dialysis).

Rheumatoid arthritis

A chronic condition, rheumatoid arthritis primarily affects the small joints of the hands and feet. The exact cause of the inflammatory changes is unknown, although the immune system plays a part in their continuance. Several features are similar to other auto-immune and connective tissue diseases.

Females are affected about three times as frequently as males, and most symptoms begin in the 20 to 40 year age group. There is one variety of rheumatoid arthritis called Still's disease that is seen in children.

Symptoms Often there is a period of fatigue, anorexia (loss of appetite), joint stiffness and aches and pains in limbs which occurs several weeks before joint swelling appears. The distribution of small joints affected initially is symmetrical, although the course from then on becomes variable, and virtually any joint of the body may become involved. Some sufferers have very mild symptoms whereas a small group undergo rapid deterioration, often resulting in marked limitation of mobility and function. In most, however, a prolonged course with some degree of progression ensues.

The membrane lining the joint, called the synovium, thickens and the joints become tender and swollen. Inflammatory tissue called the *pannus*, formed as a result of expansion of the synovium, causes erosion of the cartilage within the joint and at times parts of the underlying bone. The outer joint capsule, ligaments and muscles may also become involved. This results in joint deformities, limitation of movements and loss of function. During the 'flare-ups' of activity that are typical of this disease, the duration of joint stiffness that is present upon awakening often

The effects of rheumatoid arthritis. (Abbottempo)

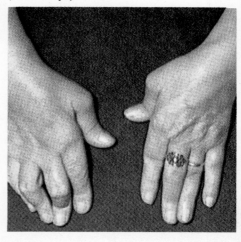

Smaller stones may be removed with a special instrument that is passed through the urethra and bladder into the ureter, larger stones generally require a surgical operation.

A new non-invasive treatment known as lithotripsy is now available in some centers. A special machine generates ultrasonic waves which are focussed on the kidney stone causing it to disintegrate. This may replace surgery in selected cases.

Renal failure

Kidney failure may be acute or chronic.

The disruption to kidney function may be temporary and reversible or the damage to kidney tissue may be permanent, frequently as a result of the regular use of analgesics.

Symptoms may include tiredness, confusion, vomiting and abdominal pain as waste products normally excreted in the urine accumulate in the bloodstream. There may be serious complications affecting muscles, the nervous system and the heart and blood vessels.

reflects the degree of active imflammation.

Nodules under the skin, most frequently at the back of the elbow but also at other pressure areas, occur in about one in five with rheumatoid arthritis.

Although it is mainly the joints of the hands and feet that are involved, no joint is immune and the upper part of the vertebral column is often affected. In severe cases, the joints may become weakened enough to cause slipping of the vertebral bones, leading to compression of the spinal cord. This in turn may cause problems with bowel and bladder control.

Treatment It is important that the patient should understand the long-term nature of the illness and its tendency to flare up. The main aim of treatment is to ensure maximum functioning, and a number of methods are used to that end. Rest, joint splintage and support during a flare-up are important and physical therapy, drugs and various surgical procedures all have their place.

Many drugs are available to control pain and limit inflammation within the joints. Aspirin is still one of the most widely used, and indomethacin and gold (given as an injection) are others that have been used for many years. Newer and more specific medications are now being introduced, including naprosyn, sundilac and penicillamine, the last being reserved for particularly severe cases.

Shingles

The infectious disease herpes zoster or shingles is caused by a virus. The virus affects the nerve root and causes severe pain and a rash along the affected nerve. The nerve roots of the eye, the face, the legs, the arms, or around the trunk can be affected.

Evidence suggests that the same virus causes both shingles and chicken pox. The skin blisters in the two diseases are similar microscopically. A person with shingles can transmit chicken pox to someone else but shingles cannot be contracted directly from a person with chicken pox.

Unlike chicken pox, which is one of the common epidemic diseases of childhood, shingles occurs sporadically, chiefly in adults. Those who have already had chicken pox in childhood can get shingles later. In this case it is thought that shingles is caused by a reactivation of the (varicella-zoster) virus which has remained dormant in the cells of the spinal cord after a previous attack of chicken pox.

Symptoms A symptom prior to shingles is usually a severe continuous pain for three or four days before the skin of the painful area becomes reddened and a blistery rash appears. The rash dries up after about a week and leaves scars. The pain often subsides when the rash appears, but in elderly people it may persist as a nagging pain for months or years (post-herpetic neuralgia).

In some people the area affected may be permanently anesthetized and there may also be wasting of the muscles. Herpes zoster of the eye can lead to blindness or partial loss of vision due to scarring of the cornea. Inflammation of the brain (encephalitis) or the spinal cord (myelitis) can also occur.

Treatment For severe attacks of herpes zoster a number of new antiviral drugs have been tried locally on the skin and in the eyes and by mouth. Some of these are quite toxic and the benefits are arguable. Pain-killing drugs are nearly always required in the acute phase. Pain persisting after the acute attack is called post-herpetic neuralgia. It is often difficult to treat. Sometimes drugs usually used for epilepsy will succeed if simple analgesics are ineffective.

Sinusitis

Inflammation of a sinus, particularly one of the paranasal sinuses, is known as sinusitis. Because their lining is continuous with that of the nasal cavity, any cause of rhinitis may also lead to sinusitis.

Although the maxillary sinuses are affected most frequently, the frontal sinuses are often involved as well because their drainage channels are long, narrow and easily blocked.

Viral rhinitis, as part of the common cold, is often associated with sinusitis. Pain and tenderness over the affected area, together with fever and malaise, are the usual features. Often these symptoms will settle down over a

Allergies (*Zefa*)

few days but become more severe and persistent if secondary bacterial infection follows. Purulent (pus-containing) nasal discharge coming from the sinus is then common unless the ostium, the opening into the nostril, is closed completely. Pain tends to be worse on arising in the morning and is often aggravated by stooping.

Persistent or recurrent sinusitis is often associated with some other problem. Septal deviation, nasal polyps, allergic rhinitis and longstanding irritation from dusts and fumes are possible causes. Allergies and irritants not only cause sinusitis in their own right, but also predispose to secondary infection.

Repeated attacks of acute sinusitis lead to chronic sinusitis when the swollen, infected lining of the sinuses helps to block the drainage into the back of the nose.

Initially, the diagnosis is made by the history and physical features.

Treatment is undertaken with analgesics for pain relief, decongestants and inhalations, and broad spectrum antibiotics if bacterial infection is likely. When these measures are unsuccessful, a sinus x-ray is usually taken, and this may be followed by an antral puncture. This latter procedure is performed by passing a thin tube into the sinus, usually the maxillary one, through the lowest segment of its wall. This assists drainage of accumulated secretions, allows the causative organism to be identified accurately and its sensitivity to particular antibiotics determined.

Anti-histamines, beclomethasone and sodium cromoglycate may be of use when allergies are important predisposing or precipitating causes. Avoidance of irritants, removal of polyps, correction of nasal abnormalities such as septal deviation, and treatment of any associated infection like a dental abscess, are other measures that may be required. About one in ten cases of maxillary sinusitis emanate from dental infections.

Occasionally more radical surgery than antral puncture is required, although this is restricted to particularly severe or resistant cases.

Sore throat

Inflammation of the pharynx at the back of the mouth, spreading sometimes to the larynx, a sore throat may be caused by a cold or other viral infection such as measles or mononucleosis, or by bacterial infection, specially with streptococci. Very rarely a sore throat may be caused by blood disorders such as absence of white cells (agranulocytosis) or cancerous white cells (leukemia). Diphtheria is now a rare throat infection. Certain drugs such as antithyroid drugs and gold injections can also cause a sore throat because of lack of white blood cells as a side-effect of the drug.

A sore throat is often accompanied by a fever and cough. Hoarseness indicates infection of the larynx.

It is difficult for a doctor to tell by examining a sore throat whether the infection is viral or streptococcal, although infants are more likely to be affected by viral infection. Treatment of the symptoms is all that is required, acetaminophen or aspirin being the drugs commonly used.

If a streptococcal infection is suspected — and this may be confirmed by microscopic examination of a throat swab — it is usual to treat it with penicillin by mouth to speed recovery and reduce the danger of rheumatic fever and acute nephritis, which are possible complications.

Throat infection, both viral and streptococcal, can involve the tonsils. A rare complication of tonsillitis is a quinsy or abscess behind the tonsil.

A sore throat persisting for several days, in spite of treatment, may be caused by mononucleosis. The diagnosis can be confirmed by the detection of an enlarged

Septic sore throat is generally accompanied by high fever and difficulty in swallowing. *(PAF International)*

spleen or lymph gland or by blood tests. A blood count will detect the rare case of leukemia or other serious blood disorder.

Tennis elbow

Lateral epicondylitis, or tennis elbow, is characterized by local tenderness and pain on the outer side, or lateral aspect, of the elbow region. The pain sometimes extends down the back of the forearm and is aggravated by movements such as twisting and flexing the wrist. A small knob just above the elbow joint, the lateral epicondyle is the site where several muscles of the forearm come together and attach. They bend the wrist back, extend the fingers and are stretched whenever the wrist is twisted and flexed.

Although tennis is the sport classically blamed for the condition, many other activities may also cause it. A straining, and subsequent inflammation, of some of the muscle fibers at their insertion is the exact cause of the pain.

Treatment The degree and duration of pain is variable, but occasionally it can be quite incapacitating and may last for several years. In most cases rest, time and mild analgesics are all that is required. The injection of corticosteroid drugs into the tender spot, physical therapy, encasement of the arm in plaster for a

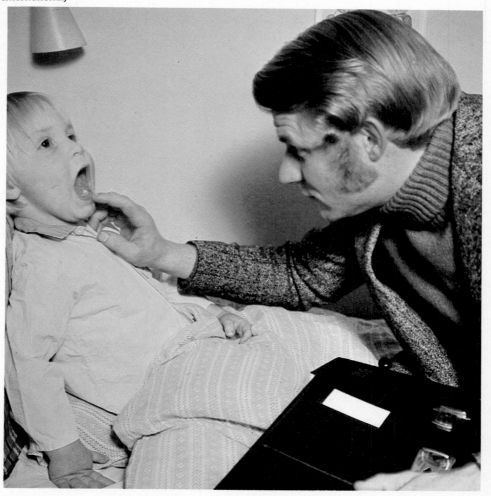

number of weeks and rarely, surgically dividing some of the offending muscle fibers at the site of attachment, are other methods of treatment sometimes employed.

Using a racquet with a wider handle, and coaching to modify some of the wrist movements may assist the keen tennis player who has developed the condition.

A similar condition may develop on the inner surface of the elbow affecting the muscles that flex the wrist downwards. It is known as golfer's elbow or medial epicondylitis.

Thrombosis

The formation of a clot of blood in a vein, artery or the heart, thrombosis is usually caused by damage to the lining of the blood vessel. Other causes are a stagnation of blood and an increased clotting tendency in the blood.

Damage to a blood vessel wall causes the blood platelets to stick together and release prothrombin, a substance which causes strands of fibrin to be laid down; these strands entangle blood cells and a clot or thrombus is formed.

Damage to veins is usually from inflammation (phlebitis); damage to arteries is from atherosclerosis; and damage to the lining of the heart is from a heart attack in which the damage to heart muscle (infarct) extends to the interior of the heart.

Tennis elbow is caused by straining and subsequent inflammation of muscle fibers in the elbow. *(Zefa)*

The danger of thrombosis lies in its threat to the circulation; a clot may block an artery and cut off the blood supply to tissue such as heart or brain (infarction) or may be detached and swept along in the bloodstream to a distant artery, and block it (embolism).

Thrombosis in a pile, or hemorrhoid, is painful but not dangerous. Thrombosis in a varicose vein may be curative; in the injection treatment of varicose veins, the injected substance irritates the lining of the

A thrombus may block the flow of blood, or an embolus may become detached and cause a blockage elsewhere. *(Westmead Center)*

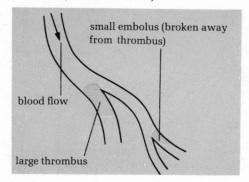

small embolus (broken away from thrombus)

blood flow

large thrombus

vein, causing thrombosis and leading to destruction of the unwanted varicose vein. But thrombosis in an artery supplying a vital organ is serious; a clot in a cerebral artery causes a stroke and one in a coronary artery a heart attack.

Occasionally a heart attack or cardiac infarction is followed by the development of a thrombus on the damaged inner wall of the heart. Such a thrombus may become detached and travel to the brain (an uncommon cause of stroke). If a clot in a deep vein becomes detached, it will be carried to the lungs (pulmonary embolism), causing pain, breathlessness and even death.

Prevention of thrombosis in an artery is based on following measures to avoid atherosclerosis including regular exercise, no smoking, control of blood pressure and avoidance of obesity.

In women taking the pill, the risk of thrombosis leading to lung embolus is increased about four times. Women older than 35 and women smokers older than 30 are at even greater risk and are advised to use another method of contraception.

Prevention of thrombosis after surgical operations has been based for many years on the principle of getting the patient out of bed at an early stage to combat stagnation of blood in the leg veins. Recently it has been shown that the risk of thrombosis is greatly reduced by small injections of the anticoagulant heparin and by intermittent compressions of the calf muscles.

To prevent thrombosis after a heart attack, sulphinpyrazone may be recommended, and for some severe cases, the oral anticoagulant warfarin. This drug is also given together with dipyridamole to patients with artificial heart valves to prevent a clot forming on the foreign implant.

When deep vein thrombosis occurs the superficial veins may become distended since they have to carry a greater than normal flow of blood. *(Westmead Center)*

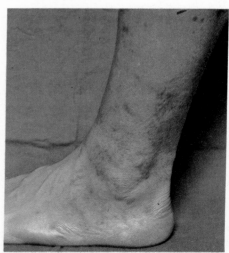

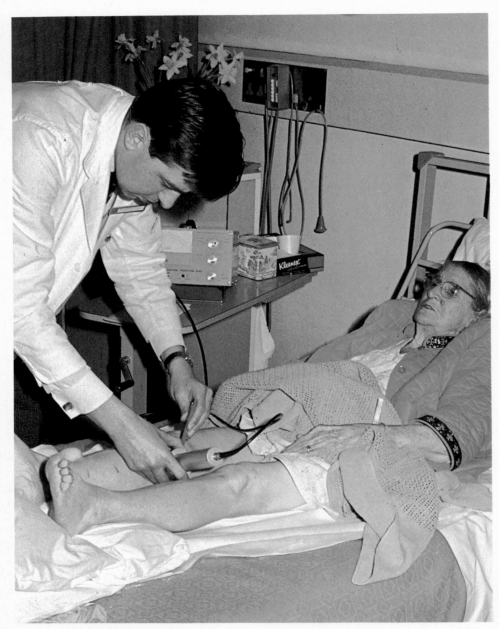

A venous thrombosis can be located by injecting radioactive fibrinogen and determining where it has concentrated. (John Watney Photo Library)

Treatment with warfarin, however, requires regular blood tests in order to determine the right dose and the avoidance of drugs which alter its effect. One such drug is aspirin which, by virtue of its mild anticlotting action, finds a place in the prevention of minor strokes (transient cerebral ischemia).

Treatment of thromboembolism is with the rapidly acting heparin, given intravenously for a week or so and followed by warfarin tablets for several months. Other drugs used are those which break down fibrin, the fibrinolytic agents such as streptokinase and urokinase; injected into the affected vessel, they may dissolve a fresh thrombus.

Tinea

The Latin for gnawing worm, tinea is the name of a group of fungal infections of the skin, more popularly known as ringworm because the lesion produced is usually elliptical with a reddened, raised scaly edge.

Initially there is a redness of the skin, soon followed by scaling. The active edge is redder than the relatively pale center and it spreads out, causing soreness and irritation. Moisture, warmth and poor hygiene aggravate the condition, and spread usually occurs through direct contact from an infected part of the body or another person.

Tinea of the foot (tinea pedis) The feet are the site most frequently affected, with the classical ring seen in other areas being absent. There are three types of rash: soggy reddish inflamed areas between the toes

which slough off leaving a raw area beneath; a reddish rash on the side of the foot with blisters; and a localized crusting red lesion on the top of the foot. The first type of rash, often called athlete's foot, is most common.

The infection is frequently spread by contact with the wet floor of communal showers, such as at beaches, swimming pools or squash courts. To help prevent infection it is advisable to wear sandals at all times in these areas, right up to the edge of the shower or pool. Close fitting footwear and nylon socks in hot weather aid the growth of the fungus.

Tinea of the groin (tinea cruris) is an infection frequently found in men and boys. It is also becoming more prevalent among women who wear step-ins and nylon pantyhose as these garments do not allow the free flow of air in the groin making sweating more likely.

The red weeping areas may have blisters or scaling and may extend down the thighs and over the buttocks at the back. Sometimes there is a ring pattern.

Tinea of the body (tinea corporis) can have a concentric ring-like edge, it can be widespread and general, or resemble plaque. There are many different diagnostic possibilities for these types of rashes so a doctor's advice should be sought.

Tinea of the nails may affect either the toe or finger nails. The nail becomes discoloured, brown and soft, fractures, thickens and eventually is completely destroyed, with separation from the nail bed.

Prevention of tinea includes keeping the feet dry and exposed to the air as much as possible.

Removal of the nail is often necessary as well as treatment with antifungal tablets. It takes about two years to heal.

Tinea of the scalp (tinea capitis) causes either a type of baldness where the hairs can still be seen broken on the surface of the scalp, or a patchy hair loss.

Tinea of the beard (tinea barbae) affects the bearded areas of the neck and face.

Tinea versicolor is a common condition affecting mainly the trunk and is most frequent in the hot tropical areas. Patches of skin with slight scaling are the predominant features. Because these patches do not pigment in sunshine, they are paler than the surrounding skin, particularly if the skin is suntanned.

Diagnosis and treatment Scrapings of the affected skin can be examined and the fungus thus identified.

Locally applied treatments containing tolnafate or the newer drugs miconazole and clotrimazole are often effective. When the scalp or the nails become affected, griseofulvin taken by mouth is the most appropriate treatment. Tinea versicolor can be treated with twice weekly applications of selenium sulphide shampoo.

Toxic shock syndrome

The condition known as toxic shock syndrome was first described in 1978 and is related to an infection caused by the bacterium *staphylococcus aureus*. It is confined largely to females, although sporadic cases affecting children and adult males have been reported.

Symptoms Over 90 per cent of women who have develped toxic shock syndrome were using tampons at or shortly before the time that symptoms commenced. These appear most frequently around the third day of the menstrual flow, with headache, fever, malaise and sore eyes being the most common initial symptoms. Nausea, vomiting diarrhea and a rash often follow. Symptoms of shock (inadequate circulation of blood throughout the body) occur several days later, both as a result of the infection and of the diarrhea. Any system of the body may become involved and at least three different sets of symptoms, such as those related to the gastrointestinal, urinary and nervous systems, have to be present before the diagnosis is made.

The initial focus of infection is not always the vagina — the nose, throat or other tissues may be primarily involved.

Treatment of the symptoms is necessary with cultures being taken to identify the strain of *Staphylococcus* and its sensitivity to various antibiotics. The replacement of fluids and electrolytes is required when significant dehydration is present. Broad-spectrum antibiotics are usually commenced immediately and changed if necessary when the culture results are available.

Clearer guidelines about prevention and control of this condition will emerge as research yields more information.

Results of research Although tampons have been in use since the 1940s the condition was not identified until 1978 and the association with tampons noted still later. A change in manufacturing methods saw the introduction of high absorbency synthetic materials to the cotton previously used. It appears the new materials may have enhanced the production of toxins. Many manufacturers have ceased use of these synthetic materials.

One theory is that there has developed a strain or strains of *Staphylococcus* that grow readily in stagnant menstrual secretions. In recent years there has been research into this aspect, together with assessment of the manufacture of tampons themselves to see if this could be a contributing factor.

Prevention Some authorities recommend that women who use tampons should wash their hands thoroughly before inserting them, change them every three or four hours and use pads instead during the night.

Trigeminal neuralgia

Also known as tic douloureux and facial neuralgia, trigeminal neuralgia is a disorder of the trigeminal nerve. The trigeminal nerve is the sensory nerve of the face. It is divided into three, the first division supplying the eye and forehead, the second division the cheek and upper jaw, and the third division the lower jaw.

Symptoms The pain of trigeminal neuralgia is stabbing and severe, with spasms of the face during a paroxysm of pain. The brief paroxysms sometimes follow each other rapidly, causing a prolonged pain. After a few weeks the pain may disappear but unfortunately is likely to recur. During an attack there may be a dull ache and a paroxysm may be triggered by even a slight stimulus such as touching the face, brushing the teeth, chewing, smiling or laughing, or by exposure to a cold breeze.

The pain is usually in the second or third division of the nerve, striking each with equal frequency; only in 5–10 per cent of cases does it affect the first division. Sometimes more than one division is involved but it is rare for both sides of the face to be affected.

Cause The onset of the complaint usually occurs after the age of fifty. It is now thought that the cause is compression or irritation of the nerve near its entry to the pons (part of the brain) usually by an artery — the superior cerebellar artery — which has become tortuous with age. In young people, trigeminal neuralgia arouses suspicion of a tumor within the skull or, more importantly, multiple sclerosis.

Treatment The usual treatment is with the anti-epileptic drug carbamezepine, taken in a dose sufficient to control pain without causing the side effects of drowsiness and clumsiness (ataxia). This dose is generally 0.007–0.014 ounce (200–400 mg), taken three times a day. In some cases, however, carbamezepine may cause a rash or a drop in white blood cells (leukopenia), and other drugs such as phenytoin and clonazepam are then given.

Surgery includes injection of alcohol or phenol into the nerve root, its coagulation by heat, or its excision within the skull. These procedures can eliminate pain, but they will produce numbness (anesthesia) which may be a problem, particularly if it involves the eye.

Tuberculosis

An acute or chronic condition, tuberculosis is an infection with the bacterium *Mycobacterium tuberculosis*, a thin straight rod (or bacillus) about 0.4 x 3 microns in size. Discovered by Robert Koch in 1882, this bacillus is acid fast and a strict aerobe, which means it grows best in plenty of oxygen. This may be why it seems to grow best in the lungs, and why it becomes dormant when encased in a tubercle. Although it commonly infects the lungs, tuberculosis may infect any tissue or organ in the body and produce a wide variety of symptoms.

Incidence Tuberculosis is endemic throughout the world and, with malaria, is one of the most prevalent of all infections. Of the 50 million people infected, about 5 million die annually. It affects all ages including babies and children but usually begins in young to middle-aged adults and produces a protracted, crippling disease which causes much misery and socio-economic loss, both to the sufferers and to the community.

Methods of infection The organism may spread in a variety of ways. Although congenital tuberculosis is rare, the infection may pass from the mother to the fetus through the placenta. People who handle infected material may contract the disease through the skin. The bacilli contained in contaminated milk from infected cows may also pass through the mouth, tonsils, stomach and intestines.

Inhalation of contaminated dust may also result in tuberculosis. Although the tuberculosis bacilli are killed by sunlight, they can withstand drying and may survive a long time away from the sun. People living in the same house as someone who has tuberculosis and who spits on the floor are in real danger of infection because the sputum dries and, with its contained bacilli, becomes air-borne as dust.

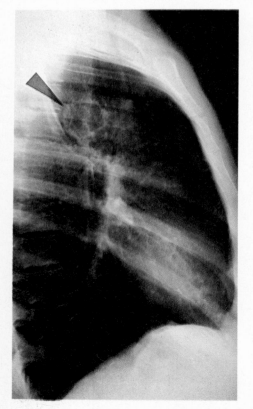

Pasteurization of milk has reduced the incidence of tuberculosis.
Left
Radiography reveals an area of tubercular infection. *(Salmer)*

Probably the main source of infection in the adult is inhalation of droplets. A person with open tuberculosis who coughs into the air sprays his environment with millions of tuberculosis bacilli contained in tiny droplets of water. Exposure to a person who takes no precautions when coughing can be followed by a massive infection.

The primary infection usually occurs in childhood through inhaling infected droplets or drinking infected milk and consists of an acute inflammatory reaction at the site of infection (for example the tonsils, lung or intestine). The bacilli spread rapidly to the regional lymph nodes which become enlarged. Usually the primary infection clears up without a diagnosis of tuberculosis being made. The involved lymph nodes degenerate and calcify and may be detected later on an x-ray. Sometimes not all the bacilli are destroyed, but lie dormant in the calcified lymph nodes to begin a secondary infection on some future occasion when body resistance is low.

The secondary infection In many infections, the invading organism stimulates the immune system of the body to produce antibodies that destroy the invaders, clearing up the initial infection and preventing the organisms becoming established when they infect the body on subsequent occasions. Vaccines of live non-pathogenic organisms (as in smallpox vaccine) or dead organisms (as in typhoid vaccine) may then be produced to stimulate antibody production and prevent people from ever getting the particular disease.

This does not occur with *Mycobacterium tuberculosis*, although the primary infection does produce a degree of hypersensitivity and increased resistance that causes the body to deal with a subsequent, or secondary, infection in a very different way. Instead of an acute inflammatory reaction which rapidly spreads through lymph vessels to the regional lymph nodes, a profuse proliferation of granular tissue cells occurs to surround and localise the invading bacilli.

Because these granulomas have a very specific appearance they are termed 'tubercles'. As the tubercles grow, they degenerate in the center into an amorphous pink cheese-like material: a process called caseation. In time, the cheese-like material softens and liquefies and, if in the lung, ruptures into an air passage (bronchus) and is coughed up with its contained bacilli, leaving a cavity in the lung. This is termed 'open' tuberculosis because such people are infectious to others. The cavities may bleed, staining the sputum with blood. The infected sputum can spread into parts of the patient's own lungs, causing further infection and, if swallowed, may infect the gastrointestinal tract.

Although without treatment tuberculosis usually runs a chronic protracted course, because of the interplay between destruction and repair, some people do recover and some die. The outcome depends on the number and the virulence of the infecting bacilli, and the resistance and hypersensitivity of the body. Poor nutrition, old age, the presence of other diseases (such as diabetes), inadequate housing, alcoholism and poor hygiene all tend to lower resistance. Tuberculosis is thus more prominent in poor countries and among the old, the poor and the alcoholic in more affluent nations.

Miliary tuberculosis When the number of bacilli is large or the resistance of the person is very low, the bacilli may spread quickly through the tissues from the site of infection and may invade the bloodstream. This produces an acute toxic infection in which tiny miliary tubercles spread throughout every organ in the body and which is rapidly fatal.

Hypersensitivity The nature of the resistance and hypersensitivity generated by the host as a result of a primary infection is not understood, but it does give the body an increased capacity to localize the bacilli, to retard their multiplication and even to destroy them.

Tuberculin (Mantoux) test An extract of broth in which tuberculosis bacilli have grown for six weeks is injected into the skin of the front of the forearm. People who have never contracted tuberculosis have no reaction. Within 24 to 48 hours, a person who has had tuberculosis (whether diagnosed or not) develops an area of redness, swelling and hardened tissue exceeding 10 mm in diameter. A positive Mantoux test indicates a past or present infection. If a person known to have had a previous negative reaction suddenly reacts positively, he must have had a recent infection, and requires treatment.

Symptoms Since tuberculosis can involve every organ system, its manifestations are many and varied. Fatigue, weight loss, weakness and fever usually occur. If the lungs are involved there is usually a chronic cough and sometimes sputum which may be blood stained.

Although x-rays are useful in diagnosis, tuberculosis can only be proven by isolating the bacilli from sputum, gastric washings or urine, or from biopsy material.

Prevention Over the past fifty years, as a result of preventive measures, the incidence of tuberculosis has decreased remarkably.

As well as improvements in living conditions and nutrition, eradication of tuberculosis in cattle and pasteurization of milk have limited the spread of organisms. Active cases have been isolated and close contacts of diagnosed patients have received regular examinations. People whose tuberculin test has recently converted from negative to positive are given routine treatment. Mass miniature chest x-rays have further controlled the spread of the disease.

BCG vaccination is generally given to people such as nurses and doctors who are heavily exposed to infection. BCG vaccine contains live bacilli of a less virulent weakened bovine strain which offers some protection to tuberculin-negative persons.

Treatment aims at curing the patient as quickly as possible while preventing him from spreading the disease, and minimizing disruptions to employment and lifestyle.

A good diet and rest are essential. Open cases are usually hospitalized until treatment renders them non-infectious. There is little evidence that climate is significant. Education about the disease and how to cover the mouth when coughing and sneezing are very important.

Chemotherapy. Because *Mycobacterium tuberculosis* rapidly develops resistance to drugs, treatment is commenced with three drugs given simultaneously. The initial three drugs are selected from isoniazid, rifampicin, ethambutol, streptomycin and pyrazinamide and are taken for three months. One drug is then discontinued and the other two taken for a further 6 to 9 months. The drugs must be taken strictly as prescribed and careful supervision is essential. A person who has been treated with anti-tuberculous drugs on a previous occasion and who is likely to have resistant bacilli is treated with four drugs for 4 months and then three drugs for 9 months. Clinical examination, x-rays and sputum cultures are performed monthly.

Symptoms usually improve within two or three weeks of starting treatment; x-rays show improvement after about four weeks; and sputum becomes negative within three months. Very few people die of pulmonary tuberculosis when modern treatment methods are started before the disease reaches a very advanced stage. Most people, including those with advanced disease, can be restored to normal health within 12 months.

Tuberculosis tends to recur six to twelve months after treatment ceases. Although patients are examined, x-rayed and bacteriologically tested every two months for two years and then annually for at least five years, life-long surveillance is recommended.

Tumor

A tumor is a growth of new cells resembling the parent tissue, which proliferate in an uncontrolled way. Most body cells have the capacity to proliferate to repair damage to an organ (for example, skin) or to replace worn out cells (for example, blood cells). This normal proliferation is controlled and ceases when the damage is restored. Neoplasia begins when changes inside a cell compel it to proliferate and render it unresponsive to body controls. The growing mass of cells forms a nodule which continues to expand, compressing the surrounding tissue.

Tumors can easily be divided into two main types, benign and malignant.

Benign tumors tend to grow slowly, their cells are of uniform size and appearance and resemble the cells of their tissue of origin. They are surrounded by a fibrous capsule, and do not infiltrate surrounding tissues or spread to other parts of the body. They cause harm only by the pressure they exert on some vital organ or duct; they do not recur when excised.

Benign breast tumors are fairly common but rarely cause pain or discomfort.

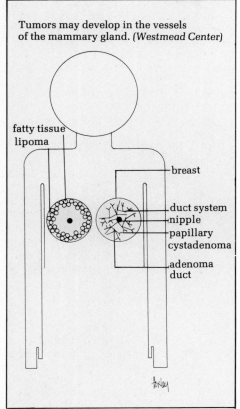

Tumors may develop in the vessels of the mammary gland. (Westmead Center)

fatty tissue
lipoma

breast

duct system
nipple
papillary
cystadenoma

adenoma
duct

foxley

Benign tumors are usually named by attaching the suffix 'oma' to the name of the organ or tissue from which they have arisen (for example, a fibroma from fibrous tissue, angioma from blood vessels, and meningioma from the meninges). Benign tumors of epithelial surfaces (for example, skin or the lining of organs like the bowel) may be named according to their appearance (for example, a papilloma is a warty outgrowth from a surface, and an adenoma is a mass of gland-like tissue developing from a glandular organ).

Malignant tumors (commonly called cancer) usually grow more rapidly, their cells vary in size and appearance and have little or no resemblance to their tissue of origin. They are not restrained by a capsule, but infiltrate surrounding tissue and invade and grow along blood and lymph vessels, in which groups of cells become detached to be swept to distant parts of the body where they seed satellite tumors (or metastases). Malignant tumors tend to recur following surgical excision.

Malignant tumors are called carcinomas when they arise from epithelial surfaces (for example, gastric carcinoma arises from the lining of the stomach and rectal carcinoma from the lining of the rectum). When a malignant tumor originates from fibrous or related tissue it is called a sarcoma (for example a fibrosarcoma from fibrous tissue and chondrosarcoma from cartilage).

Causes Many factors combine to cause a tumor. There are varying degrees of inherited predisposition or susceptibility on which various environmental influences act (for example, chronic inflammation, or chemicals, drugs, food or radiation which we inhale or ingest or to which we are exposed). The greater a person's susceptibility, the shorter the time and the lower the dose needed to stimulate tumor formation. Examples of tumors are the tumors of mouth and lung induced by tobacco smoke, the cancers of skin caused by radiation from the sun or by tar from the coal and bitumen industries.

Treatment Benign tumors are usually cured by surgical removal and do not recur. The treatment of cancer is less satisfactory and every effort should be made to promote a healthy lifestyle, industrial safety and early detection. The usual treatment for cancer is its removal by radical surgery and then, when needed, radiotherapy and/or treatment with cancer-destroying drugs. Occasionally hormone treatment helps when the cancer is hormone-dependent (for example, some tumors of breast and prostate).

Cancer tends to be most prevalent in the very young and the very old, when the body's immunological defences are inactive. It is thought that the immune system has some ability to detect and destroy cancer cells, and that it is cancers that develop at times when physical and emotional factors depress the activity of the immune system which grow and spread. Research into the ways in which the immune systems work and destroy cancer is providing hope for new forms of treatment.

Ulcer

An area of total loss of the superficial layer of skin or mucous membrane is described as an ulcer. The organs that can be affected are the digestive, respiratory and urinary tracts. Large arterial blood vessels such as the aorta also may be affected in certain types of arterial disease.

Ulceration of the body surface may follow trauma, pressure, infection, chemical irritation, burns, benign and malignant tumor formation, blood vessel disease, diabetes and blood disorders.

Common skin ulcers include basal cell carcinoma, locally malignant tumors such as the squamous cell cancer, malignant mole or melanoma, pressure sores in the bedridden patient, lower limb venous ulcers and those caused by infections such as syphilis, herpes and chicken-pox.

Mouth ulcers are very common and are caused by viral infections, badly fitting dentures, occasional malignant tumors and chemicals such as those in betel nuts in primitive cultures. They range from the trivial but painful superficial aphthous ulcers, thrush ulcers and *Candida albicans* infection, to those that are a sign of serious general illness.

Rodent ulcers A basal cell carcinoma of the skin that has a central ulcer or breakdown of the surface cells is known as a rodent ulcer. This is the most common tumor or cancer of the skin in people of Caucasian race, and is thought to arise from the basal cells that are situated in the deepest layer of the epidermis.

Sunshine is an important initiating factor in the formation of rodent ulcers, which occur most commonly in the elderly, especially in people with fair complexions. They usually occur on those areas exposed to sunshine, for example the face and neck. People who have lived for many years in tropical or subtropical areas are most prone to these tumors.

Symptoms Rodent ulcers may be multiple and they tend to grow very slowly, forming a small, smooth, translucent or pearly nodule. (The surface is smooth because basal cells are unable to form keratin, the outermost proteinous layer of skin.) As the growth enlarges, the surface at the center of the tumor tends to sink inwards and eventually break down, resulting in the classical appearance of the 'rodent ulcer' with its elevated margin. Blood vessels are often prominent above this rim. The surface of the ulcer is soon covered by a thin crust, which may periodically break down and then reform. Any crusty ulcer or sore on the skin that does not heal completely (over a period of six weeks) should be examined by a doctor because of the possibility of its being a tumor.

Rodent ulcers almost never spread to distant tissues although they may slowly erode underlying structures, and can even burrow through bone and cartilage. Treatment involves removal of the offending tissue. A complete cure is achieved in almost all cases, especially if the lesion is detected when it is fairly small.

Surgical excision, radiotherapy, and curetting of the lesion and then cauterizing the base are the most frequent methods of treatment. The treatment chosen depends on the site and size of the tumor.

Protection against excessive sunshine with hats and sunscreen are important preventive measures.

Leg ulcers Crater-like in appearance, leg ulcers are generally caused by impaired blood circulation or by a local cancer. Ulcers associated with vein problems are known as venous, varicose or gravitational ulcers. A skin ulcer which persists for more than four to five weeks without obvious healing should be medically examined.

Causes of leg ulcers Valves in the leg muscles force blood through the vein in one direction and prevent it retreating. If the valves are destroyed or damaged, because of thrombosis or clot formation within the deep veins, skin ulcers may develop, causing the superficial veins (just below the skin) to become dilated and varicose because of the increased pressure and greater volume of blood that initially flows through them. Blood also stagnates, producing an increase in pressure extending back to the capillaries.

As a result, fluid may leak into the surrounding tissues causing edema which, combined with general reduction in blood flow, may affect the skin's vitality, particularly the lower inside surface of the leg.

Arterial disease such as hypertension (high blood pressure) and atherosclerosis, collagen diseases such as disseminated lupus erythematosus, and arterial thrombosis may restrict the supply of blood and cause leg ulcers. Symptoms are cold, white feet and pain while walking (claudication). The parts most often affected are the feet and the outer side of the legs.

Diabetes mellitus may cause leg ulcers, partly through arterial disease and also through nerve degeneration (neuropathy) which leads to a loss of feeling in the skin surfaces. Neuropathy may also occur after advanced alcoholism, leprosy and advanced syphilis, or even through wearing tight shoes. It may develop unnoticed because of the lack of sensation in the skin.

Elderly people, or those who are bedridden, may develop bed or pressure sores on their heels, buttocks or over their ankles, as the skin is 'squeezed' between bone and the surface on which the person is lying.

Other causes include infections such as leishmaniasis or 'tropical ulcers', gout which creates hard nodules around the knee that cause skin breakdown, and self-inflicted skin damage. Heavy patients are especially vulnerable.

If the cause is cancer, this will generally be treated with radiotherapy or by surgical removal. If infection is involved, specific antibiotics may be needed.

Healing of varicose ulcers may be accelerated by keeping the leg elevated and wearing supportive elastic stockings. Infections must be treated to allow the healing process to progress unimpeded, while scabs, serum or other debris should be removed periodically. To prevent recurrence of the ulcers, the varicose veins may have to be removed surgically, and incompetent, perforating veins tied.

Arterial ulcers are difficult to treat as the whole arterial system is usually diseased. Controlling diabetes or hypertension when they are present is worthwhile. In selected cases surgical procedures to widen the arteries or bypass blockages may be feasible. However, if the blood supply is severely restricted localized amputation may be necessary to prevent the spread of gangrene.

Special care of the feet and frequent checking of the limbs for skin injury is required when there is reduced sensation. Lamb-skin covers and frequent turning of the patient by nursing staff can minimize bedsores.

Valvular heart disease

The term valvular heart disease describes acquired or congenital defects in the valves of the heart. The human heart has four such valves, the tricuspid, pulmonary, mitral and aortic valves, separating its four chambers and normally allowing blood to flow through them in one direction only.

Rheumatic fever was once the most common cause of acquired valve defects, but since there has been a significant decline in the incidence of rheumatic fever in countries with high living standards there has been some reduction in the overall incidence of valvular heart disease. A lower incidence of syphilis and its effective early treatment have also contributed to a reduction in aortic valve disease.

Congenital heart defects continue to be responsible for most cases of pulmonary valve disease, with occasional involvement of the other valves. The program for the eradication of German measles (rubella) during pregnancy by immunization of all women before child-bearing age should contribute to a lower incidence of congenital heart disease, including valve defects.

Infection of damaged valves (bacterial endocarditis) can compound the problems of valvular disease by causing further structural and functional deterioration. Diseased valves are particularly vulnerable to this type of infection from circulating bacterial invasion, such as that which may occur as a result of dental and genito-urinary procedures.

The tricuspid valve separates the two right-sided chambers of the heart and is so named because it has three flaps or cusps.

The most common cause of acquired disease of the tricuspid valve was rheumatic fever, usually involving the mitral valve as well. Other less common causes include traumatic valve injury, infection (for example in drug addicts), and stretching of the right ventricle caused by a form of lung disease (pulmonary hypertension), with or without mitral valve dysfunction.

Congenital causes are usually associated with multiple defects such as those in Ebstein's anomaly. The valve may either be narrowed or made weak and incompetent by these defects. In both cases there are murmurs from the disturbance in pressure and flow patterns across the valve, elevated venous pressure and varying degrees of congestive cardiac failure.

Treatment may involve rest, drugs and other medical treatment or, in particular cases, surgery. The pulmonary valve separates the right ventricle from the pulmonary artery, taking venous blood to the lungs for oxygenation. The valve is composed of three cusps of semilunar shape and may become narrowed as a single congenital defect or in association with more complex multiple defects. Pulmonary incompetence is usually a result of high pressure in the pulmonary blood vessels in certain types of lung disease.

Murmurs result from both types, with varying compensatory dilatation and thickening of the right ventricular wall, and congestive heart failure in some cases.

Valve surgery is required for severe defects.

The mitral valve separates the left atrium from the powerful thick-walled left ventricle and is composed of a two flap arrangement.

Narrowing of this valve (mitral stenosis) is occasionally the result of a congenital defect but rheumatic fever is still the most common cause in many countries. The initial attack may be clinically unrecognized but is followed years later by the classical symptoms and signs. Repeated attacks of rheumatic fever cause further damage and narrowing.

Symptoms result when a critical degree of narrowing has been reached, with gradually increasing lung congestion, and include breathlessness on exertion and later at rest, recurrent or winter bronchitis, blood-stained sputum and lassitude. Complications include cardiac rhythm disturbances and thrombotic events (embolism). Characteristic murmurs, clinical signs, and electrocardiogram and chest x-ray changes also occur.

Mitral incompetence is usually the result of previous rheumatic valvulitis but may also be caused by congenital or acquired defects in valve function, or disease of surrounding cardiac muscle. Symptoms are similar to those of mitral stenosis but there is less lung congestion and a greater risk of infective endocarditis.

Treatment may be medical with drugs for treatment of heart failure, or surgical with valve replacement in suitable cases. Antibiotic cover is required for dental and other surgical procedures.

The aortic valve, separating the left ventricle from the aorta, conveys oxygenated blood to the general circulation. It is a three cusp semilunar valve like the pulmonary. Narrowing of this valve, aortic stenosis, may be congenital or acquired as a result of rheumatic fever or degenerative changes with thickening and calcification of the valve. There may be no symptoms for many years until the sudden development of anginal pain, breathlessness, loss of consciousness on effort and dizziness on standing, with a risk of sudden death.

Aortic incompetence was previously caused by rheumatic fever and syphilis in most cases.

Both types of aortic valve disease show characteristic murmurs, electrocardiogram and chest x-ray changes with cardiac enlargement.

Treatment involves drugs for angina and surgical valve replacement in appropriate cases.

Varicocele

A varicocele is a varicose condition of the veins within the spermatic cord (pampiniform plexus) which normally drain the testes. When varicose, they feel like a 'bag of worms' when the person stands up and the veins fill. Over 90 per cent of varicoceles occur on the left side and are usually first noticed during adolescence. In most cases they are symptomless.

Because of their position in the scrotum, the testes remain about 1°C cooler than the body temperature. This slightly lower temperature is the ideal one for sperm production. Larger varicoceles, which contain a greater volume of blood that is at body temperature, may elevate the temperature in the scrotum and thus reduce the amount of sperm production. In such cases, removal of the varicocele usually allows a return to full fertility.

Varicose veins

Veins which are tortuous, dilated and lengthened, varicose veins or varices are most commonly seen in the legs, but also occur in the rectum (hemorrhoids), the esophagus (esophageal varices) and the spermatic cord (a varicocele). However, the term varicose veins is usually taken to mean those in the legs. They affect up to 20 per cent of the population; nearly half the people over 50 years have some degree of varicose veins of the legs, and they are four times as common in women as in men, probably as a result of the effects of pregnancy.

Gravity causes blood to accumulate in the veins in the legs, which contain small valves that permit blood to flow in one direction only: towards the heart. Healthy valves prevent blood flowing downwards through the veins in the legs. Blood which the heart pumps into the legs through the leg arteries perfuses the tissues of the legs through the blood capillaries and is collected in the veins. Then in the erect posture, this blood is returned to the heart by the movements of the leg muscles squeezing it up the veins and the valves prevent it falling back down again between squeezes.

Causes An increase in pressure inside the abdomen such as occurs with pregnancy, an abdominal tumor, obesity, persistent coughing, heavy lifting, or the straining accompanying constipation increases the pressure on the blood being squeezed up the leg veins toward the heart. In some people (whose vein valves are possibly a little weaker than the average through heredity) this increased pressure in the leg veins causes some of the venous valves to rupture, rendering them incapable of preventing the blood running back down the veins. The blood then pools in the leg veins, causing them to widen and lengthen and develop the characteristic tortuosity.

The pressure in the veins distends the capillary blood vessels which flow into them and spidery *telangiectases* and staining develops in the skin. The stagnation of blood in the leg tissues tends to deprive them of nutrients and oxygen, and this causes itching and scaliness of the skin. The pressure of blood within the veins causes swelling of the ankles and an aching tiredness which is felt in the whole lower leg toward the end of the day or after prolonged standing.

Complications A common complication of varicose veins is an inflammatory reaction accompanied by thrombosis which is called *thrombophlebitis*. This turns the veins into painful tender inflamed cords, and may be precipitated by injury to the veins, prolonged rest or immobility or by another illness. Extension of this process into the deep veins of the legs is unusual but can be potentially dangerous, since pieces of newly-formed clot can break away and travel up the veins and through the right chambers of the heart to lodge in arteries in the lungs (pulmonary emboli).

Chronic dermatitis of the lower legs is often a complication of varicose veins. The area is very itchy, and scratching tends to introduce infection. Treatment is with hydrocortisone cream and antibiotics for infection.

Large ulcerated areas (gravitational or stasis ulcers) may also develop, especially on the inner sides of the lower legs. Appropriate dressings and strappings provide only temporary relief. As with the dermatitis, permanent cure is unlikely unless the varicose veins are cured.

Treatment The best treatment for varicose veins is surgical. The internal saphenous vein is tied off and cut just below the groin. A flexible probe or *stripper* is then fed down several inches of the vein being removed, and its lower end brought out through a cut in the skin. The vein is tied to the lower end of the stripper so that when the top of the stripper is pulled, that section of vein is pulled inside out and torn from the leg. This process is repeated until all the varicose veins are removed, and their branches communicating with the deep veins of the leg tied off.

With the large veins gone, blood from the legs is returned to the heart through the thousands of small veins, the larger of which expand and become large veins.

Unfortunately, the valves in the new large veins are also prone to rupture, giving rise to a new set of varicose veins. Thus it is wise to try to eliminate prior to surgery the causes of increased venous pressure in the legs, such as chronic cough and constipation. Some women defer operation until after their final pregnancy. Pregnancy is a major factor in producing varicose veins in women, because it not only increases abdominal pressure and venous pressure in the legs, but the circulating hormones have a softening effect on ligaments and a dilating effect on blood vessels.

Another form of treatment involves injecting a sclerosing fluid into the veins to damage their lining, which makes the blood in them clot and results in their permanent obliteration. Because of various problems and dangers, this method is usually reserved for minor branch varicosities missed during stripping, and for minor recurrences.

People who do not want an operation or are unfit for surgery can control their varicose veins by firm elastic bandages and strapping.

Women's special problems

Disease may affect the structure or function of the female sexual organs; the breasts, the ovaries, the fallopian tubes, the uterus and cervix, the vagina and the external genital area (the vulva and perineum). Obstetrics is concerned with the care of women during pregnancy and childbirth while gynecology is the study of disease affecting all the female sexual organs.

The menstrual cycle is monthly evidence that conception has not occurred. The thick uterine lining that gradually builds up during the month under hormonal control and stimulation, breaks down when the hormone levels fall, and is shed with a certain amount of blood. Variations in cycle length, volume and duration of flow are the commonest disorders and are the result of an imbalance in the amounts of estrogen and progesterone hormones produced by the ovaries. Ovarian function is influenced by various areas in the brain and by the pituitary gland. Thyroid and adrenal disorders can also affect menstrual function.

The menstrual cycle may also be marked by other disorders such as depression, painful menstruation and premenstrual tension syndrome with weight gain.

Abnormal uterine bleeding may be either excessive or prolonged bleeding at the normal time, or any bleeding during the time between menstrual periods. Common causes of heavy menstrual flow are fibroids and polyps of the uterus, blood clotting disorders and hormonal imbalance. Irregular blood flow between periods may be caused by hormonal imbalance or abnormal conditions of the pelvic organs, such as tumors.

Although vaginal bleeding after the menopause always needs immediate investigation to exclude a tumor of the genital tract it may also be caused by estrogen administration, trauma, atrophic vaginitis and blood clotting disorders.

Amenorrhea or absence of the menstrual cycle during the reproductive years may be the result of many causes other than pregnancy. These include emotional crisis, serious illness, surgery, anorexia nervosa, thyroid disorder, an ovarian cyst or tumor, other glandular disorders, previous use of the oral contraceptive pill and certain drugs. In women who have never menstruated, developmental abnormalities of the uterus and vagina, chromosomal disorders and glandular disturbances have to be considered.

Cervicitis Inflammation of the cervix or neck of the womb is called cervicitis, a condition which may be acute or chronic. *Acute cervicitis* usually follows an abortion or childbirth, when an acute infection by staphylococcal, streptococcal or coliform bacteria invades the cervix. Fever, pain in the lower abdomen and vaginal discharge are the main symptoms. Acute cervicitis can also occur in gonorrhea with a profuse vaginal discharge. All forms of acute cervicitis respond quickly and are completely cured by antibiotics.

Chronic cervicitis is a term used to describe a variety of conditions, some of which are not truly inflammatory. If the cervix has a chronic infection and inflammation, there is a white or greenish vaginal discharge. On examination, this may be seen to be due to an infected laceration or erosion of the cervix.

Before treatment with diathermy cautery under anesthetic, it is advisable to take a smear of the cervical cells to look for any cancerous change. After cauterization the discharge becomes worse for about seven days after which there is complete healing.

Endometriosis is a disorder where islands of the specialized lining tissue of the uterus (endometrium) are found in unexpected sites in the pelvis such as the bowel wall, an ovary or a tube. Similar invasion of the muscular uterine wall by endometrium is termed adenomyosis. These areas of invasive endometrium respond in the usual way to the influence of estrogen and progesterone hormones, increasing in cellular and glandular activity and breaking down and bleeding at the end of each cycle. However, as the blood and cellular debris cannot escape, pressure builds up inside a cystic formation, causing local pain and discomfort before and at the time of menstruation. These cystic areas are sometimes termed chocolate cysts because of the appearance of the old blood contents. The condition is slowed by pregnancy and by treatment with drugs related to progesterone hormone. In many cases the affected areas may be surgically removed.

Fibroids Also known as fibromyoma, fibroid tumors or fibroids are nonmalignant masses that develop in the female uterus (womb). They are composed primarily of muscle cells with strands of fibrous tissue. They are one of the most common tumors in women, occurring in about one in four women of middle age.

The cause of their development is not

Fibroid tumors enlarge and soften during pregnancy but generally have no adverse effects during this period.

known, but they appear to be dependent upon estrogen (hormone substance) for their growth. From the time of puberty they tend to enlarge slowly, and to regress after the menopause.

They vary greatly in their size, ranging from millimetres to about 20 inches (50 cm) in diameter. They are classified according to the direction in which they grow. All fibroids begin to develop within the muscular wall or myometrium and most of them remain intramural. About one in five grow towards the outer surface and are described as subserosal, the serosa being the outer covering of the uterus. Half this number again grow inwards, distending the inner lining of the uterus (the endometrium), and these are known as submucosal.

Symptoms depend upon the site and the size of the tumors. Because their growth is relatively slow and occurs over a period of years, most of these tumors are found only on routine examination. Fibroids that grow inwards or outwards may develop a stalk, thereby becoming pedunculated. If a subserosal tumor twists upon itself to block blood supply, or bleeds from one of its vessels, a very serious condition develops with quite severe symptoms. Fortunately such occurrences are very rare.

Most frequently, symptoms occur after the age of 35. Large fibroids can produce a bulky uterus which causes a feeling of heaviness or discomfort within the pelvis. Sometimes pressure on the bladder may cause frequency of urination. Pressure on the rectum can cause constipation. Submucosal fibroids most often affect the menstrual cycle. An increase in the heaviness of bleeding, known as menorrhagia,

may result from blood loss from the endometrium that covers the offending fibroid. If clots occur as a result of particularly heavy bleeding, painful periods or dysmenorrhea often results, as may an iron-deficiency anemia.

Often it is only when the uterus is enlarged that the presence of fibroids is detected. In such circumstances, pregnancy must be excluded as the cause of the enlargement.

During pregnancy, fibroids enlarge and soften as the tissues of the uterus grow and become more pliable. Generally, pregnancy is unaffected by their presence. If the cavity of the uterus is, however, significantly distorted in shape, there is an associated reduction in fertility, and an increase in the occurrence of spontaneous abortion and premature labor. On rare occasions there may be obstruction to the delivery and occasionally bleeding in the postpartum period (after birth).

Treatment depends on the extent of fibroid development, and on the presence of symptoms or complications. Most frequently no treatment is required, except for annual assessment to detect the degree of change in size of the fibroids. Surgery may be required if there are pressure symptoms, menstrual problems that are not controlled adequately by hormones, extreme enlargement of the uterus, and significant distortion of the uterine cavity in someone who wishes to have children. In most cases of younger women, especially if they want to preserve their reproductive capacity, myomectomy is possible. This involves removal of the fibroids only. Almost half of the women who have undergone this operation are able to conceive and undertake pregnancy satisfactorily.

The recurrence of the growths or persistence of symptoms such as menorrhagia occur occasionally. A hysterectomy or removal of the uterus is undertaken most frequently in those over the age of 40 or in those who have completed their families. This procedure has the advantage of complete cure and it does not affect a person's sexuality, capacity to have sexual intercourse, or body weight, three common misconceptions.

A curettage (scraping the interior wall of the uterus) is usually performed prior to fibroid surgery to remove endometrial tumors or abnormalities. Malignant changes in fibroids are very uncommon.

Infection of the vagina or vaginitis is the most common genital tract infection and, in most cases, is easily diagnosed and treated. However, infection of the tubes (salpingitis) may be difficult to diagnose and treat and may lead to infertility. Gonorrheal infection in particular may cause significant tubal scarring if untreated. An intra-uterine device may act as a focus for infection. It may also cause heavier menstrual bleeding.

Thrush, the commonest cause of vaginitis, is the fungal organism *Candida*, previously called *Monilia*. It causes a marked itch, soreness, irritation and a creamy white, offensive smelling discharge. The common *Trichomonas* parasite can also cause a painful irritating vaginits with an offensive discharge. Both respond promptly to treatment.

Genital herpes virus infection, which causes crops of small blisters, is a very painful infection of the external genital area or vulva. If the cervix is infected during late pregnancy, the virus may pass to the infant during delivery causing severe encephalitis.

Genital wart virus infection of the vulva and vagina causes the development of multiple small warty tumors, which can be removed by chemical treatment or heat from a high frequency current (diathermy). Infection of the cervix or neck of the womb can result in an atypical PAP smear which is usually temporary.

Gonorrhea and other infections often involve Bartholin's duct and gland, causing pain and swelling on one side of the vulva. Antibiotics, and surgical treatment to drain any abscess which forms, are usually effective but symptoms may recur, requiring further surgery.

Involuntary leakage of urine during moments of coughing, sneezing or laughing, is another common complaint which may be caused by congenital or acquired disorders of the urinary tract, pelvic floor muscles or nervous system. Outside pressure on the bladder from pregnancy or a pelvic tumor may reduce the amount of urine the bladder can retain.

The most common cause of this distressing symptom is undue stretching and consequent weakness of the pelvic floor muscles aggravated by lack of exercise, age changes, obesity, generalized muscle weakness and prolapse of the uterus and vaginal wall.

Treatment may be medical or surgical. Exercises to strengthen pelvic floor muscles are important, both as a means of prevention and as treatment.

Painful intercourse may be caused by psychological or structural organic problems, or a combination of both. The problem may be transient or longstanding, affecting the vaginal opening or an area deep inside the vagina. External causes include local trauma, inflammation and infection, for example *Herpes* infection of the vulva or vagina causes severe local discomfort and painful intercourse. Internal discomfort may be the result of vaginal abnormalities, inflammation of the neck of the womb, a uterine prolapse, a tumor, an ovarian cyst or endometriosis.

Treatment of organic disorders is often easier than that of psychosexual problems which may require much time, patience and skilled counseling.

Premenstrual tension, experienced by some women, has unpleasant physical symptoms leading to an increase in irritability and aggressiveness. *(Salmer)*

Polyps of the cervix and uterine fibroids are common benign tumors which may cause abnormal bleeding. A large variety of ovarian cysts and tumors, may cause many different symptoms. Because early diagnosis is vital, regular, preferably annual, pelvic examinations are recommended for all women. Any persistent or enlarging swelling of an ovary may then be diagnosed early and treated.

Premenstrual tension Affecting over 50 per cent of women but mostly those in the 30–40 age group, premenstrual tension is characterized by both physical and psychological symptoms.

Physical signs include breast tenderness, lower abdominal discomfort, bloated feelings, change in bowel habit, lower limb pain or discomfort, ankle swelling, and marked periodic weight gain. Psychological evidence includes anxiety, irritability, inability to concentrate, depression prior to menstruation and aggressive feelings.

Treatment varies with the severity of the symptoms. Explanation of the reason for the symptoms (generally regarded as a reaction to temporarily disordered hormonal levels), correction of weight problems, encouragement of an active lifestyle, and low salt intake and discouragement of hypochondriac tendencies are all important. If active treatment is required, maximum fluid excretion in the premenstrual week can be promoted by diuretic drugs. Daily thiamine (vitamin B_1) also appears to be useful in prevention of breast tenderness. Marked changes of mood are occasionally treated with tranquilizers and anti-depressants if other treatment fails. Diuretic therapy at the start of the menstrual period may relieve tension.

Prolapse or sagging of the uterus or vaginal wall is a common condition which often occurs as a delayed result of injury to the pelvic floor muscles and ligaments during childbirth. This tendency is aggravated by degenerative muscle changes brought on by aging, physical debility and tumors which increase the weight of the uterus. The condition may be mild,

moderate or severe with heaviness in the pelvis, low backache and urinary and bowel symptoms. Surgery is required for moderate and severe symptoms.

Trichomoniasis A common cause of irritating vaginal discharge in adult females, trichomoniasis, caused by the small parasite *Trichomonas vaginalis* is generally transmitted by sexual contact.

Symptoms are usually minimal in the male. In the female the parasite often remains dormant in the spaces between the cells lining the vagina, with symptoms occurring when there is a reduction in the acidity of the vagina. This leads to rapid multiplication of the *Trichomonas vaginalis* organisms, which may occur during a general illness or during the menstrual flow. Apart from an irritating vaginal discharge, there may also be dyspareunia (pain during intercourse), an intolerable itch around the vulva, and urethritis.

Vaginal examination often reveals a frothy vaginal discharge, diagnosis being

confirmed by examining a sample under the microscope or by culturing the organism from a swab. Successful treatment is usually by the oral administration of tinidazole or metronidazole, sometimes combined with vaginal creams.

At times trichomoniasis may be associated with candidiasis or other sexually transmitted diseases such as gonorrhea.

Tumors Growths in the breast, uterus and ovary account for a large percentage of tumors in women. Breast tumors, benign and malignant, are the most common, followed by cancer of the neck of the uterus (the cervix). Cervical cancer is usually diagnosed before symptoms appear, following an annual PAP smear and cone biopsy. Cancer of the body of the uterus occurs with greater frequency in older women following the menopause. Abnormal uterine bleeding is usually the first sign and the PAP smear is very often normal. A PAP smear only tests for cancer of the cervix and not for malignancy in the interior or body of the uterus.

7 The Later Years

Aging — the Physical and Psychological Process

It is not fully understood how aging occurs and there are several theories which try to explain it. The process begins quite early in life and proceeds gradually until middle age when it accelerates. Advances in medical care, nutrition and general living conditions have resulted in longer life expectancy and therefore a higher proportion of old people and chronic illness than before. In many Western societies there is now a greater awareness of the needs of the elderly, and many research and educational programs in geriatrics have been established.

The gradual deterioration of living tissues, generally known as aging, is inevitable, but why the changes that bring it about occur is not well established.

With age, collagen and elastin, proteins that bind tissues together, become less elastic, causing sagging of body tissues and wrinkling of the skin. Most cell types become less efficient over time, probably due to some deterioration in the normal process of cell division.

Specific cells, such as those in the brain and heart muscles, are unable to divide, so that any damage they suffer results in the laying down of fibrous connective tissue in their place. These cells, once lost, do not regenerate.

The extent to which these processes occur varies greatly in different body tissues and organs. For example, hearing is at its peak during adolescence, whereas heart function does not start to deteriorate noticeably until the fourth decade.

Changes in the body systems

The first major body system that shows changes with age is the locomotor system, which is responsible for movement. Muscle strength and speed of reflexes begin to decline relatively early in life and slight deterioration has usually commenced by the age of twenty-five. Increasing rigidity of joints and loss of elasticity of ligaments also begins comparatively early.

Many elderly people remain physically active and mentally alert.

In fact, most body systems show some signs of reduced efficiency by the age of forty. The heart, kidneys, lungs and other organs all have less reserves. Fortunately the human body can function adequately even with a significant reduction in the efficiency of many organs. With age there is still a significant reserve and it is only when the body is subjected to prolonged or severe stress (such as infection or considerable exertion) that limitations become noticeable.

Changes in appearance and activity

The age of a person is generally reflected in the appearance. As age increases, there is continued degeneration of the skin with thinning of the epidermis and subcutaneous tissue, a loss of collagen fibers and a breakdown of the elastic fibers. This latter change, combined with the general disorganization of the dermis, leads to the formation of wrinkles.

Exposure to the elements, particularly the sun, hastens the process of skin degeneration. Drying of the skin that results from the excessive use of detergents and soaps is another cause. Smoking may also cause an increase in wrinkling, although it is not certain whether this is caused by chemicals circulating in the bloodstream, a local effect of the smoke on the skin surface, or a combination of both.

The forehead and outer corners of the eyes are among the first areas to develop noticeable wrinkles. They have usually begun to appear by the age of thirty.

Sexual activity may decline with increasing age, but the changes are related more to performance than desire. There are, of course, great variations among individuals. The female menopause, while associated with several body changes that result from reduced hormone levels, seems not to affect sexuality directly.

Mental capacity usually remains fully effective far longer than physical powers. This is partly because deterioration in creative thinking and innovation may be offset by increased experience and the ability to draw upon this when contemplating particular problems. Concentration is the first mental faculty that tarnishes a little.

Premature aging. Sometimes the aging process obviously occurs earlier or apparently more rapidly in an individual than would be expected in a person of that same age, way of life and family. When this occurs it is referred to as premature aging.

Excessive exposure to the sun may have the effect that the skin of a person of 35 years may resemble that of a 50 or 60 year old person living under more sheltered circumstances. A person may look much older after some severe acute illness like pneumonia or a major operation like a hysterectomy. The changes associated with old age are apparently accelerated; the person looks 'greyer', walks more slowly, reminisces more than before the illness.

Acute emotional or physical crisis, hardship or suffering, as prison camp inmates can attest, may also lead to obvious premature aging.

Psychological aspects of aging

As people grow older many adjustments have to be made; in some cases these adjustments are adequate, in others they are inadequate, and problems may arise. The changing state of health is an important factor. Most chronic diseases tend to begin in later years, and generally all result in some loss of mobility. This may lead to increasing isolation and to a general introversion or mental withdrawal which aggravates the situation.

The restricted world of the elderly person often leads to a more rigid, dogmatic view of life. A general lack of tolerance to any change is a common feature of old age. There is often a change in sex role with increasing age, particularly after retirement. The previously dominant male now loses the status of family provider,

As aging progresses, changes which occur in the body contribute to dry hair, loss of skin elasticity, fragile bones and stiff joints. (*Zefa*)

and the female partner often becomes 'caretaker'. Several studies have shown that the female copes better with a sudden loss of a partner than the male.

Depression among the aged may be associated with a particular cause (reactive depression) or arise *de novo* (endogenous depression). Suicide is also more common in the aged, and is often associated with a period of depression.

An increasing problem with memory is another psychological change of aging. Long-term memory tends to be affected much less than the memory of recent events. The elderly often appear to outsiders as 'living in the past'. It is open to conjecture whether this is the result of a definite physical change in the brain, a reduction in motivation to learn new things, or a combination of the two.

Areas of need in the aged are being increasingly defined and dealt with, but there is still much that can be done, and there are still many elderly people whose difficulties are not being cared for adequately.

Life expectancy

A long life, longevity is usually determined by a combination of factors, including heredity, nutrition, freedom from stress and good health care.

Retirement may become a time of social isolation but if adequate attention is paid to health and moderate activity, the psychological problems may be minimized. (Zefa)

sanitation and hygiene, which include adequate sewerage systems, clean drinking water and a higher standard of personal hygiene. These are thought to be largely responsible for the elimination of plagues and epidemics which at one time wiped out whole communities.

Another major factor has been immunization, including vaccination against the once deadly diseases of diphtheria, polio, tuberculosis and whooping cough. The use of antibiotics, especially in the treatment of pneumonias and tuberculosis, has also contributed to the increase in life expectancy.

The life expectancy of individuals will be affected by factors such as very stressful work and excessive alcohol consumption and cigarette smoking.

Heredity also may determine how long a person will live. An individual who had parents and grandparents who all lived into their eighties and nineties is likely to do the same. And someone whose predecessors died much earlier than normal, from strokes or heart attacks, is also likely to die earlier than the community average. It is extremely difficult to make satisfactory predictions for the life expectancy of the individual or a community as a whole, though average expectations for various age, cultural and socio-economic groups, such as may be employed for insurance purposes or medical care financing are readily calculated.

Whatever your age or circumstances, one of life's greatest pleasures is talking to a friend.

The average life expectancy of people has gradually increased over time. The early hunters and food gatherers often had a life expectancy of no more than forty-five years. In the last century life expectancy was probably not much more than sixty-five years, with a large proportion of children not reaching their fifth birthday. Present life expectancy in Westernized societies is 70 years for men, and longer for women. In rural societies in Third World countries the average life expectancy is only about fifty-five years.

Increase in life expectancy in advanced countries in modern times is attributed to many reasons. The principal ones are the improvements in public and personal

Health and old age

The effects of aging manifest themselves very differently, varying enormously between societies as well as individuals. The contented longevity of the Hunzas of the Himalayas is well known, and other isolated communities close to nature sometimes show remarkable cases of healthy individuals of extreme age.

Diet Elderly people living alone often need to be reminded to take a conscious interest in their diet. Within the possibilities of each household situation, sensible nutrition should be of first importance.

Positive attitudes Though medical science can as yet do little to combat the natural aging process, observation suggests that maintaining a basically sound diet and a balanced exercise program, the avoidance of excessive stress and the development of a commonsense attitude to the use of tobacco, alcohol and drugs are all factors in the slowing of the aging process or, at least, the moderation of its inevitable effects.

Both physical and mental capacities tend to maintain themselves by activity rather than inactivity, and a positive attitude to life, especially in the years of maturity, is of the greatest importance. The maintenance of purposeful interests and activities of value to oneself and the community is probably a major factor in achieving a healthy old age.

Above
Many people now enjoy a long retirement. (*Zefa*)

Below
Hobbies provide much enjoyment for older people.

Left
Bill Brandt, well known for his photography of social contrasts in the thirties, was still working in the seventies, constantly branching out into new and original avenues. *(The Sunday Times Magazine)*

Below
It is never too late to begin something new. This smiling swimmer took up the sport in her middle sixties. She is also proficient in yoga. *(The Sunday Times Magazine)*

Above
At the age of 87 this energetic Londoner, a champion cyclist in his youth, was still riding a bicycle, enabling him to lead an active, useful and interesting life, regularly visiting several schools in his capacity as governor. *(The Sunday Times Magazine)*

Care of the Aged

It is difficult to determine when middle age ends and old age begins; some people grow old at a much earlier stage of life than others. The aging process is the gradual deterioration of living tissues, which begins early in life, proceeds gradually until middle age and then accelerates.

Geriatrics

The branch of medicine that deals with the illnesses of the elderly is generally known as geriatrics. It includes the prevention of disease, rehabilitation, and social problems of the aged, as well as the actual physical treatment of disease. The British Geriatrics Society defines geriatrics as being 'concerned with the clinical, preventative, remedial and social aspects of illness in the elderly'.

What constitutes 'elderly' is hard to define. Often an arbitrary lower limit of 70 years is set.

The recognition of geriatrics as a major medical specialty has only occurred in the last twenty years and there is now an increasing awareness of the importance of teaching geriatrics in medical schools. Today most medical schools have set up departments specifically for this purpose. As geriatrics encompasses such a wide area, those people training to become gerontologists study both general medicine (diseases and their treatment) and rehabilitation in depth.

Geriatric services, much more than other specialties, operate with a 'team' approach. Most teams are based at hospitals, with specific geriatric units under the care of the gerontologist. In general, geriatric units tend to deal with patients with long-term problems. Short-term conditions, such as those requiring operations, are dealt with in general hospital wards, but the patient may subsequently be transferred to a geriatric unit should a period of rehabilitation be required.

The initial assessment of the patient may include both the medical condition, and the overall social condition, which is largely the responsibility of a social worker.

Most geriatric services are directly associated with rehabilitation units. Rehabilitation can be described as the 'physical' treatment of disability and includes the use of physical therapy and occupational therapy. The aim of this rehabilitation is to mobilize the particular patient as much as possible to allow him to either return home or to be able to live where less intensive assistance is available, for example a nursing home or retirement village.

Specific day-care centers have also been developed to allow people to live at home and still be able to have treatment during the day. Services provided at these centers may involve continuation of rehabilitation, the provision of minor medical procedures (for example, redressing a skin ul-

Practical aids to everyday living are available for those who are partially paralyzed. The dish sits on a non-slip mat, the food guard and 'rocker' knives make one-handed eating feasible. *(Westmead Center)*

Egg-cup has suction base to keep it steady. *(Westmead Center)*

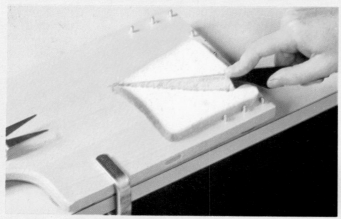

Special sandwich board clamped to the kitchen bench has pegs to stop bread falling to the floor, and a spike to anchor meat, cheese or vegetables for slicing. *(Westmead Center)*

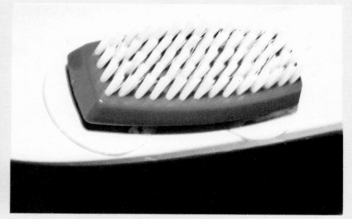

Nail brush is held to the bathroom shelf with suction caps. *(Westmead Center)*

Rehabilitation services help the elderly after hospitalization. *(John Watney Photo Library)*

cer), and sometimes follow-up of any social (family, economic, housing) problems.

Western societies are 'slowly aging', that is, there is an ever-increasing proportion of people in the community over the age of 70. This results in a greater need for geriatric services in the future, when the specialty of geriatrics will become even more important within the structure of medical care.

Gerontology

The study of the psychological, social and biological aspects of aging, gerontology differs from geriatrics in that the latter is a specific medical specialty concerned with the treatment of disorders of the elderly, disorders which can be medical, psychological or social.

Increasing proportion of elderly people Undoubtedly the most altered factor in gerontology is the increased proportion of elderly people in society. This change has occurred mainly because of the considerable reduction in the number of deaths from diseases affecting children and younger adults. A greater number of people now live to their full life expectancy. This is a trend in all Western societies.

The term 'senility' is often used to describe the feebleness of old age, particularly if associated with mental deterioration. Senility is difficult to define precisely, although the decreasing ability of a person to know how to care for himself adequately is probably a reasonable indicator of its onset.

Social aspects of aging One of the main problems associated with aging is the decreasing ability to carry out activities and functions that were once a normal part of life. Although in most cases the physical and mental changes occur very slowly (and vary greatly amongst individuals), society still tends to set rigid standards, particularly as to compulsory retirement.

Only in the last two decades has it become apparent that this inflexible attitude to the age of retirement is inappropriate. Many businessmen are quite able to function well into their seventies. On the other hand, with the increase in mechanization and in unemployment among younger people, some companies tend to make the retirement age earlier, as early as 55 in some cases.

Malnutrition in the elderly may be caused by an internal disorder or by nutritional imbalance.

Nutrition for the elderly

In this age of affluence, far too many senior citizens suffer from malnutrition. This is not always just a matter of too little of one or several nutrients. It may be a matter of too much of a good thing, excess of a particular vitamin for example. Sensitivity to substances harmless to most people can cause malnutrition in old people.

Malnutrition can result from a variety of internal disorders: diabetes mellitus and chronic bowel disease among them. It can be undernutrition, overnutrition or wrong nutrition. Nutritional imbalance may be a convenient term.

What does nutritional imbalance, or malnutrition, do to the aging individual? Obviously, since it constitutes an additional stress, and since stress itself causes aging, malnutrition hastens aging. At the same time, it weakens the organism as a whole, thereby creating fertile ground for a wide variety of ailments.

But it does a great deal more. It can, and does frequently, create specific deficiencies in the elderly: protein deficiencies, when the intake of the keystone nutrient is decreased; beriberi from deficiency of thiamine; pellagra from deficiency of nicotinic acid and other B vitamins (almost invariably associated with chronic alcoholism); scurvy from a prolonged, grossly inadequate intake of ascorbic acid.

The key nutrient, protein The most common deficiency in the elderly is deficiency of protein foods. There are good reasons for this. The protein foods, meat, eggs, fish, cheese (milk is a relatively dilute source of protein), for the most part require special preparation. They are more difficult to chew than are the high carbohydrate foods. Perhaps they pose more problems for the sensitive digestive tracts of some elderly persons.

Protein foods are not as palatable to most people as are the sweet, flavourful carbohydrate foods; and, finally, they tend to be more expensive. The latter objection is more apparent than real since cottage cheese and hamburger, superb sources of protein, are relatively inexpensive.

Lack of dietary proteins is a major factor in senile osteoporosis, and this disease is a common complaint in aged people. It can reasonably be estimated that the quantity of protein required should be 100 g daily.

The elderly may often have a deficiency of protein because meals which include meat or fish are more difficult to prepare and chew and can also be expensive.

Minerals Further problems may include deficiences of minerals. A deficit of potassium, the chief electrolyte of the cells, can result from a poor diet, but it also is brought about by a wide variety of conditions. Potassium deficit is favored by the fact that the body's conservation mechanisms for this mineral are either inefficient or non-existent.

Calcium deficiency probably occurs, although there is much disagreement as to how prevalent and important it is in the elderly. A poor intake of calcium may play a role in the development of senile osteoporosis. Good sources of calcium are milk and cheese, which certainly contribute to a satisfactory nutritional balance in the aged.

Magnesium deficiency is rare, but has been reported in association with chronic disease of the liver or intestinal tract. Iodine deficiency was frequent before salt was iodized. There is no syndrome of fluorine deficiency, but it appears probable that a generous intake of fluorine early in life helps preserve the teeth later in life.

Iron deficiency, and the anemia that it causes, can readily develop when there is blood loss from chronic infection or other causes, particularly if the dietary intake has been poor. Hypoferric anemia is far from being uncommon in the elderly, even in the absence of gastrointestinal bleeding. Green vegetables, peas, beans, prunes and figs are sources of iron.

Lack of adequate roughage in the diet favors constipation as does inadequate intake of water. Adequate water is also needed for optimal renal function.

Nutrient excess An important group of diseases is brought on by excesses of certain nutrients. Obesity, so strongly correlated with shortening of the life span, can be caused simply by excessive food intake or by eating a diet excessively high in carbohydrate, especially by those individuals who have been called 'carboholics'. ('Carboholics' have both an inordinate taste for carbohydrates and a tendency to put on weight, possibly because of an abnormally active mechanism for the synthesis of fat from carbohydrate.)

Fats Much attention has been focused on dietary fat in recent years; considerable evidence indicates that excessive intake of saturated fats (fats of milk, cheese, meat and eggs — in general, animal fats) favors atherosclerosis and its dismal train of cerebrovascular accidents, angina pectoris, coronary thrombosis and impaired circulation of the extremities.

Ingestion of a high proportion of unsaturated fats (soybean oil, corn oil, peanut oil — in general, vegetable fats, provided they are not hydrogenated) may reduce the incidence of atherosclerosis.

Although the precise role of cholesterol, which is derived not only from the diet but is also produced within the human organism, remains somewhat controversial it does appear to be positively correlated with atherosclerosis, at least in many persons. A high intake of saturated fats raises the blood cholesterol, while a high intake of polyunsaturated fats, plus restriction of saturated fats, appears to lower it. There is also something to be said for restriction of fat intake in general.

Diabetes mellitus is aggravated by excessive food intake, particularly excessive carbohydrate intake.

Salt Increased intake of sodium is correlated with an increased incidence of essential hypertension in susceptible persons. Obviously, moderation in the sodium intake is desirable. Those with essential hypertension, especially the hypertension associated with sodium retention,

A high protein diet based on fresh foods helps maintain vitality in old age.

should follow a strict low-sodium diet of approximately 250 milligrams of sodium a day. The availability of a large variety of palatable low-sodium foods and the modern art of cooking with herbs, wines and spices has removed the dreariness from the low-sodium diet. Excessive purines, which result from breakdown of protein, bring on gout in the predisposed.

Learning about sound nutrition How do the elderly become malnourished? Many older folk are sadly lacking in nutritional knowledge. Others are burdened with fad ideas. Many older people, particularly retired persons without vital interests, lack the will to go to the trouble of maintaining an adequate diet. Many live alone. Some, resenting deeply the lack of companionship, should be advised to enter institutions for old people.

Economic factors often enter the problem of malnutrition. Flour and sugar are the cheapest foodstuffs. Many old folk are plagued with poor teeth and uncertain digestions. The bland, palatable, low-protein foods go down well and without protest.

The steps in establishing and maintaining a proper diet for the elderly may include:

1 Education in the basic principles of nutrition Emphasize a balanced diet with a generous helping of protein, such as meat, cheese or fish, for every meal; generous intake of vegetables, not forgetting the legumes and the green, leafy vegetables; fruit; whole grain, enriched or restored bread and cereals; milk in moderation, and a vitamin supplement when the adequacy of the patient's total intake is questionable.

Most physicians would suggest limited intake of fat meat, gravy, ice cream and other fat mixtures; substitutions of highly unsaturated margarine for butter, vegetable oils for animal fats, avoidance of yolks of eggs, and skim or whole milk for cream. These limitations are indicated particularly if the elderly patient is overweight, has disease of the heart or blood vessels or has these diseases in the family.

2 Correction of physical ailments or inadequacies leading to ingestion of an improper diet.

3 Motivation of the individual, through hobbies and interests, to restore pleasure in living.

4 Consideration of economic factors, including instructions on how to make money go the farthest in terms of a balanced menu.

Nutrition for the elderly is reprinted, adapted, with permission, from 'Food for the Aged', *Abbottempo* magazine, Vol. 3, Book 4, published for Abbott Laboratories. Contributed by Harold Swanberg, M.D., President, Gerontology Foundation for America at the time of writing and W. D. Snively, Jr., M.D.

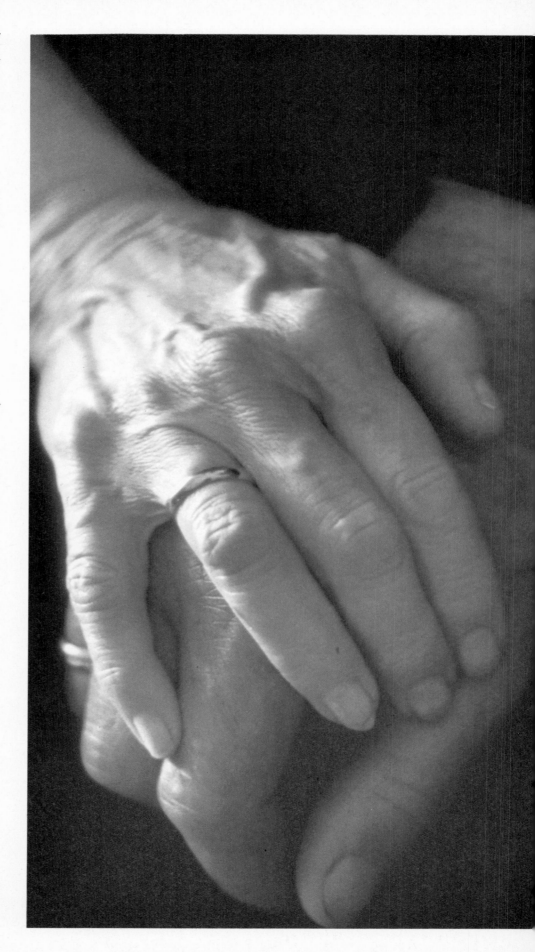

Growing old together brings its own
tranquility with a continuation of
shared pleasures.
(*Austral-International*)

Planning and coping with retirement

Withdrawal from the regular workforce as
a natural consequence of advancing age
often takes on the nature of a crisis in the
life of the individual. The overwhelming
importance of the economic aspects of
modern urban life, and the association of
personal status with economic standing
are major causes. More and more attention is therefore being given to educating
people adequately in preparation for retirement, especially as the average age of
retirement falls and employment opportunities are reduced.

Financial support is a key area that requires planning. Ideally, superannuation
and funding arrangements should be commenced at least ten years before the estimated time of retirement. Professional advice about investment as well as general
financial matters is advisable. If major expenses can be foreseen, such as moving to

a new house or replacing a car, they are
usually best undertaken prior to retirement.

Wise financial planning may mean the
difference between enjoyment and mere
existence during retirement. Range of
leisure activities and adequacy of diet may
both be impaired by poverty.

Social isolation As workmates provide the
principal companionship for many people
and by the time of retirement children
have often left home to establish their own
families, social isolation among retired
people is frequent. Death of a spouse and
general restriction of mobility because of
poor health are other factors that may contribute. Many elderly people living alone
in small dwellings or single rooms are isolated from the remainder of the community.

If the immediate or extended family is
close-knit, grandparents can play a family
role, but if people plan to move nearer
their children, such a change should be
implemented while they are young
enough to establish social contacts in
their new neighborhood.

Below
Sometimes the elderly live in social
isolation unless they have the
opportunity to be involved with
their family or social groups.

Retirement should include some
activities which provide interest
and a sense of purpose.

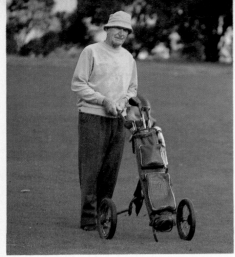

Above
For those who are enjoying good health in retirement the local golf club is a good leisure time activity.

Below
Nursing homes provide care for elderly people who are unable to look after themselves at home.

Loss of prestige or status associated with retirement can be considerable, and may be accompanied by depression and other psychological problems. Adequate socialization and appropriate leisure activities help to minimize such problems.

Keeping active Many old people derive pleasure and a sense of purpose from activities such as voluntary social work, hobbies and interests like fishing, bowling, caring for the garden, and handicrafts. Interaction with others is important as the children have usually left home, and sometimes a husband or wife dies some years before the partner. For some there is interaction with others in the form of babysitting and the extended family, for others it is gained through various clubs and senior citizens' groups.

Health Attention to physical and mental health is important at all ages, but especially for the elderly. About one person in four over the age of 65 will have some form of chronic or long-standing illness, but the effect on overall lifestyle can often be minimized by minor adjustments, such as new glasses or the acquisition of a hearing aid. Meals-on-wheels, Visiting Nurses and a number of other agencies are available for retired people with particular problems.

'Grey power' As the percentage of the population over the age of 60 increases, greater dissatisfaction is expressed about set ages of retirement. Many successful politicians, writers, philosophers and businessmen are still very active well into their seventies, although certain areas of employment are obviously more appropriate for younger workers.

With the growing recognition of the extent of the under-utilized resources of such people, the term 'grey power' has been coined to describe the political influence of people over sixty, particularly when directly related to their own lives.

Retirement villages Increasing attention is being given to providing suitable accommodation for older people.

Retirement villages have various types of dwellings in which residents may live quite independently, and for those who are unable to cope completely without assistance, communal meals, cleaning and other services are provided.

Although a sizeable initial payment is sometimes required, weekly expenses are usually below the pension level so that other items can be purchased and outings taken. Because these centers are extremely popular, there is generally a very long waiting list.

Nursing homes Elderly people are cared for in nursing homes when they are no longer able to live at home and look after themselves, but do not need specialized hospital care.

The inability to look after oneself may be the result of a stroke, or because of inability to walk, dress and eat, or to think clearly. There are also those who use the nursing home to convalesce after a major illness, and those whose regular home nurse or help has gone on holiday.

Complete or partial nursing care is provided depending on the requirements of the individual. Some homes are visited by experienced geriatric and medical specialists who advise on rehabilitation programs. Family doctors supervise medical care. Physical therapists and occupational therapists may also be attached to homes or private sessions can be arranged. As facilities vary widely, it is wise to visit several homes and make inquiries before choosing one, whether for oneself or for a relative.

It is an advantage if people can remain in their familiar home environment provided help is available to make this possible. Most elderly and disabled people prefer to remain independent for as long as possible in their own homes.

Most communities offer a number of services for senior citizens, such as adult day care programs; home health services; special transportation to shopping and 'meals-on-wheels' programs.

Problems and Diseases

More adjustments to changing circumstances occur in old age than at any other stage of life with the exception of adolescence. Physical deterioration and illness are major problems. About one in four people between the ages of 65 and 74 suffer from some form of chronic or long-standing illness, and these figures almost double among those aged 75 and over. Conditions such as hearing difficulties, visual impairment as a result of cataracts and arthritis of the hands and legs may restrict mobility and activities which once were a source of enjoyment.

On the positive side, however, medical knowledge is advancing rapidly, and many once feared conditions can now be cured or at least greatly alleviated.

Arthritis

This is an ancient disease, though it has not always been known as arthritis. Until the end of the nineteenth century, when arthritis was known as rheumatism, it was regarded as gout. It was not until World War II that the term 'arthritis' was established and distinctions were clearly made between the different kinds of arthritis. More than 32 million Americans suffer from one of the many forms of arthritis. The disease tends to occur more frequently among low-income groups than high-income groups and is much more common among women than men. Much research is now being done on arthritis.

Arthritis is one of the main causes of chronic disablement in all civilized countries, especially among people over 50 years of age. There are many different types of arthritis, which is the inflammation of a joint, usually causing pain, swelling and restriction of movement. In general parlance, the term arthritis includes rheumatism of all sorts, whether the joint is involved or not.

Diseases like fibrositis and lumbago are not regarded as types of arthritis by the medical profession; nor are joint pains that are caused by torn cartilage, foreign bodies or fractures involving the joint surface.

Forms of arthritis The main types of arthritis are rheumatoid arthritis, osteoarthritis, gouty arthritis, arthritis caused by infections, the arthritis of rheumatic fever, and ankylosing spondylitis.

Of the latter two, arthritis of rheumatic fever occurs in children and the joints return to normal when the fever is over, whilst ankylosing spondylitis most commonly affects young men. A progressive inflammatory arthritis of the spine, it becomes a great handicap as the whole spine stiffens gradually over the years, finally becoming rigid. Pain-relieving drugs and radiotherapy appear to stop the progress of the disease in some cases so early treatment is desirable.

Rheumatoid arthritis and osteoarthritis are by far the most common types.

Arthritis is also a feature of the following diseases, psoriasis, Reiter's syndrome, systemic lupus erythematosus, scleroderma, polyarteritis nodosa, ulcerative colitis, sarcoidosis, regional ileitis (Crohn's disease), Henoch-Schönlein syndrome, Sjögren's syndrome, diabetes, hemophilia, syringomyelia, Gaucher's disease, scurvy, acromegaly, amyloidosis, erythema nodosum and Behçet's syndrome.

Symptoms and effects A particular type of arthritis may involve only one joint at a time or many joints. The size and distribution of the joints attacked can also be typical of the arthritis in question; for example, small joints of the hand are affected in rheumatoid arthritis.

The onset of arthritis may be sudden, in a matter of hours, or slow, during several days or weeks. The illness may be short and self-limiting, recur in bouts or progress to a chronic disabling stage. The joints may be left unchanged after the acute episode, as in rheumatic fever; or be

1 Rheumatoid arthritis commonly begins in the finger joints, which become swollen.

2 Swollen joints caused by gouty arthritis. *(Westmead Center)*

1

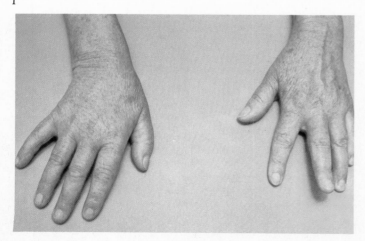

2

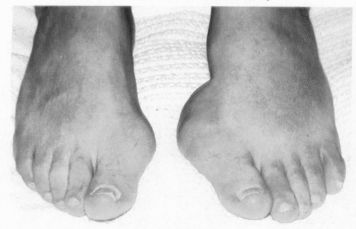

so damaged with each attack as to become almost immobile and deformed, as in severe rheumatoid arthritis or severe ankylosing spondylitis. The arthritis may be only part of a disease picture, as in hemophilia; or it may be the only feature, as in osteoarthritis. Frequently the joint disorder is accompanied by a fever and a feeling of being unwell.

Rheumatoid arthritis A chronic disease mainly affecting the joints of the limbs although all joints can be involved, rheumatoid arthritis occurs three times more frequently in women than in men. Although the disease can start insidiously at any age, it is more common about the age of forty years, when it seems to be precipitated by excessive and continuing worry and overwork.

The most common beginning of rheumatoid arthritis is swollen, painful, stiff joints at the bottom of the fingers, sometimes accompanied by a fever, loss of appetite, a headache and a general feeling of being unwell.

The disease progresses in a series of acute episodes alternating with periods of stiffness only in the mornings, until the wrist, elbows and shoulders, ankles and knees are involved. The arthritis so damages the joints that increasing stiffness, pain and swelling persist between attacks resulting in marked deformities and increasing disability. Although some become bedridden, in many it is a mild disease with little incapacity.

Bed rest, physical therapy and pain-relieving drugs like aspirin and butazolidine are the mainstay of treatment. Cortisone-like drugs and gold injections are used in severe rheumatoid arthritis. In the individual case, the earlier proper treatment is begun the better the results will be.

Osteoarthritis Sometimes called *osteoarthrosis* because it is not an inflammatory disease of the joints but a degenerative change in the gristle or cartilage inside the joint, osteoarthritis causes bony outgrowths at the edge of the joint. It is extremely common and, to some degree, almost inevitable in the aged.

Many people with osteoarthritis have very little pain or stiffness and the disease causes little inconvenience. It affects joints that have been injured, often a long time before, or joints that have had a lot of wear and tear because of the person's occupation or long-term overweight. Large joints, like the hips or back, or small joints in the toe or thumb are often affected.

The person with osteoarthritis is generally over fifty years of age and feels an aching pain with stiffness and limited movement in the involved joint. A cracking noise is often heard and felt on movement. There is no general illness.

As there is no cure, the treatment for osteoarthritis aims to relieve the symptoms with rest, avoidance of undue stress on the joint in question and pain-relieving drugs. Overweight patients should lose weight, especially if the ankles, knees, hips or back are involved. Severe osteoarthritis of the hip can be treated successfully by replacing the hip joint surgically with an artificial joint.

Gouty arthritis The person who suffers sudden severe pain in a joint which is obviously red, exceptionally tender to touch and is at the base of the big toe (the metatarsophalangeal joint), is almost certainly suffering from the metabolic disease gouty arthritis or acute gout. Although repeated attacks tend to occur in other joints as well, between attacks the joints may be perfectly normal. In some people with chronic gout there is persistent pain and stiffness resulting in the joint deformities and deposits of hard chalky lumps called tophi.

Infectious arthritis When caused by pus-forming organisms like streptococcus, staphylococcus, gonococcus or pneumococcus, infectious arthritis starts suddenly over 24 hours with pain, swelling and restricted movement in one joint. There is a marked fever and the person usually looks and feels very ill. A source of infection like a boil or wound can be found if diligently sought, in the genital tract in the case of the gonococcus. If rest in bed and local and general appropriate antibiotics are given, the outcome is excellent, with the joints returning to normal function in a few weeks.

Tuberculous arthritis of the hips or spine has a slow onset and a slow recovery with antituberculous drugs.

Arthritis caused by a virus, like German measles, usually has a sudden onset but is a self-limiting disorder and complete recovery follows.

Cancer

Cancer in its manifold forms is a major threat to life and well-being in all the advanced civilizations of the world today. Medical historical studies have revealed that ancient civilizations knew cancer too, and the tenth-century Arab physician Abulcasis commented on the necessity for total surgical removal of cancer, advising against surgery where this was not possible.

Research into causes, treatment and prevention of cancer is a major activity of medical science the world over, focusing especially on the attempt to identify exactly the process of cell growth malignancy.

The various modes of treatment, principally surgery, radiation treatment and chemotherapy, achieve varying degrees of success, according to the particular case.

A comprehensive overview of cancer occurrence and treatment at the present time is given here, followed by a detailed description of bowel cancer, as the latter occurs most frequently in people over the age of 50.

The word cancer is used in everyday language to describe any form of malignancy, although in precise medical terms it refers to an epithelial cell growth or carcinoma. When the normal control mechanisms that regulate the growth of cells fail, a neoplasm ('new formation') or tumor occurs. If this altered growth is totally out of control and causes the cells to invade other tissues, it is described as malignant. Malignant tumors from connective tissue cells are called sarcomas, and those from the blood cells are called leukemias or lymphomas.

Spread of malignancy may be by direct invasion of neighboring tissues, or by cancer cells entering the bloodstream and becoming established in a distant organ or tissue, or when cancer cells are spread by the lymphatic system to involve nearby glands (lymph nodes). Occasionally spread occurs along natural body passages or cavities. For example, cancer cells from the stomach may travel to a pouch within the abdomen between the rectum and vagina. Symptoms resulting from cancer may be due either to a direct effect of the invasion of surrounding tissues or to the more distant spread.

A site at which a cancer first develops is called the primary site. The sites to which cancer may seed are called secondary sites.

How cancer develops The exact mechanism by which normal cells become malignant is not fully understood. It is assumed that there is a spontaneous failure of a certain percentage of cells to remain 'normal'. The percentage increases when there is an hereditary tendency to certain types of cancer within families, and also when the amount of irritation or damage done to a cell is excessive.

The relationship between long-term exposure to sunlight and the development of skin cancers; between exposure to nuclear radiation and leukemia development, and between smoking and lung cancer are well known examples of this type of cell irritation. Viruses are thought to play a role in the development of some tumors.

It appears that the immune system of the body normally counteracts malignant cells. In situations where the immune system becomes ineffective, due to old age, severe illness, or the use of special immunosuppressive drugs in kidney transplants, tumors are much more frequent.

Disease distribution The relative occurrence of different types of cancer varies according to sex, age and geographical distribution. Cancer appears to be more common in today's population, but this is partly because people are living longer and because other problems of infection and nutritional disturbance are now more adequately controlled.

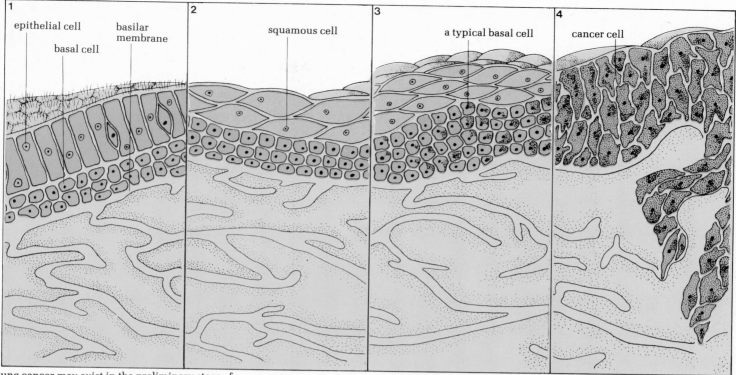

1 epithelial cell basal cell basilar membrane

2 squamous cell

3 a typical basal cell

4 cancer cell

Lung cancer may exist in the preliminary stages for some years.

1 First stage. The basal cells which lie beneath the epithelial layer of the lung tissue undergo excessive multiplication in the early stage.

2 Second stage. The epithelial cells are replaced by capsule-shaped squamous cells which form in response to chronic local irritation.

3 Third stage. Basal cells resume rapid multiplication but have changed character, probably indicating an altered genetic structure.

4 Fourth stage. The basal cells invade all surrounding tissue and the disease has reached an advanced and probably fatal stage.

The most common cancers in adult males are those of the skin, lung, large bowel, stomach and prostate, and leukemias and lymphomas; in adult females those of the breast, uterus, large bowel, skin and stomach, and lymphomas and leukemia. Children are less prone than adults to develop cancer; leukemias, lymphomas and kidney and brain tumors are most common malignancies in this age group.

Symptoms Various symptoms may be early indications of a developing cancer, and although in most cases the particular symptom will prove to be the result of some other condition, medical assessment is needed to rule out the possibilities of cancer. Eight warning signs of a developing cancer are:

1. Any new lump or swelling that persists for more than 4–6 weeks, especially in the breast.

2. Abnormal bleeding, particularly from the bowel, breast or vagina.

3. Indigestion or other abdominal symptoms that persist for more than 4–6 weeks.

4. Constipation or diarrhea (or alternation of the two) that has been present for more than 4–6 weeks.

5. Hoarseness of the voice or difficulty in swallowing present for more than 4–6

weeks.

6. Any sore in the skin or lining of the mouth that has not healed within 4–6 weeks.

7. Any change in the size and shape of any mole or wart; persistent bleeding or itching should also be checked.

8. Sudden or unexplained loss of weight.

Early diagnosis is the key to successful treatment of cancer. The often quoted statement 'cancer is a diagnosis, not a sentence' is certainly true, and it should be remembered that cancers can be detected before they cause symptoms, either by the patient (as with cancer of the breast) or by the examining doctor (as with cancer of the cervix).

Cancer prevention The two main areas of cancer prevention are the avoidance of certain factors that increase the likelihood of developing cancer (such factors are called carcinogens), and the detection of a cancer at a very early stage before it has spread significantly to other tissues.

Carcinogenic factors to be avoided include long-term, extensive exposure to sunlight which increases the risk of contracting skin cancer. The use of sunscreen creams and lotions, sun hats with wide brims to protect the face, and protective

clothing are all helpful in reducing the risk of skin cancer.

The relationship of cigarette smoking to lung cancer is well documented, and public health education programs designed to dissuade people from smoking can be regarded as a form of cancer prevention.

Industries now take special precautions to minimize the exposure of workers to various chemical carcinogens. Miners and other workers exposed to asbestos wear special protective clothes because of the increased risk of lung cancer, and precautions are also taken with radiation and radioactive materials which cause a greater incidence of leukemia, as well as other health problems. Aniline dyes, once used in great quantities in the rubber industry, have been modified chemically because of a risk of bladder cancer.

Another aspect of cancer prevention in the community is regular examination or screening, to detect a malignancy in its early stages when the chances of complete cure are at a maximum. Some tests are made only when certain symptoms develop (such as blood in the urine which usually indicates the need for kidney x-rays), while other tests are routine even if symptoms are absent (such as the Papanicolaou smear to detect changes in the cervix of the uterus).

Most authorities recommend that the 'Pap test' be done on all women every one to three years once sexual intercourse is commenced. The procedure involves scraping cells from the surface of the cervix and examining them under the microscope for any cancerous change, a state that may develop several years before the disease spreads to other parts of the body.

It is wise to use some form of
protection against the sun's rays,
such as an umbrella or a sun hat
with sunglasses and sun block
cream.

Self-examination of breasts by women
is an important screening test. A small tumor in the breast may be detected before
it spreads to other parts of the body and
regular self-examination reduces the
chance of such a tumor remaining
undetected. A similar annual examination
by a doctor is also recommended.

Mammography (an x-ray that shows up
the breast tissues), regular chest x-rays,
and chemical testing for blood in the feces are other screening tests that may be
used in patients at risk. Tubes that view
the inside lining of the stomach (gastro-
scopes) are often used in Japan as screening tests for cancer because of the great
incidence of stomach tumors in that
country.

Cancer will become an increasingly important health problem in the community
as the average age of the population increases and other illnesses, such as infections and nutritional problems are controlled more effectively. The degree of
success achieved by cancer prevention
procedures depends on public education,
but continual research into effective and
practical screening tests will enable risks
to be decreased even further.

Oncology is the general term used to describe both the study and treatment of
cancers. Once a cancer is suspected,
confirmation of the diagnosis and determination of the type, as well as the extent
of spread of the tumor, is important.
X-rays, CAT (computerized axial
tomography) scans, radioisotope scans
and sometimes procedures such as bron-
choscopy and laparotomy may be used,
and tissue may be removed and examined
under a miscroscope to determine exactly
what it is, as with lymph glands (nodes)
and breast lumps.

The three main types of cancer treatment are surgery, radiotherapy and
chemotherapy, often used in combination. The particular method chosen depends on many factors, including the type
of malignancy, the extent to which it has
spread, the site of the tumor, and the general health of the patient concerned.

Surgery It has been estimated that about
one in three patients who have a malignant tumor can be cured by surgery. The
aim of surgery is to remove all malignant
cells from the body if possible; and to relieve symptoms and delay complications
when it is not. Common situations where
non-curative surgery may be of value is in
the relief of obstruction (such as in cancer
of the bowel), the control of bleeding
(such as in stomach cancer), and in pain
relief (such as when a tumor is pressing
on a nerve). Removal of an infected tumor
is also necessary sometimes.

The growth of some cancers, such as
those of the breast, may be influenced by
hormones. Destruction or removal of certain hormone-producing glands, such as
the ovaries, the adrenals, and parts of the
pituitary gland, may stop or reverse the
cancer growth for a while. Malignant
cells from a cancer may spread to nearby
lymph glands and they are often removed
during surgery to prevent the possibility
of contamination.

Radiotherapy Radio or x-ray therapy can
be given with special ray-making
machines or by radioactive needles embedded directly into the cancer tissue.
The latter method is used particularly to
treat cancers of the womb (uterus).

Radiation damages all tissues, but tumor cells, which multiply more rapidly
than normal cells, are more sensitive to
radiation and do not recover as quickly.
Tumors of the skin, bladder and cervix
are examples of growths that are often
treated by irradiation. Hyperbaric
chambers with a high pressure of oxygen,
and microwave heating of tissue are two
means of increasing the relative sensitivity of tumor cells to the irradiation.

Gamma camera used in cancer
diagnosis. (Westmead Center)

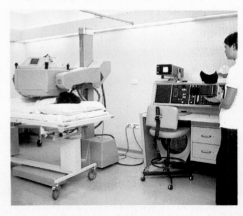

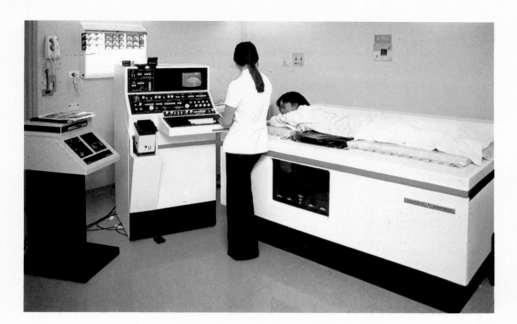

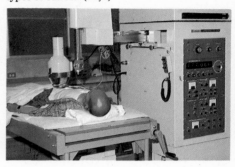

Left
The octason or ultrasound 'camera' is a medical application of the principle of sonar. The sound waves bounce off the interfaces between organs. Ultrasound is useful in the diagnosis of cancer. *(Westmead Center)*

Below
Cobalt treatment is used for some types of cancer. *(Zefa)*

Right
A radiopharmacist preparing a dose of a radioactive tracer for gamma photography. *(Westmead Center)*

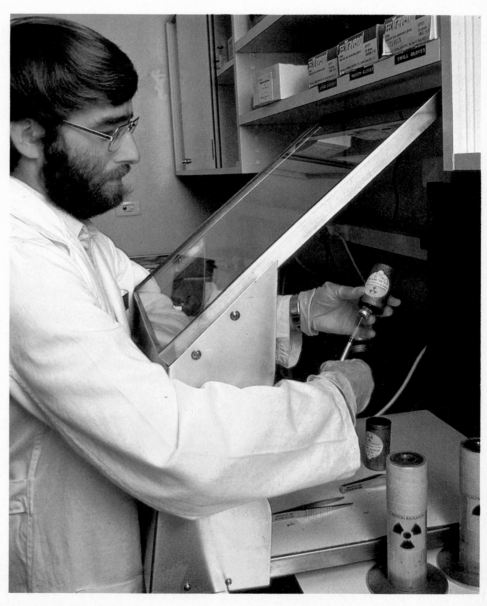

Chemotherapy The use of drugs (chemotherapy) is the third major form of cancer treatment and many advances have been made in the last 20 years in this area. Cytotoxic drugs are used to control the growth of malignant tumor cells, generally in advanced cases of cancer when surgery is not possible, but also as the mainstay of treatment of tumors of the blood cells, for example in leukemia.

General care Other things to be considered when planning the overall care of a patient with cancer include an explanation of what is going to be done, including expected complications. Information was sometimes withheld in the past, but few health professionals would now advocate this.

Physical support is needed for such things as pain relief, treating infection, and ensuring that adequate nursing, nutrition and assistance are available. Symptoms need to be treated as they become apparent, especially important if the condition has become incurable.

Emotional and psychological needs and social problems should not be ignored; they may become especially complex and severe as death approaches. Availability of appropriate resources is essential, and if the person is being nursed at home, the family general practitioner often acts as co-ordinator for the various skilled people involved.

Specially equipped hospices that look after terminally ill patients have been set up in many cities to provide ready access to the professional help that may be needed by the patient and his family.

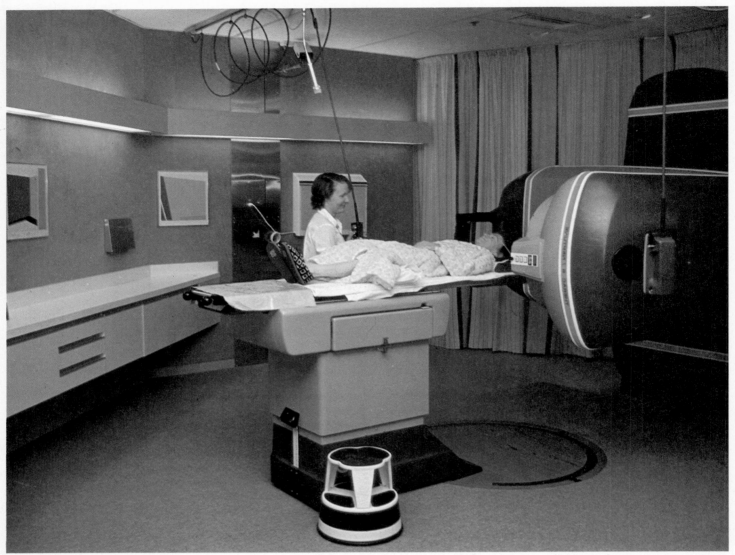

Linear accelerator used to treat
malignant tumors by radiation.
(Westmead Center)

Cancer of the bowel

The bowel includes that part of the digestive system extending from the stomach to the anus, and cancer of the bowel is an extremely common form of malignant tumor in adults. It is equally common in men and women, and is usually noted in people more than 50 years of age.

Most bowel growths occur in the colon and rectum. Cancers of the small bowel are quite rare, possibly partly because of the more rapid turnover of the lining cells in the small bowel. Although the rectum constitutes only a small portion of the large bowel, it is the site of approximately 50 per cent of all bowel tumors.

Symptoms and diagnosis The clinical features associated with bowel cancer depend largely on its site and size. Cancers on the right side (ascending and transverse colon) of the large bowel generally do not become apparent until the disease is well advanced because the feces in this section are still quite watery, and obstruction will not occur unless constriction or narrowing is very severe. Often these tumors will bleed so slowly that blood mixed with the feces is not noticed. In such cases anemia often develops.

The contents of the colon harden as they pass down the bowel (due to absorption of water) so that obstruction occurs more readily on the left side (descending colon, sigmoid colon and rectum) and the presence of tumors is usually apparent at an early stage. Bleeding, and therefore anemia, is less common. Tumors of the rectum, being close to the external orifice, produce more symptoms than those in other parts of the large bowel. The passage of blood, a feeling of discomfort, and sometimes pain are symptoms of the disease being present in this area.

A cancer can sometimes be felt through the abdominal wall as a hard lump. Manual examination by palpation or visual examination by means of the proctoscope may detect an abnormal mass. The special technique of sigmoidoscopy, in which a special viewing tube is passed up the bowel via the rectum, allows direct visualization of the last 10 inches (25 cm) of the large bowel, an area that accounts for two-thirds of all bowel tumors.

Treatment Surgical removal of growths to cure, or reduce the risk of later complications such as obstruction or bleeding, is normally carried out. The exact type of procedure depends on the site, size and extent of spread of the cancer.

A colostomy (when a permanent or temporary artificial opening is made in the abdominal wall) is often performed when the cancer is removed, and the two cut pieces of bowel are rejoined at a later date. This technique minimizes the possibility of infection from the bowel at the time of the operation and allows some healing prior to subsequent rejoining of the bowel.

Radiotherapy may be used either before or after the operation. The presence of spread of the cancer to distant tissues or organs is considered when deciding

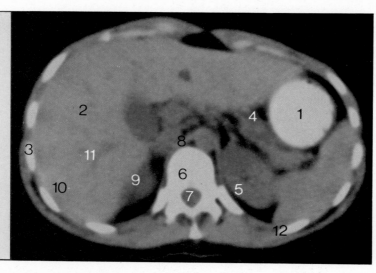

CAT scanner image of the body.

1 liver
2 stomach
3 ribs
4 gall bladder
5 top of right kidney
6 spine
7 spinal canal
8 aorta
9 left kidney
10 spleen
11 pancreas
12 ribs

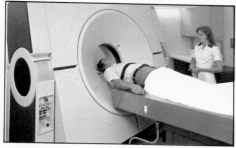

Cancer diagnosis. CAT scanner used for precision diagnosis of cancer. The image of the area under examination is projected on a screen. Refined computer control allows contrast to be altered to bring particular areas into special prominence for examination. *(Westmead Center)*

whether to use this form of treatment. Cyto-toxic drugs are also used occasionally.

Predisposing conditions Some conditions frequently become cancerous. Growths from the inside bowel wall (polyps), which are normally non-malignant, may later become cancerous and therefore should be removed if detected. Polyposis coli is an inherited condition in which an affected person has literally thousands of polyps in the bowel. The chance of one of these becoming malignant is virtually 100 per cent, and routine removal of all the colon is recommended.

Ulcerative colitis is another condition which, if chronically active, may give rise to the development of a cancer. Patients with this condition should be checked regularly.

Routine testing of the feces for blood has been recommended recently as a 'screening test' for bowel cancer. The test may detect polyps that are bleeding prior to malignant change, as well as detecting early cancers. Several curable cases have been detected by this method but the value and cost-effectiveness of the technique is yet to be established.

Very little can be done to prevent bowel cancer, except for removing the colon in patients with polyposis coli. Bowel cancer is more common in some cultures than in others, and some authorities believe that low fiber content in the diet is a reason for its increased prevalence in Western society. 'Roughage' or fiber in food has long been recommended to promote regular bowel habits and avoidance of constipation, which is commonly believed to contribute to the condition. The full explanation of the causes of bowel cancer involves factors which are yet to be clearly determined.

Cardiovascular disease

Diseases of the heart and blood vessels, particularly high blood pressure (hypertension) and restriction of blood flow caused by narrowing of the arteries (from atherosclerosis), are major causes of death in the Western world.

High blood pressure Arteries are the blood vessels conveying blood from the heart. The thick muscular left ventricle of the heart receives oxygenated blood from the lungs and pumps it through the arteries leading to the tissues of the body. The right ventricle pumps de-oxygenated blood returning from the tissues to the lungs.

Because the left ventricle pumps blood through the aorta, the main artery, to the entire body, fairly high pressure is needed to propel the blood along its course.

The peak pressure when the heart contracts is called *systolic* pressure. The lower pressure maintained during the resting phase of the heart by the elasticity of the arteries and the resistance of the terminal arteries is described as *diastolic* pressure. The different levels of pressure are represented by two numbers. For instance, the numbers 120/80 indicate that the first number is the higher pressure, the systolic, and the second number the lower pressure, the diastolic. The normal range of blood pressure is 100 to 140 for systolic and 70 to 90 for diastolic.

During the heart's relaxation phase, or diastole, the distended arteries contract and force the blood along. If the arteries lose elasticity then, with each beat of the heart, the blood pressure will reach higher levels.

'High blood pressure', or hypertension, refers to both systolic and diastolic pressure. Although 'blood pressure' as commonly used usually refers to high blood pressure, low blood pressure may occasionally indicate a medical condition, for example the rare Addison's disease; the state of shock following severe hemorrhage; or an excessive dose of drugs that lower blood pressure.

Although high blood pressure can be caused by diseases of the kidneys or adrenal glands, in the most usual condition, essential hypertension, the cause is unknown. However, it does tend to occur in particular families and may be aggravated by lack of exercise, obesity, excessive salt in the diet and emotional stress.

High blood pressure damages the arteries, stresses the heart and may precipitate a burst blood vessel in the brain causing a stroke. Blood pressure can only be assessed by measuring it. Although blood pressure may be dangerously high, a person may feel perfectly well.

Treatment for high blood pressure is usually given when the systolic or diastolic pressure exceeds a certain level; the level depends on the patient's age.

A wide choice of safe and effective drugs is available for the treatment of high blood pressure. If one sort of drug gives an unpleasant side effect, another one can almost certainly be used satisfactorily. Usually two or more drugs are used together.

Cardiovascular conditions such as high blood pressure may be aggravated by overweight.

The risk of developing coronary disease may be lowered if a healthy lifestyle is maintained.

If medications are taken regularly and the blood pressure is checked from time to time, the results of treatment are usually good. If drugs are not necessary, or unsatisfactory for some reason, a low-salt diet, regular exercise and the avoidance of overweight may help.

Atherosclerosis Hypertension increases the likelihood of developing atherosclerosis, a condition which tends to occur as one gets older, and in which the walls of arteries thicken and harden. By narrowing the arteries with deposits of atheroma, a fatty substance, atherosclerosis reduces the blood flow. The coronary arteries, supplying the muscular tissue of the heart, may be easily blocked and if the narrowing is severe enough, the heart muscle is deprived of blood. As a result, pain on exertion, described as angina, or a heart attack where the blood clots in the blocked artery resulting in coronary thrombosis may occur.

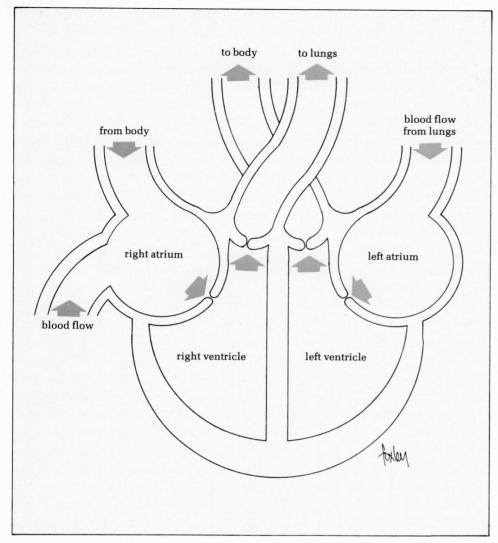

to body

to lungs

from body

blood flow from lungs

right atrium

left atrium

blood flow

right ventricle

left ventricle

Cross section of the heart. The arrows indicate the direction of blood flow. (Westmead Center)

Cataracts

An opacity in the lens of the eye, a cataract interferes with vision by interrupting the light waves entering the eye. The opacity may be a single large area or several small spots.

Cataracts are the most common eye problem in adults over the age of fifty. The person notices a gradual painless failure in sight, sometimes with blurring of vision. At first the vision can be restored with glasses but, sometimes after years, and sometimes within months, the lens becomes completely opaque and the sight is severely impaired. When this happens a light shone in the pupil of the eye reveals a white opacity.

Causes The lens of the eye has no blood supply and the majority of its cells cannot divide. Their only function is to remain transparent, but their response to damage or a defect, be it disordered metabolism, radiation, inflammation or a fault in development, is to become opaque. However, the large majority of cataracts are a result of simple senile degenerative change rather like the whitening of hair which is due to degeneration of the epithelial cells of the hair. In the majority of people over 60 years old there is some degree of lens opacity but in only a few of them does the opacity become sufficient to be called a cataract.

The other causes of cataract are numerous and varied. The incidence of these causes varies greatly from country to country. The causes include accidents, such as a perforating wound involving the lens capsule, or protracted inflammation of the iris and the ciliary body producing toxins. Diabetics are particularly liable to earlier development of cataracts of the senile variety.

If there is a low blood calcium caused by deficiency of the parathyroid gland, cataracts may develop. In industry, prolonged excessive exposure to infra-red radiation, gamma radiation or heat may cause cataracts, so appropriate precautions such as wearing protective goggles should be taken. Drugs which cause cataracts include prolonged high doses of corticosteroids including phenothiazines such as chlorpromazine.

Babies may be born with cataracts which affect one or both eyes. Often the cause of these cataracts is not known but German measles (rubella) in the mother in the first three months of pregnancy and a metabolic disorder called galactosemia are known causes. Generally speaking it is accepted that although some congenital cataracts are hereditary many more are a result of some intra-uterine influence present during the formation of the lens.

Victims of heart attack often respond well to exercise programs carried out under supervision. (Westmead Center)

By depriving the brain of blood, atherosclerosis may also cause a stroke. The kidneys may respond to atherosclerosis by producing a hormone, renin, which constricts blood vessels and further raises the blood pressure. If the arteries of the legs become narrowed, atherosclerosis causes severe pain in the calf muscles during walking which improves with rest.

Atherosclerosis and subsequent coronary thrombosis have been statistically linked with cigarette smoking, hypertension, obesity, diabetes, the fatty substances (the lipids) in the blood and cholesterol.

A Coronary Risk Profile, worked out in Framingham, Massachusetts describes the type of person likely to develop coronary heart disease: an over-weight, 65 year-old man, who smokes cigarettes, has high blood pressure, an enlarged heart, diabetes and high blood cholesterol, has almost a 50 per cent chance of developing coronary disease. By comparison a 45 year-old woman, if she is a non-smoker and free from hypertension and other risk factors has only a 0.4 per cent chance of developing it.

The development of atherosclerosis may be lessened by correcting some of the risk factors. It may be worthwhile to give up cigarettes, to exercise regularly, to avoid obesity and to have hypertension or diabetes controlled. In spite of numerous world-wide trials, prevention of atherosclerosis by lowering the blood cholesterol level through alteration of the diet has not produced any convincing results.

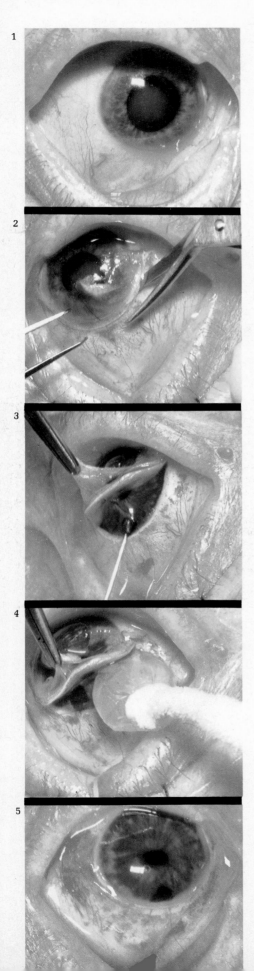

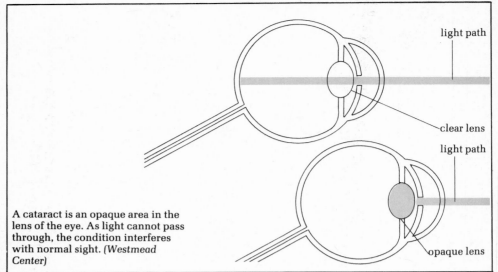

A cataract is an opaque area in the lens of the eye. As light cannot pass through, the condition interferes with normal sight. (*Westmead Center*)

Left
A brilliant series of photographs of a cataract removal operation at the Westmead Center.

1 The cloudy appearance of the cataract

2 The cornea incised

3 The iris is now visible

4 The cataract is removed using a cryoprobe

5 The corneal incision is sutured

Babies with congenital cataract often have some other defect within the eye.
Treatment The usual treatment of cataracts in adults is to remove them surgically. In the operation the lens is removed from the lens capsule. Methods first employed in the 1950s use pancreatic enzymes to release the lens from its attachments so it is more easily removed. Freezing techniques and ultrasonic probes are also employed.

Recently lenses have been replaced by an artificial lens, but some have caused reactions within the eye. Lens implants are gaining more favor. Techniques which dissolve the lens contents and suck them out have also been pioneered, and research continues.

Cataract removal is 95 per cent successful in that some, though not normal, vision is regained. The treatment and removal of cataracts is a delicate operation and a task for an eye surgeon (ophthalmologist).

On the whole, surgical treatment is not undertaken unless the vision loss is significant and the cataracts 'mature'; however ophthalmologists differ in their criteria. Congenital cataracts in babies are often not treated surgically unless they are bilateral, there is no other eye disorder and they are sufficiently severe to cause complete blindness.

Cerebral arteriosclerosis

When tissues degenerate with age, arteriosclerosis occurs in the middle and inner coat of the arteries. When this process occurs in the cerebral circulation it is called cerebral arteriosclerosis. The middle coat, or media, becomes thickened and the inner coat, or intima, splits; fibrous thickening of the vessel wall reduces its elastic quality.

Atherosclerosis further diminishes the lumen, or space within the artery, when a deposit of fatty material (atheroma) occurs in patches within the degenerated intima. When it occurs in the cerebral circulation it is called cerebral atherosclerosis. Cerebral arteriosclerosis and atherosclerosis are usually part of a condition which is generally present throughout all arteries of the body.

Effects Mental deterioration which occurs as a result of diminished blood supply to the brain may be gradual, for example memory loss for recent events. A sudden increase in blood pressure in an already hypertensive patient may cause hemorrhage as the weakened vessel wall ruptures. A few warning leaks may produce transient symptoms before a large hemorrhage results in permanent brain damage or sudden death.

When a vessel damaged with arteriosclerosis and patchy atheroma, becomes blocked or narrowed, preliminary warning symptoms lasting only a few minutes sometimes occur. These transient ischemic attacks may preface a complete blockage which causes death of the brain cells (infarction). A transient fall in blood pressure may precipitate such a blockage or thrombosis.

When thickening of the lumen is present for some time, the tissue may be partially or completely supplied by secondary blood vessels which may compensate for the blocked artery. Control of hypertension may help reduce the effects of arteriosclerosis.

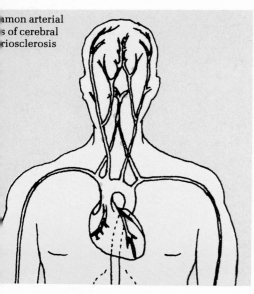

common arterial
...s of cerebral
...riosclerosis

If the arteries of the cerebral
circulatory system become affected
by arteriosclerosis, a degenerative
condition of the arterial walls, blood
supply to the brain is likely to be
diminished.

Cerebrovascular accident

The sudden 'stroke' which may convert
an active, coherent, elderly person into a
partly paralyzed one who has difficulty
speaking and communicating is a common family tragedy.

When the blood supply to the cerebrum
of the brain is interrupted by a blood clot
in a vessel or a burst blood vessel, it is
called a cerebrovascular accident (CVA)
or 'stroke'. Sometimes strokes are very
minor and short lived, leaving no disability within 24 hours (transient cerebral
ischemic attacks). In other strokes the
damage to the brain results in paralysis of
one half of the body or in the loss of
speech or some other faculty. Strokes
rarely occur before 50 years of age.

Signs and symptoms If a burst blood
vessel is the cause, as is often the case in
a person with high blood pressure, the incident is very sudden, often during exertion and sometimes preceded with a
severe headache. Loss of consciousness
often follows and sometimes fits occur. If
a large vessel has been burst the coma
deepens and the person may die without
recovering consciousness. Others survive
with one half of the body paralyzed. Repeated small bleeds cause repeated progressive deterioration in function and
deepening coma.

If a part of the brain has died because
of a blocked blood vessel the affected person may wake up in the morning with a
stroke, or the stroke may occur at any
time during the day. A mild headache for
the previous day or two is common. The
person feels drowsy but complete loss of
consciousness is not common. The
drowsiness is accompanied by weakness
on one side of the body, perhaps slurring

of speech, difficulty in swallowing,
disorientation and confusion, or loss of
sight. The situation may evolve over one
or two hours or it may go on for two or
three days before a stable state is reached.

Many minor strokes may occur over a
period of a few years. The victim may
have progressively impaired mental
ability, walking and talking or may simply
lose interest in personal appearance or in
life itself. Sometimes relatives say of such
people that they are 'aging rapidly'. After
major strokes a right handed person who
is paralyzed down the right side will also
lose the ability to speak.

Treatment The treatment of stroke begins
with the making of the correct diagnosis,
and this involves determining whether the
stroke was caused by a ruptured blood
vessel, the bursting of an aneurism, or the
blockage of a blood vessel by a clot or by
a piece of atheromatous plaque from a diseased artery.

The importance of determining the
cause rests with the treatment. For
example, a ruptured aneurism may
require surgical intervention, while a clot
may now be attacked with intravenously
administered enzymes. If the diagnosis is
not correctly made, then treatment inappropriate to the condition may be administered with inadequate results.

Most stroke is the result of blood vessel
rupture due to long standing hypertension, and the control of this hypertension
is fundamental to successful treatment.

Immediately after a stroke, the area of
brain which surrounds areas of irrepar-
able damage is also not functioning normally, and this area of impaired function
is said to be in 'brain shock'. As a result
of this, the degree of impairment or deficit
immediately after the stroke is much
worse than the result seen days or weeks
later. As time passes, and the body cleans
up and repairs the damage done, the area
of brain shock slowly returns to normal,
and, as brain swelling subsides, still more
function returns. Thus, day by day, gross
clinical improvement is seen, and the
return of functions which were thought
lost.

For this reason, the determination of
the residual deficit after a stroke is not
performed until at least three months after
the event. The treatment consists of intervention and correction of causative factors such as hypertension, and the administration of aspirin to 'thin' the blood and
allow easier perfusion of tiny capillaries.
The other treatment is popularly termed
'rehabilitation' and consists of physiotherapy with active and passive exercises
to get affected muscles moving. There is
also a degree of re-education, where damaged areas of the brain that no longer
function are 'replaced' by other areas
which are re-educated to perform new
tasks. Speech therapy is also very important, and the aim of treatment is to get the
patient to return to a life which is as near
normal as possible.

This arteriogram reveals a large
brain aneurysm. *(Abbottempo)*

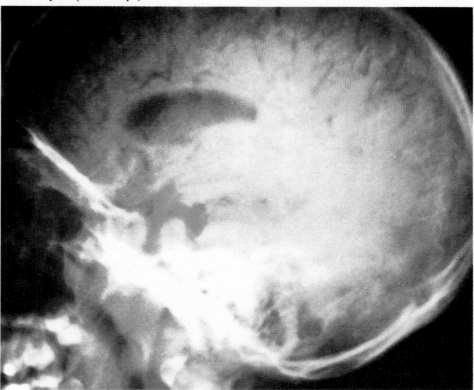

The outlook in a cerebrovascular accident is grave when the stroke is due to a hemorrhage. Eighty per cent of those affected die. In strokes caused by a clot of blood 30 per cent die within the first month. About a tenth of those who have had one stroke have another within a year and about a fifth have another within five years. In people who have had a transient cerebral ischemic attack approximately one-third have a stroke within three years.

Cervical spondylosis

A degenerative condition of the spinal column usually occurring in the aged, cervical spondylosis is characterized by degeneration of the discs between the vertebrae and by the formation of bony outgrowths, or osteophytes, which may project into the opening through which the spinal nerves pass. Although the condition may exist without any symptoms at all, damage to nerves or the spinal cord may cause pain and other neurological signs depending on the site of damage.

Treatment Bed rest, pain relief, traction, drugs, physical therapy or the use of a collar may bring some relief. Various surgical procedures also exist to alleviate the different manifestations of the problem.

Coronary heart disease

The coronary arteries supply the muscle of the heart (myocardium) with blood, and if these arteries become damaged or are in some way abnormal, the condition known as coronary heart disease occurs.

Causes The most common cause is damage from the formation of plaques in the walls of the arteries (atheroma, arteriosclerosis). These plaques have been seen in their earliest form as yellow streaks on the artery walls in autopsy specimens and at operation in children only two and three years of age. The streaks are abnormal collections of fats, producing inflammation and subsequent swelling which causes clots to form and attach to the wall of the artery, causing gradual narrowing over the years. This only becomes a problem when the demands of activity exceed the ability of the narrowed artery to supply the necessary amount of blood and oxygen.

There are also some congenital abnormalities of the coronary arteries although these are less common. *Coronary arteriovenous fistula* is a condition in which oxygenated blood from the lungs becomes mingled with de-oxygenated blood from the body, and gets shunted back to the lungs again. It may go undetected until the fifth or sixth decades when the manifestations of coronary heart disease lead the sufferer to seek medical attention.

During an autopsy or operation the coronary arteries are occasionally found to be abnormally small. The family histories of such patients often reveal relatives who have died of heart disease at an early age. In these cases minimal formation of plaques would significantly compromise

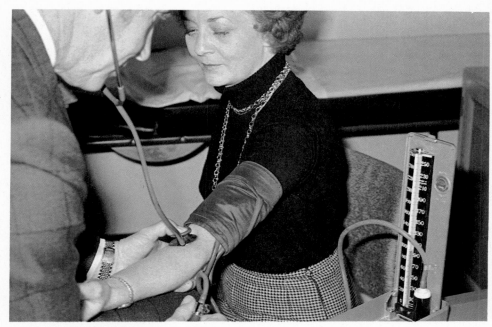

Regular check-ups in middle age, particularly to assess blood pressure, will help avoid problems later on. (*John Watney Photo Library*)

the heart's blood supply.

Manifestations of coronary heart disease Sudden death may be the first and only sign, but there is usually some warning, often in the form of pain. This pain may be temporary and intermittent (angina pectoris) or a sign of permanent damage from heart attack. The most common cause of a heart attack is a complete blockage in the artery from a clot (coronary thrombosis), although spasm of the artery or embolization (a piece of previously formed clot or plaque breaking off and lodging downstream) are other causes.

When the artery becomes blocked, blood supply to the heart muscle ceases. The muscle dies and is replaced by fibrous scar tissue, which is not able to contract like muscle, thus reducing the heart's pumping ability. Repeated or severe attacks of this nature will produce so much scarring that another stage in the disease is reached, that of heart failure. The damaged heart simply cannot cope with the load placed upon it and this results in a backlog of fluid in the lungs causing shortness of breath, swelling of feet, legs and abdomen, and gradually increasing debility. The patient may never have had a heart attack but severe narrowing of the arteries may have so affected the heart's oxygen supply that minute scarring has occurred throughout the muscle.

Investigations Prior to treatment, certain investigations are necessary. All patients with heart disease must have an electrocardiogram (ECG) which will reveal to the trained eye areas of old and recent heart damage and the abnormal rhythms which occur where the arteries supplying the ex-

citation centers of the heart are affected by disease. A stress test will confirm or deny that chest pain is originating from the heart. Following this, coronary angiography is performed, whereby dye injected into the bloodstream is traced through the coronary arteries by x-ray and the exact sites of blockages located. If at any point along its course an artery's diameter is decreased by 40 to 50 per cent, meaning a decrease of 80 per cent or more of blood flow, then operation is advisable.

Treatment The treatment of coronary artery disease falls into two categories, medical and surgical. Medical treatment consists of administering drugs which will reverse or ameliorate the disease in the coronary artery, which is basically clogging or narrowing, and which interferes with the steady supply of blood to the heart muscle. Today, the medications that are effective in this regard are numerous, and include medicines like the beta-blockers, ACE inhibitors (angiotensin converting enzyme inhibitors), calcium blocking agents, and many 'older' medications which include positive inotropic agents like digitalis and nitroglycerine.

Surgical treatment has made great advances in the last ten years or so, and now includes very sophisticated procedures like intraluminal balloon angioplasty, where a blockage in a coronary artery is visualised on x-ray, a thin tube or catheter is passed to that point, and then a balloon on the end of the catheter is inflated to dilate or stretch the narrowed vessel.

In vessels that are too physically small to allow the passage of a catheter, a laser is now being used to clear blockages.

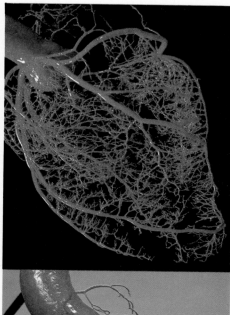

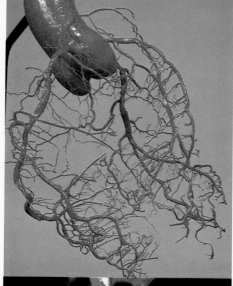

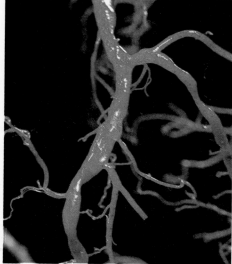

The blood vessels of the heart are shown in normal formation (1), displaying the effects of artherosclerosis (2), and some blocked vessels (3). (*John Watney Photo Library*)

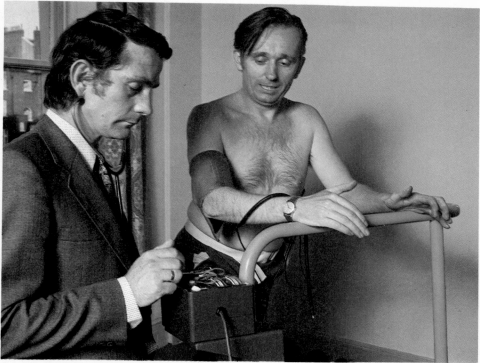

The rehabilitation of patients who suffer from coronary disease may involve supervised exercise. (*John Watney Photo Library*)

More commonly used is the procedure called coronary artery bypass surgery. This has now become routine in most big centres, and involves the replacement or bypassing of diseased coronary arteries using healthy veins from the patient's legs. This allows greatly increased blood flow to the heart which was previously starved of nutrition by diseased and narrowed vessels.

Factors involved in coronary heart disease
There are several factors which are known to influence coronary heart disease. These include high blood pressure; obesity; smoking, which is a significant factor in causing spasm of the coronary arteries; and blood fat levels (especially cholesterol), important in the formation of plaques. Correction of these factors by promotion of proper diet and exercise programs in the community should continue the downward trend in the incidence of the disease in both men and women since its peak in 1967 and 1968.

However, one important factor which is very prominent in Western culture is stress, and it is widely accepted that individuals of the 'type A' personality, typified by the successful business or professional person, have a higher incidence of coronary heart disease. It is interesting to observe that in a primitive low stress culture such as that of the Masai in Africa, coronary artery disease is virtually unknown, although their diet consists mainly of the high animal fat (cholesterol in particular) products of their cattle.

Osteoporosis
The term osteoporosis describes a group of common conditions in which there is a reduction in the mass of bone present per unit volume, that is, the bones become less dense and the outer layer of bone (cortex) thinner. The condition can develop locally, in only one particular bone, or it may be widespread, affecting the whole skeleton.

Causes The most common cause of local osteoporosis is immobilization or lack of any activity, such as following fracture, inflammation or cancer in a particular bone.

There are many causes of generalized osteoporosis. It appears to be a normal aging change, but in some people it tends to occur earlier and is more serious.

A number of factors have been associated with osteoporosis, but its exact mechanism remains in doubt. It has been observed that osteoporosis occurs more often in women who have passed the menopause. This has led to the theory that the decrease in the secretion of certain hormones may be one of the contributing factors. Another is the amount of calcium present; attempts have been made to control the condition by modifying the calcium and phosphorus intake.

It is also believed that too little physical activity may hasten the development of the condition, a view which is consistent with the observation that immobilization often causes local osteoporosis. Some drugs have been associated with the development of osteoporosis, as well as certain hormonal conditions such as Cushing's disease and acromegaly.

An active life and well-balanced
diet help to prevent osteoporosis.

Signs and symptoms There may be no
symptoms despite changes on x-ray, or
there may be great pain and easy fractur-
ing of the bone. The pain is often relieved
by rest and aggravated by movement.
There may be a decrease in body height
because of a collapse of the vertebrae.

Osteoporotic bone appears qualitatively
normal under the microscope; it is just
that there is less of it. This is in contrast
to other disorders of bone such as *osteomalacia* (softening of the bones).

Treatment of the disease once it has begun is difficult and there are conflicting
results with different studies. Many treatments revolve around modifying the diet
and giving hormones in the hope of slowing down progress of the disease.

With the knowledge of the relationship
between immobility and the development
of osteoporosis, it is important not to allow too much bed rest; activity is to be
encouraged. Obesity is to be discouraged
as extra weight provides an extra strain on
the already weakened bones. A brace may
be required for backache and pain-killing
tablets to relieve pain. Preventive
measures in the form of an active life and
a well-balanced diet are encouraged.

Parkinson's disease

Definitively described by James Parkinson
(1755–1824) in 1817, Parkinson's disease
(also called paralysis agitans, shaking
palsy and Parkinsonism) occurs when a
small group of nerve cells in the brain no
longer function as they should.

Symptoms are varied and may not all be
present in the one individual. A slowly
progressive disease, a patient may remain
at the same stage for long periods of time.
The most common features are muscular
rigidity, a slowly spreading tremor, most
often beginning in the hands, and a slowness and difficulty in starting movements
(bradykinesia).

Often beginning on one side and involving the index finger and thumb, the
tremor has been described as the 'pill rolling tremor'. It is usually most pronounced
when the person is at rest, it disappears
during sleep and often lessens during voluntary movement. Anxiety, such as embarrassment, may intensify the symptom.

Rigidity causes the typical expression-
less face and immobile posture of the
Parkinsonian sufferer, and makes fine
movement difficult. The stiff muscles can
also precipitate vague pain. Bradykinesia
is apparent in the lack of associated movements when walking (for example, the
lack of hand swinging) and an affected
person often takes short shuffling steps
and tends to lose balance easily. In an attempt to maintain balance, an individual
may find that he is propelling himself forward at an ever increasing rate. Those
who suffer from Parkinsonism often tire

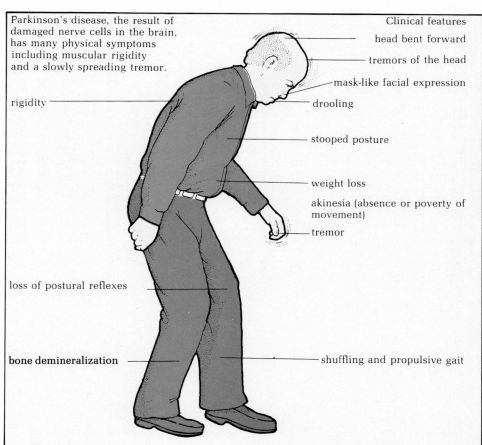

Parkinson's disease, the result of
damaged nerve cells in the brain,
has many physical symptoms
including muscular rigidity
and a slowly spreading tremor.

Clinical features
head bent forward
tremors of the head
mask-like facial expression
rigidity
drooling
stooped posture
weight loss
akinesia (absence or poverty of
movement)
tremor
loss of postural reflexes
bone demineralization
shuffling and propulsive gait

easily and have a slow, monotonous speech although their intellect is usually unaffected. Dribbling, scaly, greasy skin and constipation can also develop.

Causes Brain damage may occur, so that transmitter substances necessary for proper brain cell function are no longer released. However, in a minority of cases similar syndromes develop as the result of certain conditions, which include post-encephalitic Parkinsonism and arteriosclerotic Parkinsonism. The overall incidence of Parkinson's disease is one in a thousand, with men and women being equally affected.

Treatment Although the disease is incurable, there are several drugs which give complete or partial relief from symptoms. However, as these drugs may produce side-effects, it may be necessary to vary dosages or tablets. Surgery is sometimes used for younger patients who have tremor and rigidity on only one side of their body. Parkinsonian sufferers are usually encouraged to function as independently as possible. A society exists to help Parkinson's disease sufferers and their families.

Polymyalgia rheumatica

A rheumatic condition of the elderly, polymyalgia rheumatica involves aching and stiffness of the neck and shoulder muscle and sometimes of the thighs. The pain is aggravated by movement and extends to associated joints.

Symptoms include a mild fever, some weight loss, and headache. If there is associated temporal arteritis (joint cell arteritis) the headache tends to be more severe, and there is throbbing and local tenderness over the temple region of the scalp. The main concern about the arteritis is that the roughened and inflamed innermost layer may result in thrombus (clot) formation, which may in turn block the blood supply to the eyes, resulting in permanent blindness.

However, not all people with polymyalgia rheumatica suffer involvement of their temporal arteries.

Apart from the changes in the artery, a very high erythrocyte sedimentation rate (ESR) is common and a help in diagnosis. **Treatment** involves high doses of corticosteroids such as prednisone, and analgesic drugs may be required to reduce the rheumatic pain. Relief is usually prompt but treatment may need to be continued for some years.

Prostatectomy

The surgical removal of the prostate or prostatectomy is required in two conditions: benign prostatic enlargement (hypertrophy) and early prostatic cancer (prostatic carcinoma) which has not spread.

Prostatic hypertrophy is a benign tumor, the incidence of which is rare before the age of 40, but steadily increases after this time. By 80 years of age, 70 per cent of males have some degree of prostatic hypertrophy.

The indications for surgical intervention include difficulty in voiding and retention of urine in the bladder (residual urine), frequency, nocturia and persistent infection.

The usual prostatectomy performed today, especially in elderly patients, is the transurethral (T-U-R) prostatectomy; this has the lowest incidence of side-effects. An instrument is passed up the penis, and a high-frequency current is applied to a wire loop at the end of the instrument; multiple fragments of the obstructive tissue are removed by successive cuts under direct vision.

The other type of prostatectomy is the open type (usually a suprapubic) where an incision is made in the lower abdomen, through the bladder. The prostate is then separated from its capsule and removed. This operation has a much higher risk but may be required if there are bladder stones.

The main complication of either operation is continued hemorrhage. If hemorrhage is severe, a clot of blood blocking urine flow may develop. Adequate irrigation and drainage of the area will prevent this and the use of antibiotics decreases the risk of infection.

The post-operative stay in hospital is five days for a T-U-R and nine days for an open prostatectomy. The recurrence rate of obstructive symptoms is approximately 10 per cent.

Prostatic carcinoma In contrast to prostatic hypertrophy, early prostatic cancer must be treated with a total open prostatectomy associated with removal of seminal vesicles. In more advanced cases, a prostatectomy will not be curative but may relieve symptoms such as mechanical obstruction of urine.

Temporal arteritis

A disorder affecting older people, temporal (giant cell or cranial) arteritis is a chronic inflammation of medium and small arteries, mainly those of the head. The cause is unknown, but the disorder results in the degeneration of affected arteries and the progressive narrowing of their central channels (lumens). The arteries of the head, and especially the temporal arteries of the side of the head are most affected, although in severe forms of the disease, arteries throughout the body may be damaged.

Symptoms A severe headache, localized in one or both temporal regions, is common and is usually accompanied by a mild fever, malaise, and weight loss. Pain, tenderness and swelling along the artery develop, the overlying skin appears red and swollen, and the artery ceases to pulsate. The inflamed innermost layer of the artery may form a clot which blocks the blood supply to the eye resulting in permanent blindness. The more severely affected may also develop deafness, loss of balance, brain damage or other symptoms indicating involvement of arteries in other parts of the body.

Treatment Temporal arteritis is a self-limiting illness which may last for a few months or for several years. Meanwhile the patient needs general support and pain relief. Removing a section of the artery may ease the pain and can prove the diagnosis (classical 'giant cells' will show up under the microscope). Adrenocorticosteroid drugs, such as cortisone, may also provide relief from symptoms.

8 Maintaining a Healthy Lifestyle
— Environmental Health and Preventive Medicine

Environment and Health

The development and general health of a person is greatly influenced by the environment, which consists of all the external aspects of a person's surroundings.

The environment can be described in terms of the physical environment, that is, climate, geography, housing, sanitation and water supply; the biological environment which includes all living matter apart from other humans, that is, bacteria, viruses, insects, plants and animals; and the social environment, that is, other people and our relationship with them. These environment areas and their influence on health are naturally very much interrelated and tend to overlap. Often a change in one part of the environment will produce change in another part.

From the moment of conception we are exposed to environmental influences. The fetus is most vulnerable during the first three months of development in the womb. If there is interference with this stage of development, marked deformities may occur. The development of the fetus may be affected by infections such as syphilis and rubella, toxic agents like the drug thalidomide, and cigarette smoking, excessive alcohol consumption and inadequate nutrition. In these cases there is interaction between the physical and social environments.

Another example of the interaction of environments is the improvement in housing sanitation, nutrition and health care which has resulted in a very high overall standard of health in urban industrialized societies.

The effect of environment on an individual early in life may last a lifetime. On a physical level, for example, use of fluoridated drinking water in childhood greatly reduces the prospect of tooth decay later in life. On a psychic level, emotional deprivation or lack of adequate nurturing may result in the inability to form warm and caring relationships later in life.

Climate

Human adaptation to climate results from normal physiological responses as well as from conscious attention to changes in environment.

Physiological adaptation involves the normal mechanisms that compensate for changes in function in response to both the internal and external environment. For instance, the amount of urine produced by the body can vary according to the concentration of the blood. Therefore when the climate causes the loss of large amounts of body water, the kidneys compensate by producing less urine. Similarly, the body has various mechanisms for conserving or producing heat according to climatic and individual requirements.

In addition to such physiological mechanisms, adjustments of dress and lifestyle in accordance with environment may be made to favour health. Such modifications may make it easier for the physiological mechanisms to cope with climatic changes.

Desert-dwelling Australian Aboriginals can withstand daily temperature extremes with a minimum of protection.

A person may remain healthy in different extremes of temperature and climate by adaptation; many techniques useful for survival and to maintain health can be borrowed and modified from the customs of indigenous peoples. For example, the long, flowing robes worn by some desert people allow air to circulate around the body and cool it, as well as giving protection against wind and sun. Desert dwellers also move about during the cool

Life in an area of extreme temperature range can impose strains on the body's ability to adapt.

of the late afternoon and early morning, which minimizes their energy expenditure and body heat gain. Similarly, the dwellings of people living in climatic extremes may compensate for the climate.

In polar regions, Western man has adopted habits from the Eskimos in order to survive and remain healthy. Modern Arctic and Antarctic clothing which tends to minimize bulk and allow air circulation, borrows its principles from Eskimo clothing.

The Mediterranean dwellers' habit of having a siesta during the hottest time of the day, when energy demand is at a maximum, can be a healthy adaptation to the climate.

Early European settlers in the tropics often failed to adopt the local customs and practices suitable to the climate, often to the detriment of their health. For example, heat rashes are much more frequent when clothing is tight and restrictive. Similarly, failure to bathe regularly may be relatively unimportant in a temperate environment but a hazard in a tropical climate.

Epidemiology studies the relationship between climate and health, and specific diseases are known to be more prevalent in certain climates. When about to travel abroad it is sensible to be inoculated against any particular disease which is known to be endemic in the country to be visited. For example, vaccination against cholera is considered essential before visiting India.

Before the development of domestic air conditioning and of drugs such as antibiotics, a change of climate was often a major part of health treatment. People with a variety of ailments were sent to the country or seaside, and those with tuberculosis were sometimes sent to dry climates.

Many infectious bacterial and parasitic conditions are more frequent in tropical and subtropical regions. In these areas there is often an interplay between the biological and physical factors. For instance, the *Anopheles* mosquito, which transmits malaria, breeds only in such areas.

Below
Sunny climates are ideal for sunbaking, but exposure to the sun may result in skin cancer.

Bottom
This tent will provide reasonable comfort for a night spent on the snow.

Malignant melanoma and skin cancers in general occur more frequently in tropical areas where the ultraviolet rays, the main irritant, are stronger. Multiple sclerosis occurs more frequently in colder climates, but the reason is unknown.

Asthma and other respiratory disorders are affected by the presence of allergens, which in turn may be affected by changes in weather. The release of pollen is triggered by a fall in relative humidity. Conversely, high humidity may mean that moisture forms on airborne particles and accelerates their deposition. Asthma and hay fever tend to be worse in spring.

Some diseases occur more frequently in certain seasons. In Switzerland, for example, scarlet fever, diphtheria and jaundice occur mainly in winter, while measles, influenza and chicken pox are most common in spring. In England and Australia respiratory and heart conditions are more common in late winter and early spring. Gastroenteritis is most frequent during spring and summer.

Diseases transmitted by animals and insects, such as bubonic plague, very much depend on the weather, for climate affects the breeding and survival of insects. In Vietnam the plague is transmitted by a flea carried by a rat. These fleas are far more numerous in dry weather, when the monthly rainfall is less than 100mm.

Below
Pale plumes in Lake Michigan show where treated sewage is released into the lake.

Above
Overpopulation of any area can strain the available resources and lead to spoiling of the environment.
(John Watney Photo Library)

Housing

When people live together in a community it is of considerable importance that they should be properly housed.

The houses should have a clean water supply and be adequately sewered so that there is no overt contamination of the immediate vicinity with sewage. Without these measures there is a greatly increased incidence of enteric diseases like cholera, typhoid and dysentery, diseases which spread rapidly in communities with poor sanitation.

Overcrowding in houses should be avoided where possible. Ideally, each person should have a separate bed or sleeping place which is dry and clean and no more than two people should sleep in any one bedroom unless it is very large. Infectious diseases such as tuberculosis, respiratory virus infections, fungus infections and all airborne infections spread more rapidly and are more prevalent in overcrowded houses.

Adequate facilities for bathing, showering and washing the hands will greatly reduce the likelihood of skin infections and

In large cities and towns physical or biological methods are used to treat sewage, rendering it safe for disposal into the ocean.

Where modern sewage systems are not available basic facilities can be devised and used without disadvantage to health.

diseases, and of contamination to food. Intestinal infestations like threadworm and roundworm cannot be acquired so easily if hands are washed after using the lavatory, and before eating.

Insect- and animal-borne diseases are avoided by keeping the house scrupulously clean, and by using fly screens on windows and doors to ensure that plenty of fresh air can circulate without allowing insects to enter.

Sewage disposal The large-scale sewage disposal methods in use today are comparatively recent developments. No modern metropolitan city could exist without them, and their size, complexity and cost would have been unimaginable a century ago.

Consisting of many integrated parts, modern sewerage systems have networks of underground pipes which range in size from small diameter conduits beneath suburban backyards to cavernous submains so large that they must be inspected by boat. These interconnect with hundreds of pumping stations, and with the treatment plants which purify the sewage before its disposal.

Essentially sewage consists of 99.9 per cent water, with solids, including human wastes, forming a very small part of the total. An average suburban household discharges about one ton into the sewers each day.

Physical or biochemical treatment, which can be achieved by a variety of methods, is necessary before sewage is allowed to enter water courses or the ocean.

Most processes for treating sewage use micro-organisms which digest the solid matter, changing it into substances no longer harmful to human health, and thus fit for disposal.

Septic tanks can be constructed where mains sewage is not available. They may be prefabricated or built on the spot. It is important that any seepage or surface run off will go into the disposal area and not elsewhere, so the tank should be placed carefully with regard to the fall of the land and the proximity of the property boundaries. A septic tank is essentially a large cavity made of asbestos cement impregnated with PVC, of fibreglass or of concrete. A filter is formed by sandy gravel and soil which lines the base of the tank and surrounds it on the outside.

If the site is unable to drain septic tank effluent satisfactorily, a collection well may be installed. This simply collects and contains all the household sewage. The collected sewage is emptied at intervals by pump-out tankers.

Population

The very rapid increase in world population that we are accustomed to today appears to be a quite recent phenomenon. It was not until 1850 that the world's population reached 1000 million but only 75 years later it was 2000 million and less than 40 years after that it reached 3000 million.

Prior to 1920 the populations with the highest rates of increase were those of the

highly developed, industrialized countries where living standards were rising rapidly. Since 1920 the developing countries have had a faster growing population rate then the developed countries.

Many simple societies have high mortality rates, which encourage prolific reproduction. When mortality is reduced in such societies, population numbers explode, overtaxing slender resources and again reducing the standard of nutrition and hygiene. Over-population produces starvation, malnutrition and low resistance to infection. Nutritional deficiency conditions such as kwashiorkor, beri-beri, pellagra and rickets are likely to occur.

Where food and water are contaminated and animal reservoirs of infection and insect vectors are uncontrolled, infectious diseases like yaws, hookworm, cholera, typhus, typhoid fever, sleeping sickness, malaria, trachoma, affect so many people that other diseases go unnoticed. Under such conditions about 25 per cent of children die in infancy and another 25 per cent before age 15. The average life expectancy in some developing countries is only 30 to 40 years, although most deaths are due to diseases which can be prevented and cured.

Social change A study of the changes in disease patterns as societies become industrialized and control their rate of population growth confirms that a society's degree of social development influences its health status. All the developed countries once had patterns of death and disease similar to those the developing countries now experience. In Western Europe life expectancy in 1700 was 33 years, in 1900 it was 45–50 years and in 1960 it was about 70 years. As a society develops it can institute measures to overcome malnutrition and infection and lower the death rate. Examples of the impact of social organization on health are seen in countries like Australia and South Africa where both peasant and industrial communities can be found living together in the same environment. In some areas, white Australians enjoying the amenities and health of an affluent economy can be found living close to a community of Aboriginals with the culture and diseases of a peasant economy: high infant mortality, poor hygiene and nutrition and a high incidence of infectious disease.

Population control and a highly organized social structure have provided good food, clean water, effective sewage disposal and immunization against infection. The result is a considerable reduction in nutritional and infective diseases, and a greatly reduced death rate. The combination of a low birth rate and a low death rate has changed the age structure of the

Infections are more common and spread more easily in conditions of poverty, poor nutrition and inadequate sanitation. (*Zefa*)

Most Western people enjoy a healthy lifestyle.

changes affect both the physical and mental well-being of the people and cause a number of social problems. The stability and security of rural life centered round the extended family. Nowadays land ownership is often lost and an increasing dependence upon social security, and governmental provision of health, education, transport and other needs follows.

Most government-initiated health and social programs relating to increasing industrialization were initiated in the nineteenth century, often motivated by the desire to improve productivity and reduce the expenses associated with the care of the infirm. Improved public health facilities had a significant impact, with a marked reduction in the incidence of, and deaths caused by, infectious diseases such as pneumonia and dysentery. These changes occurred long before the discovery of antibiotics.

Health in the Third World On a worldwide basis poverty, malnutrition, overcrowding and lack of education and general facilities are still realities for the majority of people today. Self-help programs and education are considered to be the most appropriate ways of dealing with this situation.

An increasing appreciation of the importance of cultural and religious factors has occurred in recent years and has influenced the policies and effectiveness of agencies such as the World Health Organization. Medical training and instruction is now being given at the 'grass roots' or village level by trained indigenous people and has proved to be much more effective than health care delivered only by foreigners based at large hospital centers.

In Somalia poverty and malnutrition have combined with devastating effect on the health of these people. *(Campbell/Unicef)*

population, so that there are now fewer children, many more old people and a large working age group.

The decrease in infectious and nutritional diseases, together with an older population, completely changes the disease picture. It is now the chronic and degenerative diseases such as cancer, coronary artery disease, strokes, arthritis, diabetes mellitus, and peptic ulcer which are prevalent and cause most ill-health and deaths.

A lifestyle which emphasizes competition creates new tensions and anxieties and leads to psychological and psychosomatic illness. The elderly, once the objects of respect and veneration as in the peasant society, may lack self-esteem and occupation and so become anxious about their declining capabilities. This creates depression and leads to dependence on health services.

Sociological factors and health

The way in which society is structured, the cultural mores, the level of affluence and the degree of industrialization and urbanization are just some of the many sociological factors that influence the health of the individual and the community. Social conditions and problems are extensively and intimately related to problems of illness and disease.

This relationship has been recognized throughout the world for thousands of years. The ancient Roman civilization, for example, was one which developed general systems of public health, and the Aztecs of Central America had facilities such as drainage systems, public latrines, the collection of refuse and regular street cleaning. These measures apparently kept this empire free of epidemics until after the Spanish invasion of the sixteenth century.

In the Middle Ages, however, Europe suffered many devastating epidemics. High proportions of the population succumbed to plague, smallpox, typhus and various other infections; lack of adequate personal hygiene and sanitation facilitated their spread. Little was known about such matters and even basic public health facilities were not considered important by most governments.

The Industrial Revolution that began in the eighteenth century caused great sociological changes. The development of factories led to rapid expansion of towns and cities where overcrowding was often common. Fewer people lived off the land, a trend which still occurs and is becoming increasingly important in many Third World countries. Such sociological

Below
The diet of people in Western
countries frequently creates health
problems such as obesity and heart
disease. In poorer countries health
problems are more likely to be the
result of malnutrition. *(Zefa)*

Common health problems found in
most developing countries can be
prevented or cured by health
workers with limited training and
simple equipment and supplies.
(WHO/Unicef)

Health in industrialized nations Whilst
poverty and malnutrition increase the
chances of many infections, accidents,
and various nutritional deficiency states,
affluence also has its specific health problems.

The diet of most people in Western industrialized nations is of increasing concern. For example, over 20 per cent of
Americans are significantly overweight, a
situation that is associated with increased
risks of stroke, heart disease, joint disorders and a general reduction in health.
Too many calories are consumed, and the
percentage of these obtained from fats is
excessive. There is also evidence that inadequate dietary fiber intake, as occurs in
affluent societies, is associated with an increased frequency of diverticular disease,
bowel cancer, appendicitis and a number
of other conditions.

At more subtle levels, the changing of
attitudes and expectations within society,
altered roles of the extended family, increased governmental responsibility for
support and provision, and the reduced
influence of the church within society
have all had a significant impact during
this century.

The degree of change in all societies has
been increasing over the last thirty years.
An increasing acceptance of people from
different cultures, and an enrichment of

our society by their contributions are positive changes. Unfortunately, problems
such as a greater number of broken
homes, unwanted pregnancies, and an increased frequency of sexually transmitted
diseases have also emerged. The long-
term impact of the unemployment and
inflation of recent years is yet to be
evaluated.

An individual is described as obese
when he is 20–30 per cent over
average weight for his age, sex and
height.

Exercise and Sport

Physical exercise is important to the well-being of every individual. People who have a very active lifestyle, have less chance of contracting coronary artery disease, especially if they have a diet low in saturated fats. Regular exercise improves the heart's own blood supply, and in some studies the incidence of heart attacks appears to have been reduced by exercise. The whole body becomes a more co-ordinated and efficient machine, it is able to do more work for the same amount of energy expenditure. Blood pressure readings are lower and there are also changes in the blood chemistry that enable the blood to flow more easily and not to clot.

Many psychological effects related to the improvement of mood and better ability to cope with life and with stress situations are relatable to the taking of adequate exercise.

Inactivity from prolonged confinement to bed, leads to loss of calcium from bones and may result in stone formation in the kidneys. The sluggish blood flow in the leg veins after surgery or childbirth carries the risk of clotting (thrombosis) and to avoid this, early activity is encouraged.

For physical fitness, regular activity is recommended, the exercise being vigorous enough to increase the heart rate (or pulse) to over 100 beats a minute.

The training effect of a regular program of exercise lasts for 24 hours and for optimum improvement should be carried out at least every second day.

A regular program of exercise promotes healthy muscle tone.

Top
Moderate exercise is a wise measure for the elderly.

Right (John Watney Photo Library)
Exercise bicycles can be used in any weather.

Physiological effects of exercise

The movement of muscles requires energy. There are two main processes from which this energy derives: *Aerobic oxidative phosphorylation* where oxygen and glucose are consumed to produce large amounts of energy (carbon dioxide is the waste product of this oxidation reaction), and *anaerobic glycosis* which is inefficient and cannot produce large amounts of energy.

After a period of anaerobic metabolism, lactic acids build up in the muscle. In a sprint race the muscles rely solely on anaerobic metabolism, which limits the time that the activity can be sustained because the products of metabolism build up. When muscles are contracting almost continuously there is not enough relaxation time to allow for the blood to flow freely. The build up of these acids causes a cramp which is a condition of sustained contraction of the muscles. In longer runs, the muscles' blood flow catches up to restore the balance, repaying the oxygen debt and washing away the waste acids.

To deliver these large quantities of oxygen to working muscles, the body must have an efficient delivery system as well as continuous input of oxygen. These are supplied by the heart and lungs. The measure of the efficiency of the pump is called the cardiac output (the volume of blood that is delivered into the circulation within one minute). With training the heart improves its efficiency by increasing the volume of blood for each beat.

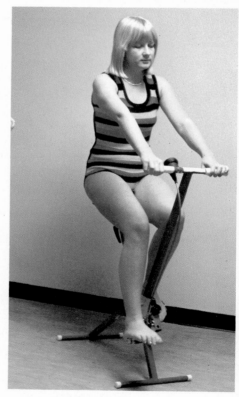

Effects of training

At rest, the athlete's heart rate is slower than the average. Rates down to forty beats per minute are not unusual and the maximum heart rates during exercise are faster than that of the normal population. Heart muscle develops increasing power with increasing stretch of the muscle fibers, which happens when there is a greater volume in the ventricle before it contracts.

Good lung function is important, because it is through the air sacs that the oxygen diffuses in and the carbon dioxide diffuses out. The amount of oxygen picked up per minute is proportional to the amount of blood flowing through the lungs per minute. The tidal volume or depth of breathing increases in the trained athlete and the lung volume itself also increases. This is the value of swimming for asthmatics (as well as teaching them to control their breathing).

The changes that occur with exercise are governed by the sympathetic nervous system and adrenalin. As the muscles start to work, the products of metabolism build up and the available oxygen is used up. The blood vessels in the muscle dilate, leading to an increased flow. This causes a lowering of blood pressure, which the heart responds to by increasing its rate.

Exercise produces carbon dioxide and lactic acid which makes the blood more acidic, resulting in an increase in the depth and rate of breathing. Adrenalin activates the enzymes in the liver that cause the breakdown of the large storage molecules of glycogen into glucose and also stimulates the breakdown of fat storage molecules.

Aerobic exercise

Resulting in an increase in the amount of oxygen that the body can process, aerobic exercise describes various types of regular exercise which stimulate heart and lung activity to a degree that promotes beneficial changes in the body. The most popular forms of aerobic exercise are jogging, running, walking, cycling and swimming.

Since the mid-1970s forms of aerobic exercise have largely dominated personal physical fitness programs. A large part of the wide interest in aerobics (as such exercise programs are popularly called) arose from the publication of *The New Aerobics* by Dr. Kenneth H. Cooper. The book describes the benefits of aerobic exercise, how to gauge present levels of fitness, what exercise goals are appropriate according to fitness and age, how to commence and develop training and how to maintain the desired standard. The format described by Cooper is the official exercise program for the United States Air Force and Navy and for the Royal Canadian Air Force.

Heavy smokers, heart-disease patients, chronically ill or overweight persons should begin an aerobic exercise program with a walking routine, for several weeks at least, before progressing to more strenuous forms of aerobics.

Any person who is unfit or suffers from a major and persistent health problem will probably have impaired aerobic capacity. Some such people have embarked on aerobics programs with the idea of getting fit quickly. This has invariably been to their detriment and a few such joggers have had fatal heart attacks as a result of trying to do too much too soon. Overtraining can also produce stiff muscles, sore feet and dehydration, which in turn will discourage the person from continuing. Some soreness and tiredness is inevitable, but if it is overwhelming it can be an indication of attempting too much.

Most men and women embarking on an aerobics program will find it encouraging and stimulating to do so with a family member or friend, or as part of a group. Jogging and swimming clubs as well as cycling groups usually have a medical or training supervisor who can check progress and perhaps spot potential problems. Alternatively, the lone enthusiast could purchase a manual containing a medically verified program. Choice of an aerobics program from the many forms available depends upon present fitness levels or ill health, time available, location and personal preference.

Jogging An extremely popular form of aerobic exercise now practiced by thousands of people, young and old, jogging is an inexpensive exercise that can be practiced almost anywhere — on roads, on beaches, in parks and on sports ovals — though health-wise it is better practiced in pleasant surroundings. Jogging along busy roads where the air is heavily polluted reduces some of the health benefits.

Only people who are invalided or recovering from major surgery or who have serious conditions such as a stroke, heart disease, hypertension, breathing difficulties or actual restriction or problems with limbs or the musculo-skeletal system are unable to jog. Anyone of indifferent health wishing to jog regularly may be well advised first to have a health check by the family doctor.

Jogging is so beneficial to the cardio-respiratory system that along with other aerobic exercise it may be an effective deterrent to heart disease.

Participants of all ages in a road race. *(Australian Picture Library)*

This series of exercises will help to reduce flabbiness at the midriff, waist and abdomen.

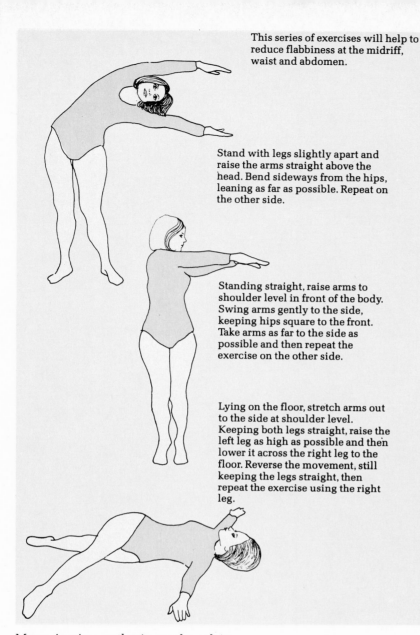

Stand with legs slightly apart and raise the arms straight above the head. Bend sideways from the hips, leaning as far as possible. Repeat on the other side.

Standing straight, raise arms to shoulder level in front of the body. Swing arms gently to the side, keeping hips square to the front. Take arms as far to the side as possible and then repeat the exercise on the other side.

Lying on the floor, stretch arms out to the side at shoulder level. Keeping both legs straight, raise the left leg as high as possible and then lower it across the right leg to the floor. Reverse the movement, still keeping the legs straight, then repeat the exercise using the right leg.

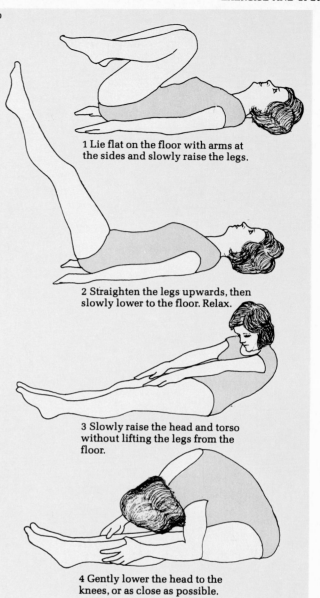

1 Lie flat on the floor with arms at the sides and slowly raise the legs.

2 Straighten the legs upwards, then slowly lower to the floor. Relax.

3 Slowly raise the head and torso without lifting the legs from the floor.

4 Gently lower the head to the knees, or as close as possible.

Many jogging enthusiasts also claim that it reduces emotional tension. Much has been said about the so-called 'runner's high', which undoubtedly exists for some if not for all. Perhaps the level of tension prior to taking up jogging is relevant. Certainly virtually all regular joggers report greater clarity of thought, improved concentration and refreshing sleep as a result of their efforts.

Sport

The relationship of sport with medicine dates from the times of Ancient Greece, where the early Olympic competitors usually had medical advisors who supervised their diet and training. When nations industrialized, there arose large cities with few areas available for sport. Most people, therefore, had to be content with team games which few people played and the majority watched.

Daily exercise such as jogging can be fun as well as healthy.

Regular runners report greater
clarity of thought, improved
concentration and refreshing sleep.

Left
People in sedentary occupations
should exercise in their free time.

Since World War II a scientific approach to sport has resulted in a better understanding of its physiology, biochemistry and biomechanics. By understanding heart function and oxygen delivery and utilization, an athlete can be trained to perform to the stage of just entering his anaerobic phase of metabolism, thus using his maximum potential. This has achieved such performances as the running of a 26 mile marathon at a rate of less than 5 minutes per mile. Attention is also being given to the psychological make-up of competitors and training is available to increase their aggression and competitive drive, and their ability to withstand pain and physical abuse.

Medical problems All this has resulted in young people voluntarily subjecting themselves for prolonged periods to intense physical activity at levels previously unknown even under conditions of slavery, and a whole range of new physiological and medical problems are arising.

Because of the particular stresses they place on the body, certain injuries predominate in various sports. In football, cuts, bruises and fractures to the head, neck, face and nose are common, as well as injuries to the brain, spine and knees. Cricket produces damage to the fingers. Tennis players place excessive strains on the forearm muscles at their elbow insertions, causing 'tennis elbow', a severe constant pain in the elbow which is made worse by moving the forearm and wrist. Boxing is notorious for serious brain damage resulting from repeated blows to the head as well as disfigurement of the face.

Below
The painful condition known as tennis elbow results from excessive strain on the forearm muscles.

Below right
Baseball players often injure shoulders and knees.

Swimmers and rowers are subject to muscle cramps and high divers can damage their ears and sometimes their spines. Scuba diving predisposes to pressure damage to ears and sinuses, vertigo, hypothermia, nitrogen narcosis, air embolism and decompression sickness ('the bends'). Water skiers risk chronic back conditions, especially when ski-jumping, and also sprains and fractures of the ankles. Snow skiers have accidents which result in sprains and fractures of their ankles and legs.

Power boat enthusiasts damage their spines and knees because of their cramped driving position and the vibrations of the boat. Water polo players have trouble with their finger joints because of trauma and cold. Volley ball also damages bones, tendons and joints of the hands. The hands of gymnasts develop callosities and areas of induration because of intense pressure and friction. Hurdlers tend to damage their feet and spine, and golfers suffer strains to their knees and shoulders.

Enthusiasts of sports such as skateboarding and trail bike riding need to wear protective clothing to help them avoid serious injury.
(Zefa)

Leg injuries are common in body contact sports. Intensive ice pack therapy, followed up by physical therapy and stretching exercises, is used to accelerate healing of sprains. (*Zefa*)

Treatment In the acute stage, muscular injuries are usually treated with ice, compression and elevation to minimize swelling and bleeding into the muscle. The part must be rested and supported by a bandage or splint. Injections of local anesthetic and cortisone are sometimes employed, and physical therapy and painkilling drugs are useful. Surgical repair is occasionally necessary. Rehabilitation is a gradual process of reconditioning the healing parts to resuming customary activity.

Precautions The people most at risk of sports injuries are holiday-makers and weekend athletes, sedentary people who try to become physically active overnight. Sports injuries can be prevented by maintaining physical fitness and training; an adequate warm-up period; using proper equipment (for example padded head gear, molded mouth guards in body contact sports); carefully observing the rules of the game; training on proper surfaces with special footwear (athletics and running); strapping vulnerable joints; adequate supervision of the game by referees and coaches; and medical supervision of players, before, during and after the match.

During prolonged vigorous exercise, sweat is lost at a rate of 2–4 pints (1–2 L) an hour, and it has been shown that it is preferable to replace it by drinking an electrolyte solution containing 20 mmol per liter of sodium, 10 mmol per liter of potassium and 13 grams per liter of glucose rather than plain water. Suitably balanced commercial drinks are available. Dehydration and heat exhaustion in marathon events can be avoided by holding the event in cool weather, and seeing that all competitors drink sufficient fluid before, during and after the event.

Diet Regular physical exercise increases the appetite because more energy is required. It is important for the increased food intake to be in the form of a balanced diet with adequate protein, minerals and vitamins. It is also important to remember that should this physical activity cease, the food intake must be drastically reduced. The grossly obese ex-sportsman is a common, if not a pretty, sight.

Drugs and sport There is evidence that even as far back as the ancient Olympic games athletes have sought artificial means of boosting their performance. The present widespread use of drugs is, therefore not a new phenomenon. Stimulants such as amphetamine and ephedrine are used because they give a subjective impression of increasing alertness, decreasing fatigue, elevating mood and boosting performance. In reality they increase aggression and hostility and impair thinking, judgement, coordination and performance. They have occasionally caused collapse and death.

Anabolic steroids are used over a long period of time to build up muscle bulk, but they do not appear to increase performance. Being similar to the male sex hormone testosterone, anabolic steroids have a masculinizing effect on women. Drugs can be detected by analyzing a sample of urine collected under supervision after the event.

Drugs such as alcohol and tobacco considerably impair performance, and no serious sportsman can afford their indulgence.

Health Care and Preventive Medicine

The World Health Organization defines health as 'a state of complete physical, mental and social well-being, and not merely the absence of disease'. Incorporated into this definition is the concept of personal satisfaction with achievements and relationships and the ability to cope with and relate appropriately to the environment. There are many people with no specific diagnosable disease who cope poorly, are continually listless, and do not enjoy life; whereas others with specific diseases or physical and mental disabilities relate well to the environment, and lead a satisfying and fulfilling life. Indeed, individual health is dependent on a number of factors.

Hereditary and familial factors Some diseases such as hemophilia, cystic fibrosis and Huntington's chorea are clearly inherited, being passed on from parents to children. Such conditions are associated with abnormalities in the genes which are contained on the chromosomes, structures that duplicate themselves and enable hereditary traits to be passed on.

Other conditions tend to run in families without having a definite pattern of inheritance. Asthma, eczema, schizophrenia and hypertension (high blood pressure) are examples of such diseases, which are known as familial disorders. It is postulated that there is an inherited predisposition to the condition that needs to be triggered by one or a number of environmental stimuli in order to appear.

Many more subtle attributes to health are also involved in the hereditary process. Character, personality, coping patterns, intelligence, and resistance to disease or illness all have inherited, as well as environmental, components.

Environmental factors Early environmental influences are crucial to the future development of the individual, and to the attainment of full inherited potentials of functioning and maintaining health. This is particularly so during the period between conception and birth. Certain conditions that affect fetal development may therefore have implications for the health of an individual throughout his life. Rubella (German measles) and the drug thalidomide are two well-known examples of adverse intrauterine influences. If a woman contracts rubella in the first trimester (third) of pregnancy, the rubella virus may cross the placenta and affect the developing fetus, possibly causing deafness, cataracts, or mental and growth retardation. The most noticeable effect of thalidomide is *phocomelia*, in which the hands and feet are attached almost directly to the trunk.

When a woman smokes or consumes excessive alcohol during pregnancy, fetal growth and development may also be adversely affected.

The first years after birth are also crucial to the development of a sense of emotional well-being and security and the subsequent ability to function comfortably

Modern medicine enables most people in developed countries to reach full life expectancy. *(Zefa)*

The health care observed by a woman during pregnancy directly affects the development of her baby. Diagnostic tests such as this ultrasound fetal scan can help to detect certain health problems. *(John Watney Photo Library)*

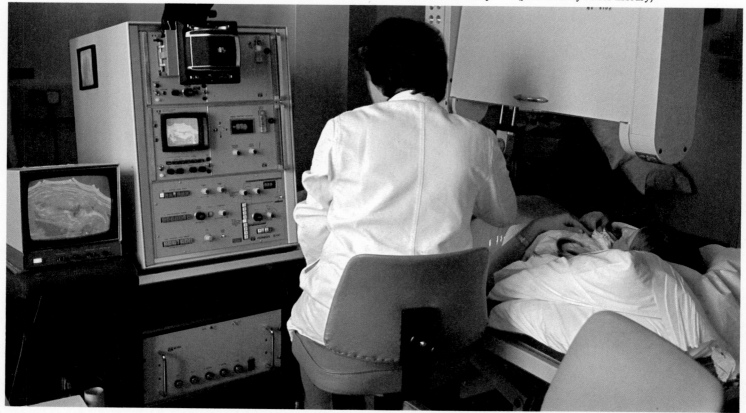

and satisfactorily in society throughout life. A caring and loving mother figure and adequate nurture, stimulation and body contact all contribute to an individual's future emotional and social development. Malnutrition in this period may also result in later difficulties as full growth and development may never occur if dietary deficiencies are severe.

An individual's present environment and lifestyle also contain many factors that influence health, for example inadequate or excessive food intake, lack of exercise, obesity, smoking, excessive alcohol and stresses related to work or home.
Health in the past Patterns of health in the community and the measures undertaken by authorities to influence these have changed throughout the ages, as have attitudes and beliefs. However, most of the diseases present today have plagued man since early civilization.

Hippocrates, the 'father of medicine', was one of the first to document the states of health and disease systematically. Some of his records still survive. At the time, most people believed that loss of health was caused by evil spirits or by the anger of gods. Nevertheless, surgery, though crude and simple by modern standards, and medications derived from plants and herbs, were regularly used. About 3000 B.C. the ancient Greeks had a pharmaceutical list containing over 700 medicinal recipes which were claimed to cure conditions such as dropsy, constipation and vomiting.

Control of infection was the main thrust in the improvement of public health which occurred in the period from the ancient Greek and Roman civilizations to the eighteenth century. Improvements in public hygiene, water supply and sanitation greatly reduced the incidence of epidemic and pandemic outbreaks of infection, the effect of which could be devastating. For example, three-quarters of the people in the Athenian empire died during the plague in 430 B.C., and millions died during the Black Death (1346–1361) and the Great Plague of London (1665–1666).

Health today Modern medicine has enabled the vast majority of people in highly developed countries to reach full life expectancy. In America in 1980, for example, official statistics indicated that the average life of a female was 77.2 years and of a male 70.2 years. At the turn of the previous century these figures were 54.8 and 51.1 years respectively.

Apart from the benefits of immunization, medications and quarantine, the environmental, occupational, educational and social aspects of health are now receiving more attention. Measures to protect the environment include car and factory emission controls, regulations concerning water pollution and restrictions on excessive noise.

The health of factory workers is improved by the control of noise within factories, and by techniques that reduce dust and carcinogens (cancer-producing agents) such as asbestos fibers.

Health is improved and illness and injury prevented through education programs about healthy lifestyle, the dangers of drinking and driving, and the advantages of using a seat belt.

There is a belief that the increased pace and stresses of modern life, particularly since the last world war, have led to a decline in the social aspects of health.
Health in the Third World In other parts of the world, health needs are different. A quarter of the world's population is starving; overcrowded conditions, poverty and squalor all affect the health of millions. Some of the attempts at improving the health of people in the Third World involve providing adequate food, education, generally improving the level of medical care and living standards, and providing the means of birth control.

Hygiene

The word 'hygiene' is derived from the Greek *hygieia*, health. Hygiene is the science of health and its maintenance, and involves all aspects of preventive medicine and health promotion.
Personal hygiene As it concerns the individual, personal hygiene is distinct from public or environmental hygiene, though they overlap considerably in some areas.

Cities depend on cleaning services to prevent spread of disease.

Attention to personal hygiene is part of the everyday routine for most families in developed countries. (*Zefa*)

Proper nutrition, exercise and leisure contribute to a healthy lifestyle, and to the prevention of obesity, heart disease, and other illnesses. In this regard health education is extremely important.

Physical hygiene such as washing the hands after using the toilet and before preparing or eating food, and regular bathing, are important. These are usually learnt at an early age.

Oral hygiene is the care of the teeth and gums to prevent problems such as cavities, halitosis ('bad breath') and gingivitis.

Mental hygiene deals with the development of mental and emotional health. Early childhood experiences have an important influence on this, particularly in the ability to trust and form healthy interpersonal relationships.
Public hygiene The question of industrial hygiene has grown considerably in importance during the last 10 to 20 years with the activities of environmentalists and the introduction of green bans opposed to certain commercial and industrial developments. During this period a considerable amount of legislation has been introduced covering matters such as factory and machinery design, control of the disposal of industrial waste, control of industrial noise and dust (in an attempt to reduce noise-induced deafness and dust

diseases) and protection against radiation in those industries using materials such as uranium.

The extent and quality of public sanitation and water supply has a crucial effect on the health of a community. In many underdeveloped countries, the overcrowding, poor sanitation and inadequate water supplies significantly contribute to the high incidence of illness and disease. In highly developed industrial societies the quality of public sanitation and water supply is regularly checked as part of the program for maintaining the good health of the community.

In many countries legislation ensures the hygienic preparation and distribution of foodstuffs, and public health inspectors regularly check the premises in which food is manufactured or prepared.

The incidence of many diseases has been significantly reduced by medical advances and the improvements in the environment and in public health facilities. For example, pasteurization of milk has greatly reduced the incidence of diseases such as tuberculosis and brucellosis, and fluoridation of the water supplies has significantly reduced tooth decay. In the future there is likely to be action to control or eliminate lead in petrol and toxic substances such as the defoliant dioxin which may have a harmful effect on pregnant mothers and their unborn children.

Community health facilities such as hospitals, health centers and private practice of health all contribute to the hygiene of the community.

Preventive medicine

The application of medical and scientific knowledge and techniques to prevent disease or its progression is called preventive medicine. Over the last century the medical profession has systematically applied itself to improving methods of avoiding disease and a great deal of progress has been made. Diseases such as smallpox have been eradicated, others like leprosy and malaria brought under relative control and the general level of nutrition has been markedly improved in many countries.

Community involvement is crucial and the quality of the environment as affecting health must be studied. Doctors are not alone in promoting public health, as social workers, nurses, teachers, administrators and others all practise preventive medicine by ensuring that public water supplies, waste disposal, food purity, overcrowding and excessive radiation are all regularly observed to pre-empt possible health dangers. Aesthetic concerns have led to incidental health benefits, such as improved methods of town sanitation, less overcrowding and better ventilation, all of which reduce the likelihood of typhoid and other enteric diseases.

Immunization Vaccination against smallpox, introduced during the late eighteenth

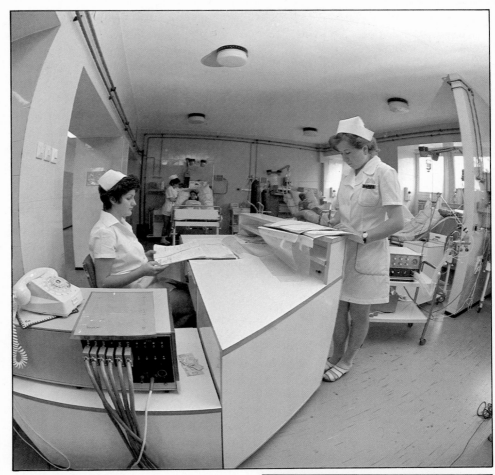

Hospital discharge statistics provide useful information on medical treatment. (Zefa)

century, led to immunization against many other infectious diseases. Tetanus declined dramatically between the two world wars following immunization, as have diptheria, whooping cough, poliomyelitis, measles, German measles (rubella), mumps and even common flu.

Quarantine stations and services have reduced the spread of human, animal and crop diseases. Diseases may be quickly discovered, traced and even eliminated. The progress of communicable diseases can be traced and subsequently countered as they spread through communities.

Pollution control Problems caused by chemical poisons, such as lead in house paint, smog in the atmosphere and industrial pollution of the sea may be pinpointed and eliminated where possible.

Child welfare has become a basic concern of most preventive health programs. Pregnant mothers are offered free health checks and advice and specialized obstetric services if necessary, as well as assistance with nutrition. Breast-feeding, now known to protect infants from many illnesses, is actively encouraged. The addition of vitamins, particularly C and D, to foodstuffs to combat rickets and scurvy, and fluoride to water to reduce tooth decay have also improved child

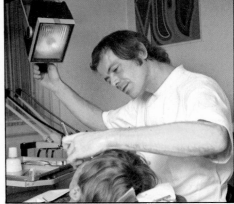

The addition of fluoride to drinking water is an effective protection against tooth decay. (PAF International)

health. Various government agencies and health inspectors advise on nutrition generally and scrutinize the quality and purity of both food and drugs.

Clinics exist to offer advice concerning child-rearing and behavior problems. The study of child abuse has helped to reduce it while much education has been aimed at parents to try and reduce child deaths through accident. Fencing of family pools, campaigns to teach children to swim and child-proof medicine cabinets have all helped.

The action of sunlight on the body is necessary for the formation of vitamin D, so some time spent out of doors each day is valuable.

Regular moderate exercise such as daily jogging promotes fitness and helps avoid some health problems. *(Zefa)*

Adult health services have developed radically on a world-wide basis since World War II. These include routine physical examinations, cancer screening, annual chest x-rays to detect tuberculosis or lung cancer, and blood tests and cardiographs to anticipate heart disease. Appropriate diets may be prescribed for obesity, thus lessening the risk of strokes, heart attacks and diabetes, while regular exercise is usually encouraged.

Keep fit campaigns widely promote jogging, swimming and regular sporting activities. Government propaganda campaigns in the media helped alert the public to the dangers of drug misuse, including alcohol and tobacco.

Industry has been obliged to take increased steps to prevent accidents and ill-health. Pre-employment medical checks, to determine a potential employee's suitability and ability to cope with his prospective job, are common. Equipment that could endanger health is monitored. Excessive noise that might cause permanent deafness is eliminated where possible and close checks are kept on radiation levels where relevant. Where the risk of silicosis of the lungs exists many industries insist on regular x-rays for their staff. Repetitive and mind-destroying procedures are made more interesting or varied wherever possible, reducing accidents and absenteeism and raising morale.

Mental illness has come within the sphere of preventive medicine. Increasingly, individuals are encouraged to join the community instead of being relegated to institutions. Halfway houses for those leaving institutions enable them to regain confidence in their own abilities before being integrated into the community.

Nutrition

The process of consuming, digesting, and absorbing food to maintain life is known as nutrition. It is vital for the growth and adequate functioning of all body tissues and organs, and for the production of energy. The science of nutrition requires an understanding of the relationship between diet and health, the appropriate foods and their nutrient values, and the processes involved in their use.

Derived from the Greek *diaita*, way of living, diet may describe the general nourishment a person receives or a modified eating regimen made necessary by some medical condition. Although dieting often refers to a regimen which is designed to reduce excess body weight, special diets for other conditions are also available.

Daily nutritional requirements vary considerably, depending on age, sex, health and general level of physical activity. Food provides the energy and the basic chemicals necessary to enable the body to function, move, remain warm, grow and heal damaged tissue. A balanced diet must contain a sufficient amount of energy and have adequate proteins, carbohydrates, fats, vitamins, minerals and water. Roughage, or food residue, is also an essential component of a balanced diet.

Measuring energy needs

The amount of energy that the body can extract from various foodstuffs was for many years expressed as Calories, a unit of heat energy. One calorie, written with

Nutritional requirements vary from person to person and depend on age, weight, sex and lifestyle. Children have special energy needs corresponding to their growth rate. *(Zefa)*

Daily energy requirements vary according to age and activity.

a small *c*, is defined as the amount of energy required, under standardized conditions, to raise the temperature of 0.35 fluid ounce (1 mL) of water through one degree Celsius. One thousand calories, known also as one kilocalorie, equals one Calorie, written with a capital C.

Ideally the energy put into the body should balance the energy used. The body needs energy for basic functions, for work or physical activity and for growth. When the energy input exceeds these needs, the excess is converted to fatty tissue and body weight increases. Each additional 0.35 ounce (1 g) of body weight represents an energy excess of about 8 calories.

The basal metabolic rate (BMR) is the amount of energy required per hour or day to maintain the body's ongoing processes such as blood circulation, breathing and digestion. A man needs about 5000 kilojoules per day when he is completely at rest and in surroundings that are at a comfortable temperature. In cold weather an increase in the BMR may be required to maintain body temperature.

Apart from external temperatures, physical and chemical changes within the body also affect the basal metabolic rate. Because muscle tissue has a higher rate of metabolism, or energy utilization, than fatty tissue, a lean person will have a significantly higher basal metabolic rate. Tall people who have a larger body surface area for a set weight, also have a higher basal metabolic rate because heat loss is proportional to the surface area of the body. Females have a relatively higher proportion of body fat than males and therefore have a slower rate of metabolism. Once adulthood has been reached, the basal metabolic rate declines with increasing age.

Daily dietary needs

The amount of work or physical activity affects dietary energy requirements. Someone undertaking a normal daily routine of dressing, moving around and participating in a sedentary lifestyle may require about 2200 calories per day, whereas someone involved in heavy manual labor may require more than twice that amount of energy. Because more energy is required for a heavy person to walk 1 mile than for a light person, the heavy person may compensate by undertaking less exertion.

Generally, women need less energy-giving food than men.

Growth allowances have to be considered when calculating energy requirements. At birth, an infant requires about 225 calories per pound weight per day, whereas an average adult needs only about 17 calories per pound per day. During the first year of life when the body weight may treble and during the adolescent growth spurt, energy needs per pound are at their greatest. During pregnancy fetal growth plus the increased body weight of the mother may require up to 300 extra calories per day and, during the period of lactation, four times this excess may be needed. Even taking into account all these variables, the individual energy needs of people show a great deal of variation.

Proteins, carbohydrates, fats, vitamins, minerals and water are essential components of the diet required for the metabolic and chemical reactions which produce energy for use in the body.

Proteins

Proteins are found in every animal and plant cell. They are complex organic chemical structures that are essential to life. Although nitrogen, carbon, hydrogen and oxygen are the main components of protein, small amounts of sulphur and phosphorus are also present.

All plant and animal cells contain protein. In general, animal-derived products such as meat, fish, cheese, milk and eggs

have a higher concentration than plants. However, some plants, such as the soy bean, also contain a high proportion of protein. Although soy bean may provide 4 calories of energy per 0.35 ounce (1 g) of protein, other nutrients in the diet, such as fats, provide more energy per ounce. In America and other developed countries, most people eat a considerable excess of protein: only 1.6 ounce–1.9 ounce (45–55 g) are needed each day.

Proteins break down into organic com-

The energy needs of a man doing laboring work in a cold climate exceed those of a man working in an air-conditioned office.

pounds called amino acids which are absorbed from the intestine into the bloodstream. Once within the tissues, the amino acids are relinked to form the many proteins of the body. Of the twenty-two amino acids found in human tissues, most can be manufactured in the body from other protein. The eight amino acids which the body cannot make, the *essential amino acids*, must be obtained from food.

Protein, which comprises 10 to 15 per cent of body weight, is important for growth and the repair of damaged tissues. It is the major component, not only of muscle and bone, but also of hair and nails. Within the bloodstream, hemo-

globin, the pigment that carries oxygen to all tissues, as well as albumin, fibrinogen and the globulins are all composed of protein. Albumin, the main plasma protein, helps to maintain the osmotic pressure of blood. Fibrinogen is important in blood clotting, and globulins include antibodies which are important components of the immune system. Hormones, such as pituitary hormones and insulin, are proteins, as are all the body's enzymes. Enzymes act as catalysts or facilitators of the many complex and essential chemical reactions occurring within the body.

Excess protein within the body is also broken down: nitrogen is removed by the liver and excreted in the urine as urea and the remainder is converted to fats and sugars for energy.

Over half the world's population has inadequate dietary protein levels. Kwashiorkor is a condition that occurs in children as a result of protein deficiency. It tends to develop during the second year of life after the baby has been weaned. Symptoms include growth failure, anemia, apathy or reduced mental functioning.

Athletes use extraordinary amounts of energy, so their diet must contain foods which supply this need. *(Zefa)*

Carbohydrates

The main energy source in the diet is carbohydrates. Grains, vegetables, fruits and plant foods in general are the main sources of carbohydrates. Flour-based products such as pastries, cakes and bread are especially rich in calories and carbohydrates.

Carbohydrates are organic compounds that contain carbon, hydrogen and oxygen. They are formed primarily by plants which use the energy from the sun to combine carbon dioxide and water, a process known as photosynthesis. Within the body, 0.35 ounce (1 g) of carbohydrate provides 4 calories of energy when glucose is oxidized back to carbon dioxide and water. The three main groups of carbohydrates are sugars, starches and non-digestible carbohydrates.

A sugar, the smallest carbohydrate molecule, is a white crystalline solid which may dissolve in water. Complex carbohydrate is broken down by digestive enzymes to form monosaccharides which are subsequently absorbed across the wall of the intestine. A monosaccharide, which has six carbon atoms, is the basic carbohydrate unit. The three main monosaccharides are glucose, fructose and galactose.

Energy value of food

	Weight (edible portion)		Calories (average figures)
Milk			
1 glass	8	oz	154
Meat group			
Cooked meats, average fat	3.5	oz	303
Egg, 1	1.5	oz	72
Vegetables and fruit			
Fresh fruit, average piece	3.5	oz	46
Salad vegetables	3.5	oz	26
Potatoes, corn, broad beans, ½ cup	3.5	oz	81
Bread and cereals			
Bread, 1 slice	.8	oz	56
Cereal, prepared, 1 cup	1	oz	100
Fats			
Butter	1	oz	217
Oil, dripping	1	oz	265
Other			
Sugar, 1 teaspoon	.18	oz	19
Meat or yeast extract	.18	oz	9
Cookies , 2	.5	oz	68

Common sources of protein

Food	Weight edible portion		Protein content (ounces)
Animal protein			
Meat, medium fat, cooked	3.5	oz	0.9
Fish, cooked	3.5	oz	0.74
Whole milk, 1 glass	8	oz	0.3
Cheese, 1 cube (2·5 cm)	.7	oz	0.24
Egg, one	1.5	oz	0.21
Vegetable protein			
Beans, lima or haricot, cooked, ½ cup, 30 g dry	4	oz	2.85
Nuts, shelled	1	oz	0.24
Bread, 1 slice	.8	oz	0.002
Ready-to-eat cereal (1 cup cornflakes or 2 wheat biscuits)	1	oz	0.10
Flour, 1 cup	4	oz	0.45
Potato, cooked, 1 medium	3	oz	0.002

A disaccharide, formed from the linkage of two monosaccharides, is the main form of sugar in the diet. Sucrose, derived from sugar cane, consists of glucose and fructose and is the sugar commonly used to sweeten foods and drinks. Lactose or milk sugar is made up of glucose and galactose molecules, and maltose or malt sugar is comprised of two glucose molecules.

Polysaccharides, which include starch and glycogen, are formed by the combination of ten or more monosaccharides. Unlike sugars, they are not sweet and do not dissolve in water.

Starch is the main form of storage of plant energy and is present in vegetables including roots and in unripe fruit. When eaten by man, starch is broken down into glucose molecules which are then absorbed.

Glycogen is a polysaccharide that is sometimes referred to as animal starch because animals, and man, may store carbohydrate in the form of glycogen. Found in the liver, and to a lesser extent in muscle tissue, glycogen may be converted readily into glucose should a sudden source of energy be required. Only a small amount of carbohydrate is stored as glycogen which comprises less than 3 per cent of the body weight. Excessive carbohydrate is mainly converted to fat which is then stored under the skin and in other tissues.

Carbohydrate intolerance In the digestive tract the starches and sugars are broken down into simple sugars by chemicals called enzymes and are then absorbed by the body. In certain people this normal absorption does not occur, due to the relative or absolute deficiency of the enzymes in the intestine.

The most common deficiency is that of the enzyme lactase which breaks down

Many vegetables and fruits can be included in the diet of people who suffer from carbohydrate intolerance.

lactose found primarily in milk and dairy products. This enzyme deficiency can be either primary or secondary. The primary deficiency is hereditary and much more common in Oriental and black races than in Caucasians. Secondary deficiency often follows diseases of the intestine such as gastroenteritis and celiac disease.

Symptoms associated with carbohydrate intolerance are diarrhea, cramping abdominal pain and flatulence following ingestion of carbohydrate (milk or dairy products in the case of lactase deficiency).

Diagnosis is made by a lactose tolerance test which involves giving the patient a test dose of lactose and measuring blood sugar levels. The treatment is simply to avoid foods which contain lactose such as milk and milk products. Milk substitutes and other suitable foods are available for those affected.

Fats

Lipids or fats are a series of substances composed of carbon, hydrogen and oxygen and comprising an important part of the diet. The major dietary sources of fats are butter, margarine, cooking oils, dairy products and fatty meats. The first three of these foods contain over 90 per cent fat. With increasing affluence the level of fat, as well as the level of protein, in the diet is usually increased.

However, the excessive dietary energy which is stored as fat in adipose tissue just under the skin is mostly derived from biochemical conversion of excessive carbohydrate rather than directly from fat in the diet. In lean people about 15 per cent of the body weight is fat whereas the percentage may rise to over 60 in the obese.

Fats are the most efficient source of energy per unit of weight, providing more energy per gram (9 c/g) than the same amount each of protein and carbohydrate combined. Because of this concentrated energy only small amounts of fat are necessary in the diet. Fats also store and aid in the absorption of essential fat-soluble vitamins, and supply essential fatty acids.

Fatty acids, several of which are essential to metabolism, are composed of chains of carbon and hydrogen atoms. Saturated fatty acids have carbon atoms linked by single bonds while polyunsaturated fatty acids have double or triple bonds. Because they are unable to be manufactured in the body, they must be obtained from the diet and are therefore termed essential fatty acids, the main ones being linoleic and arachidonic acids. As only very small quantities are needed, and they are plentiful in food, deficiency states are very uncommon.

Cholesterol The role of fats and cholesterol in the development of atheroma and coronary artery disease has received much publicity in recent years. Cholesterol is a component of fat, especially that derived from animals, as well as an important chemical produced within the body and present in all cells. Vitamin D and a number of hormones are manufactured from cholesterol which also has a number of other functions.

Although the blood level of cholesterol has been shown to have a close correlation with the prevalence of coronary artery disease, whether it is a cause or a result of the condition is still uncertain. Currently about 35 per cent of energy in Western diets comes from fats. Because of their direct effect of lowering blood cholesterol and evidence that heart disease is also reduced, some authorities have suggested that at least 10 per cent of an individual's energy needs should be derived from polyunsaturated fats (particularly from margarines and cooking oils derived from plants).

Vitamins

Vitamins are a series of organic compounds which are required in very small quantities for the regulation of chemical reactions in the body. They are not a direct source of energy and are effective in very small amounts.

Vitamin A, which is soluble fat, is mostly formed in the body from carotenes, particularly beta carotenes which are chemicals found in food. As well as spinach, carrots and cabbages, dairy products and fish oil are good sources of vitamin A. The average daily requirement is estimated to be about 750 micrograms (μg).

A deficiency of vitamin A is uncommon in adulthood as the body may store up to a year's supply in the liver. Because formation of new skin is affected by vitamin A, inadequate levels affect the skin and eyes, which become dry as sweat, sebaceous and tear gland secretions diminish. Night blindness, or an inability to see properly in subdued light, occurs because the retina, the light-sensitive membrane at the rear of the eye, requires vitamin A to maintain the normal chemical reaction that changes light waves into nerve impulses.

B group vitamins tend to be found to-

Fresh oranges are a valuable source of vitamin C.

Green vegetables are a valuable source of folic acid, which is an essential nutrient for man.

gether in food and, because they are water soluble, are readily excreted from the body rather than stored.

Vitamin B_1 or thiamine is found in all plant and animal tissues, although it is most concentrated in the outer husks of grain and in yeast. The daily requirement is about 1 milligram. Vitamin B_1 completes the oxidation of glucose into carbon dioxide and water and the energy produced is distributed to the various tissues. Although deficiency states which cause beri beri are uncommon in developed countries, adults who suffer from alcoholism may be affected. Swelling of the legs caused by heart failure and muscle weakness are the most common features.

Vitamin B_2 or riboflavine is also distributed widely among animal and plant tissues and has a similar role to thiamine in the breakdown of glucose. About 1.3 milligrams are required each day. A deficiency state is very uncommon but, when it occurs, causes dermatitis and inflammation of the tongue and lining of the mouth.

Nicotinic acid (niacin) and nicotinamide are closely related compounds that are also part of the B group vitamins. Meat, particularly liver and kidney, and wholemeal cereal, provide these vitamins. Some is also produced within the body from the amino acid tryptophan. About 15 milligrams are required each day to enable carbohydrates, fats and proteins to produce satisfactory levels of energy.

A deficiency state, known as pellagra, may occur in underdeveloped countries where maize, which is low in both niacin and tryptophan, is the major cereal. Symptoms of the deficiency include diarrhea, dermatitis and mental disturbances. Vitamin B_6 is a group of closely related compounds that are found in virtually all plant and animal foods. The primary function of pyridoxine, the main one, is in the metabolism of a number of amino acids, including the conversion of tryptophan to niacin. About 2 milligrams are required each day but, as other nutritional problems tend to occur first, deficiency states are very rare. Some drugs may affect chemical reactions that involve pyridoxine, causing symptoms such as dermatitis. Pyridoxine injections and tablets are used with varying success in the treatment of morning sickness, dysmenorrhea, menopausal symptoms, and depression resulting from use of the oral contraceptive pill.

Biotin is present in many foods, but especially in kidneys, liver, milk and some fruits. It is probably an essential vitamin in man although its function is not fully understood. This B group vitamin may be bound by the chemical avidin which is present in raw egg-white, rendering it unavailable for absorption. Dermatitis, weight loss and muscle weakness are the main symptoms of prolonged biotin deficiency.

Pantothenic acid is derived from a wide variety of foods and from bacterial action on food residue within the colon. An essential B group vitamin for many of the chemical reactions of the body, deficiencies of pantothenic acid have not been noted.

Folic acid is found especially in liver, kidney and green vegetables, although some is present in virtually all foods. As an essential nutrient for man, folic acid is necessary for the activity of a number of enzymes and for the correct functioning of cells. About 0.4 milligram is required each day.

Deficiency leads to the development of anemia, characterized by enlarged red blood cells. Elderly people, pregnant women and alcoholics who have an inadequate diet are most likely to be affected. Although during pregnancy more folic acid is used, the average Western diet usually contains enough of the vitamin to compensate.

Vitamin B₁₂ or cyanocobalamin refers to closely related chemical substances which are found in significant quantities only in foods derived from animals. Vitamin B_{12} is necessary for the production of red blood cells. The average daily requirement is about 5 micrograms and deficiency states are uncommon in Western countries. Vegetarians, pregnant women and those people with pernicious anemia are most likely to develop symptoms of deficiency.

Pernicious anemia results from an absence of *intrinsic factor*, a chemical which is produced by the stomach and which is essential for the absorption of vitamin B_{12}. Protein production is also dependent upon adequate levels of vitamin B_{12}. Prolonged inadequate blood levels of vitamin B_{12} may cause anemia characterized by large red blood cells, inflammation of the tongue and abnormalities of the spinal cord and peripheral nerves.

Vitamin C or ascorbic acid is primarily

Common sources of vitamin A

Food	Weight edible portion	Retinol activity (micrograms)
Egg, 1 medium	1.5 oz	130
Cheese	.7 oz	85
Whole milk, 1 glass	8 oz	95
Butter	2 tablespoons	380
Table margarine	2 tablespoons	245
Carrots	3.5 oz	1,170
Silver beet, spinach	3.5 oz	1,010
Broccoli, pumpkin	3.5 oz	475
Green peas, beans	3.5 oz	65
Brussel sprouts, corn	3.5 oz	35
Lettuce, raw, 2 small leaves	.7 oz	60
Mango, 1 small	3.5 oz	805
Apricots, 3 medium	3.5 oz	245
Tomato, 1 medium	3.8 oz	130
Pineapple, 1 slice	2.8 oz	35
Banana, 1 medium	3.5 oz	35
Orange, 1 medium	4.5 oz	30

Common sources of thiamine (vitamin B₁)

Food	Weight edible portion	Thiamine content (milligrams)
Meats, cooked		
Pork	3.5 oz	0·400
Bacon, 2 strips (15 cm)	.7 oz	0·080
Beef and mutton	3.5 oz	0·100
Fish	3.5 oz	0·060
Milk		
Whole milk, 1 glass	8 oz	0·085
Cheese	.7 oz	0·050
Cereals		
Bread, white, 1 slice	.8 oz	0·030
Bread, wholemeal, 1 slice	1.1 oz	0·087
Oatmeal, cooked, 1 cup	8 oz	0·180
Cornflakes, enriched, 1 cup	1 oz	0·400
Wheat biscuits, enriched, 2	1.2 oz	0·160
Vegetables		
Vegetables, cooked, average, ½ cup	3.5 oz	0·120
Fruit		
Fruit, raw, average, 1 piece	3.5 oz	0·030
Spreads, etc		
Peanut butter, 1 tablespoon	.1 oz	0·210
	.7 oz	0·010

found in fresh fruit and vegetables. A deficiency of vitamin C causes scurvy which results in bleeding into the skin and gums, general skin changes and fatigue. Severe deprivation may cause death. Infants without vitamin C supplementation and elderly people on poor diets are most often affected. In previous years sailors undertaking long journeys with little access to fresh fruit and vegetables were particularly susceptible to scurvy.

Vitamin C promotes healing and tissue growth and about 10 milligrams are required each day to prevent the symptoms of scurvy. Over recent years some controversy has existed about the efficacy of much higher doses of vitamin C in protecting the body against the common cold as well as a number of other conditions.

Vitamin D exists in two chemical forms — vitamin D_2 or ergocalciferol and vitamin D_3 or cholecalciferol. The original compound designated vitamin D_1 was found to be a mixture of the other two forms. Most vitamin D is produced by substances in food which are absorbed into the body, enter the fatty tissues of the skin and are then converted to vitamin D by the action of sunlight.

Some vitamin D is found in food, primarily in fish liver oils. It is acted upon chemically by the liver and kidney before transferring to bone and intestinal tissues where it assists in the absorption and bone deposition of calcium. About 1 microgram is required daily.

Deficiency of vitamin D most frequently occurs in young children who have not been exposed to sufficient sunshine. The

Common sources of vitamin C (ascorbic acid)

Food	Weight edible portion	Vitamin C content (milligrams)
Fruit, average, raw, 1 piece or ½ cup	3.5 oz	8
Fruit, average cooked or canned, ½ cup	3.5 oz	4
Vegetables, average, salad, raw, large plate	6 oz	25
Potatoes, boiled, baked, mashed or fried, 1 small or ½ cup	3 oz	10
Selected fruits, raw, average serving—		
Cantaloupe	4.5 oz	50
Apple, apricot, banana, nectarine, peach, pineapple	3.5 oz	15
Watermelon, cherry, plum, pear, fig	3.5 oz	50
Fruit juices, fresh or canned, ½ cup		
Orange, grapefruit	4 oz	55
Tomato	4 oz	20
Selected vegetables, average serving, ½ cup		
Capsicums (peppers), raw	3.5 oz	300
Broccoli, cooked	3.5 oz	90
Tomato, raw or cooked	3.5 oz	20
Asparagus, cabbage, cauliflower, sweet potato, cooked	3.5 oz	35
Beans (French), beetroot, carrots, onion, parsnips, pumpkin, turnips, cooked	3.5 oz	5

condition is called rickets and results in abnormalities of bones which soon become deformed. Osteomalacia is a similar condition which occurs in adults who suffer from vitamin D deficiency.

Vitamin E consists of a group of chemical substances known as tocopherols. They are fat soluble and are present in milk and any plant foods, especially vegetable oils and whole grain cereals. Although the action of these substances varies from species to species, in man they appear to strengthen cell membranes and aid the metabolism of fats. Although a deficiency is rare, when it occurs anemia, skin rashes and edema (accumulation of fluid in the tissues) result.

The average daily requirement is 10 to 15 milligrams. If a person has a normal diet and blood levels of vitamin E are satisfactory, extra quantities of the vitamin are not required. Authorities differ about whether fertility is promoted, aging slowed, or healing processes accelerated by this substance.

Vitamin K or phytomenadione, an oil found in liver and in leafy vegetables, is essential for the normal blood clotting process. Because it is present in foods and may also be manufactured by bacteria in the intestine, deficiency states are very uncommon. Bleeding disorders may occur if levels of vitamin K in the body are inadequate.

Minerals

Minerals or mineral salts consist of a group of elements necessary for normal human body functioning. As they are excreted from the body daily, sufficient quantities, contained in water and food, must be replaced.

The main elements are calcium, phosphorus, sulphur, potassium, sodium, chlorine, magnesium, iron, iodine and fluorine. Other trace elements include zinc, manganese, copper, cobalt, molybdenum and selenium but their function is

Most body calcium is in the bones and teeth. All mineral salts are water soluble and can be excreted from the body, so an adequate daily intake is necessary.

not fully understood. Although some other elements like chromium and cadmium are found in the body, it is not known whether they have any specific or important function.

Calcium salts are the most common mineral in the body, particularly in the bones and teeth. Dairy products, fish and green vegetables are all important sources of calcium in the diet. Although 99 per cent of body calcium is in the skeleton, some aids blood clotting and the contraction and relaxation of muscle and heart. Calcium also transmits nerve impulses and activates many enzymes. Vitamin D is essential for the adequate absorption and utilization of calcium, the blood level of which is maintained by the parathyroid glands. Deficiency states are uncommon but bony disorders, such as osteomalacia, are the main results of inadequate calcium.

Phosphorus in various forms, occurs in most tissues of the body. As well as its many other functions, phosphorus combines with calcium to give strength to bone and teeth. As cereals and many other foods such as nuts, cheese, eggs, liver and milk contain phosphorus,

deficiency states are uncommon.

Sulphur, a common mineral of the human body, is mainly found in protein as a component of the amino acids cystine and methionine. Deficiency states are extremely rare.

Potassium is found in all body tissues, especially within the cells. One of its many uses is to aid in the functioning of nerves and muscles. Because it is present in most foods, particularly fruits and vegetables, deficiency is very rare unless potassium is lost from the body as may occur with persistent diarrhea or when diuretic drugs increase urine flow. In such circumstances potassium in the diet may need to be supplemented.

Sodium and chlorine are usually absorbed together as sodium chloride or common salt. They are present in all foods and tissues of the body, particularly in the bloodstream and the fluid surrounding cells. Changes in sodium and chlorine concentration affect the function of muscles and nerves as well as fluid distribution within various parts of the body, for example the bloodstream. As only about 1 gram of each is required daily, deficiency states are very rare. Although more than twelve times the amount is often absorbed, the excess is rapidly excreted by the kidney.

Magnesium is present in bone and other tissues. Tetany, or muscle spasm, occurs when levels are reduced. Enzymes that control many chemical reactions in the body are dependent upon this mineral. Plant foods provide an abundant supply of magnesium and deficiency states are quite uncommon.

Iron is an important element in the body. Hemoglobin, the red pigment in blood cells that carries oxygen to the tissues, contains iron. Although most foods, especially meat, cereals and green vegetables, contain iron, milk and cheese are poor sources. The diet often contains little in excess of body requirements, so that during pregnancy or after blood loss, iron-deficiency anemia may occur. Dietary supplements are often taken during these periods.

Iodine is required by the thyroid gland for the production of the hormone thyroxine. If blood levels of iodine are inadequate, this gland enlarges to form a goiter. Sea foods, or milk and vegetables from areas where the soil has an adequate level of iodine are good dietary sources, but in many countries where the soil is deficient in this element, iodine is added to table salt.

Fluorine which may occur in tea and some sea foods, is found naturally in only some water supplies. It replaces some chloride in tooth enamel and to a lesser extent in bone. Because such teeth become much more resistant to tooth decay, many cities have added fluoride to their water supplies.

Water and the diet

Approximately two-thirds of the body is composed of water. Each individual requires about 2½ quarts (2½ L) of water a day: a percentage of this comes from the break-down of food within the intestine and the rest from water-based drinks.

An adequate fluid intake in the diet is important as water is an essential component of most functions within the body. Water enables chemical reactions to occur and humidifies the air that is breathed in and out. It enables excretion of waste products via the kidneys, aids nutrient transport via the bloodstream and provides a medium for all gland secretions.

An adequate intake of water daily is essential to good health. (Rex Features)

The kidney maintains body fluids at a constant level. Although the average daily output is about 2.6 pints (1.5 L), excretion may range from as little as 1 fluid ounce (300 mL) to 3.9 pints (2.2 L) per day. Excess loss of fluid occurs with vomiting, diarrhea and increased perspiration. Usually the loss can be counteracted by taking in more fluid but if this is not possible, dehydration will develop. Once more than 5 per cent of the body weight is lost in the form of fluid, replacement by means of an intravenous drip may become necessary.

Common sources of calcium

Food	Weight edible portion	Calcium content (milligrams)
Liquid whole milk, 1 glass	8 oz	264
Cheese, 1 cube (2·5 cm)	.7 oz	172
Ice cream, 1 scoop	1 oz	42
Fish		
Cooked fish	3.5 oz	35
Canned salmon, with bones	2 oz	110
Egg, 1	1.5 oz	24
Butter, 2 tablespoons	1.5 oz	6
Bread		
Ordinary, white or brown	.8 oz	3
Breakfast cereals		
Cornflakes, 1 cup	1 oz	1
Wheat biscuits, 2	1 oz	18
Vegetables		
Broccoli	3.5 oz	98
Potato	3.1 oz	8
Fruit, average, raw, 1 piece	3.5 oz	20

Common sources of iron

Food	Weight edible portion	Iron content (milligrams)
Liver	3.5 oz	14·2
Kidney	3.5 oz	14·1
Meat, cooked	3.5 oz	3·5
Egg, 1	1.5 oz	1·1
Green leafy vegetables (silver beet, spinach), ½ cup	3 oz	2·1
Dried beans, cooked, ½ cup	2.5 oz	1·8
Other vegetables, average, ½ cup	2.5 oz	0·4
Wholemeal bread, 1 slice	1 oz	0·8
White bread, 1 slice	.8 oz	0·3
Cooked oatmeal, 1 cup	8 oz	1·4
Fruit, average, ½ cup	3 oz	0·3
Prunes, cooked, ½ cup	1 oz (dry)	0·9
Other dried fruits	1 oz	0·7

Fiber in the diet

Food residue, which is excreted as feces, consists primarily of indigestible fiber or roughage. Most of this comes from plant-derived food and is made up of cellulose and hemicellulose, and to a lesser extent pectin, all of which are large carbohydrate molecules. This fiber absorbs water from the linings of the intestine and produces softer and more voluminous stools.

Cabbage, turnips, corn, peas, beans, onions, parsnips, nuts, wholegrain cereals and fruits are the main sources of fiber or roughage. Defining an acceptable level of fiber in the diet is difficult. An adequate regimen, however, would be to have plenty of fruit and vegetables and to use wholemeal bread and brown rice in preference to the refined varieties. Unprocessed wheat bran with, or in preference to, other breakfast cereals is also helpful.

Bran, an important source of fiber, is the outer husk of grains like wheat.

In recent years increasing evidence has shown that a high residue diet significantly benefits a person's overall health. Constipation and diverticular disease are eased or prevented by such a diet. Appendicitis and cancer of the large bowel may also be less likely in people who have a high fiber content in their food: as the feces of people on a high residue diet move more quickly through the bowel, the bowel lining may be less exposed to potential cancer-producing agents.

Some studies have suggested that increased dietary fiber leads to a lowering of the blood levels of cholesterol, which is thought to be related to some forms of heart disease. Reduction of cholesterol may occur because such diets tend to have a higher proportion of polyunsaturated fats which also lower the blood cholesterol. The increased fiber also absorbs more bile which carries fatty substances, reducing their reabsorption into the bloodstream.

Food for special situations

Because of differing nutritional needs, a particular diet may be required during such periods as childhood, adolescence, and pregnancy and lactation. A special or therapeutic diet may be prescribed to maintain or improve nutrition; to increase or decrease body weight; to eliminate foods which produce an allergic reaction; or to compensate for a particular disease or abnormality.

The most beneficial diet takes into account not only the nutritional and physical properties of the food but also the food preferences of the individual. Requirements for energy, protein, fat, carbohydrate, fiber, minerals and vitamins will be determined by the individual's age, weight, activity and state of health. A dietitian may instruct the person about the importance of the diet in the treatment of the medical condition, and may also suggest how the food may be prepared and presented.

Growing children, sportsmen or people convalescing after an illness require diets high in calories or energy. Other conditions require restricted calories, fat, cholesterol, carbohydrate or other nutrients. In some disorders, such as phenylketonuria, some foods containing a particular substance which cannot be metabolized by the individual must be completely eliminated from the diet. Many other conditions also require special dietary control.

Weight-reducing diet

Low energy diets are usually prescribed for people who are overweight. The reduced intake gradually reduces body weight by using up stored body fat. Once considered a sign of prosperity and success, obesity is now known to place unnecessary strain on the body, increasing

Indigestible vegetable fiber, which can be included in the diet by eating raw vegetables or unprocessed bran, may play a valuable part in the avoidance of intestinal disorders.

susceptibility to infection, diabetes, heart disease, stroke and other disorders.

Accurately defining obesity is not easy as body weight fluctuates daily by 2 to 5 pounds and the ideal weight is dependent on the sex, age, height and bone structure of a person. For any height the difference between a lightly framed and heavily framed individual may be almost 20 pounds. A similar weight gain is usual for those in the 40 to 50 year age group. Athletes rapidly become aware of the effects of even small weight changes which cause loss of energy and loss of speed depending on whether weight is gained or lost from the ideal level.

Suggested reducing diet

Milk: ½ pint

Lean meat, fish, egg or cheese
2 servings per day but preferably a serving at each meal.

Potato: One small (cooked without fat)

Vegetables: Two or more servings (prepared without fat or flour)

Fruit: 2–4 pieces

Bread: 2–4 slices

Butter or table margarine: ½ oz
(The calorie range of this diet is 1200–1800 calories according to the quantities of food eaten.)

Avoid: glucose, honey, chocolates, sweets, soft drinks, dried fruits, jellies, ice cream, cakes and biscuits.

Obesity may be defined as a body weight that is 20 per cent or more above that expected for a person's height, age, sex and physique.
The causes of obesity are more complex than merely overeating, as some obese people eat less than thin ones; in exper-

iments, some volunteers have doubled their energy intake with little gain in weight. Genetic and childhood feeding patterns are often relevant. If a child becomes obese during the first two years of life, he will have more fat cells than normal children of the same age. The size of each fat cell is also greater. Normally a further increase in the number of fat cells only occurs in the pre-adolescent to mid-teenage growth spurt but, in obese toddlers, fat cell numbers increase throughout childhood. The correlation between childhood and adult obesity is therefore very high.

Psychological factors are also important. The way in which a child's dietary needs are met by the mother figure often has lifelong consequences on the person's attitudes to food. If food is used as the main, or only, expression of maternal love, excessive eating, especially during times of stress or depression, is far more likely later on.

Specific diseases such as cretinism are only occasionally responsible for obesity.

The desire to look attractive can be a significant motivation for people who need a slimming diet.

Restricting intake One aim of dieting is to change long-established eating habits so that energy intake from food does not exceed the use of energy. A woman requires from 1000–1500 calories (4000–6000 kj) per day and a man needs from 1500–2200 calories (6000–9000 kj).

A reducing diet should contain 480–700 calories (2000–3000 kj) per day less than the daily needs (12–15 calories (49–63 kj) per pound of body weight for sedentary men and women) so that the body has to burn up stored fat for some of its energy needs. While the diet must contain recommended quantities of protein, vitamins and minerals, it is essential to eat foods which are low in calories and to eat regularly without nibbling between meals. Starvation diets, especially when more than 5 pounds are lost each week, are not recommended. Although many special weight-reducing diets have been constructed, none appear to have any great advantages. As foods that are fattening are primarily those rich in carbohydrates, most diets aim to reduce the intake of such substances.

It may be necessary to change existing eating habits before any weight can be lost.

Foods suitable for a reducing diet are milk, cottage cheese, lean meat, bulky low-calorie fruits and vegetables, small amounts of wholegrain bread and enriched cereal products, tea and coffee without cream or sugar, low-calorie dark green and yellow vegetables and fruits high in vitamin C, and fat-free broth.

Foods to avoid are salad dressing, gravy, fat meat, bacon, sauces, creamed dishes, rich and sweet desserts, fried food, bottled drinks, high-carbohydrate vegetables, sweets, jam, jellies, sweetened fruits and alcoholic beverages.

Prepackaged foods containing essential nutrients but a limited number of calories are available. The foods are often chocolates or milk shakes, appealing to the dieter at first but soon becoming boring. Some have a high protein content which may not be advantageous. The dieter should develop good eating habits rather than continue with such a selective and expensive diet.

Exercise Increased exertion, to accompany changes in food intake, is also important. The initial fluid loss which occurs at the beginning of a diet does not continue. As food is restricted, the body's overall basal metabolic rate slows so that the rate of weight loss is reduced. A further slowing of weight loss may occur for several other reasons. The amount of energy used by a person walking a certain distance is reduced because, as weight is lost, fewer calories are being transported. The person dieting may tend to exercise less.

A gradually increasing program of physical activity should be organized. Because of excessive strain on the heart, extreme or unaccustomed physical activity can be dangerous and is, therefore, not recommended.

Changing eating habits Although many plans for reducing weight have been tried, the percentage of successes is uniformly disappointing. Adequate motivation is required for a person to change an habitual eating pattern and lose weight. Education about diet is necessary so that new eating habits can be continued and weight loss maintained.

A researcher once stated that the bikini and blue jeans did more to reduce adolescent obesity than any prohibition. Such principles of self-mastery, as well as peer group support and encouragement, enable people to take more responsibility for, and pride in, their successful weight loss, a method used by self-help groups such as Weight Watchers. Mastering such a significant problem as obesity requires important lifestyle changes. For many obese people, the chances of success are increased by the opportunities to receive and give constructive feedback about dietary efforts and by the example given by leaders and other successful weight losers. Motivation may be less effective when treatment is given by a professionally-trained person such as a dietitian where the person dieting may be more passive.

Motivation, enhanced by initial success, may be increased further by continued interest, encouragement and support from others, particularly family and close friends. Realistic goals for weight loss should be set. The diet should have sufficient energy content to satisfy basic nutritional needs and to avoid hunger pangs; and it should contain enough variety to meet the psychological needs that the person has in relation to food.

Dietary education is important. The relationship of gross obesity to the significantly increased risks of premature death and to the occurrence of many diseases, such as diabetes and coronary artery problems is usually given. Special dietary charts and booklets are also available. Some people eat excessively when upset or depressed, while others tend to nibble between meals, particularly when they have nothing to do. Once these patterns are understood, plans to change them, by developing other ways of dealing with stress or undertaking other activities, assist greatly.

Behavior modification techniques have been used increasingly over recent years to improve weight loss and general control. After a detailed dietary history is taken, an individual program to modify food consumption is designed. Specific instructions may include eating meals at the same time each day, undertaking no other activities during meals, and replacing eating utensils on the table each time a bite of food has been taken. Such procedures increase the likelihood of eating only at meal times, and not eating when other activities are being undertaken. Slowing the rate of eating and concentrating more on the food often leads to increased satisfaction with decreased intake.

Low-salt diet

Sodium or salt is an essential mineral, required daily in small amounts and found in nearly all plants and animals used as food. Large amounts of sodium occur naturally in meat, fish, poultry, milk, eggs and drinking water. Smaller amounts are present in vegetables and very little occurs in fruit.

As well as being a natural component of food, sodium is added during processing and cooking, usually as table salt (sodium chloride), monosodium glutamate or baking soda (sodium bicarbonate). Some processed foods have a particularly high salt content.

An average diet contains 0.1–0.25 ounces (3–7 mg) of sodium per day. A Westernized diet contains a higher salt content than the body requires. Although the excess is excreted by the kidneys, the excess salt may contribute to high blood pressure.

A low-salt or sodium-restricted diet may be beneficial to people with edema and fluid retention caused by heart or kidney failure, and to people with high blood pressure. When the heart or kidneys fail to function adequately, water and sodium are retained in the body. If the daily intake of sodium is reduced to the amount required so that no sodium is accumulated in the body, less water is retained. The amount of salt allowed in the diet may be as much as 0.08–0.15 ounces (2.5–4.5 mg) of sodium per day or as little as 0.01 ounce (0.5 g) per day. Published tables which display the sodium content of all foods are used in the formulation of diets with a specific sodium content.

Diet during pregnancy and lactation

Apart from an increased energy requirement of 170–250 calories (700–1000 kj) per day in the second half of pregnancy when rapid fetal growth occurs, a number of other nutrients are also required in increased quantities. The developing fetus absorbs the various nutrients required for tissue development from the mother via the placenta.

Protein, a major component of body tissue, should be increased by about 0.28 ounce (8 g) per day. The percentage of carbohydrate in the diet needs to be reduced a little to allow for the protein increase and to ensure that the total energy intake, and therefore weight, does not become excessive. Excessive weight during pregnancy can create its own difficulties.

The minerals, iron and calcium, should be increased the most. During pregnancy the mother increases her blood volume and iron stores and the fetal circulation also needs iron. Calcium is required for the formation of bone. Vitamins A, C, D and folic acid are utilized in increased amounts.

Iron tablets are often taken by the pregnant woman to ensure that the increased needs of 3 milligrams per day are met. Although folic acid is sometimes given as well, other requirements can be incorporated easily within the diet.

The daily diet should include about 1¾ pints (1 L) of milk, which provides calcium and protein; two small or one large serve of meat or fish to provide protein and iron; vegetables and fruit twice a day to provide folic acid, minerals and vitamin C; and cereals to provide minerals, fiber and the B group vitamins.

During lactation more energy than during pregnancy is required. As well as twice as much protein, increased levels of vitamins and minerals, particularly calcium, are needed.

Active, growing children need plenty of milk, fruit and vegetables.

Diet for the expectant mother

Milk: 20–30 oz. 1 oz cheese = 8 oz milk. Use as a plain drink, milk coffee, or dessert.

Meat, fish, poultry, egg, cheese: 2–3 servings.

Vegetables: 3 servings or more (e.g. potato, peas, and a lettuce and tomato salad).

Fruits: 3–4 pieces, raw or stewed. Oranges, tomatoes and grapefruit are fruits rich in vitamin C. Try to have one serving from this group of fruits every day.

Bread and cereals: 3–4 slices of bread. One serving cereal if desired. Preferably wholemeal or brown bread and wholegrain cereals.

Butter or table margarine: ½–1 oz. The diet must be well balanced in order to ensure an adequate thiamine intake. Large amounts of sweet and starchy foods should therefore be avoided.

Daily nutritional needs of the child

Milk: 20 oz (1 oz of cheese contains the same calcium as one cup of milk).

Meat, poultry, eggs, fish or cheese: 1–2 servings.

Vegetables and fruit: 4 servings, including 1 serving raw, preferably citrus fruit or tomato.

Bread and cereals: Amount depends on age, sex and activity.

Butter or table margarine: ½–1 oz.

Diet during infancy and adolescence

Energy requirements per pound of body weight are at a maximum during the first year of life, and they increase again during the adolescent growth spurt. Protein and vitamin needs also increase proportionally.

Milk provides an adequate diet in the initial months of life for most infants, although sometimes additional vitamin C, vitamin D and iron supplementation may be required. By the second year of life the child's diet has become essentially the same as the adult's and no specific additives are required. During growth, an adequate but not excessive energy supply will prevent obesity. If water fluoridation is not present to minimize dental cavities, fluoride tablets are desirable.

High energy diet

High energy foods rich in carbohydrate and fat, such as nuts, eggs and dairy food, may be added to a standard menu to provide a high energy diet. Various high energy powder additives to be taken with milk may further supplement the diet.

A person who is underweight, for example following a major operation, is most likely to be given such a regimen. Malnutrition may also be a result of chronic alcoholism or anorexia nervosa. Once the weight has returned to normal, a standard diet is recommended to minimize the risk of unwanted obesity.

Diet in digestive disorders

Although some disorders of the digestive tract require special diets, other digestive disorders do not respond and the diet seems to have little proven value at all.

Reflux esophagitis Small amounts of gastric juice enter the lower part of the esophagus (which takes food from the mouth to the stomach) and set up an inflammation of the esophagus. Certain foods, including chocolate and coffee, aggravate the condition and should be avoided.

Peptic ulcer A bland milk diet, which once provided the mainstay of treatment for peptic ulcer, does not relieve the condition. Although a patient may be advised to avoid any food that is found to give pain and to eat small frequent meals, a restrictive diet is no longer considered effective.

Acute gastroenteritis A clear fluid diet allows the digestive system to rest but must provide adequate fluid to prevent dehydration and must contain sufficient calories for energy needs. When the condition is very severe, the patient may not be able to take any fluids by mouth. In this case intravenous fluid may be necessary. As the condition improves, diet is still important. A low-fiber, semi-fluid diet which excludes fatty foods, milk products and raw fruit and vegetables is recommended. A full diet may be introduced gradually.

Malabsorption syndromes In some diseases of the intestine, the body does not absorb certain necessary foostuffs or vitamins. In celiac disease, because of the inability to digest gluten, an ingredient of flour, a gluten-free diet is necessary. Gluten-free flour and bread products are available. Although treatment is directed toward the underlying disorder, dietary supplements may have to be given by other means, such as by injection.

Other disorders of digestion Some disorders of the intestine, including diverticular disease, irritable colon and chronic constipation, respond to a high roughage diet. The addition of unprocessed bran to the diet provides the necessary fiber content.

Diseases of the gall bladder, pancreas and liver may also respond to a modification of diet.

High protein diet

Large amounts of meat, fish and dairy products provide a diet high in protein. A high protein diet may be necessary in kidney diseases where protein is lost in the urine, after burns and during recovery from wasting diseases.

Low-fat diet

People with liver or gall bladder disease need to reduce the intake of fat in the diet.

When significant levels of fat from food enter the small intestine, certain hormones cause the gall bladder to contract, releasing extra quantities of bile. If the gall bladder is inflamed (cholecystitis) or gallstones are present (cholelithiasis), such contractions may aggravate the symptoms of pain, nausea and vomiting. People with liver disease, especially hepatitis, may also be adversely affected by fatty foods.

Those with some forms of heart and arterial disease may also need less fat. In atherosclerosis, fatty substances which are deposited on the inside of arterial walls sometimes obstruct blood flow. In hyperlipidemia, the blood levels of cholesterol or triglycerides are increased. Polyunsaturated fats, which are found in vegetable products, are preferred, and the overall level of fat in the diet is also reduced. Eggs, liver, shellfish, cream, butter, fatty meat and chocolate may be restricted. Drugs such as cholestyramine and clofibrate are sometimes used to lower blood fat levels further.

Diet and diabetes

Diabetes is a condition in which the hormone insulin is reduced or absent, resulting in an increased level of glucose in the blood. The blood level of glucose may be controlled by monitoring the intake of carbohydrate in the diet. Not only is the total amount of carbohydrate controlled but the exact time of consumption is also controlled to ensure maximum efficiency of the insulin when it is given by injection.

The Feingold diet

A special regimen that eliminates artificial coloring, preservatives and other food additives from the diet, the Feingold diet is primarily used in the treatment of overactive or hyperkinetic children. Although controversy exists as to the efficacy of these dietary changes, a percentage of such children do show definite improvements.

Vegetarian diets

In recent years diets that are free of animal products have been popular. A strict vegetarian diet excludes eggs and dairy products as well as meat and fish. A carefully selected mixture of vegetables and cereals provides adequate amounts of energy and nutrients. Many vegetables, such as potatoes, are rich in starch and vitamin C, and nuts and grains are quite rich in fat and protein.

Although the body often contains several years supply of vitamin B_{12}, a strictly vegetarian diet may produce a deficiency state, as this vitamin is derived solely from animal products.

Vegetarians eating extreme diets are much more likely to have nutritional deficiencies than those who also eat eggs and dairy products. Various dietary supplements may be necessary, especially during pregnancy or if the diet is strictly adhered to for years.

Deficiency diseases

The conditions described as deficiency diseases are caused either by a lack of essential nutrients in the diet or by the inability of the body to absorb and use the essential nutrients from an adequate diet.

Usually these diseases do not occur alone as most deficient diets have low levels of several nutrients. Those most prone to develop a deficiency disease are the very young, the old, pregnant women or those who already have a chronic disease. Once affected, infections and complications develop.

Important elements in human nutrition are calcium, phosphorus, iron, iodine, fluoride, zinc and copper. Lack of calcium leads to soft bones (osteomalacia); lack of phosphorus to weakness, lack of appetite and bone pains; lack of iron to anemia; lack of iodine to a goiter (enlarged thyroid gland); lack of fluoride to cavities in teeth; lack of zinc to dwarfism and small testes in boys; lack of copper produces anemia.

Starvation The condition of starvation is the result of not getting enough food to eat, usually in a famine. Severe disease of the intestine, in which the nutrients cannot be absorbed, results in starvation also. There is a marked loss (up to 75 per cent) of body weight, the skin is loose, dry and dull. The hair is dry and dull and the eyes sunken. There tends to be a marked accumulation of fluid in the tissues (edema) in the legs, back and abdomen. The starving person is apathetic, indifferent and irritable. Starvation affects all age groups.

Kwashiorkor A disease of young children who have a diet deficient mainly in protein and calories, kwashiorkor is the most important dietary deficient disease in the world, affecting tens of millions of children in India, South East Asia, most parts of Africa, the Middle East, the Caribbean Islands and South and Central America.

It affects children who have been weaned on a diet with virtually no protein in it, especially no milk or milk product. Cassava or local yams may be the main food. The disease often starts before the harvesting season or when the child has some other disorder like measles, malaria or gastroenteritis.

The apathetic, miserable child is underweight but looks larger because of swell-

Iron-deficiency anemia may produce flat, brittle nails.
(*Westmead Center*)

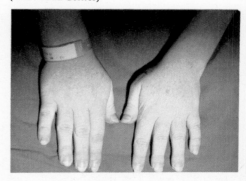

ing of the abdomen and legs. The muscles are wasted and the skin pigmented, flaky and ulcerated. The hair is straight, sparse and changed in color from curly black to grey, brownish-red or white.

The treatment is an easily digested milk based diet which is high in protein and vitamins. It can only be prevented through patient education of mothers and the use of powdered milk supplements.

Vitamin deficiencies Vitamins are organic substances in food which are required in small amounts by the human body. They cannot be made by the body in adequate quantities. Without vitamins a variety of deficiency diseases occur.

The lack of vitamin A (retinol) normally found in milk, butter, cheese, egg yolk and liver, leads to an inability to see shapes in the dark, a dry, thickened outside layer of the eye and an ulcerated cornea. This condition causes blindness. It occurs frequently in association with kwashiorkor in the rice eaters of Asia, in Africa, Latin America and the Middle East.

Beri beri is caused by lack of vitamin B_1 (thiamine). This disease usually occurs where a diet of polished rice provides most of the calories. Beri beri is not often seen now in the developing Asian countries.

The disease starts insidiously with loss of appetite and feeling, with heaviness and weakness in the legs. Sometimes the legs become filled with fluid and enlarged (edematous), and the patient feels numbness and pins and needles in them. The calf muscles are tender. Breathlessness and palpitations with more marked fluid accumulation in the face, chest and abdomen result in eventual heart failure. In some patients, there is no edema of the legs only progressive weakness and wasting so that the affected person at first needs the aid of a walking stick but finally becomes bedridden.

The treatment for mild cases is relatively small amounts of thiamine daily, for acute cases much larger doses are required.

Pellagra is caused by lack of vitamin B_2 (nicotinic acid). It is found among poor people who live mainly on maize (sweet corn). With pellagra there is diarrhea, loss of appetite, nausea, a sore mouth and a swollen painful tongue, with a marked skin redness in the parts exposed to sunlight which later blister, crack and ulcerate. The afflicted person becomes depressed and anxious, cannot concentrate and can become delirious and may require admission to a mental hospital.

The treatment is a combination of niacin and a diet rich in B complex vitamins. If there are skin lesions these can be treated with antibiotics.

Too little of the vitamin riboflavin in the diet leads to redness and cracking of the skin at an angle of the mouth (angular stomatitis) and a redness and cracking of

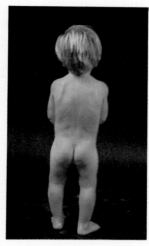

A deficiency of vitamin D may lead to rickets, a condition of bone abnormalities. *(Royal Alexandra Hospital)*

the lips (cheilosis).

Scurvy is caused by lack of vitamin C (ascorbic acid). It is a disease which affected many sailors on long voyages in the time of sailing ships. The usual signs of scurvy are spongy, bleeding, swollen gums, loose teeth, spontaneous bruising of the skin and bleeding from the intestine. Wounds fail to heal and old wounds tend to open up again.

The treatment involves administering large doses of vitamin C.

Rickets occurs in children who lack vitamin D and calcium. The child suffers delayed development and is fretful, restless and pale. The skull has little areas which are not bony but which pop like a ping pong ball when under pressure. Above the wrist, the bones are enlarged and there are lumps on the ribs in the front of the chest wall. The bones are soft so when the child walks, bowing of the legs and curvature of the spine develops.

Anemia, a condition in which normal red cells are partly replaced by larger malformed red cells (megalocytes) occurs when there is too little folate or vitamin B_{12} (cyanocobalamin) in the diet. Folate deficiency anemias occur commonly in pregnancy. B_{12} deficiencies usually happen as a result of an inability to absorb vitamin B_{12} but can occur on a strictly vegetarian diet.

The folate deficiency can be replaced by tablets but if the anemia is due to a B_{12} deficiency injections are required at weekly and later monthly intervals. These injections may have to continue for life.

Food and drink additives

In Western societies most people ingest some additives in food and drink, unless they habitually consume only fresh, unprocessed foods and drink only rain or mineral water, milk straight from the cow or goat, and fresh juices. Most of us, eating a balanced range of foods, have a surprisingly high intake of additives.

In recent years there has been a major public swing away from highly processed foods and a trend towards unrefined, raw and so-called 'health' foods. This is a healthy attitude that has stemmed in part from concern about the quantity of chemical or refined flavoring and preserving agents that are being ingested, providing the individual is well-versed in basic nutrition and does not become fanatical. Whether the trend represents an overreaction will be shown only as more controlled tests are performed. While it would appear that a small or moderate amount of additives in the daily diet is comparatively harmless, it is obvious that the less that we have the better.

Sugar An examination of many food items, including baby foods, canned fruits, frozen pies and soft drinks, reveals a high proportion of sugar. However, in the area of commercial baby foods (including vitamin supplements) manufacturers have introduced unsweetened varieties. As a 'sweet tooth' is very much an acquired habit, often leading to the problems of obesity and dental decay, babies and toddlers should not be subjected to sweetened foods for the sake of convenience.

Salt is one of the oldest additives used in food, particularly for its preservative qualities.

When cooking food, a modicum of salt is usually added to enhance the flavor, and this is sufficient for most people's taste during a meal. However, there are people who habitually add as much as half a spoonful or more of salt to each plate of food, in addition to the cook's contribution. Such a practice is liable to increase the circulating blood volume and raise the blood pressure.

Kidney and heart specialists have widely differing opinions as to the effect of a large salt intake on normal persons. Some think it causes hypertension, kidney and heart damage, others do not. However, if a person already suffers from hypertension, it is advisable not to add any extra salt to food at the table, and a very high salt intake should be avoided even by those with no hypertension problems.

Vinegar is another additive that has been used for many years. Its active ingredient — acetic acid — retards spoilage by preventing the increase of micro-organisms. Other ancient and traditional additives used mainly for flavoring originate from the root, bark, seed, flower or fruit of plants, and include pepper, mustard, cloves, ginger and garlic. These are often dehydrated and added to foods such as soups, jams and TV dinners and, although 'natural' in origin are nevertheless, additives. In the same category are hops which, in addition to making beer palatable, have antibacterial properties.

Monosodium glutamate is the most widely known of the so-called 'modern'

additives. Many people are unaware that the acid it contains, glutamic acid, is quite natural, in that it is a by-product of protein breakdown within the body. Monosodium glutamate has been the subject of much publicity following American tests in which mice were injected with very large doses and subsequently died of brain damage. No harmful effects have been recorded on persons eating food containing monosodium glutamate in normal amounts, though some susceptible persons do suffer unpleasant effects from what is often called the 'Chinese Restaurant Syndrome', developing a headache, flushed face, abdominal pain and diarrhea after eating a Chinese meal, with monosodium glutamate supposedly the culprit. If a reaction like this occurs, it is probably best to try a different Chinese restaurant next time.

Monosodium glutamate has the capacity to enhance existing flavors, particularly those associated with protein foods. It is an ingredient in many packaged foods and it is surprising that no adverse monosodium glutamate reactions

Monosodium glutamate is frequently encountered in Chinese foods.

Below, left and right
Natural foods free from additives are generally regarded as best.

have been recorded from eating, say, soups, sauces, fish or cheese spreads.

Coloring matter and preservatives are added by some manufacturers to food and drink to make them more attractive looking and give them a longer shelf life. It has been postulated by some authorities that these orange/yellow and green colorings cause hyperactivity as they are not metabolized but accumulate in the tissues. (Hyperactivity is manifested by a reduced attention span, inattention and continual uncontrolled fidgeting and movement.) There is some evidence that this may be so in some but not all hyperactive children, but the evidence is not conclusive at present.

Preservatives Some widely used modern additives are basically preservatives: these include sorbic acid, which inhibits mould in cheese; sodium diacetate to preserve baked products; sulphur dioxide to preserve dried fruits; and complex synthetic compounds such as butylated hydroxytolene (BHT) and nordihydroguaiaretic acid (NDGA), used to inhibit oxidation of foods, particularly oil and fats.

Cyclamates Chemical substances used to sweeten food and drinks, cyclamates are used in place of sugar, as in saccharin, and are therefore much favored by both diabetics and dieters. In the last five years, because of action by the United States Federal Drug Administration, there has been a 'cyclamate scare' throughout much of the Western world. The FDA banned the sale of cyclamate-containing products in America and though such food and drink items continued to be sold in Australia and New Zealand, consumption dropped rapidly and there was considerable concern and uncertainty.

The most recent evidence indicates that earlier reports (including those which motivated the FDA) implicating cyclamates as a cause of cancer, particularly bladder cancer, were inconclusive. Research on rats had indicated that massive doses of cyclamates caused cancer but present thinking is that it would be virtually impossible for a person to consume the human equivalent amount of the substance as fed to the test animals. The National Health and Medical Research Council in Australia conducted tests and concluded that the value of cyclamates in artificial sweeteners was far greater than the risk factor.

Cyclamate-containing sweeteners are a substitute for sugar; sugar itself is implicated in such diverse conditions as obesity, hyperglycemia and dental decay. A moderate usage of artificial sweeteners would appear no more harmful than the over-use of sugar in the diet.

Other additives Starch, in one form or another, is used in packet and canned soups and sauces; emulsifiers are added to ice-cream, margarines and salad dressings. Lecithin was once widely used as a natu-

ral emulsifier but has largely been replaced by glycerol monostearate (GMS). Chlorine dioxide or Dyox is used in bread as a 'flour improver' in addition to bleaching the loaf. As well, there are the vitamin and mineral additives (some synthetic) added to breakfast cereals, margarines and fruit juices and some milk-based drinks. Even our drinking water often contains added fluoride. In other words it is extremely difficult to avoid additives completely in the daily diet.

Consumer resistance can force manufacturers to restrict the use of additives and preservatives. Although it is considered to be normal procedure to rely on laboratory testing as having declared safe the additives ingested in food and drink, the *long term* effects of some additives cannot be known as they have not been part of our diet for long enough to allow realistic evaluation.

Insecticides Although they are not 'additives' in the strict sense, a word of caution on insecticides is advisable. It is virtually universal practice to apply insecticides to fruit and vegetables during growth to avoid loss of the crop and to achieve unmarked produce. The substances applied sometimes stay on the outer skin of the produce but some are absorbed into its tissue.

Although regulations prohibit harvesting before at least two or three weeks have elapsed since application of insecticides, these are not always enforced. It is therefore advisable at least to wash, and preferably to remove the outer skin, of apples, plums, pears, tomatoes and the like before eating.

Occupational Health

Occupational health is a special field of medicine concerned with the health of man in relation to his work and working environment. Interest was originally limited to diseases or injuries directly attributable to work. It had the limited objective of providing treatment and control of the more obvious hazards, for instance intoxication from inhaled fumes, gases or vapors, skin diseases from irritating substances, noise-induced deafness, and mechanical hazards.

Gradually the scope broadened with the development of scientific methods for measuring the working environment and its effects on health. It now includes studies on all factors relating to work that may lead to any deviation from health, including maladjustment to work, the effects of physical and mental strain from heavy or monotonous work, morale, human relationships at work, and productivity.

At its first session in 1950, the Joint ILO/WHO Committee on Occupational Health decided that 'Occupational Health should aim at:

1 The promotion and maintenance of the highest degree of physical, mental and social well-being of workers in all occupations;

Workers in dangerous occupations may be at risk if their health is impaired. *(Salmer)*

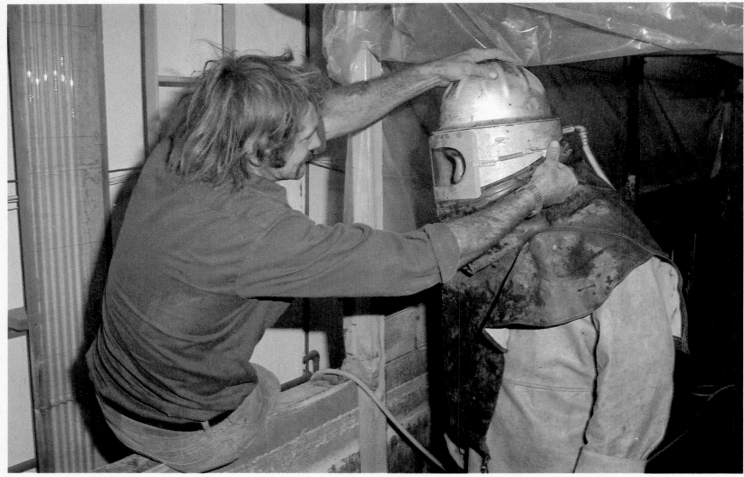

2 the prevention among workers of departures from health caused by their working conditions;

3 the protection of workers in their employment from risks resulting from factors adverse to health;

4 the placing and maintenance of the worker in an occupational environment adapted to his physiological and psychological equipment, and, to summarize,

5 the adaptation of work to man and of each man to his job.'

In 1959, the ILO Occupational Health Services Recommendations (No. 112), went on to define the functions of an occupational health service in places of employment:

1 Medical examination of workers — pre-employment and other special examinations, such as those of women and young persons;

2 supervision of the working environment — with emphasis on industrial hygiene and safety;

3 advice to management and workers' representatives — on matters such as working environment, ergonomics, placing and reassignment of workers, prevention of accidents and occupational diseases, welfare, vocational rehabilitation and training;

4 health education and training — in hygiene and first aid;

5 compilation and periodic review of statistics relating to health conditions in the undertaking — maintenance of records, recording and analysis of absenteeism due to accidents and sickness, notification of occupational diseases;

6 medical treatment — first aid and emergency treatment, ambulatory treatment of workers who have not been absent from work or who have returned after absence, medical rehabilitation;

7 health counseling — on an individual basis; on nutrition, family planning and general health matters;

8 research in occupational health;

9 co-operation with other services in the undertaking, in particular those concerned with personnel matters, conditions of employment, job training, accident prevention, welfare, industrial hygiene, engineering and vocational rehabilitation;

10 collaboration with external services, for example the factory inspectorate.

It is clear from the foregoing that occupational health covers a wide field. It calls for specialized knowledge from many disciplines — for example, medicine, engineering, chemistry, toxicology, psy-

Above and opposite
The use of safety helmets and protective clothing is essential in some occupations.

chology, physiology, and statistics, and close team-work between workers in these different spheres is essential.

Although the primary purpose of occupational health is to protect the workers' health at work, it implies not only health protection, but also health promotion, a concept which includes everything that can promote the health and working capacity of the worker. In its widest sense, occupational health deals with the total health of employed persons.

As in other fields of medicine, specialization in occupational health has led to sub-divisions such as the following:

a Occupational physiology, which deals with physiological reactions to factors at work, such as heavy work and heat stress, and the study of different types of fatigue;

b occupational psychology, which deals with the psychological and mental demands of the job and the evaluation of the mental capacity of different individuals in order to achieve a proper placement from the health point of view;

c ergonomics, which is the applied science for adjusting work to man, in the light of his anatomy, physiology and psychology;

d occupational pathology, which deals with occupational diseases caused by chemical factors, for example intoxication from metallic or non-metallic poisons, inhaled dusts, and contact dermatitis, and by physical factors such as deafness from noise and noxious effects of ionizing radiation;

e occupational hygiene, which involves methods of measuring the occupational hazards present, for example the concentration of gases and dusts, the intensity and frequency of noise and vibrations, and the techniques of elimination of these hazards;

f industrial safety, which is concerned with the prevention of accidents at work, where not only mechanical but also human factors are considered;

g occupational psychiatry, which deals with factors at work which may cause or contribute to nervous diseases or deviations from mental health;

h occupational sociology, which helps increase our knowledge of man's behaviour at work, and his attitudes to work, working conditions, management and workmates.

Byssinosis, a dust disease of the lungs, may develop in people who handle raw cotton.

Factors affecting health in the workplace include the psychological and mental demands of a particular job. (*Zefa*)

In most industrialized countries the health needs of the employed are met mainly by the national authorities or by organizations not directly connected with the employers.

Legislation relating to occupational health lays down minimum standards of health and safety at work and is usually enforced by the factory inspectorate.

Improvements in the working environment, in the mutual adaptation of men and jobs, and in the health and welfare of workers are the main advantages derived from occupational health services. This should lead to a lower rate of morbidity, mortality, and sickness absenteeism, to higher productivity and a happier and healthier working population.

Occupational dust diseases

House dust is by far the most common organic dust. It is a mixture of particles of dust, textile fibers, hair, fur and house dust mites. Inhaling house dust is often found to be the cause of allergic asthmatic (wheezing) attacks. The avoidance of this type of asthma involves trying to get another person to vacuum carpets and empty the vacuum cleaner. Desensitization may be effective, with many injections.

Byssinosis begins with wheezing and difficulty in breathing and coughing (initially on Mondays and Tuesdays after the weekend break) in cotton, flax and hemp mill workers. It is the result of inflammation of the smallest lung tubes (acute bronchiolitis) caused by inhaling cotton, flax or hemp dust. Eventually the person has symptoms all week. Once a sufferer from byssinosis has left the mill and is no longer exposed to the dust, symptoms cease and recovery is complete.

Above left
The house dust mite. Inhalation of house dust, which comprises dust mites and particles of dust, fur, fibers and hair, can cause asthma attacks. (*The Sunday Times Magazine*)

Above
Unacceptable concentrations of dust in the atmosphere can be detected by regular checks of dust levels near industrial sites. (*Zefa*)

People exposed to dust inhalation will further increase the risk of contracting lung disease if they are smokers.

Bagassosis, farmer's lung, malt worker's lung, mushroom worker's lung and pigeon fancier's lung are found respectively in cane sugar mill workers (bagasse is the sugar cane waste), and in people who work near moldy hay, malting barley, mushroom compost and pigeon droppings. The substances involved all have some fungus or mold growing in them. Two or three hours after exposure a dry cough and breathlessness develops. Repeated exposure leads to continuous breathlessness and cough until the patient is blue with a fever and breathless at rest. Inflammation of an allergic nature in the air sacs of the lung is found and this may lead to an irreversible fibrosis and lung stiffening. The mild form of the disease is cured when exposure to the dust ceases. Severe forms require steroid drug treatment and oxygen may be needed. Some residual disability remains.

Coal worker's pneumoconiosis causes a chronic cough and almost black sputum. The miner becomes increasingly breathless on exercise until eventually he is also breathless at rest. Death due to respiratory or heart failure eventually occurs in some people. The treatment is to bring the miner away from a dusty job at the coal face and give him above-ground employment. This does not cure the pneumoconiosis but it stops the progression of the disease. Some types of coal cause a form of severe pneumoconiosis called progressive massive fibrosis where even if the miner no longer mines the disease progresses.

Silicosis occurs in workers involved in mining gold, tin and other minerals where free crystalline silica dust or quartz particles are inhaled. Quarriers, miners and dressers of sandstone or granite, potters, ceramic workers, silica brick workers, abrasive soap makers, iron and steel foundrymen, sand blasters, metal grinders and boiler scalers are all at risk. The symptoms are similar to those of coal miner's pneumoconiosis and the disease progresses even after exposure to the silica has ceased. Tuberculosis is an added complication in some cases.

Asbestosis occurs in miners and millers of chrysolite and crocidolite and in people whose occupations involve dealing with asbestos, such as pipe laggers and limpet asbestos sprayers, and also demolition workers, joiners, painters and electricians who work in similar conditions. There are two main forms of the disease: a progressive fibrosis with increasing shortness of breath and cough with clubbing of the fingers, usually the result of long exposure

293

to dust; and a rapidly fatal tumor of the pleura (the membrane which covers the lung) which afflicts people who have had an apparently trivial exposure to crocidolite. The latter condition has been known to affect miners' wives or people who live in the vicinity of the mill but who do not work in it. Asbestosis in both forms continues to progress after exposure to asbestos ceases. There is no curative treatment.

Siderosis and stannosis Siderosis occurs in arc welders and is the result of inhaling iron oxide dust; stannosis occurs in tin ore miners from inhaling tin dioxide dust. Both these pneumoconioses cause no symptoms but the minerals are deposited in the lungs.

Prevention of dust diseases

The prevention of the dust induced diseases lies in increasing and maintaining standards of industrial hygiene. Using exhaust systems to remove the dusts, wearing respirators or masks, damping dusts and modifying cutting machinery so that less dust is produced are all methods which have helped to make these diseases less common today than they used to be.

Government controlled safety standards have been introduced into many industries. Each worker should have an initial (and thereafter regular periodic) medical examination and x-ray of the chest so that any disease is diagnosed as early as possible and the worker transferred from that particular occupation. However, not all pneumoconioses have specific x-ray changes and by the time they are noticed it may be already too late to avoid serious lung damage.

Opposite
Canadian asbestos mine. Inhalation of mineral dusts can cause the lung disease pneumoconiosis. (*Zefa*)

Left
Regulations usually require that work noise levels be kept below 115 decibels.

Heavy traffic has a noise level of 80–90 decibels, while a car horn may register 100 decibels.

Noise-induced deafness

In recent years there has been increasing concern about the physical and psychological problems caused by noise, problems such as deafness, interference with sleep and concentration, increase in anxiety or tension, 'annoyance', and tinnitus (ringing in the ears). Most of these problems occur in an industrial environment, and many occur in the home and in certain recreational environments. Noise-induced hearing loss and occupational deafness are now well established medical problems. The word 'socioacusis' is used to describe hearing loss directly caused by environmental noise.

Sounds vary in both pitch and intensity.

The higher the pitch, the more rapid the vibration of the sound waves. The pitch, or frequency of the sound, is measured in cycles per second (cps) or Hertz (Hz). A young child can hear sounds between 20 and 20,000 Hz, with the upper limit declining rapidly with increasing age. The intensity of a sound is measured in decibels (dB). The decibel scale is logarithmic, that is, if there is an increase in the noise level of 10 decibels the sound is ten times as loud. The decibel levels for various sounds are: whispering 25, normal conversation 60, heavy traffic 80-90, a car horn 100-110, a disco 90-100. Heavy traffic at 80-90 decibels is 100 to 1000 times louder than normal conversation at 60 decibels.

Cause of noise-induced deafness is probably direct trauma to the delicate hearing mechanisms in the cochlea, the fluid-filled organ situated in the inner ear. Short-term exposure to loud noise may cause a temporary disturbance in hearing. If exposure to the noise continues, the damage and resultant hearing loss will be irreversible.

The main factors that increase the likelihood of hearing loss are loudness of the noise, the pitch, the duration of the sound, the surroundings and personal susceptibility.

The pitch of noise that causes hearing loss is about 4000 Hz.

Hearing loss is expressed in decibels. Initially the hearing loss may be only about 20 dB, but this may rise to as high as 60-70 dB if there is continued exposure to the excessive noise. As the damage and hearing loss increases, so does the range of frequencies affected. The vocal sounds like 'th' and 's' are the first sounds that become difficult to hear.

Treatment is mainly directed at minimizing the progress of the problem and using hearing aids. There is no way to reverse the damage. Further exposure to excessive noise should be avoided.

Because the lower range of frequencies of sound is little affected, the effort to amplify the higher-pitched sounds may result in distortion of the former. This difficulty has been partially overcome in recent years as advances in electronic circuitry have led to the development of special hearing aids that operate maximally in the higher frequencies.

When there are early signs of hearing loss, such as tinnitus, fatigue, mental trauma or temporary hearing loss, rest and rehabilitation is desirable to prevent further damage.

Psittacosis is a viral infection transmitted by members of the parrot family. *(Zefa)*

Improvements in sound insulation, and quieter machines or silencers for noisy ones, hopefully will reduce the incidence of industrial deafness.

Ear plugs are an effective means of reducing the level of noise and therefore of preventing hearing loss. Dry cotton wool is of little value, but waxed wool or ear plugs reduce noise levels by about 20 dB. Ear muffs are the most effective, reducing noise levels by 25 to 40 dB.

Pets and Pests

Contact with animals and insects, from the common domestic pets like dogs and cats to insect pests such as flies and mosquitoes, can bring problems if common-sense precautions are not observed. There are only a very small number of serious diseases associated with the common domestic pet, provided the animal is properly cared for and vaccinated against disease. However, people should be aware of certain pet-related diseases so that they can prevent or treat them.

Birds

Generally there are no problems with owning one or two birds, but there are two quite serious conditions which can occur when large numbers are kept.

Bird-breeders lung is caused through inhalation of the dried droppings of birds, which in turn causes an allergic reaction in the lungs. Symptoms generally involve a feeling of debility, fever, difficulty in breathing and a severe and persistent cough. It is rare in children.

Psittacosis is a severe infectious disease with the same symptoms as pneumonia. It is a viral condition transmitted mainly by parrots and parakeets, but may also be transmitted by smaller birds like canaries. It is more serious than bird-breeders lung.

Both diseases require prompt and effective treatment; for bird-breeders lung corticosteroids are used, and for psittacosis antibiotics are generally prescribed. Birds carrying psittocosis may have to be isolated, as may the patient himself and it is often necessary to destroy birds (and their cages) affected by the disease. Illegal trafficking in exotic birds between Australia, America and Europe is likely to increase the incidence of psittacosis overseas, something unlikely to occur in the case of legal transportation which is controlled by strict quarantine requirements.

Dogs

Worms are the most common problem in dogs. Roundworms are particularly prevalent, but can be prevented easily by worming the dog once a year with anti-helminthic drugs (which cause no discomfort to the animal).

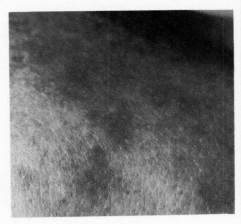

The bites of bird lice can cause extremely uncomfortable inflammation. *(Westmead Centre)*

The extremely dangerous hydatid disease, caused by the tapeworm, *Taenia echinococcus*, can be prevented by correct and regular worming of the dog, by not feeding the dog offal (specifically sheep offal) and by observing the basic rules of animal hygiene.

Hydatid cysts produce fairly unmistakable symptoms in an affected person; if they have lodged in the brain, for example, they may cause fits and paralysis. They are most commonly found in the liver or lungs. The disease occurs most frequently in rural areas where sheep are raised, although fortunately the practice of feeding dogs with the slaughtered animals' organs is decreasing.

Cats

Cats are relatively easy to care for, remarkably disease-free and present relatively few hazards to human beings. A quite rare disease called cat-scratch fever may result from a bite or scratch, generally around a week to three weeks after its occurrence. There is fever and swelling of the local lymphatic glands and the diagnosis can be confirmed by a simple skin test. Treatment depends on the severity of the illness and the site of the wound; fortunately the condition is self-limiting. The infective agent is presumed to be a virus. If scratched by a cat, promptly clean and disinfect the area, no matter how small the injury.

Other common sources of infection

Aside from the specific diseases already mentioned, the most common illnesses in humans caused by domestic pets are *allergic reactions*. These include skin disorders and irritations and respiratory/asthmatic reactions which may be the result of an allergic sensitivity to certain pets. Some people may react to cats but not to dogs, and vice-versa, or only to a particular animal.

In severe cases, when sensitivity cannot be reduced, sometimes antihistamine preparations and increasing 'doses' of ex-

Cats are generally disease-free, but if scratched by a cat it is important to clean and disinfect the area if cat scratch fever is to be avoided. *(Zefa)*

posure to the particular pet can produce a cure.

The only other common condition that human beings 'catch' from animals is ringworm which affects the skin. It is more often transmitted from one person to another, but may be passed on by domestic animals.

Rarer infections

Papular urticaria is a severe rash resulting from an allergy to flea or tick bites (from birds or animals).

Certain other serious diseases are transmitted by or emanate from animals; for example, *anthrax* may affect those working with products derived from farm animals and *trichinosis*, a parasitic disease, may result from eating undercooked pork, but these are not conditions passed on from domestic pets to their owners.

Prevention of pet-transmitted diseases

Common-sense hygiene is particularly important for children and their pets. Children and adults should wash their hands with hot water and soap after fondling a pet, or after contact with its bedding or belongings. Dogs should not be allowed to lick or 'kiss' their owners, eat from dinner plates used by people, or breathe over

food intended for human consumption. Combined with a recommended vaccination regime and a worming program (for dogs and cats), these simple measures reduce the risk of disease being spread from the animals to humans.

Insects

Insects are responsible for spreading some serious diseases. For example, flies contaminate food and transmit intestinal infection where sanitation is poor; some insects, such as the mite of scabies, infest the skin and hair; certain mosquitoes are carriers (vectors) of malaria and some carry yellow fever or filariasis; fleas carry plague and typhus, and lice and ticks carry typhus and relapsing fever.

Controlling with care Not only insecticides, but all pesticides, are dangerous to humans. Extreme care should be exercised when using them. These poisons, if handled carelessly, may be absorbed through the lungs or skin, or may be mistakenly swallowed by children who are unaware of the dangers. Accidental poisoning can also occur when these poisons, used for agricultural purposes, affect the food eventually consumed by humans.

Aim for prevention by screening windows and doors, and using mosquito nets, fly swatters and insect traps.

Rodents
Particular care should be exercised if attempting to get rid of rats by means other than trapping, especially if warfarin is used. There will be no symptoms from a single accidental dose of warfarin-based rat or roach poison, but if it appears that regular doses, however small, have been ingested, or if bleeding (first from scratches, sores or from the gums, then generalized) occurs, urgent medical help should be obtained.

Left
Rabbits may carry fleas and their fur may cause hay fever reactions.
Below
Insecticides, often used to control garden pests, should be handled with great care.

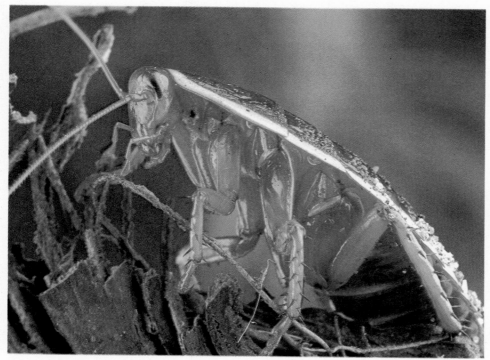

Cockroaches not only carry disease but are difficult to eradicate.

Worms and other parasites

The transmission of worms by domestic animals has, in the USA, been greatly reduced by the increased use of commercially prepared and packaged pet food, which has largely replaced the feeding of offal to domestic animals. Strict quarantine regulations and the inspection of meat and meat products has also reduced disease spread.

However, exceptions still exist and worm and other parasite infections are still seen. Because one can never be sure that a family pet is free from infection, it is still wise to maintain good hygiene and always wash after handling animals.

Nematodes or roundworms are parasites which can cause diseases such as hookworm, ascariasis (common roundworm infection), entrobiasis (pinworm or threadworm infestation) and filariasis (filarial worm infestation). Different species of roundworm are categorized as intestinal or tissue nematodes depending on where they live within the body.

Swallowed eggs usually hatch within the small intestine and most nematodes develop there, obtaining nourishment from partially digested food. The females release thousands of eggs in the feces. Human symptoms include abdominal discomfort, nausea, diarrhea and occasionally malabsorption when infections are particularly severe. Nematodes develop in tissues less often. However, symptoms are more variable as they often relate to the parasites' migration through, or development in, various organs or tissues.

Platyhelminths or flatworms form the other major parasitic group. They include cestodes or tapeworms and trematodes or flukes, both of which infest humans.

Both types are generally hermaphroditic and vary in length from less than 1 inch to 26 feet (1 cm to 8 meters). Their heads are equipped with suckers and sometimes hooks, with which they attach themselves to the inner wall of the intestine. They are able to dispense with a digestive tract by absorbing food through their entire surface. Segments or proglottids, which contain fertilized eggs that are periodically released and excreted in the feces, develop from their necks.

Tapeworms and flukes The tapeworm *Echinococcus granulosus* is responsible for hydatid disease.

Virtually all tapeworms and flukes require an intermediate host to complete their life cycle when they leave the main host. *Echinococcus* uses dogs as its definitive host, and sheep, cattle, and occasionally man, as its intermediate hosts. Cysts form in the liver, brain and lungs of the latter. The beef tapeworm (*Taenia saginata*) and the pork tapeworm (*T. solium*) are also medically important tapeworms.

Flukes usually choose water snails as their intermediate hosts. Although most flukes are hermaphroditic, the three closely related species of *Schistosoma* have separate male and female forms. These 'blood flukes' cause bilharziasis (schistomosomiasis), which affects over 150 million people world wide. The male and female worms mate in veins within the abdomen and release their eggs at that site. Eggs may penetrate through the blood vessels into the bowel or bladder, or alternatively may travel to the liver or lungs, causing localized inflammatory reactions. Varying symptoms ensue.

Treatment of worm infestations For many years worm infestations were primarily treated by using purgatives, which literally cleared the bowel of the offending parasites. But this sometimes caused unwelcome side effects. Consequently many anti-helminthic drugs have been developed to kill specific worms.

Worm infestations can be prevented by personal hygiene, ensuring there is adequate sanitation, and by dosing intermediate hosts. These measures help to prevent infestations, such as those caused by roundworms, which are spread by faecal contamination. Strict health regulations regarding the preparation of meat for human consumption has reduced the risk of tapeworm infestation while thorough boiling or disposal of offal at abattoirs has reduced the incidence of hydatid disease.

Scabies The parasitic skin infestation known as scabies is caused by the mite *Sarcoptes scabiei*. It is transmitted by direct contact, sometimes by sexual intercourse, and it may reach epidemic proportions in areas with poor hygiene.

The main symptom is an intense itch caused by an allergic reaction to the saliva of the mite or to the eggs that the female lays in the burrow made in the outer layers of the skin. Loose skin is most suitable for the burrowing, the web spaces between the fingers, the wrists, the elbows, the buttocks and the external genitalia of males being most frequently affected.

Mating of mites occurs on the surface, and the pregnant female enters the skin to lay several eggs each day. Larvae hatch within four to five days, surface once more and develop into adults and then mate. The cycle takes about two weeks.

A red, fine rash is produced, and the burrow lines are not always visible. Severe or repeated infections produce a more generalized rash that extends beyond the areas of skin penetration.

Prolonged scratching may lead to a rash resembling eczema, and secondary bacterial infection may cause pustules or ulcers.

Often a whole household is treated simultaneously to prevent reinfection of those initially infested. Because eggs may be harboured in clothes and bedding, they need to be treated as well. Commonly

Roundworms are a common problem in dogs, so children should always be encouraged to wash their hands after playing with a pet.

used anti-scabies preparations include lindane, benzyl benzoate and crotamiton. A standard treatment is as follows:

1 Prior to applying the anti-scabies lotion have a warm bath or shower gently scrubbing affected areas to open up the burrows.

2 Apply the liquid all over the body, particularly between the fingers and toes, and over the genitals. Take care not to allow the liquid to get into the eyes.

3 Leave the liquid on for 24 hours and wear the same clothes during this period.

4 Have a warm bath or shower after 24 hours. All clothes and underclothes should be washed vigorously, using hot water where appropriate. Bedding should be washed in the same way.

5 The treatment regime should be repeated within one to two weeks.

6 All children should remain home from school until the rash has cleared.

Tetanus

It is particularly important that those people who work with animals or keep them as pets should be fully aware of the dangers of tetanus which is an acute and often fatal disease, caused by toxin produced in a wound by the organism *Clostridium tetanii*. It is mobile and rod-shaped, developing in an oxygen-free or anaerobic environment.

Causes Characterized by a generalized increase of rigidity and intermittent convulsive spasms of the voluntary or skeletal muscles, tetanus is fatal in over 45 per cent of cases. The disease usually follows damage leading to the destruction and death of living tissue, such as occurs in severe injury and puncture wounds.

The tetanus spore is found most frequently in the superficial layers of soil and also occurs in moderate numbers as saprophytes living on dead matter, particularly in the gut of humans and other mammals. The spores are highly resistant to heat and antiseptics and may survive for many years.

Although it is estimated that 500 000 cases occur annually around the world, it is relatively rare in colder countries such as Russia and the United States. Males are more frequently affected, and almost half of all cases occur amongst the newborn, where unsterile circumcision and tying of the umbilical cord is carried out in primitive societies. The disease is also common among narcotic addicts.

The most common cause is a puncture wound, although the condition has been known to follow dental and middle ear infections, burns, abortion and pregnancy. In over 20 per cent of cases no apparent cause is discovered. Rarely, the spores may survive in the body for years after an injury or an operation before tetanus develops.

The incubation period ranges from two to 56 days but is usually under 14 days. The shorter the period, the more serious the disease and the less likely the recovery.

Following the introduction of the spores, a toxin is developed which enters the central nervous system through the neural or nerve pathways. Known as tetanospasmin, it interferes with the normal function of nerve and muscle control. A less damaging toxin, tetanolysis is also developed.

Symptoms In the earliest phases of the condition the patient becomes restless and irritable, complaining often of headaches. Pain in the muscles and spasm of the jaw leading to rismus (lockjaw), are associated with, or often followed rapidly by, spasms involving the muscles of the abdominal wall and the back. Difficulty in swallowing is a frequent problem. Where the muscles of the face undergo sustained contractions, a grotesque expression, *risus* *sardonicus* (bitter or sardonic smile) develops.

Reflex spasms occur with little stimulation and, when severe, can lead to sudden blocking of the larynx or airways. There is usually a low grade temperature and associated excessive sweating. The patient remains fully conscious and lucid.

Usually, progressive worsening of the condition is spread over three or four days and then a period of stability follows lasting about a week. Thereafter, for those who survive, gradual improvement leads to complete recovery after two weeks, without either complications or long-term sequelae. The most frequent cause of death in tetanus is associated pneumonia.

Treatment is carried out in an intensive care unit where possible, in quiet and unstimulating surroundings. Any foreign matter and dead tissue is removed surgically; human tetanus immune globulin is given in high dosage by injection

The combustion of fuels in large industrial plants contributes to air pollution in most large cities.

to limit the activity of the toxin; the muscles may be relaxed with various drugs and an antibiotic, usually penicillin, is prescribed.

To avoid suffocation from spasm of the airways, a tracheotomy, in which a breathing tube is placed in the trachea or windpipe through a surgical incision, is usually undertaken. Intravenous feeding of fluids and nourishment may be needed.

Prevention It is most important that all children should be immunized against tetanus in childhood. The anti-tetanus vaccine is included in the triple antigen injections given at two, four and six months of age and again at 18 months and five years. Children who have been immunized against tetanus should be given a tetanus toxoid injection after a deep wound or burn.

Adults should consult their family doctors about regular tetanus booster shots. This is particularly important for people such as gardeners and horse-riders whose work involves contact with soil and manure.

Pollution

The contamination of the environment by chemicals, biological wastes and harmful vibrations, pollution has been a feature of human life ever since primitive man began to live in groups and use fire. In more recent times, the development of cities and industry and the discovery of new, complex chemicals, has increased both the quantities and the range of polluting materials released by man. Pollution problems have been aggravated by the explosive growth in human population and now some scientists are concerned that vital global mechanisms may be disrupted by this increasing pollution load.

The health effects of pollution vary from minor psychological disorders caused by noise from aircraft and traffic, to serious illness and death brought about by polluted water, air and food. Often the effects are subtle and do not become apparent for some time, for instance cancer caused by pollutants such as asbestos may take 30 years to develop.

Air pollution over industrial areas
or any large city can have a
damaging effect.

Air pollution

Air pollution, which mainly affects urban
areas, comes from two main sources: the
combustion of fuels and the operation of
industrial processes.

Smoke and smog One of the earliest recorded anti-pollution laws was the prohibition of coal-burning in London in 1273
for health reasons. This ban was clearly
ineffective, since in 1661 the diarist John
Evelyn produced his famous tract
Fumifugium in which he described graphi-
cally the severe air pollution suffered by
Londoners as a result of coal-burning.

London's air pollution problem reached
a peak in December 1952 when a layer of
still air trapped over the city became filled
with smog, a lethal combination of smoke,
motor exhaust fumes, industrial pollutants
and fog, which caused the death of some
4000 people during the week-long episode,
either by suffocation or by extreme lung
irritation. This led to the introduction of
the Clean Air Act in 1956, which enabled
many British cities to ban the use of
smoky fuels.

Today the term smog is usually applied
to the hazy, often irritating atmosphere
hanging over most industrial cities.

Motor vehicle pollution Other cities, such
as Los Angeles, Sydney and Tokyo, suffer
from a type of smog called photochemical
smog, caused by the action of strong sunlight on the combustion products emitted
by motor vehicle exhausts. Irritant gases

such as ozone are formed and can cause
streaming eyes and respiratory problems
in people exposed to them, particularly
the elderly.

Motor vehicles emit another, more
dangerous pollutant, lead. This toxic
metal is added to gasoline to improve its
performance in high compression engines
and is emitted from exhausts as small,
easily inhaled particles.

Recent studies have shown that about
20 per cent of urban children in those
countries using large amounts of lead additives are suffering some mental impairment caused by lead. This has prompted
several countries to ban or restrict gasoline lead; for example, all new cars sold
have to be able to run on lead-free fuel.

Photochemical smog develops
where strong sunlight occurs in
conjunction with the fumes from
car exhaust systems.

Acid rain The burning of most fossil fuels
releases a gas called sulphur dioxide. This
is one of the harmful ingredients of smog
and it combines with water in the atmosphere to form highly corrosive sulphuric
acid. Acidic droplets and particles formed
in this way can be carried long distances
before falling to the ground as *acid rain*.

In order to reduce local pollution,
power stations and factories producing
large amounts of this gas are often fitted
with tall stacks which enable the pollutants to be carried long distances before
descending; however this does not solve
the problem but merely transfers it somewhere else. As a result, Scandinavian
lakes are now dying from excess acidity
caused by sulphur dioxide emissions elsewhere in Europe while Canada is receiving a similar acid rain problem from the
northern United States.

Water pollution

Rivers have long been regarded as convenient drains for the disposal of man's
wastes. Even before proper sewage systems were established, cities polluted the
rivers running through them with excre-
ment and debris, giving scant attention to
the fact that the same rivers were also
used as water sources. The realization of
the hazards involved came slowly and it
was not until outbreaks of diseases such
as cholera in nineteenth century Europe
were linked to contaminated water that
water pollution was recognized as a
problem.

This thick foam on an ocean beach
represents serious pollution.

In the developed world, sewage systems and water treatment have removed the threat of water-borne diseases but this is not the case in developing countries where millions die each year from infections such as dysentery, cholera and poliomyelitis through drinking contaminated water.

Many of the rivers and streams of Europe and North America are still badly polluted. Sewage effluent, after varying degrees of treatment, and industrial wastes still pour into them in enormous quantities. Some rivers, such as the Rhine contain so much toxic matter that they are lifeless for miles. Others have shown remarkable recoveries in recent years; in London's River Thames, sensitive fish such as salmon have been found in stretches which were incapable of supporting life two decades ago.

Deoxygenation One of the most common effects of pollution in rivers is the removal of oxygen from the water. Adequate supplies of dissolved oxygen are vital for the survival of fish and other aquatic creatures. Effluents containing organic matter such as sewage, brewing wastes and paper mill discharges are used as food by bacteria, which consume the oxygen as they break down the wastes. Unless these effluents are well diluted, the river into which they are discharged quickly becomes lifeless and foul-smelling.

Right and below
In countries where many people live in or near waterways, pollution can affect health.

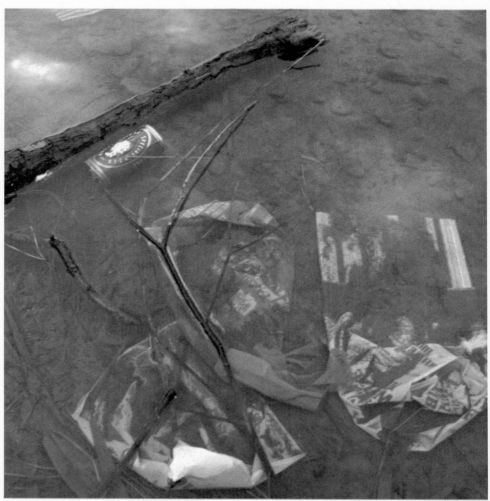

Careless disposal of dangerous
rubbish such as glass can lead to
problems for those living nearby.

The deoxygenation of rivers is often aggravated by warm water discharged from
power station cooling systems. This ther-
mal pollution stimulates the bacteria in
the water to break down organic matter
more quickly and also reduces the amount
of oxygen which the water can hold, since
gases dissolve better in cold water than in
hot.

Toxic chemicals In addition to organic
wastes, industrial plants frequently release poisonous chemicals into rivers.
Acids, alkalis, heavy metals and pesticides
cause damage to water life and some
chemicals can render river water unfit for
human consumption even after processing. For instance, the contamination of
water supplies by very small quantities of
phenol gives the water an unpleasant antiseptic taste when it is chlorinated for public supply.

More serious effects can occur. In
Japan, hundreds of people living around
Minamata Bay became seriously ill in the
1950s and 1960s when mercury effluent
from a factory caused a build-up of this
toxic metal in the fish which formed the
staple diet of the community.

Land pollution

The dumping and burial of wastes on land
has been a traditional activity since
civilization started. More recently this
practice has caused serious pollution
problems. A famous land pollution
case is Love Canal in New York. Thousands of tons of highly toxic chemicals
were dumped in an old canal and a
housing development was later built

Strict regulations govern the use of
herbicides. *(Zefa)*

on the site. Soon after, residents found
poisonous liquids bubbling up in their
gardens and seeping into their cellars. A
dramatic increase in medical problems,
such as liver and kidney disease, occurred
in the locality, which has now been declared a Federal Disaster Area. Similar
problems are now being experienced in
the Netherlands and may also occur in
Britain where a number of old waste
dumps are suspect.

Pesticides The careless use of pesticides
has also polluted the land in many

countries. Long-lasting chemicals such as
DDT and dieldrin have built up in the environment and contaminated food chains.
In Europe and America, the use of these
materials has caused drastic declines in
the populations of birds of prey, which
have become infertile through absorbing
residues from their food. Stricter controls
on the use of these chemicals are now in
force but some of their residues will remain in the environment for many years
to come.

Pesticides are known to have harmed
human beings who have absorbed them,
either deliberately or accidentally. The
herbicide paraquat, irresponsibly stored
in lemonade bottles, has been mistaken by

children for a soft drink on many occasions, with fatal results. Wheat treated with a highly toxic mercury fungicide killed hundreds of people in Iraq when it was baked into bread instead of sown and there have been numerous cases of workers using pesticides becoming ill after splashing themselves with the liquid or breathing toxic vapours.

Great concern has been expressed about pesticide contamination of food, particularly by DDT. Although no one has died as a result of DDT residues, strict limits are now set in many countries. At one time even breast milk of some American mothers was found to have a high DDT content.

Fertilizers Modern farming techniques have led to another pollution problem: the fertilizers which the farmer uses often run off the land into rivers where they stimulate excessive plant growth. When these plants die, their decomposition uses up the oxygen in the water and the river can become lifeless; this process is called *eutrophication*. Excessive fertilizer use can damage the structure of the soil and imperil the fertility and stability of the land in the long term.

One particular type of fertilizer, nitrate, can pose a hazard to humans. When very young children absorb nitrate, it is converted in their stomach into a similar chemical called nitrite which can combine with hemoglobin in the blood, blocking its capacity to carry oxygen, a condition known as *methemoglobinemia*. In severe cases, this condition can be fatal.

There is considerable concern in Britain about the large quantities of nitrates which have been released into rivers and groundwater used for public water supplies. The number of water supplies affected is increasing — some already exceed the World Health Organisation's recommended limit for nitrate — and expensive water treatment plants may be necessary to remove the nitrate before the water is distributed.

Global pollution problems

Although some pollution problems are localized, affecting one stretch of a river or a small part of a town near a factory, others have international, even global, implications. Persistent pesticide residues can be detected nearly everywhere on earth and there are fears in some quarters that these may have long-term effects on wildlife and the small algae in the oceans which produce much of the world's oxygen.

Toxic metals such as lead, mercury and cadmium are also widely distributed as a result of human activities. The air even in rural areas contains between ten and a thousand times as much lead as there would be naturally, and the contamination of food by these substances appears to be increasing.

The release of certain aerosol propellants, called chlorofluorocarbons, may be damaging the atmospheric ozone layer which protects us from cancer-causing solar radiation.

Finally, the combustion of fossil fuels at an ever increasing rate, coupled with the destruction of much of the planet's tropical forest, is causing an increase in the amount of carbon dioxide in the atmosphere. Some scientists believe that this could cause the earth to warm up, since carbon dioxide traps heat, and result in disastrous effects on climate and food production.

The difficulty with most of these global problems is that many of their effects are initially subtle and hard to detect. By the time it can be confirmed that they exist, it may be too late to take remedial action. Some countries have recognized the potential hazards and have taken steps to prevent problems from arising. America, for instance, has banned chlorofluorocarbons in aerosols, but most countries have decided to wait for conclusive proof before acting. This may be the easiest response, both politically and economically, but it is hardly wise.

Large gatherings of sports spectators lead to litter problems.

T raveling

One of the major problems in our hectic modern lifestyle is that of getting safely from place to place. Despite efforts to reduce the road toll, traffic accidents remain a major cause of death and personal suffering. In particular, road accidents have become a major destroyer of the young adult.

Local travel

The Australian State of Victoria was the first place in the world to introduce the compulsory wearing of seat belts. Several states in the U.S. and many other countries have since followed suit. Stricter 'drunk-driving' legislation, including the setting of legal blood alcohol limits for driving, the use of motorbike helmets that extend downwards to protect the neck and jaw, and better road conditions including more overpasses, have each had significant effects.

Changes in car design have also helped to reduce injuries. A collapsible steering column minimizes the chances of a driver receiving severe crush injuries to the chest, and a special bumper bar and collapsible compartment are recent and effective modifications designed to absorb the impact of a collision.

Alcohol Problem drinkers are now known to be associated with a third of all severe or fatal crashes. It is only recently that the degree of incompetence in relation to the actual alcohol intake has been properly assessed. Much more sophisticated testing has proved conclusively that even one drink affects reflexes and judgement.

Drugs The effects of drugs, particularly when combined with alcohol, have also been analyzed. Sedatives and tranquilizers certainly dull the acuteness of a driver's reflexes but many other medications also have harmful effects. For instance, most antihistamine drugs taken for hay fever are mildly sedating and can become dangerous when combined with alcohol.

Long distance drivers who take amphetamines to make them more alert tend to take undue risks and occasionally become confused when driving. Marijuana smokers are suspected of causing many accidents but, despite research, no specific test is yet available to measure particular blood levels of this drug.

Smoking increases the dangers of driving to the extent that one insurance company offers lower premiums to non-smokers. Dropping and then picking up a lighted cigarette when driving, sudden bouts of coughing and, surprisingly, a refusal by a significantly large number of drivers to wear seat belts, makes smoking a considerable hazard.

Seat belts Despite occasional criticism that belts may cause liver damage or trap

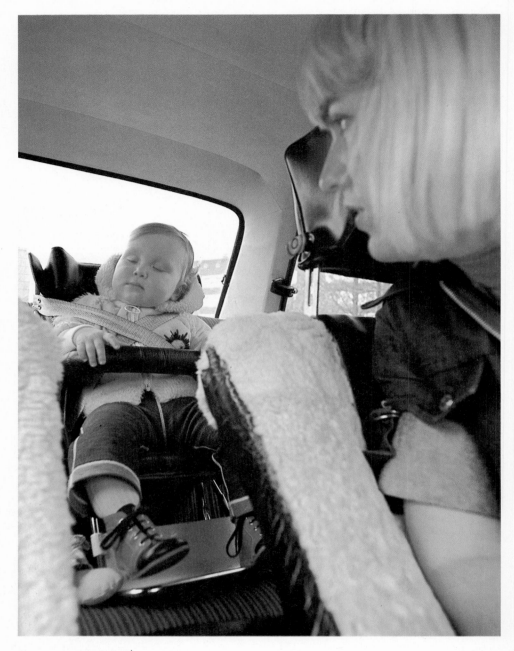

The wearing of seat belts substantially improves chances of surviving a car accident. *(Zefa)*

people in crashes, the advantages outweigh the disadvantages. In the case of children, injuries frequently occur because of inappropriateness of the seats, so that there is now intensive research into developing the ideal car seat for children. Children should always travel in the back seat, securely strapped into approved child safety seats.

Pedestrians Almost a quarter of road deaths involve pedestrians, mostly young children and the elderly. Besides educating children about road safety and suggesting the wearing of light colored clothing at night, cars themselves have been analyzed. It is recognized that many

gross disfiguring injuries to pedestrians are due essentially to various fittings which protrude from the body of the car. Metal insignias and sharply pointed mudguards have been eliminated and modifications, including rubber coverings, incorporated into the design of bumpers.

Human factors are increasingly recognized. Emotional people have more accidents after an argument. The elderly, through worsening sight and hearing, slowing reflexes and an inability to keep up with the increasing complexity of traffic flow, cause problems on the road even though they may not be directly involved in the accidents.

The physically handicapped driver has many modifications built into his car for, rather than ban him from driving, it is recognized that he should have the right to control his own car.

Bicyclists and motor cyclists have a particularly bad record of death and injury on the road. Limiting the power available to novice cyclists has no doubt saved lives. However, making compulsory the wearing of helmets which provide a high level of protection has achieved considerably more.

At the scene of a motor vehicle accident, sufficient traffic control should be arranged to minimize the risk of further vehicles colliding with those that have already crashed. Adequate illumination of the crash scene is also of benefit. An attitude of quiet confidence on the part of the rescuer is very important to reassure those injured while arranging for help to come. In most cases it is best not to move an injured person unnecessarily as this may precipitate further injury. Such duties should be left to ambulance officers and to medically trained personnel.

Continuing research Whether such measures as driver education, both before and after the granting of a license, periodic re-testing of motorists and the annual testing of motor vehicles are desirable or effective in reducing the road toll, remains controversial. Meanwhile research into a wide range of problem areas, such as pollution control and improvement of braking, continues within traffic medicine units.

Overseas travel

The vast majority of those who travel overseas have no significant health problems, but taking appropriate precautions can minimize the risks of an expensive and pleasurable journey being spoilt by illness.

People on long-term treatment, as in the case of hypertension, should take adequate supplies of medications, or ensure that they will be readily available at the destinations. Bracelets or tags with information about diseases suffered from, particularly diabetes and epilepsy, and current treatment, are also particularly useful when traveling.

Prolonged airplane flights present no health hazards to fit people, but some pre-existing conditions may be aggravated. Sitting for long periods, especially in cramped conditions, may cause discomfort to those with advanced arthritis, and aggravate any predisposition to deep venous thrombosis (blood clot in a vein that lies deep in muscle tissue).

As the oxygen level and air pressure within an airplane are lower than at sea level, those with significant heart disease (heart failure, angina pectoris, ischemic heart disease) and lung disorders (particularly advanced emphysema and chronic bronchitis), may develop symptoms of their illness.

Soon after taking off and during descent, 'popping' of the ears generally occurs. This is caused by unequal pressures between the air in the middle ear and the air outside. The popping represents the equilibration of the pressures as the eustachian tube (from the middle ear to the back of the throat) opens up. Swallowing or blowing out the cheeks whilst blocking the nose will help this to occur. Some people with middle ear disorders or blocked eustachian tubes may have difficulties as a result of an inability to equilibrate pressures. Decongestant medications that open up the eustachian tube to a greater extent may be required approximately one hour before taking off, and at a similar time before landing.

Airlines do not usually allow pregnant women to travel by air once they have reached the 34 to 36 week stage of pregnancy. Reduced air pressure is associated with a greater incidence of premature labour.

Anyone unsure of his — or her — fitness to travel should consult his family medical practitioner. Many airlines request people with significant medical problems to obtain a certificate of 'air worthiness' from their family doctor.

Floating markets in Thailand. Overseas travellers should check immunization requirements with a doctor or travel agent.

It is sensible to be immunized against possible infections prior to going overseas. Some countries require certain vaccinations, the requirements being dependent primarily on the countries that have been or are to be visited. Doctors and travel agents have up-to-date lists of appropriate immunization requirements.

The need for smallpox vaccination has been reduced in recent years since the world has been declared free of smallpox by the World Health Organization. By 1980 very few countries still required a smallpox vaccination.

Travelers visiting malaria-infected areas should take regular medications to prevent infection. Virtually all the tropical and sub-tropical regions of the world, including South East Asia, Africa, Central and South America, and various countries in the Mediterranean region, are malaria infected.

The standard regime for malaria prevention involves the regular ingestion of one or two tablets on the same day each week, from two weeks before entry till four to six weeks after leaving the malaria-infested area. The drug most commonly used is chloroquine. In recent years chloroquine-resistant parasites have developed in certain areas, and alternative drugs may be required. Details can be obtained from the family doctor or from travel agents.

Motion sickness and jet lag Two problems may be associated with the actual journey. Motion sickness is relatively common, and may be related to any form of transport — car sickness, sea sickness or air sickness. The other problem is related primarily to long air travel, and is known as 'jet lag'.

Motion sickness is apparently related to a disturbance of the balance system of the inner ear, caused by the travel, which results in nausea, vomiting and a general feeling of malaise. Sweating and rigors (shaking episodes) often occur. It is much more common in rough weather, but can also occur on smooth trips. The condition is uncommon in young children. Some people become sick on every trip, while others suddenly develop the condition after many years of regular trouble-free travel.

Several medications are available to help prevent motion sickness, usually antihistamines. It is advisable to consult a medical practitioner about the most appropriate one to use. Those who are prone to motion sickness should avoid alcohol and fatty or spicy foods.

Jet lag has become more of a problem since the beginning of long flights with few stops. On these flights, the change of time zones often upsets the internal body rhythms that are geared to a usual 24-hour cycle.

The main features of jet lag are general tiredness, irritability, and difficulty in adjusting to sleeping hours. It is a special problem for the businessman who has to conduct his business within hours of arriving at his destination.

Jet lag can be minimized by following a few general principles. The traveler should avoid a hectic schedule for the first day or two before and after the flight. During the flight rest as much as possible and eat and drink moderately.

Traveler's diarrhea The major cause of traveler's diarrhea, also known by such names as 'Delhi belly' and 'Montezuma's revenge', is a strain of bacteria, particularly *Escherichia coli*, to which the traveler is not immune.

Diarrhea is the most prominent symptom, but sweating, abdominal cramps, nausea, and sometimes vomiting may also occur. There are many possible sources of infection, including ice cream, seafood, and sometimes the local water. The diarrhea usually only lasts about one or two days, but it can often cause great inconvenience to the traveller. Treatment primarily involves a fluid-only diet for 24 hours. The water in suspect areas should be boiled and allowed to cool before being drunk. Special anti-diarrheal tablets may be of value in more severe cases.

Traveling in hot climates. Hot climates tend to cause much more trouble to the traveler than cold ones. The symptoms of excessive heat exposure often take several hours to develop.

The speed of jet travel means that people can travel from a cold climate to a hot humid one within 24 hours, adding to the problem of adjustment.

In a hot climate the basic principles of general health care are, firstly, to allow adequate perspiration, which in turn facilitates heat loss, and, secondly, to ensure an adequate fluid and salt intake.

The body's need for fluid is greater in hot climates. In general, a feeling of thirst and a dry mouth indicate a need for more fluid. At temperatures persistently high, the daily fluid needs are as high as 1 gallon (5 L) (this includes fluid in solid food). Extra salt to compensate for that lost by sweating may also be needed.

Clothing should be loose, and preferably of cotton or other lightweight natural material. Adequate protection from the burning rays of the sun is also important, and can be achieved by staying indoors or in the shade during 'siesta' time, wearing a broad-brimmed hat and keeping the shirt sleeves rolled down.

Many of the parasitic and other infectious diseases are more prevalent in tropical and sub-tropical areas. Specific drugs used to prevent malaria have already been mentioned. General protection against mosquito and other insect bites is possible by wearing long-sleeved shirts during the early evening when the insects tend to emerge, and the use of flyscreens, mosquito netting and repellent sprays.

Swimming or bathing in fluke-infested areas is not advised. In some tropical countries it is unwise to walk about in bare feet as hookworm can be contracted from infected soil.

Medical kit for overseas travel Most well-known tourist areas have adequate facilities for any medical problem that may arise. However, it is advisable for the traveler to carry a small supply of medicines and other materials. Possible items are simple pain-killers (aspirin or acetaminophen), anti-diarrheal tablets and anti-vomiting and motion sickness tablets. A tube of antiseptic cream, a couple of bandages and some safety pins are also worth taking. Other supplies depend on the area being visited. Some of the drugs mentioned above can be obtained only on prescription from the family doctor.

While the possible medical problems that could occur during travel are numerous, they occur only rarely. By following the advice and guidance of the family doctor, the travel agent and other appropriate authorities, the risks are small.

9 The Human Mind

Emotion

A state of mental excitement which alters a person's feelings is an emotion. There are five basic emotions: joy, love, anger, fear and grief. Joy and love are sometimes called positive emotions because they are aroused by something the individual likes. Anger, fear and grief are called negative emotions as they cause the individual to be unhappy and dissatisfied.

Emotions can be aroused by the individual's thinking about something or by something happening outside him. Some psychologists believe the human mind is not a blank slate at birth, but that emotional and intellectual development evolve through the interaction between biological processes and the environment. Others, however, believe that all emotions are learned from babyhood onwards and modified by maternal behavior and reaction as well as by personal experiences.

Emotions cause physical changes in the body by releasing hormones and activating nerves. Fear, for example, dries the mouth, produces a more rapid pulse and raises the blood pressure. Blood flow increases to the muscles and decreases to the gut, and the body is taut and ready for action.

The carnival clown evokes a warm response from his audience but has his own emotional needs as well.

The child who cannot adjust readily to the company of others tends to avoid social experiences. (Zefa)

Emotional deprivation

The isolation of an individual, especially a baby or young child, from a normal emotional environment is known as emotional deprivation. Providing a warm, loving and secure environment is an essential factor in the healthy development of a child; lack of such an environment may produce impairment of mental and physical development. Although there are many influences that may affect an individual's personality throughout life, the first five years of life are of special significance.

In the first few months, an infant's primary needs are food, warmth, body contact and gentle handling. From about six months of age, however, a child begins to discern specific people independently, and from then a caring relationship with at least one person is essential. A balance

must be kept between an excessive restriction of the child's activities on the one hand and a lack of guidelines and the reinforcement of appropriate behavior on the other.

When no guidelines are provided at all, a child may develop the conviction that the world is there expressly for him. A 'spoiled child' often has a number of difficult lessons to learn later in life. Appropriate restrictions provide a framework by which he can be guided while still allowing him to develop and learn. Overzealous regulation and discipline leads to problems such as repression of feelings and failure to develop independence.

Opposite
Emotional expressions are learned from babyhood *(Zefa)*

Crowd reaction to exciting events may prompt strong emotions. *(Zefa)*

Physical, psychological and mental development are all impaired when deprivation is severe. The effects of emotional deprivation depend on the severity and the extent of traumatic experiences, such as separation from a mother figure, and the inherited components of the temperament of the child. It has been observed that babies and young children growing up almost unattended in makeshift wartime orphanages or refugee camps do not develop the ability to relate to others, having been deprived of loving relationships while small.

Children who are emotionally deprived often have a low sense of self-worth and a low frustration tolerance. Their attention span is often limited and their insecurity may manifest as a persistent desire for attention and recognition. The child may purposefully do things that are unaccept-

able to the parents solely to gain attention, even though it means probable physical punishment.

Emotional disorders

Emotional disorders or disturbances include a wide range of conditions and are probably the most common type of psychological disorder seen in children.

Fears or phobias are present to some degree in virtually everyone. Fears such as those of height or small enclosed spaces are common, but in most cases do not cause significant problems or restrictions in lifestyle. Children have vivid imaginations, and fears, such as of the dark or certain animals, occur more frequently than in adults. School phobias and nightmares are other conditions that are common in emotional disorders of childhood.

As emotion incorporates feelings,

moods, and associated actions, most psychological disturbances have some degree of emotional disturbance. The term is used, however, primarily to cover anxieties, phobias, and mood changes such as depression.

Causes are frequently major changes in environment, especially in the case of reactive depression but also are related to past experiences, particularly relating to self-esteem and confidence, such as seen in school phobia. It is in this context that the early years of life are considered to be especially important.

Symptoms Depression, anxiety or phobias often have physical symptoms. Tension headache, abdominal pain, and alterations in sleeping and eating habits are common.

Regression to more childlike behavior may occur in more significant emotional disorders. In children, enuresis (bed wetting), and encopresis (soiling) may recommence after a period of complete bowel and bladder control.

Treatment depends mainly on the particular situation, but a full psychological assessment is necessary. Appropriate changes in the patient's environment are often helpful. Psychotherapy is often used to improve the ability to cope with the situation, and also to provide some insight into the processes involved in the abnormal condition. Specific behavioral modification techniques may also be employed.

Anger

Usually precipitated by frustration, anger is accompanied by physiological changes in the body; the heart rate speeds up, muscle tension builds and blood pressure rises.

It is not clear which part of the brain is responsible for the control of emotions in man, although it is known that stimulation of a certain part of the brain, the hypothalamus, will produce a rage response in animals. In man, the brain is complex and

Most psychological disturbances are in some part emotional. Psychotherapy forms part of the treatment.

In extreme cases of emotion the response to events such as a religious festival may be a state of trance. (*Zefa*)

emotions and behavior are modified by the higher centers (those parts of the brain from which impulses founded on conscious feelings or wishes emanate), and are therefore a reflection of basic temperament and experiences.

In any normal population marked differences in individual temperament may be observed. For example, some people are, throughout their life, cheerful, gregarious, optimistic and free from worry, whereas others are just the opposite. There are also those people with an explosive or aggressive personality, who are unable to control their anger and chronically overreact to difficult situations.

Still others, 'passive-aggressive' people, outwardly may exhibit a passive character and be unable to assert themselves but beneath the unassuming façade may lie a great deal of hostility and resentment. Such people may covertly express angry feelings by being stubborn, obstructionist or intentionally inefficient.

It is healthy to be able to give vent to anger insofar as the degree of expression is controlled and appropriate to the situation.

Fear

An emotion stimulated by danger, fear triggers a physical response involving the production of adrenalin, a quickening of heart rate, a heightening of senses, and the flexing of muscles. This response is a protective mechanism.

Unfounded and irrational fears can be emotionally crippling. They include the intense, unreasoned fears known as phobias (for example, agoraphobia, the fear of open spaces), the fears based on superstition and false dogma taught in childhood, and other fears acquired in childhood, such as the fear of the dark.

Some fears develop from painful experience, as in the case of a child who develops a fear of doctors or dentists.

Fear of failure is widespread and powerful, so powerful at times that it can be a reason for suicide, as in fear of failing exams or fear of bankruptcy. This may suggest that in at least some of these cases the fear of failure is stronger than the fear of death. A considerably milder response to fear is the desire to conform socially rather than risk ridicule.

Coping with fear People react to fear in various ways. Some become arrogant and aggressive, others seek refuge in superstition and carry lucky charms. Some are comforted by religion. Some seek distraction in other activities or try to escape from their fears by getting drunk or taking tranquilizers.

Most dangers are best coped with by reason and caution rather than fear. If one is afraid of being killed in the car, the rational precaution is to drive soberly and wear a safety belt.

Greater knowledge may dispel a fear based on ignorance. For example, women fearful of childbirth may be encouraged by a sober account of the process. Similarly, the fear of death may be lessened by a calm contemplation of the fact of its natural inevitability, though this is unlikely to be within the realm of all. Mental relaxation is another way of coping with fear and anxiety.

In some cases, psychiatric treatment may be required, for many fears have their origins in forgotten experiences, and the individual may need to re-confront these in order to begin to overcome a long-standing, deep-seated habitual fear. Medical treatment may be necessary if fear is associated with a condition such as alcoholism or depression.

This skilled climber may experience less fear than people watching his ascent. *(John Watney Photo Library)*

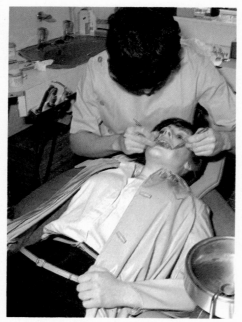

Even with modern anesthetics, fear of dentistry is common. *(Zefa)*

Below
People with low self-esteem are likely to deal with frustration poorly, perhaps ultimately with behavior problems. *(Zefa)*

Frustration

Derived from the Latin *frustratus*, disappointment, frustration is the state which arises when an individual's attempts to achieve a goal are thwarted or prevented. The term is also often used in a sexual sense, meaning the failure of the sex drive to find adequate expression. Frustration may arise as a result of unrealistic expectations, lack of foresight, or external circumstances.

The way in which frustration is coped with depends upon the nature of the goal, the person's previous experiences and capacity to cope at the time. Those with a history of repeated failure and low self-esteem are more likely to deal with frustration poorly. A sense of resignation or failure, or of difference from others, and the channeling of energies into violent or antisocial behavior may follow.

Preventing such feelings of failure is an important aspect of the treatment of some childhood conditions that may lead to behavioral problems. For example, in dyslexia (a learning difficulty which affects reading skills) an intelligent child may have great difficulty in coping with his continued inability to match his classmates in reading skills.

The sympathetic concern and patience of others, and the individual's own powers of persistence and preparedness

Temper tantrums may result from
tension and frustration experienced
by young children. (*Zefa*)

to modify expectations of himself and
others overcome or control most of the
less critical frustrations of daily life. Professional help is usually sought only when
more serious psychological consequences
become evident in antisocial behavior,
psychological withdrawal or a resort to
drugs.

Stress

Physical and emotional factors that promote tension of body or mind, as well as
the tension itself, are labeled stress.
Although the body tries to maintain a
steady internal environment, as with body
temperatures, each individual is still susceptible to the environment, which can
produce a number of stresses.

These may be prompted by injuries, disease, deprivations and particularly by
emotional disturbances, such as divorce,
marriage, death and changes in occupation and residence. Overstimulation of
the senses and emotions, especially by
noise, precipitates nervous tension and
stress. The outstanding characteristic of
modern stress is that it combines
emotional stimulation with physical inactivity — people are frequently unable to do
anything about factors which annoy them.

Anger and other emotions release the
hormones noradrenalin and adrenalin.
The former increases the supply of blood

to the muscles, which raises blood pressure, constricts arterioles to the gut and
skin and dilates arterioles to the muscles.
Adrenalin mobilizes glucose from the
liver, increases the heart rate, dilates the
bronchial tubes and causes sweating.
These changes all promote increases in
physical activity.

Over a prolonged period overstimulation of the senses and the
emotions, rapid and substantial changes
in circumstances that strain the person's
ability to adapt, and a bewildering choice
of decisions to be made, combine to cause
irritability, fatigue and apathy so that the
sufferer becomes indecisive.

Stress is often linked to the development of disease and, using coronary disease and its effects on life as a model, researchers have produced a stress index.
This index rose in the two years before a
heart attack, gradually at first, then
steeply in the last six months. It also rose
prior to the appearance of any coronary
disease symptoms, reaching a higher level
in those who eventually suffered severe or
fatal attacks. Relevant stresses were
troubles or changes at work, family upsets
and minor law-breaking. About 50 per
cent of fatal heart attacks are preceded by
several months of depression leading to
sudden activity, anger or anxiety.

Women experience some natural stress
related to their monthly period and
swings in blood hormone levels. During
this phase accidents and suicides may be
more likely. Childbirth is likely to be followed by depression, again probably a
hormonal effect. Emotional crisis may result in a breakdown in health, usually with
symptoms of anxiety or depression.

Stress as experienced in modern
lifestyles frequently occurs in
situations where there is little
physical activity.

Prevention of stress Studies of Japanese
have demonstrated that the social support
given in traditional Japanese society protects the individual against stresses harmful to the heart, while those Japanese in
Hawaii enjoy no such support and have a
higher prevalence of heart disease.

If modern stress is caused by emotional
stimulation and physical inactivity it can
be avoided by reducing emotional stimulation, such as loud noise and increasing
muscular activity. Numerous simultaneous stimulating changes should be
avoided as one stressful situation is
enough at a time, and a person should recover from one stress before undergoing
another. Leisure and regular physical exercise provide an opportunity for recovering from the effects of stress. Exercise
consumes the fatty substances in the
blood, thus lowering the blood pressure,
which helps to prevent heart disease, improve sleep, promote relaxation and ease
tension. It also deals with the effects of
adrenal hormones released by stress.

Nervous breakdown is a non-medical
term used to describe a period of time in
which a person is unable to cope properly
because of emotional or psychological
stress.

The causes of nervous breakdowns include a personal crisis such as bereavement, depression, anxiety, or a psychosis
(a severe mental illness) such as mania or
schizophrenia. The common features are
listlessness, withdrawal, loss of appetite
and a lack of interest in the surroundings.

Treatment involves time, rest, general
support and encouragement. For severe
depression specific treatment such as
antidepressant medication is important.
In the case of mental exhaustion caused
by a period of extremely heavy workload
the treatment simply may be a long
holiday.

Human Personality and its Problems

The unique mental characteristics, traits and modes of behavior that distinguish a person from others, and determine the way in which he relates to people and to the general environment, comprise that individual's personality.

Personality development involves a combination of inherited and environmental factors. An individual's formative years significantly affect personality as do all experiences, causing personality to change with time. Major environmental or personal changes such as bereavement, personal illness, disfigurement, or other major events may profoundly alter an individual's outlook on life and behavior pattern. With increasing age the impact of current environmental changes declines.

The basic personality is formed in childhood; it is considerably adjusted in adolescence and it is open to changes in adulthood only if the individual is sufficiently motivated in therapy.

The relative roles of heredity and environment on the development of personality have always been contentious. In the fifth century B.C. Hippocrates equated personality traits and characteristics with various bodily appearances and builds. Comparisons of twins, who were raised together or separately, have shown that both influences are important. However certain aspects, such as the level of intelligence, have a higher hereditary factor than others, such as a person's degree of self-assurance.

Characteristic patterns of behavior are labeled personality traits and personalities are often categorized by assessing an individual's traits as well as their predominance. Extroversion and introversion are examples of this. An extrovert is someone who is particularly outward looking, sociable and often impulsive, whereas an introvert is more inward-looking, shy and relatively cautious.

The adults with whom a small child has regular contact can influence the development of the child's personality. *(Zefa)*

Specific personality tests, to decide upon a career or to assist psychological or psychiatric treatment, often necessitate a more detailed assessment. Tests such as the Rorschach test, where the things that a person sees in the cards (which depict inkblots of various shapes and colors) are assessed and evaluated, are used. There are also various questionnaires to assess the personality profile of an individual.

Extreme responses to these tests may suggest an aberrant personality trait or personality disorder.

Personality disorders

Conditions where normal personality traits are exaggerated so that abnormal behavior becomes prominent are labeled personality disorders. These behavior patterns are usually established before adolescence and are often life-long. They are characterized by pathological trends in an individual's interpersonal relationships that usually result in distress for both parties involved.

Symptoms are, commonly, longstanding immaturity, and difficulties in relating to surrounding people and situations, particularly during times of stress. As these behavior patterns constitute a person's coping mechanism, change is not easy and personality adjustment and growth take years.

Causes These are not fully understood. Early parental influences and emotional deprivation may sometimes be important, as may constitutional or inherited predispositions. Most individuals with mild personality disorders cope adequately with society but the more severe disorders require long-term psychological help.

Treatment Psychotherapy is often beneficial if the individual is sufficiently motivated.

Below
The person who has extreme difficulty in relating to people may have a personality disorder.

Above
Adolescence may contribute to some changes in personality.

Persons with personality disorders also learn from models; constant, repeated, and accurate feed-back about the effects of their abnormal behaviour pattern on those around them is important.

Sexual deviation usually requires no treatment unless the law requires it or if the individual is concerned about his deviant behaviour.

Drug and alcohol dependence is regarded as a form of mental disorder and may respond to a combination of social and psychological treatment. Results are extremely variable.

Extroverts and introverts

The psychiatrist Carl Jung (1875–1961) first devised the concept of the opposite personality types characterized by the terms introversion and extroversion.

Above left
Attracting attention will rarely embarrass an extrovert. *(Zefa)*

Above right
The introvert is usually a shy, self-contained person.

Right
Low self-esteem may bring periods of depression.

The person who characteristically likes interacting with other people is usually described as extroverted; 'outward-going' is another term often used to describe such people. Other features of the typically extroverted person are impulsiveness and a general tendency to be a 'man of action'.

The introvert is inward-looking, is preoccupied with his own thoughts and feelings and avoids social contact with others.

To think of people merely in terms of introversion and extroversion is an oversimplification. People vary greatly in their degree of sociability and interaction with others, and this depends upon the company and their mood at the time, as well as many other factors. As with many other characteristics, when people have undergone psychological testing to assess their degree of extroversion a wide range has emerged. Few people are fully extroverted or fully introverted; the vast majority lie somewhere in the middle.

Inhibition

In general, inhibition describes the repression of an action or reaction.
Sexual inhibition basically means that an individual's personality, psychological make-up, upbringing and general way of life prevents full sexual expression.

Everyone is to some extent sexually inhibited, but this is only a problem if it is total or if it causes excessive anxiety. Total sexual inhibition occurs when an individual desires but is unable to engage in

any sexual activity. This is caused generally by being brought up to regard sexual intercourse as unclean or improper. Relative sexual inhibition becomes a problem only when an individual feels a need for a particular form of sexuality but is unable to engage in it.

Psychiatric help is often very effective in remedying sexual inhibition.

Inferiority complex

Alfred Adler (1870–1937) was a psychoanalyst who postulated that much mental disease resulted from a sense of inferiority and that the mind attempted to overcome this by overcompensation. Aspects of this process were considered to be most often subconscious (that is, the person was not fully aware of them). The asthma sufferer who became a champion swimmer or the man of short stature who became a long-distance runner are often-quoted examples. A conscious feeling of inferiority is often a powerful motivating force to succeed in some other area.

An exaggerated sense of inferiority or lack of worth may frequently lead to more negative behavior. The origins of inferiority usually go back to experiences in the first three years of life. Lack of love, or parental favoritism towards a sibling are thought sometimes to be the foundations of a long-standing problem. In susceptible people who go through life with low self-esteem, problems are aggravated greatly by any loss concerned with health, employment or family, through bereavement or divorce. Prolonged periods of depression are relatively common.

The development of physical ailments such as abdominal pain, tension headaches, diarrhea and other gastrointestinal upsets, or migraine attacks may accompany this state. Aggressive and dominating behavior may occur occasionally.

When the problem becomes severe, psychotherapy is generally required to assist the sufferer to realize that the feeling of inferiority is more imaginary than real.

Maladjusted child

Children showing unsettled or disturbed behavior and unable to adapt to their normal environment, or even to change

'Difficult' behavior may indicate unresolved emotional needs.

and stress may be described as maladjusted. Normal children commonly show a particular symptom of atypical behavior or development from time to time, but persistence of several behavior problems often indicates maladjustment.

Symptoms In the infant, feeding difficulties, disturbed sleeping/waking patterns and persistent irritability and crying may be signs of maladjustment.

In the young child, maladjustment may be expressed as temper tantrums, dietary fussiness, undue anxiety when separated from the mother, sleep disturbance, night terrors, toilet training difficulties, or just being 'difficult'.

The older child will often reveal adjustment difficulties at school in the form of learning problems, disruptive behavior, truancy, stealing, shoplifting, headaches, recurrent abdominal pains, phobias, withdrawal and depression.

In the adolescent, the combination of unresolved childhood turmoil and anxieties may appear in the form of delinquent behavior, school failure, truancy, isolated solitary tendency, aggression and other forms of 'acting out' behavior, sexual adventures, drug experimentation, migraine or a rude surly manner. Other serious cases involving suicide threats or attempts, severe depression and marked phobias about school will need urgent treatment.

Causes The child's previous and present emotional environments create these problems. They often depend on the child's stage of development and on the strengths and weaknesses of personality. A disturbed child's personality-forming experiences may influence his response to stress, which may result in the child forgetting recently learned developmental skills, such as bladder control at night.

Maladjustment can be caused by family expectations for the child, tensions in the home, divorce, serious illness and death in the family, child abuse, frequent changes of address and school, and lack of opportunity for play with other children.

Emotional maladjustment is frequently caused by physical disability, particularly when children suffer from obvious defects such as deafness, blindness, spasticity in cerebral palsy, spina bifida, blemishes, severe burns, facial disfigurement and from chronic illness, such as diabetes and leukemia.

Distressing experiences such as a stay in hospital or an unhappy school situation may also result in expressions of maladjustment.

Delinquent behavior is one of the more damaging results of a child's maladjustment. (Zefa)

Excessive anxiety at the prospect of separation from his mother appears to show that this child has not reached the level of adjustment normal for his age.

Treatment Before treating physical problems consideration should be given to the psychological and emotional effects of the treatment on the child.

The child's close emotional relationships, and the stresses created by them, need to be clearly understood. The child's relationships outside the family can then be evaluated and problems dealt with.

Professional help is provided by a family doctor, child specialist (pediatrician), schoolteacher and counselor, and by baby health clinics, which may also involve government child health facilities, area health centers, social workers, clinical psychologists or child psychiatrists.

Long-term outlook Deprivation of warm, affectionate and close relationships in the early years reduces the likelihood of satisfactory resolution of the child's problems. Healthy early development, good peer relationships and a confident, secure family background, usually enable the child or adolescent to respond positively to support, understanding and environmental changes. In some cases teenagers leave an unhealthy home environment to find help.

Psychopathic personality

Also called antisocial personality or sociopathic personality, a psychopathic personality has a number of personality characteristics. Such a person is frequently in trouble with society and appears to have no concern for or sensitivity to others. A psychopath acts impulsively in response to his desires, repeatedly ignoring social values. His behavior seems unaffected by punishment or experience. Characteristically such a person has no compunction in blaming another when caught at some misdeed.

Psychopathic behavior may arise in an individual unable to tolerate any frustration and may be a consequence of poor or absent parenting.

Symptoms A psychopath may first come to notice in childhood or adolescence with problems including theft, cruelty to animals, truancy, running away, lying, poor work achievement, playing with fires, impulsiveness and unpleasantness.

Behavior in adulthood often includes poor personal relationships and work history, lying, impulsiveness and criminal activity leading to arrests. Such a person has great difficulty in maintaining relationships and experiences no guilt in manipulating those who become involved with him. An inability to accept the ethics and laws of the society is not related to an intellectual deficiency. A psychopathic personality may be quite intelligent and often socially charming, having developed a superficial charm which aids him in getting his own way. 'Con men' often fall into this personality classification.

Treatment of such a disorder is very limited in its success.

Schizoid personality

The type of personality described as schizoid is characterized by solitariness, extreme shyness, introversion and emotional withdrawal. The individual does not enter into deep or longstanding relationships. There is excessive daydreaming and sometimes eccentric behavior.

A schizoid personality occurs more commonly in the blood relatives of people with schizophrenia. About a quarter to a third of those with schizophrenia will have developed the characteristics of a schizoid personality before they become schizophrenic. Inherited and environmental factors are thought to be important in the development of both conditions.

The ability to sustain good interpersonal relationships may be one indication of stable mental health. (*Zefa*)

Psychotic Illness

Psychotic illness may be caused by an accident, poison, tumor, infection or some similar organic cause. If no disease or impairment in brain function is obvious it is called a functional psychosis. Schizophrenia and the manic-depressive psychoses are functional psychoses. A person with a psychosis may have strange thoughts and behave in strange and inappropriate ways. He may forget things easily, become confused or have inappropriate emotional reactions, for example crying or laughing for no good reason.

Treatment of organic psychosis is directed at the cause. Functional psychosis may be treated with a combination of drugs, and sometimes with a short stay in hospital if the illness is acute. Follow-up care is essential to prevent any relapse and to help the patient to resume a normal life.

Schizophrenias

Mental illnesses of varying severity and symptoms, schizophrenias affect over 1 per cent of the population and account for more than a quarter of psychiatric hospital admissions. The term was introduced in 1911 by the Swiss psychiatrist Eugene Bleuler (1857–1939). It is derived from the Greek *schizein*, divide or split, and *phren*, mind. Bleuler thought that the features of the disorder were caused by a splitting of the mind or the personality as a result of abnormal thought processes. However, more recent theories on the phenomenonology of schizophrenia are much more complicated and extensive.

Symptoms Schizophrenia is characterized by changes in thought, mood and behavior. Specific symptoms include inappropriate emotional responses, hallucinations such as the hearing of non-existent voices, looseness of association of ideas resulting in the inability to maintain logical trains of thought, and autistic thinking which is

inward-looking and out of touch with reality.

Schizophrenia may be classified into one of four types depending upon the predominant symptoms.

Simple schizophrenia can often be traced back to adolescence when there was slow progressive withdrawal and failure to function properly in a social sense. The more bizarre features of hallucinations and marked abnormalities of behavior are not prominent.

Hebephrenic schizophrenia often commences in young adulthood and is associated with a rapid deterioration. Thought processes are grossly disorganized, the symptoms are very dramatic, and hospitalization is usually required quite early.

Catatonic schizophrenia is not a common form, although it is one in which the features are striking. Withdrawal is marked with the development of periods of apparent stupor in which movement and speech are absent. There is, however, awareness of what is being said or done nearby. Periods of marked excitement may also develop.

Paranoid schizophrenia usually becomes apparent in adult life. There are hallucinations and delusions of persecution, but these may affect only a circumscribed part of the person's life. The overall personality tends to be quite unchanged.

Causes There are many different causes of schizophrenia. Genetics play a significant part. An identical twin of someone with schizophrenia has a 70 per cent chance of developing the condition and the chances of a son or daughter of an affected person becoming schizophrenic are about one in seven.

Schizophrenia has been found to occur more commonly in impoverished people living in overcrowded city dwellings. Also, there is some evidence to suggest that abnormalities in the limbic system of the forebrain and of the chemical transmitters within the brain may also play a

Forming loving relationships is important for mental health.

role.

The outcome of schizophrenia is variable. Sometimes there is only one attack, although more frequently there is a series of attacks and remissions. Increasing deterioration and worsening social functioning between each flare-up is a feature in some cases, and long-term hospitalization may be required in the malignant cases.

Treatment The main treatment is with phenothiazine drugs such as chlorpromazine. Electroconvulsive (shock) therapy is still used for some severe attacks of a type which do not respond to drug therapy alone. After the acute phase has settled, socialization and vocational rehabilitation programs are instituted. Inpatient or day-care facilities enable planned activities to be undertaken in a setting in which personal integration or improvement of self-esteem is enhanced. Over the last twenty years there has been an increasing emphasis on re-integrating people with schizophrenia into society, and shortening periods of hospitalization.

Manic-depressive psychosis

The specific form of psychosis known as manic depressive or affective psychosis is characterized by extreme swings of mood, ranging from extreme depression to great elation.

The features of severe depression are usually marked withdrawal, loss of interest in activities, loss of appetite, and marked weight loss. At this stage there is a great risk of the depressed person attempting suicide.

The features of elation (or mania) are usually rapid, non-stop talkativeness, and a marked expenditure of energy, often with the affected person doing things almost 24 hours a day. Thinking is usually very rapid and becomes disorganized, with flitting from one idea to the next (flight of ideas). The person may have delusions of grandeur and act on grandiose but totally impractical ideas, losing interest as soon as another thought comes to mind.

These phases may last for a long time, or be interrupted by long periods of stability. Sedation is often required during the manic phase, and antidepressant drugs, or even shock treatment, during the depressive phase. Lithium is the most common form of medication used to minimize swings of mood. For those who have had several relapses, lithium therapy is used for life-long treatment. In these cases the level of lithium in the bloodstream has to be checked periodically.

Paranoid state

Paranoid state is a type of psychosis, in which persecutory or grandiose delusions occur with or without hallucinations. Significantly, intellectual functions are often not affected and emotional responses and behavior remain consistent

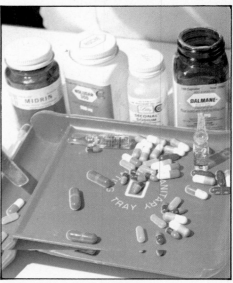

Organic psychosis, caused by disease which alters brain function, may be the result of drug intoxication. *(Salmer)*

with the ideas held.

Reactive psychosis

A psychotic state, reactive psychosis is precipitated by severe environmental stress. There is an absence of any previous history of other types of psychoses and usually recovery is good and complete when the stress is overcome and the underlying issues resolved.

Organic psychosis

Also called an organic brain syndrome, an organic psychosis is brought about by the effects of disease which ultimately change brain function. This diffuse or local impairment of brain tissue function results in disturbances in memory, orientation, judgement, intellectual functions and mood.

Primary brain diseases include senile and pre-senile dementias and Huntington's chorea. Other physical illnesses producing psychosis include tumors or lesions which occupy space in the brain, infections, drug or poison intoxications, cardiovascular diseases, anoxia (lack of oxygen), metabolic, endocrine or nutritional disorders, trauma, epilepsy and any other physical damage to the brain.

Dementia

The term dementia describes a general deterioration of mental faculties, primarily involving the intellect, although emotional and behavioral aspects are also affected to varying degrees. Dementia appears to develop mainly from a slowly progressive degeneration of brain function, usually commencing in old age. Here little can be done to slow the process. However, there are a wide range of causes, many of which do have some form of treatment; therefore, it is important to take into account the causes when diagnosing dementia.

Causes The sort of condition which can

cause dementia includes endocrine disorders, such as reduced thyroid function (myxedema), Cushing's syndrome, some vitamin and other nutritional deficiencies (for example, vitamin B_{12} deficiency), chronic drug abuse, and syphilis affecting the brain.

Others include trauma that has caused a long-standing blood clot between the brain and the skull, brain tumor and hydrocephalus (where problems of circulation of the fluid bathing the brain cause changes in pressure and affect brain function).

Dementia has been divided into two classifications, depending on the age at which symptoms first appear.

Pre-senile dementia begins in those aged between 40 and 60. A number of hereditary conditions, such as Huntington's chorea, are present in this age group. These genetically linked illnesses have no specific treatment, but discussion should be held with the younger members of the family so that they are fully informed about the mode of inheritance.

Senile dementias are the most common and occur in people over the age of 60. For many years it was thought that hardening and narrowing of the arteries, leading to reduced blood supply to the brain and associated loss of cells (cerebral arteriosclerosis), was the main cause. Recent studies have raised some doubts about this theory; however, an adequate alternative explanation is yet to be put forward.

Symptoms The early signs of the condition are impaired memory of recent events and some disorientation about times and places. The changes that occur are often at first quite subtle, with a person simply not performing to their usual standard. Irritability, lack of initiative, unstable emotions (such as easily becoming tearful) and abnormal behavior may develop. If the deterioration progresses, thinking becomes more disorganized, and delusions may appear. Paranoia often becomes a feature of the condition. Speech and day-to-day functions, such as dressing, feeding and hygiene, may also deteriorate, giving rise to considerable difficulties.

Several other diseases may appear similar to dementia, particularly in old people. Schizophrenia and severe depression are two examples of this. However, other features help to distinguish these conditions and their onset of symptoms is usually more rapid than in dementia.

Treatment In order to exclude all specifically treatable causes of dementia, a short stay in hospital for investigation is desirable. This also enables a full assessment to be made of the patient's capacity to function sufficiently well and of the capacity of the family to cope with and support the patient.

Where possible, continued care in fam-

Healthy outdoor activities encourage a positive attitude to life.
(*Australian Picture Library*)

iliar surroundings by people who show patience and care enable someone with dementia to cope independently often much longer than they would in other circumstances. With an increasing percentage of old people in the population, care of them will become more of an issue. Support for members of the family caring for someone with dementia is important, and occasional periods of residential care to allow the family to have a break may be advantageous.

If the deterioration becomes marked, continuous nursing home care is usually necessary.

Depression

True depression is a severe and persisting lowering of mood. Other lowerings of mood which last for only a short time are not abnormal. Even longer periods which often occur when there is some significant loss are important in themselves but do not represent true depressive illness. For instance, the loss of a loved one, a decline in health, loss of employment, and the loss of children when they leave home.

Melancholia is a term sometimes still used to describe severe depression, and the term involutional melancholia is used when agitation and hypochondriasis (over-concern with one's own health and body) are among the prominent features.

Causes The true depressive illness may occur for no apparent reason (endogenous depression) or it may occur as a reaction to a triggering factor in the environment (exogenous or reactive depression). Here the depression is longer-lasting and more severe than would be usually expected in the circumstances.

Sometimes depression will be part of rather than a reaction to another illness, as, for example, during recovery from a viral infection such as influenza, or as part of multiple sclerosis.

Depression sometimes accompanies changes that take place at certain times in a person's life. Some examples are hormonal changes, adolescence, puerperium (the period just after childbirth), the immediate premenstrual period, and the menopause.

Sigmund Freud's view was that depression results from a person suppressing feelings of anger towards others, and that this aggression is bottled up and turned inward upon the person himself. This theory of depression is accepted by some authorities, however, others see a lack of self-esteem and self-worth as the central, crippling aspect, and that almost all other features, including the turning inwards of aggressive and angry impulses, develop from this.

The actual mechanism of depression is still not fully understood, but, like the treatment, it appears to have definite chemical as well as psychological aspects.

A number of studies have demonstrated a decrease in the levels of specific chemicals within parts of the brains of people with depression. These chemicals are involved in the production of noradrenalin, depamine and serotonin, all of which have a role in normal nerve cell function, particularly in the transmission of impulses. In some cases of depression the levels of sodium salt within the body cells are increased and this may have a role in causing depression.

Symptoms In many ways depression is like looking at the world through dark glasses, with the inability to interpret things correctly. A painful sense of worthlessness and low self-esteem are present to varying degrees. When a person is depressed and preoccupied with his 'badness', mild rebuffs are often taken as major rejections, and other people's anxiety or preoccupations with their own

Children who are depressed often lose interest in many of their normal activities.

problems are sometimes misinterpreted as personal animosity.

Depression is often revealed through physical symptoms. Some of the most common are tiredness, aches and pains (especially in the head, neck or abdomen), loss of appetite or loss of weight, difficulty in sleeping, constipation and the cessation of menstrual periods. Some people actually overeat and put on weight when they are depressed.

Some of the psychological features of depression are a sense of hopelessness and the inability to obtain pleasure from those things that used to be a source of enjoyment; for instance the loss of interest in sex, housework, gardening, sports and hobbies. Other features which add to the difficulties of depression are the inability to concentrate, anxiety, and irritability, which are often aggravated in a family setting. In certain cases the depression will be revealed through a general difficulty in coping with life rather than through a specific symptom or set of symptoms.

In severe depression guilt feelings and persistent suicidal thoughts are often present. Suicidal thoughts follow from a deep sense of hopelessness about life and its joylessness for which there seems no solution.

When people become depressed for the first time after middle age, particularly in the absence of a triggering factor or event, they should be assessed thoroughly as the depression may be the symptom of another condition such as a brain tumor.

Treatment A sympathetic listener who shows interest and concern is very important in the treatment of the depressed person.

Encouragement and reassurance are important in the care of depressed patients, who are often unable to see 'the light at the other end of the tunnel'.

It is generally advantageous to have other members of the family actively involved in treatment, as they often have the best opportunity to support and encourage the affected person. The doctor or counselor dealing with the depressed person cannot provide the continuity of support that those in the home environment can.

Psychotherapy provides verbal support and encouragement to the patient; and sometimes even more intensive work is undertaken. The different forms of psychotherapy have different aims, which range from increasing the patient's insight into deeper underlying conflicts that may be present, through improving coping mechanisms and self-esteem, to the use of specific behavior-modifying techniques that alter some of the person's actions.

The development of antidepressant drugs after the 1950s has had a significant impact on the treatment of depressive illness. Although these drugs usually are of

less value in treating the reactive than the endogenous forms of depression, they do have a role in both forms, particularly when the depression is severe.

There are two main groups of antidepressant drugs: the tricyclic antidepressants and the monoamine oxidase inhibitors (MAO inhibitors). Although they have different ways of acting, both increase the level of specific chemical substances (known as amines) in the brain. As they take several weeks to become fully effective, and because low doses are generally used initially to minimize side-effects, they usually have to be taken for at least four weeks before a final decision can be made regarding their efficacy.

Tricyclic antidepressants are usually preferred because of the lower incidence of severe side-effects than that of the MAO inhibitors. The most common side-effects of the tricyclic group are constipation, drowsiness, blurring of vision, and dry mouth. In most cases these unwanted effects settle fairly rapidly, and this should be explained to the patient prior to treatment. A recent advance is the development of chemically related compounds called 'tetracyclic antidepressants', apparently with reduced risk of side-effects. Their advantages over the established drugs have still to be fully evaluated.

MAO inhibitors sometimes cause a sudden rise in blood pressure, sometimes with serious consequences. Severe headaches are generally the first symptom of these occurrences. As certain foods interact with these drugs strict control of diet is necessary while being treated with these medications. These drugs can also interact with several other medications, so care has to be taken in this regard as well.

Shock treatment has been used less frequently since the introduction of antidepressant medications, however it still has a definite role. For people with psychotic depression (severe depression associated with delusions and other features of grossly disordered thinking), and those with marked physical retardation (little movement, unable to eat, and usually bed-fast) it is the best and most effective treatment. It may also be used in slightly less severely affected people who have failed to respond to full courses of antidepressant therapy.

Social impact Depression has a great impact on the lives of the sufferers and their families. When someone is significantly depressed, work efficiency, family life and relationships all suffer. If untreated, severe depression may lead the victim to commit suicide.

Opposite
Periods of solitude are sought by most people, but those who suffer a severe emotional crisis may withdraw from reality and in some cases psychiatric help may be needed. (*Zefa*)

Psychoneuroses

Neurosis or psychoneurosis is an emotional disturbance arising out of the different and abnormal ways people handle the anxiety which results from underlying conflicts within the personality. Hence, the main characteristic of neurosis is anxiety which may be felt directly as such or expressed unconsciously as various subtypes of neurosis, depending on the psychological defences used. There is minimal or no loss of contact with reality, but there may be evidence of behavior problems of varying degrees in early life.

Most, if not all, people are 'neurotic' in some respects but are usually able, in most areas, to lead reasonably satisfying and normal lives using a range of healthy defences. On the other hand, some people, when subject to stress, may develop specific neuroses which then interfere to a marked extent with their ability to work or to maintain harmonious relationships. People differ, however, in their wish to seek help so that some, in spite of severe neurosis, may never see themselves as being abnormal in any way. On the other hand, individuals who may be mildly or moderately neurotic may have sufficient motivation to want to improve their quality of life and, therefore, actively seek psychological help to be rid of their underlying anxieties.

Causes It is generally accepted that experiences and relationships in infancy and childhood are the major contributing cause of the later development of neurosis. It is rare for a single cause or a specific disturbing incident to cause a neurotic illness. Usually it is the combination of developmental experiences in childhood and current social-cultural influences which together precipitate a neurosis.

Heredity usually has little effect on neurotic behavior although some scanty research suggests that behavior is largely guided by genes. Almost invariably precipitating incidents are linked with characteristics in the individual's personality which together trigger the neurosis.

Anxiety states are states of excessive worry and fear. There is over-activity of the sympathetic nervous system causing symptoms such as palpitations, tremor of the hands and diarrhea. There may be a feeling of 'butterflies in the stomach' or indigestion, and a tendency to overbreathe causing tingling and cramps in the hands and feet from excessive loss of carbon dioxide in the blood. The mouth may become dry and the muscles tense, with excessive tension in those muscles attached to the skull causing a tension headache.

Some patients become worried about their palpitations or other symptoms and imagine they have a disease of the heart or some other organ. They may become hypochondriacs, preoccupied with every sensation and activity of their body.

Hysterical neurosis is characterized by loss of function; there may be paralysis, loss of sensation, blindness or loss of memory. There is an unconscious reason for the symptoms, symptoms to which the patient seems to be indifferent.

Obsessional neurosis is a type of anxiety associated with unwanted ideas and repetitive impulses. The patient often thinks these ideas and actions unreasonable but nevertheless is compelled to experience them.

Phobic neurosis is anxiety provoked by specific situations or objects such as enclosed spaces, open spaces, heights or particular animals.

Depressive neurosis is a mild form of depression, sometimes called reactive depression to signify that it is more a reaction to unpleasant circumstances than a spontaneous (endogenous) depression.

Neurasthenia is a condition in which the patient becomes easily exhausted as a result of emotional conflicts. There is no organic disease.

Depersonalization syndrome is a frightening feeling of not being oneself. It may follow bereavement, or may occur in a form of epilepsy (temporal lobe epilepsy), in schizophrenia or in depression. It can also be caused by certain drugs, particularly LSD.

Physical treatment of neuroses is based mostly on the use of minor tranquilizers and, in rare and severe instances, psychosurgery involving leucotomy (cutting the connections of the front lobes of the brain). Tranquilizing drugs effectively calm the anxious patient but unfortunately some patients may become dependent on them. Hence the importance of exploring the use of psychological methods of treatment such as psychotherapy.

Psychiatric treatment Psychotherapy is the best form of treatment to solve the underlying problems in a neurotic individual. The criteria for psychotherapy include relatively young age, strength to tolerate the stress of looking at oneself and, of course, motivation. During insight-oriented psychotherapy the psychoanalytically trained psychiatrist helps the patient work through his underlying conflicts with significant people (usually parental figures) in the past. This helps the individual to adapt better in his interpersonal relationships as he has less need for pathological defences.

Anxiety

A feeling of unpleasant anticipation or fear, anxiety is described differently by different individuals. As a normal feeling response, it occurs in all individuals at various times. It serves as a danger signal to the body and arouses a number of physiological responses which mobilize the person to react to the perceived danger.

It can be difficult to separate normal from abnormal anxiety. The distinction will be made according to the circumstances causing the anxiety and the intensity and duration of the response of anxiety, against the background of the individual's prior experience of anxiety. In medical practice it has become common to differentiate fear from anxiety; anxiety is defined as a response to obscure, unknown or irrational causes while fear is seen to be a response to a known, real, danger. The distinction can be hard to maintain. When anxiety becomes so severe as to paralyze the individual or cause severe disorganization it becomes panic.

The anxious person usually feels tense and restless. This may lead to a feeling of helplessness, possibly so acute that fear of collapse may become an added burden. Anxiety may be described as free-floating when the individual is unaware of the cause.

People who are anxious are usually aware of unpleasant feelings and even bizarre sensations in their bodies. Many of these can be explained by physiological mechanisms, including increased release of the hormones adrenalin and noradrenalin. Other sensations can be difficult to explain. They include such phenomena as chest pain or peculiar sensations in the head including a feeling of swelling, of trickling or of crackling.

It is not unusual for the sufferer of these anxiety sensations to fail to recognize them as emotional or psychosomatic in

Anxiety can become a neurosis if the problems which cause it begin to have a marked effect on a person's normal life. (*Zefa*)

A pregnant woman may experience anxiety simply because of concern over the health of her unborn child.

origin. Such a person often decides he is physically ill and becomes concerned about the strange physical feelings he is experiencing. He then has a basis for his anxiety and it can be very difficult to tell him otherwise.

Physical symptoms The physical changes that may be produced by anxiety are numerous. They include palpitations, an awareness of heart beat, faintness, impotence, frigidity, a need to urinate frequently, pain in the pelvis in women, excessive perspiration, headache, backache, a quavering voice, shaking of the hands, a 'sinking' feeling in the stomach, 'butterflies', bloating, diarrhea, constipation, a strange taste in the mouth, loss of appetite, abdominal pain, nausea, vomiting, sighing respiration, loss of breath, dizziness and tingling in the fingers.

Effects An anxious person often becomes irritable, very alert and uncertain. Such a person will often have difficulty making decisions, may be restless or may be tensely still. Difficulty in sleeping and sexual problems are not uncommon. Severe anxiety can make it difficult to work properly and can impair memory, abstract reasoning, concentration and the ability to calculate and to perform other tasks.

Psychological basis There are many theories as to the mechanism of anxiety. These include the psychoanalytical theory which sees anxiety as a continuing conflict between inner forbidden impulses and temptations. This theory further maintains that if the anxious person can be made aware of the conflict and can resolve it at a conscious level then the anxiety will lessen.

A behaviorist theory would see anxiety as a learned response. For example if a certain stimulus, such as a smell, arouses anxiety, then it is probably linked in the person's mind with an earlier experience of anxiety, possibly a person who had that smell. The person who experiences the anxiety has made the relationship between the anxiety and the smell and bypasses the original cause. This conditioned response causes an experience of anxiety whenever the particular smell occurs.

Learned cultural values, which may help determine the feelings of guilt and conflict a person has, can also contribute to anxiety.

Treatment Various treatments have been used to alleviate anxiety. These include tranquilizing drugs, alcohol, relaxation, hypnotic and meditative techniques, self-help groups, psychoanalysis and counseling. All methods have some degree of success.

Hypochondria

In medicine hypochrondria is a preoccupation with real or imaginary medical illness, and is linked to anxiety and fear of serious illness. The hypochondriac can be very trying for his relatives, friends and especially his doctor. There is usually a minor psychiatric or a moderate to major social illness underlying the complaints.

An example is anxiety neurosis, that is, a state of fear producing inner tension and physical manifestations such as tense muscles, sweating, tremor and fast heart rate. Approximately 7 per cent of the population are 'anxious types' and often their anxiety is expressed in imagining and complaining of serious bodily diseases or malfunctions.

The social illnesses include loneliness, poor living conditions, poverty, unemployment and boredom. Sometimes the hypochondriac is simply seeking a sympathetic counselor, the one most often available being the doctor. In order to have a reason for visiting the doctor, the hypochondriac will feign various vague aches and pains that everyone suffers from time to time. This perpetuates the problem because the actual problem — the social disease — is not discussed or resolved. The patient returns whenever there are further problems.

Symptoms Some of the classic symptoms are a stabbing left chest pain (where they think the heart is situated) which comes and goes at random (which is atypical of the chest pain of heart disease), a bad back (which again gets better and worse), a vague stabbing abdominal pain in any or all locations not associated with any nausea, vomiting or change in bowel habit. Agitated hypochondriacs often demand that the doctor find the cause of these pains and insist on various expensive x-rays and tests.

Treatment of hypochondria is very difficult. If it is part of a general anxiety neurosis, the psychotherapy and psychiatric help can be of great value. This may help the patient realize the true nature of his problem and help him overcome it. In the case of social problems, hypochondria is almost impossible to treat, simply because the doctor is powerless to change the patient's social situation. Often sympathetic listening and the firm reassurance that there is nothing physically wrong is all that can be offered.

Hysteria

In psychiatry, hysteria is a form of neurosis in which a physical or mental function is lost. Physical loss is also described as conversion. Examples are the loss of motor function, as in paralysis or the inability to speak, and loss of sensation, as in blindness or the inability to feel pain. A loss of mental function, also known as dissociation, occurs in a variety of forms as faints, trances, amnesia and as a 'split personality'.

The condition is often accompanied by emotional indifference, known as 'La belle indifference', in which the person seems relatively unperturbed by the disability. There is often some indirect benefit from the condition, known as a secondary gain. A common symptom of hysteria is a lump in the throat (globus hystericus).

Hysteria is believed to represent a buried conflict that threatens to erupt completely and is only prevented from doing so by the psychological defences constructed by the individual. It is believed that the symptoms symbolize some subconscious motivation. For example, blindness symbolizes the hesitation 'to see' a true situation, muteness represents a silence that protects, and paralysis of the legs is seen as an inability to face up to a problem.

Major hysteria seems to be less common in Western societies. When it is associated with hallucination, and bizarre symptoms occur, it may be difficult to distinguish from schizophrenia.

There are various techniques to treat hysteria, the result of which may be the abandonment of the symptom, however other defences such as depression often appear. Treatment by psychotherapy attempts to increase understanding of the self in order to produce a beneficial change.

Above
Frequent and compulsive washing may be a sign of obsessional neurosis.

Below
Phobic neurosis may develop in a situation which revives memories of an unpleasant experience.

Obsessional neurosis

A nervous disorder in which a person has persistently unwelcome thoughts and repetitive impulses is described as an obsessional neurosis. The individual is sane and realizes that these thoughts and impulses are unreasonable. For example, a person may be obsessed with his hands being dirty and will compulsively wash them repeatedly.

An obsessional neurosis probably develops only in a certain type of personality, characterized by introversion and over-conscientiousness. Such a person is rigid in outlook and stubborn in character, tending to be a stickler for precision and readily bogged down by attention to detail.

Obsessional neuroses can lead to anxiety, depression and inability to carry out the ordinary activities of life.

Treatment by psychotherapy, including a close examination of current problems and stresses in a person's life, will usually bring about an improvement in the condition but compulsions are rarely completely cured.

Phobias

A condition in which a person is abnormally fearful of a particular situation or object and actively tries to avoid it is called a phobia. If the sufferer constantly comes into contact with the feared object or situation then considerable hardship may ensue. Phobias are fairly common and can vary in severity.

Causes and types Various reasons are given to explain why phobias occur. They may have been acquired through learning, a theory that has precipitated the development of behavioral modification and desensitization techniques. Common phobias include agoraphobia (fear of open places), claustrophobia (fear of being enclosed), acrophobia (fear of high places), aquaphobia (fear of water), zoophobia (fear of animals), subway phobia and airplane phobia.

Phobic states may also be provoked by social situations and lead to victims actively avoiding social situations which they feel might cause them to blush, tremble, vomit, urinate or make some sort of embarrassing scene. Separation anxiety is also thought to stimulate some phobic syndromes: agoraphobia may represent a fear of separation from the protective home environment while claustrophobia may be a fear of losing one's decision-making power.

Opposite
Workers in situations such as this cannot afford to suffer from fear of heights, but a bad experience may give rise to such a phobia. (*Zefa*)

For the agoraphobic, the thought of even such simple tasks as shopping is daunting.

Although it isn't clear what determines a particular phobic symptom its initial appearance can often be pinpointed by behavioral interpretation. It is often not evident why a particular situation should become paramount in a sufferer's imagination.

Whatever the cause, the sufferer should be encouraged to participate in life as normally as possible. Once this becomes difficult the patient's family has to decide how to react and, as this can be a delicate task, professional guidance is necessary. Often a person's phobia may not be outwardly obvious and some sufferers learn personally to confront and overcome their phobia.

Those who need external help usually contact their general practitioner who may decide to consult a specialist, such as a psychiatrist or psychologist. Mental discomfort varies among sufferers and may severely disrupt their lives. The level of discomfort at which a person seeks help differs with each individual.

Treatment includes psychotherapy, the use of drugs and desensitization to modify the person's behavior. Psychotherapeutic treatment helps the patient to work through the underlying psychological conflicts as the therapist helps the patient to gain intellectual and emotional insight. This may be painful but can help a victim adapt to and eliminate his or her phobia while giving vent to suppressed wishes, if only in fantasy.

Behavior modifications. Techniques using systematic desensitization include: (1) teaching the patient to relax, (2) constructing a hierarchy of increasing anxiety with the phobic object, and (3) allowing the patient, in a relaxed state gradually to imagine increasing steps in the hierarchy and hence desensitize himself to them. The success rate with a combination of these techniques is fairly good.

Agoraphobia Deriving from the Greek words *agora*, market place, and phobia, *fear*, agoraphobia is a psychological condition characterized by an uncontrollable fear and sense of impending panic in open spaces. It occurs more frequently in women than in men and appears to be most common amongst house-bound women in the 20–45 year age group. Victims often suffer to such a degree that they are unable to leave their own home even to do such simple things as the weekly shopping.

The scope of this psychologically crippling condition is not always limited to open spaces as commonly understood, for some people who are quite relaxed and balanced until they find themselves in a space such as an open field or a large empty sports arena may then exhibit classic symptoms of agoraphobia.

With the latter type of sufferer the simplest solution may be avoidance of the situation that provokes the response, unless this affects the social or work situation. The more advanced and generalized

Leisure activities such as bushwalking and camping can change from a pleasurable relaxation to a cause of panic for the sufferer from agoraphobia.

form of agoraphobia is regarded as a neurotic condition, and treatment by a psychiatrist or psychotherapist is required.

The most successful form of therapy developed so far has centred on slow but steady steps which take the patient into agoraphobic situations. From small beginnings such as a solo trip to the post office or a walk around the block, confidence is built up until eventually the neurosis is removed.

Dr Claire Weekes of Melbourne, Australia, has had considerable success with the treatment of agoraphobics and is regarded as an authority on the subject. She encourages her patients to 'go with' their feelings of fear and panic in trigger situations, rather than trying to muster their limited supply of courage to conquer these overwhelming emotions. Dr Weekes and other specialists have prepared cassette recordings giving step-by-step guidance and encouragement for those victims who are geographically isolated, or who are so much in the grip of the condition that they are unable even to venture out to seek specialist care.

Anyone who has been mentally or physically ill and has been in a protective environment for some time is liable to feel a little tremulous about venturing into the mainstream of life again. Such feelings are entirely natural and can be overcome readily. The agoraphobic, on the other hand, needs expert treatment which may take some time but which does have a high success rate.

Mental Retardation

Mental retardation or subnormality limits an individual's ability to learn and may be caused by a number of conditions in which heredity and environment may be important.

Causes Specific disorders which may cause mental retardation include underactivity of the thyroid gland, Down's syndrome and phenylketonuria. Other less common disorders may also cause brain damage.

Conditions before, during and after birth may impede mental development. During pregnancy, heavy smoking or drinking, infections such as rubella (German measles) or maternal conditions, such as rhesus incompatibility or uncontrolled hypertension, may damage the fetus, in some instances severely.

During and immediately after birth, the brain may be easily damaged by lack of oxygen, particularly if breathing and normal blood circulation are not established promptly.

After birth, a stimulating environment of care, nutrition, warmth and body contact is important for a child to develop fully. Although prevention of mental subnormality is not possible, genetic counseling where appropriate, dietary control of phenylketonuria and optimal prenatal care may eliminate some of the causes. In very many of those with mild mental retardation, no specific cause can be found.

Diagnosis Parents are often concerned about the developmental progress of their child. Children vary considerably in the skills they develop at a particular age, and a child often lags a little behind in one area of skill development while he is concentrating on another. For example, a child concentrating on walking may not improve his vocabulary at all for a while, but when walking is mastered, speech may start to develop. For a child to be considered mentally retarded, all areas of development must be delayed.

Medical practitioners and baby health center nurses are trained to assess the developmental progress of babies and young children and, in most cases, problems are recognized early.

Testing and classification Intelligence tests, which are designed to measure an individual's intellectual capacity, are used to determine whether the individual's skills fall within the mild, moderate or severe classification of retardation. However educational progress and social adjustment will depend not only on the IQ (intelligence quotient) but more importantly on family attitudes, personality and suitable schooling or work opportunities.

The distinction between mild retardation and low 'normal' intelligence is not definite. During school years when educational expectations are high, studies have shown that a significant proportion of students would benefit from some form of remedial tuition. However, a much smaller percentage of adults require continuing assistance because of mental retardation. In less technical or agricultural environments, where a high level of education is not so essential, the number of retarded adults requiring special assistance is even smaller.

Educational and work expectations Once a child has been fully assessed and diagnosed as mentally retarded, the family usually needs assistance and support in accepting and adapting to the situation. Children who are affected mildly usually live at home and attend a local school, possibly in a class where special tuition is available. Most are able to find appropriate work and can expect to live independently in the community.

Some may require special schools or sheltered workshops which provide an opportunity to learn skills or work in a sympathetic and encouraging environment. Special schools and workshops are particularly valuable when inability to compete with a more able peer group leads to rejection and loss of self-esteem. The emphasis is on social development and life skills; learning about shopping and using money, reading signs and developing practical skills take precedence over subjects designed for secondary and tertiary education. Some institutions provide residential and long-term care for those more severely affected who are unable to live independently.

Cretinism

Cretinism is caused by a deficiency of thyroid hormone (needed for growth) when the thyroid gland is underactive, because of malfunction or because of inadequacy in the diet, especially a lack of iodine. If the condition is untreated, development will be abnormal.

The condition may be diagnosed at birth, although the diagnosis is often not suspected or confirmed till a few months later.

In the first few weeks of life a cretinous child may show the following features: persistent jaundice, a large tongue, feeding problems, excessive sleeping, constipation, or a hoarse cry, all of which may lead to the supicion of cretinism.

After a few months an untreated child will usually be identified by the typical physical appearance and by the delay in reaching the normal childhood milestones.

Typical physical appearance of a cretinous child include coarse features, a broad flattish nose, shortness, thin hair, eyes widely spaced, dry skin and a protruding abdomen often with a hernia at the umbilicus. Such a child will be mentally retarded, an x-ray examination will show a bone age less than that of the age of the child and there will be delay in the development of teeth.

Various biochemical tests are available to check the level of thyroid hormone and the functioning of the thyroid gland. These tests are used to confirm the diagnosis of cretinism.

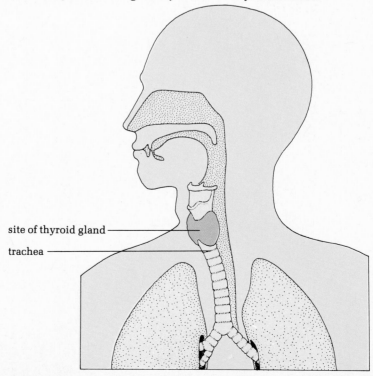

The thyroid gland is situated in the neck just in front of the trachea. Cretinism is caused by deficiency of thyroid hormone.

site of thyroid gland

trachea

The most common difficulty in diagnosing a cretin on physical appearance alone arises from confusing the appearance with that of a mongoloid child.

Once cretinism has been diagnosed it is most important that the child be given thyroid hormone as a substitute for the hormone that the body has failed to produce. If dosage is begun early enough and continued adequately the chances of normal intellectual development and growth are very good.

Down's syndrome

The congenital condition described as Down's syndrome is characterized by mental retardation and certain physical abnormalities. The name is derived from that of Langdon Down, an English physician, who first described the condition in 1866. The condition is also known as 'mongolism' because the features of the affected person resemble those of Mongol people.

Approximately 1 in 700 babies has Down's syndrome. The risk of producing a child with Down's syndrome increases progressively with the mother's age. The chance is 1 in 1500 in a mother under 30, 1 in 750 between 30 and 34 years, then rising slowly until the risk is approximately 1 in 50 in mothers older than 45 years.

Cause Down's syndrome is not caused by something going wrong during pregnancy. The event that produces it happens at about the time the pregnancy begins, in the development of the egg or sperm at the time of conception. At this time an extra chromosome appears in the cell from

Music appeals to all children and is of particular benefit in the education of a child with Down's syndrome.

which the baby grows. The child with Down's syndrome has an extra chromosome in every cell of the body and it is this extra chromosome which produces the alterations in physical and mental development.

Chromosomes are tiny structures found in the nucleus of every cell in the body. Each normal cell has 23 matching pairs numbered from 1 to 23 making a total of 46 chromosomes. A child with Down's syndrome usually has 47 chromosomes, one extra chromosome being added to the type known as number 21. This is called trisomy 21.

Chromosomes are made up of thousands of genes, and it is these genes which program the code the body uses to grow, develop and give the child its individual characteristics. The extra 21 chromosome with its genetic material upsets the genetic balance and thus alters the way the child develops.

The fertilized egg starts off as a single cell, grows by dividing into two identical cells which divide into four, then four divide into eight and so on. As the cells divide they change to form the different tissues and organs. When the extra chromosome appears at the time of fertilization it is reproduced in every cell of the body as the baby is formed.

In about 4 per cent of children with Down's syndrome the error which causes the extra 21 chromosome may occur in the second or third cell division of the newly developing child. As a result, some of the cells will develop normally while those with the extra chromosome will continue to duplicate each with an extra chromosome. This mixture is known as mosaic Down's syndrome because some of the cells contain trisomy 21 while others are normal. Because these children have some normal chromosomes they may have fewer of the physical characteristics and somewhat better mental performance than a child with trisomy 21 in every cell.

Another 4 per cent of children with Down's syndrome have a form known as translocation 21 trisomy. Translocation occurs when the extra number 21 chromosome has broken and is attached to the broken end of another chromosome. In about one-third of translocation trisomy cases one of the parents, who is quite normal physically and mentally, can carry the translocation chromosome and pass it to a child.

These last two forms of Down's syndrome are quite rare and can be detected by chromosome studies on the child and parents, carried out by special techniques on a small blood sample.

It is now possible to do a chromosome study early in pregnancy to determine whether the developing fetus has normal chromosomes. This may be recommended for mothers who have already

This little boy has the cheerful good humor characteristic of Down's syndrome children.

had one child with Down's syndrome, where the possibility of it happening again is about one chance in a hundred, and in women over 30, where the risk starts to increase. To do this test, the amniotic fluid which surrounds the fetus in the uterus is sampled by inserting a needle through the pregnant woman's lower abdominal wall. This procedure, called amniocentesis, can be done between the twelfth and fourteenth week of pregnancy. Chromosome studies on the cells will give a result within two or three weeks and the parents can then decide whether they wish the pregnancy to be terminated or not.

All the features that make up Down's syndrome occur because of genetic imbalance. This produces a particular blend of physical and mental characteristics, and personality and behavior, that is unique to Down's syndrome children. However, just as they have certain characteristics in common, each child with Down's syndrome has his own particular personality and set of capabilities like any other person. There is also a range of abilities among children with Down's syndrome so that some of the children may be well below the average and others above.

Physical characteristics A number of physical features are characteristic of Down's syndrome. Most of these are minor and do not affect the child's health in any major way. Babies with Down's syndrome have diminished muscle tone and tend to be floppy and loose jointed compared with other babies. The back of the head is less prominent and the soft spot on the baby's head may be large and close later than usual. The nose is often small and the eyes slant slightly, often with small folds of the skin in the inside corners of the eyes. The tongue is normal in size but the mouth is sometimes small and for this reason, and because of the poor muscle tone, the tongue often protrudes. The voice is often deep. The hands often appear small with relatively short fingers, particularly the fifth finger, and there is usually a single crease across the upper palm instead of the more usual two skin creases.

About 40 per cent of children with Down's syndrome have a defect in the development of the heart. Occasionally other, much rarer, problems occur.

Mental characteristics The most worrying problem in Down's syndrome is the rate of mental development, which is slower than average. In the early years the child will achieve some of the basic motor skills at a slower, but not too retarded pace. The later learning of more advanced skills becomes difficult as the potential for intellectual development is lower than average. However, it is difficult to make accurate predictions about any child.

Although the potential of a child with Down's syndrome is limited, it is important that each child be helped to reach his full potential. This means that each child should be encouraged to develop in all areas and to learn and achieve as much as possible. This will be greatly helped by a loving, stimulating environment with exposure to language, play, music, other children and appropriate educational facilities.

It is important for the child to be assessed by an appropriately experienced pediatrician and for plans to be made for a suitable education program. The parents generally need frequent support, explanation and encouragement in coping with the problems of bringing up a handicapped child.

The child will usually acquire such skills as walking, speech, self-care and often simple reading. Children with Down's syndrome take great pleasure in their surroundings, their families and friends. Throughout life they often maintain a child-like good humor. As the child grows older education will usually need to be directed to teaching useful skills and simple trades to provide the opportunity to become partially self-supporting and to live usefully in the community under some supervision.

Most communities have special programs to teach the Down's syndrome child or adult special skills and many organizations will accept some handicapped workers. It is important to check with the local hospital or medical center for information about such programs.

Minimal brain damage

A term used by psychologists and educational personnel, minimal brain damage or dysfunction describes the condition of children who have several abnormalities of behavior or brain functioning caused by developmental factors as well as cerebral damage.

Symptoms Children with minimal brain damage can be overactive; have poor concentration, a short attention span; be easily distracted, impulsive, or clumsy; have bad writing, not learn properly, have defects in perception; be stubborn, obstinate, bossy, disobedient, aggressive, negative, accident-prone; have sexual behavior disorders, fecal incontinence, be liars, commit arson, steal, be destructive, impulsive and fidget. Also they are liable to trantrums, displays of extrovert behavior and wide mood fluctuations, are often resistant to social demands and unwilling to follow the rules of the group. Almost every possible behavior disorder and many learning difficulties in children are covered by this umbrella-like term.

Medically there are usually a few physical signs of actual brain damage. A traumatic birth, a breech or forceps delivery

The effects of minimal brain damage may be seen in socially unacceptable behavior which is generally observed by parents and teachers. (Zefa)

may have caused the condition but it is difficult to prove this medically. Hence the term minimal brain 'dysfunction', which does not imply damage to the tissues of the brain as the cause of the disorder, is preferable.

Treatment Children with minimal brain damage are often put in special classes in schools or sent to a series of schools without a real physical, medical or psychological diagnosis having been made. Some may simply have an inherited personality trait which makes them difficult to educate in the normal classroom situation.

They should be allowed to live as normally as possible in the same classes as other children. With love and security at home and tolerance, understanding and patience at school they will slowly respond and become successful members of society.

Phenylketonuria

An inherited biochemical abnormality causing many physical defects, plus mental retardation of moderate to severe degree, phenylketonuria is also known as PKU and phenylpyruvic oligophrenia.

Cause The condition is caused by the body being unable to cope adequately with phenylalanine, one of several essential amino acids derived from protein in the normal diet. The case is almost invariably a congenital lack of a catalyst (enzyme) in the liver, phenylalanine hydroxalase, so that when protein is eaten, phenylalanine cannot be adequately broken down for digestion and instead accumulates in the body in excess. However, some of it partially breaks down and is excreted in the urine as phenylpyruvic and phenylacetic acids, or phenylketones.

The condition is not common, occurring only once every 14 000 births. It is transmitted when both parents are carriers of the defective gene, assumed to be present once in every 60 persons in the normal population. In these cases a child has a one in four chance of being affected and a one in two chance of being a carrier of the gene, like his parents.

Symptoms The affected child has a general deficiency of pigment, with blond hair, blue eyes and skin which is fairer than that of other children in the family. The child will have a peculiar musty body odor. A greasy form of eczema (seborrhea) frequently occurs and is resistant to routine eczema therapies but responds to special diets. Brain growth is interrupted, or stopped from about the age of four months, with the child becoming progressively retarded. The personality becomes schizophrenic-like, and overactivity is a feature. One-third of affected children develop epilepsy with generalized convulsions and many have larger heads than normal.

Diagnosis The Guthrie screening test is used in diagnosis. The procedure involves taking a drop of blood from the baby's heel following at least three days of consuming food containing protein. This is placed in contact with a culture of actively growing bacteria organisms (Bacillus subtilis). When the test is positive and phenylalanine is present in excessive amounts, the bacteria cease to multiply. If that occurs, more accurate testing is imperative to measure the exact amount of phenylalanine present in the blood and other tissues. The level, though raised, may not be concentrated enough to cause damage. Occasionally, an excess of phenylalanine is found in the blood associated with a similar rise in the amounts of other amino acids (amino acidureas)

The urine also can be tested for the phenylketones, phenylpyruvic and phenylacetic acids. Known as the PKU test, it may be demonstrated by adding ferric chloride drops or dipping a piece of absorbent paper soaked in ferric chloride (dipsticks) into the urine to be tested. A characteristic color change appears when phenylketonuria is present. However, there are many variable factors which tend to make the test unreliable.

Treatment is based on limiting the amount of phenylalanine in the diet. To this end, a special milk formula has been devised. As a child grows, other foodstuffs low in phenylalanine are introduced into the diet. The actual amounts depend on repeated blood tests which are used to monitor the level of phenylalanine, keeping it below the level at which it would be poisonous. Once brain growth has reached its maximum level, generally by the age of five or six years, a free diet can usually be introduced. However, some investigators doubt the wisdom of the practice. If there is any uncertainty, the advice of the pediatrician should be sought.

Recent observations indicate that mothers known to suffer from phenylketonuria but who are no longer restricting their diets, are very likely to give birth to babies with brain damage. In general, these infants have small brains and heads and are more likely to have heart defects. Because of this it is extremely important that the mother is restricted to a special phenylalanine-low diet throughout her pregnancy.

In sufferers of phenylketonuria, the amino acid phenylalanine, here magnified 40 times, cannot be adequately broken down for digestion but builds up to toxic levels. (*Science Photo Library*)

Forms of Therapy

Mental disorder may last for a short time or for a long time. Many kinds of mental disorder or psychiatric illness are treated adequately and simply by counseling by family doctors and specialists. Only one in twenty people with a psychiatric illness visits a psychiatrist. It is therefore important that all family doctors have some training in the symptoms and signs of mental disorder to enable them to use drugs and other treatments effectively.

Hospitalization The decline in the number of people in mental hospitals in recent years has been caused partly by an improvement in the treatment of functional psychoses (schizophrenia and manic-depressive states) by the antidepressants, phenothiazine and lithium carbonate, and partly by the increased awareness that keeping the mentally ill in the hospital is not only undesirable at times but may be harmful. Now the policy is for a patient to live at home if possible in his usual environment, or in hostel accommodation, and attend an outpatient clinic. Some accommodation and psychiatric treatment are also available through private mental hospitals and clinics.

The large crowded institutions built at the turn of the century are gradually being replaced by smaller psychiatric units, often attached to a general hospital. In addition to a small number of beds needed for the acutely disturbed or for those who require a detailed assessment, the unit has an outpatient clinic staffed by psychiatrists and a day hospital where patients are treated during the day and spend the nights and weekends at home. Continuity of after-care is maintained by outpatient visits and hostel and rehabilitation services.

Most mental hospitals are run and staffed by governments. Traditionally they cater to insane criminals, the mentally retarded, people committed for alcohol and drug abuse, involuntary patients sent by judges on medical evidence of serious mental illness, and voluntary patients who sign that they wish to stay in a mental hospital to be diagnosed and treated. In practice many of the patients have only a short stay in hospital followed by suitable outpatient after-care. Long-term patients are usually totally unable to cope with normal life because of their mental state. Involuntary patients are committed to a hospital according to the law which provides for a review of their mental state by qualified personnel at specified intervals.

Art therapy in a mental hospital. *(John Watney Photo Library)*

Psychoanalysis A highly specialized form of psychiatric treatment, psychoanalysis is appropriate only for selected patients. It usually takes about an hour of therapy once or several times per week for several years and it demands considerable motivation from the patient and sufficient strength to tolerate the deep searching that is involved in working through psychological conflicts.

A psychoanalyst receives extensive training and has usually had many years experience in helping the emotionally ill. There are psychiatrists and other professionals with specialized training who can offer this form of therapy.

Psychoanalytic treatment has changed little from the model established by Sigmund Freud. Usually the patient lies on a coach or sofa with the analyst sitting out of direct vision, usually by the side or behind him and intruding minimally into the patient's thought processes. The fundamental rule in psychoanalysis is that the patient speaks about his thoughts, feelings or whatever comes to his mind during the session without suppression or censorship of any kind.

For those who are motivated and who require this long-term treatment, psychoanalysis may have considerable beneficial results.

Psychotherapy A range of techniques used in the treatment of mental illness, psychotherapy may be a less intense and briefer therapy than psychoanalysis and more suitable for a greater range of conditions.

A technique known as a brief psychotherapy involves a shorter course of sessions which focus more on immediate problems than on a detailed discovery of the past. The therapist is likely to take a more active and directive role.

As with other forms of treatment for emotional and behavioral problems, a patient undergoing psychotherapy must be motivated. Success is more likely if some of the following criteria are present: good reality orientation; stable interpersonal relationships; an ability to develop insight; no language barrier between the patient and therapist; average intelligence; and the ability to tolerate frustration and other negative emotions. Reduced motivation is more likely when a patient is deriving certain advantages from his symptoms, for example by avoiding unpleasant responsibilities or gaining extra attention.

During psychotherapy the patient talks of his ideas and feelings while the therapist listens and tries to understand what is happening to the patient. The therapist then tries to tell the patient what he thinks is happening. Based on this the patient tries to change himself and adjust.

It is important that the therapist does not make decisions that the patient should be making and a therapist is often advised not to accept unreasonable dependency displayed by the patient. It is important, however, to explore conflicts if these arise.

Psychotherapy can be divided into several phases and different problems will arise at each stage. These must be explored and resolved as appropriate. Psychotherapy may be combined with drugs and the use of other techniques to lessen anxiety or depression, when present.

Psychosurgery The use of a surgical operation on the brain to treat a psychiatric condition is psychosurgery. Pioneered in the 1930s in Portugal, many different techniques are available.

The indications for psychosurgery are highly controversial and have been given dramatic coverage by the news media and in many places the criteria for its use are regulated by legal requirements.

Autosuggestion

Hypnosis in which hypnotic suggestions come from the person himself is known as autosuggestion. The relaxation that may accompany autosuggestion is usually mild; deeper trance-like states, often achieved with classical hypnosis, are not common.

Couéism In the 1920s Couéism, one form of autosuggestion, was particularly popular. Named after a French psychotherapist, Professor Emil Coué (1857–1926), it was aimed at curing bodily symptoms of psychosomatic illness by attempting to convince the conscious mind that they were not caused by any physical condition. Coué postulated that the change 'forced' upon the conscious mind, in turn, affected the subconscious mind. He claimed to have cured his own asthma by repeating the statement that he was getting better.

Self-motivation Since World War II the idea in the book by Norman Vincent Peale *The Power of Positive Thinking*, has become widely accepted. This method has similarities to Couéism but a broader application. The idea is that firmly believing something can and will occur, will help to bring it about. This process has become the basis of many 'self-motivation' programs and has been used commercially to train sales representatives. It can only be classified as real autosuggestion if it involves attempts to control bodily symptoms.

Many people today after repeating optimistic convictions, make claims of success similar to Coué. However in some illnesses that are apparently 'cured' by autosuggestion, symptoms may recur or different symptoms may appear because of significant psychological components underlying the condition.

Self-relaxation Another popular variant of autosuggestion or positive thinking is an increasingly used self-relaxation procedure. The person sits or lies in comfortable surroundings, and then, in sequence, contracts then relaxes various groups of muscles. Tape cassettes with recordings instructing people how to relax are available commercially. Imagining a particularly pleasant scene may be used to help relaxation.

Another common feature of the technique is attention to the breathing, making it slower and deeper. With practice, most people learn to relax completely without any external aids. This technique is especially useful in the treatment of tension and anxiety states.

Behavior therapy

A group of psychotherapeutic techniques which aims at altering particular behavior, which is usually socially unacceptable, behavior therapy is based on the theory that abnormal or undesirable behavior is learned, and can therefore be 'unlearned' over a period of time. This contrasts with the main concepts of other psychotherapeutic techniques which are based on the theory that subconscious processes or conflicts are responsible for producing abnormal behavior. The two major forms of behavior therapy are aversion therapy and desensitization.

Aversion therapy aims at preventing undesirable behavior or activity by giving the patient unpleasant stimuli whenever the unwanted behavior occurs. After a time the unpleasant feelings become associated with the undesired behavior, so that eventually the undesired action no longer occurs.

Physical and mental abuse of family members by one another is not uncommon. Frequently psychiatric treatment is needed. *(Westmead Center)*

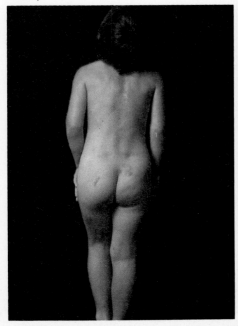

Injections of the drug apomorphine, which causes nausea and vomiting only if alcohol is consumed, was an early form of aversion therapy used to treat alcoholism. Today, disulfiram is used. It can be taken by mouth and induces vomiting only if alcohol is taken.

Electric shocks are another major form of disincentive used in aversion therapy. Their timing and power can be accurately gauged and modified and they are usually regulated so that only mild pain is experienced. Transvestism, homosexuality and fetishism are other forms of behavior against which this method has been used.

As in any form of behavior therapy, the degree of success is quite variable and many influences are important, particularly motivation. Seeking reward or avoiding punishment alone is only a medium-level motivating force. The strongest motivation comes from the desire to maintain behavior that is consistent with one's value system or morals, beliefs and convictions. Behavior therapy is far better able to modify behavior to fit it into someone's value system than it is in attempting to change the value system itself.

The person's personality and his ability to incorporate suitable alternative behavior patterns are important in replacing behavior that is being discouraged. Homosexual behavior is more likely to cease if some degree of heterosexual drive or interest is aroused.

One of the problems of aversion therapy is that it often takes much time and skill, but it is best utilized when combined with other forms of psychotherapy. Support and encouragement are important, particularly when adjustment to a significant change in lifestyle is required.

Dieting is an example where success depends on support, encouragement and motivation as well as a mild form of aversion therapy. People seeking to lose weight may be encouraged to think of chocolates, for example, as 'the enemy': 'the smell is bad, they taste horrible and are quite nauseating'. If chocolates are a person's dietary weakness, this approach may be very helpful.

Desensitization In the treatment of irrational fears, or phobias, densensitization has been found effective. The patient is taught self-relaxation which he then practices while being desensitized. A list of experiences related to the phobic object or situation is devised and arranged in order that the least threatening situation is at the top of the list. The therapist gradually works down the list, encouraging the patient to be relaxed before reminding him of the threatening situation.

For example, a patient with a dog phobia may begin by looking at canine pictures starting with a small, gentle breed and eventually progressing to pictures of German Shepherds. Moving pictures and

Sudden upheavals in personal life which leave one parent coping with a family alone, are crises suffered by many.

then actual situations involving dogs are introduced, possibly starting with meeting a quiet old pet and progressing to a walk where more aggressive dogs may be encountered with proper circumspection.

In another form of desensitization known as *flooding* the patient is immediately presented with the most feared situation while being helped to keep in touch with the problem until any induced anxiety subsides. Sedatives may be used with the flooding technique.

In *modeling*, the therapist acts out the feared situation, thereby providing a model for the patient to follow. Positive reinforcement is used by rewarding successes and ignoring failures.

Behavior therapy can be useful in the treatment of a number of conditions, and the advances achieved during the last twenty years are continuing, particularly in the area of combining behavioral modification techniques with the use of drugs and analytical psychotherapy.

Crisis intervention

To assist a person to cope with the initial stages of personal upheaval, specific forms of psychological support, known as crisis intervention, have been developed. This technique is used especially after bereavement.

In recent years great advances have been made in the establishment and use of resources related to crisis intervention.

As many people now feel more isolated, even in a crowd, they very often have no one to turn to for help. The trend in society has been away from extended families; people move home more frequently; and there has been a decline in the usual supportive role of the family doctor, family priest or 'the close friend'.

For those suffering from stress the main support has come from phone counseling, drop-in centers and various refuges such as those for women and adolescents. Help is also available in the form of general services like the well-known 'lifeline' and there is specific assistance for problem drinkers and for those who abuse their children.

The prime role of crisis intervention is sympathetic listening. However, follow-up to meet practical needs often has also to be undertaken; for instance, to avoid possible child abuse it may be necessary to place the threatened children where they can be safely looked after for some time.

People in a crisis often need formal counseling to enable them to identify and deal with their difficulties most appropriately. When the crisis is severe, the person affected is more prone to develop psychological or psychiatric problems. In addition to counseling, medical treatment,

A severe crisis can lead to psychological or psychiatric problems. Some people react by becoming withdrawn or depressed.

such as antidepressant medications, may be required. Long-term support and assistance, when needed, can be provided by the local health authorities and other bodies which continue the work done by crisis intervention agencies, many of which are voluntary.

Electric shock therapy

Electroconvulsive therapy (ECT), commonly known as shock treatment, is a form of therapy used for some mental or emotional illnesses. It was first used medically in the 1930s and, until the use of anti-depressant drugs, was the only available treatment for severe depression.

Electric shock therapy induces a convulsion or 'fit' in the patient by passing an electric current through electrodes attached to the patient's forehead. The convulsion generally lasts about one minute. The treatment is used mainly for severe depression and is often effective after therapy for 10 to 14 days. However it is not always successful.

The treatment produces a docile and vegetative state of mind, usually with loss of identity and awareness of place. This disorientation is needed to relieve the depression, but can be extremely dangerous in the case of a hospital out-patient who may leave the treatment centre with no knowledge of who he is or how to return home. ECT is therefore now rarely performed in these circumstances.

Group psychotherapy

Although the use of group psychotherapy or treatment dates from 1905, the term group psychotherapy was first introduced in 1931 by Jacob L. Moreno who believed that a group rather than an individual (as in orthodox psychoanalysis) should be treated. The substitution of the word therapy for analysis was to denote the fact that therapy was to be the main issue.

The techniques of group psychotherapy attempt to improve the behavior and personalities of the individuals through controlled group interactions. The approach may be analytical, existential, directive or non-directive. At first, group psychotherapy was controlled mainly by psychiatrists, psychologists and social workers, but as it became increasingly popular, people from various walks of life have become leaders of groups.

There are many ways of running a group. For example the evocative approach involves the individuals of the group expressing their feelings, supposedly in a mutually accepting and understanding environment. The leader avoids setting himself up as an authority and all members, including the leader, sit at the same level. In contrast, a directive group is one in which the leader asserts authority and gives advice. In this case the leader occupies a special position in the group. The didactic method aims at educating the individuals by giving them information on what is known about their problems.

Shy and lonely people and those who have become too dependent on their therapist may benefit from group psychotherapy. So also may people who have problems which are regarded as shameful, for example alcoholics, and drug addicts. Others who may benefit from group psychotherapy include obese people who support one another within weight watching groups and those who have had unsatisfactory relationships with brothers and sisters or who have difficulty relating to figures of authority. Ideally those participating in a group should not have known each other before, except when the problem involves, for example, a family or married couples.

Success in group therapy is measured in terms of increased self-confidence, personal insight, and positive change in behaviour and relationships.

Encounter groups The use of the term encounter groups originally arose out of the use of training groups (or T groups) and group therapy in the treatment of psychi-

Interaction where individuals can express their feelings is part of group psychotherapy. (Zefa)

atric patients. These groups came into existence as a means of training psychiatrists and other health professionals interested in improving their skills in dealing with people.

The T-groups and sensitivity groups extended their function into dealing with relationships and feelings among people in general and not just in the working situation.

The use of the word 'encounter' comes from the idea of encountering emotion and feeling within oneself and in relation to others.

Membership of encounter groups is thus not restricted to patients needing help, nor to special professional groups. Many different techniques are believed to be of assistance in helping people overcome alienation and to increase their self-awareness. These techniques may include acting, nudity, touching, massaging and caressing as well as verbal communication. The duration of such groups may vary from single afternoons, to weekends or full time residential groups.

Hypnotherapy

Hypnosis, or hypnotherapy as it is more correctly termed, is widely used in medicine today. It is not, however, a new phenomenon, being first used by Dr Franz Anton Mesmer ('mesmerism') in Europe in the late eighteenth century. Hypnotism is basically the inducing of an artificial trance which causes the hypnotized individual to be more open to suggestion, and

Relaxation as well as relief of pain is desirable for people who are nervous of dental treatment, so hypnotherapy may be used. (PAF International)

Hypnotherapy can be used during childbirth to assist relaxation and to relieve the awareness of pain. (*Zefa*)

in some instances, has a freeing effect on the unconscious mind thus enabling repressed thoughts or events to be brought to the surface.

Hypnotism was popularized by Mesmer in Vienna and Paris in the period between 1760 and the late 1770s. Although he successfully cured various disorders, unfortunately because his 'performances' were theatrical this tended to give the impression that hypnotism was nothing more than quackery and music-hall entertainment. This image of charlatanism persisted until the nineteenth century and to some extent until recently. Fortunately, the serious medical use of hypnosis by the French neurologist Charcot (1825–1893) in treating neuroses/hysteria gave legitimacy to hypnotism.

Hypnosis is now used most importantly in medical hypnotherapy, which is most widely used in the treatment of psychological problems (such as phobias), obesity, to assist in stopping smoking and to induce relaxation. It is also used in the treatment of illnesses such as asthma and migraine that may have a psychological basis.

Hypnotherapy is also sometimes used for the relief of pain as in the cases of childbirth and dental treatment. In both cases it assists relaxation and avoids the use of drugs for those who are anxious. However, it is time consuming for the therapist and therefore is no substitute for the usual pain relief provided in childbirth or for anesthesia which requires little preparation.

It is difficult to determine how successful hypnotism is as a medical therapy. It appears to be most useful in enabling people to stop smoking, who would otherwise find it difficult to do so. Likewise, hypnotism can be used by a qualified psychiatrist to remove psychological obstacles to recovery. It is used with some success in helping otherwise well-adjusted people to overcome phobic fears, particularly the common ones such as fear of flying and fear of dentists.

The use of hypnotherapy as a medical treatment should always be carried out by an experienced practitioner. In most countries where it is used as a form of therapy there is a national register of qualified hypnotherapists which is generally available through the offices of the national medical association.

Psychotherapeutic drugs

Recent research has suggested the possibility that many psychiatric disorders may have a biochemical cause, reaffirming the important role of chemotherapeutic agents in the treatment of psychiatric disorders. The introduction of new and more effective psychotherapeutic drugs has led to a steady decline in the number of hospital beds occupied by psychiatric patients, many of whom can now be treated on an out-patient basis. Although these drugs have not cured or altered the long-term prognosis of many psychiatric disorders, they have significantly ameliorated the symptoms, allowing the patients to function within their limitations. Drugs such as hypnotics and tranquilizers provide relief from symptoms which cause a vicious circle to be set up (for example, anxiety and tension cause insomnia and loss of weight which themselves result in increased anxiety and tension), or which hinder the establishment of normal interests, social activity or work which themselves may be therapeutic.

Although several of the psychotherapeutic drugs have multiple pharmacological effects, it is convenient to classify them as anti-psychotic drugs which have the ability to ameliorate the psychotic conditions (for example phenothiazines and thiozanthenes), antidepressants (for example tricyclics and monoamine oxidase inhibitors), antianxiety drugs (barbiturates and benzodiazepines) and anti-manic drugs (such as lithium).

Relaxation techniques

Life in modern Western society — at a hard, fast, competitive pace with a degree of social change that is totally unprecedented — has produced an excessive state of anxiety in many, but stress is not peculiar to today. It is simply that twentieth-century people are more exposed to stress and at the same time more aware of it.

A technological revolution, an increase in leisure time, a decrease in physical activity, great dependence on social drugs such as alcohol, tobacco and various 'uppers and downers', an immense shift in attitudes towards the role of the family and a similar change in the perception of women's place in society, improved public health, a highly refined diet: these are only some of the more obvious tension-inducing circumstances of today.

There are those who suffer from acute or profound anxiety states that require medical assistance as a matter of urgency. But the relaxation techniques discussed here concern the so-called 'average' person of either sex, probably aged between about 16 and 60. Anxiety, or mental tension, when it continues over a period of time and becomes chronic, opens the door to a host of serious medical and emotional conditions, including hypertension, alcoholism, obesity, phobias, ulcers and complete physical collapse. It is obvious from this that learning to relax is vitally important.

Fortunately there are many proven ways to achieve a satisfactory state of relaxation; the choice depends mainly on personal preference and state of physical fitness.

Biofeedback is especially useful for those suffering from hypertension or other physical ailments which may be partly relieved by a reduction in tension, and is very helpful for all sorts of serious stress. After one or two sessions the technique is easily mastered.

Initially, small electrodes are attached, quite painlessly, to certain parts of the skin; these record body impulses which are directed by the therapist and may include blinking, deliberately tensing certain muscles, frowning, shallow breathing and so on. The subject can observe the effect that these reactions produce by simply watching the dial on the biofeedback machine. Eventually he learns how to alter habitual tension reactions which are causing physical complaints or emotional distress. The recording equipment and electrodes are unnecessary once the subject can monitor and control his ability to tense or relax.

Biofeedback has been particularly beneficial for a stiff, sore neck caused by tensed muscles; for migraine headaches; for most forms of anxiety neurosis; and as an aid to relieve severe or intractable pain and associated depression and insomnia.

Meditation Relief from pain is also possible through the practice of deep meditation.

As a means of slowing-down, of thinking positively and of 'switching-off' from tension, meditation can induce peace of mind and an overall feeling of well-being. There are classes, books and cassettes to instruct the novice, and it can be learned in the company of others or by oneself.

There are various forms of meditation, the most common being that of learning to empty the mind of worry and extraneous thoughts while concentrating on a particular word, thought or 'sense of nothingness'. To achieve this requires continuous practice, and, although not always successful, has helped many people. Most experienced meditators acquire a better perspective of their own problems and are seldom worried by severe stress.

Deep breathing exercises and yoga Associated with meditation, although practised independent of it, are deep breathing exercises and different types of yoga.

Many people who are ill or stressed, particularly those who smoke cigarettes, develop bad breathing habits. Simple exercises to correct faulty breathing can be learned from some physical therapists and physicians, yoga teachers and some naturopaths who instruct in remedial breathing exercises known as Knowles therapy.

Breathing techniques can help those who experience tension after giving up smoking through the withdrawal period. Many people rely on simple but effective breathing techniques to help them through difficult times.

Yoga places great emphasis on the respiratory system as part of the achievement of harmony of mind and body. Some types of yoga concentrate less on bodily contortions and more on achieving a state of calm through meditation, muscular relaxation and specific breathing exercises. Movement is deliberately slow and gentle.

Physicians now sometimes suggest that patients who are tense should learn yoga.

It has helped in many cases of hypertension, muscular rigidity, 'panic', tension headache, insomnia and forms of fibrositic and rheumatic complaints that may have emotional origins.

Acupuncture Those who cannot relax through any of these methods may try acupuncture. One or two sessions with a good acupuncturist can pinpoint the areas of tension — commonly the low back, shoulders and base of the neck — so that effective remedial treatment can be given.

An acupuncturist also treats problems such as over-eating or the struggle to stop smoking; the aim is to treat the cause of the obsession or behavior, namely tension. Acupuncture is simple, virtually painless and may be used in conjunction with other relaxation techniques.

Massage When stress is merely an occasional worry, a good massage from a chiropractor, osteopath or professional masseur can work wonders. Of course,

Acupuncture may relieve symptoms of tension. (*Zefa*)

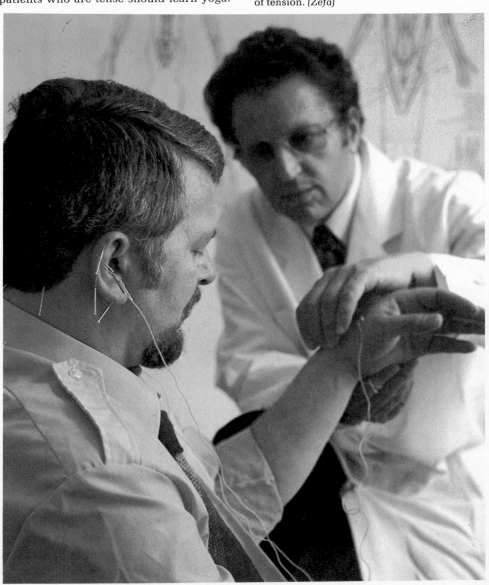

this is an extremely passive form of relaxation in contrast to physical exercise which requires effort, determination and self-discipline to achieve positive results.

Physical exercise The pleasant feelings of relaxation as a result of fairly intensive physical work-outs are frequently experienced by those such as office workers whose daily routines provide limited opportunities for physical exercise to release the inevitable build up of tension that occurs as a result of being almost continuously mentally active.

Aerobic exercise, that is, exercise which increases the heart and lung capacity, for example cycling, jogging, skipping, swimming or simply regular walking, is for many people an enjoyable way of releasing tension or pent up feelings. Regular gymnasium sessions supervised by a trained instructor also have the dual benefit of firming and toning the body while relaxing and invigorating the mind.

Any form of regular, concentrated exercise used as a relaxation technique should achieve that aim, producing a pleasant feeling of physical well-being, perhaps even tiredness. It fails if the sole aim becomes a driving competitiveness or the result is chronic exhaustion.

A carefully planned regime of regular physical exercise is an excellent combination of preventive medicine and healthy relaxation. Hostilities can be released in an entirely harmless way, muscular strength is improved, breathing capacity enlarged, and in some forms of exercise the opportunity exists to meditate as the exercises are performed.

Nutrition Some authorities, particularly those involved with alternative health practices, maintain that stress actually signals important negative changes in body chemistry which superior nutrition can relieve or cure. A radical change of daily diet is generally required; this is an individual matter as prescribed by a dietitian or naturopath.

An excess of refined sugar and other simple carbohydrates is often involved and these are usually forbidden. Herbs such as camomile, valerian and skullcap may be drunk (as teas) for their calming effects. Moreover, it is generally true that people who are tense are liable to neglect their diet and one of the best ways to restore emotional balance is to eat a palatable, balanced diet.

Professional treatment Stress is a normal reaction to many of life's strains; it is part of man's ingrained and primitive 'fight or flight' response. Though some people function better at a certain level of tension, cases of crippling tension, in which it appears to be beyond the capacity of the individual to relax, need professional help.

Physical exercise contributes to relaxation. (*Zefa*)

10 Emergency Care

— First Aid for Injury and Sudden Illness

First Aid Procedures; Resuscitation Techniques

First aid is the immediate care given to victims of sudden injury or illness, the aim being to prevent further deterioration of the casualty's condition, and to relieve suffering. Care includes reassurance and explanation to allay anxiety as well as attention to physical pain and discomfort.

Common sense is the essential component of all the principles of first aid. Clearing a blocked airway, starting artificial respiration if there is no breathing, and commencing heart massage if there is no pulse are three such principles.

The application of first aid is dependent on the circumstances in which the injury or illness has occurred. More is likely to be required of a first aider at the scene of a serious motor accident far from the nearest town than at one which occurs in a city street.

Medical information Many people suffering from a particular medical condition carry a card or wear a pendant or bracelet inscribed with their medical history and prescribed treatment. Particularly in the case of a condition which can be accompanied by a sudden loss of consciousness, such as epilepsy and diabetes, a sufferer is well advised to carry brief information as to the nature of the disease, medications used, and his name and address. In case of unexpected collapse this information will be of assistance to bystanders or those attempting first aid.

A patient in a diabetic coma, for example, can be given specific treatment once his condition is known; in the case of loss of consciousness due to epilepsy, it is reassuring for others to know that no specific treatment is required and the patient will soon regain consciousness.

Other conditions in which medical information can be helpful in the case of sudden collapse include the bleeding disorder hemophilia which requires the injection of a special blood clotting factor to control hemorrhage. Some people suffer severe allergic reactions to specific medications and information carried on the person reduces the likelihood of an unsuitable drug being administered.

Other medically related information which is sometimes carried includes the desire not to have a blood transfusion for religious reasons and, in the case of death by accident, permission for the use of organs for transplant.

The overall approach to the first aid situation

1 *Do not panic*: it not only makes you of little use but can be contagious and thus keep others from being fully useful.

2 *Take a few seconds to assess the first aid situation and the immediate surroundings.* In the long run this can save time, suffering and lives.

3 *Do not become another victim.* Beware of live electrical equipment, fumes such as smoke or coal gas, and especially passing traffic at the scene of motor vehicle accidents.

4 *Separate the victim from danger.* Have traffic controlled and deal with fire, fumes or risk of explosion. If essential have the victim moved to safety, such as to dry land when an accident occurs in the water, but unnecessary movement of the casualty may aggravate his conditon.

5 *Maximize resources that are available.* Use those people best equipped for each task, for example the lifesaver rescuing and the trained first aider attending the injured. To avoid confusion, give specific people specific tasks. If enough people are present, one may summon help, another control traffic, and others reassure any uninjured people who are in distress, depending on the situation.

6 *Assess injuries in order of priority.* Usually the most severe injuries are dealt with first, but if there are many casualities it may be necessary to treat first those injuries for which something can be done. For example, controlling hemorrhage for one victim may take precedence over attention to another's more serious crush injury for which little can be done.

7 *Be part of the team.* This includes accepting instructions from those with more experience and being as helpful as possible.

8 *Remember the aims of first aid*: to preserve life, to lessen suffering, and to prevent deterioration of the injured person. This includes continuing to help until assistance arrives or arranging for appropriate transfer of the casualty.

Essential procedures

The first step is to determine the site and nature of injuries. Bleeding, swellings and deformities should be looked for.

Unconsciousness An initial assessment of airways, breathing and circulation must be made. If appropriate, any obvious cause of the unconsciousness should be dealt with, such as gas fumes. If breathing and circulation are satisfactory and the patient is not suffering from trauma that might cause spinal injuries, place the victim in the coma position to minimize any possible blockage of the airway by the falling tongue. Anything that may obstruct breathing, such as vomitus, will come out

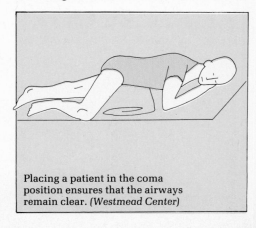

Placing a patient in the coma position ensures that the airways remain clear. *(Westmead Center)*

and not go down the lungs. A person who is unconscious should not be left unattended or given anything by mouth.

The level of consciousness should be assessed and noted. A change in the level of coma is an important sign in assessing the degree of injury and whether the condition is worsening or not. The type of stimulus required to obtain a response, and the type of response should both be noted. Treat other injuries on their own merit.

Precautions Before touching a person who has suffered electric shock switch off the current or at least drag the victim clear with a dry stick or clothing or other non-conductor. Before dealing with someone who has been gassed it is as well to remove the victim to the open air where it will be safe for the helper to start mouth-to-mouth resuscitation.

Artificial respiration, when needed, is needed at once. Delay may result in brain damage or death. The brain suffers injury if it is deprived of oxygenated blood for many minutes. Yet children have been saved despite surprisingly long immersion in water, especially cold water, without suffering permanent brain damage. One should therefore be optimistic and be ready to give artificial respiration and continue to give it until the victim recovers or a doctor certifies death.

Artificial respiration alone is not enough if the heart has stopped. Cardiac compression is then needed, for it is not enough only to send oxygen to the lungs; blood must be pumped by the heart.

Mouth-to-mouth artificial respiration

Once the supply of oxygen is cut off, the average person may die in six minutes or less. Therefore, it is important to begin artificial respiration immediately. The mouth-to-mouth or mouth-to-nose method of artificial respiration has been proven to be the most practical method of emergency ventilation for people of all ages. It is also practical in that it can be performed in any number of places (in the water, under wreckage, etc) where immediate resuscitation is necessary. The procedure involves tilting the victim's head and putting one hand under the victim's neck, gently lifting from the ground. Push the forehead down so as to move the tongue away from the back of the throat, opening the airway.

With head tilted, place your cheek and ear close to victim's mouth and nose and watch for chest movements.

Pinch victim's nose, open your mouth wide, and with a deep breath blow into victim's mouth with four quick, full breaths. With a young victim, breathe gently and do not tilt the head too far back. One breath every five seconds for an adult; one breath every four seconds for a child.

KEEP THE CASUALTY ALIVE

1. CHECK THE AIRWAY.
Clear any obvious substance which could be blocking the airway. Keep the head fully tilted back.

2. CHECK FOR BREATHING.
Look, listen and feel.

3. BREATHING ABSENT.
Quickly give 5 breaths mouth to mouth or mouth to nose. Watch for chest rising and falling. Listen and feel for air exhaling after each breath.

4. BREATHING STILL ABSENT.
Check pulse — if absent start C.P.R. if trained. If pulse present and breathing still absent continue mouth to mouth/nose at a rate of 12/minute.

Mouth-to-nose artificial respiration

Another form of expired-air resuscitation is the mouth-to-nose method where the lips of the patient are pressed together and sealed and expired air is blown into the nose. For small children and babies, cover mouth and nose with your lips. Handle infants gently and support the jaw without tilting the head backwards. A baby needs small quantities of air under low pressure; so inflate your cheeks and puff air in by the mouthful — once every couple of seconds.

The mouth-to-nose method can be used in the same sequence as mouth-to-mouth. Maintain the backward head tilt position with the hand over the victim's forehead and remove hand from under the neck. With victim's mouth held closed, blow into the nose. Open victim's mouth to look and feel for any movement.

Cardiac compression

If the heart has stopped beating there will be no pulse, the victim will be unconscious and breathing will have stopped. The first aim is to allow oxygen to reach the vital organs, especially the brain. Both mouth-to-mouth resuscitation and external cardiac massage will therefore be needed. Brain damage begins once there has been oxygen deprivation for more than three minutes. For this reason speed is essential.

Shock can make peripheral pulses, such as at the wrist, hard to find. It is best to use the neck (carotid) pulse, which can be felt in the groove beside the windpipe, in the front of the neck.

Before commencing external cardiac massage, the victim must be placed on his back and on a firm surface. This enables the heart to be squeezed between the sternum (breastbone) and the vertebral column. To get sufficient blood flowing from the heart, the sternum must be depressed about 1½–2 inches (2½ cm). A considerable amount of force is required, and if the procedure is carried out properly, ribs often break. This is a relatively minor problem for someone whose heart has stopped, but means that *the technique should be practiced only on models, not conscious people.*

Kneel beside the victim, place the heel of one hand over the lower half of the sternum, and cover it with the other hand. With locked elbows, press down by rocking forward over the victim. The hands must remain in contact with the sternum. This movement should be repeated about 80–100 times a minute. A baby or child requires less pressure, and fingertips or one hand are used respectively.

If an assistant is available, he should commence artificial respiration, breathing once every five 'heartbeats'. It is helpful for the person doing the heart massage to count aloud with each compression. This helps to co-ordinate actions so that inflation of the lungs occurs between compressions of the heart. If the first aider has to do both of these procedures without any assistance, two breaths, then fifteen heart compressions is the best method.

If there is associated bleeding, this must be treated. (See section on *Bleeding*).

External cardiac compression cannot be learned properly from a book. The only way to learn it and the best way to learn artificial respiration is by practicing on manikins under the guidance of first-aid experts.

In situations of cardiac arrest emergency treatment is of vital importance. *(John Watney Photo Library)*

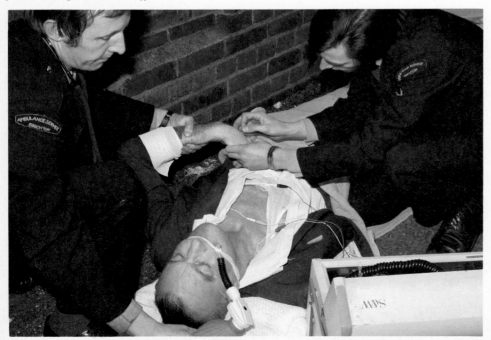

Reassessing the victim
A person who is seriously injured needs continued reassessment. It is especially important to watch the breathing, circulation and conscious state. When doing resuscitation, assess pulse and breathing about every two minutes.

Shock This is a frequent accompaniment of injury and is caused by an inadequate amount of blood circulating throughout the body. Signs of shock are a weak, rapid pulse and cold, pale and moist skin. There may also be restlessness and labored respiration.

First aid treatment of shock is important. The victim should be reassured, rested and kept warm. Pain, hemorrhage and anxiety aggravate the condition and should be kept to a minimum. Elevation of the injured part and gentleness on the part of the helper also help.

In all first aid situations, calmness, common sense, and a gentle demeanor will contribute greatly to minimizing suffering and preventing loss of life.

Bandages and dressings
Bandages can be used to apply pressure, keep dressings in position, restrict movement, and reduce swelling.

They are made from gauze or muslin material. In an emergency situation handkerchiefs, ties and belts can be used.

In general, bandages should be applied firmly, but not tightly enough to restrict circulation. A bluish color of the skin beyond the bandage indicates excessive pressure.

The triangular bandage is commonly used, and is quite adaptable. It can be folded in many different ways, and is used

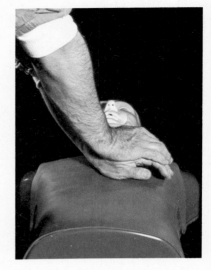

External cardiac compression can best be learnt by practising on a mannikin. *(Westmead Centre)*

in a number of situations. It can be folded to form a sling to protect an injured arm, or used to protect an injured knee and hand.

Roll bandages are used to apply firm support over a wider area, and to immobilise joints.

Dressings are protective coverings applied directly to a wound. They help to prevent infection, control bleeding, and absorb any secretions. Dressings should be as clean as possible to prevent the development of infection. Prior soaking in paraffin prevents dressings from sticking to wounds. Prepacked sterile gauze dressings are readily available for first aid use.

Compresses A pad which is pressed firmly against part of the body and which may be held in place by means of a bandage is known as a compress. It is usually made of folded layers of soft cloth, and may be used dry or wet, hot or cold.

A compress is used to exert pressure on a wound to help stop the outpouring of blood or fluid, such as serum, as well as soak up any free fluid.

A cold wet compress made of cotton material, such as folded sheets, soaked in water or normal saline or aluminium acetate solutions, is used to treat the intense irritation and weeping surface of skin diseases such as infantile eczema and contact dermatitis. The compress is applied for an hour at a time, with wetting of the pad every 15 minutes, and may be repeated three or four times a day.

Ice cold compresses are used for the first few hours of a muscle or joint injury in order to relieve the pain and allow more movement of the part. Once the injury has moved to a less acute phase hot compresses are more helpful in relieving pain. In the case of the swelling of an injured part, the use of alternating hot and cold compresses may help to reduce the swelling.

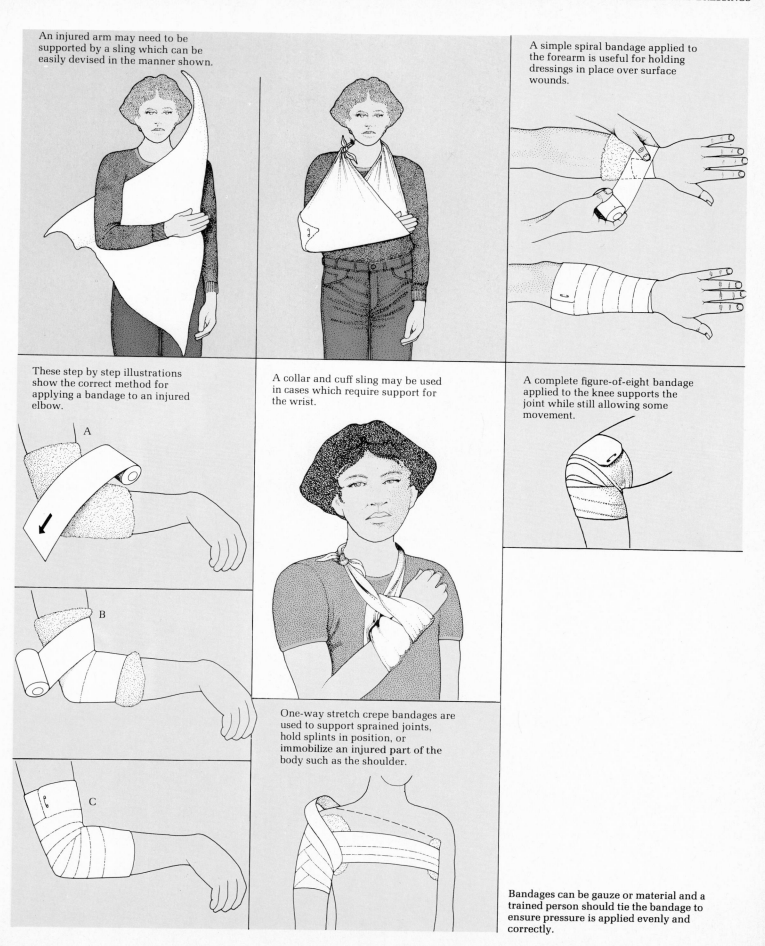

An injured arm may need to be supported by a sling which can be easily devised in the manner shown.

A simple spiral bandage applied to the forearm is useful for holding dressings in place over surface wounds.

These step by step illustrations show the correct method for applying a bandage to an injured elbow.

A

B

C

A collar and cuff sling may be used in cases which require support for the wrist.

A complete figure-of-eight bandage applied to the knee supports the joint while still allowing some movement.

One-way stretch crepe bandages are used to support sprained joints, hold splints in position, or immobilize an injured part of the body such as the shoulder.

Bandages can be gauze or material and a trained person should tie the bandage to ensure pressure is applied evenly and correctly.

343

Comfort is important for the child
with a minor injury.

ABC of Emergency Situations and How To Cope

Contents

Abdominal injuries

The abdomen contains a large number of organs, particularly those of the digestive system. Unlike the chest, the abdomen has little bony protection and is therefore more prone to crushing and penetrating injuries.

All abdominal injuries, except trivial ones, should be observed and referred for medical attention.

Pain and vomiting are frequent symptoms of abdominal injury. Symptoms may develop slowly over several hours, and it is important that a careful review of the casualty with an abdominal injury be made at least every half hour until expert help arrives. Increasing pain and tenderness to the touch plus the development of features of shock are all indicative of serious injury. Internal hemorrhage can readily occur from the spleen or liver. Leakage of bowel content may also occur, particularly in the case of penetrating injuries.

First aid entails resting the casualty, giving nothing by mouth, and arranging for immediate medical attention. Elevation of the knees slightly relaxes the muscles of the abdominal wall which often go into spasm after severe injury.

The casualty should be handled gently and treated appropriately for shock. If any bowel is protruding through a wound it should be covered with a clean soft dressing; no attempt should be made to push it back into the abdomen.

Bites and stings

Animal bites and insect stings are a frequent cause of some pain and injury, usually minor. Though injury caused by bites — and scratches — of domestic animals is usually small, medical attention is often needed, if only to ensure proper dressing of any significant wound, and protection against tetanus.

Snake and spider bites cause small skin punctures, possibly with venom injected into the wounds.

Bee farming. Some people show a severe allergic reaction to bee stings and require immediate first aid treatment when stung.

Insect bites and stings, though an almost unavoidable experience from flies, sandflies, mosquitoes and the like, are usually merely irritating.

Some caterpillars, such as the hairy caterpillar of the cupleaf moth, cause a stinging reaction when the bristles touch the skin. Although it is not dangerous the sting can be very painful. Other caterpillars can cause severe itching reactions (urticaria). A sting can be treated by rubbing the affected area with methylated spirits and placing an ice cube on it, although the pain may last for a couple of hours. Steroid creams may also alleviate pain and swelling.

Allergic reactions Some people develop allergic reactions to insect bites or stings that usually involve local pain, swelling and itchiness but occasionally extend to life-threatening effects on the breathing and the heart.

It is important for people who are known to be hypersensitive to bites and stings to take stringent precautions against being bitten. Medical aid should be sought immediately if such a person is known to be affected. The most usual serious threats are stings of bees and wasps.

Antihistamines and steroid tablets may be needed to control less severe reactions, and resuscitation and hospital treatment are necessary in more serious cases.

In most minor instances it is sufficient to clean the affected area, apply a soothing or antiseptic substance such as calamine or baking soda and apply a clean dressing.

If the area becomes weepy and inflamed, this may indicate bacterial infection and examination by a doctor is indicated, who may consider that antibiotic treatment is necessary.

Bee stings are usually very minor but an allergic reaction may develop in some people.

Ants, mosquitoes and sandflies Prevention of bites with the use of screens on doors and windows, sprays and nets is advised. When bites occur, the application of calamine lotion or an alkali solution such as ammonia or baking soda helps reduce irritation. Scratching should be avoided as this can damage the skin and cause further irritation with the possible development of sores which may become infected.

Bees, hornets and wasps Stings can be quite painful and allergic reactions which occasionally occur may require medical treatment. Usually, removal of the stinger and application of a cold water compress or a soothing lotion is all that is needed. However, the victim should be watched for signs of shock and medical help should be sought if the symptoms are severe.

The dangerous effects of bee stings usually occur in people who have had a severe local reaction to a bee sting on an earlier occasion. The complications which can result in the life-threatening situation described as 'anaphylactic shock' are manifested by a severe drop in blood pressure, swelling of the larynx and constriction of the airways, resulting in severe breathing difficulty and possible death. There may also be symptoms of nausea and vomiting.

The emergency treatment for anaphylactic shock consists of injecting 0.5 millilitres of adrenalin just below the surface of the skin, followed by an intravenous injection of 100 milligrams of hydrocortisone. Any person who has sustained a severe initial reaction to a bee sting should be supplied with the means for self-administration of the adrenalin. Mild reactions to bee stings such as moderate pain, swelling and redness can be treated successfully with antihistamines.

Domestic animals Dogs account for most bites, but cats, horses and even humans (sometimes on the sports field) also contribute. The severity of the injury varies from superficial damage to deep and jagged lacerations.

Any bleeding should be controlled by direct pressure and a clean bandage should be applied. If bleeding is significant, or if the wound is extensive enough to require stitching, medical attention should be sought.

Infection is another problem. Rabies is the most serious complication worldwide, special precautions may be necessary. Tetanus is a potential problem for any person not immunized against it. If immunity is inadequate a tetanus vaccine or a tetanus immunoglobulin (antibody) injection may be necessary. Once bleeding has been controlled, bites should always be carefully and thoroughly bathed to minimize the possibility of infection.

A common sense approach to animals is important. If a dog is obviously vicious, it should be avoided. Teasing and mishandling dogs is likely to provoke an attack.

Legislation governing the control of dogs varies from area to area and is usually under the jurisdiction of local councils. Generally, dogs must be leashed in public places, and some breeds are required to wear muzzles.

Rabies This is a potentially fatal infection to man and is usually caused by bites from animals that are themselves infected, most frequently dogs. If any animal is suspected of being infected ('rabid') it must be caught and tested for infection.

Rapid treatment is required for the victims of bites from rabid animals. Effective anti-sera are now available in most areas where rabies is present.

Animals that are potential carriers of rabies can, and should be, vaccinated against it. Pet dogs should always be vaccinated. There is no vaccine for humans.

Scorpions Scorpions inject venom through a stinger in the tail. There are many species, and a bite from one of the more dangerous species will produce marked systemic effects within 1–2 hours. Prompt medical attention is required.

A dog bite can require stitching as well as sterilization so medical assistance should be sought.

Scorpions may be highly poisonous and should not be handled.

Shark Although shark attacks attract much publicity, few fatalities are actually caused in this way. Sharks are attracted by abnormal smells, tastes and erratic vibrations transmitted through the water such as those of an injured fish. Most sharks tend to stay in a relatively small area.

Injuries are usually extensive; hemorrhage and shock being prominent. The casualty should be taken from the water and treated on the beach. Deaths have been caused by rushing the patient to hospital without adequate initial first aid. Shock is severe, and rest essential. Lay the victim on the sand head down, and control the hemorrhage with a tourniquet and by direct pressure. Maintain respiration and circulation, and reassure the casualty as much as possible. Medical assistance should be sought, and nothing given by mouth because of the likely need for emergency surgery after arrival at the hospital.

Avoid shark attack by swimming at protected beaches where possible, and never swim alone.

Preventive measures include nets around swimming beaches, spotter planes and education. Do not swim where there has been a recent shark attack or with bleeding wounds. Urinating in the water, carrying fish or swimming alone should be avoided.

Snakes Venomous snakes inhabit many areas of the world, but in the United States, Europe and Canada pose only isolated risks. However, in parts of India, Burma, and South America, for example, snakebite is a major problem.

In the United States there are approximately 45 000 incidents of snake bite each year. Of these, 20 per cent are from venomous, or poisonous snakes. These venomous snakes are most likely to be found in Texas, North Carolina, Florida, Georgia, Louisiana, and Arkansas.

The marks left on the skin after a bite vary. The puncture site is usually small — a clear mark of two fangs is rare — and there is little local reaction.

When venom is absorbed, however, the draining lymph glands become tender. This is followed by nausea, sweating, faintness, abdominal pains, blurred vision and widespread muscle weakness.

Most bites occur on the lower limbs. Do not suck or cut the wound as this is of no value. It can be washed to remove any surface venom.

Coral snake

Black-tailed rattlesnake

Copperhead snake

The most important step is to get the victim to the hospital as soon as possible. In the meantime, he should be kept calm, preferably lying down. Do not let the victim move around, as this will increase the absorption of the venom. The bitten area should be immobilized and kept at or below heart level. Reassure the victim and treat for shock.

The vast majority of bites are not fatal. Anxiety and panic aggravate the situation, so calmness is important.

If the victim can reach a hospital within 4 or 5 hours, and if no symptoms develop, no further first aid measures are necessary.

If the type of snake can be identified, antivenom specific to its venom can be given; if not, a combination antivenom is given. If the snake has been killed it can be taken to the hospital for identification.

A snake venom detection kit has been developed and is becoming widely available. Analysis of venom on the puncture site or in the body can determine which type of snake is responsible for a bite. Observation for 24–48 hours is required as symptoms may be delayed for some time after the bite. Respiratory assistance may be needed.

All snake bites should be treated as potentially dangerous.

Pit viper family. Three out of the four kinds of poisonous snakes in the United States belong to the pit viper family (Crotalinae). These are rattlensakes, copperheads, and water moccasins. These snakes can be identified by the pit between the eye and the nostril on each side of the head, oval pupils, one row of plates beneath the tail, and anywhere from one

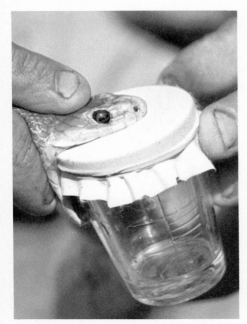

A snake is milked so that the venom can be collected for analysis and research and also for making antivenom.

to six fangs, but usually two well developed fangs. The circulatory system is affected by the venom of the pit viper family. There are 13 species of rattlesnakes, but all share the characteristics mentioned.

Coral snake. The coral snake can be identified by the red, yellow, and black rings around its body, with the red and yellow rings touching, and a black nose. It is a small snake (20–30 inches), has tubular fangs, and may have teeth behind the fangs. It also has several features of nonpoisonous snakes: round pupils and a double row of plates behind the tail. The nervous system is affected by the very toxic venom of the coral snake.

Nonpoisonous snakes can be identified by their round pupils, and a double row of plates beneath the tail. They have no fangs or pits.

Spiders Virtually all spiders are venomous, at least to some degree. But while the majority use their venom to paralyze their normal small prey, few are considered dangerous to man.

Black widow. One of two dangerous spiders in the United States is the black widow. While rarely fatal, the bite of a black widow can be extremely painful with unpleasant symptoms. These symptoms include: nausea, profuse sweating; abdominal cramps; difficulty in speaking or breathing; and severe pain produced by the spider's nerve toxin.

Brown recluse. The brown recluse, or violin spider is the other dangerous spider in the United States. A bite from this spider will produce a severe local reaction, which forms an open ulcer in one to two weeks; destruction of red cells and other blood changes; chills, fever, joint pain, nausea, and vomiting. There is also the possibility of developing a generalized rash in 24–48 hours.

Treatment is basically the same as that for snakebite. An antivenom is available and medical assistance should be sought

A tick will attach itself to any warm-blooded animal, as well as man, and in some instances can cause muscle paralysis.

as soon as possible.

Stingray The stingray usually inflicts injury by embedding a spine from its tail in the leg or foot of someone who accidentally steps on it. Stingrays bury themselves in the sand in the sea-bed; if divers shuffle their feet while walking, the ray usually moves away.

The spine is barbed and will penetrate most types of foot covering. It produces an initial severe reaction, with marked pain, and sometimes bleeding. The pain may last for several hours. Infection of the site of injury may develop several days later.

Venom is released from the spine and may cause generalized symptoms of nausea, vomiting and muscle cramps and spasm. Occasionally the heart-beat may be affected, also the control of respiration.

Observe the casualty closely and treat for shock. The venom is destroyed by heat; immersing the affected limb in very warm water until the pain has ceased is helpful. This may take up to 90 minutes. Elevation of the limb helps if heat is not available.

Delayed deterioration can occur and a period of hospitalization is appropriate. Fatalities from stingray wounds have been recorded.

Ticks are blood-sucking parasites of warm-blooded vertebrates. They usually shelter on foliage and drop on their victim when their surrounds are disturbed. Although some ticks are harmless, others carry a variety of diseases that can be potentially dangerous to humans.

Disorders caused by certain ticks include Rocky Mountain spotted fever, Colorado tick fever, Lyme disease (a form of arthritis), tularemia and relapsing fever. The wood tick and eastern dog tick are two troublesome species.

Disease-causing viruses or bacteria are transmitted in the tick's saliva during feeding. The saliva contains a toxin which is injected into the blood resulting in a wide range of symptoms. It may produce a vague nondescript illness, but occasionally muscle paralysis may occur. Slight irritation or itching is often noted at the side of the bite.

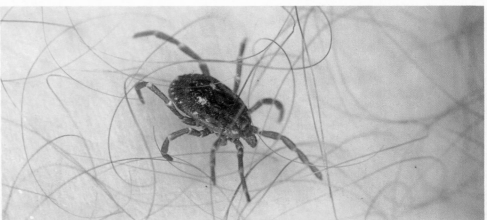

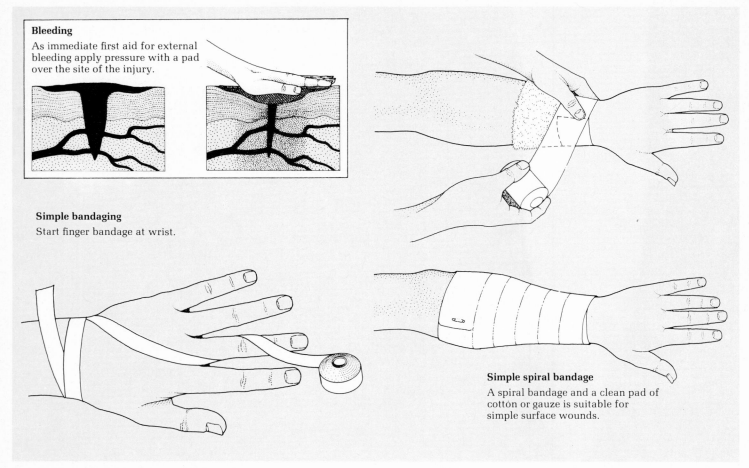

Bleeding
As immediate first aid for external bleeding apply pressure with a pad over the site of the injury.

Simple bandaging
Start finger bandage at wrist.

Simple spiral bandage
A spiral bandage and a clean pad of cotton or gauze is suitable for simple surface wounds.

At times this leads, over several days, to malaise and muscle weakness, particularly affecting the legs. In severe cases diffiiculty with swallowing and problems with circulation or respiration may occur.

Treatment involves the removal of the tick, and also checking that no others are present. The tick should be covered with heavy oil (mineral, salad, or machine). This will close its breathing pores. This may cause the tick to disengage immediately, if not, leave the oil in place for a half hour. Then remove the tick with tweezers, making sure that all parts are removed. After removing the tick, gently scrub the area with soap and water.

If symptoms persist or become severe, medical assistance should be sought. There is a specific tick antivenom available, and hospitalization may be required. Deaths are rare.

In tick-infested areas, it is advisable to have a daily body search, especially of children. Pets, particularly dogs, should also be examined.

Bleeding
Treatment of hemorrhage or bleeding is aimed at preventing further blood loss as well as maximizing the supply of remaining blood to essential organs.

Immediate control is needed for severe bleeding. Pressure over the site of hemorrhage is the best method, and the

Children suffer bruises in falls, but broken bones may also result.

fingers can be applied directly over the wound if a clean dressing is not immediately available. In most cases of bleeding a firm bandage is adequate.

There are various pressure points on the body where arteries pass over bones just under the skin, and can therefore be easily compressed. In most cases pressure applied directly to the wound is just as effective.

A tourniquet can be used as a temporary measure to control bleeding while the wound is being dressed. It can be made from any cloth tied round the limb on the side closer to the heart, and twisted by a stick. The cloth should be at least 2–3⅛ inches (5–8cm) wide to ensure that the underlying skin is not damaged.

Internal hemorrhage is the loss of blood when it escapes from the circulation into the tissues. Bleeding can occur from damaged organs such as the spleen, and into muscle tissue, particularly following the fracture of a bone.

Internal bleeding is minimized by resting the patient and keeping emotional distress to a minimum. The general principles of this are detailed below.

1 Elevate the bleeding part.
2 Rest the patient and the injured part.
3 Treat for shock.
4 Keep the casualty calm and reassured; anxiety and worry aggravate bleeding.
5 Keep the casualty warm but do not overheat as this draws blood to the skin.
6 Give nothing to the patient to eat or drink if injuries are more than minor.

7 If blood is coughed up or vomited, put the patient in the coma position immediately to reduce the possibility of inhalation into the lungs.
8 Keep a watch on respiration, level of consciousness and circulation.

Attention to these factors minimizes further bleeding and also maximizes the use of the rest of the circulation so that the heart, brain and kidneys receive an adequate supply.

Nose bleed Bleeding from the nose usually comes from a small area just inside the nostril, where several veins lie close to the surface and are therefore prone to rupture. The area is often inflamed during a cold and the veins become dilated, which also makes them more likely to rupture. Dilatation also occurs in hot weather. Local trauma to the nose will often trigger bleeding.

Bleeding can usually be controlled by pinching the soft part of the nose for five to ten minutes. The casualty should sit with the head tilted forwards as blood running back into the throat is often very irritating and may initiate vomiting. Breathing should be through the mouth and the nose not blown for a couple of hours after bleeding has ceased. Ice applied locally or to the neck can sometimes be of help if pinching the nose is unsuccessful.

If bleeding is severe or recurrent, medical attention should be sought.

Bruise

The medical term for a bruise is a contusion. Damage to small blood vessels (capillaries), causes bleeding beneath the unbroken skin, resulting in pain, dark blue discoloration and swelling. The so-called 'black eye' is a well-known example. Often sprains of ligaments and tendons accompany the bruising.

Blood tends to gravitate downwards over a period of days so that with a sprained and bruised ankle a black streak may later appear across the foot. Resorption of the blood from the tissues occurs over the following couple of weeks. Yellowing usually develops in the centre of the bruised area four to seven days after the initial injury, resulting from a chemical change in the blood pigment as it is absorbed.

Treatment The extent of bruising can be limited by applying ice soon after the injury has occurred for a few minutes every 20 minutes. A firm bandage should then be applied and if it is feasible the affected part of the body should be immobilized. Once the bruise is evident its resolution and ultimate disappearance are normally spontaneous and require no treatment.

Burns and scalds

A burn is damage to the skin and deeper tissue by dry heat (hot metals, flames) chemical agents or radiation. Scalds are burns caused by moist heat such as steam or boiling water.

Causes Almost all burns are the result of carelessness and accidents. The most common in the home is scalding caused

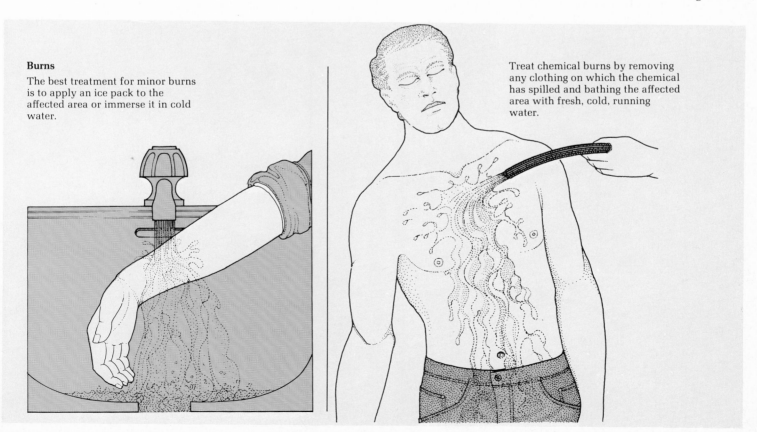

Burns

The best treatment for minor burns is to apply an ice pack to the affected area or immerse it in cold water.

Treat chemical burns by removing any clothing on which the chemical has spilled and bathing the affected area with fresh, cold, running water.

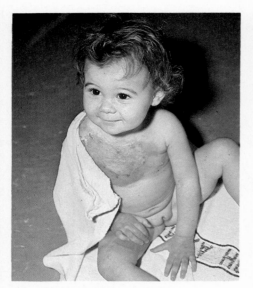

Patients with severe burns need an increased protein intake to help them recover. *(Royal Alexandra Hospital)*

Small children always need supervision while they are in the bath. *(Royal Alexandra Hospital)*

by spilling from teapots, coffee percolators and from saucepans on hot stoves. Those especially affected are children and the old and infirm.

Severe deep burns may be caused when a fire gets out of control and clothing catches fire. This most often happens when a fire is being lit with inflammable liquid and when children playing with matches catch fire and panic.

Severe widespread burns are caused in factory and car accidents, and when victims such as alcoholics and epileptics fall insensibly into an open fire.

The severity of a burn is determined by the size of the area burnt and depth of the burn.

The size of the area burnt is calculated using the rule of nines, that is, 9 per cent of the area burnt is apportioned to each of nine areas; the head, two arms (including front and back), two thighs, two lower legs, front of trunk, back of trunk. The replacement of the amount of fluid lost is calculated from the total percentage derived.

The depth of a burn is more difficult to assess. The terms first, second and third degree to denote the severity of a burn are familiar to many people. It should be remembered, however, that many burns are a combination of two or all three 'degrees'. If it is only a superficial (*first degree*) burn it will appear red, may be blistered and will be very painful. A deeper (*second degree*) burn will be mottled, will almost always be blistered or the top layer of skin will appear to be peeling.

White or charred areas with tough hard patches indicate that the full thickness of the skin (epidermis) is dead and that it is probable that the tissue below (dermis) is also burnt (*third degree* burn). These burns are not painful and the victim is usually

lucid and cooperative, though frightened.

Chemical burns. If corrosive or irritating chemicals such as strong acids or alkalis contact the skin, mucous membrane or eye, they are likely to cause chemical burns. Among the most common chemicals found in the home are drain cleaner, paint remover, battery acid and caustic soda. Industry uses many potentially dangerous chemicals.

Chemical burns should be treated immediately by running cold water over the affected area for two to five minutes to remove all trace of the chemical. The severity of the burn should then be determined.

Treatment If rapid sensible action is taken it will greatly improve the outcome of the injury. Many burns will need hospital treatment where a high standard of specialized care is needed to achieve best results.

Essential first aid. When a burn accident occurs the fire must be extinguished rapidly by smothering the flames. If any clothing is soaked in a hot fluid it should be removed immediately. In the case of an electrical burn it is important to switch off the current or use a dry wooden stick to detach the burnt person from the electrical source.

If a shower, hose or swimming pool is available the burn should be washed in clean cold water for a few minutes. This applies especially to scalds. This will greatly reduce the pain of a superficial burn and will reduce the temperature and subsequent damage to the tissues.

A clean cloth (preferably sterile) should be placed over the burn area. A clean cotton pillowcase is particularly useful for covering a whole limb in an emergency. The covering should not be removed, in case of infection, until the patient reaches the hospital.

The victim of burns to the legs and feet should be made to lie down and the feet and legs raised up on cushions. If the burns are to the hands and arms these should be held or suspended higher than the heart and any rings on the fingers should be removed.

If the face is burnt the patient should be made to sit propped up. These measures will reduce tissue swelling, loss of fluid and shock. Any home remedies, such as butter or grease, should never be applied, as they cause damage and introduce infection.

Small superficial burns can be treated at home. After first aid they should be cleaned with a mild antiseptic, and blisters should be removed carefully with gauze and clean scissors. A mild antiseptic cream should be applied to the raw area and covered with a clean dry dressing. Sterile vaseline gauze dressings are also useful in subsequent dressings and aspirin can help alleviate the pain. These burns should heal spontaneously in 7-10 days.

Hospital treatment The burns which need hospital treatment are those which: involve more than 10 per cent of the body surface, because fluid will need to be replaced; all deep burns however small, as they will need grafting; and all burns of the face, hands, feet or private parts (perineum).

Whenever there are electrical burns the victims should have hospital treatment to determine whether electrocution has damaged the heart.

If smoke has been inhaled, in the case of an explosion, hospital attention will be necessary as the lungs may be affected and oxygen may be needed.

Deep burns. Burns deeper than those described as superficial will take three to five weeks to heal, and will sometimes leave thick scars. Even deeper burns will not heal on their own and the dead tissues are best removed surgically under general anesthetic and the raw area covered with a skin graft, preferably with grafted skin taken from an unburnt part of the body. This technique reduces the time spent in hospital, and the end result is better.

Severely scarred areas also may need replacement by a skin graft, and disfigured faces will require several reconstruction plastic operations with grafts.

Throughout the acute healing stage of a burn a high protein balanced diet is needed to replace the lost tissue protein. It is advisable that a bedridden patient should also be treated with physical therapy with exercise for all the joints. The danger of scar formation is reduced by the use of splinting and pressure bandaging in some cases. At a later stage psychological and psychiatric help may be needed to complete the rehabilitation of the patient.

Complications In the case of a burn where more than 10 per cent of the body is affected, the loss of fluid, which continues for two to three days, needs to be treated by replacement; in the case of a large burn this fluid loss may produce severe shock in the patient.

The other main problem is infection. To prevent this it is necessary to cover the burn liberally with silver sulphadiazine and chlorhexidine cream at least twice a day. The patient should be nursed separately in a room with sterile techniques to prevent infection.

Prevention and safety Commonplace injuries, such as those caused by fire and hot substances, are mainly the result of carelessness; one of the primary causes of household fires is smoking in bed. Prevention is the key.

Do not smoke in bed; check all ashtrays in the house before retiring to ensure cigarettes are extinguished; do not use faulty electrical heating appliances; guard open fires well. Make sure that children do not huddle over heaters. Purchase non-flammable nightwear, especially for children and the elderly.

Take care in the kitchen where many burns occur. Turn pot handles inwards when cooking and do not let children use the stove or electric kettle until they are responsible and proficient. In the bathroom, always turn on the cold tap first when running a bath.

If possible, have a domestic fire extinguisher at home in case of emergency. Ensure that its operation is understood before it is put away; there won't be time to read the instructions if fire breaks out.

If fire breaks out in the home the most important thing is to get the people to safety. Don't rush back to get personal belongings.

Chest injuries

Difficulties in breathing can sometimes arise from injuries to the chest. For example, multiple fractures to the ribs can sometimes restrict respiration and a hole in the chest wall may result in air being sucked into the chest cavity, thereby restricting breathing.

Such wounds should be sealed firmly. Plastic or greaseproof paper is a good emergency measure. Firm bandaging can then be applied over the injured area. Associated shock should be treated, and medical assistance sought. The patient should preferably be transported lying on his side, with the injured side down.

Choking

Choking is an obstruction to respiration, usually caused by a physical blockage with a piece of food or by spasm of the larynx (voice box). Immediate action is essential for the choking victim.

The immediate first aid treatment is to remove any foreign body and then commence artificial respiration if necessary. Any visible foreign body in the throat can

Small children should never be given foods such as peanuts which could cause them to choke.

353

be removed with the fingers. If the obstruction is lower down, the methods recommended for unskilled essential first aid include four quick, hard blows with the heel of the hand between the victim's shoulder blades. If this does not expel the foreign body, then the slaps should be followed by four quick upward abdominal thrusts.

For the abdominal thrust, or Heimlich maneuver, you should stand behind the victim and wrap your arms around the waist. Place the thumb side of your fist against the victim's abdomen, slightly above the navel and below the tip of the breastbone. Grasp your fist with your other hand and press it into the victim's abdomen with four quick upward thrusts. If these procedures are not effective, repeat the sequence of four quick back blows followed by four quick upward thrusts.

An infant or small child should be turned head down over one of your forearms and given the blows between the shoulder blades. It is not recommended to give the abdominal thrusts to infants or small children. Instead, place the victim face up on your forearm with his head down. Rest your forearm on your slightly elevated thigh. Place two or three fingertips on the middle of the victim's breastbone, between the nipples, and press into the victim's chest with four quick inward thrusts.

For the unconscious victim, after the four back blows and four manual thrusts, you should open the victim's airway and sweep with the fingers. Grasp both the tongue and lower jaw between your thumbs and fingers and lift. This may relieve part of the obstruction. After you open the mouth, insert the index finger of your other hand down the inside of the cheek and deep into the throat to the base

Choking is a frightening experience for anyone. Small children especially should be reassured after the object has been removed.

of the tongue. Then use a hooking action to dislodge the foreign body and maneuver it into the mouth so it can be removed. When sweeping the mouth of an infant or small child, be extremely careful. Use a smaller finger and do not attempt to sweep if there is the risk of pushing the object further down the throat.

Children under the age of four are the most frequent victims of inhaled foreign objects, generally peanuts or small toys. It is unwise to give nuts, food containing seeds or pits to children under five, and toys for this age group should not have small detachable parts.

Concussion

If consciousness is temporarily lost due to a blow on the head the victim is said to be suffering concussion. The brain may be damaged temporarily, in which case there will be no further effects, or damage may be more severe with permanent disability.

Symptoms Concussion is distinguished by being a transient state and its onset is usually immediate following a head injury. The patient often has no memory of the actual moment of the impact. Immediately after the injury the person may momentarily show a complete loss of nervous function. The patient often suffers vomiting, headache, giddiness and nervousness after the recovery of consciousness. Patients who have suffered a head injury should be treated as though they have a spinal cord injury. They should not be moved and the head should be supported. It is very important to get medical attention.

Following a head injury signs that should be watched for include discharge

from ear and nose, loss of consciousness, headache, changes in vision, excessive vomiting and unusual or different behavior.

Concussion often occurs in motor accidents when seat belts are not worn and the head is thrown forwards forcibly with the impact. There may also be associated whiplash injuries. The violent jerking of the head often damages the muscles of the neck, and pain and stiffness follow. Sometimes the cervical (neck) vertebrae may be injured.

First aid A person with concussion should be laid down flat in bed with no pillows in a quiet, dark room.

No alcohol, tea, coffee or other stimulants should be given. Any laceration of the scalp or head should receive firm pressure with a cool, wet pad. If there is any swelling or lump forming on the head an ice pack will help to reduce further bleeding. If the head aches a dose of soluble aspirin with a glass of water may ease it and will do no harm. It will be very useful later to the doctor if the state of consciousness and behavior of the concussed person has been noted.

Medical treatment A person suffering from concussion should be examined by a doctor. Sometimes hospital observation, a skull x-ray or CAT scan (to check if the skull is fractured) may be necessary.

In more serious cases, for instance if there is evidence of intracranial hemorrhage or increasing rise in pressure of the cerebrospinal fluid, surgery to reduce the pressure may be required.

In the absence of other serious injuries, recovery from concussion is usually complete, but with frequent repetition of concussion the individual may become 'punch-drunk'. The term derives from boxing, for there is a high incidence of concussion among boxers. Common features of this condition are slurring of speech, poor concentration and forgetfulness.

Convulsions

In children, fever is the most common cause of convulsions. In adults, causes may include epilepsy, head injury or poisoning.

Collapse with loss of consciousness and writhing movements are the symptoms of convulsions. Bladder and bowel control may be lost and frothy mucus may appear around the mouth.

The aim of treatment is to protect the patient from self-inflicted injury and to provide adequate care once the actual convulsion has ceased. Moving the patient away from objects that may cause injury may be necessary, but in general movements should be restricted. Clenched teeth should not be forced open. Hard objects such as spoons forced in the mouth may damage the gums and lips, and their use should be avoided.

The convulsion usually ceases fairly

A protective helmet is required for the motor cyclist to lessen the risk of head injuries.

quickly. If consciousness is not regained, the casualty should be placed in the coma position, and not left unattended. The adequacy of breathing and level of consciousness should be continually reassessed. If cause is unknown, get medical assistance.

Confusion may remain after a convulsion, so supervision is essential until medical assistance is available.

Cramps

A cramp is a painful spasm of muscle, usually of the limbs. When the spasm is of internal structure, such as the intestine or ureter or bile duct, it is termed a colic.

Causes The cause of the common sort of cramp, which usually occurs at night, is unknown although it is often associated with old age, varicose veins, arthritis or pregnancy. Cramps can also be caused by deficient blood supply and by lack of salt.

Blood supply becomes inadequate when the arteries of the leg are narrowed by disease (atherosclerosis). On walking a certain distance, the victim suffers a pain in the calf, causing him to halt. After a short rest, the affected muscle will be cleared of the accumulated waste products resulting from activity, and the victim will be able to resume his walk.

A swimmer may experience cramps

after a prolonged swim in cold water. The cramp may be due to fatigue of the muscles and a blood supply that has become inadequate, possibly from a spasm of the limb arteries.

Vigorous activity in a hot atmosphere with consequent profuse sweating, as experienced by stokers or miners, may result in cramp due to loss of salt. Severe diarrhea and vomiting may also cause cramps from salt depletion. Writer's cramp is an occupational cramp believed to have its basis in tension.

Treatment An acute attack of cramps is best treated by stretching the painful muscle. If the muscles of the calf are in spasm, the foot must be forced upwards.

Arterial disease causing cramps on walking may need x-ray investigation; radio-opaque dye is injected into the arterial system to show the site and extent of arterial narrowing. Sometimes a severely narrowed segment can be replaced by a plastic tube but most patients do not need such radical treatment. There is a 25 per cent chance of spontaneous improvement. Daily exercise by walking up to the limit imposed by the pain is beneficial, and sufferers should not smoke.

Cramps due to lack of salt are treated by increasing the intake of salt. Workers who sweat profusely in hot surroundings should add a pinch of salt to their drinks,

rather than swallow salt tablets. In this way, the replacement of salt is kept in step with the increased need, because the heavier the sweating, the greater the thirst and, as a result, the greater the intake of salted drink.

The severe lack of salt caused by copious diarrhea and vomiting calls for a generous saline infusion into a vein. Swimmer's cramp may be combated by steady training and by avoiding prolonged swimming in cold water. It is said that a full stomach makes cramps more likely.

Cuts, abrasions and penetrating wounds

A cut or laceration is a break in the skin caused by an external injury, usually with a sharp instrument.

The degree and type of damage varies, depending on the site and severity of the injury. The common causes are knocks, falls, accidents involving broken glass and motor vehicle accidents.

Treatment Minor lacerations should be cleansed gently but thoroughly, bleeding should be controlled by direct pressure if necessary, and a clean dressing should be applied.

More severe lacerations require medical attention as there may be significant bruising and tissue damage. Treatment is mainly directed at controlling hemor-

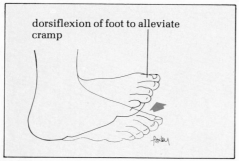

dorsiflexion of foot to alleviate cramp

When cramps are experienced the affected muscle should be stretched. *(Westmead Center)*

rhage, minimizing the risks of infection, treating shock and any other injuries, and ensuring appropriate follow-up treatment.

Shock may be aggravated by pain and loss of blood, therefore a quiet, confident and reassuring approach with gentle handling of the injury are all helpful. Bleeding is best controlled by direct pressure provided there are no foreign objects, such as glass, in the wound. An object that is deeply embedded should be left in place and pressure applied around it. Loss of blood can also be minimized by elevating, if possible, the part of the body affected. In the case of fractures the limb should first be splinted.

Gentle bathing of the injury with water, perhaps with a little soap, helps to minimize the risk of infection. Deep wounds with ingrained dirt or gravel,

however, can only be fully cleansed in a doctor's office or hospital emergency department. A sterile dressing is ideal but a clean bandage or other makeshift dressing can be applied to avoid further contamination.

Any large or gaping lacerations should be dealt with by a doctor and may require stitches (sutures). Stitches are put in after local anesthetic has been used to numb the skin surfaces. The stitches are usually of nylon or black silk and keep the skin edges together to allow rapid healing and smaller scars. They are removed after 6-10 days depending on the wound and the area of the body involved.

An alternative to stitching is the 'butterfly' or 'dumbell' adhesive closures that can be used if the cut is not gaping too much and if the adhesive is sufficient to hold the edges of the skin adequately together. This should be done by trained personnel.

If the laceration is deep, dirty or infected, tetanus immunization may be necessary. Most people are immunized as babies, and have a booster when five years old. If there has been no booster for longer than two years a tetanus toxoid booster will probably be needed. If no tetanus toxoid has been given for more than 10 years a full new course is required immediately, then in six weeks and then in six months.

Lacerations of the tongue rarely need stitching even when the tissue surfaces are widely separated. The profuse bleeding can usually be stopped by holding the tongue between the thumb and forefinger

Cramp sometimes experienced after vigorous activity may be caused by deficient blood supply or lack of salt.

with a clean pad between. The mouth should be rinsed three to four times a day in oral antiseptic and a fluid diet implemented for the next few days during healing.

Lacerations of the lip also rarely need stitching, unless very deep and gaping or if the border of the lip is cut across.

Sometimes in the case of a dirty cut with an irregular edge, when the possibility of bacterial infection is high, a course of antibiotics may be necessary to prevent infection.

Abrasions Rubbing or scraping causes loss of the upper layer or layers of skin or of the mucous membrane. It may occur following an accident or fall, particularly a motorbike accident when gravel rash could also occur.

Treatment usually consists of cleaning the wound, removing any dead tissue and applying an antiseptic or antibiotic cover if this is required.

Gravel rash is an injury to the skin often caused by falling from a moving vehicle onto a gravel road. Usually a large surface of skin is removed and thousands of fragments of gravel become embedded in the flesh beneath.

Large pieces of loose gravel may be brushed off gently but the abrasion should otherwise be undisturbed. Trying to remove small embedded pieces may introduce infection. Cover with a clean cloth

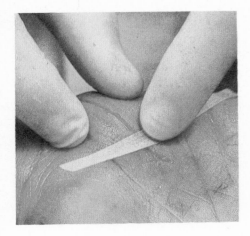

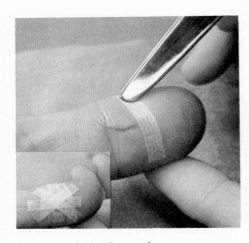

Lacerations to the skin can be
dressed with porous tape sutures
which obviate the need for stitches.
(3M Company)

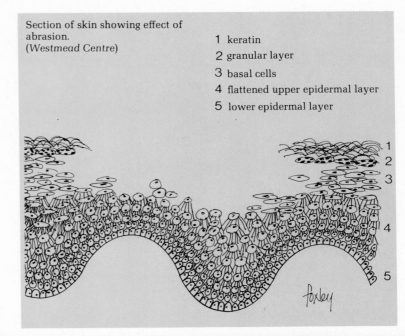

Section of skin showing effect of
abrasion.
(Westmead Centre)

1 keratin
2 granular layer
3 basal cells
4 flattened upper epidermal layer
5 lower epidermal layer

foxley

A fall from a moving vehicle can
cause severe gravel rash.

or an antiseptic dressing if available and
seek medical aid.

A penetrating wound may extend into a
body cavity such as the abdomen. All penetrating injuries should be assessed by a
medical practitioner as soon as possible
as internal organs may be damaged and
require urgent surgical repair. Although
symptoms may be minimal immediately
after the injury, they may become severe
later. Bullet wounds, stab wounds from
knives, and puncture wounds from
needles, scissors and other thin sharp objects all frequently cause penetrating injuries.

Immediate treatment should be directed at stopping hemorrhage, and treating shock if it occurs. Any impaled object
should be left intact, and kept in position
with bandages.

Bleeding is best controlled by direct
pressure. Resting and elevating the injured part of the body also help to control
blood loss and to prevent further bleeding. The risk of infection may be reduced
by washing injuries with clean water,
covering wounds with a sterile or clean
dressing and avoiding unnecessary handling. Wash hands before beginning treat-

ment and try not to breathe or sneeze directly onto the wound. A penetrating or
bleeding wound should not be bathed.

An injured person needs reassurance
and a close watch should be maintained
on breathing and circulation if shock is
likely. Other injuries such as a fractured
bone may also need prompt attention.

Tetanus germs grow best in anaerobic
conditions so that penetration into deeper
tissues, which are also bruised by the impact, creates an ideal situation for this
serious infection.

It is wise to check whether the patient
has adequate protection against tetanus

following any puncture wound, as even a
prick from a rose thorn is sufficient to
cause this disease.

Dislocation

A dislocation is the shifting of the moving
part of a joint away from its normal position. As a result, the affected joint usually
becomes immobile. As in the case of fracture, the area becomes swollen and tender
and it is often impossible to determine
whether an injury near a joint is a fracture
or a dislocation. In some cases both may
occur.

Almost any joint can be dislocated,
some more easily than others. Finger

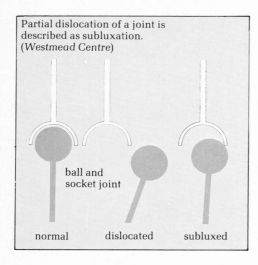

Partial dislocation of a joint is described as subluxation. (*Westmead Centre*)

normal   dislocated   subluxed

ball and socket joint

to fractures at the accident scene. Replacement of the parts of the joint back to their normal positions (called reduction) is usually done when the patient is anesthetised.

Subluxation An incomplete dislocation of a joint, a subluxation means that at least some of the bony surfaces of the joint are opposing each other.

Almost any wrenching or pulling force, or direct pressure, may result in the subluxation of a joint. Fibers within the capsule of the joint are usually torn, and there is frequently damage to the surrounding ligaments and muscles.

Symptoms are swelling, pain, bony deformity, and an overall loss of function of the joint. More severe injury usually causes a dislocation, which may also be associated with a fracture.

Treatment First aid measures involve elevating and resting the affected area. Cooling the site of subluxation with ice packs will reduce swelling as well as provide some pain relief. In most cases correction of the subluxation (called reduction) should not be attempted until x-rays have been taken to determine whether there is a fracture. Normally reduction should be done under medical supervision.

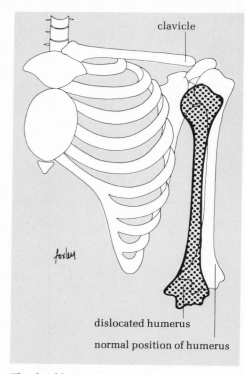

clavicle

dislocated humerus

normal position of humerus

The shoulder joint is one which is often dislocated in sporting accidents. (*Westmead Center*)

joints are easy to dislocate, especially during contact sports such as football. One of the most common dislocations is that of the shoulder. This often occurs during activities such as skiing where the force of the injury to the arm is enough to push the bone of the upper arm (humerus) out of its socket into the muscles of the shoulder joint. The affected shoulder does not sit squarely and cannot be used normally.

Dislocations should be treated similarly

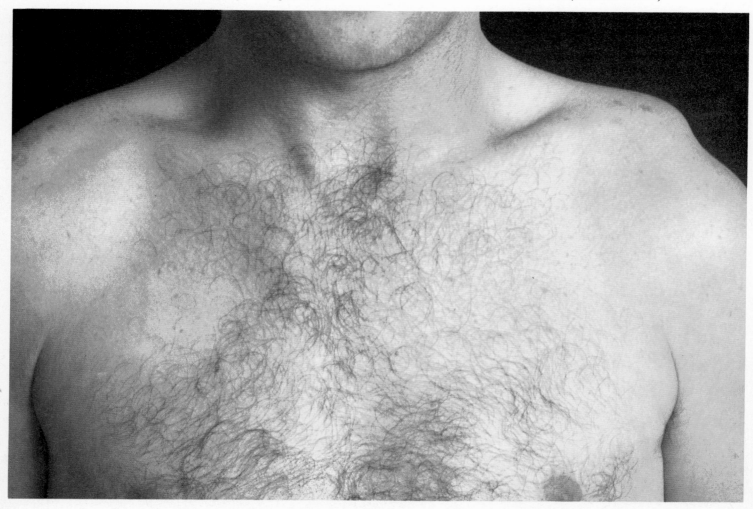

Drowning

Drowning (asphyxia caused by water blocking the passage of air to the lungs) is the cause of many deaths each summer, and almost all of these could be prevented.

Dangers Children are especially vulnerable in water. A very young child, for example, can drown in a small shallow pool. In the sea a child wearing a float, particularly water wings, can soon find himself in difficulty in rips and undercurrents. The dangers are that the water wings will not keep the child afloat in the upright position and he may drift out to sea making rescue more difficult and more protracted. It is therefore very important for children to be adequately supervised when swimming or playing near water.

Many adult drownings are partly caused by heavy consumption of alcohol just before a swim. Even a relatively small amount of alcohol inhibits body co-ordination, which is essential for swimming.

Right
Artificial respiration should begin as soon as possible if the victim is to be saved. *(John Watney Photo Library)*

Below right
Basic life-saving equipment for boating should include a lifejacket.

Below
Flotation aids may be valuable in teaching young children to swim but are not designed to prevent drowning.

The technique of mouth-to-mouth resuscitation should be learned by everyone. (Royal Life Saving Society)

The danger of drowning in fresh water is much greater than in salt water, though there is little difference if a person is submerged for more than 15 minutes. The inhalation of fresh water causes more destruction of red cells in the bloodstream and a greater change in the levels of salts (electrolytes) in the plasma. Widespread damage to other body tissues may develop several hours after inhalation of either fresh or salt water. All immersion victims, even if they appear to have recovered, should therefore be transferred to hospital for further medical examination.

Symptoms and treatment The symptoms of drowning depend on the amount of water inhaled. Both respiration (breathing) and circulation may be affected. If so, then the airway should be cleared, the head tilted back, and if breathing has ceased, artificial respiration begun. There may be a spasm of the larynx which is the normal protective mechanism the body uses to prevent water entering into the lungs. The spasm is overcome by mouth-to-mouth resuscitation. External cardiac massage may also be required if the heart has stopped beating.

Prevention Many water safety programmes are available for children. These include instructions on how to swim, the principles of water safety, and methods of rescue.

Other important safety measures include swimming with others, preferably on patrolled beaches, assessing the depth of the water, particularly before diving, and ensuring that the bottom is free of snags.

In recent years the increase in the popularity of backyard swimming pools has led to an increase in the number of water accidents and drownings, especially involving young children. The use of childproof fencing, which has been made compulsory by most local councils, around pools greatly reduces the risk.

When boating, it is important to have a reliable craft, complete with adequate supplies of water and food, and emergency equipment including flares. Each person aboard should wear a life jacket. Before setting out on a boat trip, check that weather reports are favourable and always inform someone reliable of your destination and probable arrival time.

Electrical injuries

The majority of electrical injuries can be attributed to: the use of faulty appliances, exposed wires in frayed cords, high voltage wires blown down in gales, and a lack of proper insulation in power tools.

In the home, small children are often at risk as they tend to explore electric outlets with their fingers. Infants who suck frayed electric cords or socket ends connected to a live outlet may sustain permanent injury to lips and tongue. While electrical burns and shocks are generally of an accidental nature, the accidents may occur because of inadequate parental supervision and control.

Injury caused by lightning is uncommon but can be severe. The current involved is about 20 000 amperes and thousands of millions of volts are discharged. The time taken for the passage to earth is between one-hundredth and one-thousandth of a second. Lightning does not always cause death to the person affected.

Electric burns are simply heat injuries. The tissue damage associated with such an injury occurs when electrical energy is converted to heat. The degree of injury relates to the amount of current, the length of time the victim is exposed to the current, and the degree of resistance of the local body tissues. A direct current is less harmful than an alternating current.

The degree of skin resistance to electrical injury rises in proportion to the thickness of the skin and falls if the skin is damp. More fatalities from electric shock occur in the summer months because people perspire more heavily.

Electric shock A shock sustained from either electrical current or lightning is termed electric shock. The severity varies from a mild sensation of tingling in a slight shock to severe burns, muscle spasms and even death, depending on the circumstances. Death by electrocution is most likely to occur if the victim is in contact with water, for example standing barefoot on wet grass or sitting in a bath.

It is essential that no contact is made with the casualty if there is a risk of electrocution to the rescuer. If the casualty is in contact with the household electric current, switch off the power at the power point, or at the mains box. If this is not possible push the victim away with a piece of wood. Never touch the casualty directly.

All power appliances should be kept in good condition and unsafe equipment repaired professionally. Temporary home 'repairs' may be dangerous.

Damaged high voltage wires can pose a serious threat of injury.

Small children should be carefully supervised at play and taught that electrical outlets and plugs are not toys.

The fingers and toes are particularly susceptible to frostbite so warm boots and gloves are necessary in cold conditions.

The main risk of electric current passing through the body is its effect on the heart. It may cause it to stop beating, resulting in immediate collapse. High voltage injuries also cause marked muscle spasm and severe burns. The spasm may throw the victim some distance from the site of contact. Lightning produces high voltage-type injuries.

As soon as the patient is freed from the current, you should check to see if there is breathing and a pulse. If the patient is not breathing, mouth-to-mouth resuscitation should be started. If the patient has no pulse, chest compressions should be started. Burns should be treated according to their extent. Fluids should be given, and the patient treated for shock. Immediate medical assistance should be sought.

Emergency childbirth

It normally takes several hours from the onset of labor pains to the eventual delivery of a baby, so in the vast majority of situations help can be obtained in time. It is far more dangerous to attempt to arrive at hospital a few minutes earlier by driving recklessly.

If the baby is about to be born, the mother should lie down and be made as comfortable as possible. Underclothes should be appropriately removed. Encourage and reassure the mother. Short panting breaths help the baby come out more slowly and evenly. Babies usually emerge head first and require little, if any, assistance.

There may be some bleeding from a tear at the entrance to the birth canal. This is usually minimal and is best treated after the placenta (afterbirth) and umbilical cord have been dealt with.

After the baby has been born it should be held up by the feet to clear secretions from the nose and mouth. Any remaining secretions should be gently wiped away. Breathing usually starts spontaneously; if it does not start within two minutes, artificial respiration should be *gently* applied. Once the baby has started breathing, it should be wrapped in something clean and warm and then placed on its side.

The placenta is usually expelled by further contractions of the womb (uterus). Do not attempt to pull it out by the cord. Expulsion usually occurs within 10–15 minutes. If bleeding is coming from deep inside the birth canal, gently rub the top of the womb through the skin of the abdomen just below the navel. This causes the womb to shrink in size and reduce bleeding.

It is important to keep the placenta so that it can be examined later by a doctor to check that no fragments have been left inside. Residual portions can cause continued bleeding.

The umbilical cord By this stage the umbilical cord will have ceased pulsating; it should be firmly tied in two places. It need only be cut if medical assistance is not close at hand. Infection and bleeding from the end attached to the baby are potential problems.

The baby should be kept warm, and if help is not close at hand, bathed and dried. Breathing and pulse rate of the mother should be observed. Persistent abnormalities may indicate continued bleeding.

In all cases where by reason of emergency only untrained assistance is available at childbirth, mother and child should subsequently be checked by a qualified medical practitioner as soon as possible.

Exposure to cold

Exposure to cold causes increasing physical and mental fatigue. Incoordination and drowsiness may follow. Protection from the wind and rugging up as much as possible helps. If available, a warm bath is an excellent remedy.

Prolonged exposure, particularly if in association with wind, may cause frostbite. Toes, fingers and the nose are usually affected, becoming white, hard and numb.

Treatment of frostbite involves slow warming. Use body heat or extra clothing. Hot water bottles, raylamps and massage should be avoided as rapid warming and rubbing may increase tissue damage.

Exposure to heat

The body maintains its normal temperature in a hot external environment by increasing perspiration (and subsequent evaporation) and respiration. When this mechanism fails, heat exhaustion develops. Heat exhaustion is more likely to occur in humid than dry weather.

The casualty with heat exhaustion is usually tired and feels faint. There may also be headache, nausea and cramps. Breathing is rapid and the skin moist.

Rest in the shade, tepid sponging, and plenty of drinks usually lead to rapid recovery.

Heatstroke is a much more serious condition. The medical term, hyperpyrexia, means that the body temperature has risen quite markedly as the result of a disturbance of the part of the brain that controls the body temperature. The condition is seen particularly in elderly people, and often follows heat exhaustion.

The main symptoms of heatstroke are a hot, flushed dry skin, a rapid onset of nausea, restlessness, headache and rapid breathing. Consciousness may be lost quickly. The pulse is usually strong but rapid, and the pupils dilated.

Perspiration helps the body
maintain a normal temperature in
hot conditions.

Immediate treatment of heatstroke is essential. The body temperature should be lowered as quickly as possible. Wrapping the victim in a wet blanket, showering with cool water and fanning are all mechanisms which lower the temperature. Hospitalization will almost certainly be needed to control the body levels of salt and fluid.

Eye injuries

The eye is particularly sensitive to injury, and preventive measures are as important as correct treatment.

Immediate medical attention is essential for all serious injuries. A damaged eye should never be opened or examined as the injury may easily be aggravated and the various parts of the eye further distorted. The casualty should lie down and a pad or bandage be applied lightly to the injured eye. Other general first aid measures such as reassurance and minimization of shock, if appropriate, should also be carried out.

Black eye When a blow is sustained in the eye or its general area, bleeding and bruising may occur in the soft tissues surrounding the eye. This will lead to discoloration of the skin around the eye, traditionally called a 'black eye'. The color will not only be dark but will pass through a range of colors as occurs with all bruises.

It is important to check that no damage other than bruising has been done to the eye and its surrounding structures. In severe cases, medical advice should be sought.

Ice packs or very cold compresses applied over the eye soon after the blow for a few minutes every 20 minutes for two or three hours will help to reduce the bruising. Once the black eye has appeared no treatment is necessary or of proven value, and the black coloring will disappear with time.

Chemical injuries Chemicals that have been splashed in the eye should be washed out immediately. A smoothly flowing tap is the ideal source of water. The casualty's eye should be held open and the head tilted so that the affected eye is lower. Washing of chemicals from the affected to the unaffected eye should be avoided. Medical attention should be sought.

'Flash burns' may occur after prolonged exposure to welding arc lights. Several hours after exposure, the eyes become extremely red, watery and very painful. They should be padded lightly, and medical attention sought. The use of heavily tinted protective glasses during welding prevents this condition from occurring.

Foreign bodies A foreign body in the eye is a common problem. Dust and loose particles are usually washed out by the tears, but occasionally clean tap water may be needed. If bathing the eye does not remove the foreign body, try and find the object. Foreign bodies can stick on the conjunctiva (white part) of the eye, and can be removed with a dampened cotton bud or the corner of a clean handkerchief.

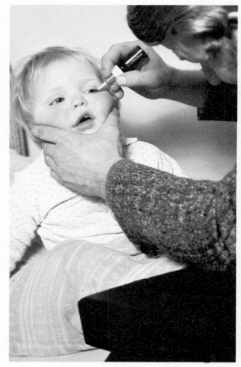

Top
Workmen in some trades are
particularly exposed to the risk of
eye injuries.
Above
Eye injuries require medical
attention. (*PAF International*)

Occasionally the foreign body may lodge on the inner surface of the eyelids.

The inner surface of the lower lid can be seen by pulling the skin downwards and slightly outwards. The inner surface of the upper eyelid is slightly harder to see, but this can be achieved by placing a Q-Tip across the lid and then pulling the eyelashes outwards and upwards so that the skin rolls gently over the match.

If foreign bodies are not easily removed by these methods, medical advice should be sought. Never attempt to remove foreign bodies that are stuck on the clear part (cornea) of the eye as these need careful removal after the application of anesthetic eye drops.

Foreign bodies that may have penetrated through the outer layer of the eye, which is very soft, should be seen by a medically trained person. These include metal filings that may have entered during high-speed grinding or hammering. The use of eye goggles during such activities reduces the likelihood of eye injuries.

Other causes of eye injury There are several medical conditions that cause red, painful eyes. A number are potentially serious if they remain untreated, and medical attention should be sought in all cases of severe or persistent eye problems.

Fainting

A temporary loss of consciousness from a reduced blood flow to the brain, fainting or syncope may be caused by a sudden emotional upset, severe pain, excessive exertion, extreme heat or a stuffy atmosphere.

The condition is not serious, and in many cases there are warning signs. The skin may become clammy, and the affected person may feel unsteady on his feet, dizzy and weak. The blood supply to the brain can be improved by getting the patient to put his head between his knees. By doing this, loss of consciousness may be prevented.

It is best to take the casualty out into the fresh air once he has regained consciousness. He should also be instructed to rest until complete recovery has occurred.

Consciousness is usually regained within a couple of minutes. In this situation all that is needed is to check that no injuries occurred during the fall and that breathing is adequate. If recovery is not rapid, the casualty should be placed in the coma position and assistance summoned.

Fire safety

Every member of a household should know exactly what to do if a fire breaks out. Needless deaths have occurred in the past because of confusion and inappropriate action.

If the fire is obviously too big to be dealt with, seal it off by closing doors and windows. Get everyone out of the house and call the fire department.

When moving through a burning building always close one door or window before moving through a second. This reduces the likelihood of wind drafts. Keep low, crawling if necessary, to avoid smoke, which is lighter than normal air. For extra protection drape something heavy, preferably wet, over your body.

Water may not always be the appropriate means of putting out a fire. Particular situations where water must be avoided are electrical fires and fires caused by flammable liquids such as petrol and oil. Special foam extinguishers are available and are marked accordingly. Smothering with sand or soil is an effective means of stopping minor fires caused by flammable liquids. A thick wet blanket may also be appropriate. In electrical fires the source of the current should be switched off if possible.

Right and below
If expert help is available to fight a fire, always ask for directions before joining in any rescue attempts.

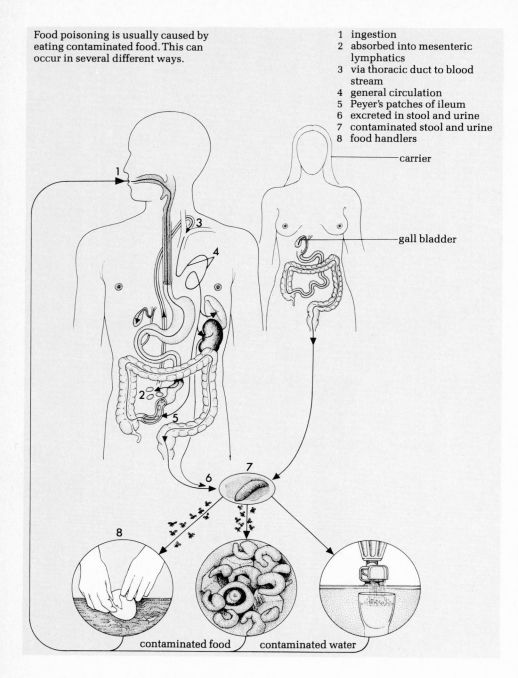

Food poisoning is usually caused by eating contaminated food. This can occur in several different ways.

1 ingestion
2 absorbed into mesenteric lymphatics
3 via thoracic duct to blood stream
4 general circulation
5 Peyer's patches of ileum
6 excreted in stool and urine
7 contaminated stool and urine
8 food handlers

carrier

gall bladder

contaminated food   contaminated water

Fractures

Bone fractures often occur in an accident, and their presence should always be suspected. Priority should always be given to the casualty's airway, breathing, and circulation (including hemorrhage), but once these are considered adequate, treatment can be directed towards the detection of fractures.

The site of a fracture is usually swollen, and may appear deformed if the broken bone has been moved out of its normal position. The casualty will complain of severe pain at the site of injury, particularly on movement. The fracture site is generally extremely tender to touch. Comparison of the affected side with the other side of the body is often useful as a means of confirming the presence of a fracture.

The immediate first aid treatment of a fracture is to prevent further damage and to minimize shock. This is primarily achieved by supporting the fracture so that there is minimal unnecessary movement of the injured site. A splint is the ideal method of achieving this immobility, particularly in the case of a fracture to the arm or leg.

Splints can be improvised from a wide range of objects including umbrellas, branches, broom handles and even tightly rolled newspaper. In a fracture in the leg, the unaffected leg can be used as a splint.

In general, splints should extend beyond the joints on either side of the fracture to ensure that movement is minimized.

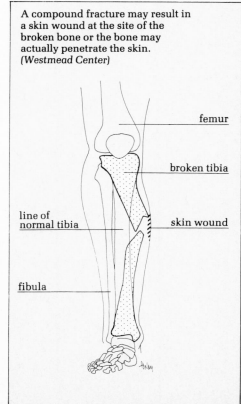

A compound fracture may result in a skin wound at the site of the broken bone or the bone may actually penetrate the skin.
(Westmead Center)

femur

broken tibia

line of normal tibia

skin wound

fibula

If the clothing catches alight, never try to remove it or move around unnecessarily as this fans the flames more. The best method is to immediately drop to the ground and roll over and over to extinguish flames. This can be taught by your local fire department.

If obviously trapped in a fire, try to seal yourself from it. Go into an unaffected room and block all the vents and the cracks under the doors with blankets to keep the smoke out. Yell for help from a window.

Food poisoning

Food poisoning is usually caused by poisons produced by bacteria (for example staphylococci and salmonella) which may grow in foods kept at warm temperatures, particularly chicken, ham, sausage, fish and milk products.

The usual symptoms of food poisoning are vomiting, diarrhea, and crampy pain in the abdomen.

The main problem of persistent diarrhea and vomiting is dehydration, particularly in the very young and the elderly; it may be increased by hot weather. Drinking an electrolyte solution (Pedialyte, Gator Aid) is the appropriate initial treatment. The intake of fluids and solids should be increased slowly, the rate being dependent on the lessening of symptoms and also on how the victim feels. Rest is also very important. If the vomiting or diarrhea is persistent or severe, medical attention should be sought.

If possible some padding such as cloth or cotton wool should be put underneath the splint, or between the limbs if they are strapped together. Once applied, splints can then be tied to the affected part with bandages or long strips of cloth above and below the site of the fracture. Always check that the circulation is still satisfactory after the splints have been applied.

Fractures of larger bones, particularly the femur (thigh bone), may be associated with internal bleeding. The loss of blood into the tissues may result in shock developing. This should be treated accordingly.

Compound fractures are those which are open to the air and are usually caused by the broken end of the bone penetrating the skin. Compound fractures should be initially covered with a clean dressing and then splinted as considered appropriate.

A fracture in which one bone is pressed against another to form a wedge-shape is known as a compression fracture. It occurs in the vertebrae of the spine, most commonly where there is the greatest movement in those parts of the spine, namely the neck (cervical) vertebrae, and at the junction of the chest (thoracic) and lower (lumbar) vertebrae.

A compressed fracture in the neck region may occur when there is excessive bending of the vertebral bones, as, for example, in the case of a car accident when the movement of the car suddenly ceases and the head of the occupant is sharply thrown forward, or in the case of a swimmer who dives into a shallow pool and strikes his head on the bottom. Compression fractures of the lumbar and the thoracic and even the cervical vertebrae may be caused by a fall from a height onto the feet or the buttocks.

Fracture of the collar-bone (clavicle) sometimes occurs. The arm on the affected side should be placed in a sling to reduce the weight dragging on the broken bone. A different type of bandage, called a 'figure eight', which wraps around the neck and shoulder is used to allow the bone to mend, but a sling is more than adequate in the initial first aid situation.

Fractures of the hip and pelvis Fractured hips are most commonly seen in elderly patients. The injury is usually the result of a breakage of the upper part of the femur (thigh bone). The pelvis is usually fractured during more severe trauma such as a motor vehicle accident.

In both cases the affected leg may be tied to the limb on the other side to achieve splinting. In a suspected fractured pelvis it is particularly important that unnecessary movement is avoided as several organs such as the bladder are nearby. Casualties with injuries to the hip or pelvis should be kept lying down and instructed not to walk as this may initiate organ damage.

Childhood tumbles can occasionally result in fractured bones. (*Zefa*)

Fractures of the ribs are particularly seen after 'punching' injuries to the chest. Splinting is usually ineffective. In more severe injuries several ribs may be broken and the bones pushed inwards. Occasionally the broken bones may get sucked inwards during breathing, a condition called 'flail chest'. This greatly reduces the effectiveness of breathing and may restrict the amount of oxygen entering the blood.

In less severe fractures to the ribs, the arm on the affected side should be placed in a sling to reduce weight on that side. The patient should be transported with the injured side facing downwards.

Fractures of the skull In most cases the fracture is a 'simple crack' in the bone. Occasionally part of the skull can be pushed inwards to form a depression in the surface. Medical attention is essential.

Fractures of the spine It is important that if fractures of the spine are suspected, the casualty should not be moved. The particular risk is that of injury to the spinal cord which extends along the vertebral column inside a bony canal.

The casualty usually complains of severe pain in the back, and if there is already some damage to the spinal cord, numbness or 'pins and needles' in the lower part of the body, or lack of motion of the arms or legs.

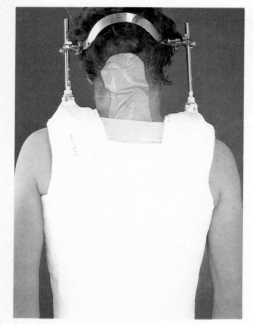

The treatment of a compression fracture of vertebrae may include this halo lumbar cast, which prevents flexing or torsion of the spine. (Westmead Centre)

Dangerous or physically demanding sports carry the risk of broken bones for the beginner.

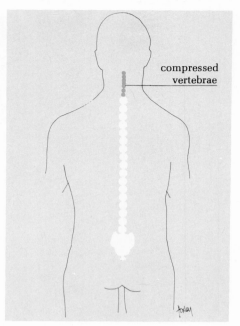

The vertebrae of the spine are susceptible to the type of fracture known as compression fracture, in which the bones are pressed against each other to form a wedge shape.

The spinal cord can be damaged in the neck region, and it is important not to move the neck if such a fracture is suspected.

Turning or twisting the head should never be attempted. Packing should be placed under the nape of the neck and on both sides of the head to act as a support until medical assistance arrives.

If a casualty with suspected injury to the spine has to be moved, the back must be kept straight. If he vomits, he should be rolled carefully over to one side.

Home safety

Homes should be sources of warmth, love and security, but they can also be dangerous. Many fatalities each year occur in or around the home, as well as about 75 per cent of non-fatal accidents. Young children and the elderly are the most prone to accidents around the home. Most home accidents can be avoided by simple precautions, knowing where the dangers are, and developing safe habits. Teach these to your children. Above all, common sense should be used.

Slippery floors, baths, loose mats and stairs can all cause falls. Cover all unused electrical outlets and try to keep long electrical cords out of the reach of children. Remove potential dangers such as matches and scissors from play areas. Frayed cords and faulty electrical gear should be fixed immediately.

The kitchen is potentially the most dangerous room in the house. Have children play elsewhere, especially when the kitchen is in use. Select saucepans with good grips on their handles, and turn them inwards on the stove. Cuts, fires and

1 Never put a knife in the toaster.

2 Always turn saucepan handles away from the edge of the stove.

3 Knives are obviously a danger to children so should be kept out of reach.

mishaps with electrical appliances are also likely to occur here, so extra care is needed.

Fires and burns Buy non-flammable children's nightwear. By law, all these garments are labelled according to their fire-resistant properties, category 1 being the safest.

Select proper fire extinguishers, and put them in easily accessible places. Always have heaters with guards. Flammable liquids should be used cautiously, and stored in a safe place. Supervision of children and making them aware of the dangers of fire are important, and adults should know how to deal with different types of fires.

Household chemicals are usually poisonous if swallowed and include cosmetics, bleaching and cleaning agents, detergents and soaps, paints, varnishes, petroleum products, photographic chemicals, fire extinguisher chemicals, insecticides and rodenticides. Most poisonings at home result from swallowing aspirin, cleaners, polishes or pesticides.

Caustic agents, such as drain and oven cleaners, are especially dangerous. They burn and destroy all tissue, whether skin, eyes, mouth, esophagus or stomach. For first aid after swallowing, give large amounts of milk or water, *never* make the patient vomit, and get him to hospital immediately.

An affected eye may be bathed under a gently-running tap for a few minutes, or with cool water poured from a tea-pot.

Ideally, caustic products should not be stored in the house. Just enough should be purchased for each occasion of use, and the empty container rinsed thoroughly under the tap before it is deposited in the garbage bin. Dangerous solutions must never be stored in drink bottles or food containers, or stored with food.

Medicines About half the fatal poisonings occur in young children. It is therefore imperative that parents teach their children at an early age the danger of touching, eating or playing with medicine, chemicals or pesticides. Even common medicines, like aspirin and iron tablets, can be fatal in overdosage, especially in children.

The family medicine cabinet needs a secure latch or lock. (*Royal Alexandra Hospital*)

Dangerous substances should be clearly labeled and kept well out of children's reach, preferably in cupboards with childproof locks.

All medicines, pesticides and chemicals should be stored in child-resistant containers and locked in a cupboard. Unused medicines and chemicals should be flushed down the toilet. Medicine should be locked away after each dose, and adults should preferably not take doses in front of children in case they imitate them later, with possibly fatal results.

Before medicine is taken or given to children the label must be read carefully and the correct dose administered. In the elderly, poor vision is a factor in many medication accidents. Clear labeling, good light in the bathroom, and correction of visual defects where possible are essential.

The tendency of small children to put everything and anything in the mouth means that extra care should be taken to keep poisonous substances locked away.

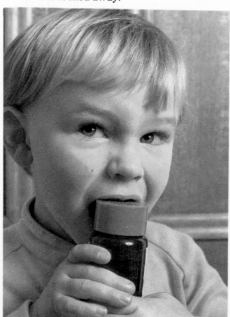

Outdoors Accidents in the garden or home surrounds frequently involve garden tools, motor mowers and noxious fluids. People step on rakes, are hit in the eye with spade handles or have their legs or eyes cut with stones thrown up from the lawn mower. There have even been cases of blindness resulting from flying stones or sharp objects. Remove stones from the ground before mowing; always wear strong shoes and never pull a mower backwards. The latter can result in gashed feet, or even the loss of toes.

Store garden and work tools, fertilizers, paint and poisons in a convenient but safe spot where children cannot reach them.

When spraying pesticides, protective clothing should be worn. The spray should be used only according to directions on the label, and neighbors should be warned of your activities in case of drift. *Never* spray on windy days.

Injuries may occur when fires are left to smoulder, or if highly flammable liquid such as methylated spirits or turpentine is thrown onto the fire to 'get it going'.

Children should be carefully supervised in the swimming pool and the supervising adult should be able to swim and to perform mouth-to-mouth resuscitation. Take care also with buckets or even puddles of water as babies and toddlers, who are un-

Even when wearing safety devices, children should never be allowed to swim without supervision.

able to right themselves quickly enough if they fall face downwards, have been known to drown in very shallow water.

Adult pool parties have sometimes ended in tragedy, generally as a result of excessive alcohol consumption. Judgement is impaired in these circumstances and intoxicated swimmers may suffer cramps or dive into the shallow end of the pool. The pool depth should be clearly marked, the area well lit and people should be discouraged from 'showing-off' or entering the water if intoxicated.

A child should be taught about poisons and warned not to eat unfamiliar berries. Adults should remember that some toadstools are extremely poisonous and sometimes difficult to distinguish from mushrooms.

Suffocation Many deaths occur, both indoors and out, through suffocation, particularly of children who play with plastic bags and are tempted to put them over their heads. Children should be warned never to play in disused refrigerators, in feed bins or in any similar 'box' situation where the door or lid may slam shut, trapping them. Playing on, and, more particularly, digging in under, sandhills is dangerous; suffocation under collapsing sand is an all too frequent vacation tragedy.

The major cause of death in persons under the age of 40 is accident. Even taking into account the fact that many such accidents occur on the roads, in industry or at sporting events, it is prudent to practice prevention at home and try to make the family as accident-proof as possible.

Home first aid and medical kit It is advisable for each home to have a first aid kit. The kit should contain equipment necessary to deal with common conditions, and to manage common illnesses.

Components of a first aid kit should be kept in one place, preferably in a child-resistant cupboard. The following items are considered to be useful components; most are included in commercially produced kits.

1 *Equipment*
   Thermometer
   Scissors
   Bandaids
   Roll of sticking plaster
   Bandages — various types and sizes
   Dressings
   Tweezers (forceps)
   Measuring glass or spoon
   Cotton wool
   Safety pins
   Tourniquet

When spraying pesticides, protective clothing should be worn. The spray should be used only according to the directions on the label and neighbors should be warned of your activities as sprays may drift, affecting nearby gardens and animals.

2 *Drugs and medicines*
  Aspirin
  Acetaminophen
  Antiseptic solution
  Antiseptic cream
  Calamine lotion
  Zinc cream
  Syrup of ipecac
  Methylated spirit
  Antiseptic gargle
3 *Other contents*
  First aid book
  Telephone numbers — doctor, ambulance, poisons center, fire department.
  Any medicines that are currently being taken by family members should also be stored safely in the cupboard.

Major disasters

Changes in society relating to housing, transport and weaponry have meant that the chance of major or 'mass' disasters occurring has greatly increased. It has been clearly demonstrated that early and adequate treatment at the scene of accidents greatly increases the likelihood of survival of the injured. Major disasters add the additional problem of deciding which of a large number of casualties most needs immediate treatment. The term 'triage' describes the classification of victims in the multiple casualty situation.

Usually the most seriously injured casualty is treated first. If there are many casualties, other factors emerge. The ages of the victims, the likelihood of the casualty dying anyway, and hemorrhage taking precedence over crush injuries are unpleasant but necessary factors that must be taken into account.

Safety at a major disaster site is important. Common risks are fire and electrocution. Fire needs three components — heat or a spark, appropriate fuel (such as gas) and air (oxygen).

If there is any possibility of fire, there should be no smoking anywhere near the disaster site; no electrical sparks, which excludes the use of power drills and saws; no oxy-cutting equipment, and minimal metal-to-metal contact, for example high speed metal saws.

The freeing of trapped people and the need to use extrication equipment can usually be left until expert help arrives. Special equipment which minimizes fire risks has been designed for these purposes.

Electric power lines should always be regarded as live until declared safe by an appropriate authority. The immediate surrounds of a high voltage wire may also be charged, particularly if wet.

Disaster plans Most major cities and towns have developed plans to be instigated in the case of a disaster. Local authorities such as the police, fire department, ambulance, and medical personnel are in-

The comfort and reassurance offered by a calm person can reduce the emotional impact of injury.

volved. The main aims of such disaster plans are to get expert help to the disaster scene as rapidly as possible, and then to set up various areas where casualties can be treated. It is important that all first aiders in a disaster scene firstly use common sense in relation to immediate treatment, and secondly follow the instructions of more highly trained personnel when they arrive.

Motor vehicle accidents

The enormous problem of injuries resulting from motor vehicle accidents is well recognized. Detailed studies have clearly demonstrated that early and adequate first aid greatly increases the chance of survival.

The basic first aid steps — rapid assessment of the overall scene, treating the immediate emergencies, and sending for help — particularly apply to the scene of a motor vehicle accident. Specific injuries should be treated as appropriate.

Casualties should not be dragged from the vehicles, as internal and spinal injuries can be made worse by unnecessary movement. Fire is unlikely to occur if it hasn't started just after the accident.

Assistance from other people should be sought, both to summon expert help and also to protect the accident scene. Waving down passing cars and arranging for adequate lighting from car headlights, if appropriate, not only help in the first aid treatment but also reduce the chance of further collisions from other vehicles.

Poisoning

When someone swallows (either accidentally or deliberately) a quantity of a medicine or chemical the basic principles of emergency treatment are: to remove or dilute the poison and delay its absorption and to maintain the victim's vital functions (breathing and circulation). You should therefore:

1. Immediately give him two glasses of milk or water to drink (both dilute the stomach contents; milk has the added advantage of delaying the emptying of the stomach).

2. Consult the Poison Control Center: specific advice can then be followed on any further treatment needed. Isolated households, and ideally everyone, should have the emetic syrup of ipecac available in their house, for use if advised by the Poison Control Center.

3. Take the victim to the nearest hospital. Do not try to make him vomit unless advised by the Poison Control Center, and not unless syrup of ipecac is available. Other methods are ineffective or dangerous. It is unwise to use salt to make an infant vomit because of its toxicity. Nor must vomiting be induced in someone who is drowsy or unconscious or who has swallowed petroleum products or a strong acid or base. In these instances vomiting carries the risk of inhalation of kerosene and petroleum products into the lungs which may cause a dangerous pneumonia. *Phone for advice before inducing vomiting.*

4. If the victim has stopped breathing, begin mouth-to-mouth resuscitation, and external cardiac massage if no pulse can be felt. These must be continued until he is put on a life support system in hospital.

Household cleaning agents should be kept out of the reach of children.

Medicines are potentially poisonous, particularly in overdosage. Medicines which are no longer required should be disposed of and those in use kept in a locked cupboard. (*Zefa*)

In hospital the victim's stomach may be washed out, but it is often unnecessary. Occasionally, poisons can be eliminated by increasing the filtration of the blood by the kidneys, and some by filtering the person's blood through an artificial kidney. Sometimes there is a direct antidote to the poison, in the form of a drug, antitoxin or antivenom which can be injected to neutralise the effects of the poison, for example tetanus antitoxin, snake antivenom and atropine sulphate which reverses the effects of poisoning by mushrooms and organic phosphate and carbamate insecticides.

It is wise to keep the telephone number of your local Poison Control Center handy by the phone and to remember that common corrosives and volatile liquids include:

Anti-rust fluids
Caustic soda
Drain cleaners
Furniture polishes
Gasoline
Kerosene
Mineral turpentine
Paint strippers
Paint thinners
Strong acids and alkalis.
(See also section on *Food poisoning*)

Poisonous plants

Although plant poisoning in people is quite rare, poisonous plants are found in virtually every garden, and many house plants and some common vegetables and fruits are poisonous under certain circumstances. For example, the cooked stalks of rhubarb are wholesome and pleasant to eat but the leaves are poisonous whether cooked or raw.

Those people most at risk of plant poisoning are: children from about one to three years old, an age when they are using taste as one means of exploring their strange new world; adults who are trying to return to nature, including the use of wild plants as food; and those who take drugs and who sometimes try garden plants or weeds in search of a 'high'. The dangers can be avoided if it is known what plants can be poisonous under which conditions.

The following list includes plants that are likely to be implicated in human poisoning. It is emphasized that, although these plants contain poisonous substances, very few of them are really dangerous unless they are actually eaten or introduced into the body in some other way; it is usually more hazardous to keep kerosene or pesticides in the cupboard, to cross the street or to ride in a motor car, than it is to have most of the plants growing in the garden.

Education and common sense are the best protection against plant poisoning. Parents should learn to identify which plants in their homes, gardens and immediate neighborhood might be poisonous. They should keep plants, seeds and bulbs away from infants, teach children at an early age to keep unknown plants out of their mouths and away from their eyes, be certain they know what plants their children use for playthings and discourage them from sucking nectar from flowers or making 'tea' from leaves. They should themselves refrain from concocting home-made medicines from wild or cultivated plants and avoid inhaling smoke from burning garden refuse.

If a child does eat some strange plant, try to find out what part has been eaten and how much, then take the child straight to the hospital emergency department of the nearest large hospital, along with a sample of the plant, including a whole twig with leaves attached and, if available, flowers, fruits and seeds. A single, detached leaf or leaf-fragment is not enough. Do not wait until symptoms develop as that may be too late. Most cities also have a Poison Control Center which is listed among the emergency numbers in the telephone directory and can be telephoned for first aid advice.

Check list of poisonous plants

Deadly nightshade All parts of *Atropa belladonna* are very poisonous. The toxin is atropine which causes dilated pupils, rapid heart-beat, blurred vision, constipation, excitement, convulsions and fever, often followed by death.

Dumb cane Chewing the leaves or stems of *Dieffenbachia* produces severe, burning pain in the mouth and throat, temporary loss of speech and difficulty in swallowing.

Foxglove The drug digoxin is derived from *Digitalis purpurea* and most cases of human poisoning have been due to overdoses. All parts of the plant are poisonous. Accidental poisoning sometimes occurs in children who eat the plants or suck nectar from the flowers. Symptoms are nausea, abdominal pain, blood-stained diarrhea, abnormal passing of urine, gross disturbance of heart-beat, mental irregularities, drowiness, sometimes tremors or convulsions.

Fungi It is safest to eat only those mushrooms known to be non-poisonous. *Psilocybe cubense* (syn. *Stropharia*, mad mushroom, golden top) is a common cause of mushroom intoxication. It produces hilarity, intoxication and hallucination, and is usually eaten in mistake for the ordinary mushroom, but sometimes is taken deliberately as a drug. The two most poisonous mushrooms known, *Amanita phalloides* (death-cap, angel-of-death, destroying angel) and *A. muscaria* (fly agaric) are northern hemisphere species.

Aspergillus flavus (golden mould) can develop on improperly dried or stored seeds and seed-meals, particularly peanuts and coarse grains. Some strains produce extremely poisonous aflatoxins that can cause cancer of the liver accompanied by impaired appetite and loss of weight. Mouldy nuts should not be eaten. Milk from cows which have eaten contaminated fodder contains toxic aflatoxins.

Holly The leaves and berries of *Ilex aquifolium* are poisonous, causing vomiting, diarrhea and stupor in children and adults.

Hyacinth *Hyacinthus orientalis* bulbs are sometimes eaten by children. They cause nausea, vomiting, diarrhea and sometimes death. Pollen from the flowers irritates the eyes.

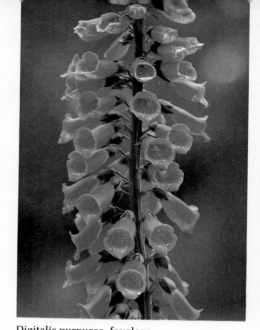

Digitalis purpurea, foxglove

The highly poisonous *Amanita muscaria*, fly agaric.

1. Ilex aquifolium, holly leaves
2. Hyacinthus orientalis, hyacinth
3. Ipomoea violacea, morning glory

Morning glory Most frequently associated with human intoxication is *Ipomoea violacea* (common morning glory). Seeds of several cultivars contain sufficient indole alkaloids to produce hallucinations.

Mountain laurel Children have been poisoned by sucking nectar from flowers of *Kalmia latifolia*, drinking tea made from the leaves or eating honey derived from the nectar. Symptoms are repeated swallowing, salivation, nausea, vomiting, staggering walk, convulsions, difficulty in breathing and paralysis.

Oleander All parts of *Nerium oleander* are very poisonous if ingested. Children have died after eating one or two flowers; adults have died after eating meat cooked on oleander sticks. Symptoms are nausea, vomiting, stomach pain, dizziness, blood-stained diarrhea, drowsiness, weakness, abnormal heart-beat and coma, usually beginning several hours after ingestion. Death may follow within thirty hours.

The so-called yellow oleander (*Thevetia peruviana* or tree daffodil) is also poisonous. All parts of the plant contain poisonous cardiac glycosides but most cases of human poisoning have been due to eating seed-kernels. One seed caused the death of a child. Symptoms are burning sensation in the mouth, tingling of the tongue, dryness in the throat, vomiting, purging, drowsiness, dilated pupils and slow, irregular pulse.

Poison ivy Perhaps the most common and most severe allergic reactions come from skin contact with the poison ivy (*rhus radicans*) family. This group includes poison ivy, poison oak (*rhus diversiloba*) and poison sumac (*rhus vernix*). Contact with these plants produces a severe rash characterized by redness, swelling, blisters and intense itching and burning. A high fever can also result. Usually the

rash will begin within a few hours after exposure, but may be delayed up to 48 hours. Poison ivy and poison oak can be identified by their leaves, which are made up of three leaflets each. Both these plants have greenish-white flowers and clusters of berries. Poison sumac grows as a woody shrub or small tree, and has feathery leaves and clusters of red berries. First aid treatment for contact with this group of plants consists of removing contaminated clothing and washing exposed areas with soap and water, followed by rubbing alcohol. If the rash is mild, apply calamine or other skin lotion. If a severe reaction occurs, or if there is a history of sensitivity to these plants, seek medical advice.

Rhododendron All parts of rhododendrons and azaleas, including the flowers, nectar and infusions of the leaves are poisonous if eaten or drunk. Symptoms are salivation, vomiting, staggering walk, convulsions, difficulty in breathing and collapse.

Rhubarb Cooked leaf-stalks of *Rheum rhaponticum* are quite wholesome but the green, expanded leaf-blades are poisonous if eaten either raw or cooked. Small amounts cause muscular weakness and twitching, slow respiration, weak pulse, coma and death. Large amounts also cause stomach pain and vomiting.

A common poisonous plant is the Rhus radicans, poison ivy.

Severed parts

Recent advances in the field of microsurgery have meant that severed limbs, toes or fingers may sometimes be replaced successfully.

If such an accident has occurred, the severed member should be kept cool and dry. The best method is to wrap the part in a plastic bag and then immerse the bag in ice and water. If this is not possible, wrapping the part in a clean cloth will suffice.

Medical assistance should be sought as soon as possible.

Shock

Generally interpreted as a circulatory collapse that effectively reduces the volume of blood in circulation, shock can also be described, when applied to nervous system functioning, as a serious emotional upset that suddenly disturbs mental functioning.

Almost any significant injury, including hemorrhage, fluid loss from burns, dehydration, severe diarrhea or vomiting, heart attacks or heart failure, poisons or infections, and nervous system reactions causing blood to collect in dilated vessels, can cause varying degrees of shock that require first aid.

Symptoms reflect the underlying cause and the body's attempts to adjust to, and overcome, blood circulation changes. Heart beat and breathing rate both accelerate while the blood vessels of skin and muscles, and those at the injury site, constrict to maintain blood pressure and ensure that essential organs, such as the brain and heart, receive adequate oxygen.

Reduced blood supply makes the skin cold, pale and clammy as the sweat glands empty their contents. Pulse rate and strength remain normal if shock is mild, but severe shock quickens the pulse followed by laboured breathing, restlessness, faintness and vomiting. If help is not at hand the affected person will lose consciousness, and will eventually die.

Treatment Immediate first aid is necessary to prevent any deterioration and to minimize the consequences of losing blood.

Direct pressure on or around the injury site controls external hemorrhage and lying the victim flat and elevating the legs will ensure maximum blood supply to the brain. The airway, breathing and level of consciousness must be continually monitored. Artificial respiration or external cardiac massage also may be required. To minimize the risk of swallowing vomit the unconscious person is best placed in the coma position.

The Nerium oleander, oleander is poisonous if digested.

Rest, warmth and reassurance will reduce anxiety, exertion and shivering, all of which can aggravate the condition. Do not warm the victim with massage as this draws blood to the skin away from the vital organs; instead use a blanket. Splinting of fractures, immobilization, elevation of the injured parts and gentle handling all help to reduce pain.

Small quantities of non-alcoholic drinks may be given if the patient is alert, able to swallow, and is not nauseous but they should not be offered if the injuries are more serious, or if an operation (including the setting of a fractured bone) seems likely.

Other injuries or conditions may require specialized assistance and blood and other fluid transfusions. Calmness, common sense and a gentle demeanor are all essential facets of first aid.

Spinal injuries

Spinal injuries include injuries to the spinal cord or to the spinal (vertebral) column. Injury to the vertebral column is serious only insofar as it impinges on the spinal cord. The roots of the spinal nerves may be irritated by a prolapsed intervertebral disc, a relatively minor injury causing pain in the region supplied by those nerve roots, commonly in the distribution of the sciatic nerve at the back of the thigh.

More serious are fractures and dislocations of the spinal vertebrae resulting in damage to the spinal cord. These injuries are usually crush fractures from forceful bending of the spine as in car accidents, falling from a height onto the feet or striking the head in a steep and reckless dive.

The results of the injury depend on the extent and level of the damage. A fracture below the level of the second lumbar vertebra will miss the spinal cord. An injury to the cord above the fourth cervical segment paralyzes the diaphragm. At the level of the fifth segment the patient will be able to rotate his humerus. At the sixth segment he can learn to feed himself with the aid of appliances attached to his wrist. At the seventh segment, he can grip effectively and may learn to feed himself, dress and drive a car again.

The cervical and the lumbar sections of the spine are the most often injured.

Injury to the lumbar spine at a high level may paralyze the legs. At a lower level, injury to the nerve roots of the lumbar and sacral nerves (the cauda equina) may cause distressing disorders of bowel, bladder and sexual function.

Paraplegia is the term for paralysis of the legs and a part or the whole of the trunk, from injury or disease of the spinal cord. Paraplegia from trauma has numerous complications, particularly aspiration pneumonia from the inability to cough, pulmonary embolism from clotting in the deep veins (a result of sluggish circulation), infection of the paralyzed bladder and bedsores. Preventive treatment includes physical therapy; sometimes a tracheotomy; anticoagulants, intermittent catheterization; and good nursing.

Although patients with spinal injuries may show some improvement in the first few days and continue to improve for a few months, it must be realized that severed nerve fibers in the spine cannot heal. The prevention of spinal injuries thus assumes great importance. This would seem to lie in the prevention of road accidents and the avoidance of diving into strange and murky waters.

First aid Also to be avoided is the unskilful movement of a person whose spine is broken. The victim is best left until expert help has arrived. In a grave emergency he may be lifted carefully, taking care that the spine does not flex and supporting the neck so that damage, or at least no further damage, is done to the spine.

Sprain

Commonly occurring during sporting activities, a sprain is an injury to a joint in which some of the fibers of the associated ligaments become stretched and torn, although the ligaments are not completely divided. The terms 'partial tear', 'rupture' and 'complete tear' are sometimes used.

The ankles and knees are the sites most frequently affected. Localized pain, swelling and a degree of loss of function are the usual symptoms, and there is often associated bruising.

Sporting activities are frequently the cause of sprains.

Treatment Initial treatment involves immobilization and elevation of the affected area and the application of ice. The ice should be wrapped in cloth rather than applied directly to the skin as excessive cold may damage the tissues. Cooling of the site of injury reduces pain, decreases the amount of swelling and reduces the degree of damage to affected tissues. The ice is generally applied at intervals for periods of 15 to 20 minutes and this treatment may be continued for 12 to 24 hours.

Other injuries need to be identified or their absence confirmed, particularly in the bones associated with the joint. In some cases a diagnostic x-ray is necessary.

Further treatment depends on the extent of the injury. Gradual mobilization is generally commenced one to two days after the injury, often together with measures such as physical therapy and the application of local heat. Strengthening exercises

The joint affected by a sprain will probably require treatment for several days.

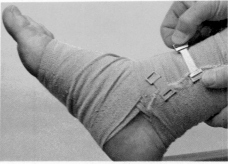

undertaken in a swimming pool are particularly helpful because excessive tension of the joints which may occur with weight-bearing is generally avoided. Care must be taken not to aggravate the initial injury. Specific anti-inflammatory or analgesic (pain-relieving) drugs may also be used.

Strain

An excessive stretching of muscle fibers leading in turn to pain, inflammation and the tearing of muscle fibers is called strain. However the term 'muscle tear' is generally restricted to a more severe separation of muscle fibers.

Commonly caused by unaccustomed or sudden exertion, especially in the absence of adequate 'warming up' exercises, strain is often characterized by severe and instantaneous pain. Any movement of the affected muscles aggravates the situation. Immediate treatment is to apply ice packs and to rest the injured muscle. Gentle exercises may usually be started after a day but care should be taken not to aggravate the initial injury. Physical therapy, ray lamps and local applications are all helpful treatment.

Mouth injuries are relatively common in contact sports.

Hong Kong, popular tourist stop. Holiday makers should take sensible precautions before travelling overseas.

Tooth and mouth injuries

Direct trauma to the mouth may cause lacerations and bleeding from the gums. Teeth may be chipped or dislodged, with resultant bleeding from the empty socket. Direct pressure usually controls the bleeding adequately. If bleeding is coming from the socket, control is best achieved by placing a small bandage or wad of cloth over the gap, and then pushing it firmly inwards with the other teeth by biting on it. The cloth should be left in place for about half an hour.

Bleeding sometimes occurs several hours after a tooth extraction, usually as a result of a dislodgement of a clot formed in the empty socket.

If a tooth has been knocked out of its socket, early replacement may enable the tooth to survive. A dentist should be seen as soon as possible.

Injuries to the mouth and teeth, such as those caused by the rim of a steering wheel during an accident, may result in obstruction of the airway and problems with respiration. Broken artificial dentures are a potential problem. Close attention needs to be given to the adequacy of breathing in these situations.

Traveling precautions

Traveling is associated with potential health problems, but the risks can be minimized by following simple precautions, such as adequate immunization prior to departure overseas, wearing of suitable protective clothing if the environment demands it, and avoidance of certain foods.

It is wise to prepare a small first aid kit prior to going overseas. Some of the preparations are available only on prescription, and it is a good idea to discuss their use and selection with your doctor. Adequate medical facilities are usually available in overseas centers, so an extensive kit is not required.

Soluble aspirin or acetaminophen are ideal pain-killers. Travel sickness may be a problem, and antihistamine tablets or other preparations to prevent this condition are available. Calamine lotion for minor itches, bites and stings and an antiseptic cream are worthwhile additions.

Travelers' diarrhea is a relatively common problem. It usually settles within 24 to 48 hours if the patient maintains a fluid-only diet, though an anti-diarrheal preparation may be needed for more severe cases.

Adhesive plasters, a couple of gauze dressings, scissors, and tweezers are also worth taking.

Unconsciousness

A patient who is unconscious is unaware of the environment and cannot be roused to consciousness by stimuli such as pain arising from inside or outside the body. As the depth of coma increases, more and more of the body's reflexes are lost until those that regulate breathing and the circulation of blood also fail.

Causes The area of the brain which governs consciousness, the ascending reticular activating system, is a network of nerve fibres in the brain stem and thalamus which relay sensation to the cortex, the site of conscious awareness of the environment. Coma may result from many causes which affect the functioning of these nerve cells.

Destruction of brain tissue may follow trauma, hemorrhage or interruption to blood supply as in infarction from a clot or embolus. Disturbance of normal metabolic processes also affects the functioning of the nerve cells such as in hypoglycemia or low blood sugar level; diabetic hyperglycemia or high blood sugar; myxedema coma resulting from untreated low production of thyroid hormone; and kidney or liver failure where substances which are toxic to the brain cells accumulate because these organs are unable to excrete or alter them into nontoxic products. External sources of toxic products may cause poisoning, for example in the ingestion of large quantities of alcohol or drugs such as barbiturates and narcotics or in the inhalation of carbon monoxide.

Epilepsy can result in transient coma because the brain cells are paralyzed following the generalized paroxysmal activity which occurs in a convulsion. Infection of the brain or its covering, tumors within the brain and certain neurological disorders such as multiple sclerosis may all result in coma.

Treatment The immediate care of the patient in a coma is to ensure that the airway is clear of the tongue and mucus. The person should be placed on his side in the 'coma' or 'recovery' position and immediate medical aid should be sought.

The care of a patient who is in a coma will initially involve placing him in the 'coma position' which ensures that the airways remain clear. *(Westmead Centre)*

Index

Dr James Witchalls MB, BS, D Obst RCOG

James Witchalls graduated from St Bartholomew's Hospital, in the City of London, in 1967. Since that time he has worked in hospital practice for three years including 18 months in the Albert Schweitzer Hospital in Gabon, West Africa, where he was mainly concerned with children. He has also worked for 10 years in General Practice in England where his main interest has been in maternity and child health. He has lectured extensively on First Aid and has participated in many conferences concerned with the health of children. He is currently involved with plans to establish a community health centre. Its concern will be the cultivation of health in a neighbourhood, rather than the investigation and treatment of disease.

First Aid
FAST & SIMPLE

Dr James Witchalls'
first-aid handbook for
childhood emergencies

Contents

Introduction

Childhood accidents are commoner today than ever before and a greater proportion of children die as a result of accidents than from any other single cause. This is partly because deaths from other causes have been drastically reduced during the past 50 years as medical science has made it possible for us to protect our children from a range of previously fatal diseases, such as diphtheria, whooping cough and pneumonia. Parallel with this desirable development, however, has been a corresponding increase in the exposure of children to mechanical and electrical appliances, such as motor cars, bicycles, electric kettles and fires, and household products which can be poisonous to children if consumed, such as disinfectants, cleaning agents and petroleum products. There has never been a greater need, therefore, for vigilance and preparedness to meet the emergency.

As a parent and doctor, with a special interest in the health and welfare of children, I find it all too common today that young parents are not sufficiently aware of the increasing sources of accidents and quite unprepared to take the necessary First Aid steps to deal with accidents until medical help is available. After all, the parent carrying out efficient First Aid is as likely to reduce injury and save the life of a child as the most skilful medical attention. Although prevention must remain our best defence against childhood injuries, nothing can, nor should, stop children from reaching out to explore their environment. Therefore accidents will happen at times, even in the safest situations.

This book, then, is designed to act as a practical guide to parents, baby-sitters, teachers and others dealing with children who at some time, usually unexpectedly, will be faced with a child who has had an accident.

The book will be most helpful to you if you familiarize yourself with the first section, Prepare Yourself, as soon as possible. **Do not wait for an accident to happen.** Always keep details of your children's medical history and a list of emergency telephone numbers and addresses – and keep them up-to-date. Use the section on the First Aid Kit as a guide to preparing your own – and keep it well stocked and easily accessible.

Mitchall

SECTION 1

Prepare yourself

Throughout this book symbols are used to indicate actions which must often be carried out in addition to basic first aid treatment. These may appear at the beginning of the sequence of actions, or at the end, depending upon the seriousness of the child's condition. They may also be used in conjunction. For example, where you are instructed to watch the child's breathing and give mouth-to-mouth resuscitation the symbols for checking breathing *and* emergency resuscitation or artificial respiration will both appear.

Remove to hospital

Check the breathing

Check the pulse

Apply heart compression

Apply artificial respiration

Clear the airway

Summon medical aid

Emergency action

First Aid consists of certain approved methods of treating a sick or injured child until he or she is placed, if necessary, in the care of a doctor or removed to hospital.

When faced with such an emergency act in the following sequence:

First Aid has three principle aims:

- To sustain life
- To prevent the condition from worsening
- To promote recovery

1 ASSESSMENT

Be calm and take charge of the situation, acting confidently and reassuring the child. Make sure that there is no further danger to the child, yourself, or any others who may be present. **Check for consciousness, breathing, pulse and bleeding.**

2 DIAGNOSIS

Find out what has happened — ask the child, if conscious, or a witness. In the event of illness, try to find out if the child has a history of illness. Examine for injury and record the level of consciousness, if necessary.

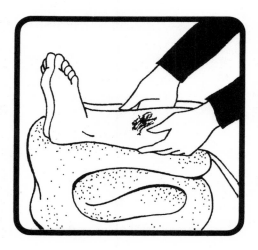

Emergency action

3 TREATMENT

Prevent the condition from becoming worse – cover wounds, immobilize fractures, place child in the correct and comfortable position. Promote recovery by reassuring, relieving pain, handling gently and carefully, protecting from cold.

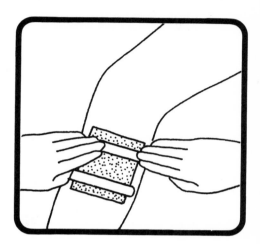

4 DISPOSAL

Ensure that the child is removed with minimum delay to home, suitable shelter or hospital. If necessary send a tactful message to the child's home stating the nature of accident or illness and where child has been removed to.

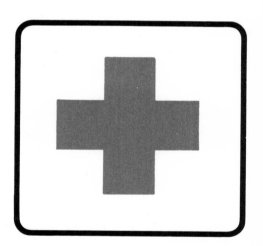

5 DO NOT

- Attempt too much
- Allow people to crowd around
- Remove the casualty's clothing unnecessarily
- Give anything by mouth to a child who is unconscious, has a suspected internal injury or may need an anaesthetic

Resuscitation

IMPORTANT

The first and most vital aim of resuscitation is artificial respiration (artificial breathing) which ensures that adequate air is getting to the lungs. Regular breathing must be established, or artificial respiration continued, to ensure that oxygen-containing blood reaches all parts of the body, especially the brain.

Make sure breathing has stopped: look at chest for movement and feel for breath from mouth — use the back of your hand or a small mirror

1 Quickly remove any obstruction from the airway; eg plastic bag, pillow, constriction around neck, teeth, blood, foreign body, vomit from mouth. Check that the airway is not blocked by the tongue.

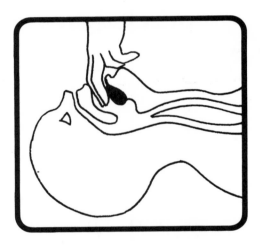

2 Lay the child flat on back on a firm surface; eg floor or table. Remove all pillows.

Resuscitation

3 SMALL CHILDREN

Slightly tilt head back, place your open mouth firmly over child's mouth and nose so that there is no air gap around the edges of your mouth.

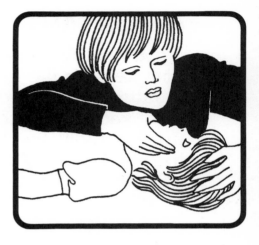

4

Gently huff air from your lungs into child until child's chest rises. Remove your mouth and watch the chest fall. Repeat 4 times taking about 2 seconds over each breath. Watch for spontaneous breathing from child. Repeat until breathing recommences.

5 OLDER CHILDREN

Carry out the above procedure but place your open mouth over the child's mouth only. With one hand firmly pinch the child's nose to prevent air escaping through his nose. Take 3 seconds over each breath.

Resuscitation

IMPORTANT

If two First Aiders are present, one compressing the heart and the other breathing into the child, maintain a strict sequence of compressions of the heart followed by breathing into the child. DO NOT CHANGE SEQUENCE OR OVERLAP YOUR ACTIONS.

Check for pulse (see page 14): if pulse is present but casualty is not breathing, continue to give artificial respiration until natural breathing recommences

1 If heart is not beating, first thump the lower part of the front of the chest firmly with the edge of your hand. Re-check the pulse. If no response to this thump, begin external heart compression at once.

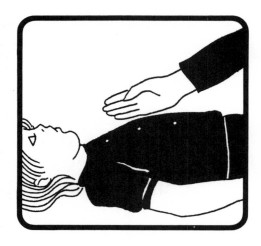

2 ## YOUNG CHILDREN

Place your index and middle fingers over the middle part of the child's breastbone.

Resuscitation

3 Make short, quick thrusts down towards the backbone, moving 12-18mm each time, 5 times every 3 seconds. After 5 compressions, if natural breathing is not yet restored, give three artificial breaths.

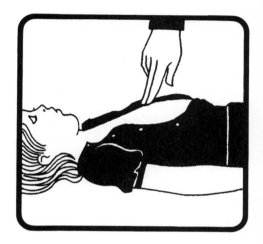

4 Check pulse. Give a further 5 compressions of the heart if necessary. Continue this sequence until medical help arrives or until the natural function of the lungs and heart returns.

5 **OLDER CHILDREN**

Use the heel of one hand to compress breastbone. Compress 5 times every 4 seconds. Otherwise the technique is the same as described for younger children.

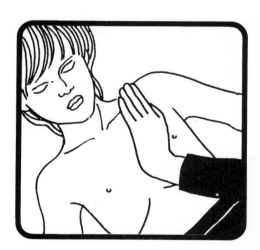

The pulse

IMPORTANT

The heart beats about 90 to 110 times each minute in a young child and about 80 to 100 times each minute in an older child. Each heartbeat forces blood around the arteries of the body and can be felt as a pressure wave over several points of the body.

There is no need to take the pulse for a whole minute. It should be sufficient to take it for 10 seconds and multiply the result by 6

1 The WRIST is the commonest place to feel the pulse. Gently press the tips of your index and middle fingers over the under side of the wrist at the base of the thumb.

2 NECK: Place your thumb around the back of the child's neck and place your index or middle finger on the side of the neck next to the windpipe and gently press towards your thumb.

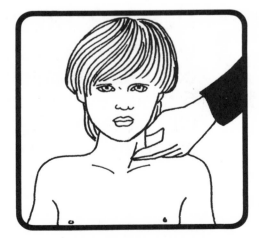

The pulse

3 Above COLLARBONE: hook your index finger over the top of the child's collarbone and gently press into the soft depression above.

4 ARM: Hold the upper arm as shown in the diagram and gently press your index and middle fingers against the arm bone.

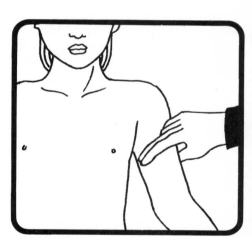

5 GROIN: Gently press your index and middle fingers over the middle of the groin fold.

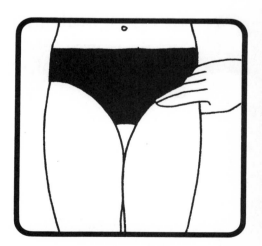

Unconsciousness

The first stage of unconsciousness is *drowsiness,* from which the child may easily be roused; the next stage is *stupor,* from which the child may be roused only with difficulty; the most serious and advanced stage is *coma,* from which the child cannot be roused at all. Unless the child is fully alert, or can be roused, treat as if unconscious.

The first aim, in dealing with any unconscious child, is to ensure an open airway and summon immediate medical aid

1 Check airway, breathing and pulse.

2 Loosen clothing around the neck, chest and waist and ensure that plenty of fresh air is available.

Unconsciousness

3 Lay child in the position shown here – the Recovery Position – preferably with the lower part of the body slightly raised above the head. This will ensure that vomit or saliva does not flow into the lungs. Do not provide pillows and keep the head flexed slightly backwards.

4 Cover with a blanket and stay with the child until medical help arrives. Never leave an unconscious child unattended.

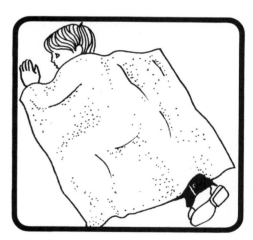

5 If consciousness returns, speak reassuringly to the child, moisten his lips and prevent him from hurting himself. Do not attempt to give a drink to an unconscious child.

Temperature

IMPORTANT

The normal body temperature is 37°C (98.4°F), but it may vary by ½°C (1°F) without indicating any abnormality. Those slight variations may occur, for example, in the early morning (lower) or in very hot weather, after severe exertion or after hot meals (higher). Feeling the skin gives only a general guide to body temperature.

If the body temperature is below 36°C (96.8°F) or above 39.5°C (103°F), seek medical advice

When warmed, the mercury in the bulb of the thermometer expands and pushes up through the narrow hollow centre of the thermometer. It shrinks on cooling. Rotate the thermometer slowly between your fingers until you see the tip of the column of mercury against the scale on the side.

UNDER THE ARM: Place the bulb of the thermometer high under the armpit and support it by pressing the child's arm against its chest. Read after about 2 minutes. *This method usually shows a temperature ½°C (1°F) lower than normal.*

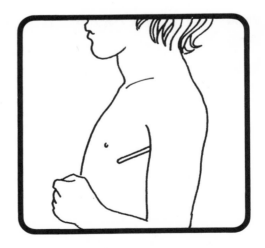

Abnormally low temperatures are frequently brought about by shock, severe bleeding or exposure

Temperature

IN THE GROIN: Place the bulb of the thermometer in the skin fold of the groin and gently hold the legs of the child together. Read after 2 minutes. *This method usually shows a temperature ½°C (1°F) lower than normal.*

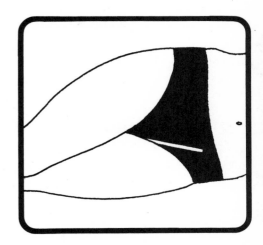

IN THE MOUTH: (Suitable in children over 5 years old.) Place the bulb of the thermometer under one side of the tongue on the floor of the mouth. Support the thermometer between gently closed lips. Read after 2 minutes.

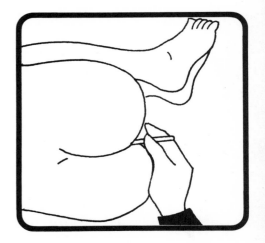

IN THE RECTUM: (At any age but especially in babies and infants.) Gently slip the bulb of the thermometer through the anus into the rectum (about 2.5 cm/1 inch) and support it there for 1 minute.
This will result in a temperature reading ½° C (1° F) higher than normal.

Abnormally high temperatures occur during 'teething' and a variety of general body infections

First aid kit

The kit shown here is recommended for *all* households. Other items, not illustrated, may be added for special purposes, but for basic First Aid requirements this kit should be adequate. Keep it well stocked and replace the disposable items as they are used. Keep a separate kit in your car or boat and for hiking and camping.

BASIC KIT

1 Absorbent cotton.
2 Adhesive strip plasters — assorted sizes.
3 Adhesive tape — 1.2 cm (½″) or 2.5 cm (1″) wide.
4 Calamine lotion.
5 Cotton tipped swabs.
6 Children's aspirin/paracetamol — according to doctor's advice — but not for infants under 1 year old.
7 Disinfectant
8 Oil of cloves — for minor toothache.
9 Rubbing alcohol or Cologne.
10 Triangular bandages — for tying splints.
11 Safety pins
12 Sharp needles — to remove splinters: sterilize first.
13 Sharp scissors with rounded ends.
14 Sterile eye pads.
15 Sterile gauze bandages — 2.5 cm (1″) and 5 cm (2″).
16 Sterile gauze pads — 5 cm (2″) and 10 cm (4″) square.
17 Thermometer.
18 Tongue depressors — wooden.
19 Tweezers.

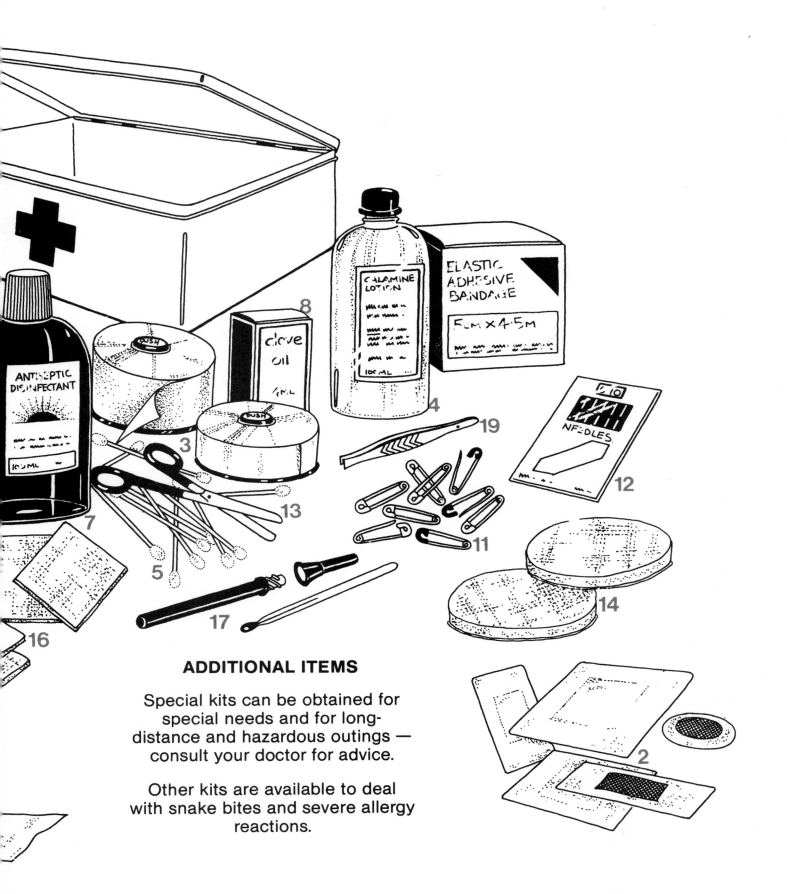

ADDITIONAL ITEMS

Special kits can be obtained for special needs and for long-distance and hazardous outings — consult your doctor for advice.

Other kits are available to deal with snake bites and severe allergy reactions.

Bandages

Bandages may be made from flannel, calico, elastic net or special paper. They can also be improvised from any of these materials or from socks, stockings, ties, belts, scarves etc.

Bandages are used chiefly to control bleeding by maintaining direct pressure over a dressing and to retain dressings and splints in position. They may also be used to prevent and reduce swellings, to give support to a limb or joint, to restrict movement and assist in lifting or carrying casualties. *Never use bandages for padding when other materials are on hand.*

APPLICATION: Bandages must be applied firmly enough to control bleeding and to prevent dressings and splints from slipping. If they are too tight, circulation will be impeded and the underlying part injured. If the toes or fingers become white or blueish, or become numb, loosen the bandage a little.

TYING BANDAGES: All bandages of this type should be tied with a reef knot, which does not slip, is flat and is easy to untie. The knot should be placed away from the injured part and should not cause discomfort. For their various uses see page 86, Fractures.

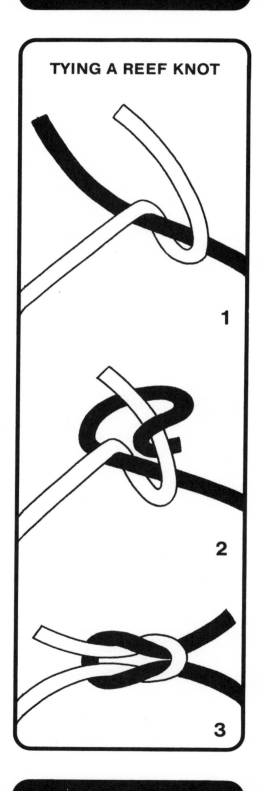

TYING A REEF KNOT

1

2

3

Bandages

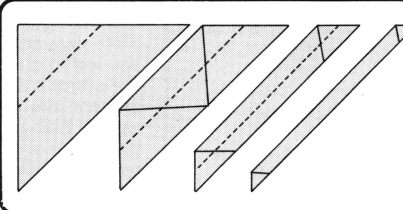

Triangular bandages can be made from squares of linen or calico – between 50 cm (20") and 1 m (3 ft.) square — cut diagonally into two pieces. They can be used as slings or folded to make either broad or narrow bandages.

Narrow bandages are not only useful for binding wounds and holding dressings in position, they are ideal for tying around splints and protective padding.

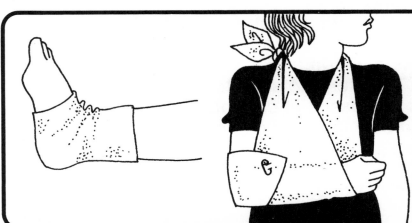

Elasticated bandages can be used to support injured joints – sprained ankles or wrists, for example. Slings can be bought ready-made or they can be adapted from triangular bandages.

Dressings

A dressing should be germ free (sterile), if possible, and able to act as a filter – restricting entry of germs but allowing air to reach the wound. It must also be very porous in order to absorb blood and sweat. If sweat cannot evaporate through it, an infection can set in. It should also be of a non-adherent material so that it will not damage the repairing wound.

> A dressing is a protective covering applied to a wound to control bleeding, prevent infection, absorb blood and discharge and prevent further damage

Adhesive dressings : These are often called 'plasters'; eg band aids and consist of a pad of absorbent gauze or cellulose with an adhesive backing which, if perforated, allows sweat to evaporate. The surrounding skin should be dry before application. When a dressing has no sticking power of its own it must be held in place by a bandage.

Prepared sterile dressings consist of layers of gauze covered by a pad of cotton wool and come with a roller bandage to tie them in position.

Plain gauze dressings come in a variety of sizes. They tend to stick to wounds but this can assist in clotting.

Vaseline gauze dressings are sold in squares in sealed packs. They are available in a number of different sizes and they do not stick to wounds.

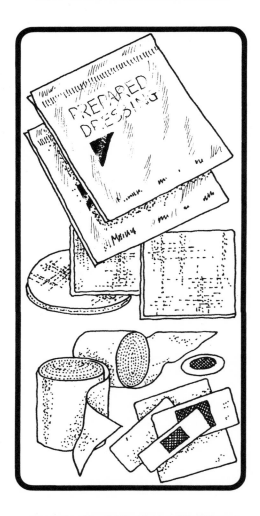

Dressings

IMPROVISED DRESSINGS

These are important because accidents tend to happen when and where ideal equipment is not available. Dressings may be improvised from clean hankies, freshly laundered towels or linen or any other clean absorbent material. Keep them in position with whatever material is to hand.

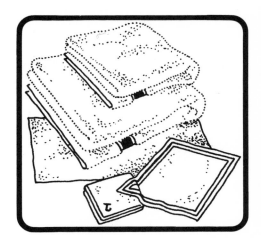

HANDLING DRESSINGS

Wash your hands before handling dressings and bandages, and avoid touching wounds with fingers. Dressings should be covered with adequate padding, extending well beyond the wound and held in place with a bandage.

CREAM AND OINTMENTS

In general, minor wounds are best cleaned with soap and water — creams and ointments should be unnecessary. Infected wounds need an antibiotic cream but these can only be obtained from your doctor.

Seek medical advice if you are in doubt about the use of any application

Aids to survival

HEAT

Do not undergo strenuous exertion during the hottest period of the day. Drink more water than usual and take salt tablets if necessary. A rest after lunch, in the shade, should be encouraged.

Acclimatize gradually before sudden exposure to heat, especially moist heat

Wear loose cotton clothing over the whole of the trunk, and a lightweight hat, preferably with a brim. Open shoes or sandals will be beneficial.

COLD

If possible, acclimatize gradually to conditions of extreme cold. Wear several layers of light woollen or cotton over-garments and soft woollen underclothing. Several light layers are better than one thick, heavy garment.

Aids to survival

Cover the extremities of the body, hands head and ears and wear comfortable, waterproof leather shoes or boots.

Do not sit or stand around in cold conditions and have plenty of warm drinks and high calorie foods.

Remove wet clothing as soon as possible and, on hikes or long walks, carry a large plastic bag – big enough to accommodate a child suffering from exposure.

Children should be encouraged to wear brightly coloured garments so that they may be easily seen

Aids to survival

Water in all forms attracts children, but any water of a greater depth than a few inches presents considerable dangers. If you always observe the following rules, however, your children should be able to enjoy water safely.

Teach your children to swim as soon as possible

- Avoid unsupervised exposure of young children to water any deeper than 5 cm (2 inches). Never leave a baby alone near water for a moment — a drowning accident can happen in seconds.
- If the telephone rings while bathing baby, wrap him in towel and carry with you to telephone. Similarly when answering the door bell.
- Never let your young children play around cesspools, puddles, ditches or wells.
- Keep swimming pools covered with hard cover during months when not in use.
- Forbid your young children to enter neighbours' swimming pools unless permission is given.
- Never let a toddler run loose near a pool.
- Know of the depth of a pool before letting your child enter the water.
- Encourage your child to use inflated tubes, rafts or armbands under supervision
- Never let your child go swimming alone.
- Never allow a child to get out of its depth unless well able to swim.
- Keep all children out of boats unless supervised.
- Supervise all fishing expeditions – never let a child go fishing alone.
- Young children should always wear a life-jacket if taken out on a boating or canoeing trip.

Rescue

1 Try to reach the child from land – using a hand, leg, clothing, pole, rope or anything that floats. If child is unconscious and not breathing, begin resuscitation at once. See page 10.

2 When rescuing older children from water, try to avoid being clutched by them as they struggle.

3 If you swim out to a child keep a close eye on the spot where you last saw the child. If possible take a life-buoy, or something that floats, with you for the child to hang on to.

Childhood illnesses

ILLNESS	SYMPTOMS	INCUBATION	DURATION
● **Appendicitis** (Unusual under the age of 2 yrs)	Sudden onset of pain in centre of stomach, which moves after some hours to the lower right side; fever; vomiting; constipation; refusal of food.	None	Seek immediate medical attention
● **Chickenpox**	Fever accompanied by itchy pink or red spots on chest, back and stomach – sometimes spreading to scalp and face. These change to blisters and then crust.	10 to 21 days	7 to 10 days
● **Croup**	Laboured breathing accompanied by loud hacking cough and hoarseness. Often comes on at night.	2 to 6 days	4 to 5 days
● **German Measles** (Rubella)	Painful swelling of glands behind the ears accompanied by low or high fever, chills and runny nose. Usually there is a fine red rash, which begins on the face and spreads over entire body.	14 to 21 days	3 to 6 days
● **Measles**	Early symptoms include low fever accompanied by slight hacking cough, fatigue, discomfort and eye irritation. Around the 4th day, fever and cough worsen and rash of faint pink spots appears on neck and cheeks then spreads to rest of body.	10 to 15 days	8 to 12 days
● **Mumps**	Swollen gland on one or both sides of the jaw accompanied by headache and fever.	12 to 24 days	6 to 10 days
● **Pneumonia**	Coughing plus fever; rapid breathing; discomfort; chills and weakness; possible nausea and vomiting; sudden fever lasting several days.	2 to 14 days	About 7 days
● **Scarlet Fever**	Painful sore throat accompanied by fever; nausea and vomiting. Within 3 days a fine rash appears on neck, armpit and groin, then spreads over body.	1 to 5 days	6 to 8 days
● **Tonsillitis** (Pharyngitis in babies)	Painful sore throat; fever; tender swollen glands under sides of jaw; refusal to eat and drink; nausea and vomiting.	2 to 5 days	About 5 to 7 days
● **Whooping Cough** (Pertussis)	Dry persistent cough for 7 to 14 days becoming a whoop in older children; watery runny nose; child distressed and exhausted; vomiting.	7 to 10 days	Several weeks

INFECTIOUS FOR	TREATMENT	PRECAUTIONS
Not infectious	Seek immediate medical attention; give nothing to eat or drink.	
1 day before spots appear to about 6 days after	Consult your doctor. Rest is essential; calamine will relieve itching.	Keep all utensils separate.
2 days before symptoms appear to 5 days after	Consult your doctor. Use a vaporizer and keep child on a light, low fat diet.	
7 days before symptoms appear to 5 days after. Dangerous to pregnant women	If the child has fever, make sure he rests and supply plenty of juice.	Keep child's hands clean. Launder linen and clothes separately.
4 days before rash appears to 5 days after	Consult your doctor. If child's eyes are sensitive to light, keep the room dim. If fever occurs make sure he rests and give him plenty of juice.	Keep all utensils and dishes separate.
7 days before symptoms appear to 5 days after	Consult your doctor. Rest is essential. Apply cool compresses to the cheeks. Do not give citrus juices.	
Varies	Consult your doctor. Make sure the child rests and give him plenty of fluids.	Keep all utensils and dishes separate
1 day before symptoms appear to 6 days after	Consult your doctor. Make sure child rests and give plenty of fluids.	Check other family members for symptoms.
From day of onset until throat clears, about 7 days	Consult your doctor. Usually antibiotics given.	Keep eating and drinking utensils and toothbrush separate.
From 4 days before onset until 28 days after onset	Seek medical attention and follow advice.	Small frequent feeds to reduce chance of vomiting.

● After infection, immunity to re-infection usually lasts through childhood

Immunization

These days all children can and should be protected against a number of serious infectious diseases. You are strongly advised to have all your children immunized against the following diseases at all times indicated. Consult your doctor, health visitor, Child Welfare Clinic or Baby Health Centre for advice.

This schedule is meant as a guide only — if in doubt seek medical advice

AGE	DISEASE	AGENT
2 months	Pertussis-Diptheria-Tetanus Poliomyelitis	Triple Antigen* Sabin Oral Vaccine
4 months	Pertussis-Diptheria-Tetanus Poliomyelitis	Triple Antigen* Sabin Oral Vaccine
6 months	Pertussis-Diptheria-Tetanus Poliomyelitis	Triple Antigen* Sabin Oral Vaccine
12 months	Measles	Measles virus vaccine, live attenuated (Schwarz strain)
18 months	Diptheria-Tetanus	Diptheria and Tetanus Toxoid Vaccine (CDT)
School entry	Diptheria-Tetanus Poliomyelitis	Diptheria and Tetanus Toxoid Vaccine (CDT) Sabin Oral Vaccine

*Pertussis (Whooping Cough) vaccine or Triple Antigen should not be used, but replaced by CDT for children with the following:
1 A previous history of neurological disease, including seizures, convulsions or cerebral irritation in the neonatal period.
2 A previous reaction to the vaccine other than minor local reactions and/or mild fever.
These children should be given CDT injections at 4 months, 6 months and 18 months of age.

- If there is a measles epidemic consult your doctor
- If you plan to travel abroad with your child consult your doctor well in advance
- If your child has a large skin wound, consult your doctor about the need for a Tetanus booster injection

SECTION 2
What to do

In this section you will find practical instruction on how to deal with a wide range of emergencies. Each important stage of treatment is accompanied by an explicit illustration or by a symbol referring to one of the life-saving methods explained in Section 1. Reading the book through *before* an emergency occurs is not only advisable, but necessary — you cannot deal with a serious burn, for example, with your First Aid manuel propped up like a cook book!

Asphyxia

SYMPTOMS OF ASPHYXIA

Breathing: Rate, depth and difficulty increase and later breathing becomes noisy with frothing at the mouth. Finally, breathing stops.

Congestion: The head and neck, face, lips and whites of eyes become red and eventually turn purple. Finger and toenail beds become purple.

Heartbeat: Becomes fast, then weak and finally stops.

Unconsciousness: Drowsiness is followed by stupor, then unrousable coma ending in death.

The commonest causes of asphyxia are spasms of the breathing tract, obstruction of the airway, suffocation and conditions which prevent oxygen use by the body. *Spasms* may be caused by food, water, smoke, irritant gases, asthma and some chest infections.
Obstruction of the airway may be caused by swallowed foreign bodies, food, teeth, blood, vomit, swellings and even the child's tongue.
Suffocation may be caused by pillows and plastic bags and *oxygen use* may be impeded by car exhausts, gas supplies, chemical fumes and smoke.

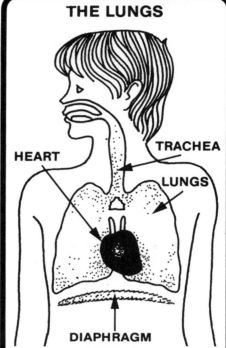

THE LUNGS

HEART

TRACHEA

LUNGS

DIAPHRAGM

In normal breathing, air passes through the windpipe into the lungs. The diaphragm, during inhaling, moves down and flattens out causing a partial vacuum in the lungs. Air is drawn in to equalize the pressure. During exhaling, the elastic tissue of the walls of the lungs enables them to deflate. Asphyxia occurs when an adequate supply of oxygen is not available to the body's blood supply. It may be due to a shortage of oxygen in the air breathed or to inadequate functioning of the heart and lungs.

Asphyxia

1 ## ACTION
CLEAR THE AIRWAY — Make sure that nothing is obstructing the air flow from the mouth and throat through to the lungs.
See page 10.

2 ENSURE AIR FLOW TO LUNGS — Begin artificial respiration without delay — seconds count.
See page 10.

3 RESTART THE HEARTBEAT — If no pulse can be felt, by artificially pumping the heart if necessary.
See page 12.

Asthma

IMPORTANT

Asthma occurs commonly in childhood and is due to exertion, emotion, allergy or infection or a combination of all three.

Symptoms: Sudden attack of tight, difficult breathing — often occurring at night; difficulty in forcing air *out* of lungs; anxiety; pale and clammy skin; rapid pulse; blueness around lips.

Common causes of asthma due to allergies are feathers, house dust, pollens and milk products

1 Sit or prop child up comfortably — leaning forward and resting on a table, pillow or back of a chair — but keep back straight.

2 Calm and reassure the child and ensure quiet surroundings. Allow plenty of fresh air — cigarette smoke, dust and cooking smells can make it worse.

Asthma

3 Give hot drinks to ease the tension.

4 Give asthma relieving drugs if these are present and the dose is known.

5 Summon medical help if severity of attack demands.
Watch the breathing: if it stops give artificial respiration — see page 10.
Check the pulse: if it stops apply heart compression – see page 12.

Bites & stings

IMPORTANT

If the skin has been penetrated, seek immediate medical advice.

Do not underestimate the severity of human bites — they can be particularly dangerous.

In countries where *rabies* may be present, all children bitten by dogs should be referred for special serum treatment. Try to capture or confine the offending animal for examination

1 Calm, reassure and lay the child down. Wash the wound well with soap and water. Gently dry. Do not apply antiseptic creams and ointments.

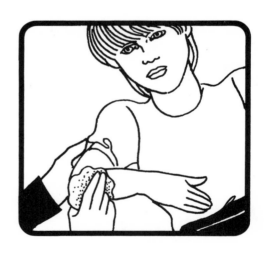

2 Cover with sterile gauze or a clean cloth and hold in place with adhesive tape or bandage.

Watch for shock — see page 116 for treatment

Bites & stings

BEDBUGS, SAND FLIES & MOSQUITOES

Symptoms: Vary from itchy red spots to mildly painful swellings.

Seek medical advice if child suffers an allergic reaction to any insect bites

1 Wash the affected area with soap and water. Apply cold compresses if swellings are present.

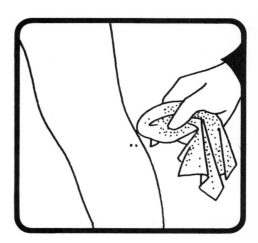

2 Apply calamine lotion, eau de Cologne or cheap perfume. Use antihistamine tablets if the bites are very itchy.

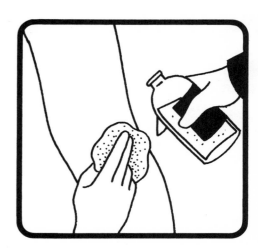

Bites & stings

BEES, HORNETS, WASPS

Symptoms: Sudden pricking pain which may become severe, local swelling, burning and itching.

Some children have an allergic reaction to bee and wasp stings. Seek medical advice if symptoms are severe

1 Remove the sting, if present, with fingernails, tweezers, forceps or the point of a sterilized needle.

2 Do not squeeze or rub the skin.

Bites & stings

3 If nothing else is available rub the fresh-cut surface of an onion over the sting or apply a cold water compress.

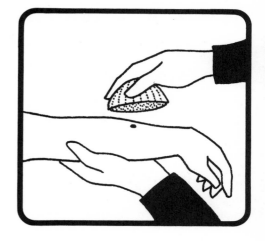

4 If the sting is in the mouth rinse well with mouthwash made up of one teaspoonful of bicarbonate of soda in a tumbler of cold water.

5 Watch for signs of shock and, if necessary give the treatment described on page 116. Watch the breathing: if it stops give artificial respiration — see page 10.

Bites & stings

BLACK WIDOW, BROWN RECLUSE & TARANTULA

Symptoms: Severe pain, profuse sweating, muscle cramps, nausea and sometimes breathing difficulties. Follow the procedure below and transport the child to hospital immediately.

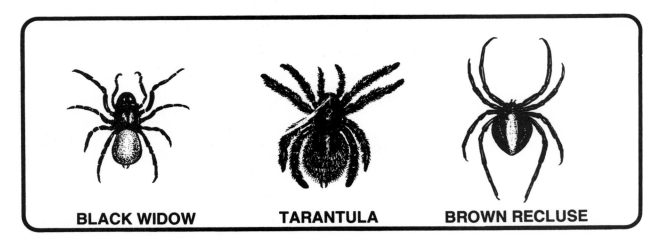

BLACK WIDOW   **TARANTULA**   **BROWN RECLUSE**

1 Calm, reassure the child and support the affected part below heart level.

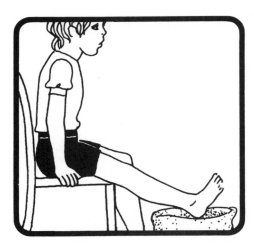

Bites & stings

2 If the bite is on the arm or leg, firmly apply a bandage, beginning at least 30 cm (12 inches) above the bite, and wind it around the site of the bite, finishing at least 30 cm (12 inches) below it. This will localize the venom to the bitten area and prevent it spreading to other parts of the body.

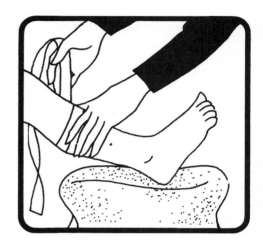

3 Splint the limb to immobilize it completely. Transport the child to hospital, moving him, and particularly the bitten limb, as little as possible.

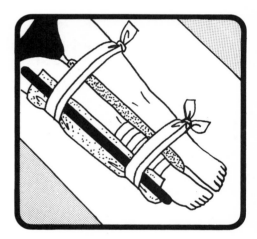

4 Watch the breathing: if it stops give artificial respiration — see page 10.
Check the pulse: if it stops apply heart compression – see page 12.
Watch for signs of shock and, if necessary give the treatment described on page 116.

Bites & stings

Seek immediate medical advice.

Symptoms: Severe pain at site of sting. Swelling, fever, nausea and stomach pains. Difficulty in speaking, convulsions and coma.

SCORPION

Treat as for spider bites on previous pages and again check breathing and pulse.

Bites & stings

Symptoms: Pin prick and irritation. The tick may be visible on the skin. Ticks, which are most active in Spring and Summer, rarely cause paralysis in humans.

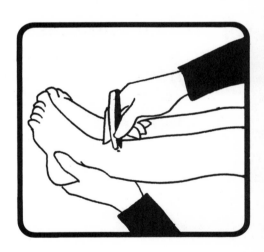

TICK

1 Do not try to remove tick from skin immediately. Apply a thick oil (eg olive oil or kerosene) to surface, then remove ticks some minutes later with tweezers.

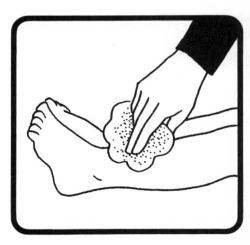

2 Wash with soap and water.

Bites & stings

CONE SHELL & SEA URCHIN

Symptoms: Vary from slight sting to severe pain, tingling and numbness, difficulty in swallowing, tightness in the chest, partial paralysis, blurring of vision and collapse.

In all cases of stings or bites from marine creatures seek immediate medical advice: it is not always possible to know the nature of the offending creature

1 Calm and reassure the child. Carry to safety and comfort. If the sting is on the arm or leg, treat as for spider bites — see page 44/5.

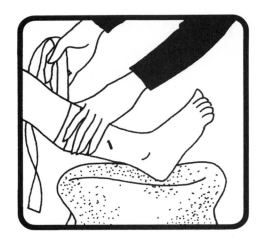

2 Transport to hospital, moving the child, and particularly the affected limb, as little as possible.

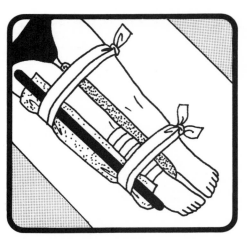

Bites & stings

JELLYFISH & PORTUGUESE MAN-OF-WAR

Symptoms: Sudden burning pain; rash and swelling; difficulty in breathing; nausea and vomiting, cramps and collapse.

ACTION: Apply vinegar to the area before attempting to remove any pieces of adherent tentacle. Make the child comfortable and give warm drinks.

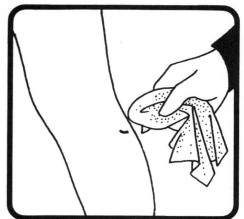

SEA ANEMONE & HYDROID

Symptoms: Sudden stinging or burning pain. Sometimes chills, stomach cramps and diarrhea.

ACTION: Soak in hot water or apply hot compresses.

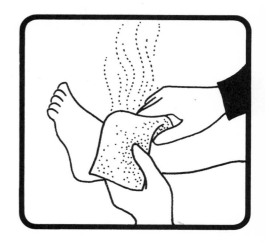

Watch the breathing: if it stops give artificial respiration — see page 10.
Check the pulse: if it stops apply heart compression – see page 12.
Watch for signs of shock and, if necessary give the treatment described on page 116.

Bites & stings

Seek immediate medical advice.

STINGING CORAL

Symptoms: Local burning or stinging pain.

ACTION: Wash with soap and water and apply alcohol or surgical spirit.

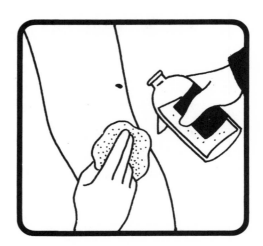

STINGRAY

Symptoms: Sudden pain, swelling and redness around wound; nausea and vomiting. Sometimes muscle spasms, convulsions and breathing difficulties.

1 Carefully remove the stinger if possible.

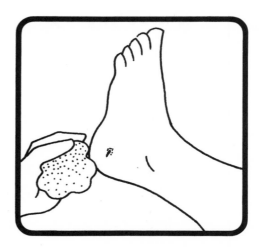

Bites & stings

2 Control bleeding if necessary (see page 54). Otherwise treat as for spider bites (see page 44).

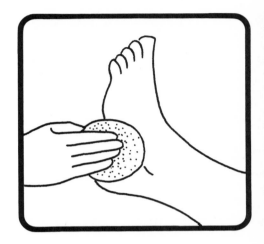

3 Watch the breathing: if it stops give artificial respiration — see page 10.
Check the pulse: if it stops apply heart compression – see page 12.
Watch for signs of shock and, if necessary give the treatment described on page 116.

OCTOPUS

Symptoms: Weakness of the muscles and numbness about the face and neck, breathing becomes progressively more difficult. As soon as this happens, begin artificial respiration (see page 10) which may have to be maintained until the paralysis wears off.

Bites & stings

IMPORTANT

In all cases of snakebite, especially if the snake is known to be poisonous, seek immediate medical attention.
Symptoms: Varying degrees of pain and swelling. Can be nausea and vomiting, weakness, blurring of vision and sweating, difficulty in breathing, slurring of speech, paralysis and convulsions.

1 Calm, reassure and lay the child down. Move the affected part as little as possible.

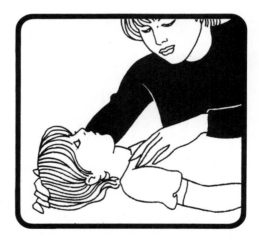

2 Firmly apply a bandage beginning at least 30 cm (12 inches) above the bite and wind it down towards the end of the limb, over the bitten area, to finish about 30 cm (12 inches) below the bite.

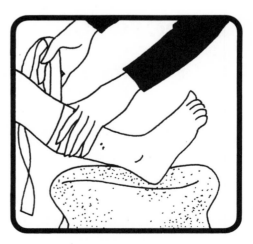

Serious poisoning is comparatively rare in man because significant quantities of venom are seldom injected

Bites & stings

3 Splint the limb to immobilize it completely. Transport the child to the nearest medical aid, moving the bitten limb as little as possible.

4 Bring the snake if it has been killed. Handle by the tail and place in a bag or sack.

5 Watch the breathing: if it stops give artificial respiration — see page 10.
Watch for signs of shock and, if necessary give the treatment described on page 116.

Fear of death is a common reaction to snakebite and tends to accelerate the effect of the venom

Bleeding

IMPORTANT

Any bleeding can look alarming — it is nature's way of shouting for help — but bleeding from a small wound will usually stop of its own accord after about 30 seconds and can be easily controlled by local pressure. Abrasions and minor cuts are best left open to the air and kept dry, unless they occur beneath clothing.

Send for medical help only if the bleeding cannot be stopped within a few minutes

1 Rest, comfort and reassure the child.

2 If the wound is dirty, gently wash for a few seconds in running water.

Bleeding

3 Press clean gauze or cloth directly over wound and dry the surrounding area if previously bathed.

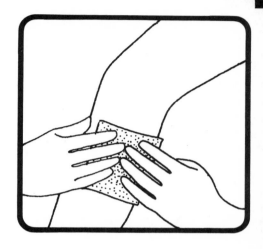

4 Replace soaked gauze with a clean dressing and attach with adhesive plaster or bandage.

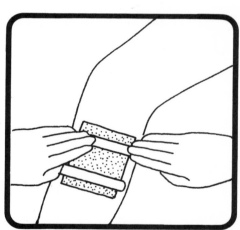

5 Elevate and support the injured part above heart level.

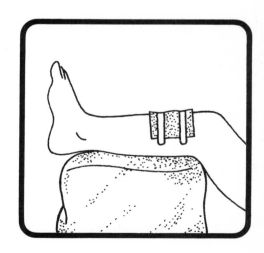

Bleeding

Aim to stop the bleeding and obtain medical help at once. Move the child as little as possible, especially if an underlying fracture is suspected.

Symptoms: Where much blood has been lost, the face and lips become pale, the skin is cold and clammy, the child feels faint or dizzy, can become restless, thirsty, sick and has a rapid, weak pulse with shallow breathing.

1 Lay the child down and give comfort and reassurance. Immediately apply direct pressure over the bleeding area with whatever clean tissue comes to hand, for 5 to 15 minutes.

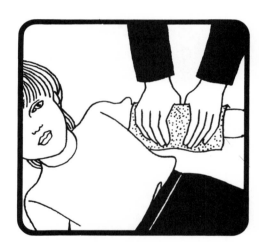

2 Raise and support the injured part, unless an underlying fracture is suspected. Any visible foreign bodies that can be picked out or wiped off should be removed.

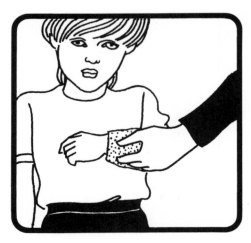

Do not give drinks — sips only — as the child may need an anaesthetic before wound is stitched

Bleeding

3 Apply a clean dressing and press this firmly over the wound. Cover this with a pad of soft material and retain in place with firm bandaging. Make sure the whole wound is covered. If bleeding continues, apply further firm dressings and bandage over the original.

4 Immobilize an arm in a sling, or a leg by tying to its fellow with adequate padding.

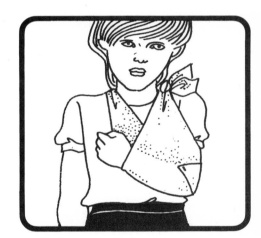

5 Watch the breathing: if it stops give emergency resuscitation – see page 10.

Check the pulse: if it stops apply heart compression – see page 12.

Watch for signs of shock and, if necessary give the treatment described on page 116.

Virtually all bleeding can be stopped by pressure upon the wound. Tourniquets are dangerous and should not be used

Bleeding

If internal bleeding is suspected, summon immediate medical aid. Internal bleeding may be suspected if a child has a broken bone or has sustained a sharp blow, knife or bullet wound to the head, chest or abdomen.

Symptoms vary according to the location of the bleeding:

* HEAD: Severe headache, dizziness, vomiting, double vision, loss of consciousness.
* CHEST: Bright red foamy blood is coughed up.
* STOMACH: Bright, dark or 'coffee-grounds' coloured vomit.
* INTESTINES: Black tar-coloured stools.
* SPLEEN, LIVER: No visible bleeding: child becomes rapidly shocked and may have stomach pain.

Internal bleeding can also occur as a result of certain medical conditions. If in doubt consult your doctor immediately

1 Place child at complete rest with legs slightly raised and loosen any tight clothing. Calm and reassure the child.

Look for other injuries and treat as necessary.

Bleeding

2 Protect from cold.

3 Give nothing to drink.

4 Watch the breathing: if it stops give artificial respiration — see page 10.
Check the pulse: if it stops apply heart compression – see page 12.

Bleeding

IMPORTANT

Bleeding from the nose is very common and does not usually denote anything serious. It is usually due to a ruptured blood vessel in the *septum* which divides the nostrils. However, it is possible that severe head injuries may cause blood to trickle from the nose.

Seek immediate medical advice if a fracture is suspected

1 Place the child in a sitting position with head slightly backward.

2 Tell him to pinch firmly the soft part of his nose for about 10 minutes and to breathe through his mouth.

Bleeding

3 Loosen any tight clothing.

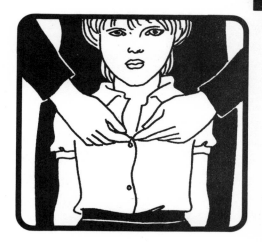

4 Apply a cold compress over forehead and bridge of nose. Warn the child not to blow his nose for some hours and not to pick it.

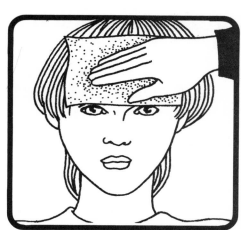

5 If the bleeding does not stop within about 15 minutes, seek prompt medical advice.

Burns & scalds

IMPORTANT

Take the child to hospital immediately if the burn is more than very slight. Burns may be **deep** or **superficial**: deep burns usually destroy nerve endings and are least painful; superficial burns, involving only the outer layers of skin, are most painful and can result in considerable fluid loss.

1 Gently flood the affected area immediately with cold water (not ice). Continue for 5-10 minutes or until the pain stops. Do not apply pressure over burned skin, or try to remove nylon clothing which has become stuck to the skin.

2 Remove promptly any tight clothing over the area, such as rings, bangles, belts and shoes. Carefully remove any clothing which has been soaked in boiling water. Do not try to remove damaged tissue or break blisters.

Burns & scalds

3 Cover loosely with a clean dry dressing, such as gauze, handkerchief, pillow case or strip of sheet. Elevate and support injured arms or legs higher than the chest. Do not apply any home remedies such as ointments and antiseptic creams.

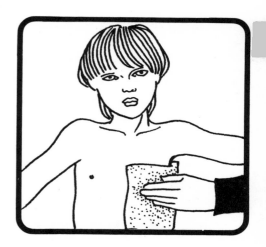

4 Give frequent small cold drinks if burns are bad. This will help to replace fluid loss.

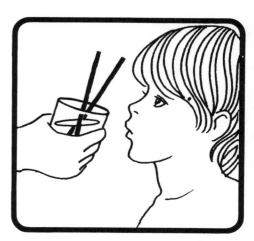

5 Watch the breathing: if it stops give artificial respiration — see page 10.

Watch for signs of shock and, if necessary give the treatment described on page 116.

Chest injuries

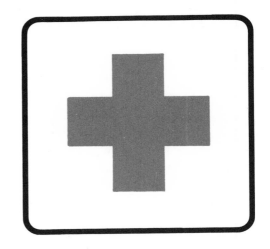

IMPORTANT

If any severe injury to chest, or fracture to rib(s) is suspected take the child to hospital immediately. Symptoms may include pain in chest on breathing and severe pain on touching the injured area. The chest may collapse rather than expand on inhaling. There may be difficulty in breathing and shock.

1 If one or two broken ribs are suspected, gently but firmly and not too tightly bind the arm on the injured side across the chest — to help immobilize injury.

2 If the injury is more severe and breathing difficult, lay child down, propped up, with head back.

Chest injuries

3 Loosen all tight clothing.

4 Facilitate fresh air, peace and calm — to reduce breathing effort.

5 Watch the breathing: if it stops give artificial respiration — see page 10.

Check the pulse: if it stops apply heart compression – see page 12.

Watch for signs of shock and if necessary give the treatment described on page 116.

Chest injuries

IMPORTANT

For all piercing wounds seek immediate medical help.
Symptoms: There will be pain associated with breathing and there is a danger that air is sucked into the chest cavity through the wound. Blood or blood-stained bubbles may ooze from wound and the child may cough up bright red, frothy blood.

1 Place the palm of the hand firmly and quickly over the wound until a dressing can be applied. The main aim is to seal the wound immediately and so prevent air entering the chest cavity.

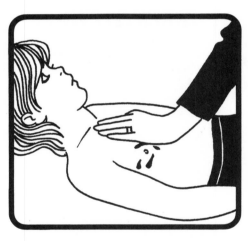

2 Plug the wound firmly with a thick dressing and retain in position by strapping or bandaging.

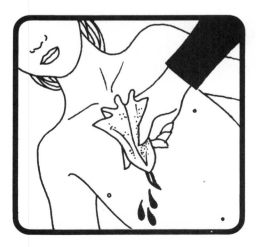

Chest injuries

3 Lay the child down with head and shoulders raised and the body inclined towards injured side.

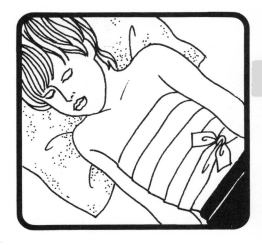

4 Loosen any tight clothing and provide fresh air and calm surroundings.

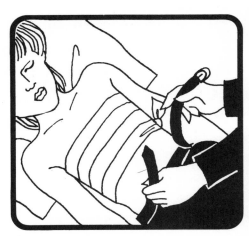

5 Keep the airway clear, see page 10.
Watch the breathing: if it stops give artificial respiration — see page 10.
Watch for signs of shock and, if necessary give the treatment described on page 116.

Choking

IMPORTANT

If choking persists or congestion becomes apparent, summon immediate medical attention.
Symptoms: Usually the first symptom is a sudden fit of coughing, the face and neck may become red turning to purple. There may be violent and alarming attempts by the child to get his breath.

1 Remove obvious obstruction; eg food, toy or nut but do not interfere with the child's own efforts to clear the obstruction.

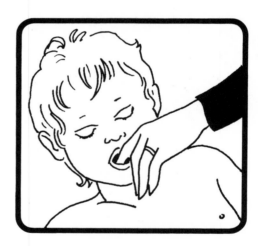

2 ## INFANTS

If the obstruction cannot be removed, or if choking continues, hold the child upside down by the legs and smack 3 or 4 times smartly between the shoulders. Repeat a few seconds later if unrelieved.

Choking

3 OLDER CHILDREN

Lay the child over your knees with head downwards and give 3 or 4 sharp slaps between the shoulders. Repeat a few seconds later if necessary.

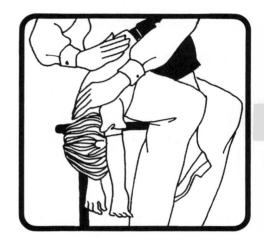

4 IF CHOKING CONTINUES

Stand behind the child and place your arms around his middle. Grip the fist of one hand, placed over the stomach between the navel and rib-cage, with your other hand. Make 3 or 4 quick and firm thrusts (squeezes) upwards. Repeat if necessary.

5

Watch the breathing: if it stops give artificial respiration — see page 10.

Convulsions

IMPORTANT

The child may fall to the ground, stiffen the whole body which may arch backwards, froth at the mouth, begin uncontrollable jerking movements and may be unconscious when the shaking is over. There may be a high temperature.

Do not try to restrain the child and offer nothing to drink during the attack

1 Clear the surroundings of hard or sharp objects that could cause harm.

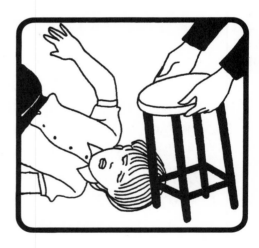

2 Loosen any tight clothing, especially around the neck, chest or waist.

Convulsions

3 When the convulsion has stopped lift the child onto a soft chair, settee or bed and lay him on one side without a pillow. Cover with a warm blanket or coat if cold.

4 If the child is hot, remove excess clothing or covers and bathe with a tepid sponge.

5 Watch the breathing: if it stops give artificial respiration — see page 10.

Cramp

Symptoms: Sudden painful tight muscle or group of muscles. Cramp commonly occurs while exercising in cold; eg swimming, or during exertion in hot conditions where a lot of sweating takes place.

In sports and games, pulled muscles may be confused with cramp. Do not stretch muscles or straighten limbs without the aid of massage

1 Forcibly but gently stretch the stiffened part until straight. Firmly rub and massage the affected muscle with your warm hands, until cramp eases.

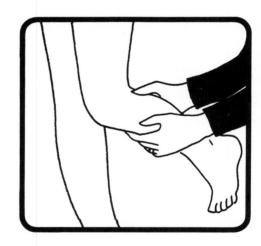

2 When there has been much sweating, and therefore much salt and water loss, give plenty of water to drink in which salt has been added: half teaspoonful salt to one large glass of water.

Drowning

IMPORTANT

Send for immediate medical aid.
Fresh water in the lungs is largely
absorbed. Sea water is less well
absorbed and more dangerous.
Sometimes spasms of the voice-box
will prevent water entering lungs.

1 On arrival on land immediately
hold child hanging over your
knee for 5 to 10 seconds to
encourage free drainage of
water from lungs. If necessary,
commence resuscitation at once.

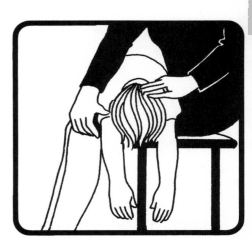

2 If the child is unconscious and
not breathing, begin immediate
resuscitation, in the water if
necessary. See page 10.

Ear injuries

Ear injuries are commonly due to cuts, foreign bodies and infection. Occasionally they may be associated with severe head injuries. If such injuries are suspected, seek immediate medical aid.

1 Control bleeding from cuts by pressing gauze or a clean cloth directly over the wound and elevate the child's head.

2 Hold the gauze in place with a bandage around the child's head.

Ear injuries

Seek medical aid in the event of foreign bodies proving to be immoveable, and in cases of infection.

Foreign bodies: Insects may be removed by gently flooding the ear with tepid water or olive oil. If the insect is alive it may be attracted from the ear by a lighted candle held 15 cm (6 inches) away. Beads, beans, nuts and other solid objects should be removed by a doctor.

Infection: Bleeding and pus from the ear usually indicates infection and possibly perforation of the ear drum. Place a wad of cotton wool loosely in the ear and hold in place with a bandage.

Electric shock

IMPORTANT

Injuries due to electric shock from low voltage contact are not usually severe, but may be more serious if the child is very young. Clinical shock (see page 116) is a likely consequence.

Avoid direct contact with child while he is in contact with the current

1 Break the contact by switching off the current, removing the plug or wrenching the cable free.

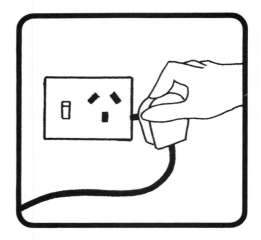

2 If the above action is not possible, stand on something dry (blanket, rubber mat, newspapers) and break the contact by pushing the child free with a wooden pole or board, or pulling with a loop of rope around an arm or leg.

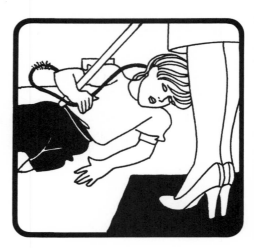

If necessary, treat the child for heat burns. See page 62

Electric shock

IMPORTANT

Injuries due to high voltage contact may be very severe — even fatal — involving burns to the skin and possibly to internal organs.
High voltage electricity is usually carried by overhead cables or conductor rails. When a main power supply is involved, contact the police immediately.

Never attempt rescue while the child is in contact with the current. Keep others away from the casualty

1 Only assist with First Aid when you are told officially that it is safe to do so — ie when the current has been switched off.

2 If the child is apparently dead, resuscitation is the first priority. See page 10.

Eye injuries

IMPORTANT

All eye injuries are potentially serious and will require medical attention.

Do not attempt to remove a foreign body which is on the pupil of the eye. Prevent the child rubbing the eye

1 Remove the foreign body from white of eye with the corner of a clean handkerchief or a moistened wisp of cotton wool. If under the lower lid, pull the lid down and remove foreign body as shown.

2 If this is unsuccessful or the object is under the upper lid, ask the child to blink with the eye under water.

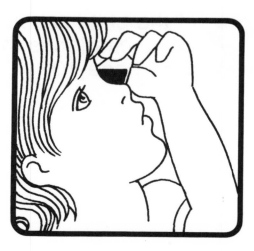

Eye injuries

CHEMICALS IN EYE

Holding the eyelid open, immediately flush the eye with gently running tepid water for 3 minutes. Make sure that the flow of water is away from the other eye. Cover the eye with gauze held in place with a bandage. and seek medical help.

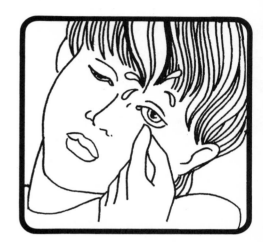

PENETRATING INJURIES

Lay the child down and give comfort and reassurance. Cover both eyes with gauze padding held in place with a light bandage around the head.

Transport to hospital immediately.

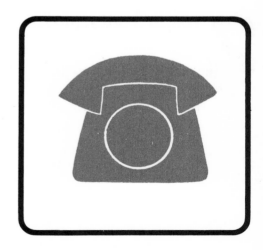

Exposure

IMPORTANT

Hypothermia is a dangerous condition in which the central part of the body cools below normal.
Symptoms: The child is usually quiet and refuses food and drinks, he is sluggish, and may be drowsy. The skin may be deceptively pink but is cold. The pulse is slow and weak. The breathing can be slow and shallow.

Do not use hot water bottles or electric blankets which could well heat the body too quickly and dangerously lower the blood pressure

1 Prevent further heat loss by removing the child from cold conditions and giving shelter.

2 Gradually warm the child by placing between warm blankets and/or cuddling him against your own body.

Infants are especially susceptible to exposure because their body temperature regulating mechanisms are not yet fully efficient

Exposure

3 Take the pulse at regular intervals.

4 If the child is conscious, give tepid or warm sweet drinks.

5 If the condition does not improve .in about ½ hour summon medical help.

Fever

IMPORTANT

Take the child's temperature (see page 18) before deciding on your course of action.

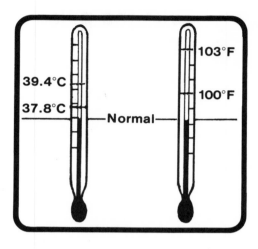

1 If the temperature is below 37.8°C (100°F) simply remove any excess clothing or bed covers. Cold drinks — fruit juice (not soda pop) milk or water — can be offered.

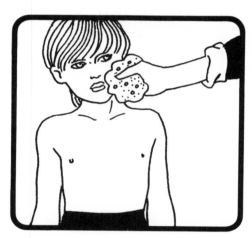

2 If the temperature is above 37.8°C (100°F), especially if it is above 39.4°C (103°F), sponge the entire body with tepid water for several minutes. This is best done in a bath of tepid water.

Fever

3 Dry the child well and cover only in light clothing or a sheet.

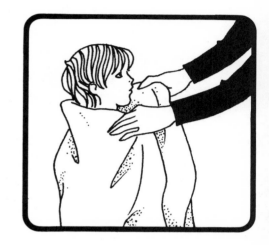

4 Keep in a cool (but not cold) room and give cold drinks. In the tropics, drinks should be salty.

5 Keep in a cool (but not cold) room and check the temperature every half hour. If the temperature remains above 39.4°C (103°F) for more than one hour or if the child is obviously distressed, seek medical advice.

Fractures

Every child with a definite or suspected fracture or dislocation should receive medical attention as soon as possible. Transport of the child should be as gentle as possible.

Fractures are often difficult to diagnose in a child. If in doubt, treat as a fracture of bone or dislocation of joint. Most fractures in children are incomplete and are called 'greenstick' fractures, (*see diagram*).

Symptoms of fractures and dislocations may vary considerably but will include one or more of the following:

Pain at or near the site of injury made worse by movement of the part.

Tenderness when gentle pressure is applied to affected part.

Swelling due to blood loss around fracture.

Loss of control – deformity of limb, inability to move, or unnatural movement of, injured part.

Coarse bony grating of broken ends of fractured bone — uncommon in young children.

Shock due to blood loss — internal or external.

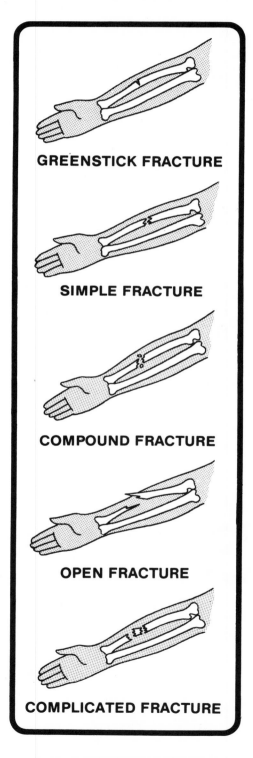

GREENSTICK FRACTURE

SIMPLE FRACTURE

COMPOUND FRACTURE

OPEN FRACTURE

COMPLICATED FRACTURE

Fractures

1 Attend to asphyxia (see page 36), bleeding and severe wounds before dealing with fracture.

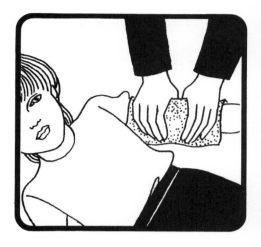

2 Move child as little as possible from site of accident — move only if life (child's or your own) is endangered. Move child by pulling him along, holding him underneath the armpits.

3 Immobilize part as soon as possible and in any case before moving the child too far, using the child's body and bandages as means of support or using splints and bandages. Raise the injured part after immobilization to reduce pain and swelling.

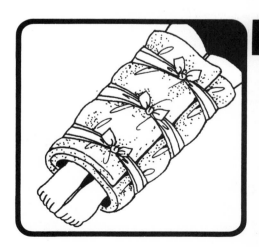

Fractures

IMPORTANT

Every child with a definite or suspected fracture or dislocation should receive medical attention as soon as possible. Transport of the child should be as gentle as possible. Care in use of bandages is essential — they must be tight enough to immobilize the part but not so tight as to interfere with the circulation.

1 Separate skin surfaces with soft padding before bandaging — this avoids chafing of skin. Tie knots over a splint or on the uninjured side.

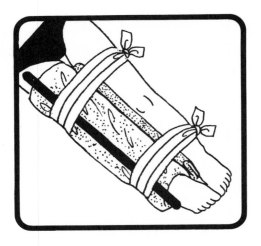

2 Check the tightness of bandaging every 10 minutes because of swelling — especially important in elbow injuries — loosen slightly when necessary.

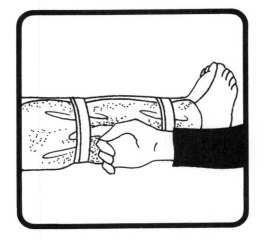

Fractures

Splints if and when used should be:

Sufficiently rigid and long enough to immobilize the joint above and the joint below a fracture.

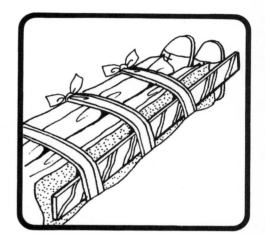

They must also be well padded, wide enough to immobilize the part and should be applied over clothing.

Splints may be improvised from walking sticks, umbrellas, broom handles, pieces of wood, cardboard or firmly folded newspapers or magazines.

Fractures

Move the child as little as possible to avoid damage to the spinal cord. Comfort the child and encourage him to lie still at all times. Give only sips of fluid, in case unconsciousness should occur. Remove to hospital as soon as possible and watch for shock.

1 If medical help is readily available, do as little as possible. Child should be lying down on flat, firm surface.

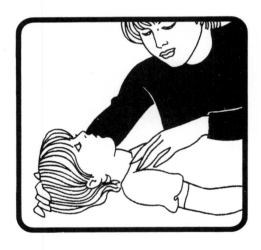

2 Instruct the child to lie still. Cover with a blanket and await the arrival of medical help.

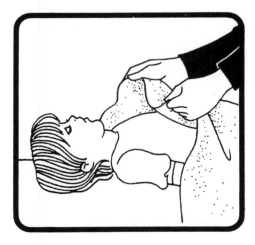

Fractures

3 If you need to transport the child to medical help, seek help in preparing the casualty. Devise a stretcher out of a sturdy board, door etc. Place the board, covered with a blanket, next to the child who should have been turned onto his side facing away from the stretcher.

4 Do not twist the child during placing onto stretcher. Move his body as single unit, keeping the head in line with the spine. On a signal from the person holding the head, roll and lift the child gently onto the stretcher without twisting the body or head.

5 Immobilize the head and spine with suitable padding and bind to stretcher with bandages, belts, scarves, etc.

Fractures

Remove child to hospital as soon as possible. Meanwhile watch for shock.

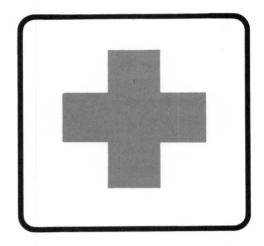

COLLARBONE, SHOULDER OR BENT ELBOW

Support the weight of the arm in a sling made from a triangular bandage. Immobilize the arm by gently tying a band over the sling and around the body.

STRAIGHT ELBOW

Do not attempt to bend elbow. Lay the child down and place the injured arm gently by child's side, palm to thigh.

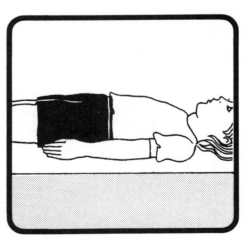

1

Fractures

2 Place adequate soft padding between the arm and the side of the body.

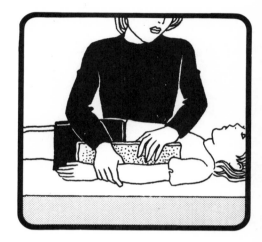

3 Secure broad bandages around the arm and body, tied on the uninjured side of the body.

4 Transport on a stretcher.

Fractures

Remove child to hospital as soon as possible and watch for shock.

1 Immobilize lower arm with padded splint — do not tie too tightly.

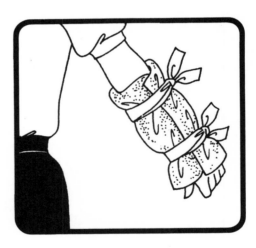

2 Support the weight of the arm in a sling made from a folded scarf or a triangular bandage. Secure the arm to the chest by a broad bandage applied over the sling.

Fractures

1 Lay the child down flat on back with legs straight. If the child wishes to bend his knees slightly, they should be supported on a folded blanket.

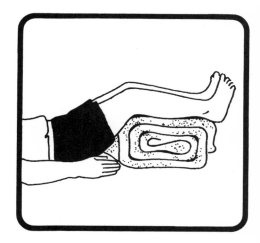

2 Place thick padding between the thighs and secure broad bandages around the pelvis, knees and ankles.

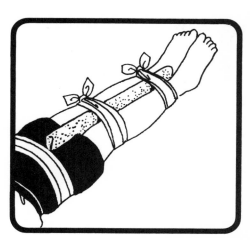

3 Transport on a stretcher.

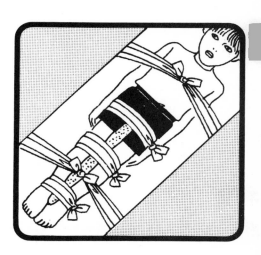

Fractures

Remove child to hospital as soon as possible. Meanwhile, watch for shock.

1 Immobilize the injured leg in the position found using padded splints. If the knee is straight, extend the splint from the buttock to the heel.

2 Transport by stretcher.

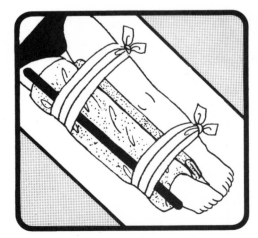

Fractures

1 Lay the child flat, with head and shoulders propped up. Lay the injured leg alongside the straightened normal leg.

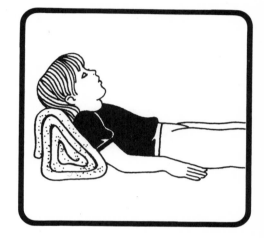

2 Immobilize with a padded splint. If it is impossible to improvise a splint, place padding between the legs and tie them together.

3 Transport by stretcher.

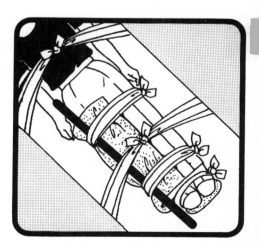

Fractures

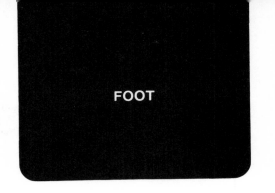

Remove child to hospital as soon as possible. Meanwhile watch for shock.

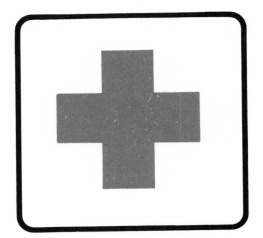

1 Carefully remove the shoe or boot and sock or stocking, cutting if necessary.

2 Treat any wounds which may be present (see page 54).

Fractures

3 Tie a well -padded support around foot.

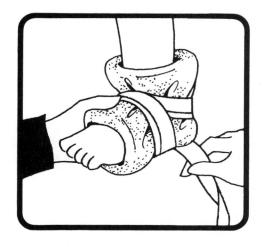

4 Support the leg and foot on a pillow, or rolled-up blanket or overcoat.

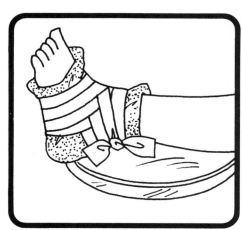

5 Transport by stretcher.

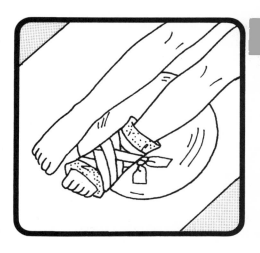

Frostbite

Frostbite occurs when part of the body is exposed for any length of time to the wind in very cold weather. The ears, nose, chin, fingers and toes are most frequently affected.
Symptoms: The affected part feels cold, numb, painful and stiff. Feeling and power of movement may be lost. The part appears stiff and white.

Do not rub the affected part. Do not apply direct heat in any form. Do not break any blisters

1 Shelter child from the weather. Give comfort and reassurance.

2 Give warm drinks if possible, but not alcohol.

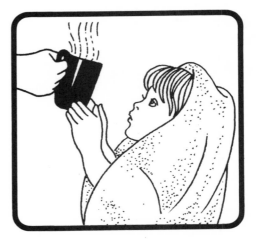

Frostbite

3 Remove constrictive clothing; eg gloves, rings, boots.

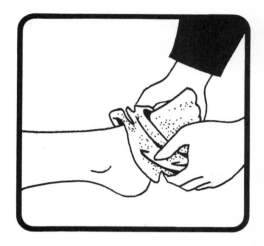

4 Thaw the affected part by warming gently with gloved hands, warm blankets or by placing the affected fingers under the armpit or wrapping in a sleeping bag. Continue until colour, sensation and warmth return to the affected parts.

5 Meanwhile, transport child to medical aid as soon as possible.

Head injuries

A moderate to severe blow on the head will usually cause a degree of concussion even if there is no damage to the underlying bone. **Symptoms** include: 'seeing stars'; temporary, partial or complete loss of consciousness; shallow breathing; nausea and vomiting; paleness; coldness and clamminess of the skin; later loss of memory.

Any case of unconsciousness must be referred to a doctor or hospital

1 Lay the child down and give warmth and comfort.

2 Do not give any drinks.

Head injuries

3 Apply a cold compress to the location of the blow or injury.

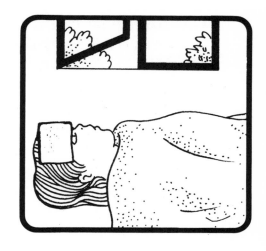

4 If unconsciousness develops, Place the casualty in the recovery position (see page 16).

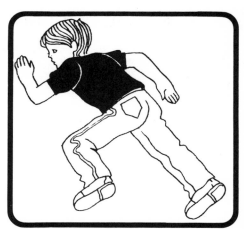

5 Observe for signs of more serious, deeper injury to the brain: deepening unconsciousness, persistent vomiting, double vision or persistent severe headache. Should any of these develop, remove child to hospital immediately.

Head injuries

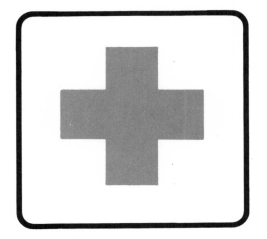

For anything but a small superficial
cut or knock to the head, remove
child to the nearest medical aid.
Any tear or cut to the scalp or face
tends to bleed heavily. Most are not
serious although they look bad.
Severe injury to the head can cause
fracture of the underlying bones and
in some cases injury to the brain.

1 Clean minor and superficial
scalp and face wounds with soap
and water.

2 Compress the bleeding point
with clean gauze or cloth until
bleeding stops.

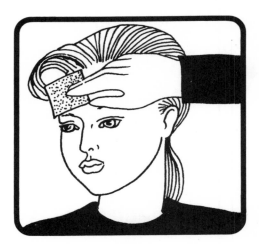

Do not give drinks after severe head
injuries — sips only can be given

Head injuries

3 Cover, if necessary (and possible), with clean adhesive plaster.

4 If the injury is more severe, lay the child down with head and shoulders propped up. Compress a large clean gauze or cloth lightly over the wound and attach with a bandage. Do not attempt to clean.

5 Watch the level of consciousness – see page 16. Check the pulse: if it stops apply heart compression – see page 12.
Watch for signs of shock and, if necessary give the treatment described on page 116.

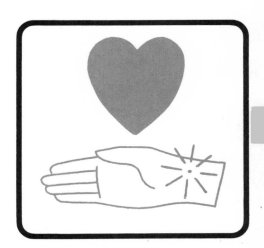

Impaled objects

Summon or transport to medical help immediately. Do not move a child off an impaling object unless his life is in imminent danger. If it is necessary, remove him as gently as possible. Do not attempt to remove the object unless it is obviously smooth and easy to do so. Otherwise, cut off any long projection 3-5 cm (1-2 in.) from the skin surface. Try not to move the object.

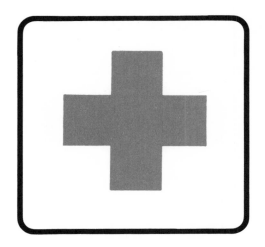

1 Cut clothing from around wound. If bleeding is severe see page 56.

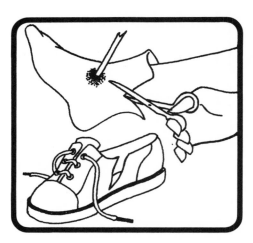

2 Place thick dry dressings around the wound and attach with bandaging.

Watch the child for signs of shock. See page 116

Impaled objects

1 Do not attempt to remove a fish hook from a child's face. In other parts of the body, push the shank through the skin until the point appears.

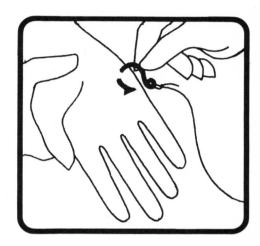

2 Cut off the barbed point with a wire-cutting tool. Retract the remaining shank from wound.

3 Clean the wound well with soap and water and cover with a clean dressing. Seek medical advice.

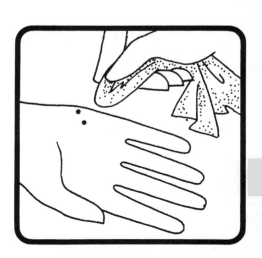

Mouth injuries

IMPORTANT

If bleeding has been severe or is not controllable, summon medical help. If the wounds are associated with other injuries see Head Injuries, page 100.

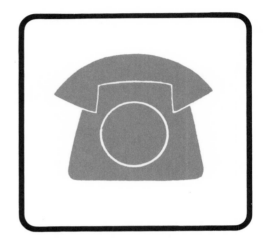

1 Clear the mouth of any broken teeth. Keep them for possible later replanting.

2 Sit the child down leaning slightly forward. Provide a bowl for the child to spit into.

Mouth injuries

3 Apply direct pressure to tooth socket or wound by placing thick gauze or cotton wool pad firmly in position.

1 **TONGUE, CHEEK OR LIP**

Compress the bleeding part between the finger and thumb, using a clean handkerchief or gauze dressing until bleeding stops. Ask the child to bite down on the pad for 5 to 10 minutes, supporting his chin with his hand.

2 Do not wash out the mouth as this can disturb the clotting. Do not attempt to plug the socket.

Poisoning

IMPORTANT

In all cases of poisoning, seek immediate medical help. Poisons may enter the body by being swallowed, inhaled, absorbed through the skin or injected under the skin. Swallowed poisons will have to be identified before the correct treatment can be given, but if in doubt, treat as corrosive poison.

1 Identify and keep safely the poison container. Save any vomit for later analysis. Do not induce vomiting.

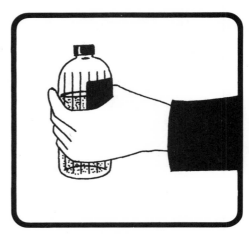

2 Telephone your local Poisons Information Centre or doctor for advice.

For a list of corrosive and non-corrosive poisons see page 121

108

Poisoning

1 If the child is conscious give plenty of milk or water to drink. Loosen tight clothing and allow plenty of fresh air.

2 If unconscious, place in the recovery position (see page 16) and call immediate help.

3 Treat for burns if necessary – see page 62.
Watch the breathing: if it stops give artificial respiration — see page 10.
Check the pulse: if it stops apply heart compression – see page 12.

Poisoning

IMPORTANT

Summon immediate medical help. A list of non-corrosive poisons is given on page 121. If you suspect that a child has swallowed one of these, or any other poison, telephone your local Poisons Information Centre.

1 If the child is conscious give plenty of milk or water to drink.

2 Attempt to induce vomiting by leaning the child over your knee and passing a spoon, knife handle or smooth stick through the mouth to touch the back of the throat.
Alternatively, use syrup of Ipecacuanha — 1 to 2 teaspoons repeated after 15 minutes.

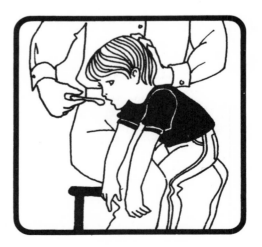

The procedure outlined on these pages also applies to swallowed poisonous plants – see page 122

Poisoning

3 Keep the child's head well down to avoid him inhaling any vomit.

4 After vomiting give further drinks of milk or water.

5 Watch the breathing: if it stops give artificial respiration — see page 10.
Check the pulse: if it stops apply heart compression – see page 12.

If there is any doubt about the poison which has been taken, act as described for corrosive poisons

Poisoning

This type of poisoning may be caused by gases, smoke from fire, solvents and certain paints.

If necessary, and possible, attach yourself to a life-line before entering a gas, or fume-filled space

1 **CAUTION:** Protect yourself — take a few deep breaths before entering a gas-filled room and take a deep breath and hold it when entering the room. A damp rag or handkerchief around your nose and mouth can help.

2 Immediately remove the child from the source of fumes and/or stop the source; eg stop car engine or turn the gas tap off.

Poisoning

3 Loosen tight clothing and allow fresh air: open doors and windows.

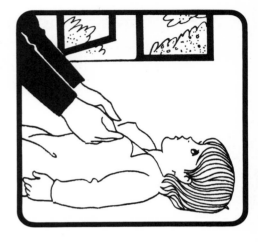

4 If child severely affected or unconscious, remove child to hospital immediately.

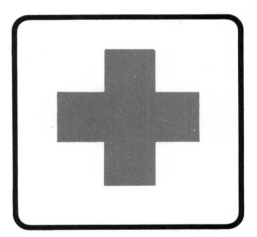

5 Watch the breathing: if it stops give artificial respiration — see page 10.
Check the pulse: if it stops apply heart compression – see page 12.
Watch for signs of shock and if necessary give the treatment described on page 116.

Poisoning

Skin contact with certain plants can
cause burning, itching, a rash,
blisters, swelling, and sometimes
headache and a fever.

For a list of
poisonous plants
see page 122

1 Remove the child from contact
with the plant.

2 Wash the affected areas well
with cold water and soap.

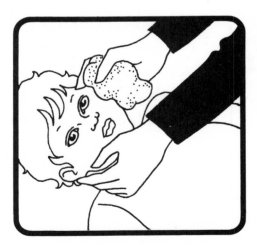

Poisoning

3 Apply calamine lotion or Cologne.

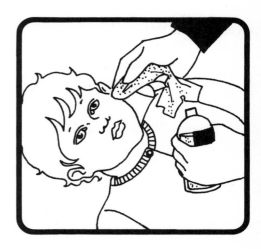

4 If the reaction is severe, seek medical advice.

5 In known susceptible children — especially in those with severe allergy – transport to hospital immediately while watching out for shock and breathing difficulties. See page 16 or 116 if necessary.

Shock

Symptoms: Usually the child becomes pale, the skin cold and clammy and there is usually sweating; sometimes giddiness, blurring of vision and vomiting. Drowsiness and unconsciousness may follow and the pulse, after becoming rapid, will be almost impossible to feel. Breathing may be rapid and shallow and may stop.

Do not overheat, as warmth draws blood into skin and away from vital organs. Do not give drinks — sips only

1 Lay the child down and deal with the immediate cause of shock. Move the child as little as possible.

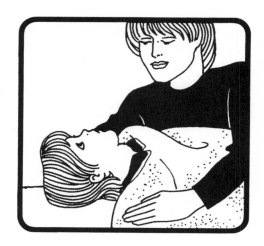

2 Loosen any tight clothing and allow plenty of fresh air.

Shock

3 Keep the child's head flat and support the legs in an elevated position — this encourages blood flow to the brain.

4 If vomiting seems likely or the child is unconscious, place in the recovery position — see page 17.
Find a suitable pot into which the child can vomit.

5 Summon medical aid as soon as possible.
Watch the breathing: if it stops give artificial respiration — see page 10.
Check the pulse: if it stops apply heart compression – see page 12.

See Unconsciousness, page 16

SECTION 3

What you need to know

Children's medical history

Keeping a record of your children's medical history can save valuable time in an emergency. The chart on this page shows the kind of information which should be recorded. Keep the information up-to-date and provide copies for teachers, camp leaders or other adults who will be responsible for your children when they are away from home.

FAMILY NAME _____

FAMILY ADDRESS _____

	FIRST CHILD	SECOND CHILD
NAME		
DATE OF BIRTH		
NATURE OF BIRTH		
BREAST FEEDING UNTIL		
IMMUNIZATIONS		
(See immunisation schedule)		
1st PDT + polio		
2nd PDT + polio		
3rd PDT + polio		
Measles		
Booster DT		
+ polio		
Booster tetanus		
VACCINATION		
BLOOD GROUP		
ALLERGIES		
MAJOR INJURIES		
HOSPITALIZATION		
OPERATIONS		
MAJOR ILLNESSES		
PSYCHIATRIC CARE		
OTHER INFORMATION		

Emergency telephone numbers

A list of emergency telephone numbers is a vital part of your First Aid equipment. It is not sufficient just to keep the numbers of the police, fire and ambulance services – you never know when you may need one of the others listed here. Keep a copy of the list next to your telephone and show it to your babysitter whenever you go out.

YOUR DOCTOR _____

   Reserve Doctor _____

AMBULANCE _____

POLICE _____

FIRE STATION _____

DISTRICT HOSPITAL _____

CHILDREN'S HOSPITAL _____

DENTIST _____

PHARMACIST: nearest all-night _____

POISON CONTROL CENTER _____

FATHER'S WORK No. _____

MOTHER'S WORK No. _____

NEIGHBOURS and FRIENDS _____

   Name _____

   Address _____

   _____

   Telephone No. _____

   Name _____

   Address _____

   _____

   Telephone No. _____

TAXI _____

GAS _____

ELECTRICITY _____

WATER _____

OTHERS _____

Household poisons

Most households contain, in the form of quite ordinary substances, a surprising number of poisonous, or potentially poisonous, items. You cannot keep your house entirely free of such dangers, but you can ensure that they are kept under lock and key or out of your children's reach. Many poisons, especially petroleum products, must be kept well away from fire or naked flames.

The list below indicates a number of poisons which are found in very many households. For treatment of corrosive poisoning, see page 109; for treatment of non-corrosive poisoning, see page 110.

CORROSIVE
Battery acid
Benzine
Brush cleaner
Caustic soda
Charcoal lighter fuel
Corn remover
Dishwasher granules
Drain cleaner
Floor polish
Furniture polish
Gasoline
Grease remover
Gun cleaner
Kerosene
Lacquer thinner
Lye
Metal cleaner
Naphtha
Oven cleaner
Paint stripper
Paint thinner
Quicklime
Shoe polish
Toilet bowl cleaner
Typewriter cleaner
Wart remover
Washing soda
Wax wood polish
White spirit
Wood preservative
Zinc compounds

NON-CORROSIVE
Acetone
After shave lotion
Alcohol
Antifreeze
Arsenic
Bichloride of mercury
Bleach
Body conditioner
Boric acid
Camphor
Carbon tetrachloride
Chlordane
Cologne
Cosmetics
DDT
Deodorant
Detergent
Fabric softeners
Fingernail polish and remover
Fireworks
Fluoride
Hair dye
Hair permanent neutralizer
Hair sprays

Hydrogen peroxide
Indelible markers
Inks
Insecticides
Iodine
Liniment
Matches (more than 20 wooden matches or 2 match books)
Mercury salts
Mothballs, flakes or cakes
Nutmeg (if eaten whole)
Oil of Wintergreen
Paint (lead)
Perfume
Pesticides
Pine oil
Rat or mouse poison
Roach poisons
Strychnine
Suntan preparations
Turpentine
Weed killer
Wick deodorizer

Poisonous plants

HOLLY

The chief problem in warning of the dangers presented by poisonous plants centers around what is meant by poisonous. The list opposite, and the illustrated plants, can all be regarded as moderately to severely toxic — many of them can be fatal to children. Those with attractive fruits are a particular hazard to children. Children under the age of three should be kept away from obvious temptation; older children should be educated to recognize dangerous plants.

If you suspect that your child has consumed a poisonous plant, take a sample of the offending plant to the hospital with the child. Take an entire stem or branch together with flowers and fruits — if it has them.

FRUITS AND SEEDS
Abrus precatorius (Rosary pea)
Argemone (Mexican poppies)
Cestrum
Clivia (Kaffir lily)
Cotoneaster
Cycadales (Cycads, zamias)
Daphne
Delphinium
Duboisia (Corkwoods)
Hedera helix (English ivy)
Ilex aquifolium (Holly)
Jatropha
Laburnum
Lathyrus odoratus (Sweet pea)
Melia azerdarach (White cedar)
Papaver somniferum (Opium poppy)
Phytolacca americana (Pokeweed)
Pimelea flava (Yellow rice-flower)
Pimelea pauciflora (Scrub kurrajong)
Ricinus communis (Castor oil plant)
Solanum (Nightshades)
Thevetia peruviana (Yellow oleander)
Wikstroemia indica (Tie-bush)
Wisteria
Ximenia americana (Yellow plum)

DEADLY NIGHTSHADE

FOXGLOVE

Poisonous plants

PRIVET

ROOTS
Aconitum (Monkshood)
Gloriosa superba (Glory lily)
Hyacinth (bulbs)
Manihot esculenta (Cassava)

FLOWERS
Gelsemium sempervirens (Yellow jasmine)
Kalmia latifolia (Mountain laurel)
Zantedeschia (Arum lily)

SHOOTS/FOLIAGE
Aesculus (Horse chestnut)
Buxus sempervirens (Boxwood)
Crinum (Spider lilies)
Dieffenbachia (Dumbcane)
Euphorbia (Spurges)
Hedera helix (English lily)
Laburnum
Philodendron
Rheum rhaponticum (Rhubarb – leaves only)

ALL PARTS POISONOUS
Atropa belladonna (Deadly nightshade)
Carissa spectabilis (Wintersweet)
Carissa acokanthera (Bushman's poison)
Conium maculatum (Hemlock)
Convallaria majalis (Lily-of-the-valley)
Datura (Thorn apples, false castor oil)
Digitalis (Foxglove)
Helleborus niger (Christmas rose)
Hyoscyamus niger (Henbane)
Ipomoea (Morning glory)
Ligustrum (Privets)
Lupinus (Lupins)
Narcissus (Daffodil, jonquil, narcissus)
Nerium oleander (Oleander)
Nicotiniana
Robinia
Taxus baccata (Yew)

POISONOUS ON CONTACT
Anacardium occidentale (Cashew)
Dendrocnide (Stinging tree)
Hoya Rhus
Sarcostemma astrale (Caustic vine)
Schinus (Pepper trees)
Synadenium granti (African milk bush)
Toxidendron (Poison ivy)

LABURNUM

DUMBCANE

Index

1 Locate the appropriate emergency tab.

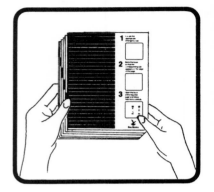

2 Bend the book so that the corresponding tab appears on the edge of the page.

3 Open the book at the required page and follow directions carefully.

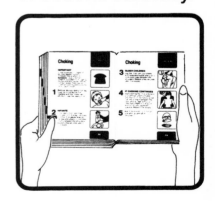